Mediation

ASPEN CASEBOOK SERIES

Mediation
The Roles of Advocate and Neutral

Second Edition

Dwight Golann

Suffolk University

Jay Folberg

University of San Francisco

Wolters Kluwer

Law & Business

AUSTIN   BOSTON   CHICAGO   NEW YORK   THE NETHERLANDS

To contact Customer Care, e-mail customer.service@aspenpublishers.com, call 1-800-234-1660, fax 1-800-901-9075, or mail correspondence to:

Aspen Publishers
Attn: Order Department
PO Box 990
Frederick, MD 21705

Printed in the United States of America.

1 2 3 4 5 6 7 8 9 0

ISBN 978-0-7355-9968-0

Library of Congress Cataloging-in-Publication Data

Golann, Dwight.
  Mediation : the roles of advocate and neutral / Dwight Golann, Jay Folberg. — 2nd ed.
      p. cm.
    Includes bibliographical references and index.
    ISBN 978-0-7355-9968-0 (alk. paper)
      1. Mediation—United States. 2. Dispute resolution (Law)—United States.
3. Compromise (Law)—United States. 4. Mediation. I. Folberg, Jay, 1941-
II. Title.

KF9084.G648 2011
347.73'9—dc22

                                                                                          2010046585

About Wolters Kluwer Law & Business

Wolters Kluwer Law & Business is a leading provider of research information and workflow solutions in key specialty areas. The strengths of the individual brands of Aspen Publishers, CCH, Kluwer Law International and Loislaw are aligned within Wolters Kluwer Law & Business to provide comprehensive, in-depth solutions and expert-authored content for the legal, professional and education markets.

CCH was founded in 1913 and has served more than four generations of business professionals and their clients. The CCH products in the Wolters Kluwer Law & Business group are highly regarded electronic and print resources for legal, securities, antitrust and trade regulation, government contracting, banking, pension, payroll, employment and labor, and healthcare reimbursement and compliance professionals.

Aspen Publishers is a leading information provider for attorneys, business professionals and law students. Written by preeminent authorities, Aspen products offer analytical and practical information in a range of specialty practice areas from securities law and intellectual property to mergers and acquisitions and pension/benefits. Aspen's trusted legal education resources provide professors and students with high-quality, up-to-date and effective resources for successful instruction and study in all areas of the law.

Kluwer Law International supplies the global business community with comprehensive English-language international legal information. Legal practitioners, corporate counsel and business executives around the world rely on the Kluwer Law International journals, loose-leafs, books and electronic products for authoritative information in many areas of international legal practice.

Loislaw is a premier provider of digitized legal content to small law firm practitioners of various specializations. Loislaw provides attorneys with the ability to quickly and efficiently find the necessary legal information they need, when and where they need it, by facilitating access to primary law as well as state-specific law, records, forms and treatises.

Wolters Kluwer Law & Business, a unit of Wolters Kluwer, is headquartered in New York and Riverwoods, Illinois. Wolters Kluwer is a leading multinational publisher and information services company.

To my wife, Helaine, who has taught me how much dispute resolution
depends on the learning of psychology and the
art of understanding people

—D.G.

To my children, Ross, Lisa, and Rachel, who taught me the necessity of
mediation

—J.F.

SUMMARY OF CONTENTS

CONTENTS

CHAPTER 3
NEGOTIATION — STEP BY STEP   37

CHAPTER 4
BARRIERS TO SETTLEMENT   69

PART II

THE MEDIATION PROCESS 87

CHAPTER 5
AN OVERVIEW OF MEDIATION 89

CHAPTER 8
EMOTIONAL ISSUES AND COGNITIVE FORCES   177

CHAPTER 9
MERITS-BASED BARRIERS   205

PART III

THE ADVOCATE'S ROLE   231

CHAPTER 10
REPRESENTING CLIENTS: PREPARATION   233

CHAPTER 11
REPRESENTING CLIENTS: DURING THE PROCESS   265

PART IV

SPECIALIZED TOPICS   293

CHAPTER 12
SPECIFIC APPLICATIONS   295

CHAPTER 13
**COURT-CONNECTED MEDIATION AND FAIRNESS
CONCERNS**   **337**

CHAPTER 15
ETHICAL ISSUES FOR ADVOCATES
AND MEDIATORS   411

CHAPTER 16
MIXED AND CHANGING ROLES
by Thomas J. Stipanowich   429

PREFACE

This book is based on three key assumptions: First, to represent clients effectively, the next generation of lawyers must be able to mediate effectively. Second, new lawyers are much more likely to encounter mediation as advocates or advisors than as professional neutrals. Finally, textbooks should be interesting to read, bring together the best writing on the process, match well with video and support interactive teaching.

Our book has a different emphasis than most other texts on mediation. It focuses on *legal* mediation — substantial disputes involving legal claims, in which the disputants are likely to hire attorneys. It also looks at mediation primarily from the perspective of a lawyer representing a client, rather than from the viewpoint of a mediator or a party.

This book includes examples drawn from actual disputes to illustrate the readings and pique students' interest. The introductory chapter on mediation, for example, features the comments of practicing lawyers about how they use mediation in a variety of settings. It also includes accounts of how two high-profile disputes were mediated, one involving a student death and the other the U.S.-Microsoft antitrust case. The readings on mediation techniques and about ethical issues are also interspersed with provocative situations drawn from practice.

The book includes questions designed to provoke critical thinking about the readings and stimulate class discussion. The text is practical, while grounded in theory, and lawyer-focused, but enriched by interdisciplinary knowledge. Accompanying roleplays allow students to apply concepts they have read about and bring the text material to life. These roleplays again center largely on the types of disputes in which students are likely to find themselves as practicing lawyers — cases with significant legal claims, as opposed to neighborhood quarrels or personal conflicts with no legal dimension. There is also on the Web site a comprehensive bibliography to give readers access to writings by scholars in the field.

This is the first mediation book to include video as an integral part of the teaching materials. Instructors will receive on request a two-hour "Teaching DVD" that contains eighteen professionally filmed video excerpts drawn from the authors' own work and leading mediation videos. The Second Edition adds to these resources with a video, "Skills of a Legal Mediator," available from the JAMS Foundation on request, which shows the mediation of an international business dispute with a diverse group of disputants and attorneys. The videos show experienced lawyers and neutrals performing in some of the same roleplays featured in the teaching materials, which allows students to see how experienced professionals deal with the challenges they have just faced.

We begin the book with an overview of the disputing universe. It shows that actual legal disputes, unlike the appellate cases that characterize first-year texts, are not neatly packaged. Instead they arise as aspects of a near-endless universe of human conflict. Because mediation is a process of assisted negotiation, we next explain the basic concepts of bargaining, analyze choices of style, and present a framework for effective negotiation. Part I of the book concludes with a chapter devoted to the strategic, cognitive, and emotional barriers that often make settlement difficult, creating a backdrop for our exploration of how mediation can assist the settlement process.

Part II, on mediation technique, begins with examples of mediation in action, then goes on to describe styles of commercial mediation that lawyers are likely to encounter, as well as no-caucus approaches. We then examine the mediation process itself in depth, focusing on the methods mediators use to deal with process-, emotional-, and merits-based barriers.

Perhaps the most practical section of the book is Part III, which focuses on how lawyers can represent clients in mediation. This unit is based on our experience conducting commercial and family mediations. Contrary to the image presented in some texts, we begin from the premise that legal mediators commonly do in fact exercise "power"; we argue that this phenomenon presents both a challenge and an opportunity for lawyers, since they can enhance their bargaining effectiveness by drawing on their neutral's influence. We describe, again with numerous actual examples, how good lawyers can become active participants in mediation, enlisting mediators to overcome common barriers to settlement and achieve a client's goals.

In Part IV we examine specialized topics. Chapter 12 shows how mediation is applied in a variety of different settings and formats, ranging from divorce cases to employment, high tech, and international disputes. We also analyze policy issues in mediation, including its impact on the development of the law and its use in situations where a disputant may be disadvantaged by culture, gender, or spousal violence. Chapter 15 delves into ethical issues, presenting situations encountered by practicing lawyers and neutrals in which the profession's standards, unimpeachable in themselves, come into seemingly irreconcilable conflict. We conclude with a look at how students entering practice are likely to see mediation evolve.

This second edition follows the same organization as the first edition and contains the same core elements. We have updated some of our narrative and included excerpts from the most recent writings on mediation, so that teachers will not need to prepare supplements in order to assign entirely up-to-date material. We also take advantage of new technology and of students' increasing preference for electronic and video formats: Items that have traditionally gone into a paper appendix now appear on the book's Web site. This makes the book more compact without sacrificing depth, allows readers to download rules and laws for discussion or study, and permits us to update the book as new rules and standards are promulgated.

A note about form: In order to focus discussion and conserve space, we have substantially edited the readings and have deleted most footnotes, references, and case citations. Deletions of material are shown by three dots, but omitted footnotes and other references are not indicated. The footnotes we have retained in excerpts carry their original numbers, while our own footnotes appear with either asterisks or sequential numbering, as appropriate.

This book is the culmination of our combined experience teaching, practicing, and shaping dispute resolution in legal contexts. Although formal acknowledgments follow, we are grateful to the students and lawyers we have had the pleasure of teaching, and from whom we have learned a great deal.

December 2010

D.G.
J.F.

ACKNOWLEDGMENTS

This mediation book evolved from our comprehensive coursebook, *Resolving Disputes: Theory, Practice, and Law*, which we wrote with Lisa Kloppenberg and Thomas Stipanowich. This Second Edition has grown to become a text of its own, but it would not exist without Lisa and Tom's collaboration in creating the survey text. We are grateful for their continuing encouragement and friendship. We benefited from their enthusiasm for this project, and we look forward to partnering with them in the future.

We are thankful for the support and assistance we have each received from the staffs and librarian of the law schools at Suffolk University and the University of San Francisco, especially from Diane D'Angelo and Richard Buckingham. Special thanks go to the anonymous reviewers, whose comments on the draft text were insightful and very helpful in refining the contents of this book. We are most grateful to the students and lawyers whom we have trained and worked with in mediation. They have inspired us and guided what we have selected here to present to the next generation of lawyers.

Finally, we are indebted to the many authors and publishers who have granted their permission for us to edit and include parts of their publications. More specifically, we thank the following sources for permission to publish excerpts of their work:

Abramson, Harold, Mediation Representation: Advocating as a Problem Solver in Any Country or Culture. Copyright © 2010 by National Institute for Trial Advocacy (NITA). Reprinted with permission from the National Institute for Trial Advocacy. Further reproduction is prohibited.

Adler, Warren, "The War of the Roses," 51-76, Stonehouse Press (1981).

Arnold, Thomas, "Client Preparation for Mediation," 15 Corporate Counsel Quarterly 2:52 (April 1999). Copyright © 1999 by Tom Arnold, Esq. Reprinted with permission.

Arnold, Tom, "20 Common Errors in Mediation Advocacy," 13 Alternatives 69 (1995). Copyright © 1995. Reprinted with permission of John Wiley & Sons, Inc.

Aaron, Marjorie, from "At First Glance: Maximizing the Mediator's Initial Contact" 20 Alternatives 167 (2002) Copyright © 2002. Reprinted with permission of John Wiley & Sons, Inc.

Bahadoran, Sina, "A Red Flag: Mediator Cultural Bias in Divorce Mediation," 18 Massachusetts Family Law Journal No. 3, 69. Copyright © 2000. Reprinted with permission of the author.

Bingham, Gail, from "The Environment in the Balance: Mediators Are Making a Difference," AC Resolution, Summer 2002. Reproduced with permission from the Association for Conflict Resolution.

Birkoff, Juliana, Robert Rack, with Judith M. Fisher, from "Points of View: Is Mediation Really a Profession?" 8 No. 1, Dispute Resolution Magazine 10, 10 (2001). Copyright © 2001 by the American Bar Association. Reprinted with permission.

Bowling, Daniel, and David Hoffman, "Bringing Peace into the Room: The Personal Qualities of the Mediator and Their Impact on the Mediation," 16 Negotiation Journal 5. Copyright © 2000 by Blackwell Publishers Ltd. Reprinted with permission.

Brazil, Wayne, "ADR in A Civil Action: What Could Have Been," Dispute Resolution, 13:4, p. 25 Copyright © 2007 by the American Bar Association. Reprinted with permission.

Brazil, Wayne D., "Why Should Courts Offer Non-Binding ADR Services?" 16 Alternatives 65 (May 1998). Copyright © 1998. Reprinted with permission of John Wiley & Sons, Inc.

Bryant, Ken, and Dana Curtis, Reframing. Reprinted with permission of the authors. Aaron Marjorie, Merits Barriers: Evalutation and Decision Analysis as a Method of Evaluating the Trial Alternative in Golann, Mediating Legal Disputes. Copyright © 2009 by Dwight Golann. Reprinted with permission.

Bush, Robert Baruch, and Sally Ganong Pope, "Transformative Mediation: Principles and Practice in Divorce Mediation," from Folberg et al., Divorce and Family Mediation. Copyright © 2004 by Guilford Press. Reprinted with permission of the Guilford Press.

Carlson, Chris, The Consensus Building Handbook: A Comprehensive Guide to Reaching agreement by Chris Carlson. Copyright 2000 by Sage Publications Inc. Books. Reproduced with permission of Sage Publications Inc. Books via Copyright Clearance Center.

Cooper, Christopher, "Police Mediators: Rethinking the Role of Law Enforcement in the New Millennium" in Dispute Resolution Magazine, American Bar Association, Fall 2000, 17. Reprinted by permission of the American Bar Association.

Curtis, Dana, and John Toker from "Representing Clients in Appellate Mediation: The Last Frontier," Dispute Resolution Alert, December 2000.

Delgado, Richard, "ADR and the Dispossessed: Recent Books About the Deformalization Movement," 13 Law & Social Inquiry 145. Copyright ©1988 by The University of Chicago Press. Reprinted with permission.

Donahey, M. Scott, "The Asian Concept of Conciliator/Arbitrator: Is It Translatable to the Western World?" 10 Foreign Investment Law Journal. 120 (1995). Reprinted with permission.

Excerpts from the American Bar Association Task Force on Improving Mediation Quality, Final Report, Copyright © 2008 by the American Bar Association.

Harr, Jonathan. From A Civil Action by Jonathan Harr. Copyright © 1995 by Jonathan Harr. Used by permission of Random House, Inc.

Haynes, John, from "Mediating Divorce: Casebook of Strategies for Successful Family Negotiations" 50, Jossey-Bass (1989). Reprinted with permission of John Wiley & Sons, Inc.

Heen, Sheila, and John Richardson, "I See a Pattern Here and the Pattern is You," Personality and Dispute Resolution in the Handbook of Dispute Resolution by M. I. Moffitt and R.C. Bordone, eds. Copyright © 2005 John Wiley & Sons, Inc. Reprinted with permission.

Hermann, Michele, "New Mexico Research Examines Impact of Gender and Ethnicity in Mediation," Dispute Resolution, 1:3, p. 10. Copyright © 1994 by the American Bar Association. Reprinted with permission.

Hoffman, David A., "Microsoft and Yahoo: Where Were the Mediators? They Help Countries and Couples, Why Not Business?" Excerpted from Christian Science Monitor. Copyright 2008 by Christian Science Monitor.

Hughes, Scott H., "A Closer Look: The Case for a Mediation Confidentiality Privilege Still Has Not Been Made," Dispute Resolution, 5:2 p. 14. Copyright © 1998 by the American Bar Association. Reprinted with permission.

Laflin, James, and Robert Werth, "Unfinished Business: Another Look at the Microsoft Mediation," 12 California Tort Reporter No. 3, 88 (April 2001). Reprinted with permission.

Lax, David A., and James K. Sebenius. "The Manager as Negotiator: Bargaining For Cooperation and Competitive Gain," Copyright © 1986 by David A. Lax and James K. Şebenius. All rights reserved.

Love, Lela, "The Top Ten Reasons Why Mediators Should Not Evalutate," 24 Fl. St. U. L. Rev. Copyright © 1997. Reprinted with permission from Florida State University Law Review.

McGuire, James E., "Certification: An Idea Whose Time Has Come," DisputeResolution, 10: 4, p. 22. Copyright © 2004 by the American Bar Association. Reprinted with permission.

Mcllwrath, Michael, "Can Mediation Evolve into a Global Profession?" Mediate.com. Copyright © 2009 by Michael Mcllwrath. Reprinted with permission.

Milne, Ann L., "Mediation and Domestic Abuse," in Folberg et al., Divorce and Family Mediation. Copyright © 2004 by Guilford Press. Reprinted with permission of the Guilford Press.

Mnookin, Robert H. from "Why Negotiations Fail: An Exploration of Barriers to the Resolution of Conflict," 8 Ohio St. J. Disp. Resol. 235 (1993).

Mnookin, Robert H., Scott R. Peppet, and Andrew S. Tulumello. Reprinted by permission of the publisher from Beyond Winning: Negotiation to Create Value in Deals and Disputes by Robert H. Mnookin, Scott R. Peppet, and Andrew S. Tulumello, pp. 37-42, 282-86, Cambridge, MA: The Belknap Press of Harvard University Press. Copyright © 2000 by the President and Fellows of Harvard College.

Nelken, Melissa, Negotiation Theory and Practice. Reprinted from Negotiation: Theory and Practice with permission. Copyright © 2007 Matthew Bender & Company, Inc., a member of the LexisNexis Group. All rights reserved.

O'Connor, Theron, "Planning and Executing an Effective Concession Strategy." Reprinted with permission of the author.

Peppet, Scott R., "Contract Formation in Imperfect Markets, Should We Use Mediators in Deals?," 19 Ohio St. J. Disp. Resol. 283 (2004).

Picker, Bennet G., Navigating Relationships: The Invisible Barriers to Resolution. 2 Amer. J of Mediation 41. Copyright © 2008 CRP Institute for Dispute Resolution. Reprinted with permission of the author.

Price, Marty, Personalizing Crime: Mediation Produces Restorative Justice for Victims and Offenders, by Marty Price in Dispute Resolution, 7:1, p. 8-11. Copyright (c) 2000 by the American Bar Association. Reprinted by permission. This information or any or portion thereof may not be copied or disseminated in any form or by any means or stored in an electronic database or retrieval system without the express written consent of the American Bar Association.

Riskin, Leonard, "Retiring and Replacing the Grid of Mediator Orientations," 21 Alternatives to the High Costs of Litigation, No. 4, *69* (April 2003). Copyright © 2003. Reprinted with permission of John Wiley & Sons, Inc.

Rosenberg, Joshua D., "Interpersonal Dynamics Helping Lawyers Learn the Skills, and the Importance of Human Relationships in the Practice of Law," 55 University of Miami Law Review. Copyright © 2004 by the University of Miami Law Review. Reprinted with permission.

Rummel, R.J., from the Conflict Helix, Copyright © 1991 by Transaction Publishers. Reprinted by permission of the publisher.

Salacuse, Jeswald, "Mediation in International Business." Copyright © Jacob Bercovitch. From Mediation in International Relations: Multiple Approaches to Conflict Management by Jacob Bercovitch. Reprinted with permission of Palgrave Macmillan.

Salem, Richard, "The Benefits of Empathic Listening" (2003). Reprinted from beyondintractability.org with permission of the Conflict Research Consortium, University of Colorado.

Shell, G. Richard, Negotiation Strategies for Reasonable People," from Bargaining for Advantage by G. Richard Shell, Copyright © 1999, 2006. Used by permission of Viking Penguin, a division of Penguin Group (USA) Inc.

Singer, Linda R. This excerpt from "The Lawyer as Neutral" is reprinted from Into the 21st Century: Thought Pieces on Lawyering, Problem Solving and ADR, 19 Alternatives (CPR Institute January 2001). Reno, Janet. This excerpt from "The Federal Government and Appropriate Dispute Resolution: Promoting Problem Solving and Peacemaking as Enduring Values in Our Society" is reprinted from Into the 21st Century: Thought Pieces on Lawyering, Problem Solving and ADR, 19 Alternatives (CPR Institute January 2001).

Smith, Pam, from Separating Opponents Key to JAMS Neutral's Success, The Recorder 4 (June 20,2006). Copyright © 2008 Incisive Media.

Smith, Robert M., "Advocacy in Mediation: A Dozen Suggestions," 26 San Francisco Attorney 14 (June/July 2000). Copyright © 2000 by the Bar Association of San Francisco. Reprinted with permission.

Technology Mediation Services, "Benefits of Mediating High Technology Disputes," www.technologymediation.com/hightech.htm. Copyright © 2004 by Technology Mediation Services. Reprinted with permission.

Welsh, Nancy A. from Making Deals in Court-Connected Mediation: What's Justice Got to Do with It? Washington University Law Quarterly, Vol 79, p. 787, (2001).

Williams, Gerald R., and Carver, Charles, "Legal Negotiation." Copyright © 2007 by The West Group. Reprinted with permission.

Wissler, Roselle, "To Evaluate or Facilitate? Parties' Perceptions of Mediation Affected by Mediator Style," 2001, Dispute Resolution, 7:2, p. 35. Copyright © 2001 by the American Bar Association. Reprinted with permission.

Wittenberg, Carol A., Susan T. Mackenzie, and Margaret L. Shaw, "Employment Disputes," in Dwight Golann, Mediating Legal Disputes. Copyright © 1996. Reprinted with permission of the author.

Mediation

PART
I

INTRODUCTION

CHAPTER
1

The Origins of Disputes

"I found the old format much more exciting."

Legend has it that the use of lawyers in court evolved from disputants hiring gladiators to fight in their place. Referring to lawyers as "modern-day gladiators" is, however, a misnomer. It is the parties who bear most of the costs, risks, and injuries of modern legal combat. Today people have options to resolve disputes other than traditional litigation, and to advise and represent clients successfully lawyers must be skilled in using these techniques. The adage that to someone with only a hammer everything looks like a nail, suggests the limitations of an attorney who only knows how to litigate or a gladiator who knows only how to fight. The purpose of this book is to provide the knowledge to counsel clients about an increasingly popular alternative to legal combat — mediation — as well as the ability to represent clients effectively in the mediation process.

A. The Nature of Disputing in America

Most of the disputes that clients will bring you will barely resemble the cases you encountered in your first-year courses in law school. In place of a clearly defined contest between named parties over narrow issues, practicing lawyers typically deal with inchoate mixtures of grievances, emotions, and justifications. Clients are usually clear about the heroes and villains in their disputes, but many of the other key facts are in doubt. Lacking a precise appellate record, attorneys typically work with, and must make decisions based on, witnesses with fallible memories and documents that are incomplete. In many situations, lawyers must rely heavily on experience and intuition to assess what a client's dispute is really about and how it may unfold in court.

The disputes that you encounter in practice will depend on the path you choose. If you become a transactional lawyer, you will help clients to evaluate and structure potential deals and then will be called on to negotiate terms that give them the greatest advantages and least possible risk. Clients will respect you for steering them away from conflict and will value your ability to bring disparate parties together into productive agreements and deal with the disagreements that are inevitable in any long-term relationship. Knowing when and how to use mediation to accomplish this will distinguish you as a lawyer.

If you become an inside counsel to a corporation or nonprofit organization, you will negotiate regularly as well, both with your counterparts in other entities and with colleagues in your own office. You may be surprised to learn that experienced corporate counsel operate not only as constant negotiators, but also at times as "mediators with a small 'm'." What this means is that many find that a major aspect of their work involves resolving disagreements and disputes between people within their organization. Inside lawyers often find that they in fact have multiple "clients," in the form of different personalities and constituencies within their company. Unless their constituencies can agree on a common course of action, it is very difficult for attorneys to produce a coherent legal policy or negotiate effectively with outsiders. Corporate lawyers thus often find themselves playing the role of honest broker, using mediative skills to forge a consensus among their multidimensional clients.

Even if you assume the traditional role of civil litigator, the disputing landscape you encounter will bear little resemblance to the case law in the typical law school textbook. First, clients seldom know the precise issue that must be resolved, the opposing arguments, or the remedies available to them. Second, most of the disputes that clients bring to litigators never become court cases. Good lawyers perform an important screening function, measuring their client's grievances against the requirements of the law and, perhaps even more critically, the client's larger interests.

Does the client have a viable legal theory? Will discovery produce factual evidence that supports his argument? Will the client be willing to persevere after his initial anger and frustration have died down, and does he have the resources to do so? Is it even in the client's long-term interest to be involved in litigation? Is a court likely to side with him, and, if it does, will the potential defendant be able to satisfy a judgment? Just as very few screenplays ever become movies, the large majority of potential legal cases fall by the wayside long before they reach a courtroom!

Indeed, the rate of trial in the United States is very small, and the absolute number of trials is declining. Of all civil cases filed in the federal court system, less than 2 percent actually reach trial. Trial rates in state courts are substantially higher, but in 2002 still averaged only 16 percent. Even allowing for cases that are decided without a trial, for example, through motions for summary judgment, *the large majority of civil cases are never adjudicated on the merits*. Indeed, professional legal groups, as well as scholars, are debating the causes and implications of what has come to be called "the vanishing trial" (see, e.g., Galanter, 2004; Lande, 2005).

There is an important qualification when considering the small percentage of disputes that are adjudicated. The possibility of going to trial has an impact on the decisions of litigants that is out of proportion to the actual frequency of courtroom decisions. The wish to avoid the "fire" of trial is a major factor in motivating parties to choose the "frying pan" of settlement. In other words, we bargain in the "shadow of the law" (Mnookin & Kornhauser, 1979). Decisions about whether, and on what terms, to settle a dispute are thus heavily influenced by predictions and concerns about what a court will do if an agreement is not reached.

B. How Disputes Arise

Where do legal disputes come from, and what determines whether a potential legal claim ever reaches a lawyer's desk? In the excerpt that follows, Professor Marc Galanter discusses how individual grievances may or may not ripen into disputes, and how only a small proportion of disputes ever become legal cases, in a process that he calls the "dispute pyramid."

❖ **Marc S. Galanter,** *Reading the Landscape of Disputes: What We Know and Don't Know (and Think We Know) About Our Allegedly Contentious and Litigious Society*

31 UCLA L. Rev. 4 (1983)

The Lower Layers: The Construction of Disputes

. . . Disputes are not discrete events like births or deaths; they are more like . . . illnesses and friendships, composed in part of the perceptions and understandings of those who participate in and observe them. Disputes are drawn from a vast sea of events, encounters, collisions, rivalries, disappointments, discomforts and injuries. The span and composition of that sea depend on the broad contours of social life. For example, the introduction of machinery brings increases in non-intentional injuries; higher population densities and cash crops bring raised expectations and rivalry for scarce land; advances in knowledge enlarge possibilities of control and expectations of care. Some things in this sea of "proto-disputes" become disputes through a process in which injuries are perceived, persons or institutions responsible for remedying them are identified, forums for presenting these claims are located and approached, claims are formulated acceptably to the forum, appropriate resources are invested, and attempts at diversion resisted. The disputes that arrive at courts can be seen as the survivors of a long and exhausting process. In this view, the arrival of matters at the doors of lawyers and courts is a late stage in an extended process by which the dispute has crystallized out of the sea of proto-disputes. . . .

We can visualize the early stages of the process as the successive layers of a vast and uneven pyramid. A pioneering inquiry by Felstiner, Abel and Sarat (1981) provides a useful conceptual map of these lower reaches. We begin, in effect, with all human experience which might be identified as injurious. This should alert us to the subjective and unstable character of the process, for what is injurious depends on current and ever-changing estimations of what enhances or impairs health, happiness, character and other desired states. Knowledge and ideology constantly send new currents through this vast ocean.

Some experiences will be perceived as injurious. (Felstiner et al. call these *perceived injurious experiences*.) Among these perceived injurious experiences, some may be seen as deserved punishment, some as the result of assumed risk or fickle fate[,] but a subset is viewed as violations of some right or entitlement caused by a human agent (individual or collective) and susceptible of remedy. These, in Felstiner's terminology[,] are *grievances*. Again, characterization of an event as a grievance will depend on the cognitive repertoire with which society supplies the injured person and his idiosyncratic adaptation of it. He may, for example, be liberally supplied with ideological lenses to focus blame or to diffuse it. When such grievances are voiced to the offending party they become *claims*. Many will be granted. Those claims not granted become *disputes*. That is, a dispute exists when a claim based on a grievance is rejected in whole or in part. Using this terminology lets us attempt a crude sketch of the lower layers of the pyramid.

First, a very large number of injuries go unperceived. Breaches of product warranties and professional malpractice may be difficult to recognize and go undiscovered. Even if the injury is discovered, the injured may not perceive that he has an entitlement that has been violated, the identity of the responsible party, or the presence of the remedy to be pursued. The perception of grievances requires cognitive resources. Thus [one study] found that both higher income and white households perceive more problems with the goods they buy and complain more both to sellers and to third parties than do poor or black households. It seems unlikely that this reflects differences in the quality of the goods purchased. Similarly, . . . better educated respondents experience more problems of infringement of their constitutional rights.

Even where injuries are perceived, a common response is resignation, that is, "lumping it." In the most comprehensive study available, Miller and Sarat (1981) report that over one-quarter of those with reported "middle range" (i.e., involving the equivalent of $1,000 or more[1]) grievances did not pursue the

---

1. [*Note:* The $1,000 threshold in the Miller and Sarat study would be roughly $2,480 today. To arrive at the current equivalent of the dollar numbers quoted in this reading, multiply by 2.5. — Eds.]

matter by making a claim. This proportion was fairly uniform across subject matters (with the striking exception of discrimination problems; almost three-quarters did not move from grievance to claim). Of course this figure is not a precise measure of the phenomen[on] of "lumping it" because it may include individuals who took other forms of unilateral action — like exit, avoidance or self-help. . . . Also, some populations have a higher proclivity for "lumping it": e.g., low income consumers. . . . "Lumping it" is done not only by naive victims who lack information about or access to remedies, but also by those who knowingly decide that the gain is too low, or the cost too high, including the psychic costs of pursuing the claim . . .

Exit and avoidance — withdrawal from a situation or relationship by moving, resigning, severing relations, etc. — are common responses to many kinds of troubles. Like "lumping it," exit is an alternative to invoking any kind of organized remedy system, although its presence as a sanction may support the working of other remedies. The use of "exit" options depends on a number of factors: on the availability of alternative opportunities or partners and information about them; on bearable costs of withdrawal, transfer, relocation, and development of new relationships; on the pull of loyalty to previous arrangements; and on the availability and cost of other remedies. Disputes are also pursued by various kinds of self-help such as physical retaliation, seizure of property, or removal of offending objects. The amount of self-help in contemporary industrial societies has not been mapped, but it evidently occurs very frequently. [S]tudies portray self-help as a major component of disputing in American neighborhoods.

The most typical response to grievances, at least to sizable ones, is to make a claim to the "other party" — the merchant, the other driver or his insurer, the ex-spouse who has not paid support, etc. Thus, Miller and Sarat found that over 70% of those who experienced "middle range" grievances made claims for redress. Aggrieved consumers make claims in about the same proportion. Some claims may be granted outright, but a large number are contested in whole or part. It is this contest that Felstiner labels a dispute. Miller and Sarat found that about two-thirds of claims lead to disputes. A large portion of disputes are resolved by negotiation between the parties. Almost half of the disputes in the Miller and Sarat survey ended in "agreement after difficulty" which I take as indicating the occurrence of negotiation. "Negotiation" ranges from that which is indistinguishable from the everyday adjustments that constitute the relationship to that which is "bracketed" as a disruption or emergency.

Some disputes are abandoned by their initiators. [A study that] coined the term "clumpit" for those who make a claim but don't persist, found that more than one-quarter of all consumers with problems abandoned their claims. Similarly, a study of medical malpractice claims found that 43% were dropped without receiving any payment.

Other disputes are heard by the school principal, the shop steward or the administrator — i.e., in forums that are part of the social setting within which the dispute arose. Such "embedded forums" range from those which are hardly distinguishable from the everyday decision making within an institution ("I'd like to see the manager") to those which are specially constituted to handle disputes which cannot be resolved by everyday processes. We know that such forums process a tremendous number of disputes. We have no count of them, but we do have some idea of the conditions under which they flourish. Resort to embedded forums is encouraged where there are continuing relations between the disputants. . . .

These data about disputing are taken from surveys of individuals or households. They tell us about the grievances, claims, and disputes of individuals in their non-business capacities (i.e., as householder, consumer, citizen, spouse, neighbor, etc.) but not in their business or professional lives. There are other disputants: businesses, organizations and units of government. We have an even dimmer picture of their patterns of disputing. . . .

The Upper Layers: Lawyers and Courts

The pyramid imagery imparts to the process of dispute construction and transformation a stability and a solidity that are illusory. Changes in perceptions of harm, in attributions of responsibility, in expectations of redress, in readiness to be assertive—all of these affect the number of grievances, claims and disputes. New activities, based on new technologies, and new knowledge may change notions of causal agency. Some parts of the pyramid are more solid than others. In matters like automobile accident claims and post-divorce disputes, there are many cues about how to perceive the problems: it is "common knowledge" how to proceed; social support for complaining is readily forthcoming; there are occupational specialists ready to receive the matter and pursue it on a routine and standardized basis. Other parts are more volatile and shifting.

We can imagine a frontier of perceived grievances moving over time. As the span of human control expands[,] so do attempts to extend accountability. Claims for compensation for rainfall from cloud seeding and "wrongful birth" claims are examples of the growing edges of the world of dispute, where the borders between fate, self-blame, and specific or shared human responsibility are blurred and disputed. These areas of blurring and contest are eventually resolved. But it should be noted that the area of recognized disputes contracts as well as expands. Claims may become subject to routine reimbursement and removed from the disputing process. Other sorts of claims may lose their standing, such as claims to honor or racial superiority, or claims to privacy by officials.

As we trace the movement of disputes up the pyramid and laterally from one forum to another, it is useful to recall that the dispute does not remain unchanged in the process. The disputes that come to courts originate elsewhere and may undergo considerable change in the course of entering and proceeding through the courts. Disputes must be reformulated in applicable legal categories. Such reformulation may restrict their scope. Diffuse disputes may become more focused in time and space, narrowed down to a set of discrete incidents involving specified individuals. Or, conversely, the original dispute may expand, becoming the vehicle for consideration of a larger set of events or relationships. The list of parties may grow or shrink; the range of normative claims may be narrowed or expanded; the remedy sought may change; the goals and audiences of the parties may alter. In short[,] the dispute that emerges in the court process may differ significantly from the dispute that arrived there, as well as from "similar" disputes that proceed through other settings.

Lawyers are often viewed as important agents of this transformation process. They help translate clients' disputes to fit into applicable legal categories. But lawyers may also act as gatekeepers, screening out claims that they are disinclined to pursue. [A Wisconsin study of the handling of consumer disputes] found that lawyers tended to defuse consumer claims, diverting them into mediative channels rather than translating them into adversary claims. Those disputes that are not resolved by negotiation or in some embedded forum may be taken to a champion or a forum external to the situation. Recourse to any such third party is relatively infrequent across the whole range of disputes. [A Milwaukee study] found that the proportion of problems that were taken to any third party was 3%. . . . As stakes increase, so does resort to third parties. . . . Yet for a very large portion of the population (47% of non-users; 40% of multiple users) lawyers are regarded as a last resort that should not be used until one has "exhausted every other possible way of solving the problem."

Some of those who consult lawyers, as well as a few who don't, get to court. Miller and Sarat report that about 11% of disputants (approximately 9% when those with post-divorce problems are excluded) took their middle range disputes to court. . . . In the mostly smaller consumer disputes . . . the use of courts virtually disappears. Overall, 9% of American adults report having had experience in a major civil court and 14% in a minor civil court. This includes parties, witnesses, jurors, and observers. . . .

There may be very little use of litigation to adjust relations among whole classes of major organizational actors such as large manufacturing corporations, financial institutions, educational and cultural institutions, political parties, etc. Macaulay found manufacturers reluctant to intrude litigation into relationships with their customers and suppliers. . . . Such potential suitors can afford, and are likely to make extensive use of, skilled professional help to channel their affairs so as to prevent trouble. Similarly, when trouble emerges, they are likely to be equipped to make sophisticated choices of alternatives to litigation to resolve difficulties through bargaining, mediation or arbitration. . . .

Like other kinds of remedy-seeking, litigation requires information and skills. Complaints to all third parties come disproportionately from the better educated, better informed and more politically active households. . . . In order to understand the distribution of litigation, we must go beyond the characteristics of individual parties to consider the relations between them. Are the parties strangers or intimates? Is their relationship episodic or enduring? Is it single-stranded or multiplex?

In the American setting, litigation tends to be between parties who are strangers. Either they never had a mutually beneficial continuing relationship, as in the typical automobile injury case, or their relationship — marital, commercial, or organizational — is ruptured. In either case, there is no anticipated future relationship. In the American setting, unlike some others, resort to litigation is viewed as an irreparable breach of the relationship. However, where parties are locked into a relationship with no chance of exit, such as divorced parents, or inmates and institutional managers, litigation may proceed side-by-side with the continuation of that relationship . . .

The Litigation Process: Attrition, Routine Processing, Bargaining and Settlement

Of those disputes which are taken to court, the vast majority are disposed of by abandonment, withdrawal, or settlement, without full-blown adjudication and often without any authoritative disposition by the court. In fact, of those cases that do reach a full authoritative disposition by a court, a large portion does not involve a contest. They are uncontested either because the dispute has been resolved, as in divorce, or because only one party appears. Over 30% of cases in American courts of general jurisdiction are not formally contested. This predominance of uncontested matters in American courts is longstanding.

Many cases are withdrawn or abandoned because the mere invocation of the court served the initiator's purpose of harassment, warning or delay. . . . The official system may be invoked, or invocation may be threatened, in order to punish or harass, to demonstrate prowess, to force an opponent to settle, or to secure compliance with the decision of another forum. The master pattern of American disputing is one in which there is actual or threatened invocation of an authoritative decision maker. This is countered by a threat of protracted or hard-fought resistance, leading to a negotiated or mediated settlement, often in the anteroom of the adjudicative institution.

Questions

1. Have you ever been asked by a family member, friend, or neighbor to give advice about a potential legal claim? Did you see a legal issue? What advice did you give, and what did your "client" do?
2. Can you think of an example of a situation in which someone might suffer a legal injury but not realize that he has been injured?
3. Can you think of a situation in which someone realizes that he has been injured but cannot identify the perpetrator? Or knows that he has a potential claim and can identify the likely defendant, but nevertheless decides to "lump it"?
4. Do you know of situations in which a case appears to have been brought for a purpose other than obtaining a court judgment? What was the apparent purpose?
5. During your childhood, how did your family deal with conflict? Do you think that your upbringing has in any way influenced your own instinctive response to disputes? In what ways?

C. The Spectrum of Dispute Resolution Options

Assuming a dispute develops far enough to reach your desk as a practicing lawyer, what options will you have to deal with it? In fact, attorneys can use a variety of processes to achieve their clients' goals. The most common options fall along a spectrum that appears in Figure 1. At one end is direct negotiation, at the other a court trial.

Figure 1.
Dispute Resolution Spectrum

Nonbinding outcomes			Binding outcomes	
Negotiation	**Mediation**	**Settlement Conference**	**Arbitration**	**Trial**

←————————————————————————————————————→

Maximum process control   Minimum process control

Negotiation and trial are polar opposites. Parties who opt for trial have relatively little control over either the process or the outcome: The proceeding is a formal and public one, conducted under detailed procedural and evidentiary rules, with a judge in control. A third party — either a judge or jury — decides the outcome and in doing so is bound to follow established legal principles. By contrast, the process at the other end of the spectrum — negotiation — gives parties maximum control over both the process and its outcome. Direct bargaining is an informal process, generally conducted in private and without set rules. Parties are free to agree to whatever outcomes they wish, subject to the limits of contract law and public policy if they seek to enforce their agreement.

In between direct negotiation and trial is a continuum of alternative dispute resolution (ADR) processes. The continuum moves from processes that have characteristics very similar to negotiation to ones that closely resemble a trial. Mediators, for example, assist negotiators in reaching a settlement but do not have the power to require disputants to reach agreement or to impose a decision on them. For that reason, mediation is on the nonbinding side of the spectrum. Judicial settlement conferences are also nonbinding, but as conducted by some judicial officers they take on a coercive, "arm-twisting" tone that makes them less than completely voluntary. Other processes, such as neutral evaluation, are also available but have become less popular than mediation in recent years.

On the other side of the divide are binding processes. In arbitration, a third-party neutral has the power to decide the outcome over the objection of a party, in essence acting as a private judge. Arbitration permits more party control than a trial, however, because the parties must agree to enter the process and can, within very broad bounds, specify the procedure the arbitrator will follow and the substantive standards on which she will base her decision. Once parties have agreed to arbitrate, however, the arbitrator's decision is fully binding.

There are several other ADR processes that could be put on the nonbinding side of this spectrum, carrying names such as "early neutral evaluation" and "mini-trial." The variety of nonbinding processes is nearly infinite, limited only by what the parties can create, agree upon, and afford. However, mediation has become by far the most popular nonbinding process aside from direct negotiation, and it is the one on which we focus in this book.

D. Conclusion

Given that lawyers have several options for dispute resolution, the challenge is to select the right approach for a particular client's problem and then to use that process effectively. Each ADR process has particular strengths and weaknesses.

Litigation culminating in a trial is still the forum of choice when it is important to know what happened — the availability of evidentiary discovery and examination of witnesses at trial are designed to find historical truth. Adjudication can provide a party with a court order to enforce a financial obligation or compel specific performance of an agreement. Judicial decisions can establish precedent, nurture the growth of the common law, and shape rules of conduct for the future. Lawsuits may also establish social values or rally people behind a principle or a cause. Finally, the litigation process can be used strategically to create the conditions for successful negotiation. Of course, the irony is that most of these advantages are potentially a two-way street: Each reason for you to pursue litigation can also be a reason for your opponent to do so. The ultimate curse may be to have a case in which both your client and the other side are sure that they are right and determined to persevere!

Mediation is a more appropriate choice when potential litigation costs are high relative to the amount in controversy, one or both parties cannot bear the risk of an adverse result, or the dispute is time sensitive. It is also likely to be appealing when standard adjudication remedies do not meet the disputants' real needs, the parties want a voice in shaping the final outcome, or confidentiality is a significant consideration. Given the rapidly shrinking number of trials and changes in the legal culture supporting ADR, you are much more likely to represent clients in mediation than at trial. Indeed, an increasing number of lawyers now say that they settle more cases through mediation than through direct negotiation. For that reason, understanding the mediation process, and how to use it effectively on behalf of clients, is important for you, whatever path your career may take.

The most direct and inexpensive path to resolving a dispute, however, remains negotiation, and mediation itself is in essence a process of assisted negotiation. Bargaining is therefore a lawyer's first option for dispute resolution and will form the foundation for our study of mediation. The next two chapters examine the process of negotiation.

CHAPTER

2

Negotiator Styles

A. Competitive and Cooperative Negotiation

We each have our own approach of how to get what we want. So it is with negotiation. Our negotiation approach or style is rooted in our values, assumptions, experiences, goals, and the situation. Even though you may have a general style, you may change your approach to a negotiation based on the specifics and the needs of your client. Many terms are used to describe different negotiating styles in a range from hard to soft. For purposes of introducing the approaches and distinguishing them, we use here two basic categories: competitive and cooperative.

Consider the following example of two different approaches applied to an intellectual property claim at different stages in the dispute.

MICROSOFT V. STAC

Stac Electronics was an engineering company founded in 1983 by seven friends at Caltech. The company developed its "Stacker" disc compression software in 1990. Bill Gates, CEO of Microsoft, wanted Stac's data compression technology and met personally with Stac's president, Gary Clow, to discuss licensing of Stac's software. The negotiations were turned over to other Microsoft executives and lawyers to negotiate. Although willing to pay Stac a modest gross license fee, Microsoft refused to pay Stac any per-user royalty for its patented compression technology. Microsoft took a hard line, saying that it could have other sources develop reliable data compression technology that could be incorporated into the MS-DOS operating system, which would have an immediate and adverse effect on the viability of Stacker and threaten Stac's continued economic viability. Microsoft had a reputation of using its huge market share and resources to negotiate in a hard fashion and favorably license software that it incorporated into its products. Negotiations broke off, and in 1993, Microsoft released MS-DOS 6.0, which included a disk compression program called Double Space. Stac was outraged, as Microsoft had previously examined the Stacker code as part of the due diligence process in their earlier negotiations and Stac believed that Microsoft infringed its patent.

Microsoft would not budge on Stac's claim, and Stac filed a patent infringement suit against Microsoft. Microsoft counterclaimed that Stac had misappropriated the Microsoft trade secret of a preloading feature that was included in Stacker 3.1. In 1994, a federal court jury in California awarded Stac $120 million in compensatory damages, coming to about $5.50 per copy of MS-DOS 6.0 that had been sold. The jury also concluded that Stac misappropriated Microsoft's trade secret and simultaneously awarded Microsoft $13.6 million on the counterclaim.

Feelings on both sides were negative and intense. Mr. Clow appeared on CBS's *Eye to Eye with Connie Chung* and described his negotiations against Microsoft Chairman Bill Gates as "like a knife fight." Bill Gates, the subject of a profile on the show, walked out of an interview when Ms. Chung asked him about Mr. Clow's charges.

A new round of negotiations commenced in the changed circumstances of the jury verdict. Both sides had the option of legal appeals over the jury verdicts. Instead, their lawyers negotiated in a more cooperative manner and created a deal that caught Wall Street off guard, favorably affecting the share price of both companies. Each side agreed to drop its claims in exchange for cross-licensing all of their existing patents, as well as future ones over the next five years. The pact called for Microsoft to pay Stac license royalties totaling $43 million over 43 months, while also investing $39.9 million for a 15 percent equity stake in Stac. The total $82.9 million outlay represented a gain for Microsoft, which had already charged off $120 million for the jury award in its fiscal third quarter and now was able to credit much of the difference in the current period. Stac also came out ahead, by getting a significant cash infusion without a long appeals process to collect money from Microsoft. Mr. Clow said that $82.9 million being turned over by Microsoft represented more than Stac would have gotten had the $120 million been paid, because income taxes and Stac's own $13.6 million penalty would have whittled the final amount to about $64 million. In addition, Stac formed an alliance with the most powerful player in the software industry. Mr. Clow stated that, "this is not personal. This makes good business sense going forward. . . . This demonstrates it is possible to do win-win deals." Microsoft's executives concurred. "This is a lot more fun than disagreeing," said Michael Brown, Microsoft's vice president of finance, referring to the more cooperative final round of negotiation.

Bill Gates became the richest man in the world by being smart, diligent, and keenly competitive. As a negotiator, he is known for being aggressive and competitive, although there are accounts of him using his considerable creative skills to negotiate value-added cooperative outcomes. In the above example, Gates played hardball when he first negotiated with Stac's Clow because he thought it was to the advantage of Microsoft. That competitive approach, which in the past had served Microsoft's interest, backfired. Gates then changed his approach, having his lawyers negotiate a cooperative deal going forward. Although the competitive and cooperative approaches are treated as separate negotiation models, a skilled negotiator may at times employ one or the other, depending on assessment of the circumstances and goals. As we will see, your choice may also be a matter of your personal style.

The *competitive* approach assumes that the purpose of bargaining is to obtain the best possible economic result for your client, usually at the expense of the other side. A competitive bargainer is likely to think that negotiation involves a limited resource or fund that must be distributed between competing parties — in effect, a fixed economic "pie." In a competitive approach, the parties' relationships and other intangibles are not of primary importance. The competitive bargainer's goal is to pay as little as possible (if a buyer or defendant) or obtain as much as possible (if a seller or plaintiff), as a dollar more for your opponent is necessarily a dollar less for you. A competitive bargainer, in other words, sees negotiation much as a litigator sees a trial: Someone must win and someone must lose, and her central mission is to win. This approach is also known as "distributive" or "zero-sum" bargaining, because the negotiators see their task as distributing a fixed, limited resource between them.

A simple example of where competitive bargaining is likely to occur is when a lawyer negotiates with an insurance adjuster in a distant city to settle a client's claim for property damage to a car caused by a falling tree limb. The client, we will assume, has since changed insurance companies, and the lawyer does not expect to do business with this adjuster again, so neither sees any interest in nurturing a relationship. In this situation both sides have a limited joint interest in conducting the bargaining process efficiently. Both the lawyer and the adjuster are likely to see their sole goal as agreeing on a dollar amount that the company will pay the insured to give up his claim, and to assume that a better settlement for one will necessarily be worse for the other.

In this negotiation, each side may posture about the dimensions of the issue or conflict, make a specific proposal to resolve the dispute, and bargain over that proposal. A competitive negotiator will attempt to persuade the other side that its case is weaker and worth less than it thought and that her case is stronger than it previously recognized. Incremental concessions are usually made, which narrow the bargaining range. Finally, a compromise settlement may be agreed upon. This approach to negotiation centers on predetermined positions and maximizing individual gain.

A *cooperative* bargainer, by contrast, does not view negotiation "pies" as fixed. Cooperative bargainers work to identify interests and examine differences in how the parties value items. They then search jointly with the other negotiator — viewed more as a partner than an opponent — for a solution that will best satisfy both parties' interests. Cooperative negotiation is marked by an effort to understand one another's perceptions and arrive at a mutually acceptable valuation. This cooperative approach is frequently called "integrative" bargaining, because it emphasizes integrating the parties' needs to find the best joint solution. It is also referred to as "interest-based" negotiation because it sees the goal of bargaining as satisfying people's underlying interests.

Rather than moving from positions to counter-positions to a compromise settlement, cooperative negotiators search for a variety of alternatives that optimize the interests that they have prioritized. The parties can then create an outcome from a combination of generated options so that a joint decision, with more benefits to all, is achieved. This collaborative approach does not necessarily produce a simple compromise between competing positions. It seeks a creative settlement not bound by predetermined positions.

A classic situation that calls for cooperative bargaining is an effort by two businesses to form a joint venture. Cooperative bargainers would first ask what special resources and capabilities each partner could bring to the deal (for example, does Partner A have special expertise in marketing, whereas Partner B has more strength in design? Does one have good access to financing, whereas the other has open office space?). The negotiators would also ask whether either partner had particular needs, for example, one for an assured stream of income and the other for cutting-edge technology. Cooperative bargainers would focus on finding terms that best exploited each partner's abilities and minimized weaknesses, creating the strongest possible future partnership.

Cooperative and competitive bargaining are not mutually exclusive. Working to "bake" the biggest possible "pie" does not, in itself, say anything about how the final pie will be divided. Savvy competitive negotiators, for example, will look earnestly for ways to "expand the pie." Competitors, however, are likely to see expanding the pie as less important than getting the largest possible piece for their clients. Cooperative bargainers must also face the pie-dividing problem, but tend to give it less significance than competitors. In the joint venture example described above, cooperatives would emphasize creating the best possible deal. They would then look for a principle for dividing the benefits (that is, the "pie") that both partners saw as fair, rather than trying to outfox their partner to get the lion's share.

In practice, cooperative and competitive approaches may be mixed or sequenced, depending on the setting, subject matter, and personalities of the negotiators. However, descriptions of cooperative and competitive styles, as well as distinctions between these two approaches, provide a paradigm for understanding the dynamics of negotiation.

There are styles of negotiating that go beyond either cooperative or competitive, which might be seen as more intense versions of each approach. Those competitive negotiators whom we label *adversarial* bargainers view negotiation as a kind of war and believe that all is fair in winning it. Extreme adversarial bargainers may be willing to renege on tentative agreements, misrepresent their authority, make empty threats, and distort facts that cannot easily be checked or challenged if such tactics seem likely to win them a better outcome.

By contrast, *problem-solving* bargainers employ intensely cooperative, interest-based tactics. Problem solvers focus almost exclusively on finding solutions that maximize the value of the deal for both parties. Problem solvers are extremely reluctant to obtain a better outcome for their client at the expense of their counterpart and insist on using genuinely neutral principles to accomplish the task of allocating benefits.

For simplicity, we follow the convention of referring to bargaining styles as *competitive* and *cooperative*, but we also separately discuss adversarial and problem-solving techniques. The distinctions between adversarial and competitive styles on the one hand, and cooperative and problem-solving styles (both used interchangeably) on the other, are not always clear. We examine below the underpinnings of the contrasting negotiation approaches and some of the strategies and tactics associated with each.

1. Competitive/Adversarial Approach

❖ **Gary Goodpaster, *A Primer on Competitive Bargaining***

J. Disp. Resol. 325 (1996)

One cannot understand negotiation without understanding competitive behavior in negotiation. It is not that competing is a good way to negotiate; it may or may not be, depending on the circumstances. Understanding competition in negotiation is important simply because many people do compete when they negotiate, either by choice or happenstance. . . .

Competitive Negotiation Strategy

In competitive negotiation or distributive bargaining, the parties' actual or perceived respective aims or goals conflict. In this context, the negotiator's aim is to maximize the realization of its goals. Since the goals conflict, either in fact or supposition, one party's gains are the other party's losses. Therefore, a negotiator's goal is to win by gaining as much value as possible from the other party. . . . Not only is the competitive negotiator out to gain as much as he or she can, but he or she will take risks, even the risk of non-agreement, to secure a significant gain.

The competitive negotiator adopts a risky strategy which involves the taking of firm, almost extreme positions, making few and small concessions, and withholding information that may be useful to the other party. The intention, and hoped-for effect, behind this basic strategy is to persuade the other party that it must make concessions if it is to get an agreement. In addition to this basic strategy, competitive negotiators may also use various ploys or tactics aimed at pressuring, unsettling, unbalancing or even misleading the other party to secure an agreement with its demands.

In an important sense, the competitive negotiator plays negotiation as an information game. In this game, the object is to get as much information from the other party as possible while disclosing as little information as possible. Alternatively, a competitive negotiator sometimes provides the other party with misleading clues, bluffs, and ambiguous assertions with multiple meanings, which are not actually false, but nevertheless mislead the other party into drawing incorrect conclusions that are beneficial to the competitor.

The information the competitive negotiator seeks is the other party's bottom line. How much he will maximally give or minimally accept to make a deal. On the other hand, the competitive negotiator wants to persuade the other side about the firmness of the negotiator's own asserted bottom line. The competitive negotiator works to convince the other party that it will settle only at some point that is higher (or lower, as the case may be) than its actual and unrevealed bottom line.

In skillful hands the bargaining position performs a double function. It conceals, and it reveals. The bargaining position is used to indicate — to unfold gradually, step by step — the maximum expectation of the negotiator, while at the same time concealing, for as long as necessary, his minimum expectation.

By indirect means, such as the manner and timing of the changes in your bargaining position, you, as a negotiator, try to convince the other side that your maximum expectation is really your minimum breaking-off point. . . . Since you have taken an appropriate bargaining position at the start of negotiations, each change in your position should give ever-clearer indications of your maximum expectation. Also, each change should be designed to encourage or pressure the other side to reciprocate with at least as much information as you give them, if not more.

Taking a firm position and conceding little will incline the other party to think the competitor has little to give. Thus, if there is to be a deal, then the other party must give or concede more.

1. Pure Bargaining, Haggling, and Just Trading Figures

When the parties are apart and have no reason, other than their mutual choice, to settle at any particular point between them, they are in a "pure bargaining" situation. It is easy to see how the simple negotiation game. . . can degenerate into a contest of haggling or just trading figures. The parties' positions — the particular dollar figures they are offering — are not connected to any reason or rationale. Basically, both buyer and seller are seeking to maximize gains. Each attempts to accomplish this by seeing how far the other party can be pushed.

Often this happens in competitive bargaining, particularly with unsophisticated competitive bargainers and usually in the late and ending stages of a negotiation. When it occurs, the "take as much as you can" grab is transparent and signals that the parties, or at least one party, is bargaining just to win as much as possible. Automobile dealers' sales practices exemplify this phenomenon. A new car dealer usually pegs an asking price to a manufacturer's suggested retail sticker price and to items the dealer adds to the car. Once those starting prices are left behind, the dealer and buyer usually just trade dollar figures until they reach one they are both comfortable with. Similarly, travelers who visit native markets or bazaars, or those who visit flea markets or garage sales in this country, sometimes experience much the same kind of trading. Offers and counteroffers are thrown back and forth, each party testing the other party's resolve to stick with a figure by refusing to budge further or threatening to walk away. In essence, bargaining in this fashion is really nothing but a contest of firmness or a game of chicken.

2. Focal Points or Mutually Prominent Alternatives

It is revealing to analyze a pure bargaining situation where two equally competitive negotiators bargain with each other. Once the bargaining parties have assured their bottom lines or reservation values and have staked out their respective positions on the bargaining range, nothing inherently seems to impel settlement at any particular point between the positions, except each party's expectations regarding what the other side in fact will accept. This is problematic, however, for with each guided by expectations and knowing that the other is too, expectations become compounded. A bargain is struck when somebody makes a final, sufficient concession. Why does he concede? Because he thinks the other will not. "I must concede because he won't. He won't because he thinks I will. He thinks I will because he thinks I think he thinks so. . . ." There is some range of alternative outcomes in which any point is better for both sides than no agreement at all. To insist on any such point is pure bargaining, since one always would take less rather than reach no agreement at all, and since one always can recede if retreat proves necessary to agreement. Yet if both parties are aware of the limits to this range, any outcome is a point from which at least one party would have been willing to retreat and the other knows it!. . .

Because people bargain competitively for various reasons, negotiators and mediators need to understand competition in negotiation in order to respond appropriately. Some people bargain competitively without giving much conscious attention to the matter. Others compete in response to the other party's competitive behavior. In this response, they follow the common pattern that a particular kind of behavior elicits a similar behavior in response. In other words, one party frames the negotiation as a contest, and the other party picks up the competitive cues and behaves accordingly. Further, people naturally incline to competitive bargaining when they are non-trusting. In such situations, in order to avoid putting themselves at risk, non-trusting people act guardedly and adopt elements of the competitive strategy, for example, withholding information or misrepresenting a position. Finally, one can readily imagine ambiguous bargaining situations, in which at least one party is non-trusting, quickly devolving into a competitive negotiation between both parties. The non-trusting party acts defensively, and the other party senses this as competitive behavior and, therefore, acts in a similar fashion.

Negotiators, however, can also consciously adopt a competitive strategy. Negotiators are most likely to compete purposefully when:

- the parties have an adversarial relationship;
- a negotiator has a bargaining power advantage and can dominate the situation;
- a negotiator perceives an opportunity for gain at the expense of the other party;
- the other party appears susceptible to competitive tactics;
- the negotiator is defending against competitive moves; or
- there is no concern for the future relationship between the parties.

This list suggests that competitive bargaining most likely occurs in situations such as labor and lawsuit negotiations, insurance and similar claims type settlements, and in one-time transactions between a relatively experienced party and a relatively inexperienced party. One would, for example, expect to see it in sales transactions where the parties will probably not see each other again.

Representative bargaining or bargaining for a constituency may also prompt competitive bargaining even when there will be future negotiations between equally sophisticated parties. The negotiator's accountability may override relationship concerns and reasons for cooperation. The concerned audience, consisting of a client, constituency, coalition partner, or other phantom party at the table, is, in effect, looking over the negotiator's shoulder. The negotiator, therefore, takes positions and makes moves she believes her client either expects or would approve. International negotiations between countries, union-management, lawsuit negotiations, and negotiations between different parties in interest-group coalition negotiations sometimes evidence this pattern.

Aside from circumstantial or situational pressures, there are some parties who bargain competitively because they believe that is the way to conduct business. There are also parties who are simply predisposed to bargain competitively and will incline to do so opportunistically in any bargaining situation if possible.

Finally, it is important to note that one can bargain competitively in a negotiation on some issues and cooperatively on others. In other words, a negotiator can selectively use competitive strategy or tactics on particular issues, while using a cooperative or problem-solving strategy on other issues. In such a case, extracting gain competitively may not greatly endanger future relationships. . . .

Obviously, competitive bargaining covers a continuum of behaviors from the simplest, unreflective adversarial actions to highly conscious and virtually scripted contests. As such, competitive bargaining moves are natural responses in some negotiation situations and advantageous or profitable actions in others. . . .

Questions

1. What are the advantages of adopting a competitive approach to bargaining?
2. What are the downsides of competitive bargaining?
3. Have you experienced competitive negotiation? What were the circumstances?

We turn now to a more aggressive form of competitive negotiation, which we refer to as *adversarial*. There is no shortage of advice about how to be a tough bargainer and how to get what you want in a negotiation. Check the self-help and business advice sections of large booksellers and you will find an array of titles on this subject, including *Guerrilla Negotiating* (1999). Although adversarial negotiation may at times be advantageous, many of these guides appear to assume that the opposing side is ignorant or gullible and will have no future opportunity to retaliate. Other books and articles catalog "hardball" tactics to warn you of what you might encounter. These writings are premised on the theory that "forewarned is forearmed." Roger Dawson, the author of *Secrets of Power Negotiating* (2001), challenges the myth of cooperative "win-win" negotiation before sharing his adversarial secrets and what you need to watch out for so you do not become the victim of others' tough moves. His list of power negotiating gambits includes the following:

- *Ask for more than you expect to get:* You can get away with an outrageous opening position if you imply some flexibility.
- *Never say yes to the first offer:* Saying yes triggers two thoughts in the other person's mind: "I could have done better," and "something must be wrong."
- *Flinch at proposals:* The other side may not expect to get what is asked for; however, if you do not show surprise you're communicating that it is a possibility.
- *Always play reluctant seller:* This is a great way to squeeze the other side's negotiating range before the negotiation even starts.
- *Use the vise technique:* "You'll have to do better than that."
- *Don't let the other side know you have the authority to make a decision:* Don't let the other person trick you into admitting that you have authority.
- *Don't fall into the trap of thinking that splitting the difference is the fair thing to do:* Splitting the difference doesn't mean down the middle, because you can do it more than once.

- *Always ask for a trade-off:* Any time the other side asks you for a concession, ask for something in return.
- *Good guy/bad guy:* It's an effective way of putting more pressure on the other person without creating confrontation.
- *Nibbling:* Using the nibbling gambit, you can get a little bit more even after you have agreed on everything.
- *Taper concessions:* Taper concessions to communicate that the other side is getting the best possible deal.
- *Withdrawing an offer:* You can do it by backing off your last price concession or by withdrawing an offer to include freight, installation, and so on.
- *The decoy:* Use a decoy to take attention away from the real issue in the negotiation.
- *Red herring:* This is a phony demand that can be withdrawn, but only in exchange for a concession.
- *Cherry picking:* Ask for alternatives and then pick the best parts from multiple choices.
- *Escalation:* Raising demands after both sides reach an agreement.
- *Time pressure:* The rule in negotiating is that 80 percent of the concessions occur in the last 20 percent of time available.
- *Being prepared to walk away:* Project to the other side that you will walk away from the negotiations if you can't get what you want.
- *The fait accompli:* This occurs when one negotiator simply assumes the other will accept an assumed settlement rather than go to the trouble of reopening the negotiations.
- *Ultimatums:* Ultimatums are very high-profile statements that tend to strike fear into inexperienced negotiators.

Questions

4. Do any of these tactics seem unethical? Negotiation presents a fertile area for ethical transgressions, with relatively little guidance as to ethical limits.
5. Is there a difference between hard, competitive negotiation and "dirty" bargaining tricks? If so, how would you distinguish them?
6. Are there any gambits or techniques that you could add to Dawson's list?
7. If the tactics listed by Dawson were used against you, what would you do? If any of these behaviors did produce an adverse result for your client, what would be your approach the next time you found yourself matched against this opponent?

Note: Responses to Competitive Hardball and Difficult People

Some of the books and articles cataloging competitive negotiation tactics also prescribe competitive antidotes that can be used in response. Most of these reactive "hardball" tactics are either responses in kind or intended to notch up the positioning in a dance of "one-upmanship." The most effective counter-move or response to sharp competitive tactics will depend on the context of the negotiation, your relationship with the other negotiator, your alternatives to continued negotiation, the strength of your own position, your goals in the negotiation, and the information available to you. The key to any effective response is being able to recognize aggressive and deceptive tactics and understanding their potential effect in distorting your perspective and masking the opposition's weaknesses.

There are alternatives to responding in kind to hardball tactics or ending the negotiation. The behavior can be recognized and labeled for what it is and then dismissed by making light of it, or you can just ignore it. You make it clear that the tactic is not working and is interfering with either of you getting what you want and that it will not be tolerated. In effect, you can discuss and set ground rules for further negotiations. Hardball tactics are most commonly used in the absence of an ongoing relationship or friendship. Taking time to become friendlier before the bargaining begins or emphasizing the likely continuing contact or repeat plays following this negotiation might discourage hardball tactics — or it might not.

The subject of responding to aggressive moves is related more generally to how we can best negotiate with people we consider difficult. Seminars and training programs are frequently offered to help us deal with "difficult people." The proliferation of these programs, including ones offered for attorneys, reflects the commonly experienced frustration most of us have had in trying to work or negotiate with others whom we perceive as being insensitive, obstinate, selfish, overly competitive, or generally unreasonable. It is an interesting paradox that experience with difficult people should be so common when few, if any, of us view ourselves as being difficult. Do you think the people you consider difficult believe themselves to be so? Studies show that opponents usually see us as more demanding and less reasonable than we view ourselves (Thomas & Pondy 1977).

William Ury, in his book *Getting Past No: Negotiating with Difficult People* (1991), outlines problem behavior from difficult people and offers five easy-to-remember counter-tactics, to which we have added our summary of his advice:

Stage One: Don't React — Go to the Balcony. This means controlling your own behavior and distancing yourself from your natural impulses and emotions. Become an observer of an opponent's bad behavior rather than being sucked into the game.

Stage Two: Disarm Them — Step to Their Side. Don't fight your opponent, join him. Defuse anger, fear, and suspicion. Feel his pain and empathize, without agreeing to his demands or conceding.

Stage Three: Change the Game — Don't Reject . . . Reframe. Ask questions to figure out what motivates the difficult behavior. Reshape the negotiation to address the issue you want to resolve and the direction you want it to move.

Stage Four: Make It Easy to Say Yes — Build Them a Golden Bridge. Make your devised outcome the opponent's idea, involve him in the solution, and help him "save face" and look good. Act more like a mediator than an adversary.

Stage Five: Make It Hard to Say No — Bring Them to Their Senses, Not Their Knees. Now that you have made it easy for the opponent to say yes, educate him so it is difficult to say no. Make it clear that his alternatives are worse than what you are offering.

2. Cooperative/Problem-Solving Approach

Cooperative or collaborative negotiation involves parties making an effort to meet each others' needs and satisfy interests. Roger Fisher, William Ury, and Bruce Patton's best-selling book *Getting to Yes* suggests that "you can change the game," so that negotiation is not positional or competitive. It prescribes an interest-based approach, with suggested tactics and the use of objective criteria for joint decisions that is referred to as "principled" negotiation or "negotiation on the merits." *Getting to Yes* is recommended reading in many courses and training classes, so you may be familiar with it. The five basic elements of principled negotiation listed in it are:

1. *Separate the people from the problem.* The negotiators should focus on attacking the problem posed by the negotiations, not each other.
2. *Focus on interests, not positions.* Distinguish positions, which are what you say you want, from interests, which are why you want it. Look for mutual or complementary interests that will make agreement possible.
3. *Invent options for mutual gain.* Even if the parties' interests differ, there may be bargaining outcomes that will advance the interests of both. The story is told of two sisters who are trying to decide which of them should get the only orange in the house. Once they realize that one sister wants to squeeze the orange for its juice, and the other wants to grate the rind to flavor a cake, a "win-win" agreement that furthers the interests of each becomes apparent.
4. *Insist on objective criteria.* Not all disputes and negotiations lend themselves to such an outcome. An insurance claim for damage to a car may create such a dispute, as each dollar paid by the insurance company is one dollar less for it. (Bargaining about issues of this nature is generally referred to as "zero-sum" bargaining.) The suggestion is that parties first attempt to agree on objective criteria to determine the outcome. Thus, instead of negotiating over the value of a car, parties might agree that the standard "blue book" price will determine the amount. "Commit yourself to reaching a solution based on principle, not pressure."
5. *Know your Best Alternative to a Negotiated Agreement (BATNA).* The reason you negotiate with someone is to produce better results than you could obtain without negotiating. If you do not think about the best result you are likely to obtain without negotiating, you might accept an offer you should reject or might reject an offer better than you can otherwise get. Your BATNA is the measure of whether you are better off agreeing to a negotiated outcome or pursuing your alternatives, whether it be a trial or a deal with someone else. Your BATNA is the basis of comparison to protect you from bad negotiating decisions.

Note: Positions vs. Interests

The central theme of cooperative negotiation is that the negotiators focus on the parties' underlying interests rather than on the positions they take. Interest-based bargainers begin with the assumption that a party's position is simply one way (and often not the most efficient or effective one) to satisfy a need or interest. In most disputes parties have multiple interests of varying intensities. *Getting to Yes* explains interests in terms of basic human needs, including security, economic well-being, a sense of belonging, recognition, and control over one's life. These needs or interests can be further explained as follows:

- *Process interests.* People have a "process" interest in having disagreements resolved in a manner they consider fair. This usually includes the opportunity to tell their story and have the feeling that they have been understood. A cooperative negotiator will sometimes address an opponent's process interest by listening quietly while he vents angry emotions, then demonstrating, for example, by summarizing what has been said, that while the listener does not agree with what the speaker has said, he has heard and made an effort to understand it — so-called active listening ("So if I understand you correctly, you believe that . . ."). Participants may also have an interest in having a negotiation proceed in an orderly and predictable way.
- *Personal interests.* Most people have a personal interest in feeling respected in their work and as human beings, and in being seen as acting consistently with what they have said in the past and in accordance with their moral standards. Negotiators might address these personal interests by treating everyone courteously and attending to "face saving" needs.
- *Relational interests.* The parties might also have an interest in preserving or creating an ongoing relationship. This is particularly true in contractual disputes, because the very existence of a contract indicates that the parties once saw a benefit in working together, but it can also be true in disputes that arise from less formal connections. Examples of situations with relational interests include divorce and child custody disputes, land use controversies between neighbors, workplace disputes, and disagreements between companies and longtime customers.
- *Economic interests.* Disputants usually have economic or substantive interests. This is where most negotiations begin and where many end unsuccessfully because interests are not addressed. Economic interests are most easy to state in the form of monetary demands and offers. These positions may be misleading because people seek money to satisfy other needs, whether material, social, or emotional. Finding out what needs money will satisfy is essential to fashioning an interest-based agreement or integrative outcome.

Fisher, Ury, and Patton recognize that it is not always easy in negotiations to identify interests, as distinguished from positions. The technique they recommend is to ask "Why?" Why do you want a particular outcome, and why does the other side take the position it does? Do not ask the person with whom you are negotiating "Why?" to seek justification of his position or challenge it, "but for an understanding of the needs, hopes, fears, or desires that it serves." If you understand why a person wants what he is insisting upon, you can better explore how his interests can be met so you can get from him what you need.

A variation of the cooperative approach, or perhaps another label for it, is *problem solving*. Problem-solving negotiators employ intensely cooperative, interest-based tactics. Problem solvers focus almost exclusively on finding solutions that will maximize the value of the deal for both parties. Problem solvers do not want to obtain a better outcome for their client at the expense of their counterpart and insist on using genuinely neutral principles to accomplish the task of allocating benefits. Negotiation is viewed as a collaboration to find opportunities for creating value through complementary interests.

Questions

8. Have you experienced situations in which you were open and cooperative initially and then felt that you might have revealed too much or been too accommodating, so that you did not get what you wanted for yourself? If you were in that same situation again, would you behave differently? What are the trade-offs?

9. Does an attorney's reputation for openness and cooperation present a particular attraction to a client willing to pay a premium for that attorney to engage in "hard bargaining" or sharp tactics on his behalf? (For an interesting real-life example, see David McKean and Douglas Frantz's *Friends in High Places: The Rise and Fall of Clark Clifford*, 1995.)

10. Can "problem-solving" negotiation occur if only one side wants to pursue this approach?

B. The Tension Between Creating Value and Claiming Value

Distributional bargaining occurs when a single, quantitative issue is being negotiated or all apparent possibilities of joint gain have been exhausted. Negotiation by a tourist over the cash price of an item from a transient merchant at a bazaar is a simple example of a zero-sum distributional game, in which a dollar more for the seller is a dollar less for the purchaser and no future relationship is anticipated. Where the possibility exists to go beyond a zero-sum situation and create additional value, such as in the Microsoft-Stac dispute reported earlier, the negotiation becomes more complex and tactical choices must be made.

The next reading, from an influential book by David Lax and James Sebenius, introduces the "negotiator's dilemma," the tension that exists between the behaviors that tend to create value and those that individually claim the value jointly created. They identify some of the sources of creating value in negotiation and suggest open communication and sharing information to avoid leaving joint gains on the table. The critique by Gerald Wetlaufer, which follows our note on differences and joint gains, is more cautionary about buying into "win-win" negotiation and advises against sharing certain information, at least for the pecuniary reasons offered by Lax and Sebenius.

❖ **David A. Lax & James K. Sebenius,** *The Manager as*
Negotiator: Bargaining for Cooperation and Competitive Gain

29 (The Free Press, 1986)

The Negotiator's Dilemma: Creating and Claiming Value

We assume that each negotiator strives to advance his interests, whether they are narrowly conceived or include such concerns as improving the relationship, acting in accord with conceptions of equity, or furthering the welfare of others. Negotiators must learn, in part from each other, what is jointly possible and desirable. To do so requires some degree of cooperation. But, at the same time, they seek to advance their individual interests. This involves some degree of competition.

That negotiation includes cooperation and competition, common and conflicting interests, is nothing new. In fact, it is typically understood that these elements are both present and can be disentangled. Deep down, however, some people believe that the elements of conflict are illusory, that meaningful communication will erase any such unfortunate misperceptions. Others see mainly competition and take the cooperative pieces to be minimal. Some overtly acknowledge the reality of each aspect but direct all their attention to one of them and wish, pretend, or act as if the other does not exist. Still others hold to a more balanced view that accepts both elements as significant but seeks to treat them separately. . . . [W]e argue that all these approaches are flawed.

A deeper analysis shows that the competitive and cooperative elements are inextricably entwined. In practice, they cannot be separated. This bonding is fundamentally important to the analysis, structuring, and conduct of negotiation. There is a central, inescapable tension between cooperative moves to create value jointly and competitive moves to gain individual advantage. This tension affects virtually all tactical and strategic choice. Analysts must come to grips with it; negotiators must manage it. Neither denial nor discomfort will make it disappear.

Warring Conceptions of Negotiation

Negotiators and analysts tend to fall into two groups that are guided by warring conceptions of the bargaining process. In the left-hand corner are the "value creators" and in the right-hand corner are the "value claimers."

Value Creators

Value creators tend to believe that, above all, successful negotiators must be inventive and cooperative enough to devise an agreement that yields considerable gain to each party, relative to no-agreement possibilities. Some speak about the need for replacing the "win-lose" image of negotiation with "win-win" negotiation, from which all parties presumably derive great value. . . .

Communication and sharing information can help negotiators to create value jointly. Consider the case of a singer negotiating with the owner of an auditorium over payment for a proposed concert. They reached impasse over the size of the fee with the performer's demands exceeding the owner's highest offer. In fact, when the amount of the fixed payment was the issue, no possibility of agreement may have existed at all. The singer, however, based his demand on the expectation that the house would certainly be filled with fans while the owner projected only a half-capacity crowd. Ironically, this difference in their beliefs about attendance provided a way out. They reached a mutually acceptable arrangement in which the performer received a modest fixed fee plus a set percentage of the ticket receipts. The singer, given his beliefs, thus expected an adequate to fairly large payment; the concert hall owner was happy with the agreement because he only expected to pay a moderate fee. This "contingent" arrangement . . . permitted the concert to occur, leaving both parties feeling better off and fully willing to live with the outcome.

In addition to information sharing and honest communication, the drive to create value by discovering joint gains can require ingenuity and may benefit from a variety of techniques and attitudes. The parties can treat the negotiation as solving a joint problem; they can organize brainstorming sessions to invent creative solutions to their problems. They may succeed by putting familiar pieces of the problem together in ways that people had not previously seen, as well as by wholesale reformulations of the problem.

Roger Fisher and Bill Ury give an example that concerns the difficult Egyptian Israeli negotiations over where to draw a boundary in the Sinai. This appeared to be an absolutely classic example of zero sum bargaining, in which each square mile lost to one party was the other side's gain. For years the negotiations proceeded inconclusively with proposed boundary lines drawn and redrawn on innumerable maps. On probing the real interests of the two sides, however, Egypt was found to care a great deal about sovereignty over the Sinai while Israel was heavily concerned with its security. As such, a creative solution could be devised to "unbundle" these different interests and give to each what it valued most. In the Sinai, this involved creating a demilitarized zone under the Egyptian flag. This had the effect of giving Egypt "sovereignty" and Israel "security." This situation exemplifies extremely common tendencies to assume that negotiators' interests are in direct opposition, a conviction that can sometimes be corrected by communicating, sharing information, and inventing solutions. . . .

We create value by finding joint gains for all negotiating parties. A joint gain represents an improvement from each party's point of view; one's gain need not be another's loss. An extremely simple example makes the point. Say that two young boys each have three pieces of fruit. Willy, who hates bananas and loves pears, has a banana and two oranges. Sam, who hates pears and loves bananas, has a pear and two apples. The first move is easy: they trade banana for pear and are both happier. But after making this deal, they realize that they can do still better. Though each has a taste both for apples and oranges, a second piece of the same fruit is less desirable than the first. So they also swap an apple for an orange. The banana-pear exchange represents an improvement over the no-trade alternative; the apple orange transaction that leaves each with three different kinds of fruit improves the original agreement — is a joint gain — for both boys.

The economist's analogy is simple: Creativity has expanded the size of the pie under negotiation. Value creators see the essence of negotiating as expanding the pie, as pursuing joint gains. This is aided by openness, clear communication, sharing information, creativity, an attitude of joint problem solving, and cultivating common interests.

Value Claimers

Value claimers, on the other hand, tend to see this drive for joint gain as naive and weak minded. For them, negotiation is hard, tough bargaining. The object of negotiation is to convince the other guy that he wants what you have to offer much more than you want what he has; moreover, you have all the time in the world while he is up against pressing deadlines. To "win" at negotiating — and thus make the other fellow "lose" — one must start high, concede slowly, exaggerate the value of concessions, minimize the benefits of the other's concessions, conceal information, argue forcefully on behalf of principles that imply favorable settlements, make commitments to accept only highly favorable agreements, and be willing to outwait the other fellow.

The hardest of bargainers will threaten to walk away or to retaliate harshly if their one-sided demands are not met; they may ridicule, attack, and intimidate their adversaries. . . . At the heart of this adversarial approach is an image of a negotiation with a winner and a loser: "We are dividing a pie of fixed size and every slice I give to you is a slice I do not get; thus, I need to claim as much of the value as possible by giving you as little as possible."

A Fundamental Tension of Negotiation

Both of these images of negotiation are incomplete and inadequate. Value creating and value claiming are linked parts of negotiation. Both processes are present. No matter how much creative problem solving enlarges the pie, it must still be divided; value that has been created must be claimed. And, if the pie is not enlarged, there will be less to divide; there is more value to be claimed if one has helped create it first. An essential tension in negotiation exists between cooperative moves to create value and competitive moves to claim it.

[T]he concert hall owner may offer the singer a percentage of the gate combined with a fixed fee that is just barely high enough to induce the singer to sign the contract. Even when the parties to a potential agreement share strong common interests, one side may claim the lion's share of the value an agreement creates. . . .

The Tension at the Tactical Level

The tension between cooperative moves to create value and competitive moves to claim it is greatly exacerbated by the interaction of the tactics used either to create or claim value.

First, tactics for claiming value (which we will call "claiming tactics") can impede its creation. Exaggerating the value of concessions and minimizing the benefit of others' concessions presents a distorted picture of one's relative preferences; thus, mutually beneficial trades may not be discovered. Making threats or commitments to highly favorable outcomes surely impedes hearing and understanding others' interests. Concealing information may also cause one to leave joint gains on the table. In fact, excessive use of tactics for claiming value may well sour the parties' relationship and reduce the trust between them. Such tactics may also evoke a variety of unhelpful interests. Conflict may escalate and make joint prospects less appealing and settlement less likely.

Second, approaches to creating value are vulnerable to tactics for claiming value. Revealing information about one's relative preferences is risky. . . . The information that a negotiator would accept position A in return for a favorable resolution on a second issue can be exploited: "So, you'll accept A. Good. Now, let's move on to discuss the merits of the second issue." The willingness to make a new, creative offer can often be taken as a sign that its proposer is able and willing to make further concessions. Thus, such offers sometimes remain undisclosed. Even purely shared interests can be held hostage in exchange for concessions on other issues. Though a divorcing husband and wife may both prefer giving the wife custody of the child, the husband may "suddenly" develop strong parental instincts to extract concessions in alimony in return for giving the wife custody.

In tactical choices, each negotiator thus has reasons not to be open and cooperative. Each also has apparent incentives to try to claim value. Moves to claim value thus tend to drive out moves to create it. Yet, if both choose to claim value, by being dishonest or less than forthcoming about preferences, beliefs, or minimum requirements, they may miss mutually beneficial terms for agreement.

Indeed, the structure of many bargaining situations suggests that negotiators will tend to leave joint gains on the table or even reach impasses when mutually acceptable agreements are available.

Note: Differences Can Create Joint Gains

Lax and Sebenius go on to summarize the differences that can lead to joint gains and creation of value. These differences can be summarized as follows:

- Differences in relative valuation or priorities can lead to exchanges, directly or by "unbundling" differently valued interests. The apple and orange fruit exchange noted in the reading is an example of differences in relative valuation that create trading value.
- Differences in tolerance for risk and *risk aversion* suggest insurance-like risk-sharing arrangements in negotiated transactions. A risk-averse litigant may be willing to discount what she will receive or pay more as a certain amount rather than bear the risk of losing at trial. If the opposing side is more risk tolerant, they can be rewarded by paying less or receiving more because they are not so averse to the risk of trial.
- Differences in *time preference* can lead to altered patterns of payments or actions over time. If a claimant needs money immediately and a defendant has a reserve set aside for settlement of the claim, a quick payment can create value for both sides and enhance the chance of an agreement.
- Different *capabilities* can be combined. Companies with complementary capabilities can negotiate deals and mergers to create value that neither could achieve alone. For example, a company with strong production capacity can combine forces with a company that has sophisticated marketing and distribution abilities to collectively enhance profitability and create value between them.
- Differences in *cost/revenue structure* can create cost-saving trades. For example, if a butcher, who gets meat wholesale, can trade meat with a shoe merchant, who gets shoes wholesale, they have created value for themselves by each getting what would not otherwise be available to them at wholesale cost.

- Differences in *forecasts* can lead to contingent agreements when the items under negotiation are uncertain and themselves subject to different probability estimates. In a negotiation over executive compensation where the prospective executive has a more optimistic view of her abilities to produce revenue than does the company, for example, the executive may agree to a lower salary with a bonus contingent on revenue increases. Both negotiating sides might feel better off because they have structured an employment deal based on their own forecasts and have, in effect, created value for themselves.
- Other differences (the importance of precedent, the value of personal reputation, constituency attitudes, conceptions of fairness, and so on) can also be fashioned into joint gains. For example, a law firm being threatened with a suit by a former clerk for sexual harassment might be willing to settle a claim for much more if it is cast as payment for wrongful termination.

These "differences" relate to the role perceptions play in understanding conflict, as explained in Chapter 3 by Rummel in his excerpt on "The Subjectivity Principle." You will note that we have come full circle in connecting the cause of conflict — different perceptions that are all in our heads — to a suggested approach for constructively resolving conflicts, recognizing the different perceptions and trading on them.

Questions

11. Are the suggestions made by Lax and Sebenius for creating value by focusing on differences equally applicable to settlement of legal disputes and to deal-making negotiations? What differences on the above list could be utilized in settling a claim for damages by an injured driver against an insurance company?
12. Do the immediate pecuniary interests of the client and the longer-term interests of the attorney in maintaining good working relations with other lawyers create a conflict of interest between attorney and client?

C. Choosing an Effective Approach

Problem

Assume that you have established yourself as an effective attorney with a good reputation for your straightforward, cooperative style. You have been a guest lecturer at local law schools about civility in the practice of law and the importance of maintaining a credible professional reputation. Your largest individual client, the president of a regional bank, which your firm also represents, has retained you to represent him in a divorce action initiated by his wife, knowing that you have experience in domestic relations practice. He explains that his highest priority is to retain total control of the bank with no share of the bank stock going to his wife, even though the law might give her a claim to some of it. He wants you to seek for him primary custody of their two middle-school-aged children, for whom he and his wife have both been active parents, so you can use that as a bargaining chip later to assure his retention of the bank stock. What would you tell him? Who should decide negotiation strategies and approaches, you or your client?

1. Negotiating Within Your Comfort Zone

Being cooperative, problem-solving, competitive, or adversarial is, at least in part, a matter of choice. The choice you make depends on a number of factors: The subject of the negotiation, the expectations of your client, ethics considerations, the customs and conventions where the negotiation occurs, the interrelation between issues, the past or anticipated future relationship between the parties and between the attorneys, your counterpart's negotiation approach, the amount of time available, and the amount at stake can all influence your approach to negotiation. The biggest factor, however, is your own comfort zone, formed by your personality and values. To the extent that how you negotiate is driven by personality and values, it could be better described as a matter of style rather than approach. Behavioral style is in large part a function of who you are. Choosing a style that does not fit your personality and values, if not a recipe for failure, is likely to make your work as a negotiator difficult and dissatisfying. To succeed as a professional and find satisfaction in what you are doing, you must negotiate within your personal comfort zone.

Defining our negotiating comfort zone is not always an easy task. It is a common desire to be liked rather than disliked. We know that we are more likely to be liked when we are cooperative and giving than when we are adversarial and taking. However, we also know that winners are admired, and we want to be respected for vigorously representing our clients' interests and succeeding when we negotiate on their behalf. Law students may hold the view of attorneys popularized in movies and television series as hard-charging, aggressive lawyers. The adversarial scenes popularly portrayed in dramatized jury trials may be transposed in our minds to all opposing lawyer interactions. As a result, many students have a latent fear that their preference for cooperation and friendliness will not serve them or their clients well in negotiation.

Other students may have thrived on competition and winning in sports and other contests. We know that law students are a self-selected group of achievers who have made it into law school through a competitive admissions process. Competition appears to be encouraged by the legal system, where cooperation and generosity may be viewed as a virtuous but less valued quality. So it is understandable that some students are conflicted about whether negotiation should be approached as a professional game in which their competitive qualities are let loose and rewarded with success.

Those of you who have enjoyed competition know that good competitors can be friendly, gracious, and ethical. Similarly, not all competitive negotiators manifest an adversarial persona. A pleasant and respectful personal style is not necessarily inconsistent with competitive negotiation, any more than being cordial in competitive sports is inconsistent with wanting to win. The style you choose in negotiation may depend on how you define the game and the relationship you want with your negotiation counterpart.

Your negotiation style might also depend in large measure on your ingrained personality pattern. If personality patterns drive how we and others approach negotiation, can we discern those patterns in ourselves and others, and how can we benefit from the information?

❖ **Sheila Heen & John Richardson,** *"I See a Pattern Here and the Pattern Is You": Personality and Dispute Resolution*

in The Handbook of Dispute Resolution 202 (M.L. Moffitt & R.C. Bordone eds., 2005)

Anyone who has more than one child knows that differences in personality are real. The first born may be quiet, eager to please, and shy in new situations. His sister comes along and is an extrovert — smiling early and befriending strangers as a toddler. These traits may remain constant throughout life as the firstborn becomes a writer and his sister makes friends easily and often as a college student, professional, and retiree. . . .

The hard question is this: are there ways to describe the differences in people's personalities that can be useful in conducting and advising negotiations? After all, negotiation is all about dealing with people, getting along with them, and persuading them. Shouldn't knowing how people are different (and what to do about it) be an integral part of negotiation theory and strategy?

One would think so. And yet, the intersection of dispute resolution and personality is a tangle of confusion and contradiction. It is not unexplored territory — scholars have tried to find answers. And it is interesting — there is fascinating work going on and much speculation about what is being learned. Yet there are few clear, satisfying answers to questions that interest dispute resolution professionals most: Are particular personalities better negotiators? Should I negotiate differently with different personalities? And what about when the people and their problematic personalities really are the problem?

[After reviewing the most widely used personality tests, their limitations, and the literature about the reported results, the authors address six questions asked about personality and negotiation.]

1. *Is there really such a thing as personality differences?* It certainly seems so. Whether hard wired by genes or chemical mix, prompted by experience or influenced by the context, two people in a similar situation will often respond differently. This may be particularly so in the pressurized context of a dispute.

Personality researchers attempt to identify and isolate traits that are consistent across situations and different between individuals. This is where things get tricky. Human beings are complex enough, and adaptable enough, that defining and tracking traits, particularly through the dynamic process of negotiation, has proven very difficult.

2. *Or are there particular personality traits that give better outcomes?* With the exception of cognitive ability (more is better), there is no strong answer in the

current research. Although you can find small-scale studies suggesting this or that trait is helpful, you can also find studies that say it does not improve outcomes.

3. *Okay, so should I negotiate differently with different personality types?* The biggest obstacle to setting your negotiation strategy based on the other person's personality is figuring out what it is. Because people act differently in different situations, researchers have found that people consistently misperceive the personality traits of those with whom they negotiate or are in dispute.

The best advice is to be aware of your own tendencies, have a broad repertoire of approaches and strategies, and be able to engage difficulties constructively as they come up. Pay attention to particular behavior you see, rather than trying to globalize how the other person "is." And if one approach doesn't seem to be working, try another.

4. *Isn't it true that some disputes are hopeless because people's personalities just aren't going to change?* It is certainly true that there are limits to what can change, and that some differences between people are harder to reconcile than others. And there are definitely limits to *your ability to change the other person's personality.*

Yet the impulse to throw up our hands and attribute the problem to the other person's personality flaws is a dangerous one. It blames the other person for the dispute, blinding us to our own contributions to the problem. It may also encourage us to give up on a relationship or dispute too easily or too quickly, when finding a way to work together with less frustration remains possible.

In addition, there are at least three paths forward that personality finger-pointing ignores. Remember that human beings' *behavior* can often change without a grand *personality* change. You might shift the context — offering a private caucus or written channel of communication, for example. You can try to influence the other person's behavior by influencing the story he or she tells about what's going on. Or you might try changing your contribution to the dynamic between you. The other person is reacting both to you and to his or her own experiences, tendencies, and stories, and that's a complex enough set of factors to suggest that progress is possible.

Finally, do not underestimate people's ability to change over time. As a person ages, encounters different life experiences, and makes the transition to new phases in life (where he or she may feel more secure or happier, or have more room for reflection for example), his or her traits and tendencies evolve. You may find that your personality gradually moves into a different era, one you would not have predicted from where you stand now.

5. *Why is personality profiling so popular, if it's so inconclusive?* People love to talk about themselves. And they especially love to talk about other people. Personality profiling also fits our interest in simplifying the world and the infinitely complex relationships in it. Researchers have long documented the effects of the fundamental attribution error, where we believe we know why people act the way they do, and tend to attribute especially bad behavior to their problematic personality.

People are so complicated that we can't really describe them with few enough variables to meet our needs for parsimony. People can only keep about seven items in their head at one time, before they go into cognitive overload. So they make up something that they can handle in their heads, whether or not it is accurate.

6. *So why pay attention to personality at all?* The fields of personality and negotiation are both relatively young. Our ability to map interaction in negotiation and dispute resolution, and to recommend paths of influence, is in its infancy. And our ability to isolate traits and trace them through complex interaction is still maturing.

Still, familiarity with common differences between individuals is useful. It reminds us that not every approach to influence works with every person. It can help us generate diagnostic hypotheses about why a negotiation is in trouble ("Ah! We may proceed to closure at different paces"), and come up with prescriptive advice to try out. It may also help us be more forgiving of others' seemingly crazy behavior if we can spot it as a difference in the way the two of us see and respond to the world.

Familiarity with personality differences can also be a self-reflection and coaching tool for yourself. It can help you identify and work on behavior that doesn't come naturally to you. It can also help you explain your behavior to others: "I've learned that I'm not very comfortable making commitments before I have a chance to think things through. Can you give me the weekend and we'll nail this down on Monday?" Becoming familiar with some of the traits that affect your ability to mediate, negotiate, or respond well to disputes can help you become more aware of the situations that bring out these traits, and other choices you might make.

2. Effectiveness and Style

As you know, negotiation is usually done in private, so there is little opportunity to compare results. How lawyers behave in negotiation and what they do is not fully known. Lawyers' tales of negotiations are filtered through the lens of the tellers' perceptions. Unless negotiations can be systematically observed on a grand scale, we will never know what really works best to produce desired negotiated outcomes. Few lawyers ever "lose" a negotiation, or tell about it if they believe they did not do well. War stories of successful negotiations are not reliable descriptions of what typically occurs, or even of what occurred in the reported negotiation. (There do not appear to be any books on "How I Failed as a Negotiator.") All this leaves new lawyers little reliable guidance on what is successful in negotiation and how to weigh the tensions they may feel between competition and cooperation, to negotiate effectively within their comfort zone.

Two studies help fill the void of information about how lawyers negotiate and which behaviors and styles are effective. Both studies are necessarily limited because they rely on attorneys responding to questionnaires and reporting their perceptions of effective and ineffective negotiation behavior by their opponents in recent negotiations. Nonetheless, both studies provide sources of information about how lawyers negotiate and what is considered effective, as well as ineffective. Because the studies were similar and conducted more than 20 years apart, we can obtain clues about changes over time in how attorneys negotiate (see Schneider 2000).

The news from the studies is both good and bad. The good news for students struggling with the tension of deciding on their negotiation comfort zone and not knowing if what they are inclined to do is the right way to negotiate is that there is no one right way.

Both competitive and cooperative styles can be effective approaches to negotiation if done well and with integrity. Being an effective competitive negotiator does not require the use of tricks or deceit. Some competitive techniques can be legitimate ways to pursue negotiation goals, provided they are not carried to extremes. Being a cooperative negotiator need not be based on naiveté or being a pushover. Cooperative attorneys, who appear from the studies to predominate in numbers and perceived effectiveness, are most successful when they are mindful of the interests they are pursuing and set limits on their cooperation.

The studies indicate that although the percentage of attorneys who are adversarial has increased, about two-thirds of lawyer negotiators are classified by counterparties as cooperative. The rating of cooperative negotiators as more effective than adversarial negotiators has increased. Again, it should be noted that adversarial attorneys are also rated as effective, but in a much lower proportion. Some admirable behaviors of negotiators (like preparation, a focus on the client's interests, and high ethical standards) are shared by effective competitive and effective cooperative attorney negotiators.

The bad news is that the more recent study reported that adversarial negotiators are becoming more extreme and unpleasant. The terms most frequently used to describe them are more negative than 20 years ago. This might not bode well for the legal profession or for clients, if the reports are accurate.

3. Cooperation vs. Competitiveness — Who Decides?

Generally, clients get to choose the objective of negotiation, and lawyers use their professional judgment in selecting the means of obtaining the client's objectives. Of course, it's not quite so simple. In matters of litigation, the lawyer may owe the client an ethical obligation of zealous advocacy in pursuit of a client's interests. Professors Robert Mnookin and Robert Gilson (1995) have written that a lawyer who wishes to pursue a cooperative approach, with sensitivity for long-term professional relationships with other attorneys, may not be able to do so in the litigation context, or at least that the client calls the negotiation shots. They also point out that the client can fire the lawyer at will if the lawyer seems more cooperative than the client wishes, but that ethical norms do not always allow the lawyer to quit if the client insists on a more aggressive strategy.

Professor Robert Condlin believes that lawyers must be substantively competitive in negotiating for clients but can choose their own personal style. Competitive attorneys can adopt a cordial and respectful persona in their negotiations, although this can be a fine and difficult distinction. Condlin refers to the tug between some clients' wish for a lawyer to behave adversarially in a particular case and the lawyer's desire to maintain a reputation for cooperation as the "bargainer's dilemma." Like the prisoners' dilemma, different negotiation tactics may be called for if the situation is viewed as a single- or multiple-round game. Clients tend to view litigation and some deals as one-round events. Lawyers usually view their negotiation with other lawyers as involving unlimited multiple rounds, where any defect may bring future retaliation and a blemished reputation (Condlin 1992). As we will see, you will encounter this tension whether you practice as a negotiator or an advocate in mediation.

CHAPTER
3

Negotiation—Step by Step

Negotiation, whether competitive, cooperative, or a mixed approach, can be viewed as occurring in stages. Even though lawyer negotiation is often not a tidy process, breaking negotiation into stages is a way to help understand and analyze it. There is, however, no script — all negotiations do not follow the same lineal staging, and each stage will not necessarily be completed in all negotiations.

Listed below are the activities typically occurring in seven stages of competitive or cooperative negotiation. The activities within each stage can be mixed or alternated between competitive and cooperative, bearing in mind the warning that cooperation is commonly driven out by competitiveness. Of course, the labels "competitive" and "cooperative," like all one-word descriptions, are too simple. Adversarial and problem-solving, positional and interest-based, or distributive and integrative may better capture the behavioral contrast. Although each pair of bipolar negotiation labels may signify nuanced differences, we will use them synonymously. Finally, note that although some of the activities and tasks within the two approaches are similar, the sequence of stages may vary between positional and interest-based approaches. For example, making demands and offers comes earlier in positional negotiation and later in interest-based negotiation, following the exchange of information, if at all.

Stage	Competitive/adversarial approach	Cooperative/problem-solving approach
1. Preparation and Setting Goals	➢ Planning and research ➢ Counseling client about negotiation ➢ Assessing power of each party ➢ Formulating positions and bottom line ➢ Setting goals	➢ Planning and research ➢ Counseling client about negotiation ➢ Assessing needs of each party ➢ Formulating best alternative to negotiated agreement (BATNA) and reservation point ➢ Setting goals
2. Initial Interactions	➢ Setting tone ➢ Establishing credentials and authority ➢ Making first demand or offer	➢ Setting tone ➢ Establishing rapport and trust ➢ Agreeing on agenda

Stage	Competitive/adversarial approach	Cooperative/problem-solving approach
3. Exchanging and Refining Information	➤ Asking questions ➤ Offering overstated or understated valuations ➤ Informational bargaining ➤ Formal discovery ➤ Stating positions (often exaggerated)	➤ Asking questions ➤ Sharing assessments or appraisals ➤ Information exchange ➤ Informal discovery (I'll show you mine, if you'll show me yours) ➤ Stating needs or interests
4. Bargaining	➤ Argument and persuasion ➤ Making concessions ➤ Forming coalitions and holding out	➤ Proposing principles ➤ Applying principled criteria ➤ Trading off priorities and brainstorming solutions
5. Moving Toward Closure	➤ Using power and threats ➤ Creating time crisis ➤ Evaluating offers	➤ Examining BATNAs ➤ Agreeing on deadlines ➤ Decision analysis
6. Reaching Impasse or Agreement	➤ Possible impasse ➤ Compromising ➤ Adding conditions	➤ Possible, but less likely, impasse ➤ Reaching mutual decisions through joint problem solving ➤ Creating alternative outcomes
7. Finalizing and Writing Agreements	➤ Preparing opposing drafts of agreement ➤ Negotiating over drafts ➤ Approval, ratification, and buy-in (if necessary)	➤ Memorializing terms ➤ Concurring on single text agreement ➤ Approval, ratification, and buy-in (if necessary)

Question

1. Have you found that negotiations in which you have been involved go through predictable stages? Did this depend on the nature of the issue, the identities of the bargainers, or something else? What seemed determinative?

A. Preparing to Negotiate

Watching a good negotiator or hearing about an effective negotiation can give the impression that negotiating skill comes easily and that success results primarily from quick thinking and intuition. However, success in negotiation, like skill in the courtroom and other disciplines, comes mainly from careful planning, research, and other preparation, especially for less-experienced practitioners. The following excerpts describe two key aspects of the planning process: identifying your alternatives to agreement and setting high goals.

1. Identifying Alternatives

One key aspect of planning is to identify the minimum terms that you will accept. As Fisher, Ury, and Patton point out, this should flow from identifying your *"Best Alternative To a Negotiated Agreement"* (BATNA) in any situation.

❖ Roger Fisher, William Ury & Bruce Patton, *GETTING TO YES*

97 (Penguin, 1991)

When you are trying to catch an airplane your goal may seem tremendously important; looking back on it, you see you could have caught the next plane. Negotiation will often present you with a similar situation. You will worry, for instance, about failing to reach agreement on an important business deal in which you have invested a great deal of yourself. Under these conditions, a major danger is that you will be too accommodating to the views of the other side — too quick to go along. The siren song of "Let's all agree and put an end to this" becomes persuasive. You may end up with a deal you should have rejected.

The Costs of Using a Bottom Line

Negotiators commonly try to protect themselves against such an outcome by establishing in advance the worst acceptable outcome — their "bottom line." If you are buying, a bottom line is the highest price you would pay. If you are selling, a bottom line is the lowest amount you would accept. You and your spouse might, for example, ask $200,000 for your house and agree between yourselves to accept no offer below $160,000.

Having a bottom line makes it easier to resist pressure and temptations of the moment. . . . But the protection afforded by adopting a bottom line involves high costs. It limits your ability to benefit from what you learn during negotiation. . . . A bottom line also inhibits imagination. It reduces the incentive to invent a tailor-made solution which would reconcile differing interests in a way more advantageous for both you and them. . . . Moreover, a bottom line is likely to be set too high. . . . In short, while adopting a bottom line may protect you from accepting a very bad agreement, it may keep you both from inventing and from agreeing to a solution it would be wise to accept. . . .

Is there an alternative to the bottom line? Is there a measure for agreements that will protect you against both accepting an agreement you should reject and rejecting an agreement you should accept? There is.

Know Your BATNA

When a family is deciding on the minimum price for their house, the right question for them to ask is not what they "ought" to be able to get, but what they will do if by a certain time they have not sold the house. Will they keep it on the market indefinitely? Will they rent it, tear it down, turn the land into a parking lot, let someone else live in it rent-free on condition they paint it, or what? Which of those alternatives is most attractive, all things considered? . . .

The reason you negotiate is to produce something better than the results you can obtain without negotiating. What are those results? What is that alternative?

What is your BATNA — your Best Alternative To a Negotiated Agreement? *That* is the standard against which any proposed agreement should be measured. That is the only standard which can protect you both from accepting terms that are too unfavorable and from rejecting terms it would be in your interest to accept.

Your BATNA not only is a better measure but also has the advantage of being flexible enough to permit the exploration of imaginative solutions. Instead of ruling out any solution which does not meet your bottom line, you can compare a proposal with your BATNA to see whether it better satisfies your interests.

The Insecurity of an Unknown BATNA

If you have not thought carefully about what you will do if you fail to reach an agreement, you are negotiating with your eyes closed. . . . Even when your alternative is fixed, you may be taking too rosy a view of the consequences of not reaching agreement. You may not be appreciating the full agony of a lawsuit, a contested divorce, a strike, an arms race, or a war. . . .

As valuable as knowing your BATNA may be, you may hesitate to explore alternatives. You hope this buyer or the next will make you an attractive offer for the house. You may avoid facing the question of what you will do if no agreement is reached. You may think to yourself, "Let's negotiate first and see what happens. If things don't work out, then I'll figure out what to do." But having at least a tentative answer to the question is absolutely essential if you are to conduct your negotiations wisely. Whether you should or should not agree on something in a negotiation depends entirely upon the attractiveness to you of the best available alternative.

Formulate a Trip Wire

Although your BATNA is the true measure by which you should judge any proposed agreement, you may want another test as well. In order to give you early warning that the content of a possible agreement is beginning to run the risk of being too unattractive, it is useful to identify one far from perfect agreement that is better than your BATNA. Before accepting any agreement worse than this trip wire package, you should take a break and reexamine the situation. Like a bottom line, a trip wire can limit the authority of an agent. "Don't sell for less than $158,000, the price I paid plus interest, until you've talked to me."

A trip wire should provide you with some margin in reserve. If after reaching the standard reflected in your trip wire you decide to call in a mediator, you have left him with something on your side to work with. You still have some room to move.

Making the Most of Your Assets

Protecting yourself against a bad agreement is one thing. Making the most of the assets you have in order to produce a good agreement is another. How do you do this? Again the answer lies in your BATNA. The better your BATNA, the greater your power. [The authors suggest that a negotiator should attempt to improve her alternative or search out a better one to increase her negotiating power.]

Consider the Other Side's BATNA

You should also think about the alternatives to a negotiated agreement available to the other side. They may be unduly optimistic about what they can do if no agreement is reached. Perhaps they have a vague notion that they have a great many alternatives and are under the influence of their cumulative total. The more you can learn of their alternatives, the better prepared you are for negotiation. Knowing their alternatives, you can realistically estimate what you can expect from the negotiation. If they appear to overestimate their BATNA, you will want to lower their expectations. . . .

When the Other Side Is Powerful

If the other side has big guns, you do not want to turn a negotiation into a gunfight. The stronger they appear in terms of physical or economic power, the more you benefit by negotiating on the merits. To the extent that they have muscle and you have principle, the larger a role you can establish for principle the better off you are.

Having a good BATNA can help you negotiate on the merits. You can convert such resources as you have into effective negotiating power by developing and improving your BATNA. Apply knowledge, time, money, people, connections, and wits into devising the best solution for you independent of the other side's assent. The more easily and happily you can walk away from a negotiation, the greater your capacity to affect its outcome.

Developing your BATNA thus not only enables you to determine what is a minimally acceptable agreement, it will probably raise that minimum. Developing your BATNA is perhaps the most effective course of action you can take in dealing with a seemingly more powerful negotiator.

Questions

2. What is your "BATNA" likely to be in litigation? Is there ever any alternative but to obtain a court judgment on the merits?
3. What alternatives might a party have in a situation in which she is bargaining to create a contract with a potential business partner?
4. In real life, should there ever be a difference between a party's BATNA and its bottom line? Can you think of a situation in which a litigant might rationally decide to accept a settlement that is not as good as the most likely outcome in adjudication, taking into account the legal costs involved in going to trial? What would explain such a decision?

2. Setting Goals

Setting high goals is identified with a competitive approach to negotiation. It is often assumed, in other words, that setting a high goal for oneself necessarily means imposing a low one on one's negotiating partner. This is not necessarily true, however. It is quite possible for negotiators jointly to set the goal of finding the potentially elusive set of terms that best satisfy each person's interests — a task that is cooperative in intent but often difficult to achieve in practice. The following reading stresses the importance of goal setting for both cooperative and competitive bargainers.

❖ **G. Richard Shell,** *Bargaining for Advantage: Negotiation Strategies for Reasonable People*

---

28 (Penguin, 2006)

Goals: You'll Never Hit the Target If You Don't Aim

In Lewis Carroll's *Alice's Adventures in Wonderland*, Alice finds herself at a crossroads where a Cheshire Cat materializes. Alice asks the Cat, "Would you tell me please, which way I ought to go from here?" The Cat replies, "That depends a good deal on where you want to get to." "I don't much care where — [,]" says Alice. "Then it doesn't matter which way you go," the Cat replies, cutting her off.

To become an effective negotiator, you must find out where you want to go — and why. That means committing yourself to specific, justifiable goals. It also means taking the time to transform your goals from simple targets into genuine — and appropriately high — expectations. . . . Our goals give us direction, but our expectations are what give weight and conviction to our statements at the bargaining table. We are most animated when we are striving to achieve what we feel we justly deserve.

Expectations in negotiation are a function of a number of factors, including our previous successes and failures in similar negotiations, prevailing market prices and standards, past practices, information about the other party's alternatives and frame of reference, our potential for a future relationship with the other side, and our basic personality. . . . The more time we spend preparing for a particular negotiation and the more information we gather that reinforces our belief that our goal is legitimate and achievable, the firmer the expectations grow. . . .

Negotiations are no different from other areas of achievement. What you aim for often determines what you get. Why? The first reason is obvious: Your goals set the upper limit of what you will ask for. You mentally concede everything beyond your goal, so you seldom do better than that benchmark.

Second, research on goals reveals that they trigger powerful psychological "striving" mechanisms. Sports psychologists and educators alike confirm that setting specific goals motivates people, focusing and concentrating their attention and psychological powers.

Third, we are more persuasive when we are committed to achieving some specific purpose, in contrast to the occasions when we ask for things half-heartedly or merely react to initiatives proposed by others. Our commitment is infectious. People around us feel drawn toward our goals. . . .

Goals versus "Bottom Lines"

Most negotiating books and experts emphasize the importance of having a "bottom line," "walkaway," or "reservation price" for negotiation. Indeed, the bottom line is a fundamental bargaining concept on which much of modern negotiation theory is built. It is the *minimum acceptable level* you require to say "yes" in a negotiation. By definition, if you cannot achieve your bottom line, you would rather seek another solution to your problem or wait until another opportunity comes your way. When two parties have bottom lines that permit an agreement at some point between them, theorists speak of there being a "positive bargaining zone." When the two bottom lines do not overlap, they speak of a "negative bargaining zone". . . .

A well-framed goal is quite different from a bottom line. As I use the word, "goal" is your *highest legitimate expectation* of what you should achieve.

Researchers have discovered that humans have a limited capacity for maintaining focus in complex, stressful situations such as negotiations. Consequently, once a negotiation is under way, we gravitate toward the single focal point that has the psychological significance for us. Once most people set a firm bottom line in a negotiation, that becomes their dominant reference point as discussions proceed. They measure success or failure with reference to their bottom line, and it is very difficult to psychologically re-orient themselves toward a more ambitious bargaining goal. . . .

What is the practical effect of having your bottom line become your dominant reference point in a negotiation? Over a lifetime of negotiating, your results will tend to hover at a point just above this minimum acceptable level. . . . Meanwhile, someone else who is more skilled at orienting himself toward ambitious goals will do much better. . . . To avoid falling into the trap of letting our bottom line become our reference point, be aware of your absolute limits, but do not focus on them. Instead, work energetically on formulating your goals — and let your bottom line take care of itself. . . .

Orient firmly toward your goal in the planning and initial stages of negotiation, then gradually re-orient toward a bottom line as that becomes necessary to close the deal. With experience, you should be able to keep both your goal and your bottom line in view at the same time without losing your goal focus. Research suggests that the best negotiators have this ability. Meanwhile, during the actual negotiation, you should strive to determine what the other side's bottom line is as best you can — and not allow yourself to be too swayed by the other party's aspirations. If, in the end, you must make adjustments to your high expectations to close a deal, you can take care of that later.

If setting goals is so vital to effective preparation, how should you do it? Use the following simple steps:

1. Think carefully about what you really want — and remember that money is often a means, not an end.
2. Set an optimistic — but justifiable — target.
3. Be specific.
4. Get committed. Write down your goal and, if possible, discuss the goal with someone else.
5. Carry your goal with you into the negotiation.

Set an Optimistic, Justifiable Target

When you set goals, think boldly and optimistically about what you would like to see happen. Research has repeatedly shown that people who have higher expectations in negotiations perform better and get more than people who have modest or "I'll do my best" goals, provided they really believe in their targets. . . .

Once you have thought about what an optimistic, challenging goal would look like, spend a few minutes permitting realism to dampen your expectations. *Optimistic goals are effective only if they are feasible; that is, only if you believe in them and they can be justified according to some standard or norm.* . . . [N]egotiation positions must usually be supported by some standard, benchmark, or precedent, or they lose their credibility. . . .

Commit to Your Goal: Write It Down and Talk About It

Your goal is only as effective as your commitment to it. There are several simple things you can do that will increase your level of psychological attachment to your goal. First, as I suggested above, you should make sure it is justified and supported by solid arguments. You must believe in your goal to be committed to it.

Second, it helps if you spend just a few moments vividly imagining the way it would look or feel to achieve your goal. Visualization helps engage our mind more fully in the achievement process and also raises our level of self- confidence and commitment. . . .

Third, psychologists and marketing professionals report that the act of writing a goal down engages our sense of commitment much more effectively than does the mere act of thinking about it. The act of writing makes a thought more "real" and objective, obligating us to follow up on it — at least in our own eyes. . . .

Questions and Note

5. Should there ever be a difference between one's goals and one's expectations in bargaining? When?
6. Does the advice to set high expectations only work if the other side does not follow the same advice? Will high expectations by both sides lead to frequent impasses? Is there a way for two highly optimistic negotiators to reach agreement?
7. If expectations in negotiation are, in part, a function of previous success and failures, as Shell suggests, how does a new lawyer set expectations? Would a client be best advised to seek out a lawyer who has had well-known success in trials and negotiations?
8. For an in-depth, scholarly discussion of the role of aspirations in settlement negotiations, see Korobkin (2002). Both Shell and Korobkin conclude that high aspirations may help negotiators reach better results, but at the cost of a greater risk of impasse and personal dissatisfaction in not fully achieving the expectations created by these aspirations.

3. A Preparation Checklist

The following checklist expands on the concepts developed in the previous excerpts and includes points from the selections that follow. Using a checklist is a way to discipline your thinking and provides an inventory of questions from which you can choose, depending on the case and the time available. Even limited preparation, you will find, is much better than none at all!

A. Strategy

1. Information:
- What data would be helpful to us in reaching a good settlement? What questions or steps will elicit it?
- What information is the other side likely to ask for?
- What information will they need to respond favorably to our proposals? Can we provide it, or help them obtain it?
- What should we be willing to reveal? What must we be careful to protect?
- Is there a basis for trading information?

2. Alternatives:
- What is our best alternative to an agreement? Can we improve the reality of that alternative?
- What is our worst outcome, if there is no agreement?
- Can we improve the other side's perception of the attractiveness of our alternative?
- What are their best alternative and their worst outcome? Can we diminish the value of their best and worst alternatives, or the way they perceive it?

3. Principles:
- What principles can we cite as to why our desired outcome is fair?
- Which principles are likely to be most persuasive to the other side?
- What standards will they cite? How can we rebut them?

4. Interests:
- What are ours? How do we rank their relative importance?
- What appear to be their interests? How do they see their relative importance?
- How do they see our interests? Should we attempt to change or enlarge their perspective?
- Are there potential solutions that would accommodate both sides' interests? What might be the best possible fit of terms?

5. Communication:
- Should we communicate with the other side, either before the first meeting or before we begin to negotiate?
- If so, should the communication be focused on building trust or on substance? What message do we want to send?
- What theme or story will best present our perspective?
- Are there special issues, such as culture or language, that we should consider?

6. Relationships:
- Will the right people be at the table? Should we seek anyone out?
- What kind of relationship do we want with the other side, at the bargaining table and afterwards?
- Should I or my client attempt to create working relationships with specific members of the other team? How?

- What message do we want to leave with the other side at the end of our first meeting?
- Are there any problems in the relationship that need to be resolved?

B. Bargaining

7. Process:
- What style of bargaining is likely to be most effective? What style is the other side likely to use? Should we change style, or expect a change, as the process goes forward?
- What process, in terms of structure or stages, do we want? What is the other side likely to expect?
- What roles should I and my client play? How should we coordinate?
- What agenda should we propose? What agenda do they expect?
- How can we influence the process, style, and agenda?

8. Goals:
- What are our goals in the process: an interest-based solution, best result for our side, or something else? What would a good overall result look like?
- What should we set as our highest achievable goal?
- How can we explain or justify it, to ourselves and to the other side? How can we strengthen our commitment to our goal?
- What is the minimum that we will accept?
- What "trip wire" should we set above the minimum?

9. Tactics:
- If we anticipate a positional process:
  - Should we make the first offer? How quickly?
  - What should it be?
  - What message do we want to send by our offer?
  - What pattern of concessions is most likely to get us to our goal?
  - What pattern is the other side likely to use?
- If we want to stimulate an interest-based solution:
  - How should we encourage a process that brings out interests?
  - That identifies good solutions?

10. Final Terms:
- Do we need any specific terms in the final agreement? Is the other side likely to insist on particular terms?
- Will we or the other side need to get approval for a settlement?

B. Initial Interaction

How we feel about those with whom we negotiate is a critical element to whether an agreement will be reached. Just as you may feel you can quickly "read" the character and trustworthiness of those you face, so others are forming a quick impression of you. The maxims that "you never get a second chance to make a first impression" and "first impressions matter" need to be considered as you prepare for and commence a negotiation.

The impression you make on an opponent will probably be formed, in part, before you meet. If the negotiation is of significance, you and your opponent will find out what you can about one another. Your reputation will precede you into the negotiation. In addition to informal inquiries among those with whom you have previously negotiated or had other professional contact, the Internet opens your public history, both accomplishments and mistakes, for all to see. So your preparation for a negotiation, in terms of the impression you make and whether you can be trusted, involves your entire professional life. Although a misimpression can be corrected, it is an uphill struggle because of what we know about self-fulfilling prophecies and the selective way we view evidence to support earlier impressions. Trust is more likely to develop between negotiators if they see one another as similar. Similarity of backgrounds, experience, values, tastes, or group identity helps develop rapport and smoothes the way to trust. There is a delicate balance when opening a negotiation session between engaging in "small talk" that might establish a shared interest, affiliation, or acquaintance for the purpose of creating rapport, and getting to the point regarding the issues in dispute. However, taking time to learn enough about your counterpart to find commonalities and the opportunity to establish a personal connection as the basis for trust is usually time well spent.

The flip side of trust, distrust, inhibits negotiation. Distrust tends to be reciprocated and becomes a self-fulfilling prophecy engendering negative behavior and selective perceptions that confirm the reasons for not trusting one another. Distrust is an obstacle to the exchange of information and collaboration or joint problem solving.

Unless negotiators know one another socially or have had positive professional experiences together, distrust is more the norm at the beginning of a negotiation because you know the other side can prevent you from getting something you want. So, setting a positive tone and early moves to build trust are important. If you can start on a positive note, you can build a momentum of trust that can carry the negotiations through difficult times. Trust initiated through good listening, sincere compliments, or small opening concessions builds upon itself through reciprocity.

Note: The Importance of "Small Talk" in Bargaining

Professor Janice Nadler has reported on an interesting experiment in which students at Northwestern and Duke Law Schools tested the impact of "small talk" on bargaining (Nadler, 2004). The following are excerpts from her comments:

> The experiment involved an e-mail negotiation over the purchase of a new car between students at the two law schools. It contained both distributive and integrative elements; although both parties were motivated to claim as much value for themselves as possible, they had different priorities as to specific terms. One set of students simply began to negotiate. Another group of students, however, were told to have an initial "getting to know you" telephone conversation with their partner lasting five to ten minutes. The participants were told that they should not talk about business (i.e., the negotiation); the goal was simply to "break the ice." The content of the chats was often trivial (e.g., "The weather is nice here in Chicago." "Yes, it is nice here, too.") Regardless of whether there was small talk, all of the negotiations took place exclusively via e-mail.
>
> The negotiators who had a "getting-to-know-you" conversation prior to negotiating via e-mail reached superior economic outcomes and markedly better social outcomes than negotiators who did not talk on the phone. . . . Only 9 per cent of

the "Small Talk" pairs failed to reach agreement, while nearly 40 per cent of the others failed to reach agreement.

Why did this occur? Negotiators who did not engage in small talk reported feeling more competitive and less cooperative toward their counterpart than negotiators who did engage in small talk. The "Small Talk" group exchanged significantly more information about their relative priorities on issues than the other group, and their information sharing was reciprocated more often.

The "Small Talk" group was also less likely to talk about their alternatives to reaching agreement (such as buying their car at another dealership). Students who did not chat first found the process of e-mail communication more difficult, ending up feeling significantly more angry, annoyed, and cold toward their opponent. In a related phenomenon, negotiators who engaged in small talk formed an impression of their counterpart as significantly more accomplished, skilled, effective, and perceptive than negotiators who did not. Finally, "Small Talk" bargainers left the negotiation with significantly more trust in their counterparts than the other group.

Nadler concluded that cooperation helped participants solve the "negotiator's dilemma." The getting-to-know-you telephone calls made the bargainers' subsequent e-mail negotiations proceed more smoothly by creating rapport that helped them trust each others' good intentions. The negotiators who engaged in small talk agreed (albeit tacitly) to share enough information to determine what kind of agreement would satisfy both their needs. In Nadler's view, the study documents the importance for lawyers of establishing rapport when negotiating with another lawyer who is an "unknown quantity."

Question

9. In her article, Professor Nadler suggests: "[O]utside of the negotiation context, social psychologists have shown that using flattery (even when people suspect the flatterer has ulterior motives) and humor, and mentioning points of similarity, can facilitate good feelings and relationship building, thereby engendering the kind of cooperation and trust that leads to discovery of mutually profitable negotiated solutions." If "schmoozing" is one form of social grease that makes deals happen, can you think of other ways to create rapport?

C. Exchanging Information

The task of finding out all that you can about the other side — their needs, their arguments, their BATNA, and other factors affecting their approach to bargaining — pervades the entire negotiation process. Similarly, disclosing and managing information in your control that may shape the other side's perceptions is also important. Exchanging information is listed as a separate step to emphasize its importance in bargaining. A hallmark of effective negotiators, whether competitive or cooperative, is their ability to listen, their propensity to ask questions, and their desire to gather information continually. Indeed, information often is power in negotiation. In one empirical study, for example, effective bargainers were found to ask more than twice as many questions as average ones (Rackham & Carlisle 1978). Good competitive lawyers devote much of the negotiation process to bargaining over information, often before they make any actual offers. Experienced cooperative lawyers also exchange information, but in an open and collaborative manner.

If you can learn what is in the mind and heart of the other bargainer, you can make a personal connection, satisfy his needs, and get what you want at the lowest possible cost. If you actively allow others to openly express themselves, they usually will give you useful data. The more you talk, the less you can listen and learn. The key lesson here is an easy one: Talk less and listen more. When you do speak in a negotiation, do so in a way that elicits information or that helps shape the process. Indeed, sometimes giving out information is the best way to encourage others to provide it to you.

❖ **Melissa L. Nelken,** *Negotiation: Theory and Practice*

41 (Anderson Publishing, 2007)

In the course of the negotiation, you will try to learn things about the other party's case, and about his perception of your case, that you don't know when the negotiation starts. He, of course, will do the same with you. Another important aspect of preparation, then, is deciding what you need to find out before you actually make a deal. Without considering what information you need to gather in the early stages of the negotiation, you will not be able to gauge how well the actual situation fits the assumptions you have made in preparing to negotiate. You may have overestimated how much the other party needs a deal with you, or underestimated the value he places on what you are selling. Only careful attention to gathering information will enable you to adjust your goals appropriately. In addition to what you want to learn, you also have to decide what information you are willing, or even eager, to divulge to the other party — for example, the large number of offers you have already received for the subject property — and what information you want to conceal — for example, the fact that none of those offers exceeds the price you paid for the property originally. Managing information is a central feature of distributive bargaining, and you have to plan to do it well.

A beginning negotiator often feels that she has to conceal as much as possible, that virtually anything she reveals will hurt her or be used against her. . . . [Y]ou are more likely to feel this way if you have not thought through your case and prepared how to present it in the best light that you realistically can. If you choose when and how you will reveal information, rather than anxiously concealing as much as possible, you gain a degree of control over the negotiation that you lack when you merely react to what your counterpart says or does. Increasing the amount of information you are prepared to reveal, and reducing the amount you feel you absolutely must conceal, will help you make a stronger case for your client. In addition, the more willing you are to share information that the other party considers useful, the more likely you are to learn what you need to know from your counterpart before you make a deal.

Using Outside Sources

As part of your preparation, you need to consult outside sources of information to help you understand the context of a given negotiation. You will need data about the subject of the negotiation — market prices, alternate sources of supply, industry standards, market factors affecting the company you are dealing with, and so on. In addition, information about the parties and their representatives from others who have negotiated with them in the past will be helpful in planning your strategy. You will also want to learn about any relevant negotiation conventions, for example, the convention in personal injury litigation that the plaintiff makes the first demand. . . .

Bargaining for Information

A central aspect of distributive bargaining is bargaining for information. In the course of planning, you have to make certain working assumptions about the motives and wishes of the other side, as well as about the factual context of the negotiation. In addition, we all have a tendency to "fill in" missing information in order to create a coherent picture of a situation. For a negotiator, it is imperative to separate out what you know to be true from what you merely believe to be true by testing your assumptions during the early stages of the negotiation. Otherwise, you risk making decisions based on inaccurate information and misunderstanding what the other side actually tells you. . . .

Many negotiators forget that they start with only a partial picture of the situation, and they push to "get down to numbers" before learning anything about the other side's point of view. Yet the relevant facts of a situation are not immutable; they are often dependent on your perspective. Knowing the other side's perspective is a valuable source of information about possibilities for settlement. The most obvious way to gather that information is by asking questions, especially about the reasons behind positions taken by the other party. Why does a deal have to be made today? How good are her alternatives to settlement with you? What is the basis for a particular offer? Asking questions allows you to test the assumptions that you bring to the negotiation about both parties' situations. Questions also permit you to gauge the firmness of stated positions by learning how well supported they are by facts. In addition, the information you gather can alert you to issues that are important (or unimportant) to your counterpart, opening up possibilities for an advantageous settlement if you value those issues differently.

In addition to asking questions, you have to learn to listen carefully to what the other party says, to look for verbal and nonverbal cues that either reinforce or contradict the surface message conveyed. If someone tells you that he wants $40,000-50,000 to settle, you can be sure that he will settle for $40,000, or less. If he starts a sentence by saying, "I'll be perfectly frank with you . . .", take whatever follows with a large grain of salt and test it against other things you have heard. Asking questions is only one way to gather information, and not always the most informative one. You also have to listen for what someone omits from an answer, for answers that are not answers or that deflect the question, for hesitations and vagueness in the responses that you get. There is no simple formula for what such things mean, but the more alert you are for ways in which you are not getting information in a straightforward way, the better able you will be to sort through the information that you get. . . .

One of the most effective and underutilized methods of bargaining for information is silence. Many inexperienced negotiators, especially lawyer-negotiators, think that they are paid to talk and are not comfortable sitting quietly. If you can teach yourself to do so, you will find that you often learn things that would never be revealed in response to a direct question. When silences occur, people tend to fill them in; and because the silence is unstructured, what they say is often more spontaneous than any answer to a question would be. Since you are interested in gathering new information in the course of the negotiation, it is useful to keep in mind that if you are talking, you probably aren't hearing anything you do not already know. Therefore, silence is truly golden. . . .

Sharing Information

All that has been said so far about integrative bargaining suggests that lawyers will only be able to do a good job if they share substantive information about their clients' needs and preferences and look for ways to make their differences work for them in the negotiation. According to [Mary Parker] Follett "the first rule . . . for obtaining integration is to put your cards on the table, face the real issue, uncover the conflict, bring the whole thing into the open." This is a far cry from the bargaining for information that characterizes distributive negotiations, where each side seeks to learn as much as possible about the other while revealing as little as it can. The more straightforward and clear the negotiators' communications are, the fewer obstacles there will be to recognizing and capitalizing on opportunities for mutual gain. This means, first, that they must be clear about their clients' goals, even if they are open as to the means of reaching those goals. In addition, there must be sufficient trust between them so that both are willing to reveal their clients' true motivations. Such trust may be based on past experience, but it may also be developed in the course of a negotiation, as the negotiators exchange information and evaluate the information they have received. It does not have to be based on an assumption that the other side has your best interest at heart, but only that he is as interested as you are in uncovering ways that you can both do better through negotiation. Self-interest can keep both sides honest in the process, even where there might be a short-term gain from misrepresentation. Of course, the need to share information in order to optimize results creates risks for the negotiators as well. . . .

Flexibility, rather than rigid positions, is key to integrative bargaining, since the outcome will depend on fitting together the parties' needs as much as possible. When the negotiators share adequate information, they may end up redefining the conflict they are trying to resolve. For example, what seemed a specific problem about failure to fulfill the terms of a contract may turn out to be a more fundamental difficulty with the structure of the contract itself. A better outcome for both sides may result if the contract is renegotiated. . . .

Strategic Use of Information

There is also anxiety because the amount of shared information needed for integrative bargaining to succeed may be more than a distributive bargainer wants to reveal. For example, a distributively-inclined buyer may prefer that his counterpart think that time of delivery, which he does not care much about, is very important to him, so that he can exact concessions on other aspects of the deal by "giving in" to a later delivery to accommodate the seller. Since it is hard to know in advance what issues will be most significant to the other side, it can be difficult to decide how much information to share and how to evaluate the quality of the information you receive about your counterpart's priorities. The fear of being taken advantage of often results in both sides' taking preemptive action focused on "winning" rather than on collaborating. Sometimes such strategies are effective; but they are also likely to impede or prevent what could be a fruitful search for joint gains.

D. Bargaining

As we noted earlier, the timing of offers and demands may vary between positional and interest-based approaches. Positional bargainers tend to make demands and offers early. Their initial interaction may commence with the presentation of a demand. The filing of a lawsuit without prior negotiation of the claim is one way to assert a demand and start negotiations. In contrast, interest-based negotiators seek information from their counterpart and prefer to establish a positive relationship before discussing proposals. One purpose of the information sought and perhaps exchanged is to discover interests that might lead to an acceptable solution that creates value, even if there might later be more competitive bargaining to allocate the added value.

Whether you prefer a competitive or cooperative approach, there will be negotiations in which you must decide if it is better to make the first offer or invite an offer from the other side. (Offers and demands are used here synonymously.) If choosing to make the first offer, should it be extreme, modestly favorable, exactly what you expect, or equitably calculated to be fair to all and maximize collective value? If the first offer is made by the other side, should you flinch, as recommended by Dawson, counteroffer immediately, or process the offer and come back with an exaggerated counteroffer or one closer to your reservation point? How does formulating the initial offer relate to what we have learned about perceptions, ripeness, anchoring, preparation, the role of expectations, and trust?

The negotiation guidebooks are full of advice on making offers, much of it contradictory. There appears to be consensus that in distributive negotiations, more extreme or aggressive offers result in more favorable outcomes. (However, an exaggerated offer can come before or after learning the other side's opening position.) This consensus, focused on distributive negotiation, doesn't help you on how to start an integrative negotiation.

❖ **Gerald R. Williams & Charles Craver, LEGAL NEGOTIATION**

79 (West Publishing, 2007)

. . . The lawyers articulate their opening positions. At this early stage in the dispute, that exchange is not as simple as it appears. The facts are not all in, the legal questions are not fully researched, and unforeseen developments loom on the horizon. In the face of these uncertainties, the negotiators must leave themselves a certain amount of latitude, yet they must develop credible opening demands and offers . . .

[T]here are essentially three strategies that can be used in framing an opening position. . . . Negotiators may adopt the *maximalist strategy* of asking for more than they expect to obtain, they may adopt the *equitable strategy* of taking positions that is fair to both sides, or they may adopt the *integrative strategy* of searching for alternative solutions that would generate the most attractive combination for all concerned. Each strategy has its own strengths and weaknesses.

Maximalist Positioning

Arguments for maximalist positioning begin with the assumption that the opening position is a bargaining position, and that no matter how long bargainers may deny it, they expect to come down from them to find agreements. Maximalist positioning has several advantages. These position statements effectively hide the bargainer's real or minimum expectations, they eliminate the danger of committing to an overly modest case evaluation, they provide covers for them while they seek to learn real opponent positions, and will very likely induce opponents to reduce their expectations. They also provide negotiators with something to give up, with concessions they can make, to come to terms with opponents. This last factor may be especially important when opponents also open high, and negotiators are required to trade concessions as they move toward mutually agreeable terms. These advantages may lead many to believe that negotiators who make high opening demands, have high expectations, make relatively small and infrequent concessions, and are perceptive and unyielding fare better in the long run than their opponents.

The potential benefits of the maximalist position need to be weighed against its potential demerits, which are those associated with competitive/adversarial strategies. . . . The most important weakness is the increased risk of bargaining stalemates. Competent opponents will prefer their non-settlement alternatives to the unreasonable demands and supporting tactics of the maximalist negotiators, unless the opponents themselves can devise effective strategies to counter such maximalist behaviors. We observe in the data that competitive attorneys at all levels of effectiveness are rated as making high opening demands. Yet, by definition, effective competitive/adversarials use the strategy proficiently, while ineffective competitive adversarials do not. We are forced to conclude that in the legal context the maximalist strategy does not consistently bring high returns for those who use it — only for those who employ it effectively. How high demands can be without losing their effectiveness depends on several considerations. One is the nature of the remedy being sought. By their nature, contract damages are less inflatable than personal injury damages, for example, and negotiators who multiply their contract damages as they do their personal injury claims will undermine their own credibility. Another consideration is local custom. Specialized groups within the bar develop norms and customs that provide measures against which the reasonableness or extremism of demands can be evaluated. Not all high demands are the same. Some demands lack credibility on their face by their inappropriateness and lack of congruity in the context in which they are made. But the level of demands is not the sole factor. The data suggest that effective competitive/adversarial negotiators are able to establish the credibility and plausibility of high demands by relying on convincing legal argumentation. Ineffective competitive/adversarials lack the skills to do this, and, in the absence of convincing support, their high demands lack credibility.

Finally, it should be noted that the effectiveness of high demands will depend upon the opponents against whom the high demands are made. In cases where opponents are unsure of the actual case values, high opening demands by maximizing negotiators have the desired effect. The opponents, unsure of case values, use the maximizer's high opening demands as standards against which to set their own goals. However, when the opponents have evaluated their cases and arrived at appropriate value judgments, the opponents interpreted maximizer high opening demands as evidence of unreasonableness. This causes maximizer credibility to be diminished, and the likelihood of bargaining breakdowns increases.

Equitable Positioning

Equitable positions are calculated to be fair to both sides. Their most notable proponent, O. Bartos, challenged the assumption of maximalist theorists that both sides to negotiations are trying to maximize their own payoffs or benefits. He argued that a competing value is also operative — that negotiators feel a cooperative desire to arrive at solutions fair to both sides. . . .

This equitable approach is considered as the most economical and efficient method of conflict resolution. It minimizes the risk of deadlock and avoids the costs of delay occasioned by extreme bargaining positions. Bartos recommended that negotiators be scrupulously fair and that they avoid the temptation to take advantage of naive opponents. He cautioned that the equitable approach requires trust, which allows both sides to believe they are being treated fairly. Nonetheless, trust must be tempered with realism. It is out of trust that negotiators make concessions, but if their trust is not rewarded or returned in fair fashion, further concessions should be withheld until their opponents reciprocate. Equitable negotiators do not always open negotiations with statements specifying their desires to achieve mutually beneficial solutions. Rather, they open with positions that show they are serious about finding fair agreement, and they trustingly work toward mid-points between their reasonable opening position and the reasonable opening positions of their opponents.

Unless both sides come forward with reasonable opening positions, it will be difficult for one side to compel the other to move toward an equitable resolution. Referring back to the data on cooperative/problem-solving and competitive/adversarial negotiators, we intuitively suspect that Bartos' equitable negotiators are cooperative/problem-solvers. . . . We must conclude that the positioning strategy, whether maximalist or equitable, does not guarantee success. Whichever approach is used, it must be employed with care and acumen or it will not be effective.

Integrative Positioning

Integrative Positioning involves more than opening demands and offers. It describes an attitude or approach that carries through the other stages of the negotiation, and is an alternative to pure positional bargaining. The most effective advocates of this method have been Roger Fisher and William Ury who advise negotiators to avoid positioning completely. Among business people, the method is seen as the art of problem solving. Integrative negotiators view cases as presenting alternative solutions, and they believe that chances for reaching agreements are enhanced by discovering innovative alternatives reflecting the underlying interests of the parties, and seeking to arrange the alternatives in packages that yield maximum benefit to both parties. This strategy is often identified with exchange transactions involving many variables, and is generally seen as having limited utility in personal injury actions, for example, where the fundamental issue is how much money defendants are going to pay plaintiffs — a classic distributive problem. . . .

❖ **Jonathan Harr,** *A Civil Action*

277 (Vintage Books, 1996)

After a few minutes, the lawyers took their assigned seats at the table. Schlichtmann began talking about how he and his partners took only a few select cases and worked to the exclusion of all else on those. (This was Schlichtmann's way of saying there was no stopping them.) He said he wanted a settlement that would provide for the economic security of the families, and for their medical bills in the future. The families, he continued, weren't in this case just for money. They wanted an acknowledgment of the companies' wrongdoing, Schlichtmann said, a full disclosure of all the dumping activities.

"Are you suggesting there hasn't been a full disclosure?" Facher asked. "No," said Schlichtmann, who was suggesting exactly that, but now made an effort to avoid confrontation. "But as part of a settlement, we want a disclosure that the judge will bless." Another condition of settlement, he added, was an agreement that the companies clean their land of the toxic wastes, and pay the costs for cleaning the aquifer.

None of the defense lawyers had touched any of the food or drink. As Schlichtmann spoke, he saw Facher reach for a bowl of mints on the table and slowly unwrap the foil from one. Facher popped the mint into his mouth and sucked on it, watching Schlichtmann watch him.

Schlichtmann talked for fifteen minutes. Then Gordon laid out the financial terms of the settlement: an annual payment of $1.5 million to each of the eight families for the next thirty years; $25 million to establish a research foundation that would investigate the links between hazardous wastes and illness; and another $25 million in cash.

Cheeseman and his partners took notes on legal pads as Gordon spoke. Facher examined the pen provided courtesy of the Four Seasons, but he did not write anything on his pad. Facher studied the gilt inscription on the pen. It looked like a good-quality pen. These figures, he thought, were preposterous. They meant that Schlichtmann did not want to settle the case, or else he was crazy. Maybe Schlichtmann simply wanted to go to trial. This opulent setting, and Schlichtmann sitting at the table flanked by his disciples like a Last Supper scene, annoyed Facher. Where was Schlichtmann getting the money for all this?

When Gordon finished, silence descended.

Finally Facher stopped studying the pen. He looked up, and said, "If I wasn't being polite, I'd tell you what you could do with this demand."

Cheeseman had added up Gordon's figures. By Cheeseman's calculations, Schlichtmann was asking a total of four hundred ten million over thirty years. "How much is that at present value?" Cheeseman asked Gordon.

Gordon replied that he would rather not say. "Your own structured-settlement people can tell you that."

Facher took a croissant from the plate in front of him, wrapped it in a napkin, and put it into his pocket. That and the mint he had consumed were the only items the defense lawyers had taken from the sumptuous banquet that Gordon had ordered.

Cheeseman and his partners asked a few more perfunctory questions about the terms of disclosure, which Schlichtmann answered. Facher had gone back to studying the pen. "Can I have this?" he said abruptly, looking at Schlichtmann.

Schlichtmann, appearing surprised, nodded. Facher put the pen into his breast pocket. "Nice pen," he said. "Thank you."

Then Facher got up, put on his coat, and walked out the door. Frederico, who had not uttered a word, followed him.

Cheeseman and his partners stood, too, and in a moment, they followed Facher.

Schlichtmann and his colleagues sat alone on their side of the table. Gordon looked at his watch. The meeting had lasted exactly thirty-seven minutes, he announced. "I guess we're going to trial," Gordon added.

Schlichtmann was surprised, but only for a moment. He looked at his colleagues and shrugged. "We're going to get a jury in two weeks," he said. "The pressure's on them."

Conway got up and paced the room and smoked a cigarette. He didn't feel like talking. There was nothing to discuss. They'd gotten nothing out of this so-called settlement conference, not even information from the other side. He put on his coat and, along with Crowley, walked up Tremont Street back to the office.

Questions

10. How did Schlichtmann go wrong? What advice offered by Shell and by Williams and Craver might have been helpful for Schlichtmann in making his demand?

11. Might local custom and the experience of opposing counsel, as well as the evaluation done by the other side, have been contributing factors to the defense walkout in the above scene? What would you have done differently than Schlichtmann in this situation?

In formulating your first proposal, whether it be a demand or offer, it is advised that you determine the most aggressive proposal for which you can state a credible justification. Never demand so much or offer so little that you can't explain the reason for it. Be able to phrase your first offer as "I propose this because . . ." This will minimize the "Schlichtmann effect."

Bargaining takes many forms and is not confined to a specific stage in the negotiation process. The term "bargaining" is more associated with the competitive/distributive approach. Phrases like "searching for solutions" and "problem solving" are frequently used to describe a more cooperative/integrative approach. However, at some point in any negotiation there must be movement from the differences that brought the parties to the table toward agreement. Whether the movement results from arguments and persuasion or from proposed principles and criteria may be more a matter of semantics and tone than of real difference.

For example, lawyers in negotiating a settlement of a lawsuit may agree, expressly or implicitly, that legal principles will be the criteria for settlement. Does this reduce the role of argument regarding what case precedent is most applicable? A hallmark of integrative negotiation is trading off a lower priority to satisfy one more personally important. Is this not a form of bargaining concession?

1. Managing Concessions

Concessions are the compromises you make after your opening offer to move the negotiation forward, particularly in competitive bargaining. Usually the concessions you make are offered in return for those your negotiation opponent offers. Making concessions can be done strategically in recognition that the timing, amount, and nature of concessions are a form of communication by which each side sends signals about priorities and reservation points. The pattern of concessions forms a message. By carefully considering what you want to communicate you can manage concessions to shape the message, particularly about how close you are to your reservation point.

Diminishing concessions signal that you are reaching your limit. The timing of concessions can also be telling. Concessions given in rapid succession early on may signal risk aversion or desperation. Giving away too much in the initial stages also depletes the reserve of concessions that can be offered later, when they may be more appreciated.

By planning and using concessions strategically, you can influence the outcome of negotiation, but a similar might strategy be used to manipulate you. Be aware that the concession signals from a competitive bargainer can be deceptive.

❖ **Theron O'Connor,** *Planning and Executing*
an Effective Concession Strategy

(Bay Group International, 2003)

Concessions and the Negotiating Process

It is the concession piece of the negotiation process — the bargaining, the give-and-take, the "horse-trading," what the parties are willing to give up in order to reach an agreement — that will be discussed here. There are two principal sets of tasks to consider. The first is how to create the most advantageous negotiation context within which a concession strategy can be implemented. The techniques to establish a favorable negotiation context are discussed elsewhere in this volume. The second critical consideration is how to effectively handle the *execution* of the concession strategy or plan once the context has been established. This piece will focus upon the execution phase.

It should be noted that the many parts of the negotiation process are not strictly sequential. Rather, they occur and reoccur throughout the negotiation and must be attended to iteratively. That is particularly true of concession patterns. Often attention to concessions is mistakenly deferred until late in the game and concessions are used tactically, rather than strategically, as a closing tool.

Planning and Executing an Effective Concession Strategy

Once a desirable negotiating context has been established, the concession strategy can be executed. Whether to concede, when to concede, what to concede, how to concede are among a number of important considerations to keep in mind in dealing with concessions. Skilled negotiators develop plans for managing the process of making concessions, and thereby exert more control over the negotiation process. Conceding without a plan can doom you to failure in negotiation.

Concessions Should Be Made Only as Required

Notwithstanding that a sophisticated concession strategy has been developed — replete with creative and cost effective negotiables — no concessions should be made unless they are demanded by the other side. If the other side is willing to accept the initial proposal, then there has probably been a failure to accurately gauge the unexpectedly high value perception of the other side and a failure to take a sufficiently ambitious opening position. That error ought not to be compounded by then freely granting concessions from the largesse that has been built into the plan. While this should go without saying, there is often the temptation to "throw something in" simply because it is unexpectedly still there.

Concessions Should Be Made Slowly and Reluctantly

At the early stages of the negotiation, the focus should be on continuing to shape and influence the value perception of the other side and continuing to uncover and evaluate their wants and needs. With the range of reason advantageously set, it is imperative to hold the line and show resolve with respect to the value proposition and opening position. Reluctance to make concessions early on tends to increase their value in the mind of the other negotiator when they are in fact granted. Care should be taken, however, not to communicate too aggressive and inflexible a stance.

Try Not to Be the First to Make a Concession

If possible, get the other party to move first. Take the time to test the resolve of the other side by asking for concessions and suggesting ways that interests might be satisfied by them. First concessions can carry strong signals as to the flexibility of the other negotiator and can help calibrate the distance between the party's positions. Do not hesitate to make a concession, however, if it seems necessary to keep the negotiation going.

Get Something in Return for Any Concession

Concessions should be made in the context of trades or exchanges rather than given simply to see if the other side's point of satisfaction might be found. Demanding a concession in return both reinforces the value of what is being conceded and signals the resolve of the negotiator making the concession. It also helps to build the process of give and take and stimulate movement toward agreement.

First Concede Low Cost Negotiables That Represent High Value to the Other Side and Vice Versa

Having prioritized and ranked those things which might be offered to satisfy the wants and needs of the parties, it is important to evaluate each opportunity in terms of what might be offered that would be perceived to provide the highest possible value to the other side at the lowest cost. Likewise, in seeking concessions from the other side, it is important to seek concessions of high perceived value at comparatively low cost to them.

Use a Concession Pattern Designed to Leverage Fundamental Interests

Concession patterns communicate predictable messages to the other side. Holding firm and making one big concession at the end sends one message; making one large early concession and then holding firm sends another message. Making incremental but growing concessions sends one message; making incremental but diminishing concessions sends another message. Driving value early on and then executing a concession pattern of a large concession first and then progressively smaller ones often can be the most powerful pattern of all. It communicates resolve, then flexibility, and then diminishing returns moving toward closure.

Conclusion

It is critical to the ultimate success of the negotiation to deal with the concession process early on — even prior to initial contact — both to build the most advantageous context and to develop a strategy for execution of the concession plan. The context-building activities, anchoring, framing, positioning, setting high opening targets, discovering interests and negotiables, and managing emotions and behaviors, help to develop a robust value proposition and to stretch the range-of-reason within which an optimal outcome can be achieved.

Concession execution guidelines help to ensure that the negotiator will not give up too much too soon and that an appropriate balance will be maintained between self-interested competitiveness on the one hand and relational collaboration on the other. The concession execution guidelines are:

- No Concession Unless Needed
- Get the Other Party to Make First Concession
- Concede Slowly and Reluctantly
- Get Something in Return
- Concede to High Value from Low Cost/Vice-Versa
- Use Advantageous Pattern

Rigorous integration of both phases, building context and concession execution—from beginning to end—create the highest likelihood of successful negotiation.

Problem

Assume you are negotiating a personal injury claim on behalf of an injured pedestrian, and liability is not clear. You have spoken with the insurance claims adjuster five times. Each time you have conceded an additional $1,000 off your initial written demand of $80,000, while offering new information or arguments in support of your claim. What do you think the adjuster might be communicating to you with each of the following concession patterns (he would use only one of these four patterns), and how would each pattern influence your recommendation to your risk-averse client about accepting a $47,000 settlement after your fifth round of negotiation?

	A	B	C	D
1.	$0	$3,000	$40,000	$47,000
2.	$0	$6,000	$45,000	$47,000
3.	$0	$12,500	$46,500	$47,000
4.	$0	$25,000	$47,000	$47,000
5.	$47,000	$47,000	$47,000	$47,000

---

2. Value-Creating Trades and Brainstorming

A type of bargaining also occurs in cooperative, problem-solving negotiation. The focus is more on finding the best fit of interests rather than on gaining a one-sided advantage. The following reading proposes a way to generate value-creating options and trade-offs. The technique of brainstorming to generate more creative options based on different interests and values is described.

❖ Robert H. Mnookin, Scott R. Peppet & Andrew S. Tulumello, *Beyond Winning: Negotiating to Create Value in Deals and Disputes*

37 (Harvard University Press, 2000)

Generate Value-Creating Options

Now . . . look for value-creating trades. But this is not as easy as it might appear. Many negotiators jump into a negotiation process that inhibits value creation. One side suggests a solution and the other negotiator shoots it down. The second negotiator proposes an option, only to be told by the first why it can't work. After a few minutes of this, neither side is willing to propose anything but the most conventional solutions. This method mistakenly conflates two processes that should be engaged in separately: generating options and evaluating them.

It often helps to engage in some sort of brainstorming. The most effective brainstorming requires real freedom — however momentary — from practical constraints. . . . [There are two ground rules for brainstorming.]

- No evaluation
- No ownership

Premature evaluation inhibits creativity. We are all self-critical enough, and adding to our natural inhibitions only makes matters worse. When brainstorming, avoid the temptation to critique ideas as they are being generated. . . . There will be time enough for evaluation. The idea behind brainstorming is that evaluation should be a separate activity, not mixed with the process of generating ideas.

The second ground rule of brainstorming is: *no ownership of ideas*. Those at the table should feel free to suggest anything they can think of, without fear that their ideas will be attributed to them or used against them. Avoid comments such as: "John, I'm surprised to hear you suggest that; I didn't think you believed that idea made much sense." John should be able to suggest an idea *without believing it*. Indeed, those at the table should feel free to suggest ideas that are not in their best interests, purely to stimulate discussion, without fear that others at the table will later take those ideas as offers. [I]t may feel very dangerous to engage in this activity with someone on the other side. Our own experience suggests, nevertheless, that by negotiating process clearly, brainstorming can also be productive across the table.

How do you convey these ground rules to the other side? You can get the point across without sounding dictatorial or rule-obsessed. Just explain what you're trying to achieve and then lead by example. . . . Generating these possible options may broaden the parties' thinking about the terms of their negotiated agreement. . . .

What happens to interest-based, collaborative problem-solving when you turn to distributive issues? Some negotiators act as if problem-solving has to be tossed overboard when the going gets tough. We could not disagree more. In our experience, it's when distributive issues are at the forefront that problem-solving skills are most desperately needed . . .

Sometimes, of course, you won't be able to find a solution that satisfies both sides. No matter how hard you try, you will continue to disagree about salary, the amount to be paid in a bonus, or some aspect of a dispute settlement. Norms may have helped move you closer together, but there's still a big gap between the two sides. What should you do?

Think about process. How can you design a process that would fairly resolve this impasse? In a dispute settlement, you might be able to hire a mediator to address the distributive issues that are still open. Is there anyone both sides trust enough to decide the issue? Could you put five possible agreements into a hat and pick one at random?

Procedural solutions can often rescue a distributive negotiation that has reached an impasse. They need not involve complicated alternative dispute resolution procedures that cost money and time. Instead, you can often come up with simple process solutions that will resolve a distributive deadlock and allow you to move forward.

Changing the Game

Not everyone approaches negotiation from a problem-solving perspective. The basic approach described in this chapter — with its emphasis on the sources of value creation and the importance of a problem-solving process — obviously departs from the norm of adversarial haggling. To be a problem-solver, a negotiator must often lead the way and change the game. . . .

Conclusion

The tension between value creation and value distribution exists in almost all negotiations. . . . The problem-solving approach we have suggested here will not make distributive issues go away. . . . But it does outline an approach that will help you find value-creating opportunities when they exist and resolve distributive issues efficiently and as a shared problem. . . .

Question

12. Assume you represent the plaintiff family suing for wrongful death of a husband/father killed by a drunk driver. Bargaining has reached an impasse, with your last demand at $1 million and the defendant's last offer at $800,000 (combining a $500,000 insurance limit and defendant's personal funds). Would you consider brainstorming? If you knew that the affluent defendant was facing sentencing for vehicular manslaughter and a letter from your client could be beneficial to her, would this open the door to value creation? The following letter was written to the sentencing judge following brainstorming, which resulted in settlement of the case. (All names have been changed.) Is an ethical problem raised by the use of this letter to settle a wrongful death claim against a drunk driver?

> To whom it may concern:
> We are the mother and surviving widow of the deceased, David Baron, whose death has left us and his three young sons behind. We write this letter to request leniency for Ms. Dorian.
> Mistakes were made by both Ms. Dorian and David, and we have all paid an enormous price. At this point, we do not believe that these consequences should be further multiplied by sending Ms. Dorian to jail.
> We understand that this was an isolated incident of drinking and driving for Ms. Dorian and she seems truly sorry for what happened. She has taken steps to deal with the drinking problem and she has done her best to compensate us and the three boys for our loss. We believe it is time for everyone to put this tragedy behind them and to begin building new lives in its aftermath.
> We want to ask that Ms. Dorian be placed on probation for a period of time. We would like to see her participate in programs and organizations for victims and substance abusers in the criminal justice system. We think David would agree.

> Thank you for your time and consideration.
> Sincerely,
> Judith Baron and Martha Baron

E. Moving Toward Closure

As the bargaining process continues, negotiators often find it more and more difficult to make concessions or identify additional value-creating trades. All the easy, obvious moves have been made, and yet a gap may well remain. There are many ways to manage the process of bridging the final gap between bargainers. This section explores two of the most common methods.

1. Planning for Closure

❖ **Roger Fisher, William Ury & Bruce Patton,** *GETTING TO YES*

171-75 (Penguin, 1991)

[H]ow do you reach closure on issues? We don't believe that there is any one best process, but here are some general principles worth considering:

Think about closure from the beginning. Before you even begin to negotiate, it makes sense to envision what a successful agreement might look like. This will help you figure out what issues will need to be dealt with in the negotiation and what it might take to resolve them. Imagine what it might be like to implement an agreement. What issues would need to be resolved? Then work backwards. Ask yourself how the other side might successfully explain and justify an agreement to their constituents. ("We will be in the top 10 percent of all electrical workers in Ontario." "We are paying less than the value given by two out of three appraisers.") Think about what it will take for you to do the same. Then ask yourself what kind of an agreement would allow you both to say such things. Finally, think about what it might take to persuade the other side — and you — to accept a proposed agreement, rather than continuing to negotiate.

Keep these questions in mind as your negotiation progresses, reshaping and filling in your vision as more information becomes available. Focusing on your goal in this way will help to keep your negotiation on a productive track.

Consider crafting a framework agreement. In negotiations that will produce a written agreement, it is usually a good idea to sketch the outlines of what an agreement might look like as part of your preparation. Such a "framework agreement" is a document in the form of an agreement, but with blank spaces for each term to be resolved by negotiation. . . .

Whether or not you start your negotiation with a framework agreement, it makes sense to draft possible terms of an agreement as you go. Working on a draft helps to keep discussions focused, tends to surface important issues that might otherwise be overlooked, and gives a sense of progress. Drafting as you go also provides a record of discussions, reducing the chance of later misunderstanding. If you are working with a framework agreement, drafting may involve no more than filling in the blanks as you discuss each term; or, if you have yet to reach consensus, it may involve drafting alternative provisions.

Move toward commitment gradually. As the negotiation proceeds and you discuss options and standards for each issue, you should be seeking a consensus proposal that reflects all the points made and meets each side's interests on that issue as well as possible. If you are as yet unable to reach consensus on a single option, try at least to narrow the range of options under consideration and then go on to another issue. Perhaps a better option or a trade-off possibility will occur later. ("All right. So perhaps something like $28,000 or $30,000 might make sense on salary. What about the starting date?"). . . .

The process of moving toward agreement is seldom linear. Be prepared to move through the list of issues several times, going back and forth between looking at particular issues and the total package. Difficult issues may be revisited frequently or set aside until the end, depending on whether incremental progress seems possible. Along the way, avoid demands or locking in. Instead, offer options and ask for criticism. ("What would you think of an agreement along the lines of this draft? I am not sure I could sell it to my people, but it might be in the ballpark. Could something like this work for you? If not, what would be wrong with it?")

Be persistent in pursuing your interests but not rigid in pursuing any particular solution. One way to be firm without being positional is to separate your interests from ways to meet them. When a proposal is challenged, don't defend the proposal; rather explain again your underlying interests. Ask if the other side can think of a better way to meet those interests, as well as their own. If there appears to be an irresolvable conflict, ask if there is any reason why one side's interests should have priority over the other's.

Unless the other side makes a persuasive case for why your thinking is incomplete and should be changed, stick to your analysis. When and if you are persuaded, modify your thinking accordingly, presenting the logic first. ("Well, that's a good point. One way to measure that factor would be to . . .") If you have prepared well, you should have anticipated most arguments the other side might raise and thought through how you think they should affect the result.

Throughout, the goal is to avoid useless quarreling. Where disagreements persist, seek second-order agreement—agreement on where you disagree. Make sure that each side's interests and reasoning are clear. Seek differing assumptions and ways to test them. As always seek to reconcile conflicting interests with external standards or creative options. Seek to reconcile conflicting standards with criteria for evaluating which is more appropriate or with creative trade-offs. Be persistent.

2. Splitting the Difference and Dealing with Impasse

A deceptively simple concluding technique often used in both competitive and cooperative negotiations is splitting the difference.

❖ **G. Richard Shell,** *Bargaining for Advantage: Negotiation Strategies for Reasonable People*

185 (Penguin, 2006)

Perhaps the most frequently used closing technique is splitting the difference. Bargaining research tells us that the most likely settlement point in any given transaction is the midpoint between the two opening offers. People who instinctively prefer a compromise style like to cut through the whole bargaining process by getting the two opening numbers on the table and then splitting them right down the middle.

Even in cases in which the parties have gone through several rounds of bargaining, there often comes a time when one side or the other suggests that the parties meet halfway between their last position. In situations in which the relationship between the parties is important, this is a perfectly appropriate, smooth way to close.

Why is splitting the difference so popular? First, it appeals to our sense of fairness and reciprocity, thus, setting a good precedent for future dealings between the parties. . . . Each side makes an equal concession simultaneously. What could be fairer than that?

Second, it is simple and easy to understand. It requires no elaborate justification or explanation. The other side sees exactly what you are doing.

Third, it is quick. For people who do not like to negotiate or are in a hurry, splitting the difference offers a way out of the potentially messy interpersonal conflict that looms whenever a negotiation occurs.

Splitting the difference is such a common closing tactic that it often seems rude and unreasonable to refuse, regardless of the situation. This is taking a good thing too far, however. There are at least two important situations in which I would hesitate to split the difference.

First, you should be careful that the midpoint being suggested is genuinely fair to your side. If you have opened at a reasonable price and the other party opened at an aggressive one, the midpoint is likely to favor the other party by a big margin. So don't split the difference at the end if there was a lack of balance at the beginning. Second, when a lot of money or an important principle is on the line and relationships matter, quickly resorting to a splitting may leave opportunities for additional, creative options on the table. . . .

When the gap between offers is too wide to split, another friendly way to close is to obtain a neutral valuation or appraisal. If the parties cannot agree on a single appraiser, they can each pick one and agree to split the difference between the two numbers given by the experts.

What Happens if Negotiations Break Down?

The concession-making stage of bargaining sometimes ends with no deal rather than an agreement. The parties reach an impasse. In fact, a no deal result is sometimes the right answer. No deal is better than a bad deal. . . .

In addition to escalation problems, the parties may start too far apart to close the gap. Many times there are miscommunications, misunderstanding, and simple bad chemistry that the parties fail to overcome. Now what?

Jump-Starting the Negotiation Process

Perhaps the easiest way to overcome impasse is to leave yourself a back door through which to return to the table when you get up to leave it. "In light of the position you have taken," you might say as you pack your bags, "we are unable to continue negotiations at this time." An attentive opponent will pick up on your use of the words "at this time" and tactfully ask you later if the time has come to reinitiate talks. This back door also allows you to contact the other side at a later date without losing face.

If the other negotiator leaves in a genuine fit of anger, he may not be very careful about leaving a back door open. If so, you should consider how you can let him back in without unnecessary loss of face. You must, in one expert's phrase, build him a "golden bridge" across which to return to the table. Such bridges include "forgetting" that he made his ultimatum in the first place or recalling his last statement in a way that gives him an excuse for returning.

When miscommunication is the problem, a simple apology may be enough to get the parties back on track. If the relationship has deteriorated beyond apologies, changing negotiators or getting rid of intermediaries altogether may be necessary.

In America, the sport of professional baseball lost nearly two full seasons in the 1990s because of an impasse in negotiations between the players' union and the club owners. The team owners from the big cities wanted to limit the size of team payrolls. The team owners from smaller cities wanted the team owners from big cities to subsidize their franchises. The players wanted more money. It was a three-ring circus. The breakthrough came when the owners hired a new negotiator — a lawyer named Randy Levine — to represent them at the table. Levine acted in the role of mediator as much as advocate and brought a high degree of both credibility and creativity to the process that, according to one participant, "broke the dam of mistrust" that had built up between the parties. Another move that helped move the talks beyond impasse was getting all parties to agree to stop talking to the press and taking public positions that made it hard for them to compromise at the table. . . . [P]ublic commitments can help you stick to your goals, but there comes a time when it is in everyone's interest to get unstuck from their positions. In a high stakes negotiation such as a labor strike, this often means getting the parties out of the spotlight so they can work in private.

The worst impasses are the products of emotional escalation that builds on itself: My anger makes you angry, and your response makes me even angrier. . . . The solution to this sort of collision, in business deals as well as wars, is what I call the "one small step" procedure. One side needs to make a very small, visible move in the other side's direction, then wait for reciprocation. If the other party responds, the two can repeat the cycle again, and so on. Commentator Charles Osgood, writing about the Cold War in the early 1960s, created an acronym for this process: GRIT (Graduated and Reciprocated Initiatives in Tension Reduction).

Egypt's late prime minister, Anwar Sadat, used the "one small step" technique to deescalate the Arab-Israeli conflict when he flew to Jerusalem on November 19, 1977 and later met with Prime Minister Menachem Begin. By simply getting off a plane in Israel — a very small step indeed — Sadat demonstrated his willingness to recognize Israel's existence. This move eventually led to the Camp David peace accords and Israel's return of the Sinai Peninsula to Egypt.

An executive once told me a bargaining story that nicely sums up how the "one small step" process can work in everyday life. Two parties were in a complex business negotiation. Both were convinced that they had leverage, and both thought that the best arguments favored their own view of the deal. After a few rounds, neither side would make a move.

Finally one of the women at the table reached in her purse and pulled out a bag of M&M's. She opened the bag and poured the M&M's into a pile in the middle of the table.

"What are those for?" asked her counterparts.

"They are to keep score," she said.

Then she announced a small concession on the deal — and pulled an M&M out of the pile and put it on her side of the table.

"Now it's your turn," she said to the men sitting opposite.

Not to be outdone, her opponents put their heads together, came up with a concession of their own — and pulled out two M&M's. "Our concession was bigger than yours," they said.

The instigator of the process wisely let the other side win this little argument and then made another concession of her own, taking another M&M for herself.

It wasn't long before the parties were working closely together to close the final terms of the deal. Call this the M&M version of the GRIT process. Any similar mechanism that restarts the norm of reciprocity within the bargaining relationship will have a similar, helpful effect.

Overall, when parties reach an impasse, it is usually because each sees the other's demands as leaving it below its legitimate expectations. Eventually, if the parties are to make any progress, they must change their frame of reference and begin seeing that they will be worse off with no deal than they would be accepting a deal that falls below their original expectations.

Sometimes this transition takes time. The impasse must be allowed to last long enough that one or both parties actually alter their expectations. A final agreement must be seen as a gain compared with available alternatives.

Questions

13. Have you ever "split the difference" to conclude a negotiation or sale? Looking back, was that the best way to close the deal? Are you now sure you were not manipulated into an outcome or price that was more favorable to the other side? Have you used this closing tactic to your advantage?
14. Do you agree with Shell that impasse can often be helpful? If so, when? Why would anyone plan an impasse as part of their negotiating strategy?

F. Finalizing an Agreement

After you reach decisions about how a case will be settled or a deal will be structured, your work as a lawyer is not complete. The relief you feel in reaching an agreement can induce you to neglect the important task of how the agreement will be worded and how the remaining details will be determined. Issues of implementation and execution may remain to be determined. The old maxim that "the devil is in the details" is an apt warning. Often, a negotiated settlement about the amount to be paid or an agreement "in principle" triggers another set of negotiations, this time over the formal terms of the settlement agreement itself. Lack of clarity about the terms of the agreement can result in perceptual differences about what was decided and the unraveling of the agreement. Inattention to how the agreement is written can also put your client's interests at risk of intentional overreaching by the other side or unintentional differences of interpretation that do not favor your client. Not memorializing the agreement in writing as quickly as possible can lead to unnecessary expenses if more time is required to reconstruct exactly what was agreed or if uncertainty develops about the outcome. If you did well negotiating, the favorable result for your client can lead to buyer's remorse, causing the other side to look for ways to change the non-finalized terms or reject the not yet enforceable agreement.

A negotiated business transaction is usually memorialized in the form of a written contract that incorporates the terms of the deal and follows general contract principles. An agreement to settle a legal claim may have different characteristics and requirements. A release of claims, a dismissal or other disposition of the underlying lawsuit, enforceability by entry of judgment or liquidated damages, how and when money will be paid or performance of obligations will occur, costs, expenses, and tax aspects — all of these issues must be considered when writing an agreement to settle a lawsuit. Ambiguities must be avoided; a settlement document is written to resolve an existing dispute, not foster a future one.

It is also important to attend to the psychological and relationship aspects of closing the deal. Never celebrate a victory in the presence of an opponent. If you can leave the other side feeling they did well, there will be fewer questions regarding implementation of the agreement. The relationship is also strengthened if no one feels they were bested and if clients on both sides have reason to think they were well represented. (It is for this reason that a good negotiator on the other side will not give you an honest critique or tell you that you could have done better.) Even if the parties will not have an ongoing relationship, the attorneys may have future professional contact. There is value in the rapport that carries forward to future negotiations when each side is satisfied with the outcome and great cost if an opponent feels compelled to "get even" at the next opportunity because of regret over an outcome.

This ends our brief introduction to the complex and fascinating process of negotiation. We now explore the hidden barriers and obstacles that often frustrate the settlement of legal disputes.

CHAPTER
4

Barriers to Settlement

If all negotiations were successful, then the dispute resolution pyramid described by Professor Galanter in Chapter 1 would have its top half lopped off. Either disputants would reach an accommodation with their opponents directly, or lawyers would negotiate satisfactory resolutions on their behalf, making it unnecessary for a party ever to file a case in court, much less go to trial. However, conflicts — in particular, legal disputes — often do fail to settle initially, leading to many court cases being filed. We now know that the large majority of legal cases are never adjudicated, implying that most litigants do eventually reach some kind of resolution short of trial. However, this often does not occur for months or years, and while the dispute is pending, all the parties are likely to incur significant costs, both directly in terms of fees for legal services and indirectly in anxiety and disruption of their personal or business lives.

Negotiations fail, or stall, for a wide variety of reasons. In thinking about how to settle disputes, it is very helpful to focus on the specific barriers that make it difficult for lawyers and clients to bargain effectively. In the readings that follow, we examine four common types of barriers to successful negotiation: strategic, principal-agent, cognitive, and emotional.

A. Strategic and Principal-Agent Barriers

❖ **Robert H. Mnookin,** *WHY NEGOTIATIONS FAIL:*
AN EXPLORATION OF BARRIERS TO THE RESOLUTION OF CONFLICT

8 Ohio St. J. Disp. Resol. 235 (1993)

Conflict is inevitable, but efficient and fair resolution is not. Conflicts can persist even though there may be any number of possible resolutions that would better serve the interests of the parties. . . . In our everyday personal and professional lives, we have all witnessed disputes where the absence of a resolution imposes substantial and avoidable costs on all parties. Moreover, many resolutions that are achieved — whether through negotiation or imposition — conspicuously fail to satisfy the economist's criterion of Pareto efficiency. Let me offer a few examples where, at least with the benefit of hindsight, it is easy to identify alternative resolutions that might have left both parties better off.

My first example involves a divorcing family in California who were part of a longitudinal study carried out by Stanford psychologist Eleanor Maccoby and me. Mary and Paul Templeton spent three years fighting over the custody of their seven-year-old daughter Tracy after Mary filed for divorce. . . .Mary wanted sole custody; Paul wanted joint physical custody. This middle-income family spent over [$75,000 in current dollars] on lawyers and experts. In the process, they traumatized Tracy and inflicted great emotional pain on each other. More to the point, the conflict over who would best care for their daughter damaged each parent's relationship with Tracy, who has suffered terribly by being caught in the middle of her parents' conflict. Ultimately the divorce decree provided that Mary would have primary physical custody of Tracy, and Paul would be entitled to reasonable weekend visitation. The parents' inability to negotiate with one another led to a result in which mother, father, and daughter were all losers.

A conflict between Eastern Airlines and its unions represents another conspicuous example of a lose-lose outcome. In 1986, Frank Lorenzo took over Eastern, then the eighth largest American airline, with over 42,000 employees and about 1,000 daily flights to seventy cities. For the next three years, Lorenzo, considered a union buster by organized labor, pressed the airline's unions for various concessions, and laid off workers to reduce costs. The unions retaliated in a variety of ways, including a public relations campaign suggesting Eastern's airplanes were being improperly maintained because Lorenzo was inappropriately cutting costs. In March 1989, labor-management skirmishes turned into all-out war. Eastern's machinists went on strike, and the pilots and flight attendants initially joined in. The ensuing "no holds barred" battle between Lorenzo and the machinists led to losses on both sides.

Soon after the strike began, to put pressure on the unions and to avoid creditor claims, Eastern's management filed for bankruptcy, hired permanent replacements for the strikers, and began to sell off assets. While the pilots and flight attendants held out only a few months, the machinists union persisted in its strike, determined to get rid of Lorenzo at whatever cost. In one sense, they succeeded, for in 1990 the bankruptcy court forced Lorenzo to relinquish control of Eastern. It turned out to be a pyrrhic victory for the union, however, for on January 18, 1991, Eastern Airlines permanently shut down operations.

The titanic struggle between Texaco and Pennzoil over Getty Oil provides another example of a bargaining failure, although of a somewhat more subtle sort. Here, both corporations survived, with a clear winner and loser; Texaco paid Pennzoil $3 billion in cash to end the dispute in 1988. The parties reached settlement, however, only after a year-long bankruptcy proceeding for Texaco and protracted legal wrangling in various courts. While the dispute dragged on, the combined equity value of the two companies was reduced by some $3.4 billion. A settlement before Texaco filed for bankruptcy would have used up fewer social resources and would have been more valuable to the shareholders of both companies than the resolution created by the bankruptcy court about a year later.

My last example is an Art Buchwald story — but it isn't a laughing matter, at least, not for Buchwald. He and his partner, Alain Bernheim, submitted Buchwald's two and a half page "treatment" for a story called "King for a Day" to Paramount Pictures pursuant to contracts providing that Bernheim would produce any film based on the story idea and that Buchwald and Bernheim would each share in the profits. In 1989, Buchwald and Bernheim sued Paramount for breach of contract. They claimed that the studio had based Eddie Murphy's film, "Coming to America[,]" on their treatment but had failed to give them their due. After three years of bitter litigation, a trial judge awarded Buchwald $150,000 and Bernheim $750,000. In the initial newspaper accounts, both sides claimed victory, but this is hardly an example of "win-win." Paramount claimed to be the winner because the legal fees of the plaintiffs' lawyers exceeded $2.5 million and the total recovery of only $900,000 was a small fraction of the $6.2 million Buchwald and Bernheim had requested in their final arguments. As it turns out, Buchwald and Bernheim will not have to pay the full legal fees because of a contingency arrangement with their law firm, but Buchwald has acknowledged that his share of out-of-pocket expenses alone exceeds $200,000 and that as a consequence, he will have no net recovery. On the other hand, Buchwald ridiculed Paramount's claim of victory. How, he asked, could it be a victory for a defendant to pay out nearly $1 million in damages, and, in addition, have legal fees of its own in excess of $3 million? Seems like lose-lose to me.

On her death bed, Gertrude Stein was asked by Alice B. Toklas, "What is the answer? What is the answer?" After a long silence, Stein responded: "No, what is the question?" Examples like these, and I am sure you could add many more of your own, suggest a central question for those of us concerned with dispute resolution: Why is it that under circumstances where there are resolutions that better serve disputants, negotiations often fail to achieve efficient resolutions? In other words, what are the barriers to the negotiated resolution of conflict?

Barriers to the Negotiated Resolution of Conflict

. . . I am not attempting [here] to provide a comprehensive list of barriers or an all-encompassing classification scheme. Instead, my purpose is to show that the concept of barriers provides a useful and necessarily interdisciplinary vantage point for exploring why negotiations sometimes fail. After describing these barriers and their relevance to the study of negotiation, I will briefly suggest a variety of ways that neutral third parties might help overcome each of these barriers.

Strategic Barriers

The first barrier to the negotiated resolution of conflict is inherent in a central characteristic of negotiation. Negotiation can be metaphorically compared to making a pie and then dividing it up. The process of conflict resolution affects both the size of the pie, and who gets what size slice.

The disputants' behavior may affect the size of the pie in a variety of ways. On the one hand, spending on avoidable legal fees and other process costs shrinks the pie. On the other hand, negotiators can together "create value" and make the pie bigger by discovering resolutions in which each party contributes special complementary skills that can be combined in a synergistic way, or by exploiting differences in relative preferences that permit trades that make both parties better off. Books like "Getting to Yes" and proponents of "win-win negotiation" emphasize the potential benefits of collaborative problem-solving approaches to negotiation which allow parties to maximize the size of the pie.

Negotiation also involves issues concerning the distribution of benefits, and, with respect to pure distribution, both parties cannot be made better off at the same time. Given a pie of fixed size, a larger slice for you means a smaller one for me. Because bargaining typically entails both efficiency issues (that is, how big the pie can be made) and distributive issues (that is, who gets what size slice), negotiation involves an inherent tension — one that [has been] dubbed the "negotiator's dilemma." In order to create value, it is critically important that options be created in light of both parties' underlying interests and preferences. This suggests the importance of openness and disclosure, so that a variety of options can be analyzed and compared from the perspectives of all concerned. However, when it comes to the distributive aspects of bargaining, full disclosure — particularly if unreciprocated by the other side — can often lead to outcomes in which the more open party receives a comparatively smaller slice. To put it another way, unreciprocated approaches to creating value leave their maker vulnerable to claiming tactics. On the other hand, focusing on the distributive aspects of bargaining can often lead to unnecessary deadlocks and, more fundamentally, a failure to discover options or alternatives that make both sides better off. A simple example can expose the dilemma. The first involves what game theorists call "information asymmetry." This simply means each side to a negotiation characteristically knows some relevant facts that the other side does not know.

Suppose I have ten apples and no oranges, and Nancy Rogers has ten oranges and no apples. (Assume apples and oranges are otherwise unavailable to either of us.) I love oranges and hate apples. Nancy likes them both equally well. I suggest to Nancy that we might both be made better off through a trade. If I disclose to Nancy that I love oranges and don't eat apples, and Nancy wishes to engage in strategic bargaining, she might simply suggest that her preferences are the same as mine, although, in truth, she likes both. She might propose that I give her nine apples (which she says have little value to her) in exchange for one of her very valuable oranges. Because it is often very difficult for one party to know the underlying preferences of the other party, parties in a negotiation may puff, bluff, or lie about their underlying interests and preferences. Indeed, in many negotiations, it may never be possible to know whether the other side has honestly disclosed its interests and preferences. I have to be open to create value, but my openness may work to my disadvantage with respect to the distributive aspect of the negotiation.

Even when both parties know all the relevant information, and that potential gains may result from a negotiated deal, strategic bargaining over how to divide the pie can still lead to deadlock (with no deal at all) or protracted and expensive bargaining, thus shrinking the pie. For example, suppose Nancy has a house for sale for which she has a reservation price of $245,000. I am willing to pay up to $295,000 for the house. Any deal within a bargaining range from $245,000 to $295,000 would make both of us better off than no sale at all. Suppose we each know the other's reservation price. Will there be a deal? Not necessarily. If we disagree about how the $50,000 "surplus" should be divided (each wanting all or most of it), our negotiation may end in a deadlock. We might engage in hardball negotiation tactics in which each tried to persuade the other that he or she was committed to walking away from a beneficial deal, rather than accept less than $40,000 of the surplus. Nancy might claim that she won't take a nickel less than $285,000, or even $294,999 for that matter.

Indeed, she might go so far as to give a power of attorney to an agent to sell only at that price, and then leave town in order to make her commitment credible. Of course, I could play the same type of game and the result would then be that no deal is made and that we are both worse off. In this case, the obvious tension between the distribution of the $50,000 and the value creating possibilities inherent in any sale within the bargaining range may result in no deal.

Strategic behavior — which may be rational for a self-interested party concerned with maximizing the size of his or her own slice — can often lead to inefficient outcomes. Those subjected to claiming tactics often respond in kind, and the net result typically is to push up the cost of the dispute resolution process. (*Buchwald v. Paramount Pictures Corp.* is a good example of a case in which the economic costs of hardball litigation obviously and substantially shrunk the pie.) Parties may be tempted to engage in strategic behavior, hoping to get more. Often all they do is shrink the size of the pie. Those experienced in the civil litigation process see this all the time. One or both sides often attempt to use pre-trial discovery as leverage to force the other side into agreeing to a more favorable settlement. Often the net result, however, is simply that both sides spend unnecessary money on the dispute resolution process.

The Principal-Agent Problem

The second barrier is suggested by recent work relating to transaction cost economics, and is sometimes called the "principal-agent" problem. Notwithstanding the jargon, the basic idea is familiar to everyone in this room. The basic problem is that the incentives for an agent (whether it be a lawyer, employee, or officer) negotiating on behalf of a party to a dispute may induce behavior that fails to serve the interests of the principal itself. The relevant research suggests that it is no simple matter — whether by contract or custom — to align perfectly the incentives for an agent with the interests of the principal. This divergence may act as a barrier to efficient resolution of conflict.

Litigation is fraught with principal-agent problems. In civil litigation, for example — particularly where the lawyers on both sides are being paid by the hour — there is very little incentive for the opposing lawyers to cooperate, particularly if the clients have the capacity to pay for trench warfare and are angry to boot. Commentators have suggested that this is one reason many cases settle on the courthouse steps, and not before: for the lawyers, a late settlement may avoid the possible embarrassment of an extreme outcome, while at the same time providing substantial fees.

The Texaco/Pennzoil dispute may have involved a principal-agent problem of a different sort. My colleague Bob Wilson and I have argued that the interests of the Texaco officers and directors diverged from those of the Texaco shareholders in ways that may well have affected the conduct of that litigation. Although the shareholders would have benefited from an earlier settlement, the litigation was controlled by the directors, officers, and lawyers whose interests differed in important respects. A close examination of the incentives for the management of Texaco in particular suggests an explanation for the delay in settlement.

The directors and officers of Texaco were themselves defendants in fourteen lawsuits, eleven of them derivative shareholder actions, brought after the original multi-billion dollar Pennzoil verdict in the Texas trial court. These lawsuits essentially claimed that Texaco's directors and officers had violated their duty of care to the corporation by causing Texaco to acquire Getty Oil in a manner that led to the multi-billion dollar Texas judgment. After this verdict, and for the next several years, the Texaco management rationally might have preferred to appeal the Pennzoil judgment and seek complete vindication, even though a speedy settlement for the expected value of the litigation might have better served their shareholders. Because they faced the risk of personal liability, the directors and officers of Texaco acted in such a way as to suggest they would prefer to risk pursuing the case to the bitter end (with some slight chance of complete exoneration) rather than accept a negotiated resolution, even though in so doing they risked subjecting the corporation to a ten billion dollar judgment. The case ultimately did settle, but only through a bankruptcy proceeding in which the bankruptcy court eliminated the risk of personal liability for Texaco's officers and directors.

Overcoming Strategic Barriers: The Role of Negotiators and Mediators

The study of barriers can do more than simply help us understand why negotiations sometimes fail when they should not. It can also contribute to our understanding of how to overcome these barriers. Let me illustrate this by using the preceding analysis of four barriers briefly to explore the role of mediators, and to suggest why neutrals can often facilitate the efficient resolution of disputes by overcoming these specific barriers.

First, let us consider the strategic barrier. To the extent that a neutral third party is trusted by both sides, the neutral may be able to induce the parties to reveal information about their underlying interests, needs, priorities, and aspirations that they would not disclose to their adversary. This information may permit a trusted mediator to help the parties enlarge the pie in circumstances where the parties acting alone could not. Moreover, a mediator can foster a problem-solving atmosphere and lessen the temptation on the part of each side to engage in strategic behavior. A skilled mediator can often get parties to move beyond political posturing and recriminations about past wrongs and to instead consider possible gains from a fair resolution of the dispute.

A mediator also can help overcome barriers posed by principal-agent problems. A mediator may bring clients themselves to the table, and help them understand their shared interest in minimizing legal fees and costs in circumstances where the lawyers themselves might not be doing so. In circumstances where a middle manager is acting to prevent a settlement that might benefit the company, but might be harmful to the manager's own career, an astute mediator can sometimes bring another company representative to the table who does not have a personal stake in the outcome. . . .[1]

---

1. [*Note*: Professor Mnookin's article also describes cognitive and perceptual barriers, which are discussed below. — Eds.]

B. The Role of Perceptions

The key to mastering both negotiation and mediation is to be aware that those in conflict and who want something from one another often see the same situation very differently. It is these differences that give root both to the conflict and to the possibility of agreement. We assess conflict and evaluate a case or the worth of an item differently because of differing perceptions. It is because of such differences in perceptions that people bet on horse races, wage war, and pursue lawsuits.

A classic Japanese story, on which the film *Rashomon* is based, illustrates the role of perceptions and how the truth through one person's eyes may be very different from another's, as seen through the prism of the individuals' own perceptions. Through divergent narratives, the story and the film explore how perceptions distort or enhance different people's memories of a single event, in this case, the death of a Samurai warrior. Each tells the "truth" but perceives it very differently. The film, like the story, is unsettling because, as in much of life, no single truth emerges.

A popular book and film, *The War of the Roses*, by Warren Adler, and its 2004 sequel, *The Children of the Roses*, capture different truths as perceived by divorcing couples. Early in the original story, Oliver and Barbara Rose reveal to their separate lawyers their perspectives on the marriage and how their family home should be divided. Each sees the marriage relationship and what's fair differently, as filtered through his or her own experience, values, and selective vision. Is there any doubt, based on such different perceptions, that the war between the Roses would follow?

❖ Warren Adler, *THE WAR OF THE ROSES*

51 (Stonehouse Press, 1981)

[Oliver Rose's perception:] "She just upped and said, 'No more marriage.' Like her whole persona had been transformed. Maybe it's something chemical that happens as forty gets closer."

He had . . . been a good and loving husband. He had nearly offered "faithful" to complete the triad but that would have discounted his two episodes with hookers during conventions in San Francisco and Las Vegas when the children were small. My God, she had everything she could possibly want. . . .

What confused him most was that he had not been warned. Not a sign. He hated to be taken by surprise.

"And the house?" Goldstein asked.

"I don't know. Say half the value. After all, we did it together. Half of everything is okay with me. . . ."

[Barbara Rose's perception:] "He's like some kind of animal. Almost invisible. He leaves early, before we get up, and comes home late, long after we've gone to bed. He doesn't take his meals at home. . . ."

"You think it's fair for me to have devoted nearly twenty years to his career, his needs, his wants, his desires, his security. I gave up my schooling for him. I had his children. And I devoted a hell of a lot more time to that house than he did. Besides, the house is all I have to show for it. I can't match his earning power. Hell, in a few years he'll be able to replace its value. I'll just have cash. Well, that's not good enough. I want the house. I want all of it. It's not only a house. It's a symbol of a life-style. And I intend to keep it that way. That's fair. . . ."

"It's my house. I worked my ass off for it," she said.

The following reading further develops the theme that conflict is subjective and flows from different perceptions in people's minds. Rummel's "subjectivity principle" may help to explain the *War of the Roses* and many other conflicts that would otherwise defy understanding and resolution.

❖ R.J. Rummel, *The Conflict Helix*

13 (Transaction Publishers 1991)

The Subjectivity Principle

Perceived reality is your painting. You are the artist. You mix the colors, draw the lines, fix the focus, achieve the artistic balance. Reality disciplines your painting; it is your starting point. As the artist, you add here, leave out there; substitute color, simplify; and provide this reality with a point, a theme, a center of interest. You produce a thousand such paintings every moment. With unconscious artistry. Each a personal statement. Individualistic.

Now, most people realize that their perception of things can be wrong, that they may be mistaken. No doubt you have had disagreements with others on what you all saw or heard. And probably you have heard of eyewitnesses who widely disagree over the facts of a crime or accident. Some teachers who wish to dramatically illustrate such disagreement have staged mock fights or holdups in a classroom. A masked man rushes in, pointing some weapon at the teacher; demands his wallet; and with it hastily exits, leaving the class stunned. Then each member of the class is asked to write down what he saw and heard. Their versions usually differ widely.

But, of course, such are rapidly changing situations in which careful observation is difficult. Surely, you might think, if there were time to study a situation or event you would perceive it as others do. This is easy enough to test. Ask two people to describe in writing a furnished room, say your living room, or a car you may own. Then compare. You will find many similarities, but you should also find some important and interesting differences. Sometimes such differences result from error, inattentiveness. However, there is something more fundamental. Even attentive observers often will see things differently. And each can be correct.

There are a number of reasons for this. First, people may have different vantage points and their visual perspectives thus will differ. A round, flat object viewed from above will appear round, from an angle it will appear an ellipse, from the side a rectangle. This problem of perspective is acute in active, contact sports such as football or basketball. From the referee's line of sight there is no foul, but many spectators (especially the television audiences who see multiple angles and instant replays) know they saw an obvious violation.

But people can compare or change perspectives. Were this all, perception would not be a basic problem. The second reason for different perceptions is more fundamental. You endow what you sense with meaning. The outside world is an amorphous blend of a multitude of interwoven colors, lights, sounds, smells, tastes and material. You make sense of this complex by carving it into different concepts, such as table, chair, or boy. Learning a language is part of learning to perceive the world.

You also endow this reality with value. Thus what you perceive becomes good or bad, repulsive or attractive, dangerous or safe. You see a man running toward you with a knife as dangerous; a calm lake as peaceful; a child murderer as bad; a contribution to charity as good. And so on.

Cultures are systems of meanings laid onto reality; to become acculturated is to learn the language through which a culture gives the world unique shape and evaluation. A clear example of this is a cross, which to a Christian signifies the death of Jesus for mankind as well as the whole complex of values and beliefs bound up in the religion. Yet, to non–Christian cultures a cross may be meaningless: simply two pieces of wood connected at right angles. . . .

Besides varying perspectives and meanings, a third reason for different perceptions is that people have unique experiences and learning capacities, even when they share the same culture. Each person has his own background. No two people learn alike. Moreover, people have different occupations, and each occupation emphasizes and ignores different aspects of reality. Simply by virtue of their separate occupational interests, the world will be perceived dissimilarly by a philosopher, priest, engineer, union worker, or lawyer.

Two people may perceive the same thing from the same perspective, therefore, but each through their diverse languages, evaluations, experience, and occupations, may perceive it differently and endow it with personal meaning. Dissimilar perspective, meaning, and experience together explain why your perception will often differ radically from others.

There is yet an even more basic reason: what you sense is unconsciously transformed within your mental field in order to maintain a psychological balance. This mental process is familiar to you. People often perceive what they want to perceive, what they ardently hope to see. Their minds go to great pains to extract from the world that which they put there. People tend to see things consistent with their beliefs. If you believe businesspeople, politicians, or bureaucrats are bad, you will tend to see their failings. If you like a person, you tend to see the good; hate him and you tend to see the worst. Some people are optimists, usually seeing a bottle half full; others are pessimists, seeing the same bottle half empty.

Your perception is thus the result of a complex transformation of amorphous sensory stimuli. At various stages your personal experience, beliefs, and character affect what you perceive. . . .Independent of the outside world's powers to force your perception, you have power to impose a perception on reality. You can hallucinate. You can magnify some things to fill your perception in spite of what else is happening. Think of the whisper of one's name.

What you perceive in reality is a balance between these two sets of powers: the outside world's powers to make you perceive specific things and your powers to impose a certain perception on the world. This is the most basic opposition, the most basic conflict. Its outcome is what you perceive reality to be. . . .The elements of The Subjectivity Principle are perception, mental field, and balance: your perception is a balance between the powers of your mental field and the outside world. It is a balance between the perception you tend to impose on the outside world and the strength of what is out there to force its own reality on you. It is a balance between what you unconsciously want to perceive and what you cannot help but perceive. . . .

This balance that envelopes your mental field changes with your interest and concentration. Its shape and extension will depend on your personality and experience. And, of course, your culture. No wonder, then, that you are likely to perceive things differently from others. Your perception is subjective and personal. Reality does not draw its picture on a clean slate — your mind. Nor is your mind a passive movie screen on which sensory stimuli impact, to create a moving picture of the world. Rather, your mind is an active agent of perception, creating and transforming reality, while at the same time being disciplined and sometimes dominated by it. . . .

You and I may perceive reality differently and we both may be right. We are simply viewing the same thing from different perspectives and each emphasizing a deferent aspect. Blind men feeling different parts of an elephant may each believe they are correct and the others wrong about their perception. Yet, all can be correct; all can have a different part of the truth.

Questions

Rummel's subjectivity principle explains how we process the information and stimuli around us through the filters of our experience, needs, and biases. The complexity of our environment and our minds prevents us from taking it all in whole, so we focus selectively on some stimuli and ignore others. We develop shortcuts in our perceptual systems that allow us to function and process information more quickly and make timely decisions. These shortcuts, known as *heuristics*, can serve us well. However, mental shortcuts create the risk that our selectivity will distort reality as seen by others. The different ways we process information can lead to conflict based on our different realities.

1. Can you recall a conflict you have experienced that might be better understood in light of the subjectivity principle?
2. Is the conflict between Barbara and Oliver Rose really over their house, or something else? If the division or ownership of the house is the manifest or presenting conflict, what is the underlying conflict or "hidden agenda"? Can lawyers negotiate what may be the underlying conflict regarding gender roles? Can they do something about each Rose's need for recognition of his or her contribution to the house and the marriage?

C. The Impact of Fairness

Our list of selective perceptions at the beginning of this chapter included "fairness." Differing views of fairness are at the heart of many litigated conflicts and failed negotiations. Fairness, like other perceptions, is in the mind of the beholder. A client may hire you to negotiate on her behalf because she feels she has been treated unfairly and that you, as a lawyer, can help her obtain what is fair. Fairness, as perceived by clients, can also become central in assessing whether to accept or reject a negotiated settlement or deal.

An outcome that appears fair can be more important than winning or losing. Fairness may define for some whether they won or lost. Offers may be rejected even though they are economically advantageous because in the client's mind the result is not fair.

Classroom experiments with "ultimatum games" illustrate the importance of perceived fairness in negotiation. In these games, Player 1 is given a fixed sum of money or chips (for example, $100) as a windfall that she might have found on the street and is asked to propose a division of that sum with Player 2 (for example, $75 to Player 1 and $25 to Player 2). Player 1 has complete discretion to divide the money as she wishes; Player 2 can choose only whether to accept or reject Player 1's proposal. If Player 2 accepts the offer, both players will keep the money as allocated. If Player 2 rejects the offer, neither player will receive anything.

Economic theory dictates that Player 1 should offer only a little more than zero to Player 2, and that Player 2 should accept this amount as better than nothing. In fact, in classroom experiments Player 1 generally offers 30 to 50 percent of the sum to Player 2, and when less than 50 percent is offered, many recipients will reject the offer, preferring to walk away with nothing rather than accept what they perceive to be an unfair result. The results of this game reflect the importance of our innate value of being treated fairly (see Brams & Taylor 1996). Ultimatum games are not restricted to the classroom. Consider the following real-life example.

THE HOME-RUN BALL CATCH

More than 40,000 fans were at the ballpark to see the San Francisco Giants' last game of the 2001 season. Most had come to see Barry Bonds add another home run to his already record-breaking total of 72. Alex Popov and Patrick Hayashi were two fans in the right field arcade standing-room section, hoping to catch a Bonds home-run ball. Sure enough, Bonds's 73rd home-run ball came sailing over the right field bleachers into Popov's outstretched glove. Within seconds, Popov fell to the ground as a rush of people converged on him and the ball. Madness followed before security officers arrived. When Popov was pulled from the pile of fans, the ball was no longer in his glove. Patrick Hayashi emerged with the ball in hand.

Both men claimed ownership of the valuable home-run ball, temporarily in Hayashi's possession. Both thought the ball was worth more than $1 million, based on the sale of Mark McGwire's 70th home-run ball in 1998 for more than $3 million. Each man offered the other less than $100,000 to relinquish any claim on the ball. Each expressed strong public views that he was entitled to complete ownership and was making a generous offer to the other. Both Popov and Hayashi cited principles of fairness and baseball fan culture entitling them to the ball. Popov argued that first possession controls, and Hayashi believed the fan who ended up in possession owned the ball. They insulted one another as liars and thieves. They both hired lawyers and filed suit in the California superior court.

Newspaper editorials, letters, talk show hosts, Barry Bonds, and several media-tors all suggested that the ball be sold and the proceeds be split by the men or that the money be given to charity. Neither Popov nor Hayashi thought that evenly splitting what they were individually entitled to was fair, nor did they feel that they could concede anything in light of the insults cast on them by the other. Following 18 months of public bickering and litigation about what was fair, the judge ordered that the ball be sold and the proceeds evenly split. On June 25, 2003, the ball, seated on black velvet and encased in glass, was sold at auction to a comic book impresario for a final bid of $450,000. Popov and Hayashi each received $225,000, minus auction expenses, and each incurred attorneys' fees exceeding that amount. Popov was sued by his attorney for fees and expenses of $473,530, and also for $19,000 by a law professor who served as an expert witness. (The whole sorry story and background is captured in the 2004 film *Up for Grabs*.)

Perceptions of fairness consist of two components. Distributional fairness is a quantitative notion of material outcome — what you get as the result of a negotiation. Procedural fairness relates to the process used to reach the outcome — how you were treated during the negotiation. Both of these components shape people's willingness to accept settlements and their feelings of how well attorneys represented them in the negotiation process.

D. Psychological Traps and Professional Objectivity

Studying the perceptions and distortions of reasoning that immerse people in conflict helps us better understand clients' disputes. Although lawyers advocate and negotiate on behalf of clients, we are less subject to the partisan perspectives that can skew our client's perceptions. This is because although we, as lawyers, may be professional adversaries, we do not have a direct stake in the outcomes, so we can think more clearly and rationally. This is the common wisdom, but is it true?

We can often recognize our clients' partisan perceptions, but we are easily fooled by our own biases and distortions. By definition, what we believe, even if selective, is our reality. The longer we work with a client on a case or a deal, the more we share the same reality — distorted or not. We might be no more able than our clients to objectively analyze the weaknesses of their case or the strengths of the other side's arguments. It can be very helpful for you to understand some of the psychological factors likely to affect not only your client's thinking, but also your own assessment of case value and the attractiveness of offers to settle. Psychological traps and biases often lead us into disputes and influence how we negotiate.

Much of what we know about the hidden forces that create conflict and shape our decisions is attributable to work done in the 1970s and 1980s by cognitive psychologists Amos Tversky and Daniel Kahneman, whose work was recognized with a Nobel Prize in 2002 (See Tversky & Kahneman 1981; Kahneman, Slovic & Tversky 1982). They focused on heuristics — the mental shortcuts mentioned above — and found that there are consistent biases in perceptions and decision making that can be traced to these shortcuts. More recently, experiments have been conducted with law students and lawyers that confirm that cognitive traps apply to our bargaining decisions and advice.

Problem

Students at your school who had expected to attend a required lecture without charge are told after they arrive that they will each have to pay $20 to cover unexpected expenses. They can, however, spin a roulette wheel with four chances in five of paying nothing and one chance of having to pay $100. Which will most choose and why? (The answer is within the list below.)

Note: Top Ten Psychological Traps

The following is an alphabetical list of the top ten common mental traps that can create disputes or make them more difficult to resolve. Some are interrelated. We return to these cognitive shortcuts and expand the list later when we examine why negotiations fail. They also come into play in the next section on how mediators can move negotiations through an impasse to settlement.

1. *Anchoring*: A dispute over the value of an item often arises because we form an estimate of an unsure value by comparing it to something we know or to a number to which we are exposed that is then planted in our brain. The number you are exposed to as a value anchors your calculation and influences your thinking.

   For example, when a client is burnt by hot soup at a restaurant, she may think the restaurant is to blame and her claim is worth millions because she heard about a multimillion-dollar verdict against McDonald's for coffee that was served too hot. You, as a sophisticated lawyer, understand that this case is distinguishable from the McDonald's case, which was reduced on appeal as excessive, and that this client's case is much weaker and worth less than that one, so you adjust from the McDonald's verdict downward. The question is whether you adjust far enough. Research suggests that you will not adjust sufficiently because of the anchoring effect, which could also distort your analysis and expectation.

2. *Confirmation bias*: We tend to give credit to information that is consistent with our preexisting beliefs and wishes rather than information that challenges or contradicts them. This can dig us deeper into conflict when dealing with those who have different beliefs or values. We read and believe articles that confirm dark chocolate and red wine are good for us, and skim past articles that question the studies.

3. *Consensus error (Projection)*: We tend to falsely believe that others think the way we do or have values similar to ours. We also believe that others like what we like and want what we want. Those who enjoy loud music presume everyone wants to hear their amplified radio selections. Conflict can be created when we find out we were wrong.

4. *Framing*: Our thinking about an issue and our answer to a question are affected by how the question is presented. Asking a priest if you can smoke while you pray is likely to result in a different answer than asking if you can pray while you smoke.

5. *Loss aversion (Status quo bias)*: Losses tend to be felt more painfully than equivalent gains are relished, so that a dollar loss is felt greater than a dollar gain. We don't value equal trades from a neutral perspective. We tend to

overvalue what we have to give up relative to what we get, making us often regret what we have done. Also, negotiating parties are more likely to view their own concessions (losses) as more valuable than equivalent concessions they get from the other side (gains).

6. *Naive realism*: We tend to think that the way we see the world is the way it really is and anyone seeing it differently is naive. This bias is in play when your idea or offer is rejected with the preface that in the "real world" things are different.

7. *Overconfidence*: We tend to rate our abilities, chance of being right, and good luck more highly than is warranted. Because we can't always be right, disputes happen. We are also overconfident about our ability to assess uncertain data and tend to give more weight to what we know than what we don't know. As a matter of fact, we are overconfident about ourselves in general. As examples, surveys have found that 70 percent of all drivers believe that they are more competent than the average driver, and 80 percent of lawyers think that they are more ethical than the average attorney (Fox & Birke 2000). In negotiation, overconfidence can be compounded by positive illusions we have about the relative righteousness of our case or cause.

8. *Reactive devaluation*: Whatever proposal comes from the other side cannot be good for us. Anything done or suggested by them is suspect. For example, if Democrats propose legislation, Republicans are likely to reject it, and vice versa. Also, any information or offer received is perceived as less valuable than what might be withheld. This tends to escalate conflict.

9. *Selective perception*: Whenever we encounter a new situation, we must interpret a universe of unfamiliar, often conflicting data that is more than we can process. We respond by instinctively forming a hypothesis about the situation in the time available, then organizing what we see and hear with the help of that premise. Our hypothesis also operates as a filter, by automatically screening out what doesn't support it — which in turn reinforces the belief that our initial view was correct. Henry David Thoreau was probably thinking about this when he said, "We see only the world we look for."

   Selective perception is also the basis of self-fulfilling prophesies and stereotyping. For example, if you are negotiating with a lawyer you believe is hostile and not to be trusted, you may dismiss his initial friendly greeting as manipulative and selectively see him scrutinizing you with suspicion. Your stilted behavior toward him will likely result in him seeing you as antagonistic. Mutually reinforced surly behavior will be selectively observed and remembered to the exclusion of overtures of civility. You will feel that your own insight and keen ability to "read" others is confirmed, and your self-fulfilling prophecy will be realized.

10. *Self-serving biases*: We are our own best friend in justifying our actions while seeing the same behavior in someone else as a shortcoming. We know that we are personally responsible for our successes, but our failures are the result of bad luck or circumstances beyond our control. When we are late it is for good reason; others keep us waiting because of their bad planning and insensitivity. Our miscalculation or misstatement is a simple mistake, but our opponent's similar error is the result of deception.

Some of the psychological factors and biases described above may work against one another when a person is making tactical decisions in a negotiation. For example, as will be discussed later, there are differing views about the advantages and disadvantages of making the first offer. Making the first offer, particularly if the values involved are uncertain or without ready comparisons, could take advantage of anchoring bias. However, reactive devaluation could cause the other side to radically discount a first offer out of suspicion of an adversary.

Questions

3. Do you think that knowing about the potential for these cognitive errors will help you to avoid being affected by them? For example, how might you overcome, or at least minimize, selective perception in your own thinking or that of your client?

4. If a lawyer is to follow a client's wishes regarding settlement, what is the lawyer's role if he is aware that the client is suffering from cognitive distortions? Must the lawyer agree to an outcome if he believes that the client is being influenced by cognitive errors?

5. How might you counter perceptual distortion that might lead an opponent to reject a reasonable settlement, for example, the tendency to reject even a reasonable offer because of her suspicion of any offer coming from you?

E. The Role of Emotions

Cognitive and perceptual distortions affect negotiations even when everyone involved is calm and attempting to think rationally. But what if the people involved are not calm — in fact, are in the grip of strong emotions? Strong feelings are common in legal cases. Disputants often do not talk about their feelings because they are embarrassed to do so, have been told that emotions are irrelevant, or are not even conscious that an emotional issue exists. Still, feelings stirred by personal clashes between participants, combined with forces generated by the dispute itself, are the primary obstacles to settlement in many cases.

The judgment of disputants can be overwhelmed by a variety of strong emotions, ranging from guilt to frustration, sadness, and anger. An accident victim or an employer charged with discrimination, for example, is likely to have intense feelings about her case. Even if the dispute itself is not inflammatory, people often become angry over events that occur during litigation. A party may be enraged, for example, by a perceived snub, or a lawyer may become angry when an opponent uses "hardball" bargaining tactics. The *War of the Roses* excerpt is only one example of how strong feelings can disrupt communication and produce irrational decision making.

This often means that bargainers must navigate through a treacherous mixture of emotional crosscurrents. Professor Lawrence Susskind, talking about efforts to resolve public controversies (Kolb 1994), cautioned that:

I don't assume some perfect rationality from everybody in the room. I assume, first, that emotion will overcome logic during the course of the process. Almost everybody will often do things that, if they thought about them beforehand and were asked "Would you do that?" they'd say, "No." But they — we — will do it anyway, because emotion dominates logic.

In the reading below, a law professor/psychologist describes the ways in which emotions can interfere with negotiators' effectiveness, and how much of this interference is unconscious.

❖ Joshua D. Rosenberg, *Interpersonal Dynamics: Helping Lawyers Learn the Skills, and the Importance, of Human Relationships in the Practice of Law*

55 U. of Miami L. Rev. 1225 (2004)

Basically, most lawyers and academics vastly overestimate the importance of reason and logic. We tend to view them as both the primary motivator of our own behavior and the primary tool to change the thinking and behavior of others. Although they are important, they are only one part of the puzzle. There are important differences between the kind of dispassionate reasoning and analysis in which lawyers and law students engage while sitting at desks at home, in the office, or in the library, and the kind of activities in which we engage when we are dealing in real time with real people. Real time, real life interactions implicate emotions, learned patterns of behavior, habituated perspectives and frames of reference, and other human, but not reasoned, responses.

The reactions to emotions occur whether or not the person is aware of either the reaction or the emotion, and they significantly impact the outcome of most negotiations and most other interpersonal interactions. People who become anxious may tend to over-accommodate the other by inappropriately giving in on the substance of the discussion, or may tend to talk too much (or too little) in an unconscious effort to forestall that anxiety. People who become irritated may tend to become slightly belligerent or withdrawn in ways that can harm their interactions. Any feelings are likely to trigger unconscious patterns of thought and behavior that will inevitably influence an interaction. . . .

It is not just how we think about what we perceive that is tainted by our feelings. Our very perceptions themselves are determined, in part, by our feelings (and thoughts). As an initial matter, emotions precipitate changes in the autonomic nervous system. These changes include increasing the heart rate, changing breathing patterns, skin changes such as perspiration or blushing, and redirecting blood flow (anger has been found to direct blood to the hands, presumably for combat; fear has been shown to redirect blood to the legs, presumably for running). At a micro level, these changes in the autonomic nervous system change not only our ability to think, but also our ability to act and perceive. Along with our thoughts, our blood flow, and our energy, the focus of our attention and our ability to take in data are significantly changed by our emotional state. Not only our behavior, but also our perceptions become both differently focused and less accurate. . . .

The Result: Interacting Systems and Self-Fulfilling Prophecies

Basically, our thoughts, feelings, behaviors and perceptions influence each other. We react to our perceptions of the world around us while our own behavior impacts on the world. Of course, the patterns of our behavior, thoughts, perceptions and feelings are far from random. We tend to learn patterns of thought, feeling, and behavioral reactions in childhood. In adulthood we tend to engage in those patterns we learned as children, often resulting in "self-fulfilling prophecies" that tend to reinforce those same old patterns. [B]ecause of our particular frame of reference (thoughts, feelings, etc.), we expect people to act in certain ways, and we act toward them in ways that tend to precipitate the behaviors we expect. When people do act in the ways we expected, we interpret that behavior in line with our expectations, and we react in certain predictable ways (which tend to confirm to us the validity of our earlier expectations).

Negotiation experts are aware of the significant impact of self-fulfilling prophecies on negotiations, but the actual impact of these patterns extends well beyond "negotiations," to encompass most of our interactions in life. [S]elf-fulfilling prophecies and other generally unconscious learned responses significantly impact the outcome of most negotiations and most other interpersonal interactions.

Human Communication: Colliding Systems

As all of the above suggests, despite our typical estimation to the contrary, we are often unaware of the actual causes (and unintentional consequences) of our own behavior, thinking, emotions, and perceptions. We are not sufficiently self-aware to realize how many of our patterns of acting and thinking are ingrained, unconscious or triggered by our autonomic nervous system rather than by reason. Communication, of course, is a two-way street, and much of the time we are even more misguided about what is headed toward us than we are about where we ourselves are going. Just as we incorrectly believe that we understand our own behavior better than we do, we also (and to a much greater degree) wrongly believe that we understand others much better than we actually do. . . .

As an initial matter, researchers have concluded that the single greatest weakness of most negotiators is that they too often fail to even consider the thinking and emotions of others. Perhaps even more significantly, when we do attempt to consider the thinking and feelings of others, we usually get it wrong. We often attribute to them moods, goals or motivations that simply are not there, or we exaggerate the significance of one of many reactions they may be having and forget that, like our own, their reactions might be both dynamic and complex.

While we tend to be accepting of situational factors that impact our own behavior, we tend to be unaware of, and inattentive to, the impact of such situational factors on others. As a result, we tend to think of ourselves as more sympathetic, as having a better case, or as being a better person than the one with whom we are dealing. In turn, this often leads us to devalue the other's case and proposals, and to fail to reach agreements that are available and would have been in our client's (or our own, as the case may be) best interest.

Basically, we tend to assume, too often inaccurately, that the message we take from the other is actually the message they intended to send. We vastly underestimate not only the impact of our own perspectives, feelings and thinking on the message we take in, but also the role of simple miscommunication.

Compounding the problem of our misperceptions of others is the fact that we are basically unaware that the problem even exists. Research clearly shows that more than 98% of us are unable to tell when others are lying or telling the truth. We are essentially equally likely to believe those who are lying as we are to believe those who are telling the truth, and we are equally likely to disbelieve those who are actually telling the truth as we are to disbelieve those who are actually lying. Interestingly, and typically, I have never met a person who believes that she is a part of that 98% majority.

All of this obviously makes for significant misunderstandings and unnecessary conflict. Even worse, it is often self-perpetuating. Because we believe that we already understand others, we rarely take the time to try to understand them better. If they do not act as we want or hope, we tend to attribute their "failure" to act "properly" to some personality defect on their part. Rather than seek to learn more about them, we tend to dismiss them or negatively characterize them. We will in turn likely act in ways that may ultimately alienate them, and they will likely react in ways that will confirm, in our minds, our initial understanding. Human communication is then the interaction of two individuals, each of whom believes that she alone understands both herself and the other, while in fact neither really understands either herself or the other, and neither seeks to gain understanding (because each thinks she already has it). Perhaps more surprising than the amount of miscommunication and conflict in the world is the fact that, at least occasionally, accurate communication does take place. . . .

Questions

6. Have you seen any examples, in real life or in an exercise in this course, of how emotional intelligence contributed to successful negotiation?
7. Do you think that such intelligence can be taught?
8. If you served on your school's curriculum committee, how would you assess the pros and cons of offering a course on "Interpersonal Skills for Law Students"? Would you vote to create such a course?

Strategic, principal-agent, cognitive, emotional, and other issues can make it hard for bargainers to reach agreement even when they have a joint interest in doing so, as in deal-making or transactional negotiations. When people are embroiled in a dispute, however, such obstacles become much larger, often making it impossible for disputants to bargain at all. Mediation has become an increasingly popular way to overcome barriers to negotiation, making it possible for lawyers and clients to achieve settlements and avoid the cost and disruption of litigation. We now examine how the mediation process does this, and how lawyers can take advantage of its qualities.

PART II

THE MEDIATION PROCESS

CHAPTER

5

An Overview of Mediation

A. Introduction

1. The Process of Mediation

a. What Is Mediation?

Mediation is a process of assisted negotiation in which a neutral person helps people to reach agreement. The process varies depending on the style of the mediator, the nature of the dispute, and the wishes of the participants. Mediation differs from direct negotiation in that it involves the participation of an impartial third party. The process also differs from adjudication in that it is consensual, informal, and usually private. The participants need not reach agreement, and the mediator, who is usually selected by the participants, has no power to impose an outcome.

In some contexts you may find that this definition does not fully apply. The process is sometimes not voluntary, as when a judge requires litigants to participate in mediation as a precondition to trial. In addition, mediators are not always entirely neutral; a corporate lawyer, for instance, can apply mediative techniques to help colleagues resolve an internal dispute, despite the fact that he is in favor of a particular outcome. Occasionally mediation is required to be open to the public, as when a controversy involves governmental entities subject to "open meeting" laws. Finally, a mediator's goal is not always to settle a specific legal dispute; the neutral may focus instead on helping disputants improve their relationship or complete a transaction.

There is an ongoing debate within the field about what mediation should be. To some degree this results from the different goals that participants have for the process: Some focus only on settlement of a claim and seek to obtain the best possible monetary terms, whereas others seek to solve a problem, and still other participants enter mediation to improve a difficult relationship. The increasing application of mediation to areas such as family and criminal law also raises serious questions of policy. This text focuses on "civil" mediation, involving legal disputes outside the area of collective bargaining, because this is what you are most likely to encounter in law practice. However, to give you a sense of the flexibility of mediation, we also present other perspectives on the process.

b. What Do Mediators Do?

Mediators apply a wide variety of techniques. Depending on the situation, a settlement-oriented mediator may use one or more of the following approaches, among others:

- Help litigants design a process that ensures the presence of key participants and focuses their attention on finding a constructive solution to a dispute.
- Allow the principals and their attorneys to present legal arguments, raise underlying concerns, and express their feelings directly to their opponents, as well as hear the other side's perspective firsthand.
- Help the participants focus on their interests and identify imaginative settlement options.
- Moderate negotiations; coaching bargainers in effective techniques, translating communications, and reframing the disputants' positions and perceptions.
- Assist each side to assess the likely outcome if the case is litigated, and to consider the full costs of continuing the conflict.
- Work with the disputants to draft a durable agreement and, if necessary, to implement it.

c. What Is the Structure of Mediation?

Because mediation is informal, lawyers and clients have a great deal of freedom to modify the process to meet their needs. In practice, good neutrals and advocates vary their approach significantly to respond to the circumstances of particular cases. That said, a typical mediation of a legal dispute is likely to proceed through a series of stages.

Pre-Mediation

Before the disputants meet to mediate, the neutral often has conversations with the lawyers, and sometimes also with the parties, to deal with issues such as who will attend the mediation and to address emotional and other issues. Lawyers can use these contacts to start to build a working relationship with the mediator and educate him about their client's perspective on the dispute and obstacles that have made direct negotiations difficult.

The Opening Session

Many mediations begin with a session in which the parties, counsel, and mediator meet together. The content and structure of such a session varies considerably, depending on the participants' wishes and the goals of the process. When mediation is focused on reaching a monetary settlement, the joint session is likely to be dominated by arguments of lawyers, perhaps followed by questions from the neutral. If the goal of the process is to find an interest-based solution or to repair a ruptured relationship, then a mediator is much more likely to encourage the parties themselves to speak and to attempt to draw out underlying issues and emotions.

Private Caucusing

After disputants have exchanged perspectives, arguments, and questions and obtained a "read" on one another, most commercial mediators adjourn the joint session to meet with each side individually in private "caucuses." The purpose of caucusing is to permit disputants, counsel, and the mediator to talk candidly together. Keeping the parties separated, with communications channeled through the mediator, also allows the neutral to shape the disputants' dialogue in productive ways.

When the mediation process is focused on monetary bargaining, the participants usually spend most of their time separated, with the mediator shuttling back and forth between them. If, however, parties are interested in exploring an interest-based resolution or repairing a broken relationship, then the mediator is more likely to encourage disputants to meet together extensively so that they can work through emotions and learn to relate productively with each other.

Joint Discussions

Even when a mediation is conducted primarily through private caucusing, neutrals sometimes ask disputants to meet with each other for a specific purpose. This might be to examine tax issues in a business breakup, explore a licensing agreement to resolve a patent claim, or deal with a difficult emotional issue in a tort case. In most mediations, whether or not conducted through caucusing, the lawyers and perhaps also the parties meet at the end of the process to sign a memorandum of agreement or decide on future steps.

Follow-Up Contacts

Increasingly, the mediation process is not limited to the occasions on which the mediator and disputants meet together. If a dispute is not resolved at a mediation session, then the neutral is likely to follow up with the lawyers or parties, and may facilitate telephone or e-mail negotiations or convene additional face-to-face sessions if the parties wish.

Variations in Format

The model we have just discussed represents a "default" model for legal mediation, but you will encounter significant variations in the field. Mediators who handle family disputes, for example, often remain in joint session during the entire process, and some mediators are experimenting with no-caucus formats in other kinds of civil cases.

At the same time, in several states the practice of holding an opening session in legal mediations is declining. Some legal mediators, acting at the request of litigators, often begin the process with only a cursory opening session or none at all, and spend virtually all their time in private caucusing. Others meet with each side before the opening session. The advantages and disadvantages of these and other formats are discussed later.

2. *The Value of Mediation*

The growing popularity of mediation reflects an important change in the legal culture. What, in the eyes of parties and their lawyers, are the potential benefits of going to mediation? Consider the comments and data that follow.

a. Viewpoints of Lawyers

Diane Gentile, Dayton

My practice is focused on employment law. These claims deal with one of the most important aspects of peoples' identity — their work. In addition, they often involve serious allegations of wrongdoing. Both sides in these disputes often have good reason to want a confidential solution. One example [is] a case I handled involving a worker and supervisor. Several years before the two had had a consensual intimate relationship, but the worker later accused her supervisor of sexual harassment. For the employer, the claim was a potential nightmare. The fact that the supervisor had at first denied the existence of the earlier relationship made it even more difficult. Moreover, because the employer was a nonprofit organization that depended in part on public funds, the potential for negative publicity could have crippled the organization. As soon as we received notice of the plaintiff's suit we suggested mediation. After nine hours of difficult discussions we had a resolution, and the organization's relief was limitless.

Mediation is effective in part because it allows the parties to talk about many things that will never be considered relevant by a court. When they are allowed to speak freely, often in private to a mediator offering a sympathetic ear, material just spills out, and afterward people are often much more willing to compromise. Mediation also allows for nonlegal relief, which is particularly important in employment cases: changes to a file to reflect a voluntary quit rather than termination, for example, or agreement on what the company will say to a future employer asking for a reference.

Stephen Oleskey, Boston

I use mediation extensively in commercial cases to deal with a wide variety of obstacles. My goals depend on the nature of the situation. In one recent case, for example, the problem was anger: The parties had been talking off and on for two years, but both were so upset that they could not focus productively on settlement. At the same time, with several hundred million dollars at stake, neither side could bear the risk of a winner-take-all trial. Mediation created the context for a rational discussion of the merits and risks. In another case, we used mediation to get a group of corporate and political stakeholders to come to the same place and focus intensively on a case that some of them had not previously thought through.

Occasionally, I've used a mediator to give a message to a client — or the other side's client — that was hard for a lawyer to deliver. In a few cases, it's been the way that the mediator has framed the discussions: her choice of what issues to focus on, or the statement that, "We'll stay here until midnight if we have to, to get this done," that tells the parties that this is the time to make the difficult choices, put all their money on the table, and work out a deal if possible.

Mary Alexander, San Francisco

My practice focuses on personal injury cases, including auto accident, product liability, and defective design claims. Years ago we settled cases only on the courthouse steps, but courts in California now push parties to mediate long before trial. Often a case will not settle at court-ordered mediation, but the process gets lawyers talking and often leads to an agreement.

The single most useful service provided by mediators in my practice is to provide a reality check for clients. People often come into a lawyer's office with very real injuries, but unrealistic expectations about what they can obtain from the court system. They have heard somewhere about a large award and assume that it is typical, when in fact it is not. Clients are often in dire financial straits and physical pain, making it hard for them to listen to a lawyer's warnings about trial risk. When a mediator, especially a former judge, explains the realities of present-day juries — often in language that turns out to be very similar to what I had said earlier — it makes a real impression. Clients are able to become more realistic, and to accept a good offer when it appears. Even if the courts did not order it, I would elect to mediate almost every significant case.

Katherine Gurun, Former General Counsel, Bechtel Corporation

Our business involved complex construction and engineering projects. It was built around long-term relationships with suppliers and partners. Things inevitably went wrong — equipment failed, customers encountered financial problems, and so on. We had to resolve these issues, but in a way that kept our relationships healthy. Mediation became our most powerful and successful process for accomplishing this.

The flexibility of mediation is its most useful quality. In the disputes we encountered at Bechtel, the complex nature of the issues almost always required several sessions, often spread over a period of months. During adjournments, people could confer with their organizations and the mediator could work on one or both sides. Overall, ADR reduced Bechtel's litigation costs phenomenally; just as important, it avoided the management distraction caused by formal litigation.

We also used mediation in international disputes. Here cultural differences were an important consideration. Many of our foreign partners were in mediation for the first time, and it was particularly important to find a neutral who "knew both sides of the fence." Asian executives seemed especially comfortable with the mixture of joint and private meetings, because the structure accommodated their preference for conferring and reaching a consensus within the team at each point in the process. Europeans sometimes seemed troubled by mediation's lack of formality, but I found that its adaptability was what made the process so effective.

Paul Bland, Public Justice, Washington, D.C.

There are two major situations in which I find mediation helpful as a litigator for a public interest organization. The first is when we challenge widespread practices; for example, a group of HMOs flagrantly violating a statute. Inside counsel sometimes cannot believe that their organization has violated any law, simply because all of their peers are doing the same thing. In such cases I ask for mediation with a former judge or well-regarded private lawyer — someone who can convincingly tell the other lawyer that her client has a genuine problem.

Another indicator for mediation is when I suspect that defense counsel is not being candid with his own client. Many firms I encounter are completely ethical — they fight hard but fair. Some lawyers, however, seem to "milk" clients, playing on defendants' instinctive belief that they've done nothing wrong and billing them unnecessarily for a year or two. Mediation can be the best way to get the truth to an unrealistic client. I often have to work to get such cases into mediation. I have resorted to coming up to a defense counsel, in the presence of his client, and saying, "This looks like a perfect case for mediation." Or I might write to defense counsel and make an explicit request that he transmit the letter to his client. The hardest part of mediation is sometimes to get the other side into the process.

Patricia Lee Refo, Phoenix

My caseload consists primarily of large commercial disputes. We use mediation in most of our cases — I sometimes joke that we lawyers have worked ourselves into a place where we can't settle cases by ourselves anymore! I don't believe that a bad settlement is better than a good trial. I am convinced, though, that in the right situation, a mediator can add a great deal of value. Sometimes the problem is that both sides have the same facts, but they view them very differently. A mediator may not be able to convince a client to change his viewpoint, but she can make the client understand what the other side can do with the facts at trial. It's often the first time the client has heard the reaction of someone who comes to the case completely fresh.

There are also issues in business cases over which people become quite invested and emotional — for example, did someone violate an agreement in bad faith. Mediation allows clients to vent their feelings in private, making it easier for them to compromise later in the process. I recently encountered a mediator who said that he didn't "do venting." I find that aspect of the process often to be crucial, and I won't use neutrals who can't handle it. Mediators can also be helpful by "cutting to the chase," focusing on the few issues that will really matter at trial. This frees parties from arguing over every point, and moves them toward making settlement decisions.

Harry Mazadoorian, Former Assistant General Counsel and ADR Coordinator, CIGNA Corporation

I've used mediative methods often in working out business relationships. Insurers, for example, often make investments in joint venture and partnership deals. It's impossible to predict the future, and as the project goes on and circumstances change, issues often arise about how the parties should share unexpected benefits and responsibilities. I remember one alternative energy venture that nearly broke down when money ran short and additional contributions were required from the participants. At first the lawyers focused on parsing the language of the contract, but as we talked I was able to persuade them to explore options that redistributed costs so that each partner could bear them most easily, and potential benefits in ways that they would be felt most strongly. Once the partners dropped their focus on legalese and looked instead at their specific needs, the conflict was quickly resolved. The greatest music to my ears in these situations was always to hear an executive say, "I just don't know how to get this done." I knew that if I could get the attention of high-level decision makers — ideally, get top people from both sides to sit down at lunch and commit to trying to work it out — success was nearly assured.

b. Business Perspectives

In recent years, researchers have questioned companies about their use of ADR. A 2004 survey of corporate general counsel, for example, found that the respondents had mixed attitudes toward binding arbitration, but supported the use of mediation. Asked "What is your company's attitude toward nonbinding mediation clauses in its [domestic business] agreements?" the respondents gave these answers:

Strongly Favor	31%
Slightly Favor	29%
Neutral	25%
Slightly Disfavor	8%
Strongly Disfavor	7%

General counsel at large companies were more likely than others to support mediation clauses, with 35 percent strongly favoring and only 1 percent strongly disfavoring their use (*www.fulbright.com*). We discuss the issues raised by contractual mediation clauses in Chapter 14.

One of the first companies to make aggressive use of mediation was the Toro Corporation, which produces a wide variety of consumer goods including lawn mowers, snow blowers, and other power tools, and as a result is subject to personal injury claims, some of them serious and complex. Here is a description of Toro's ADR program.

❖ **Miguel A. Olivella Jr.**, *Toro's Early Intervention Program,*
After Six Years, Has Saved $50M

17 Alternatives 81 (1999)

[In 1991, the Toro Corp. implemented] a pre-litigation alternative dispute resolution program that featured nonbinding mediation as its cornerstone. . . . Most of the claims diverted to the program [at the outset arose] in the products liability or personal injury areas. . . .

How the Program Works

When Toro gets word of a claim against it or one of its many subsidiaries, a paralegal in the Toro legal department is assigned the matter. The legal assistant promptly contacts the claimant's counsel and schedules a meeting to take place as soon as possible at a location convenient to both the claimant and counsel. The purpose of the meeting is to elicit information about the claim and the claimant's expectations. Documentation supporting the claim is requested [usually in the form of medical and wage records]. An in-house Toro engineer typically accompanies the legal assistant to this initial meeting to inspect the product. . . . Following this meeting, the legal assistant . . . engages in settlement discussions with the claimant's counsel. If the negotiations don't produce a settlement, the claim is referred to Toro's national mediation counsel, who suggests to claimant's counsel . . . nonbinding mediation. This offer is almost universally accepted. The mediation is typically scheduled within one month. . . . Mediations typically last the better part of a day. . . .

The Results

After almost eight years and hundreds of claims, this process has resulted in a 95% settlement rate. [The program has gradually been expanded to include] commercial matters and breach of contract . . . It is virtually impossible to think of any form of litigable claim that the Toro legal department must confront that is not sent to the program. . . . Comparing data on costs before and after the program was implemented, the total cost of handling a claims file from the time it was opened until the time it was closed decreased from $115,620 to $30,617 . . . a 74% drop. And the average file's lifespan was reduced to three months from two years. . . . With 636 claims opened and closed between 1992 and 1996 . . . the program translates into an overall savings for Toro exceeding $50 million.

. . . That doesn't include [savings in more recent years or] the roughly $6 million in insurance savings realized during the first three years of the program. We're just getting warmed up.

Notes and Questions

1. If you were Toro's outside counsel and were consulted when the company was considering whether to implement an ADR program, what concerns might you reasonably have had about its effects? Why do you think these concerns did not materialize?

2. If you were consulted by a client injured by a Toro product, would you advise her to participate in the Toro process? What factors would be important in your decision?
3. One issue that Toro faced was to persuade plaintiff counsel that the invitation to mediate was not merely a pretext for "free discovery" or "below market" settlements. To overcome such suspicions, Toro developed a list of references — plaintiff lawyers who had worked with Toro and could vouch for its sincerity.

c. Is It Right for Every Dispute? Is It Fair?

Few would argue that mediation is appropriate for every controversy. Even those who generally favor its use agree that the process might not be effective in the following situations, among others:

- A disputant is not capable of negotiating effectively. This may occur, for example, because the person lacks legal counsel or is suffering from a personal impairment.
- One side in the controversy wants a judicial decision to use as a benchmark to settle or discourage similar cases.
- A party fears a settlement that may stimulate "copycat" claims.
- A litigant requires a court order to control an adversary's conduct.
- One of the disputants is benefiting from the existence of the controversy, for example, to inflict pain or delay making a payment.
- A party needs formal discovery to evaluate the strength of its legal case.
- A crucial stakeholder refuses to join the process.

Some commentators also see mediation as inherently unjust, arguing that the very informality of the process allows the intrusion of prejudice that is suppressed by more formal procedures. Mediation, it is argued, also facilitates case-by-case resolutions that siphon off pressure for law reform (although nothing prevents parties from mediating the content of a consent decree).

Other critics concede that ADR may be useful generally, but object to its application to specific areas such as spousal abuse cases. By suggesting that legal standards are only one point of reference, they say, ADR opens the way for the exploitation of unsophisticated parties. Such criticism is particularly strong in situations in which participation in mediation is mandatory, as when parents litigating over child custody are required to go through ADR as a precondition to obtaining a court hearing. Other writers have suggested that minorities tend to do less well in certain forms of mediation. Still another issue is whether ADR gives an advantage to "repeat players," such as corporations and insurers. Some studies have also called into question a basic premise of court-related mediation programs — that they reduce the duration of cases. All of these critiques raise significant policy issues, which are discussed in more depth in Chapter 14.

Questions

4. A later article regarding Toro Corporation's use of mediation (Jones 2004) describes the company's initial approach to injured persons as follows:

> From the moment the victims answer [the paralegal's] knock on the door, they're assaulted by nice. Kelly and Gotzian avoid business garb; instead they don Toro polo shirts and khaki pants. They explain that they're not lawyers, a point the company takes very seriously. "Bring a sharply dressed lawyer to one of these meetings, and immediately you'll see the walls go up," says Byers. "If Carol and Helen were attorneys, this program simply wouldn't work."

> Two leading professors had these comments about Toro's approach to settlement:

> "I can't imagine that the plaintiffs are truly getting what they deserve," says Laura Nader, a professor of law and anthropology at the University of California, Berkeley . . . "The [Toro] plaintiffs are giving up one of their most fundamental rights — the right to our court system." But Stephen Gillers, a legal ethics expert at New York University School of Law, retorts, "These plaintiffs are free to walk away at any time: They're not getting [coerced] into anything."

> Do you agree more with Professor Nader or Professor Gillers? Why?

5. Should potential defendants be prohibited as a general rule from approaching injured parties who do not have a lawyer? What rule would you suggest?

3. Examples of Mediation in Action

a. Death of a Student[1]

In late August, Scott Krueger arrived for his freshman year at the Massachusetts Institute of Technology. Five weeks later, he was dead. In an incident that made national headlines, Krueger died of alcohol poisoning following an initiation event at a fraternity. Nearly two years later, Krueger's parents sent MIT a demand letter stating their intent to sue. The letter alleged that MIT had caused their son's death by failing to address what they claimed were two long-standing campus problems: a housing arrangement that they said steered new students to seek rooms in fraternities, and what their lawyer called a culture of alcohol abuse at fraternities.

MIT's lawyers saw the case as one that could be won. An appellate court, they believed, would rule that a college is not legally responsible for an adult student's voluntary drinking. Moreover, under state law the university could not be required to pay more than $20,000 to the Kruegers (although that limit did

---

1. [*Note:* Confidentiality is one of the most important attributes of mediation. The facts in the following account that have not previously been published have been approved by attorneys for both parties. — EDS.]

not apply to claims against individual university administrators). MIT officials felt, however, that a narrowly drawn legal response would not be in keeping with its values. They also recognized that there were aspects of the institution's policies and practices — including those covering student use of alcohol — that could have been better. MIT's president, Charles M. Vest, was prepared to accept responsibility for these shortcomings on behalf of the university, and felt a deep personal desire for his institution to reach a resolution with the Krueger family. MIT also recognized that defending the case in court would exact a tremendous emotional toll on all concerned. The Kruegers would be subjected to a hard-hitting assessment of their son's behavior leading up to his death, whereas MIT would be exposed to equally severe scrutiny of the Institute's culture and the actions of individual administrators. Full-blown litigation in a case of this magnitude was also sure to be expensive, with estimated defense costs well in excess of $1 million.

The question, as MIT saw it, was not whether to seek to engage the Kruegers in settlement discussions, but how. The university decided to forego a traditional legal response and reply instead with a personal letter from President Vest to the Kruegers, which noted the university's belief that it had strong legal defenses to their claims, but offered to mediate.

The Kruegers responded with intense distrust. Tortuous negotiations ensued. The parents eventually agreed to mediate, but only subject to certain conditions: At least one session would have to occur in Buffalo, where the Kruegers lived. MIT would have to offer a sincere apology for its conduct; without that, no sum of money would settle the case. There would be no confidentiality agreement to prevent the parents from talking publicly about the matter, while at the same time any settlement could not be exploited by MIT for public relations purposes. The Kruegers would have the right to select the mediator. And, President Vest would have to appear personally at all the mediation sessions. The university agreed to most of the conditions, and the mediation went forward.

MIT's lawyers believed that it was important that the Kruegers' lawyers and the mediator understand the strength of the university's defenses, but plaintiff counsel knew that subjecting the Kruegers to such a presentation would make settlement impossible. To resolve the dilemma, the lawyers bifurcated the process. The first day of the mediation, which the Kruegers would not attend, would focus on presentations by lawyers and would be held in Boston. One week later, the mediation would resume at a conference center located a 40-minute drive outside Buffalo, this time with the Kruegers present. Their counsel selected that location so that "no one could leave easily." On the second day the Kruegers would personally meet President Vest, and the parties would begin to exchange settlement proposals.

Counsel had agreed that the mediator, Jeffrey Stern, should begin the day by having a private breakfast with Mr. and Mrs. Krueger and their lawyers. The Kruegers vented their anger, first to Stern and later to President Vest. "How could you do this?" they shouted at Vest, "You people killed our son!" They also challenged Vest on a point that bothered them terribly: Why, they asked him, had he come to their son's funeral but not sought them out personally to extend his condolences? Vest responded that he had consulted with people about whether or not to approach the Kruegers and was advised that, in light of their anger at the institution, it would be better not to do so. That advice was wrong, he said, and he regretted following it.

Vest went on to apologize for the university's role in what he described as a "terrible, terrible tragedy." "We failed you," he said, and then asked, "What can we do to make it right?" Mrs. Krueger cried out again at Vest, but at that point her husband turned to her and said, "The man apologized. What more is there to say?" Their counsel, Leo Boyle, later said that he felt that, "There's a moment . . . where the back of the case is broken. You can feel it. . . . And that was the moment this day." The mediator gradually channeled the discussion toward what the Kruegers wanted and what the university could do.

Hard bargaining followed, much of it conducted though shuttle diplomacy by the mediator. In the end the parties reached agreement: MIT paid the Kruegers $4.75 million to settle their claims and contributed an additional $1.25 million to a scholarship fund that the family would administer. Perhaps equally important, President Vest offered the Kruegers a personal, unconditional apology on behalf of MIT that no court could have compelled and that would not have been believed if it were. At the conclusion of the process Vest and Mrs. Krueger hugged each other. For MIT the settlement, although expensive, made sense: It minimized the harm that contested litigation would have caused to the institution. And, most important, the university felt that it was the right thing to do.

What did the mediator contribute to the process? During the first day, Stern questioned both lawyers closely about the legal and factual issues, creating a foundation for realistic assessments of case value later in the process. The initial money offers put forth by each party were far apart, but the mediator put them into context so that neither side gave up in frustration. According to plaintiff counsel Brad Henry, Stern's greatest contribution was probably the way he responded to the Kruegers' feelings: "What he did most masterfully was to allow a lot of the emotion to be directed at him. He allowed it almost to boil over when it was just him with the Kruegers, but later he very deftly let it be redirected at President Vest and the university. . . . He also prepared Charles Vest for the onslaught. . . . Mediation can be like a funeral — especially with the death of a child. He mediated the emotional part of the case, and then let the rest unfold on its own."

Questions

6. What barriers made it difficult for the parties in the Krueger case to negotiate with each other directly? In what ways was mediation likely to be more effective than direct negotiation at overcoming them?
7. What goals did the university have in proposing mediation? What did the student's family appear to be seeking from the process?
8. What did the Kruegers obtain in mediation that they could not have won at trial?

b. United States v. Microsoft Corporation

In one of the highest profile antitrust cases in U.S. history, the Justice Department, later joined by several states, sued Microsoft Corporation, arguing that it had monopolized certain markets in computer software. While the case was pending, judges twice ordered the parties into mediation processes, which are described in the following readings.

❖ **James Laflin & Robert Werth,** *UNFINISHED BUSINESS:*
ANOTHER LOOK AT THE MICROSOFT
MEDIATION: LESSONS FOR THE CIVIL LITIGATOR

12 Cal. Tort Rep. 88 (April 2001)

On November 18, 1999, twelve months into a case that was eventually to last eighteen, U.S. District Judge Thomas Penfield Jackson announced the appointment of Richard A. Posner, the Chief Judge of the Seventh Circuit Court of Appeals in Chicago, to serve as mediator in the Microsoft antitrust case. . . . Posner was neither a practiced diplomat nor experienced mediator. However, he brought other credentials to the table. He had gained recognition as one of the most capable, influential members of the federal bench, and a recognized authority in the field of antitrust law. . . .

Posner's mission as a mediator was to induce Microsoft and the government to shed what he referred to as "emotionality" and come to a rational compromise. At the outset, the parties met for lunch at a private club, in what would turn out to be the only face-to-face meeting of the entire mediation process. In attendance were lawyers representing Microsoft, the Justice Department and three attorneys general representing the nineteen states who joined as plaintiffs in the suit. In describing the protocol, Posner indicated he would refrain from evaluating the strength of either side's case, "try to deflate unrealistic expectations" and keep all talks in confidence. Each side was asked "to make a detailed presentation of the facts and remedies it would consider." Posner promised to devote himself almost full time to the process.

To mitigate "emotionality" Judge Posner ordered separate meetings for at least the first month, the government each Monday, Microsoft each Tuesday. Two months later the process had evolved into a form of shuttle diplomacy interspersed with the judge's email inquiries seeking additional information. He began, in the words of one Microsoft negotiator, "growling at the other side, growling at us." After two months of work Posner outlined the first draft of a settlement proposal. Over the next several months, some nineteen draft proposals were exchanged via Posner, who edited them into his own language and emailed them either to Microsoft's General Counsel, or the chief of the Justice Department's Antitrust Division. Copies went to the chair of the association of the nineteen state attorneys general.

By mid-February, negotiations had stalled. Neither side believed that the other was open to a compromise, and both sides were often confused. At Microsoft, this was reflected by [General Counsel] Bill Neukum[,] who said of Posner, "You keep asking yourself, 'Is he wearing his hat as a mediator, trying to motivate people to narrow their differences and come together, or is he speaking as the Chief Judge of the Seventh Circuit, who's an expert on antitrust law?"' Compounding this confusion, neither side could be sure whether, or which, terms contained in the successive draft proposals originated with Judge Posner or came directly from their adversary.

From late February 2000 through the end of March, Posner had extensive telephone conversions with Microsoft, sometimes with [Chairman William] Gates directly, and with Justice Department attorneys, in which successive draft agreements were negotiated and refined. In early March Gates seemed close to accepting the deal reflected in draft fourteen, which Posner forwarded to the Justice Department and the states. The states were given ten days to accept, or Posner would terminate the process. The state attorneys general made it clear that Joel Klein [chief of the Justice Department team] was not their spokesperson and responded separately to the proposal. The states were angry with both Posner and Klein. As one state official said, "Posner was more interested in dealing with Gates and Klein and didn't perceive that he had nineteen other parties to the lawsuit. . . . He got enamored of talking to Gates. And he's not a mediator by training, and lacked basic mediation skills."

Posner was prepared to summon the parties to Chicago for direct face-to-face negotiations starting on March 24th. Their options would be to accept the basic terms contained in the most recent draft, or face termination of the mediation. More emails and telephone conversations between Posner and the two sides ensued. Meanwhile, the states had communicated their disapproval of parts of draft eighteen and added further conditions. Posner now realized he would have to negotiate with the nineteen state attorneys general to develop a single government proposal. Then, even if that could be accomplished, he would still have to negotiate the divide between the government stakeholders and Microsoft. That night he telephoned Microsoft and Klein and announced that his mediation effort was over.

The Microsoft case went to trial and the court found that Microsoft had violated antitrust laws. Judge Jackson ordered a breakup of the company, and Microsoft appealed. Several months later the court of appeals upheld some of the trial court's findings of antitrust violations, rejected others, and disapproved the court's breakup remedy. Criticizing the conduct of the trial judge, particularly his decision to talk privately with a reporter, the appeals court appointed a new judge to preside over the case. Other changes had occurred: While the appeal was pending, a new president had taken office and the Justice Department had announced that it would no longer seek a breakup of the company. Before resuming hearings, the second trial judge again referred the Microsoft case to mediation. The following reading summarizes its results.

❖ Eric Green & Jonathan Marks,
HOW WE MEDIATED THE MICROSOFT CASE

The Boston Globe, A23 (November 15, 2001)

Mediators never kiss and tell. But within the bounds of appropriate confidentiality, lessons can be learned from the three-week mediation marathon that led to Microsoft's settlements with the Department of Justice and at least nine states. Federal District Judge Colleen Kollar-Kotelly took over the case after the Court of Appeals partially affirmed the prior judge's findings that Microsoft had violated antitrust laws. . . . Neither the mediation nor the settlements would have happened if Kollar-Kotelly had not acted to suspend litigation and order settlement negotiations. The judge's Sept. 28 mandate was blunt: "The Court expects that the parties will . . . engage in an all-out effort to settle these cases, meeting seven days a week and around the clock, acting reasonably to reach a fair resolution." The court gave the parties two weeks to negotiate on their own, ordering them to mediation if they couldn't reach agreement by then. The court bounded its "24/7" timetable by ordering the parties to complete mediation by Nov. 2. . . . Tight timetables command attention. In mediation, just as in negotiation, time used tends to expand to fit time available. A firm deadline gets the parties to focus. . . .

We are both mediators, with 40 years of combined experience. . . . But we are not experts in the applicable law or the disputed technology. . . . Even had we had such expertise, our objective would not have been to try to craft our own settlement solution and sell its merits to the parties. We believed that the only chance of getting all or most parties to a settlement was for us to work intensively to help them create their own agreement. Our "job one" was to facilitate and assist in the gestation, birth, and maturing of such an agreement. We had to be advocates for settlement — optimistic and persistent — but not advocates for any particular settlement. . . .

Reaching a settlement required working with adversarial parties with very different views about a large number of technologically and legally complicated issues. When we arrived on the scene, the parties had begun exchanging drafts of possible settlement terms. . . . After initial separate briefings, we moved the process into an extended series of joint meetings, involving representatives of the Antitrust Division, the state attorneys general and their staffs, and Microsoft. No party was left out of the negotiations. The bargaining table had three sides. . . .

Throughout most of the mediation the 19 states and the federal government worked as a combined "plaintiffs" team. We worked to ensure the right mix of people, at the table and in the background. The critical path primarily ran through managing and focusing across-the-table discussions and drafting by subject matter experts — lawyers and computer mavens — with knowledge of the technological and business complexities gained through working on the case since its inception. The critical path also required working with senior party-representatives who could make principled decisions about priorities and deal breakers.

[As a result of the mediation, Microsoft, the Justice Department and ten state attorneys general reached agreement.] Even as settlement advocates we have no quarrel with the partial settlement that was achieved. . . . Successful mediations are ones in which mediators and parties work to identify and overcome barriers to reaching agreement. . . . Successful mediations are ones in which, settle or not, senior representatives of each party have made informed and intelligent decisions. The Microsoft mediation was successful.[2]

Questions

9. Neutrals reveal their own definition of mediation by the manner in which they practice it. Looking at the techniques that Judge Posner applied, what appeared to be his concept of how mediation should work?
10. In what ways did mediators Green and Marks view the process differently?
11. Green and Marks emphasize the importance of deadlines. Do you think the judge could have achieved the same settlement result by setting a firm trial date and ordering the parties to negotiate with each other directly?

---

c. Mediating as an Interested Party

❖ **Stephen B. Goldberg,** *MEDIATING THE DEAL: HOW TO MAXIMIZE VALUE BY ENLISTING A NEUTRAL'S HELP AT AND AROUND THE BARGAINING TABLE*

24 Alternatives 147 (2006)

If you've ever been part of an organizational team preparing to negotiate an agreement with another organization, you probably have faced this frustrating task: aligning your individual interests, other team members' interests, and those of your company as a whole.

For instance, imagine that you're the sales vice president for an automobile manufacturer, and that you're in charge of the corporate team responsible for negotiating a contract for the sale of next year's models to a large car-rental firm. As sales VP, you want to boost sales by offering as many models as possible. The production representative wants to offer as few models as possible, to streamline the production process. The finance VP doesn't care how many models are offered, but wants an accelerated payment schedule to maximize this year's cash flow. Meanwhile, the legal representative wants contract terms that will maximize your company's protection in the event the buyer declares bankruptcy.

How can you coordinate these different interests while ensuring that the team meets its overall corporate goal of achieving a good deal? An obvious, though infrequently used, source of expertise can help: a professional mediator. . . .

A few years ago, I was asked to serve as a facilitator for and adviser to a corporate team from a telecommunications firm that was preparing to negotiate with five other telecom companies on the division of radio spectrum for cellular telephone relay satellites. . . . All team members were knowledgeable about the cell phone industry, and some were experts on satellite transmission. I knew little of the former and nothing of the latter. I was concerned about how

---

2. [*Note:* The remaining nine attorneys general filed objections to the settlement with the trial judge, but both the trial and appeals courts upheld its terms. — EDS.]

much I could contribute to the team's success. As the internal negotiations progressed, however, I discovered that I could perform a valuable function. . . .

Using my mediation skills, I assisted the team in developing a common position that each department regarded as sufficiently protective of its interests. . . . The bulk of my work took place prior to external negotiations. I first met separately with each team member and key personnel in that member's department to get a sense of the interests underlying each department's position and the relative importance of each interest. For example, I learned that certain aspects of the new technology were less dear to the engineers than others and could be dropped from their demands if more important aspects were protected. . . .

Once I knew the core interests of each department, I engaged in "shuttle diplomacy," trying out proposed tradeoffs with each department. I then assembled the entire team to see if the team members could agree on an overall position. With my knowledge of key interests and possible tradeoffs, [r]eaching overall agreement was not difficult. Next, the operations VP assessed whether the common position fully represented overall corporate interests. His alterations led to a further round of mediated internal negotiations that formed a corporate position acceptable to all. . . .

Mediator's Role: External Negotiations

What happened next was perhaps the most surprising aspect of the experience. During the inter-corporate negotiations among the various telecom firms, I sat silently in the back of the room. Only during recesses did I talk, advising "my" team. . . .

The other negotiating teams became curious about the silent "outsider" and began questioning me about my role. On learning that I was a professional mediator with no direct stake in the amount of spectrum gained by my team, other teams began presenting proposals to me. They asked whether I thought the proposals would appeal to my team, and made some of my suggested changes to improve their acceptability. Thus, I ended up mediating not only among different members of my team but also between my team and some of the other teams. The result was a successful negotiation leading to an agreement on most issues. . . .

There is an alternative to using an outside mediator to assist the firm, organization, or corporation in preparing for negotiation. If there exists someone in the company, perhaps in the legal department, who has no personal or departmental stake in the negotiation's outcome, is trusted by all participants, and has mediation skills and experience, that person could serve as negotiation adviser. So, too, could someone from the company's outside law firm, subject to the same qualifications — and subject to the fact that this person, too, would be a sort of outsider. . . .

Questions

12. Have you seen an example of a person who acted as a "quasi-mediator," in the sense that he or she brought people together to make agreements without any formal title or role as a mediator? What was his or her formal role?

13. Have you ever seen someone take on a quasi-mediative role in a family or community setting?

4. The Evolution of Legal Mediation

The public thinks of dispute resolution primarily in terms of court trials. Court access to remedy wrongs and enforce legal rights is central to American democracy, and we have fashioned a system of rules to ensure fair trials and provide a finely tuned system of public justice. However, litigation, with all of its procedural protections, is slow, costly, and relatively inflexible. The process is also centered on lawyers, restricting the roles and options for the disputing parties. Finally, the remedies available through adjudication are limited to what can be enforced through courts; most commonly, judicial resolutions consist of money judgments.

In part because of these limitations, alternatives to adjudication have long existed. Mediation has probably existed for nearly as long as humans have lived together — think, for example, of a village elder assisting members of a tribe or village to settle a quarrel. History offers many examples of the use of mediative processes. Thousands of years ago, Chinese villagers were accustomed to resolving disputes through the assistance of respected leaders, and commercial disputes were mediated in England before the Norman invasion.

Modern American mediation began in response to the rise of organized labor. Following initiatives in several states, Congress in 1898 authorized railroads and their unions to invoke mediation and in 1913 created a Board of Mediation and Conciliation to deal with such cases. Labor mediation expanded greatly in the first half of the twentieth century, and the process began to be applied to other legal disputes. By the early 1920s, for example, mediation programs for civil cases existed in courts in New York, Minneapolis, Cleveland, and other cities. Following World War II, legal reformers began to promote the use of mediation in other subject areas, with special emphasis on using mediation to lower the frequency of divorce.

Civil mediation received a powerful boost during the late 1970s from prominent jurists who believed that the justice system was in crisis. Although some have argued that this concern was overstated (Galanter 1983), it led judges, academics, and bar leaders to advocate increased use of ADR. During the same period, leaders at the local level argued for using mediation to deal with neighborhood disputes, and support continued to grow for applying mediation in family cases (Folberg & Taylor 1984).

During the 1980s, courts and litigators experimented with the use of mediation to resolve civil disputes outside the divorce arena. At first lawyers approached the process cautiously, concerned that their willingness to mediate would be interpreted by opponents as weakness. Bar leaders and judges, however, continued to voice support for the process and, equally important, corporations began to throw their weight behind the use of ADR to reduce the cost of litigation and the risk of uncertain verdicts. Some 4,000 companies, for example, have signed a formal pledge undertaking to consider ADR before resorting to traditional litigation, and more than 1,500 law firms have signed a similar pledge; the corporate version of the pledge appears in Chapter 20.

In 1990, Congress mandated that every federal district court create a plan that incorporated ADR to control litigation delay, and in 1998, it reaffirmed that requirement. By the mid-1990s, most state and federal courts had established court-connected ADR programs for a wide variety of civil disputes, and mediation quickly became by far the most popular process used in such programs (Stienstra et al. 1996). The 1990s also saw federal and state government agencies using mediation more frequently to resolve public disputes. As one measure of the growth of the process, by the end of the decade states had enacted more than 2,000 statutes that mentioned mediation (Cole et al. 2008).

As the use of mediation became more widespread, some commentators questioned whether the process, particularly as applied in court-connected programs, might stifle law reform, condemn low-income groups to a second-class form of justice, prejudice abused women and children, or disadvantage the powerless. At the same time, new data called into question some of the premises of the mediation movement, for example, that court ADR programs sped the processing of cases (Kakalik et al. 1996), although other studies found that mediation did generate significant savings of time and money (Stienstra et al. 1997; Stipanowich 2003). We explore these policy issues more deeply in Chapter 14. Although the recognition of these complex issues has shaped mediation debate and practice, none has prevented mediation from growing rapidly in popularity.

B. Goals and Mediator Styles

1. Goals for the Process

When you participate in mediation as an advocate, what will be your goal for the process? The answer may seem simple: to settle a legal dispute as favorably as possible. But the question is often more complex. Parties' goals in the process vary widely. For example, an organization that advocates ADR in business disputes stresses that "Mediation provides a framework for parties to . . . achieve remedies that may be outside the scope of the judicial process . . . maintain privacy . . . preserve or minimize damage to relationships and reduce the costs and delay of dispute resolution" (CPR Institute 1999). By contrast, a prominent personal injury lawyer has described the process as

> An opportunity — a time for you, as the legal representative of your client, to avoid putting your client through the litigation "mill" . . . and get results. . . . It is a means of essentially "selling" your client's lawsuit to a buyer, who buys off the expense and exposure of an ongoing lawsuit. The client has the money to begin the life restructuring process and has avoided the pressures and uncertainties of litigation. . . . (Kornblum 2004)

The goals you pursue in mediation may change greatly from one situation to another, and should influence your choices about structuring the process. As a lawyer representing clients, you might have one or more of the following purposes for electing to mediate.

a. Resolve a Legal Claim on the Best Possible Monetary Terms

When litigators enter mediation, their goal is usually to settle a legal dispute. Most trial lawyers take a narrow approach to the process, discussing only legally relevant facts and issues and setting a goal of obtaining the best possible monetary payment in return for ending the case. When litigators talk about mediation, they often reflect this perspective. One lawyer, for example, has said, "The effective advocate approaches mediation as if it were a trial . . . the overwhelming benefit of mediation is that it can reduce the cost of litigation" (Weinstein 1996).

Perhaps in response, commercial mediators often see their primary role as facilitating distributive bargaining over money. One neutral, for example, wrote that, "In the typical civil mediation, money is the primary (if not the only) issue" (Contuzzi 2000), and another has said, "The goal of resolution is always the same: allowing the parties to negotiate to a 'reasonable ballpark,' in which they, with the help of the mediator, identify 'home plate' based on what a jury will consider 'a reasonable verdict range'" (Max 1999).

In the typical commercial dispute, then, litigants and counsel are likely to enter the process assuming that it will focus primarily on legal arguments and positional bargaining over money. Although this kind of negotiation often produces less-than-optimal results, a mediator can do a great deal to assist parties even when money is the only issue over which the disputants are willing to bargain.

Example: An inexperienced plaintiff's lawyer was representing an automobile accident victim in negotiations with the defendant's insurer. The victim had suffered broken bones and had out-of-pocket damages totaling $6,000. Requested by the defendant's adjuster to make a settlement demand, the plaintiff counsel asked for $1.2 million. The adjuster was incredulous: In her experience, plaintiff lawyers rarely demanded more than ten times the "out-of-pockets." She refused to "dignify" the plaintiff's "wild number" with a response, and the result was a complete breakdown of talks.

The case went to mediation. In a private meeting with the plaintiff and his counsel, the mediator asked about their goals in the negotiation. The lawyer said that he was willing to be flexible, and the client indicated that he was seeking a much more modest amount than the $1.2 million demand might suggest. The neutral asked the plaintiff lawyer to make a new offer at a much lower level. She offered to tell the adjuster that the plaintiff had done this only to accommodate the mediator's request that both sides "cut to the chase," and that the plaintiff expected the defendant to respond in a similar vein. Three hours later the case settled at $27,500.

b. Develop a Broad, Interest-Based Resolution

As we have seen, parties to legal disputes often have interests that go far beyond money, and settlements that respond to these concerns can provide greater value to disputants than a purely monetary outcome. Some lawyers employ mediation to facilitate interest-based bargaining and obtain creative resolutions. One text for corporate attorneys, for example, emphasizes that "The process creates an opportunity to explore underlying business interests [and] offers the potential for a 'win-win' solution . . .' (Picker 2003), while another describes the process as providing "a framework for parties to . . . privately reveal to the mediator in caucus sensitive interests that may assist the mediator to facilitate broad solutions" (CPR Institute 1999).

Example: A company that processed hazardous chemical waste and one of its residential abutters had been embroiled for years in a series of disputes over the company's applications for licenses to expand its operations. They eventually agreed to mediate. Although the parties at first focused exclusively on the meaning of certain state hazardous waste regulations, the mediator noted that the abutter became most angry when he mentioned the company's practice of parking large trucks filled with waste on the street across from his house. The company insisted that such situations resulted from unpredictable traffic jams at the plant, but the abutter maintained that the problem showed the company's basic callousness about its neighbors' safety.

As he spoke with the parties, the mediator found that the company also wanted to end the practice and could do so if it could widen its driveway to accommodate two trucks at a time. This was impossible because the driveway was wedged against the abutter's land. That land was not, however, being used. As part of a settlement, the mediator convinced the abutter to convey a narrow strip of his unused land to the company. The company in turn agreed to widen its driveway, thus solving the truck parking problem for everyone and increasing the value of the abutter's remaining land.

c. Repair the Parties' Relationship

Parties sometimes enter mediation not so much to obtain specific terms of settlement as to repair their relationship. The act of filing suit is usually understood as a decision to sever any connection between the parties (Galanter 1983), but many believe that "mediation has as its primary goal the repair of the troubled relationship" (Fuller 1971).

Example: An Austrian company that marketed a process to stop soil erosion along river banks and a principal officer of its U.S. affiliate were in a dispute. The plaintiff was the founder of the company, who had trained the other protagonist, a young American woman, to create a subsidiary to sell his process in the United States. The woman modified the process in the belief that the original version would not fit the American market. This triggered a violent disagreement with the founder. Faced with the prospect of resolving the dispute or declaring bankruptcy, the shareholders and executives agreed to meet.

The founder arrived at the mediation and sat rigid and silent as others talked. When the mediator asked him to give his perspective on the situation, he refused: His position was stated in a letter that everyone had received. What else needed to be said? Still, the mediator asked if he would read the letter aloud to ensure that everyone heard him clearly. As the founder began to read, feelings began to show under his stolid exterior. The woman responded angrily, and they began to argue. It seemed to be a classic daughter/mentee-grows-up-and-challenges-father/ mentor situation. Eventually the two went to a corner and talked animatedly for more than an hour.

Afterward, in a calmer atmosphere, the mediator led the principals through a discussion of the challenges facing the firm and how they might solve them. Under the leadership of a new CEO not linked to either protagonist, painful changes were agreed to, and the company survived.

d. Change the Parties' Perspectives

In a still broader view, the purpose of the mediation process is not to obtain a specific outcome but rather to assist parties in transforming their perspectives on the dispute and each other, a change that might or might not lead to an improvement in their relationship. Advocates of this approach, known as "transformative" mediation, believe that the disputants should be allowed to take charge of the mediation process with the mediator serving simply as a resource to facilitate conversations. The transformative approach is described in more detail later.

e. Choices Among Goals

Although a particular mediation can have more than a single purpose, the process can be viewed as falling along a continuum (see Figure 5.1).

Figure 5.1

Potential Goals in Mediation

Monetary result	Interest-based solution	Repair of the relationship	Transformation of perspectives

←——————————————————————————————————→

How likely is it in practice that if an attorney seeks a goal, he will be able to achieve it—how often, in other words, can parties in civil or "commercial" mediation expect to leave the process with a purely monetary settlement, an interest-based solution, or a relationship repair?

The answer will be heavily influenced by the nature of the case, the attitudes of clients and counsel, and the skills and goals of the mediator. Relationship repair in mediation is often not feasible; in most automobile tort cases, for example, there is no prior relationship to revive. Even when a dispute does arise in a relationship, the parties often litigate bitterly before mediating, and in such situations repairing the relationship is very difficult. Sometimes, however, both sides recognize that it is in their interest to heal their rupture. This is most common in settings in which the parties' past connection has been strong and their alternatives to relating are not attractive.

One example is a quarrel between a divorcing couple over parenting their children. Relationships can be important in commercial settings as well; partners in small businesses, like the Austrian-American venture described above, may have a strong interest in seeking a repair of a troubled relationship because neither is able to buy out the other and continued conflict will destroy the enterprise. A study of mediations of civil disputes arising from relationships (excluding unionized labor and divorce cases, and large enough to justify the retention of lawyers) found a pattern of outcomes shown in Figure 5.2.

Figure 5.2
Outcomes of Legal Mediation in "Relationship" Cases

Repair of relationship	*Integrative terms and money, but no repair*	*Money terms only*	*Impasse*
17%	30%	27%	27%

Figure 5.2 shows that when parties mediate a legal dispute arising from a significant prior relationship using a professional mediator, about 15 to 20 percent of the time they are able to repair their relationship, roughly 30 percent of the time they achieve a settlement with at least one significant integrative term in addition to money,[3] there is a 25 to 30 percent probability of a simple money settlement, and there is a 25 to 30 percent likelihood of impasse. Interestingly, focusing only on cases that settled, agreements that contained a relationship repair or one integrative term totaled 47 percent, a much higher percentage than pure money settlements, which totaled 27 percent (Golann 2002). Another study found that nonmonetary terms were included in most settlements of contract disputes, but seldom in personal injury (mainly auto accident) cases (Wissler 2006).

As a lawyer you are likely to encounter many situations in which a client's only goal is to end a relationship with an adversary on the best possible terms. The data suggest, however, that in cases that arise from a prior relationship, it is feasible more often than not to obtain agreements that include at least one term of significant value to the parties apart from money, and that in a small but appreciable percentage of cases, the parties repair their relationship.

---

3. Examples of integrative terms in business disputes included an agreement among parties breaking up a partnership that one partner would have the exclusive use of certain billing software, or that the ex-partners would continue to share office space. In employment cases, companies agreed to terms such as temporarily maintaining the health coverage of a departing employee or changing records to reflect a voluntary resignation rather than a termination, and employees sometimes agreed never to apply for employment with the company again. Releases of liability and confidentiality agreements were not counted as integrative terms in the survey because they were typically assented to as a matter of course.

Question

14. In what types of disputes are the parties likely to find it difficult or costly to sever their connection? In what kinds of cases should it be relatively easy to do so?

2. Mediator Styles

One key issue that you will confront when representing clients in mediation is selecting a neutral. Most communities now have a large number of mediators, and different neutrals have widely varying styles. Depending on the dispute and the personalities and goals of the participants, you may select different types of mediators. Indeed, experienced lawyers sometimes look for a mediator who can best influence the *other* party to the dispute.

a. Classifying Styles

It is possible to classify mediators according to the goals they pursue and the methods they use to achieve them, and to show the results graphically, as in the following reading.

❖ Leonard L. Riskin, RETIRING AND REPLACING THE GRID OF MEDIATOR ORIENTATIONS

21 Alternatives 69 (April 2003) and 12 Alternatives 111 (Summer 1994)

[A decade ago, there was] a vast and diverse array of processes . . . called mediation. Yet there was no accepted system for distinguishing among the various approaches. As a result, there was great confusion in the field about what mediation is and what it should be. . . . Looking back, I like to think about this confusion in terms of three gaps between mediation theory — that is, what the well-known writings and training programs, mainly those focusing on civil, non-labor mediation, said mediators did or should do — and mediation practice — that is, what mediators actually did.

First, mediation theory held that mediators don't evaluate, make predictions about what would happen in court, or tell parties what to do. In practice, however, many mediators evaluated and told people what to do. Second, mediation theory said that mediation was intended to address the parties' underlying interests or real needs, rather than, or in addition to, their legal claims. Quite commonly, however, mediations in civil disputes — especially those that were in the litigation process, or might be — were narrow and adversarial. The third disparity between theory and practice concerned self-determination. The "experts" touted mediation's potential for enhancing self-determination. Yet in practice, many mediation processes did not fulfill that promise.

These gaps between theory and practice produced a number of problems. The most salient problem concerned evaluation [a mediator's willingness to give an opinion as to the likely outcome of a case in adjudication, or to propose terms of settlement]: Sometimes parties went into a mediation thinking they were not going to get an evaluation, but got one nevertheless — without consenting to it or preparing for it. And sometimes the reverse happened: Parties who thought they would get an evaluation, because they were analogizing mediation to some judicial settlement conferences, didn't get one. Similarly, parties who entered a mediation thinking it would focus either broadly or narrowly often were surprised to find the opposite focus. And some mediators gave short shrift to party self-determination by exercising extensive control of the focus and even the outcome.

For all these reasons, great ambiguity suffused most conversations about mediation. In addition, many parties, potential parties, lawyers, and mediators did not recognize the existence of numerous choices about what would happen in a mediation and that someone would make those choices, either explicitly or implicitly. [To address these problems, I proposed a system for classifying mediator orientations.] It focused primarily on two of the gaps: evaluation by the mediator and problem-definition (which was my vehicle for addressing the tendency of many commercial mediators to focus on positions, in the form of claims of legal entitlements, rather than underlying interests). . . .

. . . The classification system [starts] with two principal questions: 1. Does the mediator tend to define problems narrowly or broadly? 2. Does the mediator think she should evaluate — make assessments or predictions or proposals for agreements — or facilitate the parties' negotiation without evaluating? The answers reflect the mediator's beliefs about the nature and scope of mediation and her assumptions about the parties' expectations.

Problem Definition

Mediators with a narrow focus assume that the parties have come to them for help in solving a technical problem. The parties have defined this problem in advance through the positions they have asserted in negotiations or pleadings. Often it involves a question such as, "Who pays how much to whom?" or "Who can use such-and-such property?" As framed, these questions rest on "win-lose" (or "distributive") assumptions. In other words, the participants must divide a limited resource; whatever one gains, the other must lose. The likely court outcome — along with uncertainty, delay and expense — drives much of the mediation process. Parties, seeking a compromise, will bargain adversarially, emphasizing positions over interests.

A mediator who starts with a broad orientation, on the other hand, assumes that the parties can benefit if the mediation goes beyond the narrow issues that normally define legal disputes. Important interests often lie beneath the positions that the participants assert. Accordingly, the mediator should help the participants understand and fulfill those interests — at least if they wish to do so.

The Mediator's Role

The evaluative mediator assumes that the participants want and need the mediator to provide some directions as to the approximate grounds for settlement — based on law, industry practice, or technology. She also assumes that the mediator is qualified to give such direction by virtue of her experience, training, and objectivity.

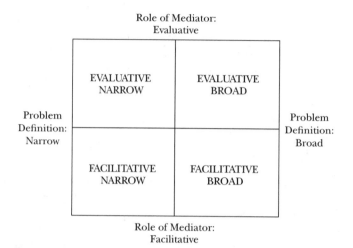

Role of Mediator:
Evaluative

EVALUATIVE NARROW	EVALUATIVE BROAD
FACILITATIVE NARROW	FACILITATIVE BROAD

Problem Definition: Narrow

Problem Definition: Broad

Role of Mediator:
Facilitative

The facilitative mediator assumes the parties are intelligent, able to work with their counterparts, and capable of understanding their situation better then either their lawyers or the mediator. So the parties may develop better solutions than any that the mediator might create. For these reasons, the facilitative mediator assumes that his principal mission is to enhance and clarify communications between the parties in order to help them decide what to do. The facilitative mediator believes it is inappropriate for the mediator to give his opinion, for at least two reasons. First, such opinions might impair the appearance of impartiality and thereby interfere with the mediator's ability to function. Second, the mediator might not know enough—about the details of the case or the relevant law, practices, or technology—to give an informed opinion.

Mediators usually have a predominant orientation, whether they know it or not, based on a combination of their personalities, experiences, education, and training. Thus, many retired judges, when they mediate, tend toward an evaluative-narrow orientation.

Yet mediators do not always behave consistently with the predominant orientations they express. . . . In addition, many mediators will depart from their orientations to respond to the dynamics of the situation. . . . [As an] example: an evaluative-narrow mediator may explore underlying interests (a technique normally associated with the broad orientation) after her accustomed narrow focus results in a deadlock. And a facilitative-broad mediator might use a mildly evaluative tactic as a last resort. For instance, he might toss out a figure that he thinks the parties might be willing to agree upon, while stating that the figure does not represent his prediction of what would happen in court. . . . Many effective mediators are versatile and can move from quadrant to quadrant (and within a quadrant), as the dynamics of the situation dictate, to help parties settle disputes. . . .

I appreciate the insight of Professor George Box: "All models are wrong. Some are useful." No graphic can capture the rich complexity of real life. Nevertheless, I hope that this grid will be useful.

Role of Mediator: Elicitive and Directive

Professor Riskin has refined his grid by replacing the word "evaluative" with "directive" and "facilitative" with "elicitive" (the "broad" versus "narrow" continuum remains the same) for the following reasons.

> First, the terms "directive" and "elicitive" more closely approximate my goals for this continuum, which [are] to focus on the impact of the mediator's behavior on party self-determination. Second, the term "directive" is more general and abstract than "evaluative" and therefore may cover a wider range of mediator behaviors. . . . Using the terms "directive" and "elicitive" also can help us recognize that mediators can direct (or push) the parties toward particular outcomes through "selective facilitation" — directing discussion of outcomes the mediator favors, while not promoting discussions of outcomes the mediator does not favor — without explicitly evaluating a particular outcome. (Riskin 2003d)

Most writing on mediator styles continues to use evaluative-facilitative terminology, and we will use those terms in this book. Students interested in exploring the issue of mediator style more deeply should read Professor Riskin's articles referenced in the bibliography.

Question

15. Have you seen a demonstration or video of the mediation process? Using the Riskin grid, how would you classify the mediators whom you observed?

---

b. Do Mediators Have a Single Style?

Do legal mediators use a single goal orientation and style throughout their practice, or at least during a single mediation? To investigate this issue, one of the authors filmed several mediators mediating the same civil case in role-play format. He found, as Professor Riskin suggests, that good neutrals do not maintain a single orientation, but instead adapt their approach to fit the circumstances of a dispute.

Indeed, the filmed mediators often changed their style repeatedly during a single meeting with a party. All began in a broadly facilitative mode, asking about the parties' business and personal interests, but were usually met with narrowly evaluative comments from the lawyers, who focused on arguing the strength of their legal cases. The mediators adjusted to the lawyers, remaining facilitative but focusing on legal issues and facts. Periodically during the process, most mediators returned to "broad" questions, asking about clients' interests and suggesting nonmonetary solutions. Some of the disputants responded by moving toward a broader focus, and others continued to remain narrowly evaluative.

The experiment confirmed Riskin's observation that successful legal mediators are not consistently either facilitative or evaluative. The neutrals in the study did become increasingly evaluative over the course of each mediation, but their advice usually focused on the bargaining situation — how the other side was probably seeing the situation and what negotiating approach was likely to be effective ("If you make that offer, I'm concerned that they will react by. . . .") rather than the legal merits.

As the process continued, mediators became more willing to ask questions and make comments that suggested a view, or at least skepticism, about the disputants' legal arguments. However, when neutrals did make an evaluative comment they almost always framed it in general terms ("The evidence on causation seems thin . . . I'm concerned that a court might. . . .").

Although commentators tend to speak in terms of a mediator's "preferred style," the stylistic changes of the mediators in the experiment seemed to be driven much more by who they were dealing with — the personalities and attitudes of the parties and lawyers — than by the tendencies of the mediators. The advocacy of the lawyers and decisions by the clients (for example, was a party representative willing to consider resuming a broken relationship?), in other words, counted for more than a mediator's orientation in happened during the process.

Question

16. What type of mediator would you select if you were a lawyer representing the following clients?
   a. The family of the deceased MIT student.
   b. The chemical company in the abutter-chemical company case.
   c. The plaintiff in the "$1.2 million demand" personal injury mediation.

---

3. Mediative Approaches and Techniques

This section examines forms of mediation that you are likely to encounter in practice. As ADR has evolved, a wide variety of approaches have gained acceptance. Most lawyer-mediators focus on civil cases — that is, disputes involving the kinds of tort, contract, property, employment, and statutory claims that you have studied in law school, compared to marital or collective bargaining disputes. These are commonly referred to as "commercial" cases and the neutrals who handle them as commercial mediators. Commercial mediators almost all use a caucus-based format, and discussions in such cases tend to focus on what courts would consider legally relevant and on exchanges of money offers.

Mediators who specialize in divorce and other disputes between family members, by contrast, usually avoid caucusing and place more emphasis on the parties' nonmonetary interests. The setting in which mediation occurs — for example, whether it is an all-day affair or a two-hour process — also affects how the process develops. The readings in this section give a flavor of several models.

a. Commercial Mediation

Mediators who focus their practice on commercial disputes tend to use similar methods to conduct the process. A legal mediator's overall goal is to stimulate constructive negotiations. If mediation is invoked, it is usually because parties are unable to negotiate effectively on their own because they are frustrated by barriers. A commercial mediator might therefore begin by seeking answers to two questions:

- What obstacles are preventing the parties from settling this dispute themselves?
- What strategy is most likely to overcome these barriers?

A mediator's understanding of what is keeping the parties apart will deepen over the course of a mediation, and the obstacles themselves may change as the process goes forward. Ideally a mediator's strategy would be attuned to each case. In practice, however, this might not be possible. Many commercial mediators use a similar sequence of techniques to deal with the barriers most likely to be present, customizing their approach as they go along. This section, written in the form of advice to a novice mediator, describes a six-step strategy:

Basic Commercial Strategy

1. Build a Foundation for Success

The challenge: Missing elements — people, data, interactions.   Negotiations often fail because some essential element is missing. One side may have the wrong people — a key decision maker may be missing, or one of the bargainers may be so emotional he cannot make good decisions. At other times, parties do not have the data they need to settle: Defense counsel may not, for instance, know how the claimed damages were computed and without this information cannot get authority to settle. Such problems are difficult to fix once mediation begins and the clock begins to run.

The response: Identify issues and address them in advance.   To identify and resolve such problems, it is best to start before the parties meet to mediate. The first step is to ask the lawyers for mediation statements and set up telephone conversations with each of them. Ask each attorney who he plans to bring and who needs to attend from the other party. If a decision maker is absent, work to bring her to the table. If key information is missing, suggest that a party provide it. Mediators can elicit information and persuade people to attend in circumstances in which the same request would be rejected if made by a party.

> *Example:* A company bought a shipping line and later sued an accounting firm for allegedly overstating the enterprise's profitability and misleading it into overpaying. The buyer's lawyer called the mediator ahead of time to warn that it was crucial for his client, the buyer's CEO, to attend the mediation. However, he said, the CEO would not come unless the managing partner of the defendant did as

well, and the plaintiff would not commit to attend first. The mediator called the defense attorney, who agreed that the principals should attend but said that his client also did not want to be the first to agree to come.

The neutral decided to ask each side to tell her privately whether its principal would come if the other did so. When they both answered positively, she announced that both decision makers had agreed to attend.

Alternatively, you might learn that one of the participants needs more time to talk, for instance, because he is in the grip of strong emotions. With the opponent's assent you can meet privately with a disputant ahead of time, allowing people to begin to work through difficult emotions and arrive at mediation more ready to make decisions. Or a lawyer might ask that you use an unusual format for the process itself.

2. Allow Participants to Argue and Express Feelings

Challenge: Unresolved process and emotional needs. If parties don't settle, it's often because someone wants something more than particular settlement terms. A litigant might be looking instead for a process: the opportunity to appear before a neutral person, state his grievances, and know he has been heard. Or a party may have a need to express strong feelings directly to an adversary.

People may enter litigation expecting to have this opportunity, only to learn that emotions are relevant only if they serve a strategic purpose, such as supporting a claim for damages. As a result, disputants can remain trapped in feelings of anger and grief for years, never having a chance to speak freely. Until they feel heard out, however, parties are often not ready to settle.

Response: An opportunity to speak and feel heard. Mediation is not a court session and mediators are not judges, but the process can give parties the experience of receiving a hearing. They can see their lawyer argue their case, or present it themselves, and listen to an opponent's arguments. The mediator will not decide the dispute and might never even express an opinion about the merits, but she can demonstrate she has heard the disputants. The experience of telling one's story and feeling heard out by a neutral person can have a surprising impact on a person's willingness to settle. Arguing the merits also focuses participants on the facts and legal principles relevant to the controversy, and knowing that a neutral person will be listening encourages them to think through their arguments and avoid extremes.

This aspect of the process often has an emotional component as well. The need to express strong feelings to one's adversary is a very human one, felt by executives and mailroom clerks alike. At various points parties can express some of their feelings about the dispute and each other.

Example: A state trooper began a high-speed chase of a drunk driver in a small New England town. The driver ran a stop sign; straining to keep up, the policeman hit a third car that was crossing the intersection. The trooper was unhurt, but the driver of the third vehicle died instantly. He was a 17-year-old boy, only weeks away from his high school graduation.

The driver's family sued the state, arguing the trooper had been negligent in ignoring the stop sign. It was a typical tort case in which a jury would have to decide whether the officer had acted carelessly. Defense counsel investigated, looking for facts to show the victim had been drinking or careless. It seemed, however, that the boy was a model student, in fact the valedictorian of his class, and had left behind a loving family. On the other hand, the trooper was showing initiative in giving chase to a dangerous driver. It was a difficult case, but one the defense thought could be won, and counsel began the usual process of discovery.

Two years later, as trial approached, the defense decided to make a settlement offer. It was rejected. Defense counsel waited a few weeks and then made a more substantial offer. The word came back from the plaintiffs' lawyer that his clients would not settle. Why, the defense counsel asked: Didn't the family understand that juries in the area had been very hard on claimants lately, and the trooper had a reasonable defense? The plaintiffs' lawyer was apologetic but said the family was adamant and refused even to make a counteroffer. Instead, he suggested they mediate and emphasized that the family wanted to begin with a meeting with the trooper.

Defense counsel agreed to mediate but resisted the idea of a joint meeting: What was the point of having angry people rehash the facts, given that the evidence was largely undisputed and the state, not the trooper, would pay for any settlement? Eventually, however, they agreed to the process.

The opening session was an extraordinary event. The victim's mother, father, and sisters came; they talked not about the case, but about their lost son and brother. The mother read a poem to the trooper describing the hopes she had had for her dead son and the life she knew they would never be able to share.

The officer surprised everyone as well. Although he maintained he had not been negligent, he said he felt awful about what had happened. He had three sons, and had thought over and over about how he would feel if one of them were killed. He had asked to be assigned to desk work, he told the family, because he could no longer do high-speed chases.

The parties did not reach an agreement that day, but as the family walked out one of the children turned to the trooper. "It's been three years since my brother died," she said, "and now I feel he's finally had a funeral." Two weeks later the defense settlement offer was accepted.

Emotional discussions are often uncomfortable for people and temporarily make them angrier, but over the course of a process difficult conversations can help disputants let go of feelings and consider settlement. You can achieve a great deal simply by allowing the parties to talk about feelings and disagreements in a controlled setting; Chapter 10 describes techniques for managing this successfully.

3. Moderate the Bargaining

Challenge: Positional tactics leading to impasse. Negotiators often have trouble reaching settlement because they use a positional approach to bargaining, trading monetary concessions until they reach agreement. We have seen that positional bargaining can be successful but that it often makes negotiators frustrated and angry, for example, when one side makes an offer that the other perceives as "insulting."

Response: Become the moderator of the process. Ideally, a mediator could avoid adversarial bargaining over money entirely by convincing parties to focus on principles and interests. In commercial mediation, however, parties usually arrive suspicious of each other, focused on legal issues, and determined to engage in money bargaining. A mediator's only practical option in such cases is often to facilitate the process the parties want while looking for an opportunity to move them toward a more effective approach.

One way to facilitate money negotiations is to act as a coach. You can, for example, ask a bargainer to support its number with an explanation ("I'll communicate it, but if they ask how you got there what should I tell them?"), or help a disputant assess how a planned tactic will work ("What do you think their response will be if you start at $10,000?").

If coaching is not enough, a mediator can become a moderator, giving bargainers advice about how to keep the process moving ("If you want them to get to $100,000 with the next round, I think your offer to them needs to be in the range of $700,000 to $800,000. . . ."). By using these steps in combination with a continuing discussion of the case, a mediator can often orchestrate a "dance" of concessions to move the parties toward settlement.

4. Seek Out and Address Hidden Issues

Challenge: Disregard of hidden issues and missed opportunities. Negotiations in legal cases are often blocked by hidden psychological obstacles, which could include the following:

Strong feelings. We have talked about the usefulness of drawing out feelings in pre-mediation discussions or the opening session, but this is often not possible. Participants in commercial mediation typically arrive with "game faces on," presenting a businesslike demeanor even as feelings boil beneath the surface. When this occurs, simply giving a disputant the chance to express emotions is often not enough.

Unexploited opportunities for gain. We know that negotiators can often create more valuable outcomes by including nonmoney terms in settlement agreements, but that parties typically enter commercial mediation focused on legal arguments and expecting to bargain solely over money.

Response: Probe for and deal with hidden issues. Even as you are carrying out other tasks, look for clues to hidden emotions and overly narrow approaches to settlement. Chapter 10 describes ways to promote more valuable settlements and deal with emotional issues.

5. Test the Parties' Alternatives; If Necessary, Evaluate the Adjudication Option

Challenge: Lack of realism about the outcome in adjudication. Participants in legal disputes often justify hard bargaining positions in terms of the merits of the dispute. They are asking for a great deal or offering little, they say, because they have a strong legal case. The problem, however, is that that both parties usually claim that they will win in court.

To some degree parties bluff about litigation options to justify their bargaining positions and do not expect to be taken literally. To a surprising degree, however, disputants actually believe their clashing predictions. Even when a mediator points out to parties that their predictions of success are inherently impossible (one believes that it has a 70 percent chance of winning, for instance, and the other thinks it has a 60 percent chance of prevailing), their confidence remains unshaken: It is the other side, they say, that is being unrealistic. There are two basic causes for disputants' distorted thinking about legal alternatives. One is lack of information; the other, an inability to interpret accurately the data disputants do have.

Response: Foster an information exchange. A first response to a disagreement over the legal merits is to help parties exchange information. Modern discovery rules are meant to require each side to disclose key evidence, but it is often surprising how little one party knows about the other's case, even after years of litigation.

As a mediator, you can be an effective facilitator of information exchange. If, for example, a plaintiff has explained its theory of liability in detail but has given no explanation for its damage claim, you can suggest it flesh out damages to help the defendant get authority to settle. Parties will often respond cooperatively to a mediator's request, although they would have refused the same inquiry coming from their opponent.

Example: A sales manager who had been fired by a computer software company sued his former employer for violating his contract. The company maintained that the termination was lawful. The case remained in discovery for years and then went to mediation. As the neutral caucused with the parties, it quickly became apparent that a major component of the manager's claims was equity options in the company. The plaintiff, however, had never been able to obtain the internal financial reports needed to value the options. He assumed that the company was concealing its wealth and intended to go public in the near future, an event that would make his options very valuable.

Questioned about this in caucus, the company CEO said that he had ordered the data withheld from the plaintiff because "It's none of his business!" In fact, the company was only marginally profitable and everyone's options were "under water" — essentially worthless.

The mediator suggested to the CEO that if there really was no pot of gold in the case, he could help settle it by letting the plaintiff know this. The CEO agreed, and the parties reviewed the financial data together. Within an hour the plaintiff was persuaded that his potential damages were much lower than he had thought, and a settlement was worked out that included verification of the company's financial representations and termination of the options.

Response: Reality test. Even when parties have the relevant information, we have seen that they often do not interpret it accurately. Another way to help to solve merits-based problems is therefore to help disputants analyze their legal case. The least intrusive way is through questions that help parties focus on evidence and issues they have missed. It is important both to ask questions pointed enough to prompt someone to confront a problem and to avoid comments so tough the disputant concludes the mediator as taken sides against her.

Questions and analysis.   Begin with open-ended questions asked in a spirit of curiosity; in this mode, you are simply trying to understand the dispute and the parties' arguments. ("Tell me what you think are the key facts here," or "Can you give me your take on the defendant's contract argument?") Your questions can progress gradually from open-ended queries ("Have you thought about . . . ?") to more pointed requests ("They are resisting making a higher offer because they believe you won't be able to prove causation . . . What should I tell them?"). You might also want to take a party through an analysis of each element in the case, using systematic questions to prevent disputants from skipping over weaknesses.

Discussing the merits can help to narrow litigants' disagreement about the likely outcome in adjudication for several reasons. For one thing, it helps counteract disputants' tendency to be overoptimistic. It also assists lawyers who are dealing with an unrealistic client, and can give a disputant a face-saving excuse for a compromise it secretly knows is necessary.

Evaluative feedback.   In some cases questions and analysis are not enough; a disputant might be wedded to an unrealistic viewpoint or require support to justify a settlement to a supervisor. In such situations a commercial mediator may go further and offer an opinion about how a court is likely to decide a key issue or even the entire case. Evaluations can be structured in a wide variety of ways; for example, "My experience with state court judges is that they usually deny summary judgment in this kind of situation," or "If the plaintiff prevails on liability, what I know of Houston juries suggests they would value damages at somewhere between $125,000 and $150,000."

> *Example:* A lawyer was pursuing a tort claim on behalf of a baseball coach at a private school who had recently died from unclear causes. The lawyer's theory was that the coach's death was due to "multiple chemical sensitivity" triggered by turf treatments. The school's position was that this theory was unfounded, but even if it was true, such a claim was barred by the state worker's compensation law, which prevented employees from suing employers in tort. The school's representatives said, however, they were willing to offer special benefits to the coach's family as a purely voluntary gesture.
>
> During the joint session, the plaintiff's lawyer played heavily on the "sympathy" card and at the same time threatened that the coach's widow was ready to rally alumni to attack the school for its stinginess. In response to the mediator's questions in caucus, the lawyer admitted privately to problems with his legal case. He asked the mediator not to opine about legal issues, however, because he thought as a tactical matter he would do better relying on a mix of threats and sympathy than his legal claim. The school, on the other hand, asked the mediator to point out to the plaintiff how weak the claim really was.
>
> The mediator carried both sides' messages to the other, but did not give either one an explicit opinion about case value. The result was an agreement.

One key point to note is that you should never say how you *personally* would decide the case, but rather you should frame your opinion as a *prediction* of the attitude of an *outside decision maker*. Expressing one's personal opinion about what is "right" or "fair" in a dispute is almost always a bad idea, because it is likely to leave a listener feeling that the mediator has taken sides against him. Properly performed, a neutral evaluation can be helpful in producing an agreement, but a poorly done or badly timed opinion can be quite harmful. This is a controversial issue that is discussed in more depth in Chapter 10.

6. Break Bargaining Impasses

Challenge: Closing the final gap. Often barriers to agreement are too high, causing bargaining to stall and provoking an impasse.

Response. A mediator has several options for dealing with a stalled bargaining process.

Persevere and project optimism. The first bit of advice might seem simple but embodies a basic truth: When in doubt, persevere. Parties get stuck at some point during a mediation, often during the late afternoon or early evening, when energy levels decline and each side has made all the compromises it feels it ought to and more. The key thing to remember at this point is that the mediation probably *will* succeed; if you can keep the parties talking, they will find a solution. The disputants will be looking for signals about whether it is worth continuing, and it is important to send positive ones if possible within the bounds of reality.

> *Example:* The dispute involved a Silicon Valley executive who sued his company after being fired. The mediator continued to work, even after each attorney told him privately the case could not settle. Finally, at 9 P.M., the parties reached agreement. As the mediator went over the settlement terms the defendant's lawyer exclaimed, "They kept beating you up and you just kept going. You were like . . . like . . . the *Energizer Bunny!*"
> At first the mediator found the idea of being compared to a drum-beating pink toy a bit demeaning. But as he thought more about it, the comparison was apt. A commercial mediator's job, he thought, is to advocate settlement until the parties tell him unequivocally to stop, and he sees no plausible way to change their minds.

Return to a prior tactic. Another option is to return to an earlier stage or tactic. You might wonder why, if an approach has not worked once, it would be successful the second time around. Surprisingly often, however, something that was rejected earlier will evoke a positive response later in the process. People's emotional states shift over the course of a mediation as they learn new facts and realize their original strategy is not working. As a result, they often become more open to compromise.

Invite the disputants to take the initiative. Another simple tactic is to ask the disputants to take the initiative. You could say, "What do you think we should do?" and then wait quietly. If disputants realize they cannot simply "hang tough" and demand that the mediator produce results, they sometimes offer surprising ideas.

Test flexibility privately. Another option is to test the disputants' flexibility in private. Parties may refuse to offer anything more to an opponent but be willing to give private hints to you. You could, for example, ask "What if?" questions ("What if I could get them down to $150,000; would that be acceptable?") or propose bracketed bargaining ("Could we agree that the parties will negotiate between $100,000 and $150,000?").

Adjourn and follow up. If the disputants are psychologically spent or have run out of authority, the best response may be to adjourn temporarily. You can follow up with shuttle diplomacy by telephone, propose a second, shorter mediation session, or set a deadline to prompt parties to make difficult decisions.

A Basic Commercial Strategy

Challenges	Responses
1. Missing elements: people, data, emotions	• Contact counsel beforehand to initiate a relationship and learn about the dispute. • Arrange for information to be exchanged and decision makers to attend. • If necessary, meet with participants ahead of time to begin working on difficult issues.
2. Lack of opportunity to present arguments and express feelings	• Provide disputants with a "day in court" to argue their case. • Create a setting in which they can express their feelings. • Encourage participants to listen to each other.
3. Positional tactics leading to impasse	• Encourage principled and interest-based approaches, but support money bargaining if parties want to use it. • Advise bargainers about the likely impact of tactics. • If necessary, coach or moderate the bargaining.
4. Hidden issues	• Probe for emotional obstacles. • Identify personal and business interests. • Treat emotional and cognitive problems. • Encourage the parties to consider imaginative terms.
5. Lack of realism about the outcome in adjudication	• Encourage exchanges of information. • Ask about legal and factual issues. • Point out neglected issues; lead an analysis of the merits. • If necessary, predict the likely court outcome on one or more issues.
6. Inability to reach agreement	• Persevere, remaining optimistic. • Invite the disputants to take the initiative. • Repeat earlier tactics. • Adjourn and follow up.

This six-step strategy will produce success in many situations, particularly when a case is relatively straightforward and the parties have a strong incentive to settle, and provides a solid foundation on which to premise a mediative effort. No single set of strategies, however, can overcome all obstacles. Experienced mediators use this basic strategy as a foundation, modifying their approach to deal with the specific obstacles they encounter in each dispute. We discuss other options in Chapter 10.

Questions

17. What goals is a mediator using the "Basic Strategy" seeking?
18. Using Professor Riskin's grid, how would you classify the style of a mediator applying the preceding advice: Broad or narrow? Facilitative or evaluative?

b. No-Caucus Approaches

Although commercial mediators typically employ a joint-session-followed-by-caucusing format, some neutrals conduct all, or almost all, of the process in joint session. Many mediators of marital disputes, for example, do most or all of their work with both parties present, in part to build a better working relationship between the spouses around issues such as parenting and in part out of concern that caucusing would exacerbate the air of suspicion that often hangs over such cases. Disputes arising from close business relationships have many of the characteristics of a family quarrel and also might lend themselves to the use of a no-caucus format. Some believe that no-caucus techniques should not be used whenever parties are seeking a better understanding of their situation and creative agreements. The following reading describes one such approach.

❖ **Gary Friedman & Jack Himmelstein, *CHALLENGING CONFLICT: MEDIATION THROUGH UNDERSTANDING***

xxv (American Bar Association, 2008)

Introduction to the Understanding-Based Model

One of the keys to the power of the Understanding-based model of mediation is that it is a real alternative . . . [W]e work from a base of four interrelated core principles.

- First, we rely heavily on the power of *understanding* rather than the power of coercion or persuasion to drive the process.
- Second, the primary *responsibility* for whether and how the dispute is resolved needs to be with the parties.
- Third, the parties are best served by *working together* and making decisions together.
- Fourth, conflicts are best resolved by *uncovering what lies under* the level at which the parties experience the problem. . . .

The Power of Understanding

In the traditional approach to resolving conflict, the coin of the realm is the power of coercion. When parties disagree, the exertion of control through the use of threat, persuasion, manipulation, or the imposition of an external authority is considered inevitable, necessary, and proper. That is true not only in the traditional adversarial model of resolving disputes but also in many of the seemingly differing models of alternative dispute resolution that have evolved.

While we do not pretend to be able to totally eliminate coercion in our approach, we try to bring the power of understanding to bear wherever possible as the gateway to resolution.

Understanding proves central along several dimensions of helping parties to deal with their conflict. One, of course, is the substance of the conflict. We support each party in gaining as full an understanding as possible of what is important to him or her in the dispute, as well as what is important to the other party. Understanding is also critical in creating a working relationship between the parties and the mediator that makes sense to all. And understanding can prove crucial in helping the parties to recognize the nature of the conflict in which they are enmeshed and how they might free themselves from its grasp. We want *everything* to be understood that may be important to the parties in resolving their differences . . .

Party Responsibility — Let the Parties Own Their Conflict

"Let the parties own their conflict" means it is important to remember and honor that it is the parties' conflict. *They* hold the key to reaching a resolution that best serves them both. And *they* have the power and responsibility, if they are willing, to work together toward that resolution. For us, that does not mean simply that the parties must ultimately agree to any final settlement of their dispute. *Party responsibility* means the parties understand what is substantively at stake for both and craft a resolution best for all. It also means the parties actively participate in shaping the mediation process by making ongoing choices, along with the mediator, as to the course it will take.

Thus, the *parties exercise responsibility* not only in determining the substantive result — the *what* of the problem, but they also participate actively in deciding the *how* — the way the mediation proceeds. For us, the *what* and the *how* are inextricably related; and the parties' active involvement in shaping the *how* is more likely to lead to their creating a better result on the *what*.

This does not mean that the mediator plays a passive role, yielding to the parties in determining the course of the mediation. Rather . . . we view the mediator's role as both active and interactive with the parties. This stands in contrast to the assumption within the traditional approach to conflict that it is the professional who needs to assume active responsibility for the resolution of the controversy.

The mediator, too, is responsible. The mediator's responsibility is directed to supporting the parties in *their ability to make choices together based on their growing understanding*. *Understanding* ensures that those choices will be informed.

Working Together

We believe that the best way for mediators to support parties in resolving their dispute is for the parties to work together and make decisions together. We appreciate that for many professionals, this is one of the most striking and questionable aspects of our approach. Most mediators regularly meet separately with the different parties ("caucusing"). Our goal is to work together with the parties directly and simultaneously. We will address at length in this book why we work in this way and how we do so. Here we highlight a few of the bases on which this core principle rests.

We work in this way because it creates better solutions for the parties. We do it also because we believe it best honors the parties while also contributing to what we view as a critical need in society for developing better ways for people. to go through conflict.

We do not believe that our approach to mediation with its emphasis on the parties working together, or any particular approach to mediation, is the answer to all conflicts. We do think that for those people who are motivated and capable of working together, there are many benefits. We have seen that succeed for thousands of individuals and organizations. . . .

Going Under the Conflict

Einstein is credited with saying that "you cannot resolve a conflict at its own level." The point for us in Einstein's words is that when it comes to dealing with conflict, we need not only breadth of understanding but depth as well. That means recognizing that conflict has an inner life and being open to that dimension. Repeatedly, we find that the basis for resolving conflict comes from examining with the parties, as best as we are all willing and able what *underlies* their dispute. . . . This deeper level of understanding can make all the difference and therefore merits a special place in our core principles. The inquiry into what lies beneath takes place in each aspect of the conflict.

First, we work with the parties to understand what *underlies the substance of the conflict*. As we noted earlier, we help both sides identify what is truly important to each in the dispute — not only *what* they want but *why* they want it . . . [T]he goal is for the parties to ultimately be able to take each other's views into account along with their own as the foundation for a solution that is individually suited to all parties. . . .

Second, we work with the parties to understand *what underlies their conflict* in terms of how it may have them trapped in their dynamic. . . . Conflict is rarely just about money, or who did what to whom. It also has a subjective dimension — the emotions, beliefs, and assumptions of the individuals caught within the conflict. This subjective dimension includes feelings, such as anger and fear, the need to assign blame, and the desire for self-justification . . .

We are not suggesting that the answer to every conflict is that a little understanding magically changes the dynamics between the parties and resolves the problem. What we are suggesting is that understanding can begin to help the parties appreciate how they have become caught in this ricocheting trap and lead to a way out . . .

The Non-Caucus Approach

Many other approaches to mediation recommend that the mediator shuttle back and forth between the parties (caucusing), gaining information that he or she holds confidential. Our central problem with caucusing is that the mediator ends up with the fullest picture of the problem and is therefore in the best position to solve it. The mediator, armed with that fuller view, can readily urge or manipulate the parties to the end he or she shapes.

The emphasis in our approach, in contrast, is on *understanding* and *voluntariness* as the basis for resolving the conflict rather than persuasion or coercion. We stress that it is the parties, not the professionals, who have the best *understanding of what underlies* the dispute and thus are in the best position to find the solution . . .

The parties' motivation and willingness to *work together* is critical to the success of this approach. Mediators often assume that the parties (and their counsel) simply do not want to work together, and therefore keep the parties apart. In our experience, many parties (and counsel) simply accept that they will not work together and that the mediator will be responsible for crafting the solution. But once educated about how staying in the same room might be valuable, many are motivated to try it. If the parties (and the mediator) are willing, *working together* throughout can be as rewarding as it is demanding, as the mediations recounted in this book illustrate.

Role of Law and Lawyers

Mediators tend to be divided in how they approach the role of law in mediation. [W]e welcome lawyers' participation *and* we view it important to include the law. We do not, however, assume that the parties will or should rely solely or primarily on the law. Rather, the importance the parties give to the law is up to them. Our goals are (1) to educate the parties about the law and possible legal outcomes and (2) to support their freedom to fashion their own creative solutions that may differ from what a court might decide. In this way, the parties learn that they can together reach agreements that respond to both their individual interests and their common goals while also being well informed about their legal rights and the judicial alternatives to a mediated settlement.

We also want to respond to a common perception and challenge that working in this way is simply not realistic for most conflicts and most people. When we hear that critique, we are reminded of similar statements three decades ago when it was the legal profession directing the challenge at the very idea of mediation where parties would decide for themselves. Now, too, the challenge is from many lawyers (not all), and they are joined, ironically, by a good number of mediators. Our response now — as it was then — is that many parties in conflict, if given the opportunity, can and want to do it. . . .

Example: A caucus-oriented mediator took on a case involving the dissolution of a design firm. One of the partners, whose specialty was marketing, had taken an inside position with a large client of the firm, while her partner, who focused on supervising the execution of projects, had decided to continue the business on her own. The two women remained friendly, but the situation had created tension around setting the terms of the remaining partner's buyout of her colleague's interest in the firm. The partner who handled production was anxious at the prospect of becoming solely responsible for the business and plainly felt somewhat abandoned. Her marketing colleague, by contrast, tended to take an everything-will-work-out approach to life, and found it hard to credit her partner's concerns.

The partnership's corporate lawyer recommended that they mediate the issues between them. In light of their long history of working together cooperatively, he suggested that they do so without lawyers present, but with each having a personal attorney available for consultations between sessions. The mediator ordinarily used a caucus-based format, but he decided in this case to keep the two women together throughout their discussions. He felt that with some assistance they could negotiate directly and was concerned that if he held separate meetings it would be taken as a signal that their disagreements were more serious than they were. Most important, the partners themselves expressed a preference for face-to-face discussions. The mediation went forward in a joint-meeting format, although each woman occasionally talked with the mediator privately by telephone. The memo of agreement was written out and initialed in an ice cream shop located under the partnership's offices.

Questions

19. What potential advantages would a no-caucus model provide, as compared to a caucus-based approach, in a typical commercial contract dispute? What drawbacks?

20. Can a no-caucus model be effective when the disputants believe that the only issue in the case is money? If they insist on limiting bargaining to money?

21. In the case example, the mediator had occasional private conversations with each party over the telephone. Although neither party appeared to feel excluded as a result, what concerns might a no-caucus mediator have about this technique?

22. In terms of the Riskin Grid, how would you chart the style of a mediator who uses an "understanding-based" process?

c. All-Caucus Mediation

While some mediators advocate spending the entire process in joint session, an increasing number of disputants in commercial mediation — civil litigators and, it appears, the parties who hire them — do not want to meet together at all. More and more mediators report that at the request of lawyers they do not hold a substantive opening session in commercial cases.

Instead, the mediator is likely to bring the parties together for a short meeting to introduce themselves to each other and permit her to explain ground rules such as confidentiality. Disputants do not make substantive statements in each other's presence, however, and after introductory comments adjourn into private caucuses, where they spend the rest of the process. Some mediators do not hold even an introductory meeting — disputants go into separate rooms on arrival, and the mediator conducts the entire process in caucus format.

❖ **Pam Smith,** *Separating Opponents Key to*
JAMS Neutral's Success

The Recorder 4 (June 20, 2006)

The lawyers who bring their cases before William Cahill . . . can't predict if they'll lay eyes on their opponents. The retired San Francisco Superior Court judge dispenses with the initial joint session practiced by many mediators. "Sometimes it takes two hours to undo the bad feelings that that creates," he said.

Instead, he meets separately with each party at the beginning of the day to assess whether to bring the attorneys, their clients or both into the same room. On rare occasions, opponents don't see much more of each other than the signatures that dress a settlement at the end of the day, Cahill said.

Litigator Michael Early first picked up on that technique in a case before Cahill, though he says he's since noticed more mediators doing away with those initial group presentations.

"Except in exceptional [cases], it tends to get more sides entrenched in their positions and starts the mediation off with the confrontation that mediation is supposed to avoid."

Questions

23. Why might counsel in a civil case prefer a pure caucus model? Why might the parties?
24. What are potential advantages and disadvantages of this model? In what kinds of cases might it work well or poorly?
25. Would Gary Friedman and Jack Himmelstein agree that mediation is "supposed to avoid . . . a confrontation"? Why do you think litigators might favor this approach?
26. Is it significant that the mediator described in the article is a former judge? What might be the pluses and minuses of selecting a former judicial officer as a mediator?

Problem

Assume you are a mediator who uses the "Basic Strategy" described above. Two lawyers ask you to mediate a contract dispute between an IT firm and a manufacturer. The dispute involves a $1.4 million contract the parties signed 18 months ago to create software for workstations that control the manufacturing of sensors used in cars' automatic braking systems.

The manufacturer says that the software was delivered late and is unreliable, stopping production and costing the company lost profits on the contract of more than $3.5 million. The developer agrees that there have been delays and problems but attributes them to "scope creep," saying that the original project was to create software to manage no more than 50 workstations performing no more than 15 operations, but over the contract life this number expanded to 175 stations and 25 operations, greatly increasing the complexity of the required software. It says it is entitled to $400,000 in unpaid fees for work it has done to date, and that the entire contract, with its larger scope, will cost nearly $2 million.

- Would you suggest a caucus or no-caucus process for this dispute? Why?
- Would you agree to use the opposite format if the lawyers in the case strongly wanted to do so? What would you tell them if you did?

4. *Is There More to Mediation Than Technique?*

The discussion so far might give the impression that while mediators' styles vary widely, the key differences involve choices of format and tactics. The mediation process, however, involves subtle personal influences that are more important than any particular format or technique.

> ❖ **Daniel Bowling & David Hoffman,** *BRINGING PEACE INTO THE ROOM: THE PERSONAL QUALITIES OF THE MEDIATOR AND THEIR IMPACT ON THE MEDIATION*
>
> **16 Negotiation J. 5 (January 2000)**

Empirical studies of the mediation process consistently show high rates of settlement, as well as high levels of participant satisfaction. These favorable results seem to occur regardless of mediation styles or the philosophical orientation of the individual mediator (e.g., evaluative vs. facilitative; transformative vs. problem-solving). Indeed, the history of mediation, as well as our own experience, shows that mediation sometimes works even when the mediator is untrained. Is there some aspect of the mediation process — wholly apart from technique or theory — that explains these results?

Some might say that mediation works because it provides a safe forum for airing grievances and venting emotion (that is, it gives people their "day in court"), and this can be done even with an unskilled mediator. Others might point to the use of active listening and reframing — skills that many people have, whether or not they have had any formal mediation training. Still others may focus on the use of caucusing and shuttle diplomacy — again, techniques that do not necessarily require specialized training.

We believe all of these techniques are important. We also believe that mediation training is vitally important. However, there is a dimension to the practice of mediation that has received insufficient attention: the combination of psychological, intellectual, and spiritual qualities that make a person who he or she is. We believe that those personal qualities have a direct impact on the mediation process and the outcome of the mediation. Indeed, this impact may be one of the most potent sources of the effectiveness of mediation. . . . As mediators, we have noticed that, when we are feeling at peace with ourselves and the world around us, we are better able to bring peace into the room. Moreover, doing so, in our experience, has a significant impact on the mediation process. . . .

Our starting point is to reflect on how we ourselves developed as mediators. For us, and for many of our fellow mediators, the process seems to involve three major "stages." Although we describe these aspects of our development sequentially, for some mediators they may occur in a different order, overlap, or occur to some degree simultaneously.

First, as beginning mediators, we studied techniques [and] looked for opportunities to practice these skills. A period of apprenticeship ensued. . . . The second stage of our development involved working toward a deeper understanding of how and why mediation works. In seeking an intellectual grasp of the mediation process, we hoped to find the tools with which to assess the effectiveness of various techniques . . . and better understand what we were doing, why we were doing it, and the meaning of the process for our clients. . . .

The third stage of our growth as mediators is the focus of this article, and we consider it to be the most challenging frontier of development. For us, the third aspect begins with the mediator's growing awareness of how his or her personal qualities — for better or worse — influence the mediation process. . . . It is about being a mediator, rather than simply doing certain prescribed steps dictated by a particular mediation school or theory. . . . More specifically, it is the mediator's being, as experienced by the parties, that sends the message. . . .

The Mediator's "Presence"

This brings us to the heart of our thesis — namely, that there are certain qualities that the mediator's presence brings to the mediation process that exert a powerful influence, and enhance the impact of the interventions employed by the mediator. . . . Central to this way of looking at mediation is the recognition that the mediator is not extrinsic to the conflict (any more than the therapist is wholly separate from the issues addressed in therapy). . . .

Subtle Influences

If we accept the view that, notwithstanding impartiality, mediators are inevitably engaged in creating a relationship with the parties, a relationship in which their personal qualities will influence the parties' ability to negotiate successfully — we are led inevitably to the next question: What are the qualities in the mediator that will contribute to a successful relationship with the parties, one that will support reorganization of this conflict "system"? . . .

In our work as mediators, integration comes in part from developing a strong identification with our role: the transition from feeling that "I am someone who mediates" to realizing that "I am a mediator" — from seeing mediation as work that we do to seeing it as an integral part of our identity. . . . [T]hese theories suggest that we as mediators "create" the conflict resolution process through our perception of the participants, the conflict, and our role in it as conflict resolvers. . . . Accordingly, who we are — i.e., the personal qualities we bring into the mediation room — begins to take on larger significance. . . . The effectiveness of our interventions often arises not from their forcefulness but instead from their authenticity. . . .

Implications for Mediation Practice

. . . Integration is a quality that we may never fully achieve but are continually developing. It is a quality which, we believe, mediators should foster because (1) it provides a model for the parties — bringing peace, if you will, into the room; and (2) by subtle means which are more easily described than understood, the "integrated" mediator's presence aligns the parties and mediation process in a more positive direction.

Questions

27. Are the qualities described in this reading more compatible with some models of mediation or negotiation you have read about than with others? Which ones?

28. In the mediations in the *Microsoft* case, what quality did Judge Posner appear to "bring into the room"? What did Green and Marks try to project?

29. Does it appear to matter that Posner conducted the process primarily by telephone and e-mail, whereas Green and Marks met with the parties in face-to-face sessions? Do you think a mediator can communicate "presence" to the parties without being physically present?

CHAPTER
6

Stages of Mediation

What a mediator does, and how disputants and their lawyers experience mediation, can be thought of in different ways: One is as a *process* that proceeds in stages, like negotiation. The other is in terms of how mediation *responds to specific obstacles* that are preventing the parties from communicating or bargaining effectively. This chapter examines mediation as a process. Later chapters focus on specific obstacles to agreement and how mediation can address them. For purposes of comparison, we look at both caucus and non-caucus models and explore the process from both the perspective of mediators and that of lawyers representing clients in the process.

A. Commercial Mediation

A mediator has almost complete freedom to improvise, and in practice, good neutrals use widely varying approaches. As mentioned previously, however, commercial mediation usually takes place in several distinct stages: pre-mediation, the opening session, private caucuses, and joint discussions. These stages, and the goals and methods appropriate to them, are discussed below.

1. Pre-Mediation

Before parties first meet together, mediators may talk with the parties' counsel to lay the ground work for a successful process. Some pre-mediation tasks are mundane, while others can be quite sensitive. They are discussed below.

Performing administrative tasks. The mediator or an assistant must carry out administrative tasks, such as arranging for the participants to sign a mediation agreement and obtaining money deposits. The participants must also agree on when and where the process will take place.

Ensuring the right people are at the table. The mediator and the participants share a common interest in having the right people present to make the process succeed. Usually the right people are those with the motivation and authority to agree to a settlement. Lawyers are the most likely to know about these issues and should bring "people" problems to the neutral's attention in advance. The mediator can then work to ensure that the necessary people are present.

Building a working relationship. The pre-mediation stage may be the first time the mediator actually meets the disputants. This is a good opportunity for lawyers to start to build a relationship with the neutral that will allow them to influence the process and ease hard decisions later on. This can be done through meetings or telephone conversations between the mediator, the lawyers, and possibly also the parties.

Starting to mediate. It may seem strange to talk about mediating before the parties have even met, but in one sense every contact between a mediator and a lawyer or client is part of the process. In certain situations — for example, an angry plaintiff in an employment case or a bereaved widower in a wrongful death action — it may be useful for the mediator to start to work with one or perhaps both parties before the sides meet to mediate. Defense counsel, for example, will often agree to a mediator having a private meeting with an emotional plaintiff or even suggest that he do so, recognizing that doing so may lay the groundwork for progress in the "formal" process.

> *Example:* A professor was stalked for years by a disturbed female student. He asked his university for assistance, but felt that the deans ignored his plight, eventually forcing him to move to a secret location. He complained to the media and then sued the university, demanding compensation for his distress and the right to teach by video in the future. It was clear to the mediator that the professor was extremely distraught over the ordeal.
>
> With the assent of the university's counsel, the mediator arranged to meet with the professor and his lawyer privately before the mediation began. He listened to the professor describe his feelings of anger and betrayal. Several days later the parties met to mediate. The professor was less upset, but still too angry to accept a compromise, and the university remained suspicious that the professor would continue to criticize them in the media even if the case was settled.
>
> Three weeks of telephone diplomacy ensued between the mediator and the lawyers. All the parties then met again, this time on campus rather than at the mediator's office. The mediator shuttled between the offices of the professor and the university president. A settlement was eventually reached that included a rearranged teaching load, a sensitization program for staff about stalking, special monitoring of the stalker when she was released from prison, and a monetary payment.

2. The Opening Session

The opening session is the first time in most mediations that the disputants meet as a group. It is often referred to as the "joint" session, but "opening session" avoids implying that this is the only time disputants will meet together. Lawyers and usually the parties are present during the opening session and the mediator moderates it.

Should there be an opening session at all?

As we have discussed, in some areas commercial mediation is now conducted almost exclusively through caucuses, and participants do not meet together at all. Even where opening sessions are customary, lawyers often suggest skipping them. Among the less persuasive reasons given for avoiding an opening session are:

- We've heard it all before (You might ask: Who is "we"? The lawyers or the clients?)
- They'll blow up (This is extremely unlikely in commercial cases)
- They'll get angry and refuse to settle (People sometimes get angry when they express feelings about disputes, but emotions tend to fade quickly, and even when not expressed openly often influence people)
- We don't have time (What's more important than talking together?)

Example: A condominium association sued a developer over major defects in construction. The developer in turn sued its architect, contractors, and insurers. The parties agreed to mediate for two days, and more than 40 people convened for the event.

The lawyers had strongly advised the mediator not to hold an opening session. Just hearing from 15 parties, they said, would chew up most of the first day, leaving little time for private discussions and bargaining, and in any case they all knew each other's arguments. The better strategy, they said, would be to caucus immediately. The mediator agreed and went directly into caucusing.

The discussions were difficult, but by the end of the second day the parties had narrowed an initial gap of $5 million to $400,000. At that point, however, the condo association directors refused to move any further. When the mediator asked why, one of them complained of years of frustration with the development company's predecessor. He insisted on explaining this to the current developer's CEO who, he said, didn't know what the unit owners had gone through.

The mediator adjourned the process, and a week later convened the plaintiffs and the developer for a special two-hour meeting. Reading from binders full of documents, the board members traced their past frustrations while the developer's CEO listened. The discussion deteriorated into thinly-veiled threats, and the meeting broke up without apparent progress. Two weeks later, however, the board agreed to an additional compromise and the case settled.

Mediators should be reluctant to eliminate an opening session for reasons such as lawyers' claims that "we've heard it all before." Even if this is true for the lawyers, it usually is not for the parties. And, as long as basic ground rules are enforced, even angry parties can talk with each other without provoking a damaging confrontation.

There are a few circumstances in which there is little risk in skipping an opening session, for instance, if each of the following factors is present:

- All of the participants are dispute professionals: lawyers, adjusters, etc.
- The professionals are the real decision makers in the case.
- Each side has received full discovery about the other's case and any underlying issues.
- No one is too angry, and it truly is largely, if not entirely, about money.

Example: A large manufacturer sued two insurers to recover the cost of remediating a large plume of pollution that had been spilled from one it its plants and entered the water table hundreds of feet below the ground. The estimated cost was more than $20 million.

Despite the large amount of money involved, none of the people at the mediation seemed emotional about the case. The spill had occurred in the late 1960s, and no one now involved with the company felt responsible for it. The adjusters representing the insurers viewed the case as a typical problem of trying to allocate risk under uncertainty: The underlying facts were buried in the past, relevant insurance policies had been lost, and so on. In addition, a nationally known venture capitalist who controlled the defendant insurance company was, by coincidence, that very day making a takeover bid for the manufacturer. As a result, both sides' negotiators knew the dispute might soon be "all in the family."

At the participants' request the mediator agreed to dispense with an opening session and go directly into caucusing. The neutral's role turned out to be a small one. The disputants had gone to mediation primarily to create a settlement event and did not need much outside help. They quickly traded concessions of $1 million or more, and within a few hours had a deal.

a. Goals

The overall goal for the opening session is to create a foundation for productive bargaining. One should structure it as a serious meeting rather than an adjudicatory proceeding.

Begin to build good working relationships.   Your primary goal from your first contact with the disputants is to build their trust and confidence so that they will accept your guidance. You need to give each party the feeling you are genuinely interested in their viewpoint and want to help them achieve a good result. The opening session is usually the first time the parties, and perhaps also the lawyers, have met you, apart perhaps from a brief chat in the waiting room. Particularly if you have a goal-oriented, "get it done" personality, this may seem pointless, but as noted in the Introduction, surveys of clients of commercial mediators show that this is crucial to success. Don't let your interest in moving the process along get in the way of trying to make a personal connection with each disputant.

Explain the process.   The opening session is also your best opportunity to explain mediation to the disputants. Often the parties are first-time participants. By describing the process you can clear away misconceptions and make them feel on more of a level playing field with experienced participants. Even lawyers who are familiar with mediation often welcome a brief explanation, both for the benefit of their clients and to confirm that key ground rules are understood by everyone.

Before reaching mediation, the parties will often have been involved in bitter litigation and failed negotiations, so you also want to set a positive tone for the process, suggesting it will be different from what has gone on before.

Give lawyers an opportunity to argue and the parties to listen.   Opening sessions can play a significant psychological function for both attorneys and clients — the opportunity to have a "day in court." Lawyers sometimes also need to demonstrate the strength of their arguments and their commitment to their clients. And the opening session allows a client to hear, often in blunt terms, what his opponent will say if the case goes to trial.

Allow the disputants to express views and feelings. The opening session allows participants, directly or through their attorney, to express feelings such as anger or grief directly to the other party. Indeed, mediation is often the only chance a party has to talk directly with its opponent during the entire litigation process. Parties are free to talk about business and personal issues, but commercial litigants usually focus on their legal case.

Exchange information. The opening session is an opportunity for disputants to exchange information. This is particularly valuable when mediation takes place at the outset of a dispute, at a point when the parties have not conducted formal discovery.

b. Techniques

Overall format

The format of an opening session is flexible, but typically follows this structure:

- The parties meet and introduce themselves.
- The mediator welcomes the participants and explains the process.
- The lawyers, and perhaps also the parties, make statements.
- Disputants exchange questions and comments, and the mediator may pose clarifying questions.
- The mediator concludes the session and transitions to caucusing.

Opening moments. Greet people as they arrive and make small talk as you would at the start of a business meeting, but don't put yourself in a position one side may interpret as bias toward the other. For example, unless it has been cleared in advance, a party should not arrive to find you talking with its opponent behind a closed door.

Follow the cues of the disputants concerning formality. If they already are on a first-name basis or doff their suit coats, you can do so. If, however, you sense a participant is uncomfortable with this, err on the side of formality at the outset. Disputants from other cultures may interpret American casualness as lack of respect.

Mediator's comments. Mediators almost always make opening comments. Experienced mediators tend to keep these relatively short, especially if the parties are professionals who have probably been briefed by their lawyers. They also know most people cannot remember more than a few minutes of oral comments when they are tense, as is often true of disputants. A transcript of suggested opening comments appears below.

Parties' statements.   After opening comments, the mediator gives each side the opportunity to speak. What a party says is in its discretion, but typically lawyers make statements, sometimes supplemented by comments from a party or an expert. As the mediator you will want to:

Set the agenda and encourage participants to listen.   The plaintiff usually speaks first as a matter of convention. Occasionally, if the plaintiff's position has been explained in advance and the defendant's views are not known, it may make sense to start with the defense. Notify the lawyers in advance if you decide to do so.

Participants often listen with a focus on rebuttal, rather than taking in what they hear. Encourage the parties to listen carefully to what their adversary says, noting that it may well be a preview of what they will hear in court if the case is not resolved.

Listen carefully, and show you are doing so.   Remain quiet but engaged. As each person speaks, turn to look at them. Demonstrate you are listening by nodding or taking notes. Intervene as moderator only if necessary: This is the disputants' chance to speak freely.

You may want to pose a clarifying question or make a comment occasionally to show you are listening or that you have "done your homework." If you sense your comments may be misinterpreted, explain your intent ("My questions are meant only to clarify what I'm hearing; I don't mean to express any view about the merits of the case, and I expect to be asking the same kinds of questions when the other side speaks.")

Encourage the parties as well as the attorneys to talk.   Lawyers' instinct is often to keep clients under wraps, and parties themselves may be reluctant to talk. Encourage them to speak, but make it clear there is no pressure to do so.

Example: A retired executive bought an antiques company, only to conclude a few months later that the seller had deceived him about its condition. He filed suit but then agreed to mediate. The mediator called each lawyer before the mediation and mentioned he would invite their clients to talk. The executive's lawyer said he thought his client would welcome the chance. The attorney for the seller, however, warned that her client was an "engineer-type" who would not want to say much.

The purchaser showed up with a four-page single-spaced text and described how he'd entered the deal in good faith, only to find himself betrayed by deceptions ranging from inflated inventory to a clientele outraged at the prior owner's failure to meet shipping dates.

After 30 minutes, the purchaser finished and the seller began to talk. Belying his counsel's prediction, he spoke articulately and at length. There was a back-and-forth discussion in which the attorneys participated but which was dominated by the principals. When the discussion became heated and repetitive, the mediator deferred to the lawyers' request they move into caucusing. Still the opening session went on for 2½ hours, and later that day the case settled.

Promote discussion but maintain order

The opening session is often the first time the principals have met since the dispute began. Parties are sometimes hostile, and lawyers sometimes feel the need to play aggressive roles. Your goal when this happens should ordinarily be to manage a "controlled confrontation." This includes confrontation — allowing participants to express conflict and emotions — and control — not permitting the process to degenerate into bitter accusations. You might think of your role as similar to a chef preparing pasta: To cook it well the water should boil vigorously, but not overflow the pot. Success in mediation also lies in having enough heat to produce change, without making a mess.

Outbursts are rare in commercial mediation, probably because disputants feel they would lose face if they were chided by a mediator in front of an opponent. (This is also a reason to be very polite when intervening, so you are not perceived to be "slapping their hand.") If a discussion starts to spin into a confrontation, a cautionary comment will restore order quickly. ("The plaintiff has the floor at the moment Mr. Smith. I'll ask you to take careful notes, and once the plaintiff is finished I want to hear how you see this.")

Information exchange.   Opening sessions are an excellent opportunity for parties to exchange information. Parties can also do this once they are in caucuses, of course, but at that stage questions and answers must be relayed through the mediator.

Once each side has made an opening statement and offered a rebuttal if it wishes, you may encourage the parties to talk directly with each other. If attorneys want to head prematurely for their caucus rooms, encourage them to stay. As a rule of thumb, do not become concerned about moving out of joint session until one-third of the expected time for mediation has gone by.

Transition to caucuses.   At some point in almost every session, one or both lawyers will suggest the parties go into caucuses. Or you may decide the joint discussion has run its course or that the participants are becoming too adversarial and decide to move into caucusing.

Confidentiality rules in caucusing.   One question is what rule of confidentiality to announce for the caucusing phase. Will everything a disputant says be confidential unless the disputant authorizes the mediator to disclose it, or will the mediator have discretion to transmit information unless a disputant affirmatively flags it as confidential? The second option is preferable because in the heat of mediating, mediators often forget to ask for permission, and in any event cannot always foresee what they will need to disclose in the other caucus room.

c. Mediator's Opening Comments

To help you anticipate what to expect in a legal mediation, here is a transcript of a typical opening statement by a commercial mediator, with comments to explain the thinking behind them:

MEDIATOR: Good morning. I'm _____. I don't know everyone, so before we go any further I'd appreciate it if you would introduce yourself and indicate who you're with.

Comment: It is often useful for counsel and the mediator to sketch the shape of the table and write down each person's name and role.

M: Some of you are probably familiar with mediation, but for others it may be a new experience. Let me describe what we'll be doing, then turn it over to you for opening comments.

Comment: Participants often are doubtful about protocol (for example, will there be a time limit on statements?). It's best for lawyers to discuss these issues with the mediator in advance, but a confirmation at the outset is also useful.

M: The purpose of mediation is to help people negotiate. My only role here is to help you find a solution to this dispute. I am not a judge, and I have no power to decide this case. By signing the mediation agreement you have agreed that I am disqualified as a witness and will never play any role in this case if it goes to trial. That leaves me entirely free to focus on one thing: helping you to find a settlement. My goal is that if an agreement is possible — and it usually is — it should not be left on the table because of an accident or misunderstanding.

In cases like this my experience and that of other mediators is that about three-quarters of the time parties *are* able to reach agreement. That means that the odds of obtaining a settlement are strongly in your favor. The fact that you have all come here is evidence that everyone wants to find a solution and that you are willing to make reasonable compromises to bring it about. However, ultimately it's up to you whether you agree or not.

Comment: Neutrals should promote optimism but not misstate the terms of anyone's participation.

M: One of the key aspects of this process is that it is confidential. You have all signed the mediation agreement and agreed not to disclose anything said during this process. You've agreed to confidentiality on two levels. First, both sides agree that nothing said here can be used at trial: No one can ask you in court, "Didn't you say 'X' at mediation, and now you're saying 'Y'?" Second, you've agreed that you won't discuss anything said here with outsiders such as a reporter or a neighbor. It's understood that if you are with an organization, you may have to talk with others to confirm a settlement, and if you are an individual you may want to talk with an advisor or family member. But aside from consultations about settlement, no one will discuss what occurs here with anyone outside this room. That gives us more freedom to talk frankly about possible solutions.

Comment: These comments focus on what the parties have agreed to, rather than what the law requires (for the law of confidentiality, see Chapter 14). A mediator cannot guarantee what legal rule may be applied in a future proceeding, and participants in a court-related program may be subject to special reporting requirements. Counsel and mediators need to think through these issues so as not to mislead clients about the degree of confidentiality protection.

M: I understand that we have as long as we need [or: until 5:00 P.M.] today, and if we keep focused I believe that we can get it done. If you don't mind, since this is an informal process, I'll proceed on a first-name basis, and I hope you'll do so with me too.

Comment: Some participants, such as a complainant in a sexual-harassment case or a foreign businessperson, may feel demeaned by being called by first names. If there is a question about this, a mediator will want to check (and a lawyer will do well to warn the neutral) ahead of time how each person wishes to be addressed. If there is doubt, it is best to proceed formally at first.

M: I would like to begin by asking each side to present its perspective on the situation. It's useful for me and for the other side to know your views on the legal issues, but I also would welcome ideas about how we can get to a resolution.

I've asked each side to present its views frankly, so everyone knows what will happen if you can't settle this case. But I've asked the lawyers not to give the kind of full-scale presentation that they would at trial. I also hope that you'll avoid personal attacks.

Comment: If the parties are represented by counsel, the attorneys will usually choose to make the opening statements. Again, counsel will want to think through carefully how large a role to take and what tone to set; Chapter 11 explores this issue in depth. Mediators may want to encourage counsel in advance to let their client or another key player speak, or even to be the primary spokesperson. A personal injury plaintiff, for instance, might be asked to describe how her injuries have affected her life. The plaintiff usually speaks first as a matter of convention.

M: Mr. [party] and Ms. [party], I will ask you to take a special role. You each have experienced lawyers who will handle the legal issues. I'd like you to sit back and simply listen. Ask yourself: If I were a judge or juror hearing this story for the first time, and didn't know what actually happened, how would it sound? As you listen, feel free to take notes but please don't interrupt. No one will take the fact that you are listening politely as meaning that you agree with anything that you're hearing. I know that you disagree, or you wouldn't be here.

Comment: In general, mediators apply a no-interruption rule. But if the participants begin to talk with each other constructively, an experienced neutral will sit back and let it happen. Counsel should think about whether they prefer a format in which each side takes turns or a less structured exchange.

d. Parties' Opening Comments

M: Does anyone have any questions about the process or what I've said so far? If not, let's go ahead. I'll ask the plaintiff to go first, and then we'll hear from the defense.

M: [If a lawyer speaks first, when she concludes the mediator might say] Mr. [party], your counsel has covered the legal aspects of this dispute, but I wonder if there is anything of a non-legal nature you'd like to say, or that you think we should have in mind as we go forward? If you'd rather not, or would like to wait until later, that's fine, but if you do want to say anything I hope you'll feel free to do so now.

e. Joint Discussion

M: [*After each side has spoken and replied to the other*] Often, especially when people mediate early in a dispute, there is information that each side needs to know to make a decision about settlement. You should keep in mind that you are each asking the other to make a very difficult decision. If there is something they need to know to make that decision, I'd encourage you to provide it. Does anyone have any questions?

Comment: This is often an ideal setting for a lawyer to gather information that the parties may need to bargain effectively, and a lawyer who needs data should prompt the mediator to mention this. Parties who "stonewall" during discovery may be more forthcoming in mediation, especially if they are encouraged by the mediator.

M: [*After any discussion has taken place, mediators might ask a few clarifying questions. When parties do not want to talk or fall into repetitive argument, a mediator might say the following*] It's clear that there is a disagreement about what happened. Given enough time we might be able to reach conclusions about the facts, but you're here with the goal of avoiding a trial. I suggest that we go forward with discussions and work to reach a resolution.

f. Transition to Caucuses

M: [*When productive discussions are over*] At this point, I suggest that we go into caucuses so that I can talk with each of you privately. We do this because it's usually easier for people to discuss the pros and cons of the legal issues and options for settling if the other side is not sitting there listening while they do it. I'll ask the plaintiff side to come with me to the other conference room and the defense to remain here.

There is an additional rule of confidentiality that applies to the caucusing process. If you tell me in caucus that something is confidential, I will not disclose it to the other side — just like a lawyer's relationship with a client. Even if you don't say anything, if I sense that something is sensitive I will check with you before discussing it with the other side. But it is much easier for me if you flag items that you want to keep confidential.

Comment: If a lawyer does reveal confidential information, she should make a note of it and remind the mediator not to disclose it at the end of the session.

M: I should warn everyone now about one basic rule of caucusing: Time always passes more slowly for whoever is waiting for the mediator! Please keep in mind, though, that if I spend a long time with the other side — and I'm sure that at some point I will — it's usually because I am explaining your point of view and they are disagreeing, or I am asking them questions so that I can bring you their responses. The first caucuses are also usually longer than later ones because there is more new information to cover. I'll be back with you as soon as I can.

3. *Private Caucuses*

Almost all commercial mediations involve some private caucusing, with the mediator moving back and forth between parties sitting in separate rooms, and in most cases disputants spend most of their time in caucuses. The typical format of commercial mediation thus contrasts sharply with family and community mediation, where parties typically remain in joint session throughout.

Should parties caucus at all?

Most commercial mediators believe the advantages of having private conversations with disputants strongly outweigh the disadvantages of separating them. Occasionally, however, even commercial mediators do not caucus, usually because the parties prefer to talk directly.

Patterns in caucusing.   A mediator's goals and techniques will change as caucusing progresses. In the first round your primary goal will usually be to allow disputants to explain their perspective, express feelings, and develop confidence in you. To do this, focus on listening and drawing people out and try not to challenge what you hear.

As the process goes on you will want to become more active, posing pointed questions and offering advice about bargaining. During the last stages of the process you will often feel it appropriate to make specific suggestions about what parties could do to achieve a settlement and perhaps to predict the likely outcome if the case is litigated.

Mediators tend to progress from a restrained to a more active role for several reasons. First, as the process goes forward participants become increasingly convinced they have been heard and gain confidence in the mediator, making them more willing to listen to suggestions. At the same time the mediator learns more about the legal issues and the parties' concerns, making the neutral more confident about giving advice. Disputants are also likely to become increasingly frustrated with the results of traditional bargaining, making them more receptive to suggestions about other ways to approach the dispute.

a. Early Caucuses

Goals

During the first round or two of caucusing, mediators usually have the following goals:

* Continue to build relationships
* Make the disputants feel fully heard
* Gather sensitive information and control negative communications
* Identify interests and probe for hidden obstacles

Continue to build relationships.   A primary goal continues to be to build a working relationship with each side. Good relationships will make you more effective later in the process as you deliver unwelcome news and suggest painful compromises. The first caucus is usually the first time you talk privately with either principal, making the interaction particularly important.

Make the disputants feel fully heard.   It is important to create an atmosphere in which disputants feel free to express feelings, perspectives, and wishes they may not have felt comfortable stating in the presence of their opponent. In the privacy of the caucus, parties can speak their minds without concern about being embarrassed. Your goal at this stage is to listen well and show you are listening; it is not to offer advice. Try to keep in mind that during the first caucus the parties and lawyers are entitled to "have it their way." There will be time later to point out the errors and inconsistencies in their case if necessary.

Gather sensitive information.   Caucuses allow a mediator to gather sensitive information the parties want to hide from an adversary. Disputants may be guarded about disclosures at first, but will often become more open as the process goes on.

Control negative communications.   The caucus format allows a mediator to translate one side's angry or provocative language into words the other party can hear. If you cannot put a statement into acceptable language, you perhaps can withhold it until the recipient is able to listen or the speaker has become calmer.

Identify interests and probe for obstacles. Because caucus discussions can be less guarded and more free-ranging than joint meetings, they are a good opportunity to look for hidden obstacles and encourage disputants to identify underlying interests.

Techniques

During the first caucus meeting with each side try to follow these guidelines:

- Ask open-ended questions
- Engage the principals
- Start slowly and listen carefully
- Show interest and empathy
- Perhaps start the bargaining process
- Keep track of time

With whom to start? The convention in mediation is to meet first with the plaintiff, if only for a few minutes. Disputants sometimes read significance into where a mediator begins, so give a reason for your decision ("It's traditional to begin with the plaintiff, so that's what I'm going to do . . ." or "Since the plaintiff made the last offer, I think I will start with the defense . . .").

Ask open-ended questions. Start with open-ended questions that invite disputants to talk freely. You might begin with: "Is there anything you didn't feel comfortable mentioning in front of the other side, but you think I should know to understand the situation?" Alternatively, if a party seems to have been in a personally trying situation, you could acknowledge this and invite the person to elaborate ("This sounds like it was an awful experience for you Ms. Smith...").

Focus your initial comments on the issues raised by the people with whom you are meeting rather than their reactions to the other side's comments. Most disputants want to know their own views have been considered before they will deal with an opponent's concerns.

Engage the principals. Focus some of your questions on the parties rather than the lawyers. To avoid making them uncomfortable, ask simple, factual questions rather than legal ones ("Mr. Yao, can you tell me where you feel the pain?" or "Ms. Green, I heard your counsel say you were seeking reinstatement. Do you know if your position has been filled?"). Or you might ask a general question such as, "Jim, how do you feel about all this?"

Start slowly and listen carefully. Resist the temptation to "cut to the chase." Unless the process is operating under a tight time constraint, be wary of directing the agenda, making suggestions, or using confrontational tactics during the first round of caucusing. Even evaluative mediators rarely offer opinions during their first caucus meeting with each side.

Show interest and empathy.   It is vital the participants feel heard out. Listen in a way that shows the speaker she has been heard and understood. You can convey this by taking notes, maintaining eye contact, and checking your understanding ("So if I understand you correctly, you feel the defendant never intended to comply with the contract?"). Suggestions about how to listen effectively appear in Chapters 7 and 8.

Perhaps start the bargaining process.   You can wait until the second round to ask for offers, or suggest a party make an offer at the end of the first caucus meeting. If there is no clear signal about the parties' wishes, you can offer the party whose turn it is to move a choice ("You could make a first offer now, or treat this round of talks as focusing on information and wait for the next round to put out a number. We probably won't get an offer from the other side until you have made one, but we have time. It's really up to you.").

Keep track of time.   Early caucus meetings are usually much longer than later ones because more information is being gathered and communicated. Disputants are sometimes frustrated at waiting as a mediator talks with the other side. You may want to warn disputants of this and, if a session extends for much more than an hour, step out and "touch base" with the side that is waiting.

b. Middle Caucuses

As the caucusing progresses, parties gradually move from exchanging data and arguments to analyzing the case and making offers. Mediators become more active participants in the discussions, for example, by pushing parties to consider the costs and uncertainties of litigation. Middle caucuses tend to mix case analysis with active bargaining and sometimes exploration of interests. During this stage you are likely to:

- Moderate the bargaining process
- Encourage information exchange
- Ask about interests and probe priorities
- Reframe disputants' views
- Change disputants' assessments of the merits

Moderate the bargaining process.   Bargaining over money, coupled with arguments over the value of each side's litigation option, take up most caucus discussions in the typical commercial case. Facilitating hard money negotiations is a frustrating and difficult task. You can play a helpful role by advising disputants how to interpret offers, predicting an opponent's likely reactions to a party's planned offer, and suggesting tactics to move the process forward.

Bear in mind that parties often come to mediation with unreasonable expectations about what the other side will be willing to do, and even realistic parties often take extreme positions for tactical reasons. Disputants often realize only gradually how much they will have to compromise to get a settlement and need time to adjust to unwelcome news. The first caucus is usually too soon to ask a party to make a real effort, but as the process progresses you will probably need to push and coach parties to compromise. Chapter 7 gives suggestions on how to facilitate "pure money" negotiations.

Encourage information exchange. We have seen that one of the main reasons people are unable to negotiate successfully is they do not have enough information, and a mediator can help negotiate exchanges of data. This process is likely to become more intense as it becomes clearer where the parties disagree.

You might, for instance, say to a defendant who has refused to disclose information: "I think the defendant is not coming up because he hasn't seen a detailed critique of his statute of limitations defense. In order to get the kind of movement you need here, I'd suggest you authorize me to explain how you plan to defeat it."

Ask about interests and probe priorities. At first, parties and their lawyers usually want to talk only about their legal case and money offers. As time goes on, however, disputants sometimes become more open to considering non-legal issues and options. The middle caucuses are a good time to suggest that disputants focus on their own business or personal interests and factors that might motivate their opponent to settle. You can also ask about the parties' relative priorities and give each side a signal about what is more or less acceptable to the other. Suggestions about how to do this appear in Chapter 7.

Reframe disputants' views. Mediators work to change disputants' views of the controversy and each other, by suggesting a different way, or "frame," in which to see a situation. For example:

> *Example:* A homeowner was bitterly opposing a neighboring business's expansion plans before a local licensing board. The company proposed a buyout of the homeowner's property. The homeowner reacted angrily, saying he could not understand why the company would try to "drive me out of my home."
>
> The mediator responded, "From what they're telling me in the other room, the company is impressed by your tenacity. They're convinced you'll fight every effort they make to grow their business. In one sense it's not too surprising that they see it that way, you've filed protests to their expansion applications for the last ten years, and succeeded in delaying a lot of them."
>
> "To them, paying you money to drop this particular objection looks like giving you a war chest to fight the next battle. I think this is what's motivating their request for a buyout. Is there anything we could tell them that would give them confidence if they settle without it they'll be able to live peacefully with you?"

Change disputants' assessments of the merits. Middle caucuses are also the time a mediator can start to push parties to assess their best alternative to settlement, which is usually to continue in litigation. The court outcome is usually the focus of these discussions, but you should seek to define "alternative" more broadly to include:

- The cost of litigation: How much will the party have to pay to pursue the adjudication option?
- The intangible costs of remaining in conflict: personal stress, business distraction, and other non-legal burdens.
- Whether the alternative is in fact adjudication. Remember that only a small percentage of cases are ever decided on the merits. Most parties who break off talks spend time and money litigating, only to find themselves back in negotiations in the future.
- The likely outcome if a court does decide the dispute.

During this stage a mediator can help parties analyze each aspect of their alternative to reaching agreement, bringing each side's arguments and perspectives to the other and asking for help responding to them. ("They are challenging your claim for emotional distress because they say there aren't any medical records to back it up. Is there anything I can give them so they will make a better offer?")

As the process goes on you can become increasingly active, explaining and emphasizing each side's key points to the other and probing assumptions about liability, damages, and the cost of litigation. Your goal will be to make each side confront, perhaps for the first time, the full costs of pursuing the dispute and the possibility that if they do so they will lose. Ideas about how to do this appear in Chapter 9.

c. Later Caucuses

As the process moves toward closure, disputants focus less on the value of their case and more on pure bargaining. Indeed, toward the end caucus sessions may last only a few minutes. Disputants are usually more willing to accept advice from the mediator at this stage, but at the same time are resistant to making additional concessions, feeling they have already given up more than they should. During the later caucuses a mediator can:

- Seek to maintain momentum
- Set up joint meetings
- Offer or initiate process options
- Commit agreements to writing
- If necessary, adjourn and try again

Seek to maintain momentum. The most basic way to maintain momentum is by keeping the mediation in session. Participants look to mediators for cues about whether there is real hope of settling, so to the extent possible you should emphasize the positive.

Set up joint meetings. Many commercial mediators stay in caucus continuously after the opening session, bringing participants together only to sign a settlement agreement. In can be helpful, however, to convene the participants to talk or bargain directly with each other. Full teams can meet, but more often one or a few members of each side gather for a private discussion. The participants may be CEOs, lawyers, or experts; what is appropriate depends on the situation.

Offer or initiate process options.   If the bargaining process falters, a mediator can suggest options to restart the process or apply them on his own initiative. For ideas about how mediators can overcome impasse, see the latter part of Chapter 11.

Commit agreements to writing.   If the parties reach agreement, the next step is to convene the lawyers to write up the terms. Usually disputants prepare a handwritten memorandum that sets out key terms and calls for the execution of formal documents and payment within a specified period of time. Lawyers may take over this process, but often the mediator will be asked to serve as the moderator or scribe; if you do, be careful to avoid acting in a way one side may interpret as biased.

4. Follow-Up Contacts

If parties are not able to reach agreement, don't give up. Instead, suggest they adjourn and think things over. Contact them a day or two later to take the temperature of each camp, and then either conduct shuttle diplomacy by telephone or e-mail or schedule another mediation session.

In conclusion, mediation is a flexible process, and good neutrals modify the usual structure to meet the needs of particular situations. That said, opening sessions and private caucuses, preceded and often followed by telephone contacts and in-person meetings, are the settings in which most commercial mediators do their work.

B. No-Caucus Processes

Even among mediators who generally work without caucusing, there is considerable variation in the structure of the process. Folberg and Taylor (1984) describe the structure of classic divorce mediation as follows:

Divorce and family mediation can be conceptualized as a multistage process. Building rapport and gaining trust pervade the early stages. A holistic family system approach, rather than a focus on the interests of one party, is a hallmark of each stage. Though writers may divide or categorize the stages differently, the following stages are most frequently listed.

- Introduction and orientation
- Fact-finding and disclosure
- Isolation and definition of issues
- Exploration and negotiation of alternatives
- Compromise and accommodation
- Reaching tentative agreement

- Review and processing settlement
- Finalization and implementation

Friedman and Himmelstein, in the no-caucus model described in Chapter 5, advocate using phases, if not rigid stages, which include:

- Contracting, in which the parties agree to ground rules and take responsibility for participating actively in the process;
- Defining the problem, bringing out all relevant issues and information, legal and non-legal;
- Working through conflict, analyzing the way they communicate and assessing interests;
- Developing and evaluating options that accommodate those interests; and
- Concluding an agreement.

The transformative model, described by Professors Bush and Pope in Chapter 12, does not follow a specific structure or agenda. "Unlike other models of mediation, the transformative mediator is not a process guide, but follows the parties by using supportive skills such as reflection, summary and checking in. [The neutral] avoids using directive interventions such as setting an agenda, normalizing, pointing out common ground, probing for underlying issues and keeping parties focused on a discussion topic." (Folberg, Milne & Salem, 2004). In the transformative model, the parties determine the nature of the conversation and the structure it takes.

Questions

1. In what kinds of disputes would you, as an advocate, advise your client to use a commercial format?
2. When, apart from divorce cases, might the approach outlined by Folberg and Taylor be most effective?

Note: Choosing the Right Process

After reading about different structures and approaches to mediation, you may be left with the impression that one model is right and the others wrong. We do believe that there are more and less effective ways of conducting mediation, but we also strongly believe that which approach is best will vary from one dispute to another. As counsel to a disputant, one of your most important tasks will be to select the process that best matches your client's needs and preferences. We explore this issue in more depth in Chapter 10. For now, however, you should be aware that decisions about the structure of the process will depend on factors such as the following:

- The client's overall goals: The best possible monetary outcome? Repair of a ruptured relationship? Something else?
- The client's preferences as to process: Is he willing, for example, to confront or at least tolerate strong and angry emotions? Would he be more comfortable in a caucusing format, or can he handle face-to-face discussions about contested issues?
- The client's role: Is she willing to mediate without a lawyer present? Will she present well? Or would she be better off if you do most of the talking?
- The other side's answers to the same questions.
- The preferences and abilities of the mediator: Although you will seek a neutral who meets your preferences, your choice often will be constrained by the need to agree with the other side on a candidate.

CHAPTER
7

Process Skills

The next three chapters probe more deeply into the mediation process, examining the techniques that mediators use to overcome obstacles to settlement and how lawyers can take advantage of a mediator's interventions. We organize the discussion around three topics: process skills, psychological and emotional forces, and merits-based barriers.

Before focusing on mediation technique, though, we should ask: How much do specific skills, whether good listening, analytic ability, or creativeness, matter to a mediator's success? The following article describes how the lawyers who hire commercial mediators answer this question.

❖ **Stephen B. Goldberg & Margaret L. Shaw,** *FURTHER INVESTIGATION INTO THE SECRETS OF SUCCESSFUL AND UNSUCCESSFUL MEDIATORS*

26 Alternatives 149 (2008)

This article reports the results of . . . a continuing research project. . . . [W]e surveyed people who had participated in mediation as representatives of disputing parties — typically attorneys — to determine their responses to the question of what led to mediation success.

The most frequently cited behavior correlated to mediator success involved the mediator's ability to gain the parties' confidence. . . . Tops on the list — referred to by an average of 60% of the mediation advocates . . . — was that the mediator was friendly, empathic, likable, etc. Examples of the respondents' comments include:

> "He is a genuinely nice guy. People like to be around other people whom they like — especially someone you have to spend hours with in a high-stakes situation."
>
> "She demonstrates compassion for the client, which makes the client feel that she is working hard on her behalf and tends to make the client trust her."

The next most frequently cited reason for mediator success — referred to by an average of 53% of the mediation advocates — was that the mediator had high integrity, as demonstrated by his or her honesty, neutrality, trustworthiness, protection of confidences, etc. Examples of these comments include:

> "He has honesty and integrity. We had absolute confidence that he would not reveal information we did not want revealed to the other side."

> "Another essential quality is her personal integrity — as it is essential to any mediator. Both sides trust that the information she relays is accurate, and that she's not putting a spin on things to help her get where she needs to go."

Rounding out the top three most frequently cited reasons for mediator success, and referred to by an average of 47% of the mediation advocates, was that the mediator was smart, well-prepared, or knew the relevant contract or law. Examples . . . include:

> "She's extremely smart. That plays out in several ways, such as creativity in finding solutions."
> "He was an extraordinarily quick study who was able to master the underlying facts and issues of a complex case well enough to be credible in his discussion of the strengths and weaknesses of each party's position."

The confidence-building attributes referred to above were cited by respondents as key elements of mediator success more frequently than various skills used by mediators to bring about agreement. The most frequently mentioned mediator skills were patience and persistence (referred to by an average of 35% of the advocates); providing useful evaluations or reality-testing regarding the likely outcome of the dispute in court or arbitration (33%); and asking good questions and listening carefully to responses (28%).

Some comments relating to the mediator's patience and persistence include: "Her patience was outstanding. The parties were very far apart: We didn't give this case a chance for success. . . . However, her patience resulted in a settlement."

Comments involving the mediators' provision of useful evaluations or reality-testing . . . include: "She readily identifies — and expresses in a non-confrontational fashion — the most significant weakness or downside in each party's position."

Comments involving the importance of asking good questions and listening carefully to responses include: "I think primarily he's a good listener, which is key for a mediator to be successful. . . . "

The central conclusion . . . is that a — if not *the* — core element in mediator success is the mediator's ability to establish a relationship of trust and confidence with the disputing parties.

———————————————

A. Pre-Mediation Contacts

You now know that a mediator can do a substantial amount before the parties first meet to create the conditions for a successful negotiation. In some contexts this is not possible: If you are a student in a clinic or a lawyer in a court-sponsored program, for instance, you may not have the ability to talk with a mediator before the process begins. If you are dealing with a busy commercial mediator, it may also be impractical to talk in advance. In many cases, however, mediators and disputants can contact each other ahead of time. If so, a neutral can do preparatory work, and lawyers have the opportunity to begin to shape the neutral's approach to the conflict.

As you read, think how you could apply these ideas in a neutral's role, or how as a lawyer you could use pre-mediation contacts to advance your bargaining agenda.

❖ **Marjorie C. Aaron,** *At First Glance: Maximizing the Mediator's Initial Contact*

20 Alternatives 167 (2002)

First moves matter. A mediator's strategic choices during the initial contact can encourage the next steps that will produce a successful mediation, or render mediation less likely or less productive. Too often, a mediator receives a telephone call from a lawyer in a case, and without much thought, gathers the essential information needed for a conflict check and scheduling. Trained to listen, the mediator does so, as the lawyer recites his or her version of the case. A tentative date is set, or opposing counsel is contacted to select a date and work out document exchange. [This response is not necessarily harmful, but it] may cause the mediator to miss significant opportunities to enhance her effectiveness, the likelihood of selection as mediator, and achieving a successful resolution.

This article suggests a set of questions a mediator might ask during the first few moments of initial conversation with a contacting lawyer. Based upon the answers to these questions, the mediator can . . . more strategically choose among next steps. . . . The following are questions for the mediator to ask the contacting lawyer.

Who is opposing counsel? Before learning anything but the paltriest information about the type of dispute and the parties, the mediator should ask for the identity of opposing counsel. . . .

I am curious, how did you get my name? Perhaps you have mediated with opposing counsel, who recommended you for this case. . . . The judge may have recommended you. A former student or law school classmate may be an associate at the firm. . . . The mediator must be acutely sensitive to instances where the referral source could raise neutrality issues. . . .

The following questions are safe for initial and for "separate" conversations — and often yield helpful information:

Have you and your client been involved in mediation before? How did it work? Does it raise any concerns for you about mediation in this case? It is very helpful to know what participants' level of experience is and their expectations are going into the mediation. You may learn [for example] that the attorneys' most recent mediations took place with no joint session — only caucusing back and forth. So that's what those attorneys understand mediation to mean.

What is the status of this dispute/case? Is it in litigation? . . . Has a trial date been set? When? This information will give you some indication of the lawyers' and parties' current mindset: the dollars that have been spent; . . . how much entrenchment there has been and whether a relationship repair is likely to be an option; what is motivating the parties; and the time constraints within which you must operate.

How did the case get to mediation? Was it referred by the court? A suggestion by counsel? Initiated by the client? The neutral may learn that only one party is anxious to settle or that the lawyers really want to settle and talked the clients into the process — or vice versa. . . .

If you and opposing counsel were negotiating, without any involvement by the clients, do you think you could settle it without need for mediation? It's so much more elegant than just asking if there's a client problem, and may prompt a richer response.

Can you describe what the dispute is about — just a bare bones description — that both parties would agree upon? Where a "little bit" of case information before a conference call won't jeopardize perceived neutrality (particularly if you have worked with opposing counsel before), you might opt to ask for a limited description. . . .

Please tell me a little bit about the personalities of the people involved and their relationships. Do counsel get along? . . . What are the dynamics between the parties? Is there any past history between them . . . ? This is extremely important information for a mediator to have, and it is best obtained in separate conversations.

A mediator can safely operate with the hypothesis that there is something or someone dysfunctional at work in a mediated dispute. Otherwise, they would have been able to settle it without mediation. Sometimes, the dysfunction is limited to the negotiation process; often it is not. The mediator is well served by the answers to questions that will help everyone avoid potential minefields created by the human dynamics in the dispute.

Who do you think should be present at the mediation? . . . Anyone who would be a disaster? The answers to these questions can be critically important. Sometimes counsel will have arranged to bring someone with the appropriate level of "authority," but who was directly involved in the decisions leading to the dispute. Counsel are generally receptive to the mediator's — not the other side's — suggestion to rethink their choice of a representative at the mediation. . . .

Although responses to Professor Aaron's questions are very helpful to a mediator, are there any that lawyers might be reluctant to answer?

Problem

1. You represent an entrepreneur who has filed a claim of fraud against a former business partner. After a year of discovery, it is becoming clear to you that your client has little evidence of fraud; the problem seems to be due more to misunderstandings, exacerbated by some less-than-fully-candid statements by the former partner. You have a shot at winning the case, but you now believe that the more likely outcome is a defense verdict. Meanwhile, as the case has continued and legal costs have accumulated, your client has become increasingly entrenched in his position. He simply will not listen to reason. It was all you could do to convince him to mediate.

   Would you be willing to provide this information to the mediator in advance? What might make you more or less inclined to do so?

B. During the Process

Among the most important ways in which mediators can help parties deal with conflict are to:

- Listen, and show that they understand
- Reframe communications
- Identify interests and develop options for settlement
- Manage positional bargaining successfully

If you are in the role of a neutral, think about how you can use these skills in your cases — and why applying them may be difficult in practice. As a lawyer selecting mediators, ask yourself whether process issues appear to be obstacles to settlement in your case and, if so, whether a particular candidate has the skills needed to overcome them.

1. Listening

Most mediators would agree that of all the skills needed to be an effective neutral, the most important is to be a good listener. This is harder than it may seem, especially for those of us who are inclined by temperament and training to identify issues, discard irrelevancies, and make decisions quickly. It is often difficult, as we listen to clashing viewpoints, to restrain our instinctive wish to pass judgment. Doing so requires us to put aside, if only temporarily, some important skills we have learned in law school in favor of a different approach to listening.

To understand the importance of listening, consider the following example drawn from America's most famous expedition. In 1804, acting on orders of President Thomas Jefferson, Meriwether Lewis and William Clark set out on an epic journey across the unexplored American continent. After wintering on the Pacific coast they began the long trip home. The party reached the Bitterroot Mountains of Idaho, where they expected to recover horses they had left behind for the winter with a local tribe, the Nez Perce. The horses were essential; without them the party could not survive their passage through the arid mountains. The following account is taken from the journal of Captain Lewis:

> The Americans met an important leader of the Nez Perce, Chief Cut Nose, and rode on with him. They then encountered another chief, Twisted Hair, who had taken their horses for the winter. Lewis and Clark were happy to see Twisted Hair, but he did not return their friendliness. Instead he began to shout and make threatening gestures to Cut Face, who reacted angrily. The explorers were baffled and disturbed — recovering the horses was a matter of life and death, and they needed the cooperation of both chiefs to accomplish this.
>
> The chiefs left, apparently still very angry, and Lewis and Clark set up camp. When their interpreter returned from hunting they invited Twisted Hair to the campfire for a smoke. He explained that the previous fall he had collected the expedition's horses, but that Cut Nose had then asserted that he was the supreme leader of the Nez Perce and should have received care of the horses rather than

Twisted Hair. Angered, Twisted Hair had ceased minding the animals, which promptly scattered. Most, however, were apparently still in the vicinity.

Lewis and Clark then invited Cut Nose to join the group. He arrived and "told us in the presents (*sic*) of the Twisted Hair that he the Twisted Hair was a bad old man that he woar two faces." Cut Nose said Twisted Hair had let his young men misuse the horses, leading Cut Nose to forbid him from managing them.

The explorers suggested they go out the next day and see how many horses they could gather. This appeared acceptable to Twisted Hair and Cut Nose, both of whom had become much calmer after talking. The expedition soon found most of the horses and about half the saddles.

Questions

1. What was the "dispute" here?
2. Did either chief change his mind about who was at fault? If not, why was the meeting helpful?
3. If this encounter had been a modern mediation, what would one call the meeting hosted by Lewis and Clark?

❖ **Richard Salem,** *THE BENEFITS OF EMPATHIC LISTENING*

Conflict Research Consortium, University of Colorado (2003)

Empathic listening (also called *active* listening or *reflective* listening) is a way of listening. Though useful for everyone involved in a conflict, the ability and willingness to listen with empathy is often what sets the mediator apart from others involved in the conflict.

How to Listen with Empathy

Empathy is the ability to project oneself into the personality of another person in order to better understand that person's emotions or feelings. Through empathic listening the listener lets the speaker know, "I understand your problem and how you feel about it, I am interested in what you are saying and I am not judging you." The listener unmistakably conveys this message through words and non-verbal behaviors, including body language. In so doing, the listener encourages the speaker to fully express herself or himself free of interruption, criticism, or being told what to do. It is neither advisable nor necessary for a mediator to agree with the speaker, even when asked to do so. It is usually sufficient to let the speaker know, "I understand you and I am interested in being a resource to help you resolve this problem." [In the words of Madelyn Burley-Allen], a skilled listener:

- takes information from others while remaining non-judgmental and empathic,
- acknowledges the speaker in a way that invites the communication to continue, and

- provides a limited but encouraging response, carrying the speaker's idea one step forward.

Empathic Listening in Mediation

Parties to volatile conflicts often feel that nobody on the other side is interested in what they have to say. The parties often have been talking at each other and past each other, but not with each other. Neither believes that their message has been listened to or understood. Nor do they feel respected. Locked into positions that they know the other will not accept, the parties tend to be close-minded, distrustful of each other, and often angry, frustrated, discouraged, or hurt.

When the mediator comes onto the scene, she continuously models good conflict-management behaviors, trying to create an environment where the parties in conflict will begin to listen to each other with clear heads. For many disputants, this may be the first time they have had an opportunity to fully present their story. During this process, the parties may hear things that they have not heard before, things that broaden their understanding of how the other party perceives the problem. This can open minds and create receptivity to new ideas that might lead to a settlement. In creating a trusting environment, it is the mediator's hope that some strands of trust will begin to connect the parties and replace the negative emotions that they brought to the table.

Mediator Nancy Ferrell questions whether mediation can work if some measure of empathy is not developed between the parties. She describes a multi-issue case involving black students and members of a white fraternity that held an annual "black-face" party at a university in Oklahoma. At the outset, the student president of the fraternity was convinced that the annual tradition was harmless and inoffensive. It wasn't until the mediator created an opportunity for him to listen to the aggrieved parties at the table that he realized the extraordinary impact his fraternity's antics had on black students. Once he recognized the problem, a solution to that part of the conflict was only a step away. . . .

Guidelines for Empathic Listening

Madelyn Burley-Allen offers these guidelines for empathic listening [the guidelines have been edited]:

1. *Be attentive.* Be interested. Be alert and not distracted.
2. *Be noncritical.* Allow the speaker to bounce ideas and feelings off you. Don't indicate your judgment.
3. *Indicate you are listening by:*
   - Making brief, noncommittal responses ("I see . . .").
   - Giving nonverbal acknowledgment, for example by nodding your head.
   - Inviting the speaker to say more: for example, "Tell me about it" or "I'd like to hear about that."
4. *Follow good listening ground rules:*
   - Don't interrupt.
   - Don't change the subject, or move in a new direction.
   - Don't rehearse a response in your own head.
   - Don't interrogate with continual questions.
   - Don't give advice.

- Do reflect back to the speaker:
    - What you understand.
    - How you think the speaker feels.
5. *Don't let the speaker "hook" you emotionally*. Don't get angry or upset or allow yourself to get involved in an argument.

The ability to listen with empathy may be the most important attribute of interveners who succeed in gaining the trust and cooperation of parties to intractable conflicts and other disputes with high emotional content. . . .

Do executives appreciate empathy? William Webster, a former federal appeals judge who also served as Director of the CIA and FBI, later became a mediator. He was once asked to name the book that he had found most useful in his work as a neutral in complex corporate disputes. Webster's response: "When my wife and I had teenagers, I found Dr. Haim Ginnott's book, *Between Parent and Child*, very helpful . . . and I find it equally useful now."

Dr. Ginnott emphasizes how important it is for parents to listen to children empathically, without expressing judgment on what they say. This, Judge Webster was suggesting, is one of the most important skills that a mediator can bring to a dispute — apparently as useful with executives as with upset children.

Problem

2. Your client is going through a difficult divorce and has engaged you to negotiate the terms of dissolution of the marriage. Your client and her husband have been separated for two months. They have two children — a boy, seven, and a girl, ten. He is a partner in a local law firm, and she is a teacher who has been a homemaker since the birth of their second child.

    Your client is extremely angry at her spouse. Her feelings are crystallized around an affair he had with a co-worker a year ago. She complains, however, that the husband was never really committed to the marriage. He enjoyed weekend golf more than spending time with their young children; neglected her emotionally; did not attend many of the children's after-school activities, pleading the press of work; and failed to give her any support during the illness and death of her father two years ago. Your client has demanded that you get the maximum possible recovery from him and "not pull punches." She calls you about every second day to describe her most recent run-in with the husband about payments for household expenses and visitation with the children, and regularly sends you documents that she thinks may be helpful in proving his neglect and ability to pay high alimony.

    a. Do you think that you would have any difficulty listening empathically to this client? Why? What might you do to deal with such a problem?
    b. Would you have any concern about sending your client into mediation? What qualities would you look for in selecting a mediator for this case?
    c. What, if anything, would you want to tell the mediator in advance?

2. Reframing

The root of many disagreements is that people see the same dispute in quite different ways. As you read in Chapter 4, the "frame" a person puts on a situation will influence, in particular, whether he will see a proposal for settlement as a net loss or gain, and this in turn will strongly affect his decision about whether to settle. Helping disputants to reach agreement often requires finding a way to modify their perspectives, or frames, on a controversy, or at least to allow them to appreciate that an opponent honestly sees the same situation differently. One powerful technique for doing so is known as "reframing."

❖ Ken Bryant & Dana L. Curtis, *REFRAMING*
(2004)

To "reframe" a statement (in mediation lingo) is to recast the statement in more neutral terms, giving the speaker, as well as his mediation partner(s), the chance to look at the problem differently, in a more positive way. The new statement offered by the mediator to accomplish this goal is the "reframe."

How It Works

Let's assume for the moment that a mediation participant has made a statement using value-laden (negative) language. The statement is guaranteed to make the other party angry or defensive if simply left floating in air. The task and challenge for the attentive mediator is to quickly find a positive, constructive interpretation of the assertion. (It helps if you simply assume that every behavior, including a rude comment, is appropriate, given some context, or frame.)

Before you can restate or paraphrase, of course, you must be certain you have heard the original statement correctly, which involves a heavy dose of active listening. Your goal is to accurately reflect the message sent by the speaker, while simultaneously molding the statement into an aid for easier communication. In other words, the speaker must be comfortable that you heard what was said, the other party must not be offended by your restatement, *and* the new version (yours) should point the conversation in a constructive direction.

Restating the Message

You might try restating the message by:

- Redirecting the thrust of the negative assertion, i.e., away from persons verbally attacked to problems inherent in the complaint.
- Narrowing or broadening the gist of the allegation by pinpointing a single problem, or generalizing the issues to include basic policy decisions.
- Forming a question: e.g., "Is there a specific issue you would like to work on? Is there another possible explanation for what happened?"
- Shifting the focus from problems to opportunities: "Recognizing that you feel the status quo is intolerable, do you have some ideas about what changes are needed?"

- Simplifying a complex statement of a dispute, by choosing a single issue which can be addressed immediately.
- Categorizing the speaker's concerns to be dealt with either on a "most important," "easiest to deal with first," or some other useful basis.
- Neutralizing the original statement by excising ad hominem attacks and generalizing the issues, while retaining the essential elements of the message.

It bears repeating: *Confirm the accuracy of your reframe*. You can confirm your reframe by simply asking "Is that what you meant?" Or, "Have I expressed your concerns accurately?" Additional, and even more effective, confirmation can be obtained by using your powers of observation of the speaker's non-verbal communication. Check the body language: posture, facial expression, muscle tension, skin coloring, and breathing pattern. Remember, studies indicate that more than ninety-three per cent of human communication is non-verbal.

Why Reframe?

Your purpose is not only to change the harsh effect of the words used by the speaker, but also to create a new dynamic in the mediation. Reframes can change the focus of the speaker's statement, and the mediation, from

- Blame and guilt, to problem-solving
- Past to future
- Judgmental to non-judgmental
- Position to interest
- Ultimatum to aspiration

It probably goes without saying that reframing can, by lowering emotional temperature, increase the efficiency of the mediation process.

Reframing as a Joke

Consider that reframing is the essence of a good joke: What seems to be one thing suddenly shifts and becomes something else. Example: "What do Alexander the Great and Smokey the Bear have in common?" (Answer: their middle names). When you reframe a statement, you shift the speaker's perception, even if just a little. The shift can get creative juices flowing and enhance discussions of options for resolution.

"Meaning" Reframe and "Context" Reframe

Meaning

There was a man who was compulsive about cleaning his house. He even dusted light bulbs. He made his family take their shoes off in their living room. His view of fulfillment as a father and husband was reflected in his home's cleanliness. The problem: He was driving his family crazy. The man was asked to visualize his living room rug, white and fluffy, not a spot anywhere. He was in seventh heaven. Then he was asked to realize that his vision meant he was totally alone, and that the people he cared for and loved were nowhere around. He ceased smiling, and felt terrible, until he was asked to visualize "a few footprints" on the carpet. Then, of course, he felt good again. This is a "meaning" reframe, where the stimulus in the world doesn't actually change, but the meaning does.

Context

A father complained that he and his wife hadn't done a very good job in raising their daughter, because the daughter was so stubborn. The father, a successful banker, acknowledged that he had acquired traits involving tenacity and a stubborn quality needed to protect himself. The father was asked to look at his daughter and to realize that he had taught her how to be stubborn and to stand up for herself, and that this gift might someday save her life. Imagine, he was asked, how valuable that quality will be when *his* daughter goes out on a date with a man who has bad intentions. This is a "context" reframe, demonstrating that every behavior in the world is appropriate in some context. Being stubborn may be judged bad in the context of a family, and becomes good in the context of banking and in the context of a man trying to take advantage of a young girl. When faced with an assertion about the meaning of an event or a person's conduct, the mediator might ask, "What *else* might that conduct mean?" A context reframe can be handled by asking, "Where would this behavior be *useful*?"

Finding the appropriate reframe for negative or non-useful assertions during mediation is hard work and takes practice. No two circumstances will be the same. More often than not, you will not be quite sure if your reframe was useful. Sometimes you will know it was not. There is, however, no such thing as failure, only feedback. You will learn as you try different approaches, and your mediation partners will benefit from your dedication to improving your skills.

Perjury, or just hardball? During mediation of a case arising from a failed partnership, the defendant's attorney argued vehemently that the plaintiff's lawyer had committed malpractice in drafting the partnership contract. This accusation inflamed the plaintiff side, requiring the mediation to be temporarily adjourned. A few days later the plaintiff lawyer produced a recently signed affidavit in which a key witness not only rebutted the defendant's version of events, but went on to say that the defense lawyer had told him that he would be given free legal counsel if he changed his story, arguably an incentive to perjure himself.

Defense counsel, told by the mediator about this in caucus, stood up and said angrily that he would not stand for being accused that way. The mediator replied that he thought the abetting-perjury innuendo was simply a "high inside fastball," thrown by the other side in response to the defense attorney's own "hardball" charge of malpractice. The defense lawyer, who did not really want to walk out and did not mind being characterized as a tough player in front of his client, accepted the reframing of his adversary's accusation as a professional sports tactic and sat down. Both the perjury and malpractice issues tacitly dropped out of the case.

3. Working with Interests

a. The Value of Interest-Based Mediation

Interest-based techniques can help frustrated disputants in several ways. Some of these are obvious and others more subtle. Among the useful impacts of value creation are to:

- Overcome hidden barriers
- Increase the value of settling
- Diminish feelings of losing
- Distract the parties from positional tactics

Overcome hidden barriers

As discussed in the context of negotiation, one of the interests of disputants is in the process itself: the chance to express emotions and to tell their story. By responding to such interests, mediators can diminish obstacles to settlement.

> *Example:* A mediator handling a construction dispute had become familiar with the parties' arguments through pre-mediation discussions. The parties, who were experienced in mediation, asked her to "cut to the chase," skipping the opening session and going directly into caucuses.
>
> After a few hours, however, the parties fell into impasse. The mediator realized that they were stuck because the CEO of the general contractor felt that he had not had the opportunity to explain why, if all the facts were fairly considered, the problems with the job were not his fault. She convened an "opening session" in the middle of the process in which the CEO explained his position at length. After presenting his arguments, the CEO became more open to considering the practicalities of the situation — for example, that litigating to trial would cost as much as a settlement. After a few hours the parties agreed to a compromise payment and settled the case.

Increase the value of settling

If negotiations were analogized to a card game, moving from competitive bargaining to an interest-based approach would amount not merely to dealing each side a new hand, but changing the game altogether. Players who cannot reach an accommodation under the rules of a positional game are often able to succeed when they apply the rules and goals of an interest-based process. As we have seen, negotiators commonly assume that their goals necessarily conflict with those of the other party and that they must therefore bargain over a "fixed pie." If mediation can increase the amount that each side expects to gain from a settlement, agreement will become more attractive. In some cases the impasse occurs at a point where the parties' positions are quite close; in these circumstances, "expanding the pie" by even a modest amount can produce a resolution.

Diminish feelings of losing

Negotiators often make decisions based on subjective perceptions rather than cold logic. In particular, as we have seen, disputants will keep fighting and take unreasonable risks if they see a settlement as a "loss" compared to their prior expectations, but will agree much more readily to results that they see as a "gain." Closely related to this is the psychological need we all have to feel in control of situations. The conflicts and tests of wills that occur during competitive bargaining often threaten negotiators' sense of control, leading them to become rigid.

By helping the parties to identify new opportunities, a mediator can give both sides the sense that they can win something through agreement and regain some control over their fate. This makes it much easier for them to compromise. This psychological effect occurs even when, from an outsider's perspective, the added value is not large.

Distract the parties from positional tactics

Another psychological obstacle to agreement is the tendency of positional bargainers, in particular, to view compromise as giving in to an opponent's will. Zero-sum bargaining often degenerates into an adversarial contest, as each side tries to avoid submitting to the other. By discussing interests rather than positions a mediator can distract the negotiators and end their psychological contest. In essence, by shifting their discussion to interests, a mediator helps negotiators to stop thinking about the positional conflicts that provoked their impasse.

b. Obstacles to Interest-Based Mediation

One of the themes of this book is that bargainers can create value and smooth the path to settlement by using interest-based techniques. It is also true, however, that competitive approaches tend to dominate settlement negotiations in legal disputes.

Why is it so difficult to use interest-based approaches in the context of a lawsuit? It is not that disputants don't know the value of such techniques. Most commercial disputes arise from contracts, and mediators report that most of the contracts they deal with contain significant interest-based terms. Litigants, in other words, arrive at mediation with a record of having created interest-based bargains in the very document over which they are now quarrelling. Once in litigation, however, they usually stop looking for creative options and focus solely on money. Why might this occur? Among the reasons for this are:

- Mutual mistrust
- Role limitations/Lack of knowledge
- Limitations of the commercial format

Mutual mistrust

The first obstacle is the air of suspicion that permeates most commercial cases. To implement interest-based solutions, litigants usually will be required to work together in the future. It is possible to reach interest-based settlements that do not involve future performance, of course: A divorcing couple, for instance, might decide to take turns in dividing their furniture, allowing each to choose the pieces he or she wants most. But the strongest interest-based settlements usually involve parties working together, or one side providing a service or product for the other, after the settlement takes effect.

The problem is that by the time two parties have become involved in a lawsuit, they are usually deeply suspicious of each other. They may distrust the other side's *competence*: An owner, for example, might mistrust a contractor's ability to complete a construction project. An even more serious problem exists when a party suspects an opponent's *intentions*. A buyer, for example, might believe that a supplier intentionally underbid a project, intending to make a profit through shoddy work.

A mediator who proposes a relationship repair to litigating parties risks being met with a response such as: "You've known these people for only a few hours. When we first met them they seemed competent, too, so we're not surprised they look that way to you. It took a lot of bad experience for us to learn what they're really like. No way are we going back into a deal with them!" This example illustrates a pervasive phenomenon, one psychologists call *attribution bias*: Litigants tend to assume the worst about their opponent's motives, viewing every ambiguous step with suspicion.

In legal conflicts, parties' suspicions are magnified by the litigation process itself. Filing suit requires a plaintiff to accuse a defendant of errors or wrong-doing, and parties often exaggerate their claims for tactical purposes. Disputants arrive at mediation, in other words, having accused an opponent or having been accused themselves of behavior unworthy of any good professional. Even if parties know that accusations against them were exaggerated for tactical purposes, they are likely to be embarrassed to admit it. The following responses can help alleviate this distrust.

Confront the issue directly. There is little point in pretending that feelings of anger or mistrust do not exist, or in asking bitter parties to let bygones be bygones. It is better to acknowledge that each side does have serious concerns about whether they can work together in the future.

Promote confidence-building measures. Having elicited confirmation that a problem exists, a mediator can begin to work on it. Most important is to change people's doubts about their adversary's intent. If parties trust an opponent they may excuse a failure of performance, but as long as they doubt the other side's good faith, repairing a relationship is extremely difficult. Sometimes explaining how the problem arose is enough to restore trust.

Example: A franchisor and franchisee were in a dispute over the franchisor's alleged inability to deliver services and the franchisee's failure to pay a $60,000 quarterly fee. It became clear any settlement would require continuing the franchise relationship. The franchisor, however, would not consider this, arguing that the franchisee was a deadbeat who had made up his allegations simply to avoid paying the fee. Asked about this, the lawyer for the franchisee explained that his client had been planning to make the payment and had only withheld it because the attorney told him to do so.

The mediator knew the opposing lawyers in the case respected each other, and asked the franchisee and his attorney if the lawyer would be willing to go into the franchisor's caucus room to explain why the payment had not been made. He suggested the lawyer go in alone, so there would be less suspicion he was simply protecting his client.

The lawyer went into the other caucus, explained that the franchisee had acted on his instructions, and answered questions. After talking privately the franchisor team told the mediator that the franchisee had gotten bad legal advice, but they were now less concerned about his good faith and willing to consider restructuring the franchise.

Provide certainty. As we will see in the next chapter, people strongly prefer certain outcomes over ones that involve even a small amount of risk — what psychologists call the "attraction to certainty." As a result, parties attach much less value to an offer if they see even a very small chance the other side will not carry it out. Interest-based settlements suffer from this, because it is usually easier to determine whether an opponent has paid a sum of money than whether it has adequately carried out a cooperative activity.

It is usually not possible to eliminate the risk of implementation entirely, but it may be possible to convince a party that a risk is manageable. To do this a mediator can analyze less-than-certain proposals carefully so that parties understand that a risk is minor in objective terms. ("What you're asked to assume here is that the defendant will make payments under the new schedule. But the proposal gives you a judgment in escrow and a guarantee of attorneys' fees if you have to collect. Do they really have any incentive not to make a payment — and if they do miss one, can't you bring them into line pretty quickly?")

Role limitations/Lack of knowledge

The next barrier flows from the people who usually attend commercial mediations. Mediation representatives can be "wrong" in two different respects: their roles and their lack of knowledge.

Consider first the problem of role. Once parties define a dispute as a matter that requires the threat or filing of a lawsuit, they usually hire litigators as their representatives, both to conduct the litigation and to discuss settlement. As a result, when parties enter mediation litigators usually act as their spokespersons. Litigators have special skills but tend to approach problems narrowly assuming they have been hired as gladiators and focusing only on the legal aspects of a dispute and money remedies. Litigators are also in a potential bind because they have been hired as legal gladiators. Unless a litigator has strong credibility with a client, she will be reluctant to mention "soft" options for fear of seeming weak or disloyal to the cause.

The most likely way to deal with this as a mediator is to talk privately with the litigators, asking how to raise interest-based issues and offering to take responsibility for promoting alternatives. Another avenue is to talk directly with the principals, relying on the lawyers not to squelch the conversation.

Even when mediation representatives are willing to consider nontraditional remedies, they often lack the necessary information to do so. Bargainers usually are either litigators or persons with checkbook authority. Interest-based solutions, however, require people who can think "outside the box" of court remedies. The more imaginative an option, the more likely it is that new people and information will have to be brought into the mediation to develop it.

Limitations of the commercial format

Knowledge and people problems are especially difficult to solve in the context of commercial mediation because it is usually scheduled for only a single day. If only litigators and "checkbook" personnel have come to the mediation, and constructing an interest-based solution requires business executives and other specialists, it is impossible to import them or in many cases even to contact them by phone the same day. Similarly, when a novel solution requires non-legal information, it is often impossible to access and evaluate the necessary data in a few hours.

A one-day format confronts mediators interested in exploring interests with a difficult choice: Encourage parties to devote time and energy to gathering data, contacting experts, and exploring an imaginative option, or seek a simple deal based only on money? One option is to hold pre-mediation conversations to begin to identify interests and assemble the information and expertise needed to explore them during the mediation. Another is to adjourn to permit a creative idea to be considered. There are drawbacks to stopping, but the following is a case in which it proved effective.

> *Example:* A computer manufacturer brought a warranty claim against a chip maker who had inadvertently supplied it with defective chips. The parties agreed that the chip maker was competent and the problem was caused by an adhesive compound supplied by an outside company. The manufacturer argued, however, that the chip maker was legally responsible for the problem.
>
> The chip maker said it did not have enough cash on hand to pay the tens of millions of dollars the manufacturer was demanding, and eventually proposed making a low-seven-figure payment and providing additional compensation in the form of discounts on future orders. The manufacturer agreed to the concept, conceding privately to the mediator that it expected to need the chip maker's products. However, none of the people at the mediation knew what kinds of products the manufacturer would need from the defendant over the next few years.
>
> The parties agreed to adjourn for a month so their product teams could confer about a new chip the defendant had under development. Two months later, a deal was worked out that included cash and a discount on future orders.

c. Methods to Identify Interests

Mediators can help disputants and counsel draw out interests by taking the following steps:

- Ask specifically about interests
- Listen carefully for clues and references
- Suggest needs, give examples, and undertake private probes
- Ask each side about the other's interests
- Advocate each side's interests to the other
- Lower the level of pressure
- Be persistent

Ask specifically about interests

It may seem obvious, but given the blinders with which many disputants approach negotiations, a mediator can often accomplish a good deal simply by looking actively for interests that could be addressed in a settlement. A mediator might see underlying issues in the parties' written statements, for example, or might ask himself what, in his own experience, people in this kind of situation want: What, aside from money, might they find attractive in a settlement?

A mediator can refer to this possibility in a general way in the opening session, but should often save specific questions for caucuses, where the principals are more likely to talk candidly. In general, by designating the topic of interests as relevant, a mediator can ease the "negotiator's dilemma," making it easier for participants to discuss interests without compromising their bargaining positions.

There is an issue of timing, however. If a mediator immediately focuses on interests instead of the legal issues in the case, the negotiators may become annoyed that he is not listening to their arguments or is not sufficiently "hardheaded" — a particular risk if the mediator is young. Litigants are often reluctant to discuss "soft" items until they have shown commitment to their legal positions.

A neutral can sometimes shorten this process by asking the parties to discuss both their legal arguments and creative solutions — and a proactive lawyer can ask a mediator to prompt both sides to do so. Often, however, mediators will wait until later in the process, after the parties feel fully heard-out on their legal arguments and realize that they are approaching an impasse. Apart from the issue of timing, mediators use open-ended questions, avoid leading ones, and tolerate silence as tools to draw out interests.

Listen carefully for clues and references

Mediators listen carefully for clues to the existence of interests — a shift in posture, a change in tone, or a gap in a party's presentation that indicates that something lies beneath the surface. A good lawyer can provide such clues or push for them by asking why the opponent is pressing an issue that appears to his side to be counterproductive or illogical.

> *Example:* A failed businessman sued the bank that had foreclosed on his property, claiming that he had been misled by the bank's president during the transaction. As the mediator caucused with the lender's lawyer, the defense attorney asked in an irritated tone why the plaintiff was even bothering to press the suit, given that he had other creditors who would quickly seize any judgment he might obtain. The defense team in fact had threatened to buy up these unsatisfied claims at a few cents on the dollar, so that it could recoup any money that it might eventually be ordered to pay the plaintiff.
>
> The mediator was intrigued, and asked the plaintiff how he planned to deal with his other creditors. The plaintiff lawyer seized on this, mentioning that the plaintiff was also attempting to buy out the debts but did not have the resources to do so, and asked whether the mediator could suggest a way to deal with the problem. A settlement was eventually reached that included the bank's agreement to buy up the plaintiff's debts at a few cents on the dollar and then cancel them.

Suggest needs, give examples, and undertake private probes

In addition to general questions, a mediator might mention an interest that she thinks a disputant would have in that situation. Or she might tell an anecdote about a situation in which non-legal interests proved to be the key to a good settlement and ask a party whether he can think of anything that might be included, if only as an "extra," in an agreement. Again, good lawyers will take advantage of the opening created by such situations to suggest or ask about underlying needs.

Ask each side to describe the other's interests

A mediator might ask each side, perhaps as homework while the mediator meets with the other party, to think about what his opponent might value other than money or a release of liability. Such a question often feels less threatening to a litigant than being asked about his own needs, and can help each side appreciate an opponent's perspective.

Advocate each side's interests to the other

In situations where the advocates are skilled and the participants have decent personal relationships, mediators — or counsel — may suggest holding a joint meeting, often in the middle of the process, in which either the principals or all of the participants can explain their interests directly to each other. If, however, parties are too hostile or suspicious to talk directly with each other, the neutral can become the channel of communication, exploring and transmitting new ideas. Again, counsel should think about asking mediators to take on this role.

Lower the level of pressure

Adjourning briefly or changing the physical setting or configuration (perhaps by having the principals talk in the lobby, or look at a whiteboard rather than at each other) may relax people, making it easier for them to think inventively. A lawyer who sees her client "freezing up" should consider prompting the mediator, perhaps in a private conversation, to propose a change or a break.

Be persistent

Good mediators are not surprised or offended to be rebuffed when they first ask about interests. It is not unusual for a question about interests to be rejected out of hand in the first caucus, only to be welcomed later in the same case. Persistence is often required to draw out disputants, and if the area seems fruitful or other approaches have hit dead ends, a mediator should be willing to raise the issue more than once.

d. Methods to Develop Settlement Options

As we have seen, a key problem in stimulating creative bargaining is disputants' suspicion that they will open themselves up to competitive demands by the other side. Mediators can help create the conditions for fruitful discussions of options using the following tactics, among others:

- Brainstorm
- Make an "unacceptable" proposal
- Promote principled techniques
- Present a proposal as the mediator's

Brainstorm

A mediator's first option is to encourage "brainstorming." Having the mediator present to moderate the process may make disputants more willing to try this technique. If the parties' relationship is good enough, it is best to discuss possible options jointly. Even when parties are not willing to brainstorm together, they may be willing to do so in private caucuses, relying on the mediator to integrate their ideas and filter them to the other side. The tension is between the advantages of exchanging information quickly and accurately and gaining the psychological "high" that occurs when parties realize that their opponent is genuinely interested in a solution, versus the reluctance that people are likely to feel about throwing out ideas in the presence of adversaries.

Make an "unacceptable" proposal

A mediator can sometimes provoke a useful discussion by making a proposal that he knows will be rejected, but which has elements that respond to the parties' interests. The mediator can then invite each side to critique and improve on the proposal.

Promote principled techniques

The basic problem, once the parties have developed options, is to discourage them from lapsing into positional bargaining over them. The suggestions made in the next section for dealing with positional tactics apply here as well. If, for example, a negotiator tries to disparage an option to get it more cheaply, a mediator might privately point out the risk that this will disrupt the process, and ask if the bargainer can suggest a neutral principle to govern the allocation.

Present a proposal as the mediator's

Another option is for a mediator to float settlement packages anonymously, for example by taking a party's proposal and presenting it in the other caucus as his own, or by formulating a settlement package himself. This tactic can be risky, however, for two reasons. First, cognitive forces often make parties perceive even neutral proposals as biased against them. Second, if the mediator becomes too active, the parties may lose their initiative and the mediator may become over-invested in his own solution. A mediator should ordinarily be careful to make it clear that he is merely putting out options for consideration, not designating any particular term as the "right" or "fair" outcome in the dispute.

4. Managing Positional Bargaining

Competitive or positional tactics are a common source of bargaining impasse. We have seen that the problem of "dividing the pie," however large it can be made, exists in almost every situation. Competitive approaches and positional bargaining are common in mediation, and a primary challenge for commercial mediators is to manage it effectively. When the process gets into difficulty, a mediator's best options are to offer information, advice, and coaching. One can, for example:

- Ask about their thinking
- Ask about the underlying message
- Ask about the likely response
- Ask for private information about goals
- Offer advice

Ask about their thinking

Often a party who uses positional tactics has not thought through its strategy or has adopted a poor one. If, for example, a party gives a mediator an extreme offer, the neutral can ask how it was formulated ("Can tell me how you got to that?") The tone should be one of curiosity, not disagreement — assuming that the bargainer has a reason and wanting to understand it. Once the neutral knows what a bargainer intends by making a tough positional offer it is possible to discuss whether there are other ways to achieve the purpose.

Ask about the underlying message

Numbers, like words, have meanings and every money offer carries an implied message. Positional bargainers may, for example, make an extreme offer to express anger ("There — *that's* what I think of your case!") or frustration ("If the court system were fair, this is what we'd be paid!"), or to suggest that the other side has not been reasonable ("Until they get realistic, we're not going above $15,000.").

When a money offer arrives without an explanation the recipient must decide what it means, and disputants' tendency is to interpret an adversary's signals in the worst light. A mediator can ask a bargainer to say explicitly what he intends to communicate by an offer and suggest less disruptive ways to send it. ("If you want me to tell them how angry you are with their behavior, I can do that. In terms of an offer that will tempt them to make serious concessions, though, I wonder. . . .")

Ask about the likely response

The next step can be to ask a party to think about, or predict, the other side's response. ("Let's try to game this out . . . If you drop to 1.675 million from 1.7 million as a first move, what do you think they'll do?") Thinking about an adversary's response can give a party some of the satisfaction of taking an extreme position without actually doing so. If a disputant is not predicting the likely reaction realistically, the mediator can offer her own assessment ("If you start at $5 million, I think they'll assume you need a settlement well into seven figures, and you may get a response in the $20,000 range.").

Ask for private information about goals

If a party insists on making a tough proposal, the mediator can ask for private information about its ultimate goal ("I understand you don't want to put any money on the table now. But just for my information, where would you be willing to go if, for example, I could get them down to actual damages?").

Offer advice

Positional bargainers are tempted to act as if they do not want an agreement at all, provoking impasse, and it can be tempting to offer advice to head off the problem. Mediators should be reluctant to do so early in the process, and should bear in mind that tone of voice and phrasing are as important as what is said. That said, in a caucus format a mediator may be able to give each side valuable suggestions about what is needed to provoke movement from the other.

CHAPTER

8

Emotional Issues and Cognitive Forces

We have seen that disputes often fail to settle because the people involved are emotionally at odds with each other. Strong feelings may be provoked by the incident that gave rise to the dispute, or by something that happened afterward. Recall, for example, how the parents of the deceased MIT student, already grief-stricken, became angry because the university president did not greet them at their son's funeral. Strong emotions can disrupt communication and produce irrational decision making. And cognitive forces can provoke disputes and prevent bargainers from making good decisions even when they are calm. We explore in this section how mediation can deal with emotional and cognitive forces.

A. Strong Feelings

1. Dealing with Emotional Issues

Both mediators and lawyers can contribute greatly to the process of settlement by dealing with emotional forces. To do this you do not have to become a pseudo-therapist or take on other inappropriate roles. You must, however, be willing and able to listen to strong expressions of feeling without becoming flustered or squelching them. The following responses can be effective in dealing with emotional issues:

- Identify the issue
- Allow venting: listen, acknowledge, empathize
- If necessary, trace the issue back to its source
- Provide, or arrange for, a response
- Treat continuing problems
- Distinguish feelings carried over from the past
- Extend the process or adjourn for a time

Identify the issue

Legal disputes almost always stimulate strong feelings, but as we have discussed, mediators often see little or no emotion when parties meet to

177

mediate. Particularly in commercial disputes, parties usually arrive at mediation with "game faces" on, not showing emotions unless they are part of the legal case. A person whose legal claim involves emotional distress, for example, may be willing to describe her feelings, but executives and lawyers typically do no more than show irritation at their opponent's unreasonableness. A mediator or advocate's first task, therefore, is often to discover what emotions are affecting the participants.

A person's feelings may be apparent from facial expressions, body language, tone of voice, or the way he relates to people on the other side of the table. Often, however, a neutral or lawyer has to ask questions to dig out emotional issues. Attorneys or parties can probe for feelings in a joint session, but it is often easier for a mediator to do so in the private setting of a caucus. Options, couched in terms of what a mediator might say, include the following:

- *Open-ended questions.* ("Is there anything you think I should know about that you didn't feel comfortable mentioning in the opening session?")
- *Mildly prompting inquiries.* ("This must have been very difficult for you, Mr. Smith. . . .")
- *Leading questions.* ("I can see that this has been very frustrating for you. . . ." or "You know, if I felt that I'd been fired because of my age, I'd be very angry. . . . Are you?")
- *References to similar events or personal experiences.* Mentioning that one has had a similar experience can make it clear that feelings are a valid topic. Sometimes it is equally persuasive to mention a situation that you have seen, which strikes the disputant as less personal and so easier to acknowledge. ("It's been my experience that when people have had this happen to them, they often feel. . . .")
- *Suggestions of possible responses.* You may want to suggest that the disputant could be experiencing a variety of feelings, indicating that the same events affect people differently. This allows listeners to explore possibilities and adopt the one that feels most true or capable of being admitted. ("Well, I wasn't exactly angry, but I guess I felt misunderstood . . . and maybe even cheated!")
- *Inquiries to lawyers.* If a party is not willing to talk about an emotional issue, one can sometimes gather information through a private chat with the party's attorney. ("Jane, I gather from what's been said that Brad is furious about the way this contract turned out. . . . ")

A mediator must be willing to accept brush-offs at the outset, remembering that a question that is turned aside at first may be answered later as the participant comes to trust the mediator. The right approach, therefore, is to be both diplomatic and persistent.

> *Example:* A mediator was attempting to settle a claim by an auto dealer that a banker had unfairly foreclosed on his loan and driven him into bankruptcy, then sold his property at a bargain price to a business associate. During the first caucus, when the mediator remarked to the plaintiff how crushing the experience must have been, his lawyer interrupted, saying, "Never mind that—I want to know what they'll offer to settle this thing." The discussion returned to the bargaining situation.

The mediator raised the emotional issue again during a second meeting a week later. This time, the auto dealer hesitated and looked at his attorney. Gesturing expansively, the attorney said, "Joe, tell him how you felt when the bank foreclosed on you. . . . " A torrent of feelings about scheming lenders, the unfair way the public views car dealers, and other angry emotions poured out.

Allow venting: listen, acknowledge, empathize

Once an emotional issue has been identified a mediator must decide how to deal with it. In some situations, simply allowing the disputants to vent their feelings directly to each other or privately to the mediator is enough to clear the air. An attorney might, for example, warn a mediator that his client has something to get off her chest and ask the neutral to make clear in opening comments that frank expressions of feelings are welcome and to be prepared to draw them out.

If a party does express a strong emotion, someone should respond. The first-level response is simply to acknowledge that the feeling exists. Beyond that, the appropriate reaction will vary depending on the nature of the issue; a lawyer's anger over an opponent's litigation tactics, for example, is very different from the feelings of a victim of sexual abuse. Whether you are in the role of lawyer or neutral, you can often accomplish a good deal by listening to the aggrieved party and simply showing that you have heard and understood her feelings. Describing how you sense or observe another person is feeling is *empathy* ("I'm hearing that this was upsetting . . ."); by contrast, describing how *you* feel about what happened to the other person is *sympathy* ("That must have been awful . . ."). As a rule mediators should empathize but be very careful about sympathizing — doing so may draw a mediator over the line of neutrality.

A listener does not need to agree with a party's view of the facts to empathize with the party's emotional reaction to them. Indeed, mediators in particular need to be careful to keep the issue of what happened separate from how a disputant feels about it. By characterizing a situation in terms of "if," one can imply gently that there might be other ways of interpreting the underlying facts. You might say, for instance, "If I felt that I'd been cheated by a business partner, I'd be very angry . . . ," or "I can understand your frustration, given your belief that the company never tried to respond to your complaints."

Finally, you do not have to *fix* the problem. This is a lawyer's (and beginning mediator's) instinctive reaction to many emotional situations; solutions, after all, are what we are inclined by temperament and training to look for. But many situations are not "fixable" in any conventional sense. It might help instead to think of the mediator's role as similar to that of a mourner at a funeral: You cannot change what has happened, but the very fact that you are present and showing concern provides solace. In summary:

- Listening is valuable in itself.
- Active listening, in which you show that you have understood the speaker, is more effective.
- Express empathy if appropriate, but except in unusual circumstances don't discuss how you personally are feeling, or commit yourself to a position on disputed facts.

• You need not have a solution to be helpful on an emotional level.

Retrace the issue to its source

Often acknowledging or empathizing with the emotion is not enough: The person remains "stuck" in the feeling. When this occurs, it can help to trace the emotion back to the events that stimulated it. The listener might, for instance, encourage a disputant to describe how the situation developed. A lawyer can sometimes do this through tactful questions, delivered in a tone that suggests that she is genuinely curious to know the answers. Again, it is easier for a mediator to do this than an opponent, because he is not viewed as an adversary.

By asking a disputant to trace the history of a dispute from her perspective, you can often discover the reasons for feelings and begin to identify areas in which emotion is affecting settlement decisions. When a mediator asks about the past, he also allows the party the opportunity to reexamine underlying assumptions.

Arrange a response

Even more can be accomplished with emotional issues if a mediator brings an adversary into the process in a constructive way. A neutral may, for example, be able to persuade one party to listen to the other express feelings and then acknowledge having heard what was said (but probably not agree with it). Disputants are sometimes able to go even further to express empathy. In fact, within the confidential setting of mediation, with the parties communicating directly with each other and with less concern about admitting liability, one disputant might even express regret or apologize to another. In arranging such encounters, one needs to consider the following questions.

Who should speak and who needs to hear?   A formal statement from one attorney to another will not have the emotional impact of a sincere statement made by one party directly to another. In some situations, however, a lawyer-to-lawyer format may be the only option available, because a direct encounter would risk causing a damaging explosion.

What form should the communication take?   If the goal is personal reconciliation, words heard in "real time" and to which the listener can respond are much more effective than letters or formal statements. Also, to seem sincere an expression of regret should be offered freely, without asking for anything in return; an offer of an apology linked to a concession ("We'll apologize, if they'll come down into five figures.") is not likely to impress the listener as sincere. (The effectiveness of apologies is discussed below.)

What needs to be said?   It is often not necessary for the defendant to admit error or guilt; the plaintiff may be seeking only an expression of sincere regret. Like Mark Twain's dog who knew the difference between being kicked and being stepped on, persons injured by someone else's negligence are less likely to insist on an apology than people who believe they have been the victims of an intentional act.

Treat continuing problems

Sometimes people are upset not by a past event, but by an opponent's current conduct. If, for example, one side is angry over what it sees as an opponent's improper tactics, the issue should be handled as a process problem. If, by contrast, the irritation is caused by a condition outside the negotiation process, a mediator can approach it as a hidden substantive issue.

Example: A mediator was moderating discussions between a man and a woman who were breaking up their partnership. The mediator pushed to wrap up the case because he knew that the man was anxious to start a new job and the woman was pregnant. The woman partner, however, canceled a session at the last minute. The mediator learned from a friend that she had been diagnosed with a serious genetic problem that would affect her unborn child, and she was agonizing over it.

Exploring the issue of scheduling gingerly with both partners, the mediator decided that it would make sense to delay the process. An adjournment would create additional issues, however, because the woman was upset that her partner was making efforts to collect the partnership's outstanding bills. The man had meant this as a gesture of assistance, but the woman interpreted it as a maneuver to change the value of the receivables and thus the sale price of the business. The mediator worked out an agreement by which the male partner would handle day-to-day finances under agreed criteria, and there would be a two-week adjournment of the mediation.

Distinguish feelings carried over from the past

Disputants may react negatively to opponents because of feelings carried over from a different situation. A plaintiff, for example, may be suspicious of assurances given by a defense attorney because she once had a bad experience with another lawyer. When experiences become obstacles to resolving the dispute at hand, a mediator can make progress by taking the following steps:

- Draw attention to the issue in a diplomatic way
- Identify the source of the inappropriate emotion
- Help the participant to distinguish the source of the feeling from the present situation

The mediator, for example, might simply acknowledge the reaction. ("It sounds like you've had a bad experience that's affecting your view of this case.") Alternatively, she might point out objective differences between the two situations, or call attention to facts that support the credibility of the person involved in the current case.

Extend the process or adjourn for a limited time

Highly emotional disputants may need time to work through their feelings. Few mediators would suggest waiting for months for feelings to cool, or sending bills, but it is sometimes sensible to adjourn a settlement process for a day or a week to give a participant time to adjust psychologically to the need to compromise.

> Questions
>
> 1. Why might a mediator find it easier to identify an emotional obstacle than a lawyer in direct bargaining?
> 2. Which of the techniques described above could a lawyer apply with an angry opponent?
> 3. Which might an attorney apply with her own emotional client?

Note: Apology in Mediation

One of the potentials of mediation is that it provides a setting in which disputants can apologize more easily than in direct negotiation. In part this is because the process is confidential, making it possible for a party to express regret without concern that the gesture will be thrown back at him if the case does not settle. In part also, it is because of the atmosphere created by the process itself — the mediator's "presence in the room," described in Chapter 5. Mediators in commercial cases report that it is very unusual for litigants to apologize to each other, but when it does occur, an expression of regret can have a major impact.

> *Example:* A famous singer wanted to refurbish an old mansion she had just purchased. She decided to hire a well-known contractor who specialized in restorations, draw her vision of what she wanted, and have the contractor execute it. The contractor gave her a price of several hundred thousand dollars for the job. She agreed, and work began. The project, however, rapidly spun out of control. Changes were made, expenses mushroomed, and the eventual cost was more than double the estimate. The singer refused to pay the final bill, and the contractor sued. The parties agreed to mediate.
>
> Each side sat stiffly at a conference table while the mediator made his opening comments. After the singer's lawyer had summarized her legal arguments, the singer herself asked to speak. Looking directly at the contractor, she said that she realized that she bore some of the responsibility for what had happened: She had very much wanted to realize a vision for her new home, but had made the mistake of not using an architect. She felt that while the contractor should have done a better job of explaining the cost of the changes in the project, part of the fault was hers. As the singer spoke, the contractor visibly relaxed. He responded that he had tried to do his best, but was willing to work to find a fair solution. After a day of hard bargaining, the case settled.

As you know from your earlier reading, how an apology is made is crucial to its effectiveness. Professor Jennifer Robbenolt (2003) found that whereas full apologies lessened the likelihood that plaintiffs in a tort case would reject offers and go to court, a partial apology—one viewed by the listener as insincere—was usually worse than nothing, lowering the chances of settlement.

One exception is when a party is focused on vindication about facts ("I just want them to admit that . . ."). Since what is at issue is the truth of what happened rather than the speaker's feelings about it, sincerity about feelings is relatively unimportant. In libel cases, for example, injured parties will often demand that a formal retraction be published. For more on the impact and legal issues involved in apologies, see the articles by Professor Jonathan Cohen and Deborah Levi in the bibliography.

Questions

4. In April 2001, a U.S. spy plane made an unauthorized emergency landing on China's Hainan Island after colliding with a Chinese fighter jet and causing the loss of the Chinese pilot. The Chinese refused to release the 24 American crew members until the United States issued an apology. The U.S. apology read:

    Both President Bush and Secretary of State Powell have expressed their sincere regret over your missing pilot and aircraft. Please convey to the Chinese people and to the family of pilot Wang Wei that we are very sorry for their loss. Although the full picture of what transpired is still unclear, according to our information, our severely crippled aircraft made an emergency landing after following international emergency procedures. We are very sorry the entering of China's airspace and the landing did not have verbal clearance, but very pleased that the crew landed safely. We appreciate China's efforts to see to the well being of our crew.

    What elements of an apology does this statement contain? How might it have contributed to the release of the U.S. crew?

5. A highly publicized apology from basketball star Kobe Bryant in 2004 played a role in the dropping of criminal rape charges by the recipient of the apology, as well as the settlement of a related civil suit. The apology is set out below. What considerations and motivations, from both sides, prompted the inclusion of the specific wording in the statement? Do the apology, the subsequent dropping of criminal charges, and a negotiated settlement in 2005 that resolved the civil suit concern you? Why?

    First, I want to apologize directly to the young woman involved in this incident. I want to apologize to her for my behavior that night and for the consequences she has suffered in the past year. Although this year has been incredibly difficult for me personally, I can only imagine the pain she has had to endure. I also want to apologize to her parents and family members, and to my family and friends and supporters, and to the citizens of Eagle, Colorado.

I also want to make it clear that I do not question the motives of this young woman. No money has been paid to this woman. She has agreed that this statement will not be used against me in the civil case. Although I truly believe this encounter between us was consensual, I recognize now that she did not and does not view this incident the same way I did. After months of reviewing discovery, listening to her attorney, and even her testimony in person, I now understand how she feels that she did not consent to this encounter.

I issue this statement today fully aware that while one part of this case ends today, another remains. I understand that the civil case against me will go forward. That part of this case will be decided by and between the parties directly involved in the incident and will no longer be a financial or emotional drain on the citizens of the state of Colorado.

6. Compare the Bryant apology with the statement made by the president of MIT in the mediation of the student death claim in Chapter 5. What differences are there between them?
7. During the 2004 Super Bowl halftime show, singer Janet Jackson experienced a notorious "wardrobe malfunction," in which her co-star, Justin Timberlake, pulled away part of her costume, exposing her breast. A week later at the Grammy Awards, Timberlake made this statement about the incident:

"I know it has been a rough week on everyone and, umm, what occurred was unintentional, completely regrettable, and I apologize if you guys were offended."

Evaluate the quality of Timberlake's statement. Do you think it accomplished its purpose? If you had been his advisor, what would you have advised him about what to say and in what setting to say it?

2. Personal Issues in Dealing with Emotion

Many attorneys and mediators find dealing with intense emotion one of the most difficult aspects of their work. As you read the following dialogue, ask yourself if the lawyer's comments describe your own reaction to emotional situations.

A Dialogue between a Lawyer and a Psychologist

Lawyer: The fact is, I sometimes don't feel that I'm being professional when I work with emotions. It's not what lawyers do.

Psychologist: That's interesting — What *does* make you feel as if you're acting like a professional?

L: Dealing with facts and arguments, analyzing issues, generating strategies and, most important, solving problems. . . .

P: Well, those are clearly professional activities, and they are often invaluable to clients. My only concern would be not to rush into them too soon. In an emotional situation — and people who feel that they've been hurt or treated unfairly are often quite emotional — people *can't really listen until they feel they've been heard.* You might think that you can predict their story because you have heard so many similar ones, but even if you are right, they won't feel heard until they've told it. In fact, they may need to review the story with you in order to hear it themselves and become open to different ways of resolving the problem. Rushing to analyze can get in the way of disputants figuring out what is important to them.

I sometimes think of people in this situation as being like a tightly closed fist: One option is to help them strike with that fist. Another is to counsel them about their chances of winning the fight. But it could be even more useful to help them uncurl their fist, so that they can grasp other possibilities. Strategizing with "closed fist" clients who don't know what they feel or why they feel it is often unproductive. The issues they present are often only a smokescreen for other, more important concerns. Lawyers or mediators who charge ahead to focus on legal or bargaining issues may find themselves going off in a direction that the client may later resist or even sabotage.

L: I think it's sitting without doing anything that often strikes us lawyers as meaningless.

P: OK, I'm hearing how important it is to feel that you are *doing something specific* to feel like a responsible professional. It's true that usually more is needed than silence; we need to find a way for lawyers to experience listening, and even encouraging the expression of emotions, as an active, professional activity in and of itself.

L: Another problem is that lawyers often feel lost in long discussions about emotions — they seem directionless.

P: It's true that exploring emotional territory makes it difficult to have a clear agenda. Your questions and interventions need to be guided by what emerges as important to the client as she tells her story. Early in my training as a psychologist, for example, I was assigned to interview a client. The session occurred in a special room fitted out with a one-way mirror and a telephone. Behind the mirror was my professor, also with a phone, and the rest of my class. A patient came in and we began to talk, but he only wanted to discuss his hobby, which was scuba diving.

After about 20 minutes of listening to his adventures while diving, I began to worry about demonstrating my therapeutic skills and interrupted the client to ask what had led him to make the appointment. Immediately the phone rang. I picked it up. It was, of course, my professor. He had one question: "*So . . .* what's the matter with scuba diving?" I took the hint and began to listen more closely to the diving talk. Almost immediately it became clear that he was talking about some complex issues, for example, his anxiety over sharing an air tank with his girlfriend. Was it something about her, about their relationship, or was it more about him and past relationships that had compromised his ability to trust? All I needed to do was reflect the questions I began to hear in his story to help him begin to formulate his own answers.

Years later, the part of me that wanted to say, "Why don't you just get a second tank and let's move on to talking about something *important?*" still occasionally rears its head. I can cringe as I review a session and recognize that I failed to hear something that was essential to my client because I was too caught up in trying to be "helpful." Shutting up and listening can be as hard for psychologists as for other professionals, but equally rewarding.

L: Actually, many of us became lawyers to avoid dealing with these messy emotional issues. I've sometimes said that hearing people out is like "draining pus from an infected wound."

P: Ugh — I can understand why you wouldn't be enthusiastic about doing it. That metaphor also helps me understand why I've rarely heard "venting" described by lawyers as anything more than a necessary evil, to be gotten out of the way as quickly as possible. But allowing people to vent emotions doesn't have to be distasteful, and it does have a purpose and goal — it's just that *you* are not the one setting the goal. It might help to imagine a litigant's experience as a dark room filled with noxious fumes; "venting" is an opportunity to open the windows, release the blinding smoke, and let in fresh air so your client can think more clearly.

L: Are you saying that venting moves inevitably toward clarity?

P: Not necessarily — people can just spin their wheels and go even deeper into the same old rut. We all know couples who've been having the same argument for years. That's where the active aspect of listening comes in. If it's not clear to you how a disputant got from point A to point B, you can ask for an explanation (for example, "I hear that A happened and then B, but I'd like to understand better how you are connecting them"). The answer may be even more clarifying for the client than it is for you. If there's a lot of fuzziness about how A led to B, that may be where unarticulated feelings are hiding.

Active listening stays focused on encouraging the client to tell her story fully, but it also offers opportunities for lawyers to use their organizational skills to bring clarity You might summarize with a statement such as "As I listen to you, I think I'm hearing at least three separate issues here. Please correct me if I'm wrong." By separating and listing the concerns in this way, you are demonstrating your attempt to understand their perspective (including their feelings), but also are introducing clarity and perhaps facilitating movement. Of course, when you ask if you are getting it right, you also have to be prepared to hear that you've got it all wrong!

L: Many of us worry that if we start to let parties express emotions, the situation will blow up. It'll be like uncapping a volcano — lava everywhere! And people will get burned.

P: In fact, no one can cap an emotional "volcano," and even if you could it might not be a wise course. The pressure is there and denying it may fuel it further. If you don't drain emotional pressures off, they will find their own escape routes — often to fuel more arguments and hardened positions.

   If you want to think of emotional release as a volcano erupting, think of your job as allowing the lava to escape, while at the same time channeling it away from the "village" and into a safe area. There are ways to channel discussion so that it does not disrupt the process of settlement or your relationship with the parties. Just by modeling respectful listening yourself and establishing ground rules for how people express themselves, you can channel emotional "lava." Perhaps the most important rule I enforce in working with families is to ask each participant to focus on his own experiences, feelings, and wishes, without accusing or analyzing the motives of the other side.

L: Again, as I think about it, the more usual problem is that most parties come to mediation with "game faces on." They act as if there is no emotional issue, when I suspect they are simmering inside.

P: Yes, in therapy, too, clamming up is by far the more common and challenging response to emotional turbulence. The listening techniques we've been discussing are the most effective ways I've found to get at buried emotions.

L: The final obstacle is litigators — the people who usually hire legal mediators. One might fairly ask: If the lawyers don't want to get into an emotional issue, how can we do it without offending them?

P: I wonder if you're reading them right? A major problem may be that a litigator's role as an advocate armored for battle often makes it hard for her to explore a client's mixed feelings. I think a mediator could make himself quite valuable as someone prepared to handle the messy emotions that some attorneys don't feel in a position to confront, yet know are preventing a resolution of the dispute.

Question

8. Could any of these factors lead you to avoid dealing with intense emotions in a legal dispute? Which seem most significant?

B. Cognitive Effects

We saw in Chapter 4 that the effect of psychology on decision making is not limited to emotions; cognitive forces often prevent persons from making good decisions even when they are calm. Of the numerous cognitive forces that affect disputing we will focus on three — selective perception, optimistic overconfidence, and the endowment effect — that impair disputants' ability to assess the merits of a case, and three others — reactive devaluation, loss aversion, and the attraction to certainty and familiar risks — that distort parties' judgment about bargaining decisions.

1. Forces That Affect Evaluation of the Legal Merits

a. Selective Perception

Example: Students at Harvard Law School are preparing to negotiate the settlement of a personal injury case. Before they begin, they are asked to make a private prediction of their chances of winning based on their confidential instructions. What the students don't know is there is nothing confidential about the instructions: Both sides have received exactly the same data, with different labels. Because both sides have the same information, they should come out with the same answers, but this is not what occurs.

In fact, hundreds of law and business students told to negotiate for the plaintiff assess her chances of winning as being nearly 20 percent higher than students who are assigned to the defense. The two sides' predictions total nearly 120 percent. Asked to estimate what damages a jury will award if the plaintiff does win, there is a similar disparity: Plaintiff law students estimate her damages at an average of $264,000, whereas defense negotiators looking at the same data estimate a verdict of only $188,000.

What caused these distortions? It was not due to disparities in information, because both sides had the same facts. Nor was it due to lack of experience: When experienced litigators training to be mediators were assigned roles in the same problem, their predictions were similarly distorted. Disagreements like these are a serious barrier to settlement, because parties understandably resist accepting an outcome worse than their honest (but inflated) estimate of the value of their case.

Selective perception most likely explains the results of the Harvard experiment, and it can pose a serious problem in mediation. A typical litigant will quickly form an opinion about who is right in a controversy, and most people instinctively assign that role to themselves. Once a disputant adopts a viewpoint, he unconsciously filters out data that conflict with his "take" on the case, and at the same time gives full weight to information that affirms it, becoming even more convinced that his initial view was correct. Mediators often encounter cases in which the facts are largely undisputed but parties disagree vehemently about who will win in court. Each litigant's perspective seems plausible to itself, because selective perception has caused it to disregard the evidence that contradicts it.

To deal with the problem of selective perception:

- Encourage the parties to speak
- Use charts and other visual aids
- Explicitly question gaps
- Ask for help in understanding the other side's points

Encourage the parties to speak

One excellent option is to encourage parties to speak for themselves, either during an opening session or in ad hoc tête-à-têtes with a counterpart on the other side. The reason is that a party is much more likely to listen to the opposing party than to a lawyer. Fairly or not, disputants tend to view the attorney on the other side as a hired gun and to disregard what she says. Listeners are often, of course, suspicious of what opponents say, but are likely to listen more carefully to them, if only to see whether the speaker makes an admission or misrepresentation about what happened. As a result, both lawyers and parties pay better attention to statements made by an opposing party.

Use charts and other visual aids

Lawyers are accustomed to dealing with printed documents, especially the proverbial "fine print." Non-lawyers, by contrast, may absorb information more effectively when it is presented in other formats. A disputant who misses information in a memo, for example, might be able to understand it if it is presented or reinforced with a chart or graph. Similarly, data that are skipped over in black and white may be remembered if highlighted in color, and information that fades out on a printed page can become clearer if written on a whiteboard.

Explicitly question gaps

The most straightforward way to deal with a gap in a disputant's assessment of data is to ask about it, in effect shining a spotlight on the omitted item. We give suggestions for how to ask questions about the merits in the next chapter.

Ask for help in understanding the other side's points

Asking disputants to summarize an opponent's argument may push them to confront its strength or focus attention on an issue. However, disputants are usually reluctant to do this in an opponent's presence. Instead, in the privacy of a caucus you can:

- Express doubt about what the other side is saying and ask for help ("I'm not sure which is their main argument on the contract issue . . . what do you understand them to be saying?").
- Note that the disputant has been living with the case much longer and so probably better appreciates the opponent's position.
- If a summary seems erroneous or incomplete, point this out diplomatically ("Hmm . . . what I thought I heard was more that . . .").

b. Optimistic Overconfidence

Assessing the value of a legal case requires predicting events that are uncertain, for example, how an unknown jury will react to evidence that may or may not be admitted. These assessments are often unreliable. For one thing, people are consistently overconfident about their ability to assess uncertain data. Why is this? The problem is that when we don't know something — even a fact that we aren't expected to have at our fingertips — we are either embarrassed to admit our ignorance or simply feel a competitive urge to be right. So we give a more precise answer than our knowledge can support.

The tendency to be overconfident becomes even stronger when a person acquires a personal stake in the outcome. In psychological experiments, for example, subjects who placed a small bet that a horse would win a race were consistently more confident about their ability to predict the outcome of the race than people who had not placed a bet: Becoming bettors made them believe they were better handicappers.

There is a related problem. When people in an uncertain situation are asked to estimate the likelihood of a good or bad outcome, they consistently underestimate the chances of an unfavorable result. The reason, it appears, is that we like to believe that we are in control of events and thus able to bring about good outcomes, even when we cannot. In addition to being overconfident of our ability to predict the future, we are overoptimistic that future events will be favorable to us.

How do these forces affect negotiations over lawsuits? Lawyers are often asked to estimate the outcome of court proceedings when they have little basis for offering an accurate assessment. Under pressure to appear expert, they are particularly likely to be overconfident about the accuracy of their estimates. To make matters worse, both lawyers and clients "bet" on cases by investing time and money in them, accentuating the tendency to be overconfident. To deal with litigants who are optimistically overconfident:

- Discuss best-case and worst-case scenarios
- Focus on the most likely outcome, a mediocre result
- Distance the "bettor" from his "horse"

Discuss best-case and worst-case scenarios

If a disputant has misevaluated a case because she is using a false point of comparison, it can be helpful to present other examples, making the risk of loss more concrete in the litigant's mind. Parties are more likely to listen to warnings about bad outcomes, however, if a mediator or advocate first acknowledges the possibility of a good one. You might begin, therefore, by admitting that a big win is possible for the party and discussing it. Having covered the best possibility, one can move on to other, less attractive but more likely outcomes, for example, by asking a lawyer if he has seen a bad result in this kind of case. Discussing adverse outcomes also harnesses the power of loss aversion, discussed later.

Focus on the most likely outcome, a mediocre result

Another option is to draw a litigant's attention to the most likely outcome in the case, which is often a mediocre result rather than a clear victory for either side. Parties who see only win-or-lose possibilities, and focus only on the better one, need to be reminded that many judgments fall in the middle. A tort case, for instance, might result in a ruling that the defendant is liable but that the plaintiff is contributorily negligent, resulting in a modest award. To the extent that a mediocre result replaces an outright win as the benchmark for evaluating a settlement, compromise will appear more attractive.

Distance the "bettor" from his "horse"

A mediator can reduce the "bettor" effect by making a party feel less invested in his prediction. You might, for instance, suggest that the money a litigant has already spent on a case — its bet — is a "sunk" cost that cannot be recovered regardless of the outcome and is therefore irrelevant to decisions about the future. The real issue is whether to spend new money — to place an additional "bet" — on a case that has not been a winner so far.

c. Endowment Effect

People who possess something typically value it more highly than people who do not, a phenomenon known in psychological literature as the "endowment effect." This is a particular problem for owners who are selling an item. The endowment effect makes sellers tend to view whatever they own as "special" and therefore worth much more than very similar items offered by others. Thus, for instance, a homeowner is likely to see his house as significantly more valuable than other homes that appear identical to a third party, car owners tend to see their vehicles as "better" than others of the same make, and so on. The endowment effect also afflicts buyers, who tend to undervalue what they are bargaining for, but data show that buyers are affected by this much less severely than sellers.

In negotiations to settle a legal claim, the plaintiff is the seller, typically offering to give up a claim in return for the "buyer" defendant paying him money. Not surprisingly, the endowment effect leads plaintiff/sellers to value their claims too highly and, to a lesser degree, encourages buyer/defendants to underestimate their worth. Faced with this a mediator can:

* Lessen the effect on plaintiffs by:
  * Framing the question as a joint problem ("How should we respond to the defense offer?").
  * Creating emotional distance between the plaintiff and the claim being sold, by treating it as an analytic problem and the claim as being in someone else's control ("How would a judge value this case?"), or alternatively by placing it in a larger group ("How do juries value this kind of claim?").
  * Offering your own opinion of how a court is likely to value the claim.

- Increase feelings of ownership in defendants by:
  - Treating terms already agreed to as "owned" by the defendant/buyer, to encourage feelings of endowment in the bargaining process itself.
  - Leading a party to imagine how it will feel to "own" the claim.

2. *Forces That Influence Bargaining Decisions*

a. Reactive Devaluation

We mentioned earlier the phenomenon of "reactive devaluation." To understand how it works, imagine that you are defense counsel in a lawsuit. Your opponent is demanding that you pay $100,000 to settle but appears sure that you will never agree. Now you decide to offer that sum. Is your adversary pleased? To the contrary, her first reaction is likely to be that she has undervalued the case: It must be worth more than $100,000, because you, the enemy, would never offer her a fair deal. A bargainer's instinctive response to an opponent's offer is reminiscent of the comedian Groucho Marx, who vowed never to join any club that would have him as a member.

> *Example:* A biotech company hired a contractor to install a state-of-the-art heating and air conditioning system in its office building. The installation went badly. In particular, individual rooms' air flow controls were apparently improperly connected to sensors. As a result, some employees had to work in offices heated to only 55 degrees, while others sweltered at 80. The biotech company, frustrated, refused to make the last two payments due under the contract. Two months ago the contractor walked off the job, claiming that the company's decision to withhold payments had prevented him from paying subcontractors. Both sides have claimed large amounts of expenses and lost profits caused by the situation.
>
> After two sessions of mediation and an exchange of expert reports, the contractor has proposed to go back and finish the work. He suggests that the work on the air flow controls be done by a different subcontractor than the one originally charged with the task and the system's performance then be checked by an agreed independent expert. The contractor also offers to warranty the system's performance for two years.
>
> To the mediator this idea seems promising. She has tentatively concluded that the original problem was due in large measure to a personality conflict between the company's chief of physical plant and the contractor's job supervisor. The contractor has been in business for more than 20 years and appears to have a real interest in salvaging his reputation, and the expert's credentials are solid. A supervised fix seems much more promising than engaging in positional bargaining over the parties' rather vague damage claims.
>
> The company representatives, however, react negatively to the idea. The contractor, they say, is a sleazy fraud who will simply make jury-rigged adjustments so that the system passes initial tests and then disappear. They note that the expert has his office in the same city as the contractor, and speculate that the two must have an arrangement to refer each other business. They reject the offer out of hand.

Probably a mediator's single greatest advantage is that he is not subject to reactive devaluation, offering ways to get around this barrier to agreement. For example, you can:

- Offer a proposal as your own
- Discuss the merits of an idea in the abstract
- Offer a disputant a choice
- Accredit an adversary's proposal

Offer a proposal as your own

If as a mediator you float a proposal, for instance, that a contractual relationship be restructured or parties agree to an expert appraisal of a disputed piece of property, the disputants are likely to listen politely. They will not devalue your proposal as quickly as they would if it came from the other side.

There are two dangers in doing so, however. First, if the listener thinks you are simply communicating an idea generated by an adversary, devaluation will apply with full force. Second, if the listener thinks you have endorsed a skewed proposal, he may decide you have taken sides against him. It is therefore important to think through not just whether an idea makes sense in the abstract, but also how a partisan listener will interpret it. Citing objective criteria or principles to support your ideas is also useful; even if the listener is not convinced by them, it will help reassure him that you are acting in good faith.

Discuss the merits of an idea in the abstract

The flip side of disputants' tendency to devalue ideas because opponents favor them is that if an opponent has not yet agreed to an option, devaluation is less likely to occur. Put another way, a hypothetical offer is not yet cursed by the fact the other side is actually willing to make it. If the party agrees that an offer not yet on the table might be acceptable, it is at least partially "inoculated" against being devalued if the other side later signs on.

Presenting an offer as out of reach also takes advantage of the so-called scarcity principle — the fact that people instinctively want things that are not available. To take advantage of this effect, test out proposals as uncertain possibilities even if you are fairly sure you can persuade the other side to agree to them ("You know, I think if we could ever get them up to $100,000, it would be worth serious consideration . . . What do you think?").

Offer a disputant a choice

If you present two or three settlement options and indicate the opponent has not opted for any of them, it is less likely they will be devalued ("I think I may be able to convince the defendant either to pay the money within 60 days or over a year at a reasonable rate of interest. Which would you prefer?"). People usually like the feeling of having a choice, even if none is very attractive. (Think of a child who is inveigled into going to bed by being asked whether he would prefer red or blue pajamas.) However, many people become indecisive if given too many options, so limit the choices to a handful at most.

Accredit an adversary's proposal

If you genuinely believe an adversary's proposal is constructive, you can say so, using your credibility to persuade the listener it is worth considering. In doing so you might want to note that the proposal has flaws from the perspective of the listener — it almost certainly will — but may be worth considering. Be careful, however, not to sacrifice your relationship with a party by advocating a solution it sees as seriously biased.

b. Loss Aversion

We have seen that disputants often develop an opinion about the "right" outcome in a case based on statements by friends, comments by attorneys, stories they see in the media about superficially similar cases, and other sources. In addition to stimulating selective perception, such opinions then become a mental benchmark for later settlement decisions.

For example, a tort plaintiff might hear on television about a $500,000 verdict in a case that seems similar to his. The plaintiff then begins to think of $500,000 as the right amount at which to settle his claim. Two years later, a mediator may suggest that information produced in discovery has lowered the chance of winning and that verdicts in this kind of case rarely exceed $100,000. The plaintiff, however, feels a strong sense of loss at being asked to settle for less than his $500,000 benchmark.

Loss aversion is both a cognitive effect and a source of emotion that distorts judgment, because feelings of loss are quite painful.

> *Example:* Students at Stanford University who had expected to attend a seminar without charge are told after they arrive they will each have to pay $20 when they leave the room to cover unexpected expenses. They can, however, spin a roulette wheel with three chances in four of paying nothing and one chance in four of paying $100. The odds thus discourage gambling — because the average cost of spinning the wheel is of $100, or $25, the smart choice is to pay $20 and leave. However, 70 percent of the students tested chose to spin the wheel. Having expected to pay nothing, they apparently experienced the demand for $20 as an unwelcome loss and were willing to take an unreasonable risk to avoid it. (Mnookin 1993)

People involved in legal disputes behave much like the Stanford students, often taking unreasonable risks to avoid what they see as a "loss." To deal with feelings of loss, consider the following:

- Identify loss benchmarks
- Recharacterize the situation
- Suggest new terms

Identify loss benchmarks

The first task is to identify the benchmarks by which disputants are measuring losses or gains. You can do so, for example, by asking parties what they think would be a fair outcome and how they arrived at their opinion. Remember not to argue with a party — your goal at this point is to identify the issue, not to resolve it.

Recharacterize the situation

Because loss calculations are inherently subjective, you can reduce feelings of loss by persuading a disputant to use a more realistic benchmark.

Example: A discharged employee brought an age discrimination claim against his employer and became convinced his claim would bring $200,000 or more. Over two years of litigation, however, he got no settlement offers at all and became increasingly frustrated with his ex-employer's bad faith.

The case eventually went to court-ordered mediation. After five hours of discussion, the employer put $40,000 on the table. From the perspective of the employee's initial goal this was extremely disappointing, and he complained about this to the mediator. In response, the mediator said, "For two years now, you've seen nothing at all. The defendant has ignored you! But now we've got his attention and there's $40,000 on the table. The challenge at this point is to find out just how far you can push him, *then* decide if you want to take it."

The employee listened, seeming to take satisfaction at having finally forced the employer to pay attention to his grievances. His focus shifted to how to "push" the employer to its limit, measuring progress from the employer's offer rather than his prior benchmark.

Suggest new terms

Feelings of loss are more painful when there is only a single issue in play, making each party's loss easily measurable. Thus, for instance, loss aversion is such a problem when parties engage in positional bargaining over money. By contrast, when there are multiple issues under consideration, losses are harder to measure. If a new issue is introduced into the mix, disputants often have no benchmark for measuring what they ought to get or seeing the outcome as a loss.

Example: Former Secretary of State Henry Kissinger is said to have ascribed his success in mediating agreements between Arabs and Israelis to the tactic of "making the deal so complicated no one could tell who was winning." In essence, he used complex proposals attuned to the parties' sensitivities to distract the parties from measuring agreements against their prior benchmarks.

c. Attraction to Certainty and Familiar Risks

Disputants are often willing to pay more if they can achieve a certain outcome and dislike even objectively minor risks. Mediators encounter this "premium for certainty" whenever they present a settlement proposal that leaves open even a minor risk in the future. Listeners often react with negativity out of proportion to the actual risk.

People also prefer familiar risks to strange ones. Most people, for example, find it much easier to take on a commonplace risk like jaywalking across a busy street than an unusual one like walking along a cliff, although the consequence is the same in either case — death — and the familiar risk is actually much more likely than the strange one to occur. Mediators and counsel confront this preference whenever a party sees a settlement involving a risk that seems unusual or out of its experience. In response, mediators can:

- Analyze less-than-certain proposals carefully, so that the listener appreciates that although a risk does exist, it is small in objective terms.
- Reframe an unusual risk in more familiar terms. ("This is really just like giving a warranty. . . .")

Finally, the attraction to certainty can work as a "deal-clincher" for a potential settlement. If a settlement does permanently settle all possible legal claims and end the matter once and for all, a mediator can use this. Disputants are more likely to agree to even a very painful concession if a lawyer or mediator can assure them that doing so will bring complete peace. ("If you can just take this one last step, you will never have to hear about this case again.")

Questions

9. Thinking back on roleplays you have negotiated in this course, does one of the cognitive factors described above appear to have affected the bargaining?
10. Have you ever encountered such reactions in real life?

3. General Responses to Cognitive Issues

Apart from the suggestions for responding to specific issues, mediators can use several general techniques to deal with the impact of cognitive forces on negotiations.

- Treat obstacles as psychological, not simply legal, issues
- Retrace the disputant's analysis
- Distance current circumstances from prior ones
- Reframe the decision
- Ask the person to play an adversary's role
- Use humor to shake a disputant out of a rigid stance

Treat obstacles as psychological, not simply legal, issues

Often when a disputant resists settlement because of a psychological issue, the instinctive response of legally trained mediators is to present more information or argue for settlement more strongly. This approach is likely to have little impact because the problem is not a lack of data or arguments. Indeed, arguing may worsen the situation by making the disputant dig in more deeply.

Instead, a mediator needs to understand the psychological reasons for the person's resistance and respond to them.

Retrace the disputant's analysis

The first step is usually to listen carefully to the explanations offered by the disputant and talk them through even if they seem illogical, as one would with a purely emotional issue. It may become apparent to the person that her reasoning is flawed, opening the way to a more realistic appraisal. At a minimum the disputant is likely to become less rigid if he feels heard. A listener could, for example, use reflective statements such as "I see, so you assumed that the documents would show . . . and that led you to estimate the damages at . . ." while refraining for the moment from pointing out data that contradict the person's assumptions.

Distance current circumstances from prior ones

Because the problem, particularly with "loss-gain" obstacles, is that a party is using an obsolete or inaccurate frame of reference to make decisions, one response is to help the person distance the situation in which she set up the internal benchmark from present circumstances. A mediator could suggest, for example, that the initial assessment was reasonable given what the person knew at the time, but that new data have since come to light. This frees the disputant from having to admit that her earlier judgment was wrong.

Reframe the decision

A mediator can also place the decision in a new context, in which the feeling of loss is not as strong. For example, changing the frame of reference from a lawsuit to a business context may make it easier for the disputant to let go of an obsolete loss benchmark.

Example: An executive was frustrated because his company was being offered only $30,000 to settle a claim for damages. The offer was far less than the company's $500,000 initial damage estimate, or even the $70,000 it had spent in legal fees. The problem was that discovery had turned up documents in the company's files that contradicted large portions of its damages and also called into question the defendant's basic liability. The case was now in court-ordered mediation.

Rather than telling the executive that his focus on the company's initial valuation of the case was wrong or the money spent on it was illogical, the mediator listened to the executive's reasons for clinging to a six-figure settlement demand. The neutral went on to ask about the history of the litigation and how the problems with the claim had become apparent. It became evident that the executive had personally advocated filing the case and was embarrassed that it now appeared to be a loser.

The mediator commiserated with the executive's situation, suggesting there was no way he could have known that records kept in a subsidiary would contradict what he was told by his staff. The neutral went on to tell a story of having gotten into a similar situation when he was a litigator. He then characterized the issue as a tough business decision: Should one put additional money into a disappointing investment, or close out the venture and move on? Will the additional costs involved in persevering be worth whatever one can reasonably expect to gain, over the current settlement offer? He suggested that he would also be willing to brief the company's management about why it made sense to settle. As the discussion went on, the executive became less tense and gradually focused on what could be done to get the best possible deal now.

Ask the person to play an adversary's role.

If a party is having difficulty understanding an adversary's perspective, a mediator can try to explain the opponent's position. A more powerful technique, however, may be to ask the recalcitrant party privately to summarize the opponent's arguments, for example, by taking on the role of lawyer for the opponent. By playing out an adversary's arguments, disputants are sometimes able to move out of their own framework and see their situation more objectively.

Use humor to shake a disputant out of a rigid stance.

Finally, a mediator can resort to humor, telling a story that illustrates the illogic of life and helps the listener let go of the feeling that the prospective "loss" has great meaning. Humor can also serve as a break in the process, helping a disputant to relax and shake loose from a rigid position. Mediators and lawyers need to be careful about how they use this technique, however; the wrong anecdote can strike a disputant as trivializing an important issue.

> *Example:* A mediator had to convince a real estate investor to contribute to a settlement of a "lender liability" case in which a bank had allegedly swindled a borrower out of a piece of land. The investor had bought the property through a private deal with his friend, the president of the defendant bank, at what he indignantly insisted was a fair-market price.
>
> In response, the mediator told the investor a story about a recent appellate case involving the trustees of a church board who were exposed to tort liability for inadvertently violating the privacy of their minister while they checked on reports that he had appeared nude in the pulpit. The implication was that one could find oneself legally liable despite the best of intentions. The investor laughed, and 20 minutes later agreed to put in the $50,000 needed to close the deal.

C. The Special Problem of Loss Reactions

There is one barrier to settlement that has both emotional and cognitive aspects. It is the strong reaction that some disputants experience at the point they are asked to make serious compromises to settle. At this point parties must, sometimes for the first time, give up a cherished hope or illusion of victory that they had preserved until now. The following reading discusses what happens in such situations, and how lawyers and mediators might respond.

"It's hard. . . . There's a finality about it. . . . When we sign, then it's done. He's really gone." — The widow of a victim of the 9-11 disaster, describing her reluctance to apply for compensation to which she is entitled

Negotiation is not a fully rational process. People in conflict feel intense emotions, and many of these feelings are negative. In order to reach a settlement disputants must compromise, often accepting terms much less favorable than the goals they set at the outset of their dispute. The experience of giving up hopes and settling below expectations is extremely painful, but in addition litigants incur both explicit expenses, in the form of lawyers' fees and other out-of-pocket costs, and implicit expenses such as lost time, distraction and worry. The longer the conflict goes on before settlement is discussed, the more severe these costs will be.

Experienced mediators often remark that the sense of loss that accompanies settlement is the most serious single obstacle they encounter. Such feelings appear in almost all litigation settlements, but they sometimes take on an unusual intensity. Consider the following example:

A sixty-year-old software engineer, James Evans, was terminated by his company. He filed suit, claiming that he had been fired simply because his young manager did not believe that an older employee could do cutting-edge work. Evans asked for more than two million dollars in damages. After more than a year of litigation the employer moved to dismiss Evans' claim, arguing that he had failed to file his charge with his state anti-discrimination agency. As the parties awaited a court hearing on the motion, the company proposed mediation and Evans agreed.

During the parties' initial session Evans and his lawyer argued strongly that there could be no reason for his firing other than age. The employer, however, maintained that it had terminated Evans based on his performance, presenting mediocre reviews that he had received from the manager. The company also argued that Evans' failure to file charges with his state anti-discrimination agency would require the court to dismiss his lawsuit, regardless of merit. The mediator's private view was that the company's failure-to-file defense was very likely to prevail. However, the employer knew that the court might well delay ruling until trial and thus had an incentive to settle. She began to work with the parties, and made some initial progress.

In the late afternoon, as the negotiations reached the point at which the disputants confronted painful concessions, Evans began to act oddly. He had voiced anger all along at what he saw as his employer's duplicity and ingratitude, but now he began to act erratically. He would discuss legal risks rationally at one point, then a short time later refuse to talk about the case at all, exclaiming that he could not believe that this was happening to him. At one point Evans authorized the mediator to make a substantial concession, but when she returned with a counteroffer he became nearly hysterical, insisting that he had been "crazy" to make any move at all. At still other times he seemed deeply withdrawn, barely responding to the mediator or his counsel's suggestions. Eventually Evans' emotions subsided, he deferred to his lawyer's advice, and the case settled.

This mediation was unusual. The typical money negotiation resembles an uphill slog, but in this case the process was more like a roller coaster. The employee's emotions were striking not merely because of their variation, but also because they followed a distinct pattern. Indeed, Mr. Evans seemed to go through phases similar to those observed in people mourning the loss of a close relative. In this case, however, the "death" was of something other than a human being.

The Psychology of Grieving

To understand how people deal with feelings of loss during settlement, it is helpful to consider how they respond to very personal losses such as the end of a close relationship. Theorists such as Sigmund Freud and Elizabeth Kubler-Ross developed models of human response to such traumas.

Freud provided the classic analysis of how people respond to the loss of a close relationship. A victim of serious loss, Freud observed, typically goes through an initial period of shock and withdrawal in which he loses all interest in the outside world: During this period the victim often clings to the fiction that the object of his affection — the lost person — continues to exist. Gradually, however, most victims begin to reconcile with reality, realize that the departed person is truly lost, and withdraw their emotional attachment. Freud saw the process of grieving as a kind of internal negotiation, in which the mind of the bereaved reluctantly works out a compromise between its wish that the relationship continue and the realization that it cannot. As this happens the victim gradually gains the ability to form new emotional attachments and go on with life.

Other clinicians have developed models of human response to loss; perhaps the best-known is Elizabeth Kubler-Ross (1969), who described patients' response to being told that they are terminally ill. She reported that such patients typically go through five distinct stages: numbness/denial, anger, bargaining, depression and acceptance.

A person's first reaction to hearing that she will soon die, said Kubler-Ross, is often numbness followed by the urge to deny what is happening — similar to the belief of Freud's patients that their lost love will somehow return. A typical patient, for example, might exclaim, "No, not me, it cannot be true." Kubler-Ross suggested that patients use denial as a defense against the overwhelming feelings of shock that they experience upon hearing their diagnosis. A patient, she reported, will later enter a second phase in which they begin to feel anger at what is happening: "The cry 'Not me!' becomes 'Why me?' In posing this question, however, the patient is not asking for an explanation, but instead is protesting her fate. . . ."

Kubler-Ross found that many terminally-ill patients enter a third stage in which they attempt to negotiate. Since death cannot be avoided, this bargaining is not realistic, but rather is another form of denial. A dying patient, for example, may offer to donate her body to science if she is allowed to extend her life. The fourth stage is depression: When the patient comes to realize that she cannot avoid death, she is likely to become deeply morose. Kubler-Ross's final stage, acceptance, occurs when people accede to the inevitability of their impending death; patients in this phase may exhibit few feelings of any kind. This series of emotions might be termed a "loss reaction."

Loss Reactions in Legal Disputes

How do these psychological findings apply to persons involved in legal disputes? Freud was clear that people can feel intense grief over the loss of an abstraction as well as another human being. He observed that "Mourning is . . . the reaction to the loss of a loved person, or to the loss of *some abstraction which has taken the place of one, such as . . . an ideal*, and so on." (Emphasis added.) Freud's observation applies readily to legal disputes. A worker who suddenly loses his job, for example, not only is deprived of income but also forfeits social status and his personal identity as a breadwinner or professional. As one writer put it, "From a grief perspective, the worker is saying, 'Two parts of me are about to die'" (Evans and Tyler-Evans, 2002). Defendants in legal disputes also feel loss; a manager charged with discrimination, for instance, might feel that regardless of the outcome, the charge alone will harm his reputation and prospects for advancement in his company.

When a person suffers the loss of an "object" such as a business relationship or an "ideal" such as her self-image, she is likely to react in much the same way as someone grieving over the loss of a personal relationship. Parties to law suits do, in fact, go through distinct phases of mourning.

Most examples arise from family disputes, perhaps because they involve disruptions of such intimate relationships. One Florida domestic relations lawyer, for example, reports that clients who are surprised by a spouse's demand for a divorce typically display feelings of denial; they may express incredulity that a demand has been made, and even suggest that their partner is suffering from mental illness.

Divorce litigants, of course, also become angry. Some parties, one practitioner says, will demand that their lawyer use scorched-earth tactics and "crucify the offending spouse." As the legal process continues, these same clients may show signs of depression and some eventually reach acceptance, coming to terms with the fact of separation. Parties may also skip over or mix these phases together. One lawyer, for instance, reports that "In one appointment I have seen a client go from anger to sadness back to anger and finally to acceptance."

Although there are virtually no published reports of litigants outside the divorce arena showing loss reactions, they certainly occur. The age discrimination claimant described at the outset, for example, appeared to go through denial, anger, unrealistic bargaining and depression. Litigants in commercial disputes sometimes also display such feelings.

Even if we accept that parties to legal disputes may react like people confronting death or a deep personal loss, however, it is still not clear why these emotions sometimes do not appear until settlement is discussed. The claimant described above, for instance, displayed symptoms during negotiations that took place more than a year after his law suit had been filed. One might think that by the time litigants got to the point of settling their feelings of loss would be substantially resolved. Why do some litigants suffer reactions so long after their loss has occurred? To answer this question, it is necessary to consider the psychology of abnormal reactions to loss.

Abnormal Responses to Loss

Freud found that while most mourners gradually work through their loss, some do not. This latter group remains "stuck," unable to deal with their feelings of deprivation and disabled from moving on. Thus some parents whose son or daughter has died will maintain their child's bedroom untouched for years, a poignant example of unresolved grief. Freud posited that a key reason for this difficulty is that some victims maintain "a strong fixation to the [lost] love-object." Anna Freud spoke of patients who maintain themselves in denial over a loss by "the substitution of a fantasy or an action, or something of that sort; the defensive use of action in order to do away with something painful and unpleasant." By adopting such a strategy — that is, by fixating on a substitute object or cause — a victim can avoid much of the pain inherent in his loss, sometimes for years.

Some civil litigants also fall into this trap. They avoid the feeling of the loss caused by a dispute by investing another "object" with their feelings. Often this object is the lawsuit itself. A terminated employee, for example, may escape some of the pain of losing his job by convincing himself that a court will compensate his injuries. Defendants may also cling to the belief that they will be vindicated in court.

What happens when such disputants must make compromises to settle? If a person has worked through feelings of loss before negotiations begin, she will be emotionally ready to compromise. If, however, the litigant pretended that a loss could be avoided, then she will confront the loss for the first time when she faces a settlement decision. This is exemplified by the poignant words of the wife who would not claim compensation for the death of her husband in the 9-11 disaster: "When we sign, it's done. He's really gone."

Implications for Bargaining

What are the implications of loss reactions for a negotiator or mediator? Most mediators see expressions of emotion as positive events, but there are reasons why both mediators and lawyers should see loss reactions as a potentially serious problem. The first issue involves interpreting the reaction. Disputants suffering from such reactions behave very similarly to adversarial bargainers. "Tough" negotiators will, for example, present cases in a distorted manner and cling stubbornly to viewpoints. Unfortunately, disputants in the grip of denial behave in much the same way. Adversarial bargainers will also sometimes pretend to agree to terms, and then renege once the other side has accepted the offer.

Disputants suffering from a loss reaction may engage in similar behavior, making proposals sincerely, but then falling prey to sudden feelings of anger or denial and withdrawing them. This, for example, is what happened in the age discrimination mediation; the plaintiff authorized the mediator to make an offer, but later denounced the same proposal as "crazy." A negotiator who encounters someone in the throes of a loss reaction may interpret his behavior as unethical bargaining, when in fact it is driven purely by emotion.

A second problem arises from the fact that loss reactions are likely to occur not at the outset of a negotiation, but much later when disputants must confront painful compromises. At that point the parties are feeling frustrated and want to wind up the process. Even the mediator may feel that the "listening to feelings" stage is, or should be, over. As a result, both mediators and other disputants may either ignore the loss reaction or become angry.

Potential Responses

How should a negotiator or mediator deal with a disputant who is "acting out" because of a loss reaction? The most useful lesson is to be aware of such responses and recognize them when they occur. If a mediator realizes that a loss reaction is happening, she will understand why a disputant is suddenly behaving in an inconsistent, even offensive manner. Opposing counsel should also bear in mind the possibility that their adversary is not being intentionally difficult or duplicitous, but may simply be unable to deal with the sudden realization that she will have to accept a serious loss in order to settle.

Mediators can treat loss reactions with techniques similar to those applied to emotional issues generally. They might, for instance, invite a person to describe the loss he has suffered, listening actively and empathizing with his feelings. A mediator could also work to reframe how a disputant views the situation. Both neutrals and opposing lawyers should bear in mind that the process of working through a loss reaction may take longer than a single day, and be ready if necessary to adjourn temporarily; this may, for example, explain why divorce mediations typically take weeks or months to complete, while commercial cases often settle in a single session. Professionals who encounter sudden, erratic behavior during bargaining should keep in mind the possibility that a disputant is going through a loss reaction, one of the many factors that make resolving disputes a less-than-fully-rational experience. (Golann, 2004).

CHAPTER
9

Merits-Based Barriers

Lawyers who negotiate over legal disputes instinctively apply one of the key lessons of good bargaining practice — not to settle for less than the value of one's best alternative to a negotiated agreement. In legal disputes each side's most obvious alternative to settlement is usually the same: to submit the case to adjudication. But the fact that disputants have the identical alternative does not mean that they agree about its value. In practice, disagreement over the likely outcome in adjudication is a major obstacle to settling disputes.

Litigators tend to assume that if they cannot settle, it is because the other side has misevaluated its case. But as we saw from the discussion of judgmental overconfidence and selective perception, *both* sides in a dispute — as well as their lawyers — commonly miss relevant information and make overoptimistic judgments about the likelihood that they will win. Given this phenomenon, it is understandable why litigants would have trouble settling. If a tort plaintiff, for example, assesses the most likely outcome at trial as a $120,000 verdict, while the defendant is convinced that the average verdict will be $80,000, they do not agree about the value of their alternative to agreement. Indeed, to the extent that a settlement above or below their projected outcome will feel to each like a "loss," strong psychological forces will motivate them to fight on.

The vast majority of cases do settle, however. Many settlements are driven by the reality that under U.S. law even a winning party cannot usually recover its costs of litigating. If each side in the above example expects to spend $30,000 to litigate, for instance, the plaintiff should be willing to accept $90,000 (120 minus 30) and the defendant to pay $110,000 (80 plus 30). Litigation costs thus transform a gap of $40,000 into an overlap, or zone of potential agreement, of $20,000 (110 versus 90). Of course, the fact that a solution between $90,000 and $110,000 makes financial sense does not mean that the disputants will regard it as fair.

Another factor inducing settlement, however, is risk aversion — the phenomenon that although sides in a case may think that they have a 60 percent chance of winning at trial, they often cannot afford, either financially or psychologically, to sustain a loss. The prospect of a loss may be devastating to the lawyer as well, particularly if she previously assured a client that his case was strong. The risk of losing is so frightening to many litigants and lawyers that they are willing to accept even what feels like an unfair bargain.

Despite the effects of litigation costs and risk aversion, disagreement about the likelihood of success in court often frustrates negotiations over legal claims. In such situations, part of the challenge for lawyers and mediators is to find ways of bringing the parties' assessments of legal issues closer together, so that a settlement will seem less unfair and cost and risk factors will induce them to agree. How can this be done?

A. Responses to Lack of Information

One key obstacle to settlement is often a simple lack of information: People sometimes assess their alternatives incorrectly because they do not have enough data, or the data that they do possess are not accurate. Lawyers express this feeling when they protest that, "It's too early to settle; I don't know the case well enough." In other situations, the negotiators claim to have all relevant data, but a neutral observer can see that their arguments are laced with gaps and assumptions. It is also possible that each side has information on all points, but their versions conflict with each other.

It is often surprising to an outsider how little litigants know about each other's claims and defenses even after years of discovery. Court rules are designed to give parties full disclosure of relevant information, but in practice litigants usually attempt to "hide the ball," concealing evidence as long as possible. Even when parties do learn legally relevant facts, they often lack information about other important issues. When a litigant meets a representative of the other side, for example, at a deposition, he is usually discouraged from volunteering any information, particularly about the underlying causes of their dispute. As a result, a mediator can often make significant progress simply by arranging for an informal exchange of information among disputants.

> *Example:* A sales manager who had been fired by a computer software company sued his former employer for violating his employment contract. The company maintained that the termination was lawful. The case remained in pretrial discovery for years, and then as trial approached went to mediation. When the neutral caucused with the parties it quickly became apparent that a major component of the manager's claims involved stock options in the company. The manager, however, had never been able to obtain the internal financial reports needed to value the options. He assumed that the company was hiding the data because it expected to "go public," an event that would make his options very valuable.
>
> Questioned about this in caucus, the company's CEO said that he had ordered the data withheld from the plaintiff because "It's none of his business." In fact, the company was only marginally profitable and the options were nearly worthless. The mediator suggested to the CEO that if there really was no pot of gold in the stock options, he could help settle the case by letting the plaintiff know this. The parties agreed to review the financial data. A settlement was quickly worked out; among its terms were verification of the company's financial representations and termination of the plaintiff's options.

To help to resolve disagreements over the legal merits that stem from information problems, a mediator can:

*   Arrange an exchange of information
*   Resolve internal obstacles
*   Moderate a joint discussion

- Serve as a channel for, or verifier of, confidential facts
- Direct attention to non-merits information

Arrange an exchange of information. As the above example shows, a mediator can often arrange for a more effective exchange of information than occurs in most discovery proceedings. Litigants are usually more forthcoming in the context of mediation because they have a realistic hope of settling the case, wish to cooperate with the neutral, and trust the mediator to shield them from unreasonable demands. In the mediation context, parties may even provide information without a quid pro quo by the other side, as occurred in the stock options case.

Information exchanges are also easier to arrange because the time-limited quality of the mediation process focuses the parties on pulling together data quickly. Finally, the special confidentiality rules that apply in mediation allow disputants to share data with less fear of being harmed if the case does not settle. Some of the techniques described earlier can also be of help: Mediators can identify information that one side lacks and ask the other party, in the interest of settlement and/or as a courtesy to the neutral, to make an effort to obtain it.

Resolve internal obstacles. Negotiators often fail to obtain data from their own side that would help in settlement. This may occur because the inside litigation contact for a corporate party does not see the case as a priority or does not have enough influence to obtain the data. A party can also encounter frustration when a co-plaintiff or co-defendant procrastinates about collecting facts. A mediator can often coax special efforts from parties that allow negotiators to get data from their own side that they need to settle.

Moderate a joint discussion. In some cases disputants have never looked at the relevant information together to understand its significance to the other side. In these situations a mediator can move the negotiation forward by helping them do so. It often makes sense to ask the participants, or a subset of them, to meet for a joint review of an issue. Even when parties are too emotional to negotiate with each other, they may still be able to talk about facts, for example to review a plot plan. Such discussions can expose ignorance and misunderstandings, as well as give parties the experience of working cooperatively.

Serve as a channel for, or verifier of, key facts. In direct negotiation facts and arguments cannot be used in bargaining without becoming known to the other side and exposed to discovery. In mediation, by contrast, confidentiality guarantees open up possibilities for exchanging sensitive data. Sophisticated negotiators and neutrals use the special confidentiality rules of mediation to communicate information while at the same time preserving "ammunition" for trial. Parties may agree, for example, to allow a mediator to show key financial documents to the other side, on the condition that no copies will be made and the originals will be returned at the end of the process.

Example: Two parties' disagreement about a claim turned in large part on the credibility of a defense witness. The defendant allowed the mediator to question the witness in caucus and then give her impressions to the other side. Since the witness had never been deposed and the time for taking depositions had expired, the defense was able to use the witness for settlement purposes without sacrificing its tactical advantage if the case had to be tried.

Direct attention to non-merits information.   We have seen that negotiators tend to define "relevance" narrowly in legal disputes, focusing on data that would be useful at trial but slighting information about non-litigation interests. Mediation, by contrast, can help parties to develop data that allow them to construct more valuable settlement packages. Even while a mediator is focusing on the merits, he can help parties exchange useful non-merits data.

B. Intermediate Techniques

Even when litigants have complete information they are likely to disagree about the value of their litigation alternative, due to cognitive forces such as selective perception. In addition to the specific responses discussed in Chapter 8, both mediators and bargainers can use the following approaches to influence disputants who have relevant information but appear to be misreading it:

* Ask questions
* Lead disputants through an analysis
* Point out worst-case scenarios
* Stress transactional costs
* Lead the parties through a decision analysis
* Form alliances with some players to convince others
* Directly challenge assumptions

Ask questions.   The safest approach to a litigant's misevaluation of an issue is to ask questions about the factual and legal assumptions that underlie his view. This is the essence of the tactic referred to as "reality testing." Asking questions is particularly useful at the outset of a case, because one does not need to have his own analysis to pose queries.

It is worth stressing that reality testing does not require a mediator to disclose her own view about an issue. By phrasing questions carefully, mediators can challenge the parties' viewpoints without appearing biased. To avoid humiliating participants, this kind of questioning is best done privately and by a neutral. It can be done in joint session, but if so, the mediator should take care that parties do not resent being pushed about sensitive issues in front of an adversary. For example, a mediator might:

* Ask a plaintiff "Can you help me understand how you calculated the figure of $5 million in lost profits? Are there any documents I could look at to flesh that out?"

- Ask a defendant "Is there a precedent for your argument that a judge will have to throw out the punitive damages claim? The plaintiff says that the circuit court ruled the other way; is there anything to the contrary I can show him?"
- Draw attention to a problem that a party has ignored: "You're looking for $2 million in damages, but I see insurance coverage of only $250,000. How do you think you can collect a judgment that favorable?"

One useful tactic is to ask each party to suggest questions to present to the other. This allows you to raise an argument as coming from the other side and offer to reply on the party's behalf ("The defense is arguing that there is no proof of emotional distress — can you give me something I can take to them on this?").

Lead disputants through an analysis. If initial questions are not enough, mediators can take an unrealistic disputant through a point-by-point analysis. A typical money damages claim, for instance, has four basic elements: the plaintiff's allegations, affirmative defenses such as statutes of limitations, proof of damages, and collection of a judgment. The mediator can break each of these elements into subquestions; for instance, proving damages may involve issues of evidence, computation, and expert opinion. He can also discuss potential counterarguments, perhaps writing the issues on a whiteboard to dramatize them. This approach can pinpoint problems that are glossed over or forgotten during informal discussion and counteract litigants' persistent tendency to filter out unfavorable information and overweight the importance of favorable facts.

Point out worst-case scenarios. Although the concept of the best alternative to a negotiated agreement (BATNA) is very useful, parties often take it too much to heart. They are likely to focus only on their *best* alternative to a settlement, which usually is seen as a win in court, ignoring the *most likely* result or what is often even more significant, the *worst* possible outcome (sometimes given the acronym "Worst Alternative to a Negotiated Agreement," or WATNA).

Given the tendency of parties to focus on best outcomes and ignore mediocre and worst-case possibilities, mediators should direct each side's attention to less-favorable scenarios. A mediator might play on risk aversion, for instance, by probing the impact of a total loss in the case and requesting each lawyer to estimate for his client the risk that it will occur. If counsel says that a complete loss is inconceivable, a mediator might ask if he has ever lost a similar case, or heard of others doing so, or cite accounts of serious losses drawn from trial reports. Focusing on WATNAs also lets a mediator harness the psychological power of loss aversion and attraction to certainty: If disputants measure an unattractive but certain settlement against the possibility of a total loss, a compromise may seem more attractive.

Mediators can also focus attention on the most likely outcome, a mediocre one. In a tort case, for instance, this might be a finding that the defendant is liable but that the plaintiff is contributorily negligent and should receive reduced damages. In doing this, a neutral is seeking to counterbalance the human tendency to focus on reports of dramatic events such as a huge victory or loss, rather than more common mediocre results.

Stress transactional costs.   We noted earlier that because of the impact of transactional costs, rejecting a settlement offer often does not make sense even if a party expects to do somewhat better in adjudication. Parties almost always understand this problem in general terms, but often have not calculated even approximately how much it will actually cost to pursue their case through trial.

A mediator can prompt disputants to discuss a budget for additional litigation using both optimistic and pessimistic scenarios. If cost estimates seem unrealistic, a mediator can use the same techniques as for miscalculations about legal issues: ask questions, go through a formal analysis, and if necessary express skepticism or offer opposing views.

In talking about costs, good mediators make special efforts to ensure that the parties are inclusive. A thorough assessment would include not only attorneys' fees, but also the cost of experts, deposition transcripts, services such as "rush" trial transcripts, and travel.

A good mediator will also help each side think through and experience more vividly the hidden costs of litigation, such as being pulled away from one's occupation and family by the demands of legal war. Participants who are not regularly involved in litigation do not know how painful the process can be; for a one-time participant, even a routine deposition can be a wrenching experience.

It is often wise to defer the issue of litigation costs until later in the mediation process. Even when negotiators have developed a realistic estimate of costs, they are often unwilling at first to acknowledge them, making comments such as, "I shouldn't have to take less than a fair result just because the justice system is inefficient!" Disputants sometimes also refuse to consider litigation costs because they feel that the other side will also save by settling, and so there is no reason for them to make a special effort to compromise. Because of this mediators do not usually focus on costs until after the merits have been fully aired.

Lead the parties through a decision analysis.   "Decision analysis" is a more formal version of the inquiry described above and is described in detail below. This method is especially helpful with numbers-oriented litigants such as engineers and CFOs. It is used both by lawyers and by mediators.

At a simple level decision analysis simply involves asking a disputant to place specific percentages on his chances of winning at various stages of the process. A skeptic might point out that if a disputant is not assessing his case accurately, putting the misestimate into numbers will not make it any more reliable. In fact, though, decision analysis can help a party think through each of the possible outcomes in a case and understand the impact of risk on case value. How to perform a decision analysis is discussed in the next section.

Form alliances with some players to convince others.   Some members of a bargaining team may be more realistic about the value of their case than others. Attorneys are likely to be most realistic because they have more experience and are less likely to be driven by emotion. Lawyers also know that they risk being held responsible for a bad result, a counterweight against the tendency to be overoptimistic. By talking with a lawyer alone a mediator can sometimes identify such disagreements. Indeed, attorneys sometimes will tell a trusted mediator that their client is being unrealistic and ask for help in dealing with him. How mediators and lawyers can work in concert to deal with unrealistic clients is explored in Chapter 11, and the ethical issues it raises in Chapter 13.

Directly challenge assumptions. If other methods fail a mediator can explicitly indicate that he disagrees with a disputant, but still avoid giving his own opinion. The neutral might emphasize his disagreement in a clear, even blunt manner; for example, "I understand you plan to argue that the company records were altered, but I'm concerned that the jury will see it as an ordinary error, rather than a cover up."

For a mediator to directly challenge an opinion after having demonstrated that he has listened to arguments can shake a litigant's confidence. Simply indicating disagreement without offering one's own opinion has the additional advantage of not locking the mediator into a position that may become an obstacle later in the process. On the spectrum of facilitation to evaluation, this technique crosses into the evaluative sector; some mediators, however, would describe it simply as a tough form of "reality testing."

As we have indicated, one option to resolve differences in case assessment is to carry out a process known as decision analysis. In the reading that follows, Marjorie Aaron explains the basics of how to do decision analysis and why it can be helpful in settling cases.

❖ Marjorie Corman Aaron, *DECISION ANALYSIS AS A METHOD OF EVALUATING THE TRIAL ALTERNATIVE*

Mediating Legal Disputes 162 (D. Golann ed., 2009)

For most of us, the logic and method underlying the method known as "decision analysis" is quite natural and accessible. When faced with a decision, we inevitably choose among paths at the proverbial fork in the road. To choose wisely, we try to anticipate options and assess probabilities associated with each path. For a businessperson, the decision might be whether to maintain high cash reserves or make investments in product development or both. He would be wise to consider the likelihood of success in product development and to estimate the consequent revenues and costs. Litigants faced with deciding between settling or pursuing a litigation path should similarly consider challenges along the way, the likelihood of success at each step, and the range of possible results. Decision analysis uses the same logic and provides a quantitative method for considering the litigation path and comparing it to settlement options.

Lawyers, clients, and mediators implicitly accept the logic of decision analysis when they argue about the merits of a case, discuss strengths and weaknesses and relate them to a "reasonable" settlement figure. A lawyer whose defense client is *just about certain* to lose, and be forced to pay *at least* $500,000 and *quite likely* between $700,000 and $1,000,000, will advise his client to offer much more in settlement than if she thinks the client has a *good chance* of avoiding liability, with a $300,000 award *most likely*, and only a *slight chance* of an award exceeding $500,000.

This lawyer is considering different uncertainties in the case, and relating his assessment of probabilities and outcomes to settlement. However, because he is using inherently vague prose to express probabilities, he cannot communicate clearly the size of each risk or the impact of cumulative risks. (If you doubt this, ask a few people each to write down in percentage terms what one of the italicized words means to them — we almost guarantee they will disagree significantly!) If the same lawyer were using decision analysis, he would assign numerical probabilities to his assessment of each risk and then estimate the monetary value of each possible case outcome, deducting the cost incurred along the way, before making a settlement recommendation.

Why work with decision analysis in mediation?

Decision analysis can help move participants toward settlement in mediation. Assigning numerical probabilities to possible twists and hard dollar estimates to potential case outcomes can prove illuminating to participants who haven't related their lawyer's assessments, expressed in prose, to settlement value. Numbers tend to capture peoples' attention, perhaps by rendering the future more concrete. Using decision analysis enables participants to understand the cumulative impact of risk in the litigation, relating various theories to a precise outcome. It enables them to see the likelihood of each possible case outcome — whether, after all is said and done, there's a 10% chance of collecting more than $150,000, or less than a 30% chance of collecting more than $75,000, etc. By mathematically discounting each case outcome by its probability, decision analysis yields a number both sides might view as "reasonable" settlement value.

Sometimes decision analysis is helpful not because of the numbers, but because discussion around the numbers helps participants detach — emotionally and personally — from their case. Decision analysis almost necessarily uses less emotional, less personal language than we often hear in mediation. No longer are parties arguing directly back to their lawyer or mediator, opposing a view that "your witness isn't very strong and you may lose this motion." Rather they are looking at the tree and discussing whether another witness, if located, could raise the percentage chance of winning a motion by 10%. The focus of attention is "mediated" by the easel, scratch pad, or computer on which the analysis is shown, and the task and tone become less oppositional and more focused on working with the problem.

Of course the end numbers calculated through decision analysis can have power. When participants accept the logic of the method and recognize that the probability and pay-off values in the decision analysis of their case are reasonably accurate, they may readjust their internal benchmark about what constitutes a fair settlement . . . providing reason or excuse for movement. . . .

Do not assume decision analysis should be limited to mediations involving engineers, MBA's, CFO's and accountants. . . . In our experience, a wide range of people, even many lacking post-high school education, can also understand it. No calculus is involved, just basic arithmetic. Most people do understand betting, and the logic of discounting for risk when making decisions. That is all you need. Even if a disputant does not follow the math, he will understand that a logical analytic method has been applied to his case, and its results may persuade him to adjust his settlement position. Whether introducing decision analysis will be productive in mediation depends less upon whether participants will understand it — they will — and more on whether it will matter to them when making settlement decisions.

Two formats: scratch pads and tree structure

There are two ways of doing decision analysis. One we'll call a basic "scratch pad" format. The other we'll refer to as "tree format," as it involves drawing horizontal tree-like structures on paper or computer to demonstrate the inter-relationship of the issues in the case. The two methods are logically identical but they appear quite different.

Scratch-pad analysis may seem more familiar to people. . . . They may not need or care to see a map of the litigation and its flow or how one issue may affect another. As the name suggests, it requires a pen and a writing pad or whiteboard and marker. For more complex cases, a [Microsoft] Excel spread-sheet can be used.

I prefer the tree format, as more elegant and effective for people who process information visually. The tree method creates a map of the possible twists and turns in a case, using horizontal tree branches, generally moving over time from left to right, with the probabilities of each possible event carried on the drawing, ending with all the possible case outcomes at the far right.

In relatively simple cases a mediator can draw the decision tree entirely by hand on a regular note pad or easel. As with the scratch pad, a calculator makes the arithmetic easier. In more complex cases, analysis is best done on a computer using decision tree software. (We use the TreeAge software available from *TreeAge.com*, but other software is available.) Printing it out is recom-mended if more than one or two participants will want to study and discuss it.

Working with Decision Trees

For legal disputes, decision analysis is used to value the parties' litigation alternatives. A typical decision tree used in litigation typically has two branches: "litigate" or "settle." The settle branch may reflect the other side's most recent offer. The litigate branch is generally an extended tree, whose branches repre-sent the different events that may transpire during litigation.

Decision trees are organized chronologically, from left to right. Events are depicted in the tree in the order they are likely to occur. Decision trees contain "nodes." [A "node" represents two or more possible outcomes or choices at a particular point in a case, such as winning or losing at trial.]

Working with Decision Trees

The following example represents a situation in which a plaintiff must decide whether to accept a settlement offer of $30,000 or proceed to trial with a chance of recovering $100,000. Assume that you represent the plaintiff, with whom you have a contingent fee arrangement in this lawsuit.

Figure A.

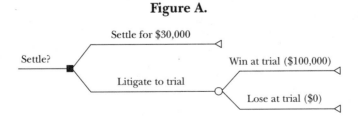

The plaintiff faces two choices — litigate or settle — which are represented by branches. If the plaintiff settles, the inquiry is complete: he will get $30,000 and the dispute will be over. If he chooses to litigate, there are two possible outcomes: win (a payoff of $100,000), and lose (a payoff of $0). For the purposes of this example, all other uncertainties associated with litigation have been ignored. To make this decision intelligently the plaintiff must assess how likely he is to win if litigation is pursued. The $30,000 settlement offer may be inadequate if the plaintiff has an excellent chance of winning $100,000. However, the offer may be attractive if the chance is low.

Assume that, in the attorney's professional judgment, the plaintiff has a 60% (.6) chance of winning at trial. This probability would be displayed beneath the chance labeled "win." Accordingly, it follows that a probability of 40% (.4) would be displayed beneath the node labeled "lose."

Figure B.

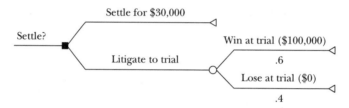

Litigation is apparently preferable to settlement (at least given the current settlement offer) in this case because the probability of winning is more than high enough to warrant gambling at trial. In simple terms, the expected value of a course of action is the average value of taking that course of action many times. If one were to try the identical case one hundred times, and there is a 60% likelihood of a plaintiff's verdict, approximately 60 trials would result in a plaintiff's verdict while 40 would result in a defense verdict. The average recovery would be 60 victories multiplied by $100,000 per victory or $6,000,000, divided by 100 cases, for an average recovery of $60,000.

Walking Through a Slightly More Complex Tree. In more complex cases there will be more than one layer of nodes, or options. Before the case goes to trial, for example, it may be heard on summary judgment. Thus, there would be a node for summary judgment (granted or denied). Assume a 10% chance that the summary judgment motion will be granted. On the branch of the tree that represents "summary judgment denied," one would find the chance node for liability at trial. Figure C below illustrates how a motion for summary judgment would be interposed between the decision to litigate and the outcome of trial.

Figure C.

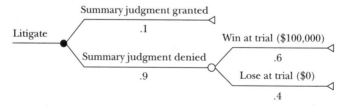

As in all decision trees, the calculations start at the right side. By multiplying the probability of defeat at trial by the payoff, and adding the two figures together, an expected value of $60,000 is calculated (or "rolled back") and displayed next to the node "Summary Judgment denied." Thus, the expected value of the case upon denial of summary judgment is $60,000.

In this case, the plaintiff's expected value of litigation must also take into account the possibility of losing on summary judgment. Thus, the expected value of the litigation is calculated by multiplying the expected value after denial of the motion for summary judgment — $60,000 — by the probability that summary judgment will be denied, 90%. As reflected in figure D below, the expected value of litigation is thus $54,000. The $6,000 difference between this expected value and the expected value in the earlier example reflects the risk that the plaintiff will lose on summary judgment.

Figure D.

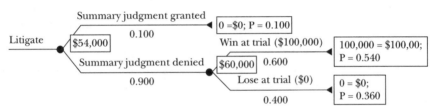

The Analysis Is Only as Good as the Data. It is important to remember that the outcome of any analysis is only as valuable as the input. One must consider carefully the numbers assigned to the range of predicted awards and associated costs at each node. For example, where a party is paying for its attorney's time (not on a contingency fee), lower legal costs should be factored in at the node where summary judgment is granted than at either of the nodes that follow trial. Depending on the level of precision required, one may design a rough-cut model, limiting the range of possibilities and making bold assumptions about damages. Or, one may develop a more refined tree, taking into account numerous possibilities (even if some have low probabilities) and assigning probabilities to different levels of damage awards.

Notwithstanding the inherent imprecision in assigning probabilities to events at trial, the process of designing a decision tree can itself assist in valuing litigation. Thinking through the hurdles to be surmounted in order to prevail can help each side organize its thinking. Furthermore, performing more advanced calculations can identify those issues that have the greatest impact on case value, which can help focus negotiation strategy and research emphasis.

Sensitivity Analysis

Particularly where the parties' assessments on one or two issues diverge widely (from each other's or from the mediator's), it is worth asking how sensitive the case's expected value is to those issues. What if one's assessment of that issue were to change? How much difference would alteration of the assessment make [to case value]? Sensitivity analysis answers such questions, whether done with formal computer-generated graphs or the ubiquitous legal pad and hand calculator.

. . . The expected value of a case is derived from its many components. However not all components are equally important; they have different degrees of influence on the expected value. For example, the parties may disagree strenuously on two issues, such as whether a particular witness's testimony would be admitted or whether lost profits would be the appropriate measure of damages. . . . Both are uncertainties in the case, and sensitivity analysis could determine how much they matter to the end result. In other words, if one were 100% certain (or 90%, or 70%, or 50%, etc.) that the lost profits measure would be applied, how would that change the expected value? If the expected value is highly sensitive to a given issue, a small change in the probability assigned that issue would lead to a large swing in the expected value of the entire case.

There are two basic and related ways to perform a sensitivity analysis. The first is simply to recalculate the tree, answering the "what if . . . ?" question. Assume that the defendant in the example described earlier disagrees strongly with the assessment of a mere 10% likelihood that the summary judgment motion will be successful. The defendant agrees that summary judgment is a "long shot," but more on the order of 25%. (After all, 10% makes it hard to justify the fees for the summary judgment motion.) The mediator might then recalculate the tree, substituting a 25% probability of summary judgment for the original 10%. The resulting change in the expected value would demonstrate its "sensitivity" to the summary judgment issue. Sensitivity analysis can be particularly useful in a mediation context, as discussed in more detail below.

Technologically Appropriate Choices

For [a lawyer or] mediator who is less than comfortable with high technology, it will be reassuring to learn that decision analysis can be performed in "scratch pad" format. Those who wish to use a computer will find comfort in simple, user-friendly decision analysis software. Using a computer with special decision-tree software is often effective in business disputes because business people tend to have confidence in the computer's ability to generate valuable information and many learned the principles of decision analysis in business school . . . For other people, who may have had some difficulty embracing the approach or who view computers as alien, the pad and the calculator may be the best choice, despite or even because of the slower pace.

C. Evaluation of the Likely Outcome in Adjudication

When bargaining reaches an impasse and the reason is disagreement over who will win in court, many lawyers expect mediators to give an opinion on the issue. Evaluation is a controversial topic, and this section explores the issue.

Keep in mind as you read that legal issues are not the only topics on which a mediator can express a viewpoint. He might, for instance, suggest what offer a party should make, how a proposal is likely to be received by an adversary, the likely meaning of an opponent's move, or whether a particular offer satisfies a person's personal interests. Doing any of these things requires that a mediator "evaluate" something. The classic form of mediator evaluation, however, is to offer an opinion about how a court will decide a legal issue or about the monetary value of a claim.

1. Should Mediators Evaluate?

No one argues that mediators should use evaluation as a first resort, and court-related ADR programs that focus on evaluating cases, like "Early Neutral Evaluation" shown in the chart at the start of Chapter 13, have declined greatly in popularity. Still, commercial mediators may think that offering advice about legal issues is part of what they have been hired to do, and there is often no clear dividing line between facilitative and evaluative interventions.

Other mediators, however, believe that evaluation should not be part of mediation at all, that for a mediator to offer advice in their view interferes with core values of the process, such as the right of parties to make their own decisions. Consider the following perspectives on this issue.

❖ **Lela P. Love,** THE TOP TEN REASONS WHY MEDIATORS
SHOULD NOT EVALUATE

24 Fla. St. U. L. Rev. 937 (1997)

. . . The debate over whether mediators should "evaluate" revolves around the confusion over what constitutes evaluation and an "evaluative" mediator. . . . An "evaluative" mediator gives advice, makes assessments, states opinions — including opinions on the likely court outcome — proposes a fair or workable resolution to an issue or the dispute, or presses the parties to accept a particular resolution. The ten reasons that follow demonstrate that those activities are inconsistent with the role of a mediator.

I. The Roles and Related Tasks of Evaluators and Facilitators Are at Odds

Evaluating, assessing, and deciding for others is radically different than helping others evaluate, assess, and decide for themselves. Judges, arbitrators, neutral experts, and advisors are evaluators. Their role is to make decisions and give opinions. To do so, they use predetermined criteria to evaluate evidence and arguments presented by adverse parties. The tasks of evaluators include: finding "the facts" by properly weighing evidence; judging credibility and allocating the burden of proof; determining and applying the relevant law, rule, or custom to the particular situation; and making an award or rendering an opinion. The adverse parties have expressly asked the evaluator — judge, arbitrator, or expert — to decide the issue or resolve the conflict.

In contrast, the role of mediators is to assist disputing parties in making their own decisions and evaluating their own situations. A mediator facilitates communications, promotes understanding, focuses the parties on their interests, and seeks creative problem-solving to enable the parties to reach their own agreement. Mediators push disputing parties to question their assumptions, reconsider their positions, and listen to each other's perspectives, stories, and arguments. They urge the parties to consider relevant law, weigh their own values, principles, and priorities, and develop an optimal outcome. In so doing, mediators facilitate evaluation by the parties.

These differences between evaluators and facilitators mean that each uses different skills and techniques, and each requires different competencies, training norms, and ethical guidelines to perform their respective functions. Further, the evaluative tasks of determining facts, applying law or custom, and delivering an opinion not only divert the mediator away from facilitation, but also can compromise the mediator's neutrality — both in actuality and in the eyes of the parties — because the mediator will be favoring one side in his judgment.

Endeavors are more likely to succeed when the goal is clear and simple and not at war with other objectives. Any task, whether it is the performance of an Olympic athlete, the advocacy of an attorney, or the negotiation assistance provided by a mediator, requires a clear and bright focus and the development of appropriate strategies, skills, and power. In most cases, should the athlete or the attorney or the mediator divert their focus to another task, it will diminish their capacity to achieve their primary goal. "No one can serve two masters." Mediators cannot effectively facilitate when they are evaluating.

   I.   *Evaluation Promotes Positioning and Polarization, Which Are Antithetical to the Goals of Mediation . . .*

   II.   *Ethical Codes Caution Mediators — and Other Neutrals — Against Assuming Additional Roles . . .*

   III.   *If Mediators Evaluate Legal Claims and Defenses, They Must Be Lawyers; Eliminating Non-Lawyers Will Weaken the Field . . .*

   IV.   *There Are Insufficient Protections Against Incorrect Mediator Evaluations . . .*

   V.   *Evaluation Abounds: The Disputing World Needs Alternative Paradigms . . .*

   VI.   *Mediator Evaluation Detracts from the Focus on Party Responsibility for Critical Evaluation, Re-Evaluation and Creative Problem Solving . . .*

   VII.   *Evaluation Can Stop Negotiation . . .*

   VIII.   *A Uniform Understanding of Mediation is Critical to the Development of the Field . . .*

   IX.   *Mixed Processes Can Be Useful, But Call Them What They Are! . . .*

❖ **Marjorie Corman Aaron,** *MERITS BARRIERS: EVALUATION*

Mediating Legal Disputes 145 (D. Golann ed., 2009)

A mediator's ultimate weapon for influencing divergent case assessments is to offer an evaluation. Evaluation is an important, risky, and controversial tactic that should be carefully considered, structured, and delivered.

To understand the difference between evaluation and other mediator interventions, consider this metaphor. If mediators were doctors, fostering an information exchange might be the equivalent of recommending exercise and diet. Helping lawyers and parties to rigorously analyze their own views on disputed issues would be like administering medicine with potentially uncomfortable side effects.

Mediator evaluation would be akin to surgery. Just as surgery can range from an arthroscopic procedure to a major operation, evaluation can vary from small and low-risk to comprehensive and potentially threatening. Most people would not choose a doctor whose first response to every illness was to bring out a scalpel. At the same time, few would feel comfortable with a physician who refused to perform surgery regardless of need. The challenge for a mediator is to know when and how to perform evaluative "surgery" in the safest possible way.

What do we mean by "evaluation"? In this context it means forming and expressing one's views regarding the likely outcome in adjudication. Evaluation can focus on single issue ("It seems doubtful the statute of limitations defense will be successful.") or the overall outcome ("The plaintiff is likely to win."). It can be expressed as a range ("I think damages could run between $125,000 and $175,000."), a numeric probability ("I would estimate a 40 percent chance of success."), or a precise number ("I predict a $500,000 award in this case in Randolph County."). An evaluation can be expressed with certainty ("I am fairly sure the plaintiff will win . . .") or left vague ("I have some doubts about how a jury might react to . . .").

The idea that parties and lawyers evaluate their own cases is not controversial. However we have seen that a party's numbers may be seriously distorted. . . .

Lawyers and parties who enter mediation often expect the neutral to evaluate the issues. Having educated a mediator about their case, disputants anticipate that she will think about what she has heard. Professional mediators are not "potted plants" and do in fact form judgments much of the time. Lawyers and parties are thus reasonable to ask a mediator "What do you think?," "How do you see this argument?" or "Where do you predict the damages will fall out?," and if a mediator refuses to answer they may feel frustrated.

On the other hand, many mediators can recount a time they provided an evaluation, were rebuffed, and soon thereafter the process ground to a halt. Experienced lawyers talk of frustration with mediators who announce a "reasonable settlement number" and then alienate or entrench clients by trying to push the outcome toward their opinion. Because evaluation can be powerful both negatively and positively, it is critical for mediators to evaluate appropriately, skillfully and with minimum collateral damage, just as a surgeon must choose the optimal technique to achieve a goal with minimum post-operative harm.

Benefits

Evaluation can cause litigants to question and reevaluate their own judgments and "bottom lines." When a neutral who has listened thoughtfully to a presentation of facts and arguments disagrees with a litigant's prediction of victory, the party may be motivated to rethink its position. Evaluation can, for example, help to overcome the impact of selective perception and other cognitive forces discussed earlier.

. . . A mediator evaluation can also satisfy a litigant's emotional desire for "my day in court." An evaluation approximates the civil justice paradigm — both sides present their stories and arguments and a neutral renders a judgment — but within the safer, non-binding confines of mediation. Having presented their cases to a neutral, even one without a black robe, parties may feel less need to do it again before a judge.

A mediator's evaluation can also provide psychological or professional cover to litigants who realize negotiation concessions are necessary, but do not want to move from an entrenched position without a rationale. Business representatives, insurance adjusters, government officials, and even individuals who feel obligated to family members, often use evaluations to protect them from after-the-fact criticism.

Disputants can use evaluation as a convenient scapegoat for a difficult decision, even when the disputant privately agrees with the assessment. ("Once the mediator said the case was worth $100,000, there was no way I was going to be able to settle it for any less. . . .")

Dangers

Mediator evaluation can also create a serious risk of harm to the process, making settlement more difficult. First and foremost, mediators who evaluate risk damaging their credibility as neutrals. As long as litigants trust a mediator is impartial, they are willing to consider options, listen to questions, and make painful compromises. When a mediator evaluates, however, a participant may conclude the mediator has "gone over to the other side," assuming that because the mediator thinks the other side will win, the mediator must want settlement to be skewed in the other side's favor. When the mediator next asks for compromise in such circumstances, the disputant is likely to resist.

If these risks are not enough, consider the following additional concerns. A "global" opinion of case value may freeze the bargaining process, because neither side wants to accept a settlement worse than the neutral's number even when it would be wise to do so. In these circumstances a mediator's evaluation becomes a take-it-or-leave-it offer to both sides.

The expectation of a mediator evaluation can also discourage bargaining. After all, why confront painful decisions about concessions when the neutral may soon vindicate one's position? Disputants may also assume the mediator will place her evaluation between their last offers, and thus be concerned that offering additional concessions will simply shrink the zone in which they can "win" in the evaluation.

The expectation of an evaluation also changes the focus of the dialogue. Participants emphasize their legal arguments, seeking to persuade the mediator as judge and jury. This, in turn, can cause parties to become even more convinced of the strength of their arguments and angry at the other side's advocacy. Evaluations also tend to distract the parties' (and perhaps also the mediator's) attention away from non-legal barriers to settlement and creative solutions. And if the real barrier to agreement is a party's unresolved feelings or a similar non-legal issue, evaluation will be irrelevant.

Given its inherent dangers, our fundamental advice regarding mediator evaluation is: "Only when necessary, and with humility." To us "necessary" means evaluation should be undertaken as a strategy of last resort, when it appears to be the only way to break a negotiation deadlock. At that point even if all the risks of evaluation come to pass they are of no ultimate consequence, because the case probably would not settle in any event.

Questions

1. Do Professor Aaron's arguments answer any of Professor Love's concerns? Which are not addressed?
2. The Federal Court for the Northern District of California has adopted the following rules for its court-connected mediation program:

   . . . As promptly as possible during the mediation the mediator should identify the issues and discuss them with the parties. . . .

   Is a mediator who does this engaging in evaluation under Professor Love's definition? Professor Aaron's?
   The rules go on to say:

   In some cases the mediator may consider suggesting specific settlement terms. Such action is not required, or even appropriate, in every case, and should generally be employed only if the parties request it and the mediator concludes it will aid the parties and counsel in reaching a settlement. Any such settlement recommendation should be based on the mediator's experience or other knowledge concerning jury verdicts and settlement value.

   If the parties request a mediator to make a suggestion about settlement terms, is doing so "evaluation"? Would Professor Love object if a mediator, responding to the parties' request, based a settlement recommendation on an assessment of their underlying interests rather than the litigation value of the case?
3. The Supreme Court of Virginia has adopted the following rule for court mediators:

   The mediator may offer legal information if all parties are present, or separately if they consent, and shall inform unrepresented parties or those parties who are not accompanied by legal counsel about the importance of reviewing the mediator's legal information with legal counsel. Also, the mediator may offer evaluation of strengths and weaknesses of positions only if such evaluation is incidental to the facilitative role and does not interfere with the mediator's impartiality or the self-determination of the parties.

   Does this rule respond to Professor Love's concerns about evaluation? Which ones?
4. To what degree are the problems of mediator evaluation lessened if the parties are represented by counsel?

2. What Is Evaluation?

One of the issues in this debate is what constitutes "evaluation," as opposed to the less controversial practice of "reality testing." Consider the following analysis of practice in Australian family mediation.

❖ **Tom Fisher,** *Advice by Any Other Name*

29 Conflict Resol. Q. 107 (2001)

Within the context of family law mediation [there is a] well documented tension in both practice and in ethical codes between listening and giving advice, between encouraging the client to make decisions, and taking over the decision making process. . . . The Australian community of family law mediators would commonly draw a distinction between providing information, which is acceptable practice, and offering advice, which is not. [However,] it is arguable whether, given the power of a mediator, her suggestions or recommendations may not carry considerable authority. . . .

For example, in a dispute about which parent a child will reside with, a mediator might suggest shared residence. How might this intervention affect the parties, particularly if they know that the mediator is also a psychologist? At first glance, it may appear that simply providing information is less directive and more impartial than offering advice for action. So the mediator might say that recent studies have shown that in general the interests of children of separated parents are best served by frequent contact with their father. Again, how might these words affect party self-determination? In both cases, how impartial might the intervention seem to the mother who has just suggested full residence with herself? . . .

Many mediators are loath to give direct advice, even to clients who indicate they are desperate for it. This reluctance, however well intentioned, may nevertheless mask intervention, used consciously or unconsciously, that is designed to accomplish similar ends. These methods include, among others, creating doubt (usually by posing questions), reframing, and selective facilitation. . . .

Creating doubt

One party might say something like, "I'd rather roast in hell than let that creep see the kids!" A lawyer advising such a client may give direct advice that, according to [legal standards,] children have the right to see both of their parents. A mediator, on the other hand, might seek to create doubt in that party's mind by asking whether the party is familiar with the relevant [law]. Or the mediator might first reframe the comment to manage the emotional content of the message and then might say something like, "I can see you're furious with him for what he's done to you. But what effect would that have on the parenting needs of the children?" In both cases, however, the force of the intervention is somewhat akin to a lawyer's saying, "I must *advise* you that such action is contrary to the interests of the children and the relevant legal principles."

Reframing

Another major formulation is reframing, which occupies an important place in the practical literature and in mediation training courses. Reframing takes the communication of a party and, without abrogating his or her meaning entirely, alters and redirects that meaning to allow for its more constructive use. For example, it can detoxify aggressive language. So when one party says to the other, "Stop sucking at the trough and get a life," the mediator might reframe the outburst as something like, "You'd like Mary to be more self-sufficient." It may shift attention from positions to interests (from "I need the car on Wednesdays" to "So, you need a way to get to the day care center every Wednesday.").

Perhaps the most frequently used and helpful mediator intervention, reframing also carries with it some danger. Because it is an opportunity for the mediator to put words into a client's mouth to forward the mediator's own agenda, the client may experience reframing as manipulative or partisan.

Selective facilitation

Selective facilitation, as originally conceived, refers to how mediator acknowledgment of a party's statement may be used to produce a specific outcome favored by the mediator. For example, there might be an argument over who gets the household appliances, which starts when one former spouse say something like "I'll take the vacuum cleaner, washing machine, microwave, and the dishwasher. You probably never noticed that we had them, since you never did a thing around the house." The other responds with a counterattack on the standard of cleanliness of the house and a homily on the importance of financial contributions to the welfare of the family.

A mediator, particularly one wishing to work in a transformative mode, might choose to ask for mutual emotional acknowledgment from the parties. Perhaps more commonly, the mediator elects to ignore the interchange and say something on the order of "It seems that one area to be dealt with in deciding who gets what is the household appliances." Mediators are almost continuously making choices about what to attend to and what to let pass.

Conclusion

An intervention that casts doubt, reframes, and selectively facilitates communication between parties obviously does not fit [the] definition of giving advice in the narrow sense by recommending a specific course of action. However, it is not simply a process intervention; it is potentially powerful. This kind of intervention forces us to confront [the] critique of the central "myth" perpetuated by mainstream guidelines to mediation practice, that the mediator is a "passive and neutral facilitator." In fact, using such tactics raises the question of the extent to which the mediator is engaging in some sort of dissimulation, using techniques of "deception and manipulation" even if they are intended to help people in conflict view and understand the world around them differently and to help release disputing parties from their self-imposed constraints of limited options. In the end, successful implementation of the balancing act lies with the individual mediator.

Questions

5. Would Professor Love agree that each of the behaviors described by Tom Fisher is "evaluation"? What might she exclude from this category?
6. Using Fisher's definition, can you think of any time in a role-play or in real life when you have "evaluated" something, even if unintentionally?

3. If a Mediator Does Evaluate, How Should It Be Done?

Assuming that a mediator does evaluate the merits, a key issue is what substantive standard he should apply. There are several possible criteria:

- A mediator can offer a *prediction of what will happen* if a particular issue or the entire matter is adjudicated. Here the mediator is not saying how he personally would decide the issue, but rather is assessing how a judge, jury, or arbitrator in that jurisdiction, with all *their* quirks and foibles, is likely to respond. To put it another way, in this model the mediator is offering a "weather forecast" about the atmosphere in some future courtroom, but not advocating rain. This is the classic form of mediator evaluation.
- Alternatively, a mediator can give an *expert judgment about what happened or a personal view of what is fair*. Here the neutral is assuming the role of advisory arbitrator in the case. This is the most dangerous form of evaluation, because the loser is likely to feel, with justification, that the neutral has taken sides against him. And the mediator's personal view of a case is irrelevant, because he is almost always disqualified from sitting in judgment on it.
- Finally, a mediator may not evaluate the legal merits at all, but instead *assess the bargaining situation*. Here the neutral is giving an estimate of what each side needs to do to get an agreement, given the current state of mind of the other party. A neutral might say, for instance, "Given how they are feeling in the other room, my sense is that you'll need to go to six figures if you want a deal today." This is probably the least dangerous form of evaluation, because the mediator is simply assessing the opponent's attitude, without indicating that he thinks that it is fair or agrees with it.

❖ **American Bar Association Task Force on Improving Mediation Quality,** *FINAL REPORT*

(2008)

"Analytical" Techniques Used by the Mediator

C. Information from Focus Groups, Surveys, and Party Interviews

The Task Force collected substantial amounts of data about user perceptions of mediators utilizing analytical techniques in mediation. We observed in our focus groups that many reasonably sophisticated mediation users in civil cases want mediators to provide certain services, including analytical techniques. A substantial majority of survey participants (80%) believe some analytical input by a mediator to be appropriate.

Other survey questions focused more specifically on user attitudes about specific kinds of input by the mediator. The following percentages of our users surveyed rated the following characteristics important, very important or essential:

- 95% — making suggestions;
- about 70% — giving opinions;

In addition, we asked survey participants to indicate the proportion of cases in which a particular activity would be helpful. The following percentages of users thought the listed activities would be helpful in about *half or more* of their cases (emphasis added):

- 95% — ask pointed questions that raise issues;
- 95% — give analysis of case, including strengths and weaknesses;
- 60% — make prediction about likely court results;
- 100% — suggest possible ways to resolve issues;
- 84% — recommend a specific settlement; and
- 74% — apply some pressure to accept a specific solution.

On the other hand, nearly half of the users surveyed indicated that there are times when it is not appropriate for a mediator to give an assessment of strengths and weaknesses, and nearly half also indicated that it is sometimes not appropriate to recommend a specific settlement. User reservations on these issues should give pause to mediators who routinely offer such analysis and opinions. . . .

There is an interesting contrast between user and mediator survey responses when asked about recommending a specific settlement.

- Eighty-four percent (84%) of users . . . but only 38% of mediators . . . thought it would be helpful in half or more cases.
- 75% [of users but only 18% of mediators] thought it would be helpful in most [to] all . . . cases.

Similarly, when asked about applying some pressure to accept a specific solution,

- 64% of the users . . . but only 24%..of mediators . . . responded favorably for most or all or almost all cases and 75% [of users] but only 30% of mediators-. . . for half or more cases.

The opinions of parties who were interviewed differed from . . . lawyers on the issue of whether mediators should state their opinions about settlement terms. While only a minority of lawyers objected to this, six parties out of twelve stated that mediator comments such as "I think this is the best offer you're going to get," are inappropriate. An even higher percentage, eight out of eleven parties, objected to mediators telling them what to do, as in "You should accept this offer," or "If I were you, I'd offer $70,000 and be done with it."

Questions

7. Why do you think a much higher proportion of attorneys than neutrals in the ABA survey favor mediators giving opinions and applying "pressure" to settle?
8. What accounts, do you think, for the differences of opinion between attorneys and clients?

Does a disputant's reaction to evaluation differ depending on what issue the mediator evaluates, or the reasons the neutral gives? Consider the following survey of parties' reactions to evaluation in court-connected mediation programs.

❖ **Roselle P. Wissler,** *To Evaluate or Facilitate? Parties' Perceptions of Mediation Affected by Mediator Style*

7 Disp. Resol. Mag. 35 (Winter 2001)

Some commentators have argued that if a mediator evaluates the merits of a case instead of using a more purely facilitative approach, the parties will feel that the mediator is less neutral. The parties will also have less opportunity to participate in the mediation process and to determine its outcome, will not gain a better understanding of the other side's position and their own interests, and will be less satisfied with mediation. Four recent studies of mediation in civil and domestic relations cases provide the opportunity to empirically test the effect of mediator style on parties' perceptions. . . . No consistent differences were observed in the pattern of findings between the studies of civil cases and the studies of domestic relations cases.

When the mediator evaluated the merits of the case, no negative effects on parties' perceptions of mediation or the mediator were observed in any of the studies. Instead . . . parties were more likely to say that the mediation process was fair and the mediator understood their views. They were also more likely to say that they had enough opportunity to express their views, had input in determining the outcome, were satisfied with the outcome and gained a better understanding of their own interests. Importantly, parties who reported that the mediator evaluated the case did not feel more pressure to settle.

In contrast, when the mediator recommended a particular settlement, parties were *less* likely to say that the mediation process was fair and the mediator was neutral [and] parties were more likely to feel pressured to settle. When the mediator suggested possible options for settlement, parties were more likely to say that the mediation process was fair and that the mediator was neutral and understood their view. By far the strongest and most consistently positive effects on parties' perceptions were observed when the mediator encouraged the parties to express their feelings and summarized what they said. (These actions were examined only in the domestic relations studies.)

In summary, if the mediators evaluated the merits of the case and even made some suggestions about possible settlements, the parties had more favorable perceptions of mediation with virtually no negative repercussions, as long as the mediators did not recommend a specific settlement.

Questions

9. According to the ABA and Professor Wissler, which evaluative interventions are more dangerous and which less so? Assuming that parties do not object to certain forms of evaluation, does this answer Professor Love's concerns?

10. Imagine that you are counsel for MIT in the student death case described in Chapter 5. Can you imagine circumstances in which you would want the mediator to give an evaluation? If so, what would you want evaluated?

11. Now assume that you are counsel for the plaintiffs in the same case. How, if at all, might an evaluation be useful to your side?

12. If you agree with Professor Love, how would you want a mediator to respond to a situation in which you and your opposing counsel disagreed vehemently about the likely outcome at trial and you thought the other lawyer was being unrealistic? What if your own client appeared to be overly optimistic?

Problem

Read the following exchanges, taken from the mediation of a commercial breach of warranty case. The plaintiff entered the mediation with a demand of $1.5 million, based on out-of-pocket damages of about $250,000, an additional $200,000 in intangible damages, and a demand for treble damages under a state unfair business practices statute. The defense had made no offer of settlement prior to the litigation. The mediator formed an initial impression that the plaintiff would face significant obstacles in proving liability and find it difficult to establish damages beyond the out-of-pocket sum. As to each exchange, ask yourself:

- Is the mediator here "evaluating" or only "reality testing"?
- If so, what issues are being evaluated?
- Is the mediator acting in a manner likely to incur resentment?

a. A Caucus Meeting with the Defense

Mediator: Well, all right, you heard the frustration from the plaintiff side, and you said you were surprised by it. What I'm hearing from [the vice president of the plaintiff company] is that he feels that there has never been a dialogue, acknowledgment of their difficulties and, most importantly to them, I guess, an offer of cash to settle this dispute. I'm hearing from you that you are not willing to make a specific settlement offer at this point. If you can't authorize me to bring back a specific number to the plaintiff . . . what I'd like to have is a feel for the range that you are in that I could communicate to them, so that they would have a sense of where things are going.

Defense counsel: We will respond if they come down to a range of reasonable-ness, but their demand of $1.5 million is just in the stratosphere. I know that you're experienced, and I'm going to rely on you to digest what our view of the damages are and speak to them and maybe tell them what the real world is like: A million five is just not the real world.

Mediator: Well, what if the plaintiff were willing at this point to accept an amount that would allow them to recoup their out-of-pocket costs, and were perhaps looking for a little bit extra to put away in case their soft damages become a reality: Would you think that was a more reasonable place for them to be?

Defense counsel: Well, that would be a more reasonable place for them to *start*, and then we have to discount that number for the risk that they won't be able to prove liability at all.

b. Meeting with the Plaintiff

Plaintiff counsel: The bottom line is — what is their bottom line? What's their offer? That's what we have been trying to get at for two years.

Mediator: I think there is a number that they would pay, which maybe will turn out to be a number that you would accept. But they haven't told me what it is yet. I don't think you're going to find out what they'll pay unless you get past this impasse. I see you as being at an impasse so far because they see you as "up in the clouds," and because you see them as completely recalcitrant "stones" who won't offer a thing. In fact, I don't see them as stones refusing to deal — I think they *will* deal. But they want to have some confidence that they are in the right universe with you, and if I can give them that confidence, then we'll get a number out of them. A better indication of what you're really looking for is what I need.

c. Second Meeting with the Defense

Mediator: What is it going to cost to try this case?

Defense counsel: Oh, about $25,000.

Mediator: Wow, that's a bargain . . . You really think you can do it for that?

Counsel: Most of the discovery is done, and my rates are reasonable.

Mediator: Well, you're going to need an expert . . . They'll get an expert . . . It'll get expensive.

d. Meeting with the Defense Late in the Process

Inside counsel: You don't have to do this now, but if at some point if you could explain to me if you think we are being too optimistic about our chances at trial. I just don't see very much risk here.

Mediator: Well, I think the following . . . So far, the court has been willing to accept the plaintiff's case on their "*res ipsa*" theory that incidents of this type just don't occur without somebody being negligent. It looks as if the judge will let the case go to the jury on that theory. As a result, I think you run the risk that the jury will seize the appealing simplicity of the plaintiff's argu-ment, and if it does it will find against you.

You have a credible, viable defense, and I think that this significantly reduces the likelihood that the plaintiff will prevail. But the likelihood that the other side will win on liability, given their *res ipsa* argument, is probably at least 50-50, and maybe better than that.

Note: Issues for Advocates

The use of evaluation also presents practical issues for lawyers. As counsel to a disputant you should think about the following questions:

- Do you want your mediator to give an evaluation at all?
- If the mediator does evaluate, at what point in the process and on what issues should she do so? Would you prefer to have the evaluation done in joint session or in caucus?
- Is the other side likely to ask for evaluative feedback? If so, how should you respond?
- Is the mediator likely to offer evaluative comments on her own initiative? What can you do to influence this?
- What do you want the mediator to see before making an evaluation?

We discuss how a lawyer can use evaluation to best advantage in Chapter 11.

PART

III

THE ADVOCATE'S ROLE

CHAPTER
10

Representing Clients: Preparation

The next two chapters focus on the lawyer's role in mediation. We have described how the mediation process can facilitate disputants' ability to communicate and bargain with each other. We now explore how advocates can use the process to best advantage.

Lawyers' expectations upon entering mediation, and the tactics they use when working with mediators, are changing in significant ways. A decade ago lawyers approached mediation like processes with which they were familiar — direct bargaining and settlement conferences conducted by a judge.

In this traditional model, assent to mediation is a signal: By committing to engage in an intensive and expensive process, parties confirm to each other that they are serious about settling. Lawyers who embrace this model often see mediation as a way to bargain competitively with less risk of impasse than direct negotiation. The process tends to be dominated by legal arguments and exchanges of money offers in a caucus format. If, as often occurs, positional tactics lead to impasse, the mediator may take the lead and evaluate the case or suggest a settlement, which often amounts to a take-it-or-leave-it offer to the litigants.

This concept of mediation is still prevalent, but lawyers increasingly approach the process in other ways. They are more likely to use mediators in a variety of roles, supporting both competitive and creative strategies. Good advocates see themselves as bargaining not only with the other side but also with the mediator in what becomes a three-sided process. Attorneys may negotiate with a mediator, for example, over what he will say to their opponent ("I'd prefer if you stressed that . . ."), ask for information ("Has he calmed down yet?"), and bargain over tactics ("We'd like you to hold off on giving an evaluation for now."). Indeed, mediated negotiations sometimes have more than three sides; a lawyer might, for example, enlist a mediator to help persuade her client to compromise. We explore the practical questions raised by attorney tactics in Chapter 11 and ethical issues in Chapter 15.

A. An Overview

1. Identify Your Goals

The first issue when planning for mediation is your client's goal in the process. Are you seeking the best possible money outcome? An imaginative solution?

Repair of a relationship? Your objective should influence the approach you take to the process and how you relate to the mediator.

If your goal is to solve a problem or repair a relationship, you can treat the mediator almost as a member of your team, revealing interests and soliciting the neutral's advice about how to achieve them, and if the focus is on relationship repair, both lawyer and mediator may gradually withdraw to give the parties an opportunity to reconnect.

If, however, your goal is to get the best possible money outcome, your relationship with a mediator will be more complex. You can continue to take advantage of the neutral's knowledge, for example, by asking about hidden obstacles, and as long as you employ principled bargaining techniques you and the neutral can work together cooperatively. At the point, however, that you begin to compete with the other side for the best possible terms, your goals and those of the neutral are no longer the same, because the mediator cannot take sides.

Legal mediators have significant power, whether or not they decide to use it. Although mediators cannot compel parties to settle, they can greatly influence the *process* of bargaining, opening opportunities for advocates to mold the process to meet their clients' needs. Whatever your goals, you can use the mediation process to your advantage by approaching it actively and exploiting its special characteristics.

Questions

1. What would you have said before taking this course was the typical goal of a lawyer settling a lawsuit? Has your perspective changed?
2. What do you think the typical client in civil litigation wants to achieve through mediation?

Problem

Your client is a business in a dispute with a supplier of software services over the quality of the supplier's performance under a contract. Given the expected costs of litigating the issue, you have recommended that the client consider mediating before a complaint is filed, and the client has reluctantly agreed.

The client sees the goal as simply to collect as much as possible for the interruptions and lost profits caused by the supplier's bad work, and has estimated damages at $1.5 million. The client would also like to recoup as much as possible of the roughly $500,000 it has paid the supplier so far, and secure cancellation of its obligation to pay $200,000 more due under the contract terms.

You see the merits of the case as doubtful. The rupture seems to have been caused more by ambiguities in the scope of work in the contract and the rather rigid approach taken by your client's IT director than by lack of competence in the supplier — although the supplier's performance can certainly be faulted. You also doubt that, as a practical matter, you could collect most of the past payments even if you won. You see ways in which the supplier could continue to provide services to your client, and think that this might be more effective as compensation than a legal judgment.

1. What problems might you encounter in raising your concerns with the client?
2. What could you say to the client about goals in this mediation and how to accomplish them?

2. An Overview of Strategy

We believe that over time more lawyers and parties will come to view mediation as a method to solve problems. At present, however, most attorneys in mediation are litigators who tend to see the process as a way to facilitate competitive bargaining over money. To prepare for what you are likely to encounter in practice, we examine how counsel can approach a legal mediation process that includes a large element of competitive bargaining. To provide you with tools to adapt to the future, we also discuss how to represent a client in a problem-solving process.

a. Commercial Mediation Processes

We begin with a reading that focuses on some errors an adversarial mindset can produce. Inherent in listing errors are messages about what lawyers can do to be effective. As you read, think about these questions.

Questions

3. Have you made any of the mistakes Arnold describes in an exercise in this course?
4. Which errors do you think you are most likely to make in an actual case?

❖ **Tom Arnold,** *Twenty Common Errors in Mediation Advocacy*

13 Alternatives 69 (1995)

Trial lawyers who are unaccustomed to being mediation advocates often miss important opportunities. Here are twenty common errors, and ways to correct them.

Problem: Wrong Client in the Room

CEOs settle more cases than vice presidents, house counsel, or other agents. Why? For one thing, they don't need to worry about criticism back at the office.

Any lesser agent, even with explicit "authority," typically must please a constituency which was not a participant in the give and take of the mediation. That makes it hard to settle cases.

A client's personality also can be a factor. A "Rambo" who is highly self-confident, aggressive, critical, unforgiving, or self-righteous doesn't tend to be conciliatory. The best peace-makers show patience, creativity and sometimes tolerance for the mistakes of others. Of course, it also helps to know the subject.

Problem: Wrong Lawyer in the Room

Many capable trial lawyers are so confident that they can persuade a jury of anything (after all, they've done it before) that they discount the importance of preserving relationships, as well as the common exorbitant costs and emotional drain of litigation. They can smell a "win" in the court room, and so approach mediation with a measure of ambivalence.

Transactional lawyers, in contrast, having less confidence in their trial outcome, sometimes are better mediation counsel. At a minimum, parties should look for sensitive, flexible, understanding people who will do their homework, no matter what their job experience. Good preparation makes for more and better settlements. A lawyer who won't prepare is the wrong lawyer. Good mediation lawyers also should be good risk evaluators and not averse to making reasonable risk assumptions.

Problem: Wrong Mediator in the Room

Some mediators are generous about lending their conference rooms, but bring nothing to the table. Some of them determine their view of the case and like an arbitrator urge the parties to accept that view without exploring likely win-win alternatives. The best mediators can work within a range of styles. . . . Ideally, mediators should fit the mediation style to the case and the parties before them, often moving from style to style as a mediation progresses, relatively more facilitative at the beginning and more instructive or directive as the end comes into view. Masters of the questioning process can render valuable services whether or not they have relevant substantive expertise.

When do the parties need an expert? When do they want an evaluative mediator, or someone of relevant technical experience who can cast meaningful lights and shadows on the merits of the case and alternative settlements? It may not always be possible to know and . . . fit the choice of mediator to your case. But the wrong mediator may fail to get a settlement another mediator might have finessed.

Problem: Wrong Case

Almost every type of case, from antitrust or patent infringement to unfair competition and employment disputes, is a likely candidate for mediation. Occasionally, cases don't fit the mold, not because of the substance of the dispute, but because one or both parties want to set a precedent. For example, a franchisor that needs a legal precedent construing a key clause that is found in 3,000 franchise agreements might not want to submit the case to mediation. Likewise, an infringement suit early in the life of an uncertain patent might be better resolved in court; getting the Federal Circuit stamp of validity could generate industry respect not obtainable from ADR.

Problem: Omitting Client Preparation

Lawyers should educate their clients about the process and the likely questions the mediator will ask. At the same time, they need to understand that the other party (rather than the mediator) should be the focus of each side's presentation.

Problem: Not Letting a Client Open for Herself

At least as often as not, letting the properly coached client do most or even all of the opening, and tell the story in her own words, works much better than lengthy openings by the lawyer.

Problem: Addressing the Mediator Instead of the Other Side

Most lawyers open the mediation with a statement directed at the mediator, comparable to opening statements to a judge or jury. Highly adversarial in tone, it overlooks the interests of the other side that gave rise to the dispute. Why is this strategy a mistake? The "judge" or "jury" you should be trying to persuade in mediation is not so much the mediator as the adversary. If you want to make the other party sympathetic to your cause, most often at least it is best not to hurt him. For the same reason, plenary sessions should demonstrate your client's humanity, respect, warmth, apologies, and sympathy. Stay away from inflammatory issues, which are better addressed by the mediator in private caucuses with the other side.

Problem: Making the Lawyer the Center of the Process

Unless the client is highly unappealing or inarticulate, the client should be the center of the process. The company representative for the other side may not have attended depositions, so is unaware of the impact your client could have on a judge or jury if the mediation fails. People pay more attention to appealing plaintiffs, so show them off.

Prepare the client to speak and be spoken to by the mediator and the adversary. He should be able to explain why he feels the way he does, why he is or is not responsible, and why any damages he *caused* are great or only peanuts. But he should also consider extending empathy to the other party.

Problem: Failure to Use Advocacy Tools Effectively

You'll want to prepare your materials for maximum persuasive impact. Exhibits, charts, and copies of relevant cases or contracts with key phrases highlighted can be valuable visual aids. A ninety-second video showing one or more key witnesses in depositions making important admissions, followed by a readable-sized copy of an important document with some relevant language underlined, can pack a punch.

Problem: Timing Mistakes

Get and give critical discovery, but don't spend exorbitant time or sums in discovery and trial prep before seeking mediation. Mediation can identify what's truly necessary discovery and avoid unnecessary discovery.

One of my own war stories: With a mediation under way and both parties relying on their perception of the views of a certain neutral vice president who had no interest in the case, I leaned over, picked up the phone, called the vice president, introduced myself as the mediator, and asked whether he could give us a deposition the following morning. "No," said he, "I've got a board meeting at 10:00." "How about 7:30 A.M., with a one-hour limit?" I asked. "It really is pretty important that this decision not be delayed." The parties took the deposition and settled the case before the 10:00 board meeting.

Problem: Failure to Listen to the Other Side

Many lawyers and clients seem incapable of giving open-minded attention to what the other side is saying. That could cost a settlement.

Problem: Failure to Identify Perceptions and Motivations

Seek first to understand, only then to be understood. [B]rainstorm to determine the other party's motivations and perceptions. Prepare a chart summarizing how your adversary sees the issues: Part of preparing for media- tion is to understand your adversary's perceptions and motivations, perhaps even listing them in chart form. Here is an example, taken from a recent technology dispute:

Plaintiff's Perceptions:	*Defendant's Perceptions:*
Defendant entered the business because of my sound analysis of the market, my good judgment and convictions about the tech- nology.	I entered the business based on my own independent analysis of the market and the appropriate technology that was different from plaintiff's. . . .
Defendant used me by pretending to be interested in doing business with me.	Plaintiff misled me with exagger- ated claims that turned out to be false.
Defendant made a low-ball offer for my valuable technology. Another company paid me my asking price.	I made plaintiff a fair offer; I later paid less for alternative technol- ogy that was better.

Problem: Hurting, Humiliating, Threatening, or Commanding

Don't poison the well from which you must drink to get a settlement. That means you don't hurt, humiliate, or ridicule the other folks. Avoid pejoratives like "malingerer," "fraud," "cheat," "crook," or "liar." You can be strong on what your evidence will be and still be a decent human being. All settlements are based upon trust to some degree. If you anger the other side, they won't trust you. This inhibits settlement.

The same can be said for threats, like a threat to get the other lawyer's license revoked for pursuing such a frivolous cause, or for his grossly inaccurate pleadings. Ultimatums destroy the process and destroy credibility. Yes, there is a time in mediation to walk out — whether or not you plan to return. But a series of ultimatums, or even one ultimatum, most often is counterproductive.

Problem: The Backwards Step

A party who offered to pay $300,000 before the mediation, but comes to the mediation table willing to offer only $200,000, injures its own credibility and engenders bad feelings from the other side. Without some clear and dramatic reasons for the reduction in the offer, it can be hard to overcome the damage done.

The backwards step is a powerful card to play at the right time — a walk away without yet walking out. But powerful devices are also dangerous. There are few productive occasions to use this one, and they tend to come late in a mediation. A rule of thumb: Unless you're an expert negotiator, don't do it.

Problem: Too Many People

Advisors — people to whom the decision-maker must display respect and courtesy, people who feel that since they are there they must put in their two bits worth — all delay mediation immeasurably. A caucus that with only one lawyer and vice president would take twenty minutes, with five people could take an hour and twenty minutes. What could have been a one-day mediation stretches to two or three.

This is one context in which I use the "one martini lunch." Once I think that everyone present understands all the issues, I will send principals who have been respectful out to negotiate alone. Most come back within three hours with an oral expression of settlement. Of course, the next step is to brush up on details they overlooked, draw up a written agreement and get it signed. But usually those finishing touches don't ruin the deal.

Problem: Closing Too Fast

A party who opens at $1 million and moves immediately to $500,000 gives the impression of having more to give. Rightly or wrongly, the other side probably will not accept the $500,000 offer because they expect more give. By contrast, moving from $1 million to $750,000, $600,000, $575,000, $560,000, $550,000, sends no message of yield below $500,000, and may induce a $500,000 proposal that can be accepted. The "dance" is part of communication. Skip the dance, lose the communication, and risk losing settlement at your own figure.

Problem: Failure to Truly Close

Unless parties have strong reasons to "sleep on" their agreement, to further evaluate the deal, or to check on possibly forgotten details, it is better to get some sort of enforceable contract written and signed before the parties separate. Too often, when left to think overnight and draft tomorrow, the parties think of new ideas that delay or prevent closing.

Problem: Breaching Confidentiality

Sometimes parties to mediation unthinkingly, or irresponsibly, disclose in open court information revealed confidentially in a mediation. When information is highly sensitive, consider keeping it confidential with the mediator. Or if revealed to the adversary in a mediation where the case did not settle, consider moving before the trial begins for an order in limine to bind both sides to the confidentiality agreement.

Problem: Lack of Patience and Perseverance

The mediation "dance" takes time. Good mediation advocates have patience and perseverance.

Problem: Misunderstanding Conflict

A dispute is a problem to be solved together, not a combat to be won.

b. Problem-Solving Approaches

> ❖ Harold Abramson, *MEDIATION REPRESENTATION: ADVOCATING AS A PROBLEM-SOLVER IN ANY COUNTRY OR CULTURE*
>
> ──────────────────────────────
>
> **1 (NITA, 2010)**

The mediation process is indisputably different from other dispute resolution processes like arbitrations and judicial trials where the third party makes decisions. The strategies and techniques that have proven effective in these other forums do not work optimally in mediation. You need a different representation approach . . . Instead of advocating as a zealous adversary, you should advocate as a zealous problem-solver.

. . . Many sophisticated and experienced litigators realize that mediation calls for a different approach, but they still muddle through the mediation sessions, guided by familiar approaches that have worked well in other forums like arbitration and court. . . .

As a problem-solver who is creative, you do more than try to merely settle the dispute. You search for solutions that go beyond the traditional ones based on rights, obligations, and precedent. [To do this you] develop a collaborative relationship with the other side and the mediator, and participate throughout the process in a way that may produce solutions that are inventive as well as enduring. . . .

You should avoid the hybrid approach [of mixing creative and positional techniques,] despite the claims of supporters that it is the best one due to its flexibility . . . You should be a persistent problem-solver. It is relatively easy to engage in simple problem-solving moves such as responding to a demand with the question "why?" in order to bring to the surface the other party's interests. But it is much more difficult to stick to this approach throughout the mediation process, especially when faced with an adversarial, positional opponent. Trust the problem-solving approach. And, when the other side engages in adversarial tactics or tricks—a frequent occurrence in practice, you should react with problem-solving responses, responses that might even convert the other side into a problem-solver.

You should even strive to create a problem-solving process when your mediator does not. Your mediator may fail to follow a problem-solving approach (despite professing to foster one) because he lacks the depth of experience or training to tenaciously maintain a consistent approach throughout the mediation process. Or, your mediator may candidly disclose his practice of deliberately switching approaches based on the needs of the parties — a philosophy that I have already suggested undermines the problem-solving approach . . .

Finally, I need to respond to the skeptics who think that problem-solving does not work for most legal cases because their cases are primarily about money, plaintiffs only want money, and the negotiation is only about how to get the most money or to pay the least amount. They see no potential to uncover creative solutions. For the skeptics, I offer four responses.

First, the endless debate about whether or not legal disputes are primarily about money is distracting. Whether a dispute is largely about money varies from case to case as experiences and studies have demonstrated. Second, you have little chance of discovering whether your client's dispute is about more than money if you approach the dispute as if it were only about money . . . Third, if the dispute or any remaining issues at the end of the day turn out to be predominately about money, then at least you followed a representation approach that may have created a hospitable environment for dealing with the moneyed issues. A hospitable environment can even be beneficial when there is no expectation of a continuing relationship between the disputing parties.

Fourth and most importantly, the problem-solving approach provides a framework for resolving money issues . . . If [it fails], you then might turn to a positional dance, but one that has been refined to serve a problem-solving process by focusing on objective standards and justifications while avoiding tricks.

Skeptics also frequently inquire whether this approach will work if the other side has not read this book. The answer is yes it can, as will be illustrated in each chapter. And, I will go one step further. Even if the other side has read this book and firmly rejected this approach, the representation framework still can work . . . In short, the problem-solving approach provides a complete approach to representation that can guide you throughout the mediation process. . . .

B. Entering the Process

1. Should You Mediate?

The first issue is whether to mediate at all. You should recommend mediation to a client if the following conditions are met:

- There is a reasonable chance that the client can obtain a more valuable result by negotiating than by litigating, considering the risk and cost of continuing the conflict;
- It is difficult or impossible for the parties to negotiate directly; and
- It appears likely that mediation can help the parties overcome the obstacles that are frustrating the bargaining process

It is worth remembering that people can elect to mediate for reasons other than settlement, for instance, to set up an efficient discovery plan or improve a relationship. The fact that complete agreement does not appear realistic, in other words, is not always a reason to reject mediation.

There are also reasons why you might reasonably recommend that a client not enter mediation, at least at the present time. These factors — for example, the need to establish a benchmark or precedent — are described in Chapter 5.

2. If So, When?

Assuming that mediation is appropriate, when is the right time to enter the process? There may be no choice, because your client is required to mediate by a contract or a court order. If you have a choice, however, the issue of timing depends on your goals. If your primary objective is to solve a problem or repair the parties' relationship, it is usually best to mediate quickly. If not, the parties' positions are likely to harden, and one party may replace the relationship with a new one, making a repair much more difficult.

If, however, your client's priority is to obtain the best possible monetary outcome, then the issue of timing is more complex. By delaying mediation a lawyer may be able to improve a client's bargaining position, for instance, by winning a decision in court. But litigating is expensive and the opponent may adopt the same strategy, increasing costs for both sides and making a settlement even more difficult.

Disputants tend to enter legal mediation at particular points, often when they face an increase in cost or a serious risk of loss. Natural points to discuss settlement are before a formal legal action is filed, after initial proceedings are complete, and in the shadow of a trial or court ruling.

Before a legal action is filed.   Parties may decide to mediate before entering litigation. By doing so each side accepts a trade-off: It has less information, but avoids the cost and disruption of legal proceedings. In recent years parties have become increasingly willing to mediate before filing a legal action.

After initial proceedings.   Another option is to file a court action and take the initial steps needed to protect one's position, gather information, and frame the issues. Once this is accomplished, however, the parties may elect to mediate. Parties may file suit and undertake limited discovery, for instance, document requests, but mediate before undertaking costly, adversarial processes such as depositions. One commentator has noted that:

> One approach . . . is to follow the 80-20 rule: 80 percent of the relevant information that parties learn from discovery often comes from the first 20 percent of the

money they spend. Tracking down the last, difficult-to-obtain data is the most expensive part. . . . If parties conduct initial core discovery, they may find all they need to know in order to resolve the case appropriately. Following this approach, parties can agree to take abbreviated depositions of the key witnesses and then proceed to ADR. . . . Often this will give them everything they need to determine their negotiation position with reasonable accuracy. (Senger 2004)

In the shadow of a significant ruling.   Lawyers traditionally have waited until just before trial or another significant litigation event to pursue settlement discussions. First, as trial approaches attorneys must prepare intensively, imposing costs on them and/or their clients. Second, trial represents the ultimate win-lose event, triggering strong feelings of loss aversion. Finally, there are cultural assumptions about the "right" time to broach settlement: In the legal community this used to mean that mentioning mediation early in a case was considered a sign of weakness, whereas raising the issue on the eve of trial was acceptable, an assumption that no longer appears true.

3. Initiating the Process

a. Convincing Clients or Opponents to Mediate

The biggest single obstacle to entering mediation is probably the concern of many parties and lawyers that their opponent will interpret an expression of interest in settlement as a signal that a party does not believe in its legal case. There are ways to avoid or lessen this concern, however.

Point out that settlement discussions are inevitable.   You might note that you like to litigate — it is your profession, after all. But since very few cases go to trial, it is very likely that the parties will talk settlement at some point. Why not explore it now and save everyone cost and delay?

Rely on a policy.   A corporation or law firm can adopt a policy of exploring settlement early in every dispute. Lawyers can then avoid the implication that they are suggesting mediation only because their legal position is weak.

Ask a provider organization to take the initiative.   Another option is to ask a mediator or a provider organization to suggest mediation to an adversary. Your opponent will probably know that you initiated the approach, but using a third party allows you to avoid having to "sell" mediation yourself.

Cite a rule.   Some courts require lawyers to negotiate or mediate before filing a case or going to trial. If so, an attorney can suggest that the parties design their own process rather than be pushed into a rigid judicial program. Even if a court does not have such a requirement, a lawyer might privately ask a court official to suggest mediation to the parties.

These suggestions assume that the challenge is to persuade the opponent to mediate. Often, however, the barrier is a lawyer's own client. In the words of litigator David Stern:

There are no hard and fast rules as to when that perfect moment has arrived to mediate, but one point is clear. Before you begin, recognize that the first obstacle to starting the dialogue early may well be your own client, particularly if you have not represented him in the past. He may wonder if you lack confidence in yourself or the case if you push for settlement too early. On the other hand, if you don't mention settlement to the more sophisticated client, he may well wonder whether you are looking to "milk" a case that will likely never be tried. Begin with the adversary only after you have reached a consensus with your own client. (Stern 1998)

b. Drafting an Effective Contract to Mediate

There are two basic situations in which a lawyer must deal with contracts concerning mediation:

- A dispute exists and the parties have agreed to mediate, but they need to decide how the process will be conducted.
- The parties have no present dispute but wish to commit to mediate any controversy that may arise in the future.

Agreements to mediate an existing dispute

If parties have agreed to mediate an existing dispute, they can benefit by entering into an agreement that covers the following issues:

- What rules of confidentiality will apply to the process?
  - Can a statement or document used in the mediation be used in a later judicial proceeding?
  - Can information provided in mediation be disclosed to anyone outside the process or the media?
- Who will pay the cost of mediation?
- How can a party terminate its participation in the process?
- What rules will apply? For example can the mediator offer an opinion about the legal merits without the parties' consent?
- Will litigation be suspended or legal claims preserved while mediation occurs?

Most mediation providers have standard forms that deal with these issues, and attorneys ordinarily execute such forms without changes. An example of a form mediation agreement appears in the Appendix.

The most common area of disagreement about terms of mediation concerns how the parties will share the cost of the process. If, for instance, a plaintiff sues three related corporations represented by one law firm, should the plaintiff bear one half and the defendants the other half, or should the defendants pay three-quarters of the cost? Mediators are usually reluctant to become involved in such disputes, but they may be willing to facilitate a discussion about allocation of the cost if the total amount is not in dispute — that is, if they do not have a personal interest in the outcome.

Agreements to mediate future disputes

Parties entering into contracts may include a provision that commits them to mediate any future dispute in their relationship. Businesses in an ongoing relationship, for example, are likely to encounter unforeseen changes and benefit if they have a process to resolve such problems quickly and amicably. Examples of a mediation clause and a "multistep" clause that calls for negotiation followed by mediation and arbitration appear in the Appendix.

Once a dispute arises, one of the parties to an agreement may wish to mediate while the other does not. The party favoring mediation may decide not to seek to enforce the obligation to mediate, reasoning that it is useless to force someone to engage in mediation against their will. Alternatively, a party that does not want to mediate may decide that it is easier to go through a mediation session than to argue about it.

If, however, one party demands to mediate and the other refuses, a court may be asked to enforce the obligation. At first courts refused to enforce mediation clauses, concluding that it would be impossible or burdensome to determine whether a party had participated in mediation in good faith. Recently, however, courts have become more willing to enforce such obligations, at least where a party has refused to participate at all. Among the sanctions courts may impose are:

- If a plaintiff fails to mediate, dismiss or suspend the legal case until the plaintiff carries out its obligation.
- If a party fails to appear at a mediation session, require the offender to pay the mediation costs and perhaps also the legal fee of the other side's attorney.
- If a party refuses to mediate and later prevails in court, deny it costs or attorneys' fees it would otherwise be awarded.

To be enforceable an agreement to mediate must be clear. To accomplish this:

- Use simple language and set clear timeframes,
- Avoid ambiguity: In particular, keep the commitment to mediate separate from any obligation to arbitrate,
- Describe specifically what remedies or penalties a party may recover if the other side violates the agreement, and
- Provide a mediation process that is fair in light of the nature of the underlying transaction. (Katz 2008)

c. Dealing with Obligations Created by Law or Judicial Order

Your client may be required to go into mediation by a law, court rule, or judicial order. If so, consider the following points:

- Will you have a role in choosing the neutral? Some programs designate a specific person, while others require parties to select a mediator from a list of candidates.

- Who will be required to attend? Some programs require parties to send representatives with "full settlement authority," which can create problems for large organizations with cases pending in several court systems.
- Will you be permitted to provide a statement of your case or documents to the mediator in advance?
- Will you be required to pay for the process? If so, how much?
- Will you be required to mediate in any specific manner or time period?
- Will statements and documents used in the mediation be confidential and not admissible in later court proceedings?

If you are not satisfied with the court's program, consider whether you can modify the process, either by agreement with the other side or through a request to the court. If you do not want to engage in court mediation at all, ask:

- Is it possible to decline to participate, or to apply for an exemption from the program?
- What is the minimum you must do to comply with the program rules?
- What penalties are likely if you do not comply?

C. Shaping the Process

1. Select the Right Mediator

a. Identify the Best Person

The most important issue in designing a mediation, apart from obtaining the presence of the right party representatives, is to select the right mediator. In many cities there is a pool of potential mediators who vary greatly in experience, background, and style of mediation. You will want to find the person whose qualities best match the needs of your case.

Begin by thinking about what is preventing the parties from negotiating effectively. If, for example, the problem is that your opponent (or your own client) has an abrasive personality, then you will want a mediator with strong process skills. If the major obstacle to agreement is that your opponent has misjudged the strength of its legal case, a former judge may be most effective. If a party is willing to settle, but needs to justify a difficult compromise, someone with a strong reputation who can endorse the decision may be the best choice. Often more than a single barrier exists, calling for a mediator with a blend of qualities.

You will remember from Chapter 7 that when researchers asked the lawyers who hire some of America's most successful business mediators what qualities they value in a neutral, the central conclusion was that "a — if not the — core element in mediator success is the mediator's ability to establish a relationship of trust and confidence with the disputing parties." (Goldberg & Shaw 2007) The single most important factor in choosing among qualified mediators is thus how well they will be able to relate to the parties, including your own client. Will your client feel more confidence in a former business executive or an experienced litigator? Will the key decision maker on the other side defer to an ex-judge? How effective will a candidate be at establishing rapport with strangers quickly?

To decide whether a candidate possesses the necessary qualities, you and the opposing attorney may wish to interview him by telephone. Some mediators refuse to talk with lawyers in advance, but many neutrals are willing to do so, feeling more freedom to discuss a case as a potential mediator than as an arbitrator

b. Bargain for Your Choice

Bargaining for a mediator is like other negotiations, except that finding the right neutral can be a "win" for both sides. Commonly, each of the lawyers prepares a list of candidates and they exchange names; sometimes a name appears on both lists, but if not, the lawyers discuss which of the listed candidates to choose or add names to the pool.

Another option is to suggest that the opposing lawyer prepare a list of candidates. If the lawyer suggests someone whom you also would nominate, you can obtain a good mediator who already enjoys the confidence of the other side. If you respect the opposing lawyer, you might even allow her to select the mediator, while you retain only the right to veto a choice. Allowing an opponent to choose your mediator may seem strange, but if your goal is to persuade the other party, the most effective mediator may be someone they themselves have chosen

Example: In the student death case described in Chapter 5, the defense attorney decided to allow the Kruegers' lawyer to select the mediator. In part this was because they insisted on the right to do so and in part because the defense respected plaintiff counsel's ability to choose wisely.

The Kruegers selected a mediator who regularly handled personal injury claims for plaintiffs, but they had other concerns as well. It was important that the mediator be willing to work to customize the process, and that he or she be respected by defense counsel so the University would listen to his or her recommendations. Plaintiff counsel also knew that the discussions would be extremely emotional, and it was therefore crucial that the mediator have the ability to absorb and manage intense anger and grief.

The mediator's final qualification was unique: In a conversation with the mediator, the plaintiff lawyer discovered that he had once lost a college-age son himself.

Questions

5. Texas mediator Eric Galton has suggested that transactional lawyers are better advocates in mediation because "they negotiate better, more creatively and are more acutely aware of business solutions which may be advantageous to their clients."
   a. Assuming this is true, in what types of legal disputes would a transactional lawyer be best suited to represent clients in mediation or serve as a mediator?
   b. What might you sacrifice by selecting a transactional lawyer rather than a litigator as your representative in mediation?

6. Assume that the other side proposes a mediator and you learn that the opponent has mediated with this neutral more than a dozen times. What should you do in response? Should it matter if it is the opposing party or lawyer who has had experience with the neutral?
7. If you wish to propose a mediator with whom you have worked repeatedly, how might be a good way to do so?
8. Assume you represent a party in a role-play assigned by your teacher. You are in the process of selecting a neutral. What qualities would you look for in a mediator for the case? Obtain biographies of actual mediators in your community, decide whom you would prefer or object to, and prioritize the candidates in terms of attractiveness.
9. Can you think of a case in which the gender or race of the mediator might make a difference? If so, how would you handle neutral selection in such cases? If not, how would you respond if the other lawyer seemed to be taking race or gender into account?

2. Ensure the Presence of Necessary Participants

The presence of the right persons at the mediation table is crucial to the success of the process; indeed, the identity of the bargainers is often more important than the identity of the mediator. We have placed this issue after selecting a mediator, however, because once you have selected a mediator, you may be able to call on her help to get the right people at the table. Consider the following example from San Francisco mediator Jerry Spolter:

This may come as a surprise, but there is nothing wrong with communicating ex parte with a mediator or prospective mediator. In fact, it's usually the smart and right thing to do to secure the best result for your client. So don't be bashful. Talk to your mediator.

A recent mediation session I conducted highlights what can happen when you leave your mediator in the dark. Everything went great for about five hours. . . . The joint session was textbook material, with lots of helpful information exchanged; the private caucuses peeled away postured "positions" to reveal the parties' real interests. And then it happened: Although the physician accused of malpractice was in the room, the doc wouldn't make a move until his personal attorney gave the OK.

Unfortunately, the personal attorney was on a chairlift in the Sierra with a dead battery in her cell phone. And since this was a malpractice case requiring the doc's consent, "my" mediation was suddenly in trouble. To make matters worse, the doc's insurance representative had to consult two "invisible-hierarchy" decision-makers to discuss increasing authority.

If only I had received a heads-up beforehand, we could have resolved the authority problems in advance and taken advantage of the momentum we had generated that day to settle the case. (Instead, the parties are now scurrying around trying to acquire the necessary authority to put Humpty Dumpty back together again.)

Who the right people are in a particular case will depend again on your objectives. They may include:

- *Principals.* If the primary goal is to repair a personal relationship, then the presence of the principals, to talk through their problems and regain the ability to relate with each other, is usually essential. The same may be true when the outcome is intensely important to a party, as in a "bet the company" case.
- *Experts.* If the objective is to work out an imaginative solution, it is necessary to have people who are capable of thinking imaginatively, as well as experts who know enough to develop and assess options. Restructuring a contract, for example, may require the participation of financial, production, or marketing executives.
- *Persons with authority.* If the parties no longer have a relationship and there are no serious emotional issues, as occurs, for instance, when a company makes a routine claim against its insurance policy, then the primary concern is usually to be sure that each side's bargainer has the authority to agree to a substantial compromise.

Lawyers must sometimes bargain to insure that the other side, or even their own client, has someone at mediation with the knowledge and authority to make difficult decisions. A mediator can help with this task. When you ask a mediator for assistance in setting up the process, you benefit from several factors. First, having agreed to mediate, your opponent will feel an interest in maintaining a good relationship with the neutral. In addition, mediators are likely to show a bias toward inclusion: Better, the neutral will think, to bring in someone who later proves unnecessary than to lack a key decision maker at an important moment.

> *Example:* A software company sued a former employee in the Italian courts, arguing that he had violated a non-competition agreement by recruiting his former development team to join him at his new company. The parties agreed to mediate.
>
> The competitor company, a Polish entity, was not a party to the litigation, but its participation was essential to any settlement because it had agreed to indemnify the employee for any liability arising from his activities in recruiting employees. However, its chief executive refused to attend the mediation, saying that Rome was too far to travel and that in any event his company was not a party to the case.
>
> The plaintiff's lawyer asked the mediator to persuade the executive to come. He stressed how important his presence would be to the success of "our" case. The mediator responded to the challenge and contacted the competitor's CEO repeatedly. Although the executive refused to attend in person he agreed to join all sessions by video, and his participation proved crucial to reaching agreement.

Negotiators routinely claim to have "full authority," but in practice their ability to agree is usually limited. Disputants also routinely conceal their authority even from mediators, for fear that admitting to authority will be interpreted as a willingness to make concessions. To deal with this, ask opposing counsel who will attend for the other side, and check with your own client about their authority; a person's title and role may offer an indication of his ability to make a hard decision. But as the following story illustrates, it is sometimes difficult even to determine who can make a decision for your own client.

❖ **Bennett G. Picker,** *NAVIGATING RELATIONSHIPS: THE INVISIBLE BARRIERS TO RESOLUTION*

2 Amer. J. of Mediation 41 (2008)

Most mediation advocates and party representatives, when preparing for mediation, primarily focus on one relationship that significantly impacts resolution — the relationship between plaintiff and defendant.

A trial lawyer will often pause in the middle of a negotiation or mediation and wonder, "Why hasn't the other side made a realistic offer? Don't they understand their risk?" The question ignores the fact that "they" — those on the other side — frequently do not function as a cohesive unit with the capacity to either make a collective decision or speak with one voice.

For example in a recent mediation involving an alleged breach of a long-term supply agreement, the corporate plaintiff's representatives each entered the process with considerably different perspectives on the "ideal outcome" for the company. As the mediator, I spent well over an hour in a private caucus session with the company's CEO, CFO, general counsel and general manager. After exploring the positions and interests of the parties, we began discussing the plaintiff's response to a proposal by the defendant. Initially, the plaintiff's several representatives stood in total disagreement with each other.

The CEO argued that the defendant should pay a large sum of money, readily admitting that the result would directly affect the size of the bonus he would receive at the end of the year. The CFO expressed concern about the timing of any payment, conscious of maximizing reported earnings in the current year. The general counsel of the company warned that everyone in the room represented the "client" — the company — and had a duty as fiduciaries to maximize shareholder value [and] Wall Street values long-term streams of revenue more highly than a one-time payment of cash. . . . The general manager who originally determined that the defendant breached the contract simply wanted a court to affirm the breach had occurred and that she had made the correct decision.

During the caucus I conducted what was, in essence, an internal mediation with the plaintiff's representatives to get all of them on the same page. . . . Even though the CEO had the ultimate decision-making power in this dispute, internal differences of opinion presented a serious potential barrier to resolution — a barrier invisible to the defendant. . . .

To maximize the opportunity for success, advocates . . . should pay extra attention to the relationships among and between the representatives of the client. [C]ounsel to the parties [should] ask who in [their] company really "owns" the dispute. They can then assemble a team to define goals, discuss "authority," and try to align the varying interests and perspectives of the key players. . . .

Sometimes the key decision makers are not parties at all. A husband, for instance, might look to his wife for advice, or a company may be unable to make a deal without permission from its insurer. There is no easy way to resolve this issue. Wise lawyers know, however, that a mediator can help them obtain the participation of key persons.

Questions

10. Neutrals come to mediation from very different careers. What back-
    ground might make a mediator more or less willing to take active steps
    to bring the right people into the process?
11. How could you test for this quality when selecting a neutral?

3. Influence the Format

We have seen that mediation can occur in a wide variety of formats. If you see a
reason to change the "default" process, alert the mediator to this in advance.
Again, the choice depends on objectives.

- If the goal is to repair a relationship, you will probably want the clients to have
  as much opportunity to talk directly as possible. This suggests a longer
  opening session, private meetings between the principals, or both.
- In a highly emotional case it might be useful for a party to meet with the
  mediator ahead of time and for the neutral to carefully structure the party's
  interactions with the other side.
- In factually complex cases it may be necessary to arrange advance meetings
  and lengthy opening statements, perhaps supported by experts.
- Where the condition of property is at issue, as in construction and environmental disputes, it might make sense to take a site view.

Example: In the MIT-Krueger mediation the lawyers modified the format in
several ways:

- They divided the process into two days, the first day involving only lawyers and
  focused on legal arguments, and the second bringing together all the stakeholders and issues.
- To satisfy the Kruegers' need to feel the University was coming to them, the
  second meeting was held near the parents' home.
- To discourage a walkout and set an informal tone, the second session was held
  at a rural conference center.
- To create an opportunity for the parents to express their anger and grief, the
  mediator began the second day by having breakfast with the Kruegers and
  their lawyer.
- The "formal" mediation began with a joint session in which the parties could
  speak directly to each other and express emotions. The process then evolved
  into caucusing.
- At the end, the Kruegers and President Vest came together and hugged.

Very few cases are as emotional as the Krueger case, but the modifications give
a sense of how much freedom imaginative lawyers have to vary the format of
mediation to achieve their objectives.

Timing.   You and your opponent must also agree on a time period for the
mediation. Should it be scheduled for a few hours, one day, several days, or a
series of sessions over a longer period? The tension here is between allowing
enough time for the process to work and not encouraging the parties to put off
tough decisions. In general:

- One day is usually appropriate for a contract dispute, although the process may continue into the evening, and the party representatives should plan for this.
- Two days or more are sometimes necessary for construction cases, because they usually include several parties and present "mini-cases" over various aspects of a project.
- Exceptionally complex disputes, either in terms of the number of parties or the nature of the issues, may require several meetings over a period of weeks or months. Examples may include antitrust cases, public controversies, and environmental contamination claims.

When in doubt err on the side of allowing more time. You will always have the option to finish early, but reassembling the parties for another session can be difficult.

4. Deal with the Special Issues of Court-Mandated Mediation

The discussion to this point has assumed that you have freedom to design the mediation process in cooperation with the other side. Sometimes, however, your client may be required to engage in mediation by a contract clause or a court. In states such as Florida, Texas, and California, for example, most civil cases must go through mediation as a precondition to trial.

Courts may order parties to mediate but leave process choices to them, with court rules available only as a default. Many jurisdictions, however, impose significant restrictions on the process. Litigants might be able to opt out of such restrictions by agreement, but in the context of litigation this can be difficult to do.

If you have a case that is subject to mandatory mediation, whether by contract or court rule, ask yourself whether the mandated process is adequate and, if not, how to respond. In assessing adequacy, think about these issues:

- Will you have a role in choosing the neutral? Some programs require parties to select a mediator from panels. Others assign a mediator to each case, or give parties the option to select a private mediator themselves.
- Who will be required to be present? Many courts require parties to send representatives with "full settlement authority," creating serious problems for organizations with cases pending in several different jurisdictions.
- Will you be able to brief the mediator in advance?
- Will you be required to pay for the process? Some programs are free, whereas others use private neutrals.
- Will you be required to mediate within a limited time frame? Court-related mediation can range from an hour or less to a full day, with the option to extend by agreement. If the process is time-limited, even good mediators will feel pressure to "cut to the chase" to produce progress quickly, limiting consideration of broad issues.
- What confidentiality guarantees does the program offer?
- Can you modify the process by agreement? If so, will the other side agree to the changes you want?

If you do not want to mediate at all, or decide that the mandated process is inadequate, you should consider these questions:

- Is it possible to opt out or apply for an exemption?
- If not, what is the minimum you have to do to comply? (See the discussion of "good faith participation" requirements in Chapter 14.)
- Are there penalties for nonparticipation or noncompliance? Can the mediator report to the court concerning the parties' cooperation? Can the court ask the mediator to recommend how it should rule on unresolved issues, as occurs in some California family courts?

To gather information, talk with a local lawyer or program administrator and review the program rules. We discuss policy and legal issues presented by court-related mediation in Chapters 13 and 14.

D. Preparing to Mediate

To plan for mediation, think not only about what you will do as an advocate, but also about the roles you want your client and other team members to take. This includes at least three issues: developing a negotiation plan, considering whether to exchange information, and coaching your client.

1. Develop a Negotiating Plan

Texts often speak of the art of "mediation advocacy," but you now know that while lawyers may make semiformal opening statements, most of the process consists of a mixture of discussion and bargaining. You should plan for mediation in much the same way as for direct negotiation, and points made in the context of negotiation about preparation apply here as well. You will want, for example, to consider the parties' alternatives to agreement, principles that each side can cite, underlying interests, and potential options for settlement.

You should also, however, plan to take advantage of the special aspects of mediation — the presence of the neutral and the format of the process. The next chapter describes several ways in which lawyers can "borrow a mediator's powers." Here is advice from competitive and cooperative perspectives.

a. A Competitive Viewpoint

❖ Robert M. Smith, *ADVOCACY IN MEDIATION: A DOZEN SUGGESTIONS*

26 San Francisco Att'y 14 (June/July 2000)

Your strongest ally, if you can make him or her an ally, is the mediator. It is the mediator's neutral voice that is most powerful in carrying your argument to the other side. This is true even if the mediator asks a lawyer to put on the chalkboard the strongest points of the case, then unveils the board to the other side.

The mediator knows you — indeed, everyone — is trying to manipulate, or con, him or her. Manipulation is as much a given as the coffee machine. But often — perhaps usually — the mediator is aware of the con. Good advocates know when to stop the con, show some trust, and make a straighter, and more reasonable, argument. Honesty can buy an advantage.

Play the Odds

When you go to a commercial mediation, there is, statistically, close to an 85 percent chance of settling the case. This means you should probably prepare as if the mediation session will be the last step in the case, and prepare your client accordingly. To tell the client, for example, that we are all just going through the motions and then find yourself in serious end-game bargaining is not prudent.

Black-Tie Affair

Often — we all know this — lawsuits bobble along like a play in search of a theater; they need a defining event before both parties and lawyers get serious.

Mediation is an event — probably the event. If the mediator is effective, everyone will focus on the matter in a way that they haven't before.

The Art of Scribbling

This is the time to do your best brief. Mediators read them — they get paid to. And this may be all they know about the case before you troop in. The mediator is likely to ensure that the parties, as well as the lawyers, see the brief and consider your most forceful arguments, or what a neutral sees as your most forceful arguments. It may be worth considering their impact on the plaintiff or the defendant when sections are pointed out to them.

Sharing Can Be Beautiful

You might consider whether you want to give a copy of the brief to the other side, as well as to the mediator. But you can give only a portion of the brief to the other side — or the whole brief, with only a secret annex going to the mediator (for instance, "I think the claims rep was himself a party to a similar squabble two years ago"). The process is what you make of it. Flexible, it bends to your imaginative sculpting.

We Don't Accept Cash Here

Some have pointed out the power of an apology, appropriately timed and tendered. But advocacy may also involve asking for a non-economic concession — even one you know you likely won't get; it may put other demands in a new, or reframed, perspective.

About Reframing

Once discussions have foundered, the mediator knows that the parties are not likely to move on their own. It is up to the mediator to step back and find a new perspective or approach. You should anticipate the possible reframing, or you may not like the suddenly unfamiliar perspective. Be reframed, not hung.

A las Cinco de la Tarde

"At five in the afternoon" is a repetitive line in a poem by Federico Garcia Lorca. It has to do with a death, not mediation. But I sometimes think of it when discussions bog down after hours of negotiation because it is about five in the afternoon that the role of poetic imagination is sometimes called into play in mediations. You hope the mediator did not lose his or her imagination in the second year of law school; part of what you are paying for is creativity. But when the clock strikes — or beeps — in a soundless room, your own imaginative suggestion may prove sublime advocacy.

b. A Problem-Solving Approach

The following reading is addressed to problem-solving advocates, but applies to other styles as well.

❖ **Harold Abramson, MEDIATION REPRESENTATION: ADVOCATING AS A PROBLEM-SOLVER IN ANY COUNTRY OR CULTURE**

283 (NITA, 2010)

[*Note:* Professor Abramson recommends that advocates begin preparation by analyzing the overall nature of the dispute, doing necessary research, and resolving issues of structure such as who will attend. Having done this, lawyers should consider the following issues. — Eds.]

Part 1

Prepare for Negotiation

1. Identify Interests to Meet

    ☐ Your Client's

Identify Interests to Accommodate

    ☐ Other Side's

2. Identify Impediments to Overcome

    ☐ Relationship
    ☐ Data
    ☐ Value

☐ Interests

☐ Structural

· · ·

8. Identify the mediator's possible contributions to resolving the dispute

Approaches to Dispute
You want the mediator to use the following approaches:

☐ a. Manage the process by primarily facilitating, primarily evaluating, or following another approach.

☐ b. View the problem broadly or narrowly.

☐ c. Involve clients actively or restrictively.

☐ d. Use caucuses extensively, selectively, or not at all.

Useful Techniques
You want the mediator to use his or her techniques to:

☐ a. Facilitate the negotiation of a problem-solving process.

☐ b. Promote communications through questioning and listening techniques.

☐ c. Deal with the emotional dimensions of the dispute.

☐ d. Clarify statements and issues through framing and reframing.

☐ e. Deal with power inequalities.

☐ f. Overcome the impediments to settlement.

☐ g. Overcome the chronic impediment of clashing views of the court outcome . . .

☐ h. Generate options for settlement (e.g., brainstorming).

☐ i. Separate process of inventing settlement options from selecting them.

☐ j. Fashion creative solutions.

☐ k. Close any final gaps (consider your preferred methods for closing gaps).

☐ l. Deal with _____

Control over Mediation Stages
You want the mediator to use his or her control over the mediation process to:

☐ a. Use the mediator's opening statement to set up a problem-solving process.

☐ b. Use the information gathering stage for venting and securing information for the specific purposes of understanding issues, interests, and impediments. . . .

☐ c. Use the stage of identifying issues, interests, and impediments to ensure that key information is clearly identified.

☐ d. Use the agenda formulation stage to ensure key issues and impediments will be addressed.

☐ e. Use the overcoming impediments stage to overcome known impediments.

☐ f. Use the generating options stage to ensure creative ideas are developed.

☐ g. Use the assessing and selecting options stage to ensure that your client's interests are met.

☐ h. Use the concluding stage to ensure that any written settlement meets your client's interests or if no settlement, a suitable exit plan is formulated.

[The checklist also covers an advocate's activities at key junctures in the process.]

Questions

12. Assume that you are a competitive advocate in an exercise assigned by your teacher. Your goal is to get the best possible money outcome for your client. How would you answer the questions on Professor Abramson's checklist?
13. Now assume that you have a problem-solving orientation in the same case. How would your answers change?

2. Exchange Information

One of the key aspects of any negotiation is exchanging information, and part of mediation's value is its ability to enhance the flow of data between the parties. What information will be relevant depends again on your goals. If the process turns on money, then legal evidence and arguments are likely to be key. If your purpose is to repair a relationship, knowing the "why" behind a disputed action will be important. If the objective is to create a new business arrangement, then financial data might be more useful. As a rule, negotiations that focus on imaginative options require a much broader base of information than discussions that revolve solely around money. You should think about two types of data:

- What information will your client need to make a good settlement decision?
- What information will help persuade your adversary to agree to the terms you are seeking?

We saw in Chapter 9 that advocates can enlist a mediator's help with an adversary; the neutral might also be able to help you explain to your client why it makes sense to give an opponent "free discovery."

a. Exchanging Data with the Other Party

Disputants usually need less data to mediate effectively than to try the same case. Still, especially if parties mediate early in a dispute, one side may lack the information necessary to assess the value of its litigation alternative or determine whether an imaginative option is viable. An insurance adjuster, for example, might not be able to obtain the authority needed to settle a claim without documents verifying the plaintiff's medical expenses, and a plaintiff lawyer might be unable to accept a reasonable settlement offer until he is satisfied there is no "smoking gun" lurking in the defendant's files.

Consider what data you and your opponent need to negotiate successfully, and whether you can arrange this through direct discussions or would benefit from the assistance of a mediator.

> *Example:* A town sued a company for negligently designing a solid-waste treatment plant. It complained that the sludge produced by the plant, which it had expected to be able to market as fertilizer, was not solid enough; not only did farmers refuse the sludge, but it could not be stored effectively. Before going forward with expensive litigation, the parties agreed to mediate.
>
> When the outside counsel for the defendant received the parties' pre-mediation statements, she realized that the town had described her client's alleged design errors in great detail, but had given no explanation of how it calculated its $3 million damages demand. Without an explanation, the lawyer could not get authority from her client's insurer to offer a significant settlement.
>
> The lawyer contacted the mediator, who explained the problem to the town's lawyer and recommended that he provide a damage calculation to the defense. A day later it arrived, totaling slightly more than $1.7 million. Counsel reviewed the document and passed it along to the insurer, who arrived at mediation with the authority to close a deal.

Questions

14. What types of data gathered before mediation might help an advocate avoid some of the "20 errors" described by Tom Arnold?
15. Assume that you are the lawyer in an exercise assigned by your teacher. What additional information would help you mediate? What data might the other attorney ask you for?

b. Educating the Mediator

In smaller cases and court-connected programs, neutrals sometimes are told almost nothing about the dispute in advance. In privately conducted mediations, however, lawyers typically make an effort to orient, and begin to persuade, the neutral before they meet to bargain. Pre-mediation communications can take at least three forms: written statements, organizing discussions, and private conversations.

Written Statements. In commercial cases parties almost always file written statements and documents with mediators in advance. As you plan for this, think about these issues:

- Do you prefer to prepare a customized statement of your case or use an existing document or pleading? A customized document has obvious advantages, but particularly in small cases or when mediation is scheduled on short notice, it may be preferable to use an existing document. Mediators may also be willing to receive statements in less formal letter or memorandum formats.
- Should you submit a statement to the mediator privately or exchange statements with opposing counsel? Mediators usually prefer that lawyers exchange statements, so they are free to discuss one side's arguments with the other. Even if you exchange statements, you may be able to discuss a sensitive issue confidentially with the mediator through a private letter or telephone call.
- Should you work with your opponent to compile a common set of documents, especially in complex cases? A single set of documents is easier for the mediator to manage, but using separate documents allows you to highlight the passages in each document that are most important to your arguments.

What should be in your mediation statement? The mediator is likely to be interested in knowing:

- How did the dispute arise?
- Who are the important actors in it?
- What are the key factual and legal issues and important points of agreement and disagreement?
- Without reciting every event, what has occurred in the legal proceedings?
- Have the parties held any direct negotiations? If so, what was the last offer on each side, and who made the last concession?
- What, in your opinion, has made it difficult to settle the dispute through direct bargaining? Are there non-legal concerns in the case?
- Is there any possibility of settlement terms that go beyond a simple monetary payment?
- Does either side need more information to mediate productively?
- What documents should the mediator review in advance? If the documents are lengthy, what parts are most relevant to your arguments?

If you do not wish to provide this information to the other side, you may be able to communicate it through a private conversation with or letter to the mediator.

In cases that involve complex facts or law, you may want to arrange for the mediator to receive a briefing from each side before the mediation session. It may also be important to provide the mediator with reports from experts or to have the mediator meet with experts in advance. If the condition of land or buildings is at issue, it may be useful for the mediator to visit the site.

Organizing Discussions. In complex legal cases, mediators often schedule joint meetings with counsel to discuss organizational questions such as who will be present at the mediation. These discussions usually occur through conference calls and are typically limited to lawyers, but clients and experts participate occasionally.

Private Conversations.   Often lawyers do not seek to talk with mediators ahead of time, or limit any conversation to legal issues. Both are mistakes. Pre-mediation conversations offer exceptional opportunities to shape a neutral's initial "take" on a dispute. As you talk with the mediator, think about covering non-legal obstacles, the personal dynamics of the participants, and potential settlement options, not merely legal points. Mediators have trouble assimilating long oral presentations about unfamiliar disputes, and will in any case get a more complete summary of the case from the written briefs.

In addition to attorney-mediator conversations, lawyers and clients may benefit from meeting, or at least talking by telephone with, the neutral before the process begins. You might seek out a meeting:

- To permit a client to work through emotions or get to know the mediator.
- To present sensitive or complex data or proposals.
- To allow the mediator to meet with a key witness or decision maker who will not be present at the mediation session.

Questions

16. You are representing a party in an exercise assigned by your teacher. What might be helpful for you or your client to tell the mediator in a private conversation before the process begins?
17. You have sent your mediation statement to your adversary and the mediator. The other side now sends its confidential statement to the mediator alone. What can you do in response? How might you have avoided this problem?

---

3. Preparing the Client

Although mediation is primarily a process of assisted bargaining, it differs from direct negotiation in several important ways.

One is in intensity. Ordinary bargaining may occur intermittently over a period of months or years, without any clear structure and often over the telephone or by e-mail. Mediation, by contrast, is usually set up as a "settlement event": Parties agree to meet on a certain date in the presence of a third party and to bargain continuously to a resolution. While mediations may be temporarily adjourned, parties usually enter the process assuming that it will be a one-time event, and that if they do not settle or at least make progress at the first session, the mediation will not continue.

It is perhaps for these reasons that 75 percent or more of all legal mediations result in settlements. As a result you should plan thoroughly, covering everything from your first offer to final terms of settlement. You should impress on your client that it is very likely entering the culminating event of the case and should prepare accordingly.

In addition, unlike direct negotiation, which is often conducted through telephones or by e-mail, participants in mediation almost always meet in person. As a result, the decision makers will observe and interact with — and be open to observation by — the opponent and the mediator.

The most important difference between mediation and direct negotiation, however, is the mediator. As we have mentioned, the presence of the neutral means that the process at times sometimes resembles a two-party facilitated negotiation and at times a three-sided interaction among the parties and the mediator. The special nature of mediation requires an attorney to cover the following topics with a client, in addition to the issues involved in preparing for an ordinary negotiation.

- How the format of mediation differs from that of a typical negotiation, including:
  - The procedure: for example, will there be an opening session?
  - The confidentiality rules that apply and any exceptions.
- How the client should interact with the mediator and the opposing party, including:
  - The mediator's background, personality, and style. Alert the client that the mediator may change style as the process moves forward, for example, by changing from an empathic listener to legal evaluator.
  - The allocation of roles between you and your client. For instance, will the client have a speaking role in the opening session? In private discussions, will you talk while the client listens, waiting to confer until the mediator leaves the room? Will the client play "good policeman" while you play a tough one?
- The role you will play in the process. Explain that your overall goal, getting the best possible outcome for the client, remains the same, but that you must adapt your tactics to the fact that you are in a bargaining session involving a neutral facilitator.
  - You may act more conciliatory in mediation than you would in a court.
  - You may not mention favorable evidence, so as not to alert your adversary
- How the client should respond to questions.
  - Note that the client is free to decline to answer questions posed by the opponent or even the mediator.
  - Warn the client that you may argue politely with the mediator.
  - Explain that you can ask the mediator to leave the room so that you and the client can talk privately.
  - Explain that the client may be invited to meet privately with the other party and the mediator outside your presence, and that she should talk with you before agreeing to this.

❖ **Thomas Arnold,** *Client Preparation for Mediation*

15 Corp. Couns. Q. 52 (April 1999)

In adjudicative processes (both arbitration and court trials), it is common for the advocacy to be an attack upon the good faith, integrity, and alleged wrongs of the other. . . . Necessarily that attack angers the other party, stirs up animosity, and interferes with any settlement effort.

In mediation the intent is to move the parties together, to treat the dispute as a problem to be solved together by respectful partners rather than a combat to be won. It is not the neutral but the other *party* and counsel that are the critical persons to be persuaded. So you don't hurt or disparage them: You seek out, you court, their good will and understanding. From this and other differences between mediation and adjudicative processes, you will see that advocacy and exhibit preparation . . . are poles apart as between mediation and adjudication. In this paper I list key client and some lawyer preparation pointers for mediation.

Who Represents the Client?

Who is the choice client representative for this mediation? A bellicose, unforgiving, inflexible, arrogant, and/or big-risk-taking personality? A wet rag personality who might give away the store? A person whose concessions at the mediation inherently imply criticism of his own prior actions, or his boss's prior actions? A temperate-mannered somebody who knows the subject matter, knows the values of the likely trade-outs? An open-minded person with quiet courage but no arrogance? Merely discussing these considerations and what available person is the best client representative with the client contact . . . becomes importantly educational . . . as to how he should undertake to conduct himself. . . .

First Impression

Upon arrival at the mediation, [the client should be cautioned to] be friendly and respectful, and attempt to build trust with the adversaries. Most settlements involve some degree of trust between client to client, client to counsel, counsel to counsel . . . so it is important to start developing trust at the first opportunity. . . .

Confidentiality

Acquaint the client with the rules and realities of confidentiality. Emphasize what not to say in plenary session, and that it's okay simply to decline to answer some questions. Only some, not all, disclosures in mediation are confidential. . . . Once learned in a mediation, . . . information can still be discovered by regular discovery processes and used, even though it may not be attributed to the . . . mediation.

Consider Strengths and Weaknesses

Counsel in a preparation session should have the client write down all of the weaknesses and strengths in his/her case, and discuss and evaluate each with counsel. It is important that counsel strain hard to be objective. . . .

Don't Argue

The client should be cautioned not to argue with the other party or try hard to "win" the . . . case. The stock in trade in most legal negotiation is the other party's (and your own) risk of a substantial loss at important expense. But arguing hard and aggressively to get an admission . . . is usually counterproductive. Just be sure the other party truly knows their risks. . . .

Know Which Questions to Answer

The client should be advised to answer questions from the other lawyer without exaggeration, honestly, carefully, and correctly. And he or she should also know which questions to quietly, simply decline to answer. Some lawyers try to use mediation as if it were primarily a discovery tool. You must make material disclosures for the process to work, but you don't have to tell the other side everything (for example, information subject to the attorney-client privilege). . . .

Become Familiar with "The Dance"

Plan with the client how you might handle the first . . . rounds of offers and counter-offers to convey subliminal messages. Plan not to be disturbed by an outlandish initial offer by the other party, but to turn it to . . . advantage by showing how ridiculous it is. . . .

Consider Speaking Out

When the parties can understand the issues, as is usual in commercial and many other disputes, encourage them to speak up during the mediation and participate in the negotiation.

End the Battle Within the Camp

Within a "party" there often are many constituencies . . . with different interests or viewpoints, for example, a partner, the vice-president . . . , the union, the board, the marketing manager. They may be represented at the mediation by one, two, or three persons, or some of them by no one. . . . Not infrequently, the most important and destructive disputes are between constituencies on the same side. In multi-faction situations, counsel and the client business representatives at the mediation must each be sure to address all internal disputes before they face the other side.

Don't Look Like a Klutz

This goes for you and the client, but the client is more likely to need the reminder. It is important to show the client off in the mediation as someone who would be an appealing witness in any court process, should mediation fail. People pay more to, and accept less from, a party with jury appeal.

Be Prepared for Down Time

There is often some idle time during mediation, while the other party meets with the mediator in private caucus, so the client should bring work or reading material. . . .

Plan for a Long Session

Let the client know that it will be necessary to make sure work and children are taken care of all day — until 7:30 in the evening or later, if need be. It is a good idea to talk to the mediator in advance about termination times. Some mediators like the pressure of late hours and work on past midnight if there is even a little movement in parties' positions; some quit at 6:00 P.M. no matter what is going on.

Bow Out Gracefully

Advise your client that when the process ends, you should each shake hands with your opposite number and say "Thank you," even if there's no settlement. Many settlements follow shortly after a mediation, when the right flavor is left in the mouth of an adversary. . . .

Questions

18. What aspects of the mediation process do you think a typical plaintiff in a personal injury case is unlikely to understand? What might a business executive find surprising in mediation of a contract dispute?

19. Tom Arnold's underlying theme is that a lawyer needs to prepare a client differently for mediation than for litigation. Which of his suggestions would you *not* follow if you were preparing a client for a hearing in court?

20. Any advice must be adapted to the needs of specific situations. As one example, Arnold advises that clients be told to assume an "empathetic" role. In what kinds of disputes would empathy be likely to be productive? Are there situations in which it might be the wrong emotion to show?

CHAPTER

11

Representing Clients: During the Process

We now focus on the stage in the mediation process at which the parties and mediator convene together to talk and bargain. This is what many lawyers think of as the "actual" mediation, but you now know that effective advocacy begins well before the parties meet in person.

There is relatively little written about advocacy outside commercial mediation. This could be due to the fact that in the traditional family-mediation format and in "transformative" mediation attorneys do not appear at mediation sessions. The most common noncommercial formats do not offer attorneys very much opportunity for advocacy. We therefore discuss advocacy in the context of commercial mediation, the form of the process in which lawyers do play significant roles.

A. Joint Meetings

1. The Opening Session

a. Should You Have an Opening Session?

Most mediators prefer to begin the process with an opening session attended by all the disputants. Lawyers, however, regularly suggest that the parties dispense with the opening stage and go directly into caucusing. Each side already knows the other's arguments, they say: What benefit could there be to repeating them? Or, they warn, the session will simply inflame their clients. Moreover, time is limited: Why not get right to the bargaining? There is often some truth to each of these concerns, and as noted, the practice of holding opening sessions seems to be dying out in some locales. Still, however repetitive or uncomfortable an opening session may appear, you should be reluctant to ask that it be omitted entirely.

The key point is that this is probably the only time in the entire litigation process that you will have the opportunity to talk directly to the principal on the other side and inform her of the facts and considerations you think she should bear in mind when deciding whether to settle the case. In ordinary litigation you will rarely encounter the opposing principal, other than in formal, adversarial settings such as depositions and court hearings. The opening session in mediation is a unique opportunity to avoid the obstructions imposed by court rules and opposing counsel and communicate directly with the person who has the authority to grant the concessions you seek.

You could, of course, send opposing counsel a letter and request that he forward it to his client, but writing has a very narrow "bandwidth" by comparison with direct, informal conversation. Don't let the opportunity pass to present your message directly to the decision maker on the other side.

> *Example:* A retired executive bought an antiques company, only to conclude a few months later that the seller had deceived him about its condition. He filed suit, then agreed to mediate. The mediator called each lawyer before the mediation to ask about process issues. The purchaser's lawyer said he thought his client would welcome the chance to talk and asked the mediator to encourage the principals to participate. The attorney for the seller, asked about this, agreed to an opening session, but warned that her client was an "engineer-type" who would not want to say much.
>
> The purchaser showed up with a four-page single-spaced text. He described how he'd entered the deal in good faith, only to find himself betrayed by deceptions ranging from inflated inventory to a clientele outraged at the prior owner's failure to meet shipping dates. After 30 minutes the purchaser finished and the seller began to talk. Belying his counsel's prediction, he spoke articulately and at length.
>
> There ensued a back-and-forth discussion between the principals in which the attorneys participated. When the discussion became heated and repetitive, the mediator deferred to the lawyers' request they move into caucusing. Still, the opening session went on for 2 hours, and later that day the case settled.

If you do have a reason for avoiding a joint meeting, raise this with the mediator in advance and work out an agreement about how to proceed. Remember, though, that you have options between complete cancellation of the opening session and the "usual format." You could, for example, ask that the session be limited to comments by parties, not attorneys, or that the mediator conduct the session entirely in "Q and A" format.

Question

1. Can you think of any type of dispute in which an early joint meeting is likely to be counterproductive? What format would you use instead?

You will want to use an opening session to best advantage. To do so, consider these questions:

- What is special about opening sessions in mediation?
- What is my goal for this stage of the process?
- How can I structure the session for maximum impact?
- What can the mediator do to help me do so?

b. What Is Special About the Opening Session?

An opening session in commercial mediation resembles a court hearing in that attorneys and parties engage in advocacy in the presence of a neutral moderator. Unlike a judicial hearing, however, mediation is a "cool" medium, and sessions usually take place in rooms much smaller and less imposing than a courtroom. Parties are seated only a few feet away from each other, and the mediator sets an informal tone. As a result, a subdued style of advocacy is usually more effective than courtroom rhetoric.

A calmer, less formal presentation also makes sense because of the nature of the audience. Unlike a court hearing, in mediation you have two quite different audiences: the opposing party and the mediator. The mediator is willing to listen but has no power to make a decision, whereas the opponent has the ability to decide but will resist agreeing with what you say. Decision makers from both sides will also be personally present at an opening session, something usually not true in direct negotiations.

c. What Is Your Goal?

Advocates' overall purpose for the opening session is usually to create the conditions for successful communication and bargaining later in the process, but beyond that their approach will depend on their ultimate objective.

Foster a working relationship

A lawyer can use an opening session, and perhaps also the casual interactions that often occur as people assemble, to foster a better working relationship with an opponent. This does not necessarily mean repairing a past connection, although that might be desirable. Instead the goal at this stage is typically more modest — to create a good framework for the parties to bargain later. You can do this, for example, by demonstrating that you are serious about settlement and are willing to make principled compromises to reach one. Or you can use the opening session to help emotional or angry participants work through feelings preventing them from bargaining well.

Gather information

You can also use the opening session to gather information. In a joint meeting, unlike discovery or court proceedings, disputants can talk informally. Attorneys and clients also have the opportunity to observe the people on the other side and perhaps also the chance to speak directly with the opposing principal. (The other side, of course, has the same opportunity to "size up" you and your client.)

Focus the discussion on key issues

Another option is to use the opening session to focus discussion on issues helpful to your case or that create a platform for effective bargaining. If, for example, you want to emphasize the evidence (or lack of it) supporting the plaintiff's damage claims, you can alert the mediator beforehand that this issue is significant and focus attention on it through your comments. If your primary goal is to explore an interest-based solution, you can use the opening session to send signals about this as well, either directly or through the mediator. Neither side can control the agenda of an opening session, but attorneys who take the initiative can significantly influence it.

Persuade an opponent

You can also use the opening session to begin the task of persuading an opponent to compromise. If this is the objective, you should usually focus your advocacy on the opposing decision maker. You will have other chances to talk with the mediator, but this could well be your only opportunity to speak directly to the other party. The goal is usually to convince the other side that it is in its own best interest to compromise. Opponents are more likely to do so if they believe that:

- You are serious about seeking a settlement; they can, therefore, probably gain something tangible by compromising, and it will not be a one-sided process.
- You are open to options that will advance their interests.
- If discussions fail, however, you believe that you have a good alternative to settlement and they do not.
- You are willing to compromise, but will accept impasse sooner than an unfair result.

d. How to Present Your Opening for Maximum Effect

How should you frame your presentation?

What format should you use?   The fluid nature of mediation gives you great freedom to customize a presentation. For example, you can:

- Speak yourself, or involve your client or other team members.
- Restrict the presentation to legal issues, focus on personal or business interests, or discuss other topics.
- Rely solely on a verbal presentation, or incorporate media such as PowerPoint slides and video. Within fairly broad limits you can take as much time as you need.

If, however, you plan to say nothing or take an unusual length of time, need special equipment, or have unusual elements in your presentation, alert the mediator to this so she can facilitate your approach and alert you to any problems it might create.

Remember that exhibits and videos are likely to have a greater impact in mediation than in a courtroom, because the room is smaller and documents can stay "on the table" for hours. Evidence also cannot be excluded: If an item is inadmissible your opponent will probably point that out, but evidence that would never get before a jury can still have an effect, especially on lay parties.

Example: A plaintiff lawyer found an embarrassing e-mail sent by the defendant's CEO. She had it blown up on a 2-by-3-foot board, which she set up as she talked. The words seemed to fill the conference room, to the evident discomfort of the defendant team.

When the lawyer turned the floor over to the other side, the defense attorney took the board down and set it facing the wall. But as the plaintiff counsel began her rebuttal she put the board back up, underlying the fact that the words would return to bedevil the defense.

Although a mediator has no power of decision, his views about a case may affect the bargaining. Bear in mind that a mediator's views will usually flow from the briefs and documents he reads, augmented by observations of the people present at the mediation. This means that like trial, mediation has:

- A *primacy effect*: The evidence and people a mediator actually observes are more vivid, and thus usually have more impact on decisions, than data the neutral only hears about.
- A *melding effect*: When a mediator cannot personally observe a witness she is likely to place the person in a category ("nurse," "retired accountant," etc.), and then make an assumption about how a fact-finder would react to a typical member of that group.

These effects apply in the opening session — it is at this point that the mediator gets his first view of people whose persuasiveness as witnesses he may have to evaluate. The opposing party and lawyer may have seen the witness before, but the mediator will not and will have to imagine whatever he cannot see.

Conversely, whereas the mediator may have reviewed key documents, the opposing decision maker might not have seen them or understood their significance. If you have a person or document that strongly supports your case, consider bringing the witness or item into the mediation room and making it part of your presentation.

Remember also that once the mediation session begins the mediator will not have much leisure time to read though new documents or court opinions. If you must present a document for the first time at the mediation, highlight or make a copy of the key passages.

Who should speak? Unlike statements at trial, openings in mediation can include several people: lawyers, parties, experts, and witnesses. Most lawyers are inclined to take the lead in the opening session and treat it like an informal pretrial hearing or business negotiation. A better approach is to take advantage of this freedom in the format to use as a spokesperson whoever is likely to have the most impact on the other side and the neutral.

Look for ways to involve your client in opening meetings. Opponents tend to "tune out" the opposing attorney, but they are usually interested in hearing from principals: They represent the "horse's mouth," and might make a mistake or offer hints about concessions. Mediators also seek out contact with parties for some of the same reasons, paying close attention to what they say. Statements by your client will therefore usually have a greater impact than the same words from you. Parties who participate effectively in an opening session can significantly affect how an opponent views them as witnesses, future partners, or negotiators.

- In a personal injury or employment case, in which pain and suffering or emotional distress is often an important element of a claim, a plaintiff who can persuasively describe how he has suffered increases the settlement value of his case. Whenever a person is likely to be a significant witness in adjudication, his participation at mediation can affect the other side's estimate of the value of the case.
- When parties wish to repair a relationship or the principals cannot avoid relating with each other, for instance, if they have children together, one party's participation in mediation can affect the other side's willingness to revive a working relationship. Again, statements made by one principal to another almost always have greater impact than comments made by a lawyer or through a mediator.
- If interests are the focus, parties can often articulate their concerns more persuasively if they speak themselves.
- If one side doubts an opponent's commitment to settling, the principal may be able to dispel those concerns by participating in the opening session.

You could, for example, summarize the legal arguments in the case and then ask the client to describe key factual events, or cover liability and let the client describe the effect of the case on her family or business. If you do want your client or the other party to speak, prompt the mediator in advance to encourage principals to comment.

All this assumes, of course, that a client presents himself positively. If a client is obnoxious, inarticulate, or unappealing, then her participation will lower an opponent's opinion and make it harder to achieve her objectives. In such situations it is better for the person to remain silent if possible.

If you don't want your client put on the spot, warn the mediator about this. If a client is inarticulate or an unattractive witness, you have no obligation to put him on display. If you do want your client to participate, go over with him in advance what he will say and how to present it, as you would with a witness at a trial or deposition. In particular:

- Remind your client that the setting is informal and that he can take a break to consult with you at any time. Discuss how you and the client will communicate, for example, how to signal a need for a break.
- Alert him that he may be asked questions or given the chance to speak in joint sessions in mediation, but that unlike in a courtroom, he has no obligation to do so even if the mediator asks.
- If you don't want your client to answer a question, intervene and respond yourself. If you don't wish to seem rude, say that you would prefer to discuss the issue in caucus.

What tone to take?

Mediation is an informal process that combines discussion with bargaining. Speakers should therefore use a conversational tone, usually focused on the key opposing decision maker.

If the speaker is discussing background facts that are familiar to the other side, he should address the neutral. If the issue involves past incidents between principals, or a party is attempting to explain a misunderstanding, apologize, or empathize with an adversary, he should speak directly to the concerned person. If the purpose is to show the client's effectiveness as a witness, then it is usually best to address the other side and the mediator at once, like a judge and jury.

If it is necessary to make an accusation, for example, that the other side has committed fraud, it is usually better to address comments to the neutral, to make listeners feel less "assaulted" and more willing to listen. Mediators with backgrounds as judges also sometimes prefer that participants speak directly to them.

Question

2. You represent a company that vacated commercial space because of dissatisfaction with the condition of the building. Your client is being sued by a corporate landlord for rent due under the lease. Both sides have agreed to mediate. Apart from the basic issue of liability, which you see as a 50-50 proposition, you believe that the landlord ignored its responsibility to maintain the building and as a result would not be awarded much even if it did establish a technical violation of the lease. How can you use the opening session to make the landlord aware of its risk at trial?

---

e. How to Take Advantage of the Mediator's Presence

Shaping the agenda

Chapter 10 described how a mediator can influence the negotiation agenda. If you would like to have an issue discussed in the opening session, ask the mediator to encourage this. If you don't want to raise the topic yourself, ask the mediator to do so. You might also want to avoid issues; it is difficult to avoid a topic entirely, but if your client will be upset by discussion of a certain issue, you can alert the mediator to discourage or contain it. Mediators can also help with issues of timing and structure; if, for example, you want a recess between an opponent's presentation and your own, ask the mediator ahead of time to suggest a break.

Muting adversarial reactions

If you need to make adversarial statements, for example, accusing the other side of intentional misconduct, a mediator can at least partially "defang" your role and make it easier to present the issue.

Example: An American pharmaceutical company terminated its Brazilian distributor, alleging that its sales were disappointing and that it had the right to cancel the contract on 90 days' notice. The distributor filed suit in Texas state court, alleging that the American company had hired away the distributor's chief salesman, persuading him to break his noncompetition agreement, and had encouraged him to begin soliciting the same clients he had developed while on the Brazilian company's payroll.

The distributor's lawyer told the mediator before the opening session that his client had e-mails showing that the American company's executives had begun talking with the disloyal salesman a full three months before he left. The lawyer planned to argue that the U.S. company had intentionally stolen the employee away, in knowing violation of his contract with the Brazilian distributor. Recognizing that the American company's executives might take umbrage at these charges, the distributor's lawyers asked the mediator to prepare them for what would happen.

In his opening comments the mediator said, "I've asked each lawyer to state their case unvarnished and with the gloves off. The parties may find what they say upsetting, but I've asked them to do this because we have to be aware of what will happen in court if this case does not settle."

Gathering information

If you want to gather information during the opening session, ask the mediator to:

• Raise certain issues himself, or
• Suggest that the parties ask each other questions or discuss the case.

Example: A contractor was sued by an owner for allegedly mispouring the concrete slab on which a building had been erected. Before the mediation the attorney warned the mediator, "We cannot figure out how the plaintiff got its number of $750,000 to fix the foundation. Even assuming it's our problem, our contractors are coming in with figures in the $300,000 range. This is the major element of their damages, and the difference is driving our assessment of what we'd pay to settle. Can you ask them to flesh out their estimate, or suggest it would be useful to have a discussion in the joint session about the calculation of repair costs?"

2. *Other Joint Formats*

We have seen that commercial mediation typically relies on private caucusing, but that does not mean that parties must spend all their time after the opening session separated from each other. Caucusing can be useful, but it also imposes significant limitations. Don't let yourself fall into a caucus format as a matter of routine without thinking first about whether other approaches might be more effective in a particular case.

Caucusing is most useful when disputants want to focus primarily on legal issues and monetary offers, or when they are too emotional or unskilled in bargaining to interact effectively. If, however, parties wish to repair a relationship or work out inventive or complex solutions, direct discussions are often effective because they allow the people most concerned or knowledgeable about a situation to talk with each other. Even when a case is "only about money," it may be useful for opponents to talk directly to deal with emotions, address complex factual issues, or clarify misunderstandings. The flexible nature of mediation allows participants to change the structure on an ad hoc basis. This creates another opportunity for sophisticated counsel to use the process to their advantage.

> *Example:* A manufacturer and a trucking company had a productive relationship for more than a decade, with the trucker distributing the manufacturer's products throughout the southern United States. Then their relationship went sour. The manufacturer sued the trucking company, claiming it had fraudulently inflated its costs by overstating mileage and padding other charges. After two years of intense litigation, the parties agreed to mediate.
>
> The mediation process began with an unusual twist: The plaintiff's lawyer called ahead of time to suggest that the mediator ask the defense whether they could dispense with the usual opening statements by lawyers and instead have the two CEOs meet privately. The mediator raised the issue with defense counsel who agreed, subject to the neutral being present during the conversation.
>
> The three retired to a room, leaving the lawyers behind. The plaintiff executive opened the discussion by retracing the companies' earlier good relationship and their later problems. He suggested the breakdown had been provoked in part by a wayward manager he had hired away from the trucking company but had recently let go. The executive then made a settlement offer. The defendant CEO said he needed to run it by his lawyers.
>
> The parties went into caucuses and bargained intensely for hours, reducing an initial $900,000 gap to $30,000 — a demand of $300,000 against an offer of $270,000. At that point, however, the defense refused to make another offer, expressing frustration at the plaintiff's unreasonableness.
>
> As the mediator searched for ways to break the impasse, the defendant CEO suddenly pulled a quarter out of his pocket. "See this?" he asked. "You check — It's an honest quarter. I'll flip him for it!" "For what?" "The 30," he replied. "Let's see if he's got the ****s to flip for it!" The mediator looked at the trucker's lawyer: Was this serious? The attorney shrugged his shoulders; "It's OK with me. Why don't you take Jim down and present it to them. But you should do the talking; Jim's feeling really frustrated by all this." Why not? the mediator thought; it was better than anything he had to suggest.
>
> The neutral led the defendant CEO into the plaintiff's conference room and, with a smile, said, "Jim has an idea to break the deadlock. It's kind of . . . unusual, but you might want to listen to it." In a calm voice and without anatomical references, the CEO repeated his coin-toss offer.
>
> The plaintiff executive grinned. "OK," he said, "But you didn't answer my last move, so the real spread is 50, between my 320 (his last offer before dropping to $300,000) and your 270." They argued over what should be the outcomes for the flip, showing some exasperation but also bits of humor. When the discussion stalled the mediator suggested options to keep it going ("Why not give the 20 to charity?"), but they could not agree and the defendant CEO walked out.
>
> As he left, the mediator walked with him down the hall. "Suppose I could get him to drop to a flat 290," he asked. "Would that do it?" As it turned out, it did.

In this mediation both attorneys' initiatives proved important to settlement. The plaintiff lawyer's proposal that the process begin with a parties-only meeting created an informal connection between the executives that smoothed their later bargaining. And the CEO's idea of a coin toss, which the mediator learned later had been concocted with his lawyer, was key to shaking the parties out of their stalemate.

As this example demonstrates, even in a process in which the parties are separated in caucuses, lawyers can advance their clients' interests by arranging meetings of subgroups of disputants. The mediator will usually be present during such sessions, but this is not always true: In a case described later, the plaintiff's inside counsel asked to meet privately with the defendant's CEO outside the presence of both the outside lawyers and the neutral. Good mediators will usually agree to ask whether people can talk directly with each other, and smart lawyers are not afraid to ask a mediator to vary the usual format. Both understand that mediation is inherently a fluid process.

B. Caucusing

Because caucusing is dominant in civil mediation outside the family law area, attorneys and mediators you encounter in practice are likely to expect to spend most of the time in caucus format. You will need either to take the initiative to change this assumption or work to reap an advantage from it.

To make the best use of caucuses, you need to prepare in two ways. First, you must adapt bargaining tactics to a situation in which you are communicating with the other side indirectly, through a third person. Second, you need to think about how to deal with the mediator.

> *Example:* During the opening session opposing counsel asks in a challenging tone whether your client, a discharged employee claiming discrimination, ever sought medical care for the emotional distress she is claiming. You immediately step in and order her not to respond, noting that this is a settlement process, not a deposition.
>
> During a later caucus discussion the mediator, in a sympathetic tone, asks your client essentially the same question, and your client begins to explain that she never obtained treatment. You might be more willing to have your client answer in this context, knowing that you could tell the mediator not to reveal what she says, but even if you were reluctant you would not wish to appear uncooperative. You might also be concerned that a failure to answer in the "nonadversarial" setting of a caucus would be interpreted by the mediator as an admission that there was no evidence to support the claim.

The nature of caucusing typically changes over the course of mediation, and we therefore focus on early and later caucuses separately.

1. Early Caucuses

Goals

During the early caucuses you are likely to have some or all of the following goals:

- Relationships:
  - Develop a good working relationship with the mediator.
  - Not harm, and perhaps improve, your relationship with the other side, unless you have decided to adopt a hard-bargainer role.
- Legal issues:
  - Focus attention on favored issues and avoid or minimize unhelpful ones.
  - Gather the data you need to bargain, and provide the other side with information that will induce it to move in your direction.
  - Persuade the other party and the neutral that you have a good alternative to settling or that its alternative is not attractive.
- Interests:
  - Identify non-legal barriers that have made settlement difficult.
  - Focus the mediator on your interests and identify the key concerns of the other side.
- Bargaining:
  - Start the process of exchanging offers.
  - Encourage or assist the mediator to pursue interest-based options.

Content

You can expect the following to occur in a first caucus meeting. The mediator will emphasize listening and gathering information, while building a working relationship with the attorney and client. He will seek to gather information to help the parties understand each other's perspectives and perhaps also to lower their confidence about prevailing in court. Attorneys pursuing a competitive strategy will want to offer data that support their legal position and perhaps some "ammunition" that the mediator can use with an opponent. Lawyers taking a cooperative, interest-based approach will want to give the mediator information about their underlying needs and those of the other side; cooperative bargainers might also ask for help identifying what is important to an opponent.

Many neutrals in early caucuses will use a principled bargaining style, trying to avoid or minimize positional tactics such as "insulting" first offers meant to jolt the other side. The mediator will invite disputants to offer ideas or concessions to help the process gain momentum, and will be looking for possible openings or at least a private indication of flexibility. Be prepared to offer the mediator something to assist the bargaining process, or to explain you do not believe that is yet appropriate.

Of the potential goals listed above, we focus on two: facilitating exchanges of information and initiating bargaining.

a. Exchange Information and Arguments

In direct negotiation good lawyers often spend considerable time exchanging information and feeling each other out before making explicit offers; it is not surprising that advocates and mediators do so in mediation as well. At this stage a lawyer might pose questions to a mediator that she wants answered by an opponent, or pass on to the neutral points to emphasize in the other room.

Neutrals, for their part, understand that disputants often arrive at mediation without the data they need to make good settlement decisions, and that smart lawyers will seek to use the mediator to convey arguments more effectively to an adversary. Indeed, to the extent that a party's questions, like queries on cross-examination, amount to disguised arguments, mediators are often happy to transmit them as part of their effort to encourage both sides to reassess the value of their case. To understand how lawyers can use mediation to assist the exchange of information, consider the following.

> *Example:* Professional mediators and litigators were put in a role-play situation as part of an experiment to film how advocates use the mediation process. The dispute involved a manufacturer's claim against a supplier for selling a defective product. The manufacturer also sued the supplier's insurer, alleging that the insurer had acted in bad faith by refusing to settle the claim and asking for treble damages. The bad-faith claim hung over the case, inflating the plaintiff's monetary demands and discouraging the defense from making a serious offer.
>
> In defense of the bad-faith allegation, the defendant's counsel pointed out to the mediator in their first caucus meeting that the insurer had a solid basis for denying the claim — the results of tests conducted by an independent expert. At the end of the first caucus meeting she elected to highlight the issue:
>
> *Defendant's inside counsel:* We hope you'll raise with them that we see the crux of settlement as hinging on the fact that we don't see any evidence to support their case on treble damages. . . .
>
> *Mediator:* But if they do have evidence, that might influence your bargaining position?
>
> *Counsel (smiling):* Yes, and if they don't, we hope it influences theirs. . . .
>
> In response, the mediator raised the issue during his meeting with the plaintiff side:
>
> *Mediator:* Suppose an outside expert reports that he found nothing in the insured's product that could have caused the damage and the insurer then denies the claim on that basis. If all that is true and the expert is credible, how would you then get the insurer into the case?
>
> *Plaintiff counsel:* Well, it's a problem, no question about it.
>
> *Mediator:* What percentage chance would you place on the bad-faith claim?
>
> *Counsel:* Twenty-five percent.
>
> At the conclusion of this caucus meeting the plaintiff agreed to heavily discount the bad-faith claim. What the defense counsel obtained by making her request through the mediator was to focus his discussion with the plaintiff on her issue. She also benefited from the plaintiff lawyer's natural inclination to be candid with the neutral.

Potential questions

The following are some specific questions a lawyer may have in planning for an early caucus.

- If I have confidential information that supports my analysis of the merits, should I disclose it early in the process or wait?

It is usually better to offer evidence early, while the mediator is focused on gathering information. If you wait until late in the process, the new data will be mixed with bargaining discussions. Recall a case, mentioned earlier, in which a Brazilian company sued an American distributor for allegedly inducing the plaintiff's chief salesman to violate his non-compete contract. To bolster his claim, the Brazilian company's lawyer might say in caucus, "We've located another salesman they tried to solicit in violation of his contract with us. They don't know about this, but it will really make them look bad at trial."

If a party waits to disclose "silver bullet" information until late in the process, when the mediator is pressing each side to make difficult concessions, it risks being heard by the neutral not as genuine data, but as an excuse for avoiding compromise. Late in the mediation a mediator is also likely to give new evidence less weight because he has shifted focus from understanding the case to finding settlement terms.

One reason not to disclose evidence early in the process might be that counsel is not yet convinced that the other side is ready to settle, and if not, wishes to preserve "good ammunition" for another day. If that is the concern, a lawyer can make her reasoning clear to the mediator, or even make settlement a quasi-condition of disclosure: "You can tell them, but only if you're confident that it will seal a deal. . . . "

- Should I direct the mediator to take a tough line with the other side, but tell him privately that we are willing to compromise?

Your strategy should flow from your goals. That said, it is usually a good idea to let the mediator know your strategy in general terms so he can warn you of problems and present it most effectively to the other side. Telling the neutral that you are delaying in offering a compromise rather than refusing to ever to do so makes you appear more cooperative.

- Who should make the first offer in mediation?

As a rule, plaintiffs come into mediation having made a demand and will not make another offer until the defense puts an offer on the table ("We won't bid against ourselves."). If a defendant has responded, however, the plaintiff is usually asked to make a concession.

- Should I make an offer during the first caucus meeting?

Assuming it is your "turn" to bid, making an offer in the first meeting might or might not be the best strategy. It depends primarily on whether you think that by simply exchanging information in the first round of caucusing you can learn something valuable or persuade the other side to be more conciliatory. If you decide to wait, don't let yourself be pushed into acting prematurely. Instead of making an offer, you could say that you prefer to wait because you want to talk more about the substantive issues or each side's larger interests before making decisions about settlement.

- Will the mediator be offended if I ask her to leave the room temporarily or don't explain my bargaining goal or strategy?

Don't be bashful about asking a mediator to leave so you can confer with your client, especially when concessions are under consideration. Mediators expect parties to talk confidentially with their lawyers. Indeed, the fact that you want to do so could be taken as evidence that you have listened to what the mediator has said. You might say, "This has given us some things to think about. Can we have a few minutes to talk?"

Mediators also understand that lawyers usually do not disclose their entire strategy, because advocates and neutrals do not have the same goal. Neutrals expect that if an attorney makes a factual representation it will be accurate, but not that lawyers will confide in them completely.

Problem

1. You represent the defense in the mediation of an employment discrimination case. A typical plaintiff's claim for damages in such a case consists of lost wages, out-of-pocket expenses, and emotional distress. Of these, the item that is often the largest, and the most subject to dispute, is emotional distress.

   Here the plaintiff is demanding $200,000 in emotional distress damages, but you think it is highly unlikely that he will recover more than a modest amount, because he never sought medical care for his alleged condition. Also there are no egregious facts, such as being ordered out of the building summarily in front of other employees, that a fact-finder would think likely to trigger serious distress.

   You are in the first round of caucusing. The mediator is coming to meet with you and your client and will then meet with the plaintiff. Outline how you would raise this issue.

---

b. Initiate Bargaining

Advocates in settlement discussions may focus either on monetary goals or creative solutions. The format of mediation allows lawyers to advance either of these goals, or both of them, more effectively.

Interest-based bargaining

Although interest-based bargaining is desirable, a basic problem, especially for plaintiffs, is that if they show a willingness to explore nonmonetary terms, their opponent could interpret this as a signal that the party is not committed to its monetary position. (Defense lawyers, by contrast, tend to be receptive to imaginative terms, because they see them as a substitute for paying money.)

Mediation can allow a lawyer to have it both ways to some extent. The advocate can press "publicly," in communications sent through the mediator or in joint session, for the best possible money outcome, and at the same time ask the neutral "privately," in a caucus discussion, to explore nonmonetary options.

Example: A large manufacturer sued a supplier of sensors, alleging that the defendant's product was defective, causing an unacceptable rate of failure in automobiles in which they were installed. The defendant supplier was interested in restoring its business relationship with the manufacturer. Not only had the contract been a source of profit, but the supplier knew that if the manufacturer resumed using its products, it was much less likely to make negative comments about the defendant to other customers.

Because the plaintiff knew that the quality failure had been a one-time event caused by a third party that provided defective wiring to the supplier, it was not necessarily opposed to this. Still, it was concerned that the defense would seize on talk of a "win-win" solution to avoid its cash demands, and it badly needed the cash it could gain from a settlement. To deal with this problem the manufacturer's lawyer continued to press for a large money settlement, while indicating to the mediator privately that the plaintiff would not object to renewing the contract if it was additional to, and not a substitute for, a cash payment.

By exploiting the structure of mediation, the plaintiff lawyer in this example was able to pursue distributive and integrative bargaining strategies simultaneously.

A "hard" bargaining strategy

One aspect of mediation not often mentioned is that it offers protection to parties who opt for a competitive approach as well as creative ones. Indeed, the structure of mediation often allows attorneys to take tougher stands than they could in direct negotiations. Because the process is seen as a one-time effort, participants in mediation are more reluctant to walk out in response to "insulting" proposals. Bargainers also know that the mediator will work to "scrape the other side off the ceiling" when it erupts at their stubbornness. Lawyers sometimes take advantage of this dynamic to play "tough cop," knowing that good mediators will instinctively take on a good-cop role to keep the process alive.

Example: A manufacturer was in a dispute with its insurer over the insurer's refusal to pay nearly $1 billion in claims against the manufacturer arising from a mass-tort class action. The parties agreed to go to mediation. The insurer's CEO prepared intensively for the process, planning to have a point-by-point discussion of the merits with the manufacturer's representatives.

When the parties convened, however, the plaintiff's inside counsel said that he wasn't interested in discussing legal issues with the CEO; he had listened carefully to his litigation team's analysis, and saw no point in having a debate. He went on to say that he would not make any concessions at all until the insurer first agreed to pay the full amount the manufacturer claimed was due under an "incontestable" section of the policy. That amount, counsel said, was just under $130 million.

The mediation was held in a conference room at a large airport, and in a direct negotiation the insurer's team would very likely have been on the next flight out. The manufacturer's lawyer knew, however, that the mediator would respond to his tactic by cajoling, even begging, the CEO to ignore his opponent's obnoxiousness, look at the big picture, examine the legal risks — and put up a very large amount of money. And that is exactly what happened.

After hours of talking, the CEO strode into the manufacturer's conference room, wrote "100" on the board, and walked out. Now it was the neutral's job to convince the plaintiff team that although $100 million might seem paltry in light of its claim, from the insurer's perspective it was a large step forward. To counter feelings of reactive devaluation, he argued that the right way to assess the offer was to count up from zero, rather than down from the plaintiff's original demand. In fact, by relying on the protection afforded by the mediation process, the manufacturer's lawyer had been able to take a hard positional stance and obtain a huge first offer from the other side.

Months later the case settled. The turning point came when the manufacturer's counsel — the same lawyer who had refused to discuss the case with the CEO — intervened to change the mediation format. He asked the mediator to invite the CEO to meet him in the lobby of the hotel where the mediation was being held. As the neutral and the lawyers sat in conference rooms, reading newspapers and speculating about what was going on, the two key players sat down over coffee and cut a deal.

As this example illustrates, good lawyers can use mediation to enhance a competitive strategy as well as a cooperative one, in the knowledge that the mediator will work to keep the process from falling apart.

2. Later Caucuses

As caucusing progresses, the tactics of the disputants and the mediator are likely to evolve. Advocates will continue to probe for information, argue the merits, and explore interests, but as the process continues these aspects usually become less dominant. Parties find themselves returning to the same facts and legal arguments, making continued discussion seem repetitive. If the process has followed a creative path, parties in later caucuses often shift their attention from identifying and communicating interests to devising options that satisfy them.

As a result, during the later stages of a process that focuses on monetary demands, caucuses are likely to become progressively shorter, as both sides focus on exchanging and interpreting offers. In one focused on interests, caucuses might actually become longer, as participants focus on finding terms that produce the best possible fit of concerns, and opposing parties or subgroups are likely to meet directly with each other to clarify issues and discuss options.

In later stages of the process, mediators also become more active in expressing viewpoints and press parties harder about the cost and risk of litigation and the resulting advantage of compromising. In part this happens because the mediator becomes increasingly confident about her assessment of the participants, the legal issues, and the obstacles blocking agreement. Parties often also become more receptive to the mediator's advice, because they realize that the neutral has listened carefully to their concerns and communicated them to the other side, and perhaps because they realize that their preferred tactics are likely to lead to an impasse. As mediators become more active in the process, lawyers should:

- Be prepared for harder reality testing. Warn clients that the mediator may ask tough questions and disagree explicitly with their arguments; assure them that this is a normal part of the process, and that the neutral is being equally frank with their opponent.
- Be ready to suggest changes in the format, for example, a joint meeting or conversations between subsets of disputants. Ask the mediator to advise you whether the other side would be receptive to such an approach.

- If your client is becoming discouraged, consider asking the mediator for an assessment of how the process is going. If your client is becoming tired or irritable or is pushed too hard, ask the mediator to arrange a break or adjournment.
- As the process nears an end, be ready to bargain with the mediator about whether and how the mediator will use evaluation and other impasse-breaking tactics (discussed below).

a. Bargaining

As the parties move into what is often difficult and competitive bargaining, lawyers can take advantage of a mediator's presence in several ways.

Use the mediator to obtain or convey information

One of the paradoxes of mediation is how mediators are expected to treat information that they gather during private caucuses. On the one hand, caucus discussions are to be kept confidential. At the same time, one of mediation's key purposes is to foster better communication, and as long as the parties are separated in caucuses this can happen only if the mediator conveys information between them. How can an advocate take advantage of this tension?

In practice most lawyers in mediation designate very few facts to be held confidential from the other side, and appear to expect a mediator to reveal at least some of what they say in private caucus. A plaintiff lawyer might tell a mediator, for example, "$500,000 is as low as we'll go at this point. You can tell them 500." The attorney knows that the neutral will interpret this to mean that he can tell the other side that the plaintiff is reducing his demand to $500,000. The mediator can also, however, offer a personal opinion — not attributed to the plaintiff — that she thinks the plaintiff will be willing to go further ("at this point") if the defendant makes an appropriate concession.

Experienced lawyers know, in other words, that although mediators will not report sensitive data to the other camp they will usually feel a license to go beyond simply repeating what a party says, to interpret its underlying message and intentions. Unless instructed otherwise, a mediator should convey such information as his own impression and not attribute it to the speaker. The result resembles the way government officials sometimes float trial balloons on a "background" basis. In mediation this tactic has two advantages. First, the listener might be left a bit unsure of whether the other side is sending a signal, giving the sender leeway either to reinforce or back away from its message later. Second, the fact that the mediator is the one making the interpretation makes it appear less manipulative, and therefore less subject to reactive devaluation, than if the signal were attributed to the opposing side.

More generally, advocates should realize that the mediator may well interpret their attitude or intentions in the other room. Lawyers should think about what they wish a mediator to say about them, and state their desires to the neutral. Mediators are not bound to follow such instructions, but the chances that a neutral will do what you want are much greater if you make your wishes known.

Advocates should also consider whether to ask the mediator about the other side's state of mind. If, for instance, a plaintiff seems agitated during an opening session, defense counsel might later ask the mediator, "Has Smith calmed down?" or "If his lawyer recommends a deal, do you think he'll listen?" Alternatively, a lawyer might ask a mediator to collect specific information, such as whether the other side has retained an expert. Lawyers can also ask mediators to explore an adversary's reaction to a potential deal without disclosing their own interest in it.

Questions about what the other side is thinking pose tricky ethical and practical issues for mediators because of the paradox mentioned previously, but that does not mean that counsel should not ask them. Lawyers should be aware, however, that if they ask a neutral for information about their opponent, the neutral may interpret this as permission to provide the other side with the same kind of data about the questioner. As in direct bargaining, in other words, information exchange is a two-way street. That does not mean, however, that asking questions is not helpful, and mediation can amplify the effectiveness of doing so.

To take advantage of the mediator's ability to gather and convey information during the caucusing process:

- Ask the mediator about the other side's attitude and intentions.
- Discuss with the mediator what he will say to your opponent about you.
- Use the mediator as a sounding board for how a potential offer might be received.

Problem

2. You are in the late afternoon of a mediation of a dispute over a large software contract; your client, the buyer of the software, experienced serious business problems because it was defective, and sued for nearly $10 million in out-of-pocket damages and lost profits. You and your client have become frustrated with the slow pace of the bargaining and the defendant's lack of realism. You began with an offer of $5 million, to which the defendant offered $200,000. Your most recent proposal was $2.75 million, with a final "bottom-line" target of $1.9 million. The defense has been inching up, their last move being only from $650,000 to $700,000.

   In a private conversation while the mediator is out of the room, your client tells you that he is willing to drop to $2.5 million, but that unless the defendant's next offer "hits seven figures" (i.e., $1 million), he's inclined to pack up and leave. How might the mediator help you? What should you and/or your client say to the neutral?

   Assume that the mediator comes back 30 minutes later with a defense offer of $900,000. What should you do now?

Take advantage of a mediator's neutrality

As we have seen, mediators have a key advantage not available to even the best advocate: the simple fact that they are seen as neutral. The phenomenon of reactive devaluation makes humans instinctively suspect anything proposed by an opponent, but mediators can deliver bargainers from at least some of its impact. Take, for example, a situation in which a defendant is stubbornly clinging to an offer of $75,000. The mediator could say to the plaintiff, "You know, I think that if we could ever get them up to $100,000, it would be worth serious consideration. What do you think?" By phrasing the issue in this way, the neutral has done two things. First, she has presented the offer as hypothetical — it is not yet "cursed" by the fact that the defendant is actually willing to make it.

Second, she has tentatively endorsed its reasonableness. If the plaintiff buys into the potential offer, the mediator will have partially "inoculated" it against being devalued if it materializes. Good lawyers instinctively work to take advantage of the advantages conferred by the mediator's neutral status.

> *Example:* In the filmed experiment described earlier, defense counsel's initial response to a high cash demand was to propose that his client provide the plaintiff with future products at a discounted price, but no actual cash. As he made this offer the lawyer was being imaginative, but he also was offering no money so as to deflate the plaintiff's expectations.
>
> *Mediator:* I've told you that the plaintiff is willing to move significantly from their opening demand. This isn't just the mediator reading tea leaves — they gave me explicit permission to tell you that. . . . But if I go back now and say, "They're willing to give you a discount but . . . *that's it*," we will have a big problem and a short afternoon, I think. . . . But I could be wrong.
>
> *Outside counsel:* David, we need you to be more . . . *creative* than that. I'm confident that you would say to them that you decided after talking to us that it wasn't fruitful to talk in terms of how many dollars we would give them to settle — that *you* came up with the suggestion for a discount program. . . .
>
> In this instance defense counsel was not able to persuade the mediator to assume authorship of the proposal; the neutral was appropriately concerned that he would seriously damage his credibility if he endorsed an offer that the plaintiff saw as unfair. But the lawyer was not bashful about asking, and in the end he got an excellent result for his client.

Take advantage of a mediator's perceived neutrality by:

- Asking a mediator to deliver unwelcome information to the other side.
- Suggesting that a mediator offer your proposal or argument as his own.
- Requesting the mediator to certify the fairness of a proposal.

Use a mediator to carry out uncomfortable tasks

Mediators are freer to use unorthodox tactics to solve bargaining impasses because they needn't worry about maintaining a judge's reserve or showing a litigator's resolve. Attorneys can take advantage of this by asking mediators to take on unconventional tasks.

Example: Two brothers were fighting over the business empire of their deceased uncle. Following years of inconclusive court proceedings, the two agreed to mediate. The parties went through a difficult first day, in part because the mediator encountered ambivalence from the plaintiff. He would make a decision, but then backpedal after the neutral left the room. The defendant's lawyer became angry over this, and the mediator hinted at what was happening.

Defense counsel told the mediator that the plaintiff couldn't decide anything without talking to his wife, and was calling her while the mediator was out of the room. The wife was not at mediation; to alleviate the family's dire financial situation she had taken a job as a bookkeeper at a local store. "Why don't you go talk to her before we meet tomorrow?" the lawyer suggested. With the assent of the plaintiff's attorney, the mediator agreed.

Early the next morning the neutral drove out to the store, walked down to the basement, and amid boxes of auto parts sat down to talk with the plaintiff's wife. After listening to a tearful story of betrayal and sacrifice, he suggested that she accompany him to the mediation — it was her family's future that was being discussed, after all. She agreed, and rode with the mediator to the mediation site. In the ensuing hours the wife proved to be more decisive than her husband, and also better with numbers. The case settled, but absent an outside-the-box suggestion from counsel and a mediator's freedom to respond to it, the process would almost certainly have foundered.

Mediators can take on a wide variety of roles to support a settlement process. They might counsel a distraught litigant, deliver a "hard sell" to a stubborn executive, or act as scapegoat for a difficult compromise. If a mediator does not see the need or seems reluctant to take ·on an unusual role to promote settlement, counsel should take the initiative to ask the neutral to do so.

Questions

3. Is there any reason that you as an advocate would feel reluctant to ask a mediator to take the kinds of initiatives described previously?
4. What kind of background would make a neutral more likely to agree to take such initiatives? Less open to doing so?

b. Impasse-Breaking Techniques

Each of the techniques described so far can help an advocate achieve more than is possible in direct negotiation. Suppose, however, that despite your best efforts the bargaining process hits an impasse because of a process issue such as lack of authority, psychological factors such as loss aversion, merits-based problems like misevaluation of the likelihood of winning in court, or some other barrier. How can you use mediation to overcome the problem?

Impasses occur most frequently when negotiators focus narrowly on monetary solutions, but they are possible even during interest-based bargaining. Two parties might agree, for example, that it would be desirable to restore their business relationship, but reach a stalemate in allocating the costs and rewards of the new arrangement. When an impasse does occur, advocates can often take advantage of a mediator's assistance to resolve it. In some instances, however, a lawyer may have to bargain with a mediator over what the neutral will do and how.

Ask the mediator for advice

The first suggestion is simple: Ask the mediator for a suggestion about what to do. Mediators have seen many settlement processes. More important, they have had a unique opportunity to observe and talk with both sides. As the process goes on they often acquire a great deal of information about each party's state of mind, approach to bargaining, and priorities for settlement. A mediator will not help one side obtain an advantage over another, and commercial mediators do have an interest in seeing each side compromise as much as possible. But they do share some goals with you and your client. If the negotiation process bogs down, consider asking the mediator for advice about how to restart it.

You can also use a mediator to educate an unsophisticated or emotional client, or to present difficult truths to either or both sides about what is achievable. Possible questions include the following:

- What seems to be the obstacle here? What can we do to resolve it?
- Would a gesture toward the other side help? What would be most effective?
- Is a new combination of terms likely to get a positive response?
- Are other process options available?

Retry an earlier step

Many of the interventions discussed earlier — reframing, drawing out difficult emotions, assessing the merits, and so on — can be useful at the end of the process as well as at earlier stages. The concept of returning to a tactic may seem strange — after all, if a particular approach wasn't successful when the participants were fresh, why should it be productive when everyone is tired and frustrated?

Necessity, however, can be the mother of invention, in mediation as elsewhere. For example, would a renewed focus on interests produce movement? Does a review of disputed facts appear capable of helping? A party who rejected an option early in the process might become more open to advice as time goes on. The fact that a particular step has been taken earlier in the process, either with or without success, does not mean that it cannot be used again.

Arrange a discussion among a subset of participants

A variant of retrying a prior technique is to go to a different format. You will recall, for example, that in the "hundred-million-dollar offer" case, the same lawyer who, during the opening session, had flatly refused to discuss issues with the defendant's CEO later asked to talk with him privately, and by doing so resolved the case. In the "$30,000 coin-toss" mediation, defense counsel asked the mediator to arrange for his client to meet the plaintiff's executive, leading to a solution.

Most common is for a person on one team to talk with his counterpart on the other side: lawyers with lawyers, VPs with VPs, experts with experts, and so on. Such discussions can produce genuine insights. Even when this does not occur, however, a new exchange could provide a party with an excuse — a "fig leaf" one might say — to take a step it knows is necessary to revive the process. If nothing else, by demanding even an inconclusive meeting, a bargainer sends the signal that further concessions will not be obtained easily.

Make a hypothetical offer

Counsel who will not make a unilateral concession will sometimes authorize a mediator to make an offer in a hypothetical, "if . . . then," format. The goal can be to test the waters, probe the other side's flexibility, or ensure that a potential move will be reciprocated. For instance, a lawyer might say to a mediator, "Given the other side's refusal to go below 250, I cannot see us getting above 100. However, you can tell them that you personally think you could get us to 125 if they would respond by breaking 200."

The hypothetical formula gains added impact if it is presented as a final resolution of the case rather than simply as a new move. By proposing an actual settlement, bargainers take advantage of the fact that disputants will often make a special effort if they can achieve complete peace — the "certainty effect" described in Chapter 8. You might say, "You can tell them that if they could get to 750, you have some optimism that you could convince my client to go there — but only if it would settle the case, once and for all." Hypothetical offers can sometimes short-circuit impasses caused by positional bargaining.

Ask the mediator to intervene

If these steps are not effective, another option is to ask a mediator to intervene directly, as described below. Good mediators will delay doing so for as long as possible, knowing that disputants could be alienated by a perception that the neutral is "taking over," or perhaps because the mediator sees intervening as inconsistent with his role. Still, many commercial mediators are prepared to intervene actively in a case if the bargaining process appears to be seriously stalled. If you prefer that a mediator maintain a restrained role in the face of impasse, make that preference known to the neutral. Alternatively, if you want the neutral to become more active, say that.

Next we discuss three interventions used by mediators to resolve impasses — confidential listener, evaluation of the merits, and the mediator's proposal. We also suggest ways in which lawyers can use each tactic to advantage.

Ask for "confidential listener"

Sometimes each side in mediation refuses to move to a reasonable position until its adversary has done so. The result is an "After you . . . No, after you" situation in which both sides remain stuck, but each would be willing to compromise if the other did so. In response a mediator may offer to play "confidential listener." This involves asking each side to disclose to the neutral privately how far it would go to settle the case. The mediator can then make a judgment about the real gap between the parties.

Often mediators will then give the lawyers a verbal statement of how far apart they are ("You are quite close — it's really worth making another effort," or "You are far apart, but the difference is less than it would cost to try this case."). The mediator's characterization is intentionally ambiguous and verbal, to preserve the confidentiality of what each side has said. However, each lawyer, knowing what he or she has told the mediator, is able to process the words and make a rough estimate of how apart the parties really are.

The first question about the confidential listener technique is whether you wish the mediator to use it. If so, suggest it; if not, ask the neutral to hold off. Sophisticated lawyers sometimes ask, for example, that a mediator delay doing so and that the parties continue to exchange offers. The next question is how to use the technique to best effect. Lawyers should realize that at this point they are in a three-sided negotiation with their opponent and the mediator. The neutral is not on anyone's side: His goal is simply to obtain a settlement.

What should an advocate tell a mediator who is playing confidential listener? Unless you are in a situation in which a mediator states explicitly that he wants each side's true bottom-line number *and* you believe that he really means it — that unless the parties' positions either touch or come very close, the mediator will terminate the mediation — it is not wise to give your client's actual bottom line. Doing so will place you at a disadvantage in the next stage of the process in which the parties continue to bargain, and might lead your client to dig prematurely into an unrealistic position. For these reasons, experienced mediators often avoid asking litigants for bottom-line numbers at all.

For a competitive bargainer, the challenge in the confidential listener process is to make an offer extreme enough to set up a favorable compromise, but realistic enough to motivate the other participants to continue. A principled bargainer, by contrast, will gravitate toward a proposal that is solidly based on neutral criteria, but also leaves them room to move. A cooperative bargainer will be inclined to answer the mediator honestly and consult about steps to keep the process alive. Parties can couple a response with an indication of intention for the mediator's private information ("Our number is $100,000. That's as far as we're willing to go at this point. Let's see what they come back with.").

One final point: If a neutral does ask for your "bottom line," how should you respond? If you are cooperative and fully trust the neutral, you can answer with complete candor. In other situations, you might want to adopt this response, suggested by a litigator:

> Based on what we currently know about the case and taking into account the arguments, we believe that the offer we have made is the best we could make. Obviously, we would like to pay less and [they] would like to receive more, but what we might like is not the issue. If you can give me a principled reason why my client should consider paying more, we will consider it; otherwise, we don't believe that any further adjustments are warranted.

[By this response,] you are conveying at least two messages. First, you are flexible. Second, your flexibility is based on principle — meaning the value of the case — not demands, extortion or other extraneous factors. With this response, you have left the door open for dialogue and you have moved the dialogue to the plane of principle rather than petulance. (Stern 1998)

Ask for an evaluation

If shuttle diplomacy fails, litigators often ask mediators to evaluate the legal merits of the case. As we have indicated, evaluation is a somewhat controversial technique but one that most lawyers surveyed think can be useful in commercial mediation. The value of an evaluation is not simply in changing opponents' minds, but also those of clients. Whenever, for example, an advocate stops a mediator in the hall and suggests that she give the client her "thoughts" about a case, the neutral knows that she is being enlisted in the difficult task of client education.

Evaluations usually focus on the legal issues in the case — who is likely to prevail in court, what the damages are likely to be, and similar issues. It is possible, however, to have a mediator evaluate broader issues as well. If, for example, a disputant is suspicious that its adversary will not carry out a proposed settlement, the mediator could offer an assessment of that risk, based on what he has observed about the opponent and his experience with other settlements.

Before requesting a mediator's evaluation on a legal issue ask yourself two basic questions. First, is the primary obstacle to settling this case really a disagreement about the outcome in court, or another issue evaluation can address? If the real barrier is something else, evaluation will not be effective. Second, if the mediator does evaluate the merits, are you confident that the result will be helpful — that you will get the opinion you want?

Once you decide to seek an evaluation, the next issue is how to structure it. The first question is what data the mediator will consider. Bear in mind that a mediator's views about a case are usually based on the briefs and documents she sees, augmented by personal observations of people at the mediation. As was mentioned earlier, this means that information presented directly to the neutral has a "primacy" effect and witnesses or evidence that the neutral only hears about tend to be "melded," that is, treated as if they were a typical member of a category of people — an electrician, for example, or police officer.

As a result, if you want a mediator to give full weight to a witness or a piece of evidence, you should show it directly to the neutral. In a construction case, for example, you might ask the mediator to visit the site, or in a commercial case have the mediator meet a key witness. Again, bear in mind that in mediation, unlike a court proceeding, you can arrange for the neutral to see evidence without having to make it available to your opponent.

Take care to ensure that the mediator takes time to give your evidence adequate consideration. Don't assume, for example, that he will read every document you give him. Mediators often receive thick piles of paper in advance, and must review them without knowing what may turn out to be relevant. A neutral who is busy or concerned about keeping costs down is likely to skim through voluminous materials and wait for the parties to tell him what is important. Once the process begins, however, mediators are often reluctant to take long breaks for fear of losing momentum.

If you have documents that are important to a mediator's evaluation, tell him what, specifically, you want him to focus on, provide highlighted copies of key passages, and ask him to examine the evidence before opining. A mediator assisted in this way is less likely to jump to an erroneous conclusion with which you will then be stuck.

A second crucial question is what, exactly, you want evaluated. Don't simply say "the case." Ten years ago mediators routinely provided global opinions about the likely outcome if a dispute were adjudicated. Increasingly, however, mediators think of evaluation as a means to jump-start a stalled negotiation — more like filling a "pothole" in which the "settlement bus" has gotten stuck, than building a road to a predetermined destination. Often a prediction limited to a single issue is enough to put the parties back on the path to settlement. The question, then, is this: What aspect of the case do you want evaluated?

As discussed in Chapter 9, you should not expect every evaluation to take the form of an explicit opinion. Good mediators see evaluation as a spectrum of interventions rather than a single event. They rely on pointed questions, raised eyebrows, and other "shadow" techniques much more than explicit statements to nudge negotiations back on track. When an advocate hears a mediator make such comments, he should realize that the evaluation process is under way, but in a form less likely to provoke resentment than an explicit conclusion. Again, your chances of getting the level of specificity you want are much higher if you ask for it.

If there is no agreement, ask the mediator to continue

If a case does not settle at the mediation session, what should an advocate do? One option is to keep trying. If your mediator loses heart, you might have to prompt him to continue. Consider this anecdote related by mediator Bennett G. Picker:

Example: An inventor sued a company for patent infringement. The company hired a large law firm to represent it. It was aware, however, that litigation costs in such a case could easily exceed $1 million, and in the meantime its business strategy would be in limbo. The company therefore decided to explore settlement, and it designated a separate lawyer in the firm as "settlement counsel," responsible for seeking an agreement while his colleagues focused on litigating. The lawyer suggested early mediation. The plaintiff agreed, and the parties selected a retired judge as mediator.

At the end of the first day of mediation, notwithstanding a defense offer of several million dollars, the mediator indicated that the parties were far apart and recommended that the process end. The settlement counsel suggested, however, that the mediator instead ask the plaintiff to think about how he would spend the millions of dollars that were on the table, and adjourn the process for a week. The hope was that loss aversion would set in, making the plaintiff reluctant to risk money that was already "his." At the second session, the defense sweetened its offer slightly and the parties reached agreement.

Questions

5. Parties are mediating a dispute concerning the amount due from a commercial real estate developer to a building contractor under a "cost-plus" contract. You represent the developer. The contract provides that the contractor will be reimbursed for its reasonable costs plus a 10 percent profit. The project is complete and all issues have been resolved except one: The contractor has demanded that the developer pay for the cost of benefits in a tax-sheltered retirement plan accrued by the contractor's employees while they were working on the project. Your client believes that the contract, which is silent on the issue, does not call for reimbursement of employee expenses other than wages and usual fringe benefits such as medical care.

The mediation proceeds through an opening session and a lengthy series of caucuses. The law and facts relevant to the issue are exhaustively discussed, but the parties continue to disagree about the merits. You privately evaluate the likely outcome in court at a $650,000 verdict for the contractor, with a potential high of $1 million and a low of zero. You expect the future defense costs in the case to be roughly $75,000. Your client is reluctantly prepared to offer up to $600,000, and if absolutely necessary would go to $700,000. He has no interest in working with this contractor again. During the afternoon the process gradually focuses on exchanges of money offers. The offers are as follows:

Contractor's demand:	Developer's offer
$1.5 million	$100,000
$1.3 million	$100,000
$1.25 million	$250,000
$1.2 million (with difficulty)	$275,000
Remains at $1.2 million	Defendant refuses to "bid against myself"

   a. Assuming that the only term at issue is money, what should you do next on behalf of the developer?

   b. Suppose that your client sees a possibility of using the contractor to do approximately $200,000 worth of work on another property. What process would you recommend?

6. You represent the plaintiff in an employment dispute. It is 5 P.M. and you have been mediating for nearly eight hours. You began with a demand of $1.5 million, and in response the defendant offered $25,000. After laborious bargaining, you have dropped to $400,000. You need at least $350,000 in a cash settlement, but could conceivably go to $200,000 if your client were offered a good job back at the company. Unfortunately, the defendant is at only $100,000, having moved there from a prior offer of $85,000. Your client is feeling very

> frustrated and has told the mediator this. The mediator has gone back to the defense and returned.
>
> a. Assume that the defendant suggests that the mediator play "confidential listener" and you agree. What should you tell the mediator?
>
> b. Assume instead that the defense suggests a "mediator's proposal." Should you agree?

If negotiations fail

Sometimes settlement is genuinely unachievable. Even in such situations a mediator can be of use by helping disputants to design an efficient process of adjudication, for example, by facilitating negotiations over a discovery plan or brokering an agreement on an expedited form of arbitration. To take advantage of mediation even when settlement is not possible:

- Ask the mediator to contact the parties periodically to urge further negotiations.
- Ask the mediator to facilitate agreement on an efficient process of adjudication.

How should an advocate leave an unsuccessful mediation process? A litigator offers the following advice:

> At some point, hours or days after you have started, the mediation process will end. If it ends with an agreement, that is fine. But if you can't reach agreement, accept that as well. Parties and lawyers often get desperate as the mediation nears conclusion, but the dispute remains unsettled. It is possible, but exceedingly unlikely, that the mediation is the last chance to settle the case. More likely, there will be multiple opportunities — at deposition, at court-ordered settlement conferences, before trial, during trial, even after trial and appeal — to settle. As such, do not despair or let your client despair if you walk away without a deal. Not all cases should be settled, and almost none should be settled on any available terms. Most will eventually settle one way or another, so if you can't settle at the mediation, ask yourself what benefits you can achieve before you part ways.
>
> Occasionally, you can agree to keep talking. Sometimes that dialogue will depend on one side or the other developing more information. Or it might depend on how well a witness does at a deposition or whether a particular motion is granted or denied. Search for partial agreements if feasible or part company respectfully so that the possibility of future negotiation remains open. In all likelihood, settlement will eventually occur and both you and your client will benefit if you keep that probability in mind. (Stern 1998)

Attorneys too often treat the mediation process simply as a safe place in which to conduct positional bargaining and mediators as mere messengers, trading arguments and offers until they reach impasse. At that point the mediator often takes over the process by making a settlement recommendation or offering an evaluation.

We hope you appreciate that whatever approach you take to bargaining, the mediation process has a great deal to offer. Lawyers who approach mediation actively, looking at a mediator as a consultant, resource, and potential ally, use the process to best effect and obtain optimal outcomes for their clients.

PART
IV

SPECIALIZED TOPICS

CHAPTER
12

Specific Applications

Mediation is used in a wide variety of subject areas. From its traditional roots in family, union, and construction disputes it has expanded to employment, environmental, high-tech, and even criminal cases. The application of mediation to specialized fields raises issues of process design, and also poses the question of whether the process is appropriate for every kind of dispute. We explore these issues here. There is a rich literature on the use of mediation in each subject area, and we invite you to read more on applications of particular interest to you.

A. Family Disputes

1. What Is Unique About Family Mediation?

Family disputes involve several factors that make them different from other civil cases. Among them are the following.

Intense emotions. Marriage is perhaps the most intimate relationship that human beings can enter. People often define themselves around being a husband or wife, and divorce thus strikes at the very heart of their sense of identity and self-worth. This is likely to provoke feelings more intense than those found in almost any other kind of conflict. Marital discord can also trigger deep and sometimes irrational emotions that stem from each spouse's own childhood.

Continuing relationships. Ordinarily when people fall into disagreement, they have the option to separate. If a couple has children, however, they usually cannot completely dissociate even when they divorce. Instead, ex-spouses remain connected in their roles as parents, often for many years. Divorced parents must find ways to share their children's physical presence, financial responsibility, teaching, socializing, and a variety of other tasks. People often find it difficult to cooperate on these issues even when they are happily married. If both parties seek custody, or if a spouse decides to use the children as a weapon in marital conflict, difficulties will multiply.

Impact on, and participation by, children.   While children are young they are completely dependent on parental decisions about their upbringing. This raises a concern that a spouse who is desperate to escape a marriage or simply not thinking clearly may sacrifice a child's best interests to his or her own wishes. For teenagers, a different problem arises. Older children often have strong wishes about where they want to live and how to lead their lives, and can become third-party actors in disputes over custody and visitation, rejecting agreements worked out by parents and complicating the process of settlement.

Potential for physical or emotional abuse.   In domestic conflicts, unlike most civil disputes, there is a real possibility that criminal acts will occur, in the form of physical or emotional abuse. Even when victims do not complain, society has a strong interest in preventing such acts or an abused spouse from giving away rights. This issue is especially acute in states that require couples to engage in mediation as a precondition to gaining access to a court, an issue discussed in Chapters 13 and 15.

Lack of legal counsel.   Despite the fact that family disputes involve some of people's most basic rights, divorcing spouses are less likely than most litigants to obtain legal advice. Businesses typically have resources to obtain counsel, and in personal injury cases contingent fees or insurance can provide parties with access to lawyers. Family disputes, however, involve disagreements between individuals who often have no means to pay legal costs. This creates a serious risk that participants in family mediation will not get good advice, making it difficult for them to negotiate effectively and putting mediators in an awkward position.

Although there can be problems with the use of mediation in family cases, the consequences of litigating such disputes can be worse. Legal proceedings are often deeply destructive, creating rather than healing emotional scars and exhausting a family's financial resources at the very time its expenses are increasing. Legal battles over custody and visitation, in particular, often have a severe impact on children.

For these reasons, family disputes were among the first cases to be mediated. Most states now mandate that disputes over child custody or visitation go through mediation before entering a courtroom.

We have seen that the process of family mediation differs from traditional civil or commercial mediation in several respects. First, the parties generally remain together throughout rather than separating into caucuses, and mediation occurs in multiple sessions spread over weeks or months. Attorneys are ordinarily not present, although the parties may consult a lawyer between sessions. Because many couples have issues regarding children, there is more need for the process to be interest based and future oriented. Finally, perhaps due to the strong emotional issues present in such cases, most family mediators have in the past been mental health professionals.

2. *The Process*

Given the special characteristics of family disputes, it is not surprising that the process differs from general civil mediation. The following is an edited transcript of a mediation session that occurred at the outset of a divorce case. As you read it, think about these questions.

Questions

1. How does this process differ from examples you have seen of commercial mediation?
2. What might have happened in this case if the parties had not gone to mediation?
3. Some commentators criticize this mediator's technique, seeing him as maneuvering disputants into going in a certain direction rather than helping them make decisions for themselves. Do you see any evidence of this in the transcript?
4. Like many mediators in this field, John Haynes was not a lawyer, instead holding a doctorate in the social sciences. Do you think his background has any impact on how he mediates?

❖ **John Haynes,** *Mediating Divorce: Casebook of Strategies for Successful Family Negotiations*

50 (Jossey-Bass, 1989)

Transcript and Annotations[*]

Mediator: [Your] counsel has asked you to come today to see if we can work out an agreement that is appropriate for both of you and in the best interest of Sarah and Daniel. I wonder if you could tell me a little bit about what's happened in the last month.[1] Perhaps if I could ask you to begin, Debbie, in terms of where the children are living currently and what the arrangements are.[2] Then we can see what differences there are between you and see where we go from there.

---

[*] [The footnotes to this reading contain comments of the mediator as he reviewed the transcript of the session. They set forth why he made certain interventions and his assessment of what the disputants were feeling at the time. — EDS.]

1. I open with this information question about the events of the last month to focus on what is current and avoid drifting into the past and the marriage. The body language of the couple throughout the session is very revealing. Michael is very closed when I talk to Debbie and tends to open when I talk to him. Debbie looks away from Michael and down [at] the floor when Michael says something she does not like. Michael frequently turns away from both Debbie and the mediator, gazing at the wall.

2. A focused question, directed at Debbie, is designed to limit the amount of space for a marital fight to develop. This future-oriented question sets the agenda for the session.

Debbie: Well, the children are with me in the matrimonial home. Michael left a month ago, and I have let him see the children on several occasions.[3] But the children aren't happy seeing their father. They said they don't want to see him. They are very unhappy about the separation.[4] When they come home, they're very upset. They're crying, and it takes me hours to settle them down. I just don't know how they're going to cope with this.

Mediator: So they're currently living in the family home with you, and they're spending time with their dad.[5] Michael, what is your feeling?

Michael: I think that Debra's a little . . . ah . . . she doesn't have a grasp on the situation. I've seen these kids now five times over the past month. They are happy to come with me; we have a good time. We've done a lot of things together; they enjoy being with me. They're obviously at strain, because when I was living at home they were seeing me daily, constantly. . . . I don't think that Debra is helping them at all. I'm having a great difficulty in coming back and watching her dissemble. When I bring the kids back home, she starts. . . .

Mediator: How old are the children?[6]

Michael: Five and seven.

Mediator: Five and seven, and the older one is . . .

Michael: Daniel.

Mediator: Daniel is seven and Sarah is five. Okay. It's not unusual for them to have this tension and lots of crying when they go back and forth. . . . So it's perfectly possible for them to have a good time when they're with you, Michael, but also express real concerns and reservations when they're with you, Debbie. That's not an unusual situation. Let me just see now what's the difference between you. What is it that brings you here?

Michael: Well, the difference basically is this: Debra says that I can be a part-time parent and I can see my kids every second weekend from Saturday morning until Sunday night, if I see them alone and so long as she maintains control over it.

Mediator: What does Michael want?

Michael: These are my children. I am one-half of their parents. I want the kids half-time. When we were living together, I was spending most of the time with the children.

Mediator: So you'd like to have the children spend half of the time with you and half the time with Debbie.[7]

Michael: I think so. I don't see that it's inappropriate in our circumstance.

Debbie: I don't think he wants to see the children. I think he's using that.[8]

Mediator: What do you want, Debbie? . . .

Debbie: I want him to come back. My children are devastated. I'm devastated. . . . We had plans for us and for our children, and he's destroyed that. He's giving me no reason. All of a sudden, after fifteen years of marriage, he says that's it, I can't stand

---

3. "I have let" indicates that Debbie believes she has the power in the situation. If Michael agrees with this assessment, it will provide me with some power-balancing information.

4. Debbie's complaint about Michael is diffuse as she stakes out a tough opening position, defining the problem as the children's unhappiness, which can be solved only by a change in Michael's behavior, as defined by Debbie.

5. This summary of the factual content makes no comment on Debbie's charges, so as not to solidify her position. If the mediator comments or argues with her about this, she will have to defend her position and thereby become more "wedded" to it.

6. As Michael continues his complaints, I cut through the "feelings" with a factual (closed) question on a different subject. This process interruption breaks the cycle Michael is about to launch.

7. The summary of Michael's proposal reframes it, to help Debbie hear that under his proposal she would also have them half of the time. She probably heard only that he wanted them. By pointing out the "half-full glass," the mediator facilitates the bargaining.

8. Debbie ignores the reframing of Michael's statement.

it any more. And I think you should know he's seeing someone else, and he's exposing our children to that other person. . . .[9]

Mediator: Help me understand, Debbie, what it is you are looking for me to do. . . .

Debbie: Well, I'm here because I don't want to go through the court system. If we're going to separate, I don't want a lawyer or judge shoving an agreement down my throat.

Mediator: That's wise. So, what you want me to do is mediate . . .?

Debbie: Yes.

Mediator: . . . I'm not going to work with you to get back together.[10] If you want to do that, there are other people competent at doing that. That's not my area. . . . What I'm going to do is to help you define the problem between the two of you, see what options there are to solve that problem, and help you solve that problem in a way that's mutually acceptable to you, and in the best interests of Sarah and Daniel. . . .

Mediator (to Michael): So you'd like to have them. Right? You'd like to have them half of the time.[11]

Michael: Yes.

Mediator: Debbie, if you were to structure the arrangement for the parenting, how would you structure it?[12]

Debbie: Well, I think the children need a home. . . . And I don't think he's prepared to give them the proper kind of a home. . . .

Mediator: . . . That's an issue; we will deal with it because it's obviously an issue between you. But assuming that was not an issue, then how much time would you want Sarah and Daniel to spend with their daddy?

Debbie: The children love their father, and I don't want to keep the children away from their father. I suppose if we could sort out other problems, I would want him to see them as much as he could and as much as their schedules would allow.[13]

Michael: . . . She's misrepresenting me to the children on a constant basis. She tells them that I'm sick, she tells them that I'm depressed, she tells them that poor daddy doesn't know what he's doing, poor daddy has a mean friend, poor daddy has a friend who's taking your daddy away from you.

Mediator: It's very, very hard when you get divorced, isn't it? To deal with all of the emotions and all of the things that happen.[14]

Michael: She's a professional woman, she's a smart lady. I have a lot of respect for her. She moves in those circles, she knows what she's doing. . . .

Debbie: Well, I don't see how the children can live one week here and one week there. I think it will be too hard on them. I don't think he's being fair to them. He's the one that broke up this family. . . .

Mediator: Are there any other problems?

Debbie: I don't think they should be exposed to this woman.[15]

Mediator: Okay . . . you're living with somebody, Michael?

---

9. Debbie sends two messages: She wants Michael back, and he is seeing another woman. I develop a hypothesis that the fight is over the other woman and devise questions to test my hypothesis.

10. I clarify my role, disclaiming responsibility for repairing the marriage.

11. The restatement of the content of Michael's proposal is designed to redirect the discussion and to emphasize "half."

12. Debbie is asked for the first position statement. Given their respective positions and the fact that hers is unlikely to be supported by community norms, I decide to look for the first concession from her.

13. Debbie makes the first significant move, acknowledging Michael's father role. She picks up my language, moving from the spousal to the parenting designation.

14. I let Michael ventilate. . . . I empathize with Michael . . . to re-engage him in the process.

15. I continue probing until all the issues are on the table. This helps to test my hypothesis and determine the order of priority of the issues. Debbie restates an untenable demand, confirming my hypothesis.

Michael: No. I have a relationship with a woman I've come to know over the last period of time. And I can honestly say this isn't the reason that I left. The reason I left is that I was sitting at home and dying, waiting to die in that house. I was sitting at home looking after the kids. Mommy's got a meeting. Mommy's at the hospital. . . . They need their mother, they love their mother. But . . . all of a sudden I'm a bad bastard. . . .

Mediator: I'm hearing Debbie say that. I'm also hearing her say they love their father and they need their father and she would like to work it out so they could be with their father.[16] That's what I'm hearing on two levels . . . and those are the issues that we need to focus on and get some agreement on. . . . What would you like?[17]

Debbie: Well, I don't think he should be sleeping — letting his girl friend sleep overnight, and sleeping in the same bedroom with her with our children in the house. I don't think it's right.

Mediator: Let me ask you now: A question, if . . . excuse me just one second, but what is her name?

Michael: Jocelyn.

Mediator: Jocelyn. If Jocelyn is not sleeping over, would you feel comfortable working out some arrangement for the children?[18]

Debbie: I'd feel more comfortable. I'd be more comfortable, as well, if he had a house not too far from ours, so the children could go back and forth on their bicycles. . . .

Michael: Tell him about what sort of car I should drive. Tell him about where I should take the kids on the afternoons. Tell him about. . . .

Mediator: And you, Michael, would like to make your own decisions about these issues?

Michael: Of course. This is ridiculous. . . .

Mediator: Okay, so you've been living apart for a month. You're both angry with each other, and that's perfectly legitimate, and that's perfectly normal, too. . . . Although, interestingly enough, so far today I've not heard any serious differences emerge between you as father and mother. There's a lot as wife and husband — there you're way apart — but not as mother and father. I'm wondering now where you want to go. . . .

Debbie: He's a good father. He's been a good father. I can't deny that. The children love him and he loves the children.

Mediator: In the short run, Michael, could you agree that Jocelyn would not sleep over when the kids are with you?

Michael: What's the short run?

Mediator: Two months. . . . Give the children a sort of chance to settle in.

Michael: I can live with that. I don't know if Jocelyn can, but I can live with that. . . .

Mediator: All right. Debbie, if, for the next two months, when the children were with Michael . . . she's not sleeping over, . . . how would you then feel about sharing the parenting? . . .

Debbie: Well, I want the children to see their dad, but why does she have to be along? . . .

Mediator: There's a lot of work to be done by all of us in terms of working out all of the details. . . . I'm wondering if we could move for just the next two months, in a sense of trying to get a little space for both of you as we think through all of the issues.

---

16. Michael moves from talking to me to talking directly to Debbie. Therefore, I permit him to continue . . . even though he begins to ventilate. Michael sends a message to Debbie that she will not be displaced. The mediator considers this directional information, indicating where Michael might move in the negotiations.

17. I am using a particularly gentle tone of voice as I pursue this line of questions and providing Debbie with a face-saving way out.

18. A reframing into a future goal, not a current impediment, in an effort to decouple the issue from Jocelyn.

Debbie: Well, maybe if he would agree not to hold her hand and kiss her in front of the children — that's just his friend, that's what he's told them. . . .
Mediator: Okay, so you're saying that if Michael would agree not to be physically affectionate with Jocelyn while the children are there, you'll feel comfortable moving off your position and sharing time for the children with both of you.
Debbie: I'm not saying fifty-fifty, but . . . I'd try.
Michael: I'll live with it.
Mediator: All right. Let's then do that for the next few weeks. Let's review it along the way, and let's get back together next week to talk about some of the other issues that are going on between you, so that we can try to get the children clearly out of the middle of your fight as spouses. Okay?
Debbie: Thanks.

The Mediator's Concluding Thoughts

It could be argued that Michael lost in this settlement. He did not achieve the 50–50 shared parenting he sought, and he did give up his girlfriend when the children slept over. It could also be argued that I had a major role in shaping the agreement. These observations are true — in the short run. Note, however, that I sought the agreement only for a couple of months; it was not a permanent agreement. I did not make a moral judgment about Jocelyn's sleeping with Michael; I made a practical one. Debbie was incapable of dealing with her displacement by Jocelyn as wife, and her possible displacement by Jocelyn as mother, while she was still dealing with her loss of Michael. . . . What this couple needed was a brief respite from the battle, to give them a chance to organize their lives for the next two months. . . . Mediation is situational. . . . The agreement provided them with a breathing space in which to collect themselves and sort out the more serious emotional issues.

---

3. An Alternative Process: Transformative Mediation

Chapter 5 mentioned a different kind of mediative process known as "transformative" mediation, which does not seek to settle disputes but is focused instead on creating a setting in which participants can, if they wish, change the way in which they view themselves and others in the dispute. The following reading describes how transformative techniques are used in divorce and family disputes.

❖ **Robert A. Baruch Bush & Sally Ganong Pope,** *TRANSFORMATIVE MEDIATION PRINCIPLES AND PRACTICES IN DIVORCE MEDIATION*

Divorce and Family Mediation 53 (Folberg et al. eds., 2004)

Why do parties come to divorce mediators, and what is it that mediators can do to best serve them? The parties themselves, as they enter mediation, give varied reasons for their choice, but most fall into the following categories. Saving money and time and avoiding the legal system are at the top of most lists. Reducing hostility and conflict for their own sake and the sake of their children, and developing effective parenting plans, are also important. One party may be more interested in the time-savings and the other in protection of the children. Most all, however, agree that staying out of the legal system is essential. Certainly, with few exceptions, all hope to achieve a fair divorce settlement agreement. . . .

How then are we to understand the "why" of divorce mediation? In our view, all of the above descriptions of clients' goals express their desire to experience a different form of conflict interaction than they have experienced in their private negotiations and than they believe they would find in the legal system. . . . Rather, they want to come out of the process feeling better about themselves and each other. . . .

This conclusion is the result of insights from the fields of communication, developmental psychology and social psychology, among others. According to that view — what we call "transformative" theory — conflict is about peoples' interaction with one another as human beings. It is not primarily about problem-solving, about satisfaction of needs and interests. Certainly there are problems to be solved at the end of a marriage — the assets to be divided, the parenting plan to be created — and certainly parties want to solve those problems. The reality is, however, that they want to do so in a way that enhances their sense of their own competence and autonomy without taking advantage of the other. They want to feel proud of themselves for how they handled this life crisis, and this means making changes in the difficult conflict interaction that is going on between them, rather than simply coming up with the "right" answers to the specific problems.

. . . When we study perceptions of and attitudes towards conflict, we find that what most people find hardest about conflict is not that it frustrates their satisfaction of some interest or project, no matter how important, but rather that it leads and even forces them to behave toward themselves and others in ways that they find uncomfortable and even repellent. . . . Before the conflict, there is some decent human interaction going on, whatever the context — between people in a family, a workplace, a community. Even divorcing couples were once engaged in some form of decent, even loving, human interaction. Then the conflict arises and, propelled by the vicious circle of disempowerment and demonization, what started as a decent interaction spirals down into one which is negative, destructive, alienating, and demonizing, on all sides. . . .

Given this view of what conflict entails and "means" to parties, where does conflict intervention come into the picture? In particular, what are divorcing couples looking for when they seek the services of a mediator? One fundamental premise of the transformative model is that what bothers parties most about conflict is the interactional degeneration itself, and therefore what they most want from an intervene — even more than help in resolving specific issue — is help in reversing the downward spiral and restoring a more humane quality to their interaction. . . .

But how do parties in conflict reverse the destructive conflict spiral? . . . The first part of an answer to this question is that the critical resource is the parties' own basic humanity: their essential strength, and their essential decency and compassion, as human beings. . . . They move from weakness to strength, becoming (in more specific terms) calmer, clearer, more confident, more articulate and more decisive. They shift from self-absorption to responsiveness, becoming more attentive, open, trusting, and more responsive toward the other party. . . . [T]hese dynamic shifts are called "Empowerment" and "Recognition." Moreover, there is also a reinforcing feedback effect. . . . The stronger I become the more open I am to you. The more open I am to you, the stronger you feel, the more open you become to me, and the stronger I feel. . . . Why "conflict transformation"? Because as the parties make empowerment and recognition shifts, and as those shifts gradually reinforce in a virtuous circle, the interaction as a whole begins to turn the corner and regenerate. . . .

What divorcing parties want from mediators, and what mediators can in fact provide — with proper focus and skills — is help and support for these small but critical shifts by each party. . . . The mediator's primary goals are: (1) to foster Empowerment shifts, by supporting but never supplanting each party's deliberation and decision-making, at every point in the session where choices arise (regarding process or outcome); and (2) to foster Recognition shifts, by encouraging and supporting but never forcing each party's freely chosen efforts to achieve new understandings of the other's perspective.

The transformative model does not ignore the significance of resolving specific issues; but it assumes that if mediators do the job just described, the parties themselves will very likely make positive changes in their interaction and, as a result, find acceptable terms of resolution for themselves where such terms genuinely exist. . . . The transformative model posits that this is the greatest value mediation offers to families in conflict: it can help people conduct conflict itself in a different way. . . .

This is what we have learned from the parties that we have worked with and studied over all these years. . . . The promise mediation offers is real . . . because wise mediators can support the parties' own work, create a space for that work to go on, and — most important — stay out of the parties' way. . . .

Translating Theory into Practice: How Does the Transformative Mediator Work?

. . . *Essential Skills: Avoiding Directive Responses.* The mediator "follows" or accompanies the parties. . . . The transformative mediator is not the director of the discussion. . . . He trusts the parties. He has confidence in them — that they know best — that they know what is right for themselves and their children. He will not attempt to substitute his judgment for theirs. He will not try to steer them in the direction of what he thinks is the best arrangement for them and their children. He will not decide what is fair for them. He respects and trusts the parties to make those decisions. The mediator is not trying "to get the parties to do anything." He is not trying to "get them" to talk to each other, to stop arguments for the sake of the children, or to stay out of court. . . . Probing for the "real, underlying issues" is leading, directive, and disrespectful of the party choice about what to talk about. Following the parties in their discussion will highlight all of the issues the parties choose to put out on the table. . . .

The skills employed by the transformative divorce mediator are simple to describe: listening, reflection, summarizing, questions used to open doors, to invite further discussion on a subject raised by the parties, and to "check in" on what the parties want to do at a choice point in the discussion. . . . They are difficult to employ. It is much easier to allow our directive impulses and positive goals for the parties to steer us into leading and guiding the discussion and, therefore, the outcomes. It is much more difficult to stay with the parties through their cycles of conversation as they develop strength and understanding and become clear about what they want to do. . . .

---

4. Policy Issues

The very elements that make divorce mediation so appealing compared to the adversarial model also create dangers and raise serious policy issues. Because mediation distinguishes itself as an approach that recognizes divorce and family disputes as both matters of the heart and of the law, there exist issues of how emotional feelings are to be weighed against and blended with legal rights and obligations and what are appropriate subjects for mediation. Because mediation is conducted in private and is less hemmed in by rules of procedure, substantive law, and precedent, questions arise of whether the process is fair and the terms of a mediated agreement are just. This concern for a fair and just result has particular applicability to custody and child support provisions because mediated bargaining occurs between parents, and children are rarely present or independently represented during mediation.

Because mediation represents an "alternative" to the adversarial system, it lacks the precise and perfected checks and balances that are the principal benefit of the adversary process. The purposeful "a-legal" character of mediation creates a constant risk of overreaching and dominance by the more knowledgeable, powerful, or less emotional party. Some argue that the a-legal character of divorce mediation requires all the more careful court scrutiny before mediated agreements are approved and incorporated into a judicial decree. Others argue against court review of mediated agreements. They reason that if the parties have utilized mediation to reach agreement, there is no need for the expense, delay, and imposition of a judge's values — all features of the judicial review process. Questions about the enforceability of agreements to mediate as well as the enforceability of mediated agreements have not been fully answered.

Fairness

In considering whether mediated settlements will be fair and just, we must ask "compared to what"? We know that the great majority of divorce cases currently go by default. The default may be a result of ignorance, guilt, or a total sense of powerlessness. The default could also be a result of an agreement between the parties on distributional questions, eliminating the need for an appearance. The question persists in our present dispute resolution system of whether such agreements are the result of unequal bargaining power due to different levels of experience, patterns of dominance, the greater emotional need of one divorcing party to get out of the marriage, or a greater desire on the part of one of the parties to avoid the expense and uncertainty of litigation.

The current adversarial approach does not require the adverse parties to be represented, nor does it impose a mediator or "audience" to point out imbalances and assure that they are recognized by the parties, as mediation should attempt to do. Pro se divorce, in which there need be no professional interven-tion prior to court review, is increasingly popular and sanctioned by our existing system. Mediation, at least, provides a knowledgeable third party to help the couple evaluate their relative positions so that they can make reasoned decisions.

The most common pattern of legal representation in divorce is for one party to retain an attorney for advice and preparation of the documents. The other party will often negotiate directly with the moving party's attorney or retain an attorney to do so without filing an appearance. If a second attorney has not been retained, the unrepresented party will often consult with an attorney to deter-mine whether the proposed settlement is "fair enough" not to contest and if all necessary items have been covered or discussed. The reviewing attorney serves as a check, informing the client of any other options to the suggested terms and whether the points of agreement fall within an acceptable range of legal norms. The likelihood of a different court outcome than the proposed agreement is weighed against the financial, time, and emotional expenses of further nego-tiation or litigation.

A similar pattern of independent legal consultation could, and should, be utilized for review of mediated agreements. Current mediation practice, influ-enced by ethical restraints, is to urge or require that each divorcing party seek independent legal counsel to review the proposed agreement before it is signed. Although the criteria for independent attorney review of a proposed mediated agreement are not clear, the purpose of the review is no less clear than it is under present "fair enough" practice. The initial mediated agreement is formed in a cooperative environment with the assistance of a neutral person who serves as a check against intimidation and overreaching. Independent legal review by an attorney for one spouse pursuant to a "fair enough" standard would assure at least as great a fairness safeguard as the common reality of our present adversary system. When both parties to the mediation obtain independent legal review, as they should be encouraged to do, there is a double check of what is fair enough. In some complex cases, other professional review, such as that of a certified public accountant, may be necessary.

Protection of children

When divorce involves minor children, some argue that the state has a responsibility beyond encouraging the speedy, private settlement of disputes between parents. The state, however, under the well-developed doctrine of *parens patriae*, has a responsibility for the welfare of children only when parents cannot agree or cannot adequately provide for them. Divorce mediation begins with the premise that parents love their children and are best able to decide how, within their resources, they will care for them.

A mediated agreement is much more likely than a judicial decision to match the parents' capacity and desires with the child's needs. Whether the parents' decision is the result of reasoned analysis or is influenced by depression, guilt, spite, or selfishness, it is usually preferable to an imposed decision that may impede cooperation and stability for the child. In any event, a resolution negotiated by attorneys or reviewed by or litigated before a court is no more likely than a mediated settlement to disclose which outcomes are the result of depression, spite, guilt, or selfishness.

The principal protection that a mediator can offer a child in the context of divorce is to ensure that the parents consider all factors that can be developed between them relative to the child's needs and their abilities to meet those needs. The mediator should be prepared to ask probing and difficult questions and to help inform the parents of available alternatives. The mediator's ethical commitment, however, is to the process of parental self-determination, not to any given outcome.

The continuing role of courts and attorneys

Increased use of divorce mediation does not remove the courts from the divorce process and would not entirely eliminate adversarial proceedings. We know that some cases cannot be settled or mediated. There must be a fair and credible forum with procedural safeguards and rules to assure the peaceful resolution of disputes for parties who are unable to recognize the benefits that may come from a less coercive process. The threat of court litigation, with all of the human and material expense that it requires, might be the very element that will help some parties cut through their egocentric near-sightedness to see that their self-interests, as well as the interest of the family, may be promoted through mediation rather than a court fight.

To conclude, divorce mediation has been touted as a replacement for the adversary system and a way of making divorce less painful. Although it should be available as an alternative for those who choose to use it, it is not a panacea that will create love where there is hate, or totally eliminate the role of the adversary system in divorce. It may, however, reduce acrimony and postdivorce litigation by promoting cooperation. It might also lessen the burden of the courts in deciding many cases that can be diverted to less hostile and less costly procedures (see Folberg et al., 2004).

Questions

5. What do you think are the primary risks to parties in mediating family disputes? Are risks larger in disputes in certain subject areas or involving particular types of litigants?
6. Would you impose any special conditions on mediation of family disputes?
7. In answering the preceding questions, would you distinguish between private mediation, in which parties or lawyers opt for mediation, and court-connected mediation, in which parties may be compelled to engage in mediation by a judge or court rule?

B. Employment Cases

One of the fastest growing areas of mediation practice is employment disputes. These range from contract claims by terminated executives to discrimination charges lodged by hourly employees. In the excerpt that follows, practicing mediators analyze the special issues likely to arise in such cases.

❖ **Carol A. Wittenberg, Susan T. Mackenzie & Margaret L. Shaw,**
EMPLOYMENT DISPUTES

Mediating Legal Disputes 279 (D. Golann ed., 2009)

The use of mediation to resolve employment disputes is on the rise. Increasingly, federal district courts are referring discrimination cases to mediation, and similarly administrative agencies charged with enforcing anti-discrimination laws are experimenting with mediation programs. Mediation is well suited to resolving employment disputes for a number of reasons

1. Special Issues

Emotionality

Employment disputes usually involve highly emotional issues. It is said that loss of one's job is the third most stressful life event, next only to death and divorce. Whether one's livelihood is at stake, as in a wrongful termination case, or the issue involves a professional relationship that has gone awry, as in a sexual harassment claim, the dispute occurs in a charged atmosphere. A mediator can help parties vent their anger and frustrations in a nonjudgmental setting that allows them to feel that their positions have been heard and to move on to a more productive, problem-solving viewpoint.

One of us, for example, had the experience of being asked by a plaintiff after several hours of mediation if a one-on-one meeting with the mediator was possible, and counsel agreed. After telling the mediator that she reminded her of a former boss who had been an important mentor, the plaintiff talked about how upset the case had made her. She also talked about how much the negotiations over dollars were leaving her feeling disassociated from the process, and from what she was personally looking to accomplish. The mediator was able to help the plaintiff identify her feelings, think through what she really wanted out of a resolution, and work within the process to accomplish that result. The case settled shortly after their caucus.

Confidentiality

The privacy and confidentiality that mediation affords may be important to employees and employers alike. For example, in many of the cases involving sexual harassment claims we mediate, a primary focus of claimants is to have an unpleasant situation stop, stop quickly, and stop permanently. Individual respondents, too, unless they are looking for vindication, may want to get on with their lives and put the incident behind them. Most employees are concerned about their reputations and want their careers to continue uninterrupted. Employers, for their part, are almost always interested in confidentiality. This is particularly true in discrimination cases since publicity can affect the employer's reputation in the marketplace. Employers are also concerned that without confidentiality, settlements will create precedents or "benchmarks" for future complainants, or encourage "me-too" complaints.

Creativity of outcomes

Mediation's creativity is particularly important in employment disputes, where the impact of the controversy can have profound effects on the parties' lives. We find that in many of the litigated disputes we mediate non-legal and non-monetary issues are barriers as significant to resolution as the financial and legal aspects of the case. For example, in one age discrimination claim we mediated, the settlement called for the employee to retain his employment status without pay for a two-year period, so as to vest certain benefits afforded retirees. In a gender discrimination case, the terms involved keeping the employee on the payroll for a period of time with a new title to assist her in securing alternative employment. In a breach of contract case involving a senior executive, part of the settlement involved a guaranteed loan to invest in a new business.

Cost savings

Practical considerations also make mediation of employment disputes an attractive alternative to litigation. The process is likely to be much less expensive than litigation, or even arbitration. One attorney who frequently represents plaintiffs in discrimination cases observed that, as of the mid-2000s, the litigation cost of a discrimination claim to individual claimants was roughly $50,000, as compared to $2,000 to $4,000 for mediation. A study in the early 1990s estimated the cost to defend a single discrimination claim at $81,000, a figure that is now almost certainly much higher.

Note also that the monetary cost of litigation does not take into account the indirect, personal, and emotional costs to all parties of a court proceeding. All workplaces have informal information channels; we often hear from individual mediation participants about the disruptive effects of the case on fellow employees. For instance, at one company with which we worked speculation was rampant about who would be let go or reassigned in the event the case resulted in the reinstatement of a discharged employee.

Speed

Mediation is also likely to be significantly faster than litigation. This is of particular importance in the employment context, given the dramatic increase in antidiscrimination claims. In our experience, mediation of a routine employment case involving an individual claimant generally can be concluded in one or sometimes two days. Although some parties are unable to reach complete closure in the mediation sessions, often additional follow up telephone conferences with one or both parties will bring about a settlement. An evaluation of the EEOC's pilot mediation program, for instance, showed that mediation resolved charges of discrimination less expensively and more quickly than traditional methods, with closure in an average of 67 days as opposed to 294 in the regular charge process

Questions

Are there disadvantages to mediation in the context of employment disputes? Of course there are, although we believe that some of the "dangers" are often overemphasized. Some employers are concerned that the availability of mediation will encourage frivolous complaints. Others are concerned that mediation simply adds a layer of time and expense when a case does not settle. Certain attorneys have also expressed a concern that an opposing party might merely be using mediation as a form of discovery. There are, of course, specific cases that are inappropriate for mediation, cases that upon analysis are without any apparent merit and call for the employer to take a firm stance.

2. Challenges for the Mediator

There are some distinctive characteristics of employment cases that can challenge a mediator and require special approaches

Disparity in Resources

While parties in other kinds of cases may have unequal resources, in employment disputes a lack of parity can make it difficult even to get the parties to the table. Employment claimants are often out of work, or face an uncertain employment future. They may balk at the added expense of a mediator, particularly when the outcome is uncertain. While some employers will agree to pay the entire mediation bill as an inducement to a plaintiff to participate, others are concerned that without some financial investment a plaintiff will not participate in the process wholeheartedly. In these circumstances, we have found several approaches effective. If, for example, the employer is worried about the employee's investment in the process, the mediator can explore the nature of that concern and whether verbal representations by the claimant or claimant's lawyer might allay them. As an alternative, a mediator can suggest having the employer assume most of the cost, while requiring the employee to pay something.

Timing

The timing of mediation can affect both the process and its outcome. Where it is attempted shortly after a claim has been raised, the claimant may need extra help in getting beyond feelings of anger or outrage, while an individual manager or subject of a claim may feel betrayed. If little or no discovery has occurred the lack of information about the facts on the part of one or both parties can hamper productive negotiations. At the other extreme, when a case has already been in litigation for an extended period of time, positions can become hardened and the parties even more determined to stop at nothing short of what they perceive to be "justice.

For instance in one case we handled, an age discrimination claim referred by the court, the plaintiff's attorney had done little investigation prior to the mediation and thus was unaware of circumstances that called into question the plaintiff's integrity during his final year of employment. Assisting the attorney to become more realistic about the chances for a recovery at trial became the challenge of this mediation. In another case that involved a sexual harassment claim, outside counsel for the employer, who had recommended mediation, was unaware of some of the conduct of the individual manager who was the subject of the allegations. That case required us to mediate between the employer and the manager, the individual manager and the claimant, and the claimant and the corporate entity as well.

Imbalances of Power

In certain employment disputes, such as those involving sexual harassment claims, a perceived or real imbalance in the power relationship between the parties may itself constitute an impediment to settlement. We have found that as a general proposition, particularly in dealing with an individual who feels at a power disadvantage in mediation, movement is better accomplished by pulling rather than by pushing. For example, in one case where the facts underlying the claim were perhaps unconscionable but not legally actionable, helping the claimant to recognize the benefits of moving forward with her life was more effective than trying to convince her that she had a weak case.

When an issue of power imbalance is articulated or apparent, it is helpful to take the time to consult with the parties before the "real" mediation begins in order to structure the process. We typically discuss, for example, whether the complainant or the attorney wants to make an opening statement. We have observed that complainants who prepare a statement for the initial joint session tend to feel a degree of participation that engenders a sense of control and dignity in the process that is not otherwise possible. At times, having a family member or close friend attend a session is helpful. We also attempt to establish in advance whether will be necessary to keep the complainant and individual respondent apart at least initially. We routinely schedule pre-mediation conference calls with all persons involved in the case to work through these kinds of issues.

Desire for Revenge

Complainants who feel they have been wronged will sometimes look for a way to make the employer or the individual charged with harassing or discriminatory behavior "pay." Such a focus on revenge can present a major obstacle to settlement. There is no simple way to deal with this in mediation. Sometimes, particularly in cases where the complaint has already prompted the employer to take preventive measures, explaining the full impact that the complaint has already had on workplace policies or on the careers of others can help the complainant recognized and change to a posture more conducive to resolution. Another approach may be to have the individual respondent contribute out of his or her own pocket to a financial settlement.

Negotiation by Numbers

In some employment mediations one or both parties may become fixed on a settlement figure and refuse to budge. Finding a new framework for analysis that appears objectively fair can help parties stuck on numbers save face and ultimately agree on a different figure to settle the case.

Non-Legal and Personal Issues

At times both parties will fail to realize that a non-legal problem is the root cause of an employment dispute. For example, in one case we handled a personality conflict between the head of accounting and his most senior employee had festered for years. The working relationship between the two had deteriorated to the point that they routinely hurled racial and sexual epithets at one another. At that point, management could see no alternative to dismissing one or both of them. With the mediator's assistance, each party was able to shift focus from placing blame on the other to recognizing their mutual interest in continuing to be employed, and mutually-acceptable procedures for personal interaction in the office were identified and reduced to writing. During the mediation, the parties also came to recognize that a contributing, if not overriding, cause of the deterioration of their relationship was an outstanding loan from the department head to the bookkeeper. While the department head had treated the loan as forgiven years ago, in reality the bookkeeper's failure to repay it had continued to bother the department head. The resolution between the parties included a repayment schedule for the loan.

In some employment cases, the real barrier to resolution may be an individual who is not a direct party to the dispute. For instance, in one case we mediated involving a disability claim by an airline manager it became clear that his spouse, who was also present, was so angered by what she perceived as unconscionable treatment that she urged rejection of all settlement offers as insulting. The mediator dealt with this situation by recognizing the spouse's feelings and helping her understand that her anger was fueled at least in part by resentment over the amount of time her spouse had spent on his job rather than with his family. The spouse was also given an opportunity to air her position directly to the corporate representatives. Once she had done this, she was able to reorient her focus from the past to the future and the elements of a mutually acceptable package fell into place.

"Outside" Barriers to Resolution

In some employment cases the real barrier to resolution may be an individual who is not a direct party to the dispute. In one case we mediated involving a disability claim by an airline manager with over 25 years of service, the claimant was moving toward resolution. However, as the mediation progressed, it became clear that his spouse, who was also present, was so angered by what she perceived as unconscionable treatment by the employer that she considered all offers of settlement by the employer insulting. Egged on by his spouse, the claimant became more obstinate and refused to budge from his initial position.

The mediator dealt with this situation by giving recognition to the wife's feelings, and by helping her understand that her anger was fueled at least in part by resentment over the amount of time her spouse had spent on his job rather than with his family over the years. The spouse was also afforded an opportunity to air her position directly to the corporate representatives who were present. Once she had communicated her feelings, she was able to reorient her focus from the past to the future, and to consider the potential impact of lengthy litigation on her husband's deteriorating health and well-being. Both she and the complainant were then able to focus on what could be accomplished in mediation, and the elements of a mutually acceptable package fell into place.

A Case Example: Wrongful Termination and Race Discrimination

Mary Beth Lee, a 28-year old African American female, was terminated from her position as make-up artist with a clothing designer after seven years of continuous employment. At the time of her termination, Mary Beth earned a base salary of $55,000 and bonus of $12,000. The clothing company is known for both its couture women's clothing and its make-up products.

Until the last eight months of her employment, Mary Beth had excelled in selling make-up at a number of the company's store locations, and developed sales in one ethnic neighborhood store to exceptional levels. Mary Beth was then transferred to a mid-town store. She accepted the transfer for two reasons: one, her boss Suzanne Kay was taking over management of the mid-town store and asked for Mary Beth to join her; and two, she would be eligible for a promotion in six months.

The mid-town store was a challenge. Historically, it had been poorly managed and sales were flat. Suzanne left the company three months after Mary Beth's transfer, as did one of Suzanne's managers. Mary Beth asked for a promotion at that time and was not interviewed for the position. Instead, the company transferred Beverly Tam, a Caucasian woman, from another store into the position Mary Beth was seeking. Beverly brought Laura Bay, another Caucasian woman, with her to the mid-town store. Laura had previously worked with Beverly as a make-up artist.

Things did not go well for Mary Beth from the time Suzanne and Laura joined the mid-town store. Mary Beth felt that she was being unfairly criticized for poor sales. In addition, her time was being scrutinized in ways she had never before experienced. Mary Beth also noticed that Suzanne started replacing other African-American make-up artists with Caucasian and Asian make-up artists. Suzanne, a demonstrative person, would often hug others, but was cold and aloof to Mary Beth. After six months at the store, Mary Beth received a mid-term performance appraisal of "less than satisfactory," the first negative performance appraisal Mary Beth had received in seven years.

Two months later, the company announced a reduction in force of 50 employees. There were two layoffs at the mid-town store and Suzanne was given the authority to select those to be laid off. Suzanne selected Mary Beth and another woman who had only joined the company within the last year. Although Mary Beth had seven years of service with the company, she had the second least seniority at the store.

Mary Beth filed suit against the company a few weeks later, charging race discrimination and wrongful termination. She opened a full-service salon in her local neighborhood, which included selling make up and providing related services. That salon has yet to turn a profit one year later. Mary Beth insisted that she looked for make-up artist jobs, but that she believed that her reputation had been harmed in the industry, making it impossible for her to find a comparable job. She also claimed that she suffered emotional distress as a result of her termination.

After the initial joint session, the mediator met separately with Mary Beth and her attorney. Mary Beth was extremely angry about her treatment by the company. She felt that she had accomplished much in her seven years, and that Suzanne set her up for termination because of her race. She was particularly upset that she had not even been interviewed for the supervisory position at the mid-town store, and pointed out that Laura had no supervisory experience when she was brought to mid-town by Suzanne.

Company representatives, who viewed Mary Beth as an employee at will and one of 50 employees who lost jobs as a result of the decline in sales, did not appear to understand Mary Beth's perspective. The company stressed Mary Beth's poor performance and claimed that she disappeared frequently from the store during the day.

The mediator spent much of the day exploring Mary Beth's goals in mediation and the basis for her anger, including her feeling that she had devoted herself to the company since college graduation and that she had been humiliated by her performance appraisal and selection for layoff. Mary Beth was seeking a significant settlement to compensate her for the start-up time it would take to make her salon successful, demanding $250,000, based in part on her belief that there were two former employees who also worked with Suzanne who would testify to the manager's racist comments.

The mediator then met with company representatives to explain Mary Beth's substantive and emotional position and to explore the company's response. The company wanted to settle the case, but also believed that it was not "a six figure" case, particularly because Mary Beth had chosen to open a salon rather than to seek other employment. The company was insistent that Suzanne was a strong and fair manager and that her performance appraisal of Mary Beth was defensible. The company acknowledged that Suzanne hired more Caucasian and Asian make-up artists for the store counter, but insisted that her actions did not constitute race discrimination. The company also questioned whether Mary Beth's witnesses would actually be willing to testify against the company. Nevertheless, the company offered Mary Beth $50,000.

The mediator returned to meet with Mary Beth and her counsel. They discussed the company's offer, which Mary Beth thought was an "insult." The mediator explored some potential weaknesses in Mary Beth's claim, including her failure to search for an equivalent position after her layoff and the lack of medical treatment for emotional distress. Mary Beth's attorney acknowledged that even if she were to prevail in court, she might not be awarded the amount she was seeking. The mediator discussed with Mary Beth the emotional toll that a trial would take and her need to move on with her life.

The mediator continued with the negotiations between the two sides. After a long day, Mary Beth agreed to accept $125,000, which she viewed as a significant compromise. She was concerned about having to wait for money she needed for her salon. The mediator was convinced that Mary Beth's position was firm. At that point, the Company had offered $100,000 and was adamant that it was not going to increase its offer because of the limited value it placed on the case. Nonetheless, the company was concerned about defending the charge of racism.

The mediator had been impressed during the day with the way Mary Beth presented herself; she was impeccably dressed and her make up was perfect. She mentioned several times that losing her job and struggling to establish a business on her own affected her ability to "dress for success." As a means to bridge the gap, the mediator discussed with the company its willingness to offer Mary Beth a gift certificate to purchase designer clothing. Because of the high mark up on couture clothing, the company could offer Mary Beth a significant benefit that would cost the company a fraction of the face value. The company agreed to the idea, but insisted that the gift certificate be no more than $15,000.

The mediator presented the idea to Mary Beth, who was excited about the prospect of being able to obtain designer clothing. She accepted the $15,000 gift certificate in addition to the $100,000. Mary Beth's attorney agreed to base his fees on the $100,000 alone and the case was settled on those terms.

Questions

8. What style would you look for in an employment mediator?
9. Would a caucus or no-caucus model be more likely to be effective in such cases?
10. The U.S. Postal Service has used a form of transformative mediation in employer-employee disputes. Why do you think that two styles as different as conventional commercial and transformative mediation have each enjoyed success in this area?
11. The U.S. Equal Employment Opportunity Commission, in an effort to address lengthy delays in processing complaints, has adopted a policy of active and early promotion of mediation of all employment claims filed with the Commission. Do you see any dangers in the EEOC policy? Any advantages for parties?

C. Environmental and Public Controversies

❖ Gail Bingham, *The Environment in the Balance: Mediators Are Making a Difference*

2 AC Resol. 21 (Summer 2002)

[T]he number and magnitude of environmental disputes is rising, and finding solutions only gets more difficult . . . there are many reasons why environmental and other public policy disputes are difficult to resolve. . . . For a mediation process to be successful, it must be designed with these challenges in mind.

Multiple Forums/Changing Incentives. Frequently, the same or related [environmental] issues may be the subjects of simultaneous action at different levels of government and in one or more administrative, legislative, or judicial forums. Disputing parties may have different advantages in different forums, creating conflicting views about the best process to use. A mediated negotiation is just one more choice among competing forums.

Multiple Parties/Issues. Because environmental disputes typically affect large numbers of interested parties and involve a multiplicity of issues, organizing the negotiation process may prove to be extremely difficult. Sometimes coalitions can be formed, allowing several parties to be represented by one negotiator. At other times, one must design ways to have conversation in large groups. . . .

Institutional Dynamics.   Environmental and resource management conflicts are more often played out between organizations or groups than between individuals. Therefore, the individuals at the table must get proposals ratified by others who are not participating directly. . . .

Complex Scientific and Technical Issues.   [P]arties to environmental disputes are often confronted with large volumes of information that require broad-based expertise and may be subject to honest differences of opinion. . . .

Inequality of Resources.   Mediation processes are resource intensive in the sense that the parties take the time to negotiate with one another up front, and need funds for travel expenses, information collection, evaluation, and expert advice. While government agencies and private corporations are generally well funded and represented by paid staff, other parties may lack the necessary financial and technical resources. . . .

Public/Political Dimension.   Environmental disputes generally involve public issues, addressed in public forums, with laws, governmental institutions, and the media all playing a significant role. Any mediation process must therefore respond with sensitivity to the press and open meeting laws and must attempt to arrive at outcomes that can withstand public scrutiny. . . .

Questions

12. What qualities would you look for in selecting a mediator for an environmental dispute, as compared with an employment case?
13. Would the basic mediative strategy described in Chapter 5 have to be modified to deal with an environmental controversy? In what respects?

One of the unique aspects of public controversies is that it is often difficult to identify all of the "parties" to the dispute. Public disputes may simmer in the community at large, and first become visible through discussions in community centers, city council meetings, and the news media rather than in formal court proceedings. In such situations, one of a mediator's challenges is to determine who the key disputants are and develop a consensual framework in which they can communicate and bargain effectively.

This task is known as "convening" and the overall resolution process as "consensus-building." The word "consensus" reflects that the goal in these processes is not necessarily to achieve agreement among all the participants, but rather to develop a solution agreed to by a large enough majority to give confidence that it will be successfully implemented.

❖ **Chris Carlson,** *CONVENING*

The Consensus Building Handbook 169 (2000)

When someone *convenes* a meeting, he or she typically finds appropriate meeting space, invites people to attend, and perhaps drafts an agenda. In a consensus building process, however, which may involve multiple meetings over the course of weeks, months, or years, convening is a more complex task. In this context, convening typically involves

- assessing a situation to determine whether or not a consensus-based approach is feasible
- identifying and inviting participants to ensure that all key interests (i.e., stakeholders) are represented;
- locating the necessary resources to help convene, conduct, and support the process; and
- planning and organizing the process with participants or working with a facilitator or mediator to do so.

It may be helpful to think of convening as Phase 1 in a consensus building process, which is followed by Phase 2, the actual negotiating or consensus building phase. . . .

The Importance of Convening: Two Examples

How the convening steps are carried out, and who carries them out, can have an impact on whether or not a consensus process will be successful. The parties who serve as convenors, whether they are government agencies, private corporations, nonprofit organizations, or individuals, need to be viewed as credible and fair-minded, especially in those cases in which issues are contentious or parties are distrustful of each other. At the community level, consensus processes are often sponsored and convened by a local leader, an organization, or a steering committee made up of representatives of different groups. At the state and federal levels, government agencies or officials often serve as sponsors, and sometimes as convenors. Let us look at two examples illustrating the importance of effective convening — one convened by an individual, the other by a federal agency.

A Community Collaboration Gets Off on the Right Foot

In the first example, a diverse conflict over logging practices and their impact on endangered species was under way in a rural community in southern Oregon. By the early 1990s, there had been numerous skirmishes between environmental interests and timber industry supporters over logging in the Applegate Valley. In 1992, the listing of the northern spotted owl on the federal endangered species list led to an injunction prohibiting logging on federal lands. There were bitter and sometimes violent protests. Yet, in the midst of the crisis, some representatives of industry and environmental groups were able to negotiate land exchanges and timber sales. These agreements seemed to signal the possibility that a consensus building approach might be useful for developing a longer-range plan for the watershed.

A local environmentalist who had been one of the architects of the earlier cooperative effort served as the sponsor and convenor. He put together a proposal to use a consensus building approach to develop a comprehensive ecosystem management plan. He distributed his proposal to all the involved and affected stakeholders. He then shuttled back and forth among them, discussing and revising the proposal, and got their agreement to start meeting. The participants included most of the major interests: government agency staff, environmentalists, timber industry representatives, farmers and ranchers, and a variety of other local residents.

The convenor decided that rather than begin with a formal meeting, complete with flip charts and facilitators, he would host a potluck at his home. The first meeting was spent reaching agreement about how the process would be organized and developing ground rules. The partnership rapidly took shape, and after several months of meetings, the group arrived at an agreement on basic objectives.

After a promising beginning, the Applegate Partnership got swept up in the national politics surrounding the spotted owl issue in Oregon. All the outside attention and publicity caused the partnership to founder, but it managed to survive because participants continued to see a need for building consensus on plans and actions to serve the community's interests. The partnership has been able to develop consensus on projects to restore watersheds, improve agricultural irrigation practices, and initiate economic development projects in the community. By almost any assessment, this convening led to successful outcomes.

A Federal Agency Convenes a Similar Process That Fails

Our second example came about as a result of the Applegate experience. Word spread quickly about the success of the Applegate Partnership. Federal officials caught wind of Applegate's success, and Interior Secretary Bruce Babbitt dropped in on one of the partnership meetings. What he saw fit nicely into the administration's plans for resolving the spotted owl issue: Getting communities involved in working out how federal policies could be implemented locally. The federal government decided that there were 10 communities in which it wanted to stimulate similar partnership efforts.

However, when the federal agency tried to convene local groups and get them to form partnerships, it failed. In each case, stakeholders attended one or two meetings, but were not willing to commit to a longer-term, consensus building process. One probable reason for the failure was that the agency's attempts were made unilaterally, without consulting local stakeholders about what should be discussed and what it would take to make the discussions "safe" for participants, among other things. When the federal government organized meetings, stakeholders came, but they participated only grudgingly. They felt compelled to be there to protect their interests.

When asked, the participants revealed a variety of concerns about how the process had been planned and convened by the federal government. They were concerned, for example, about the federal government's motives, the balance of power at the table, and the availability of resources to enable all groups to participate on an equal footing. Because these questions were not addressed during the convening stage, the groups were ultimately unable and unwilling to form partnerships to work toward consensus on watershed management. . . .

What made the difference in these two cases? The difference was not in *who* carried out the convening role. Federal agencies can convene processes just as successfully as individual community members. The difference in this case lay in how the convening role was handled.

D. Intellectual Property Disputes

❖ **Technology Mediation Services,** THE BENEFITS OF MEDIATION
IN HIGH TECH DISPUTES
_____

www.technologymediation.com (2010)

Mediation is the best method of resolving most high tech and other intellectual property disputes. Mediation is fast and helps the disputants work together to find an effective solution, with much less expense than a full lawsuit. Mediated solutions preserve goodwill and reputations, and may even lay groundwork for future business. Mediation keeps control of a business' future where it belongs — in the hands of the business executives, not judges. . . .

About Mediating Intellectual Property Disputes

Mediation is not just for simple contractual disputes. Indeed, complex intellectual property matters may be resolved best through mediation. An intellectual property dispute may be especially ripe for mediation if any of the following factors exist:

One or both parties may have an interest in cost control: Most intellectual property matters are expensive to litigate. It is not unusual for a patent infringement dispute to cost each side well over $1 million through trial, and such cases are often appealed, adding more to the cost. Moreover, they often are settled via business agreements. Much of the cost of extensive discovery, trial preparation, voluminous exhibits, expert witness testimony, and diverted executive time can be spared by using mediation at an early stage to craft an appropriate settlement.

A business resolution may solve the legal dispute: A mediator can help the parties craft a variety of business arrangements, such as licensing (or cross-licensing) agreements, joint ventures, distributor agreements, usage phase-out agreements, etc., which may lay the groundwork for future business. A mediated agreement may extend well beyond the subject matter of the pending lawsuit and accommodate larger business interests.

The decision maker may misunderstand the law or technology: If the judge, jury or arbitrator may have trouble understanding intellectual property law issues such as prior art or doctrine of equivalents, or the underlying technology, it may be best to avoid the possibility of being handed a "poor" decision. The parties can keep control of the outcome by mediating, rather than relinquishing the decision to a third party.

The defendant may feel disadvantaged in the forum chosen by the plaintiff: In complex intellectual property matters, a defendant may need lots of time (and money) to prepare its defense and cross-claims alleging invalidity of the patent, trademark or copyright. If time is short, such as in investigations before the US International Trade Commission, or in federal courts such as the "rocket docket" of the Eastern District of Virginia, it may be better to settle a dispute than to defend under such constraints. Similarly, a defendant may prefer not to defend in a jury trial in the plaintiff's "home" court, or in a jurisdiction with precedent favorable to the plaintiff. Mediation offers a sensible way to end the dispute before it's too late.

The useful life of the subject matter may be depleted before the litigation is over: Many "hot" products or technologies are covered by patents, trademarks or copyrights, and by virtue of their appeal become subject to infringement. But how good is a favorable judicial decision if the patented technology already has been superseded by another patent, or if last season's most popular toy now sits on the shelf, or if some other copyrighted software game now heads the "top 10" sales list? Mediation can resolve the dispute quickly, while the product is still commercially viable.

One or both parties are concerned about disclosure of confidential information: Many intellectual property disputes, particularly alleged trade secret misappropriation, involve confidential business and technical information. Mediation avoids disclosure of such sensitive information, to the public and to your adversary. Everything said in mediation is protected as confidential settlement discussions, and cannot be introduced in litigation or disclosed in public. Additionally, a party can disclose certain information in confidence to the mediator, who will not transmit it to the opponent.

Questions

14. Given the advantages of mediation in this area, why do you suppose every high-technology dispute that cannot be directly negotiated is not mediated?

15. If you were counsel to a company that had a claim against a competitor for infringement of a biotech patent and wished to try mediation, but the only available mediators had either strong process skills or extensive technical knowledge but not both, which type of mediator would you choose? Is there a way to obtain the presence of both qualities?

E. Criminal Matters

One of the most controversial uses of mediation is in criminal cases. The vast majority of criminal charges, ranging from small misdemeanors to capital cases, are plea bargained — that is, negotiated by prosecutors and defense counsel — rather than tried. Mediation has not, however, been used with any frequency to assist the process of plea bargaining. At the same time, the use of mediation is expanding in other areas of the criminal justice system, raising both exciting possibilities and troubling issues of justice.

Questions

16. As prosecutors and defense counsel negotiate plea bargains in criminal cases, what obstacles might they encounter? Could mediation be useful in overcoming these obstacles?
17. Why do you think lawyers in the criminal justice system so rarely use mediation to help work out plea bargains?

1. Potential Charges

❖ Christopher Cooper, *Police Mediators: Rethinking the Role of Law Enforcement in the New Millennium*

7 Disp. Resol. Mag. 17 (Fall 2000)

In the 21st century, it is time for new and fresh police strategies. One such strategy is mediation of interpersonal disputes by patrol police officers. . . . The patrol police officer is often the first person to respond to many of American society's interpersonal squabbles, including disputes between neighbors, siblings, and customers and merchants. Many of these disputes are marked by flared tempers or chaos. . . . Mediation by a patrol officer need not be carried out in an office. It can be conducted on a basketball court or in a parking lot, for example. It can be done standing up or sitting down. . . .

For calls-for-service involving an interpersonal dispute in which there are no grounds to arrest or to cite a party for a law violation, mediation by a police officer often is a sensible approach. . . . When police officers apply this approach to conflict, citizens make fewer repeat calls-for-service, including 911 calls. . . . Whereas poor conflict resolution skills and unsystematic approaches by an officer can escalate disputes, using a systematic dispute resolution process such as mediation is less likely to have such a negative effect. . . .

Poor relations, particularly between people of color and police, are at epidemic levels throughout the United States. The relationship is strained in part by police who act as arbitrators in situations in which citizens have a legitimate expectation that they should be empowered to help themselves.

. . . It makes good sense to provide police officers with the professional skills they need to empower others. . . . Mediation by patrol officers champions community policing objectives by providing . . . self-empowerment to citizens, who should expect contemporary law enforcement officers to function as a police service, rather than a police force.

Question

18. Does the use of informal mediative techniques by police officers pose any dangers?

2. Victim-Offender Cases

Mediation appears to be taking root at the post-sentencing stage of the process, involving encounters between victims and offenders. The issue at this point is not the defendant's guilt, but rather how he and the victim will deal with what has happened. We have seen that mediation can be used to help people change perspectives and restore ruptured relationships, but in the criminal context such efforts are much more controversial. As you read the following excerpt, ask yourself these questions.

Questions

19. For what purposes is mediation being used here?
20. If you were designing a victim-offender program, would you make all types of criminal cases eligible for it or exclude some categories of cases? If so, which ones?

❖ Marty Price, PERSONALIZING CRIME: MEDIATION PRODUCES RESTORATIVE JUSTICE FOR VICTIMS AND OFFENDERS

7 Disp. Resol. Mag. 8 (Fall 2000)

Our traditional criminal justice system is a system of retributive justice — a system of institutionalized vengeance. The system is based on the belief that justice is accomplished by assigning blame and administering pain. If you do the crime, you do the time, then you've paid your debt to society and justice has been done. But justice for whom? . . .

Because our society defines justice in terms of guilt and punishment, crime victims often seek the most severe possible punishment for their offenders. Victims believe this will bring them justice, but it often leaves them feeling empty and unsatisfied. Retribution cannot restore their losses, answer their questions, relieve their fears, help them make sense of their tragedy or heal their wounds. And punishment cannot mend the torn fabric of the community that has been violated. . . .

Focus on Individuals, Healing

Restorative justice has emerged as a social movement for justice reform. Virtually every state is implementing restorative justice at state, regional and/or local levels. . . . Instead of viewing crime as a violation of law, restorative justice emphasizes one fundamental fact: crime damages people, communities, and relationships.

Retributive justice asks three questions: who did it, what laws were broken and what should be done to punish or treat the offender? Contrast a restorative justice inquiry, in which three very different questions receive primary emphasis. First, what is the nature of the harm resulting from the crime? Second, what needs to be done to "make it right" or repair the harm? Third, who is responsible for the repair? . . .

As the most common application of restorative justice principles, VOM [victim-offender mediation] programs warrant examination in detail. These programs bring offenders face to face with the victims of their crimes with the assistance of a trained mediator, usually a community volunteer. Victim participation is voluntary in most programs.

In mediation, crime is personalized as offenders learn the human consequences of their actions, and victims have the opportunity to speak their minds and their feelings to the one who most ought to hear them, contributing to the victim's healing. Victims get answers to haunting questions that only the offender can answer. The most commonly asked questions are "Why did you do this to me? Was this my fault? Could I have prevented this? Were you stalking or watching me?" Victims commonly report a new peace of mind, even when the answers to their questions were worse than they had feared.

Offenders take meaningful responsibility for their actions by mediating a restitution agreement with the victim to restore the victim's losses in whatever [way is] possible. Restitution may be monetary or symbolic; it may consist of work for the victim, community service, or other actions that contribute to a sense of justice between the victim and offender.

Fulfilling Restitution

. . . There are now more than 300 programs in the United States and Canada and more than 700 in England, Germany, Scandinavia, Eastern Europe, Australia, and New Zealand. Remarkably consistent statistics from a cross-section of the North American programs show that about two-thirds of the cases referred resulted in a face-to-face mediation. More than 95 percent of the cases mediated resulted in a written restitution agreement. More than 90 percent of those restitution agreements are completed within one year. In contrast, the rate of payment of court-ordered restitution is typically only from 20 to 30 percent. Recent research has shown that juvenile offenders who participate in VOM subsequently commit fewer and less serious offenses than their counterparts in the traditional juvenile justice system. . . .

Careful Preparation Required

Mediation is not appropriate for every crime, every victim, or every offender, Individual, preliminary meetings between mediator and victim, mediator and offender permit careful screening and assessment according to established criteria. . . . At their best, mediation sessions focus upon dialogue rather than the restitution agreement (or settlement), facilitating empathy and understanding between victim and offender. Ground rules help assure safety and respect. Victims typically speak first, explaining the impact of the crime and asking questions of the offender. Offenders acknowledge and describe their participation in the offense, usually offering an explanation and/or apology. The victim's losses are discussed. Surprisingly, a dialogue-focused (rather than settlement-driven) approach produces the highest rates of agreement and compliance.

Agreements that the victim and offender make together reflect justice that is meaningful to them, not limited by narrow legal definitions. [T]he overwhelming majority of participants — both victims and offenders — have reported in post-mediation interviews and questionnaires that they obtained a just and satisfying result. Victims who feared re-victimization by the offender before the mediation typically report that this fear is now gone.

Forgiveness is not a focus of VOM, but the process provides an open space in which participants may address issues of forgiveness if they wish. Forgiveness is a process, not a goal, and it must occur according to the victim's own timing, if at all. For some victims, forgiveness may never be appropriate. Restorative justice requires an offender who is willing to admit responsibility and remorse to the victim. . . .

Different Concept of Neutrality

Neutrality, as understood in the mediation of civil disputes, requires that the mediator not take sides with either party. Judgments of right and wrong are not within the mediator's role. The mediation of most crime situations, however, presents a unique set of circumstances for a mediator and the concept of neutrality must be different. In the majority of criminal cases, the parties come to VOM as a wronged person and a wrongdoer, with a power imbalance that is appropriate to this relationship. The mediator balances power only to ensure full and meaningful participation by all parties. . . . The mediator is neutral toward the individuals, respecting both as valuable human beings and favoring neither, but the mediator is not neutral regarding the wrong. . . .

Most victim-offender programs limit their service to juvenile offenses, crimes against property, and minor assaults, but a growing number of experienced programs have found that a face-to-face encounter can be invaluable even in heinous crimes. A number of programs have now mediated violent assaults, including rapes, and mediations have taken place between murderers and the families of their victims. Mediation has been helpful in repairing the lives of surviving family members and the offender in drunk-driving fatalities. In severe crime mediations, case development may take a year or more before the mediation can take place. . . . In cases of severely violent crime, VOM has not been a substitute for a prison sentence, and prison terms have seldom been reduced following mediation. . . .

What Can We Learn?

What can attorneys and other dispute resolution professionals learn from the philosophy and successes of restorative justice? Our system, which settles most cases without trial, does so with adversarial assumptions as its foundation. Each attorney is expected to maximize her client's win at the expense of the other attorney's client's loss. In the majority of cases, the clients of both attorneys (and often the attorneys, as well) feel like losers in the settlement. . . .

Our system of money damages and financial settlements for losses and injuries has a faulty assumption at its core. We give lip service to the truth that "no amount of money can right this wrong," then we conclude that the only available measure of amends is the dollar! In contrast, a basic principle of restorative justice is that a wrong creates a singular kind of relationship — an obligation to personally right that wrong. . . . The most important lesson learned from restorative justice practice may be the realization that the key to justice is found not in laws but in the recognition and honoring of human relationships.

Questions

21. Criminal prosecutions serve important public functions. Which of these functions may not be fulfilled when cases go into a VOM program?
22. Does VOM serve functions not met by the traditional criminal justice system?

F. Deal Mediation

You now understand, as many practicing lawyers do, the potentially significant role that a mediator can play in resolving disputes, enhancing communication, and even repairing relationships. It should therefore come as no surprise that some have theorized about — and in some cases implemented — efforts to apply the same principles at points "upstream" from active disputes.

The reading by Professor Stephen Goldberg in Chapter 5 gave an example of a situation in which a mediator who had been hired to act as bargaining advisor to one side in a business negotiation became both advisor to his own team and an informal "mediator to the deal" for both sides. The next section, on international mediation, describes an international commercial negotiation in which a Hollywood agent performed a similar function. Could "true" mediators — impartial, rather than retained by one side — be helpful in creating deals? The following reading, mentioned earlier in the context of negotiation, explores this question.

❖ Scott R. Peppet, *Contract Formation in Imperfect Markets: Should We Use Mediators in Deals?*

38 Ohio St. J. Disp. Resol. 283 (2004)

[M]any of the same barriers to negotiation that plague litigation settlement exist in commercial transactions, particularly during the closing stage of a deal when lawyers attempt to negotiate terms and conditions. [A] transactional mediator could help lawyers and clients to overcome such barriers.

[O]ccasionally transacting parties fail to "close the deal" because of strategic posturing. [Moreover] . . . empirical analysis of contracts shows that parties often do not trade risk in complex — yet value-creating — ways. Instead, in many domains contracts are simpler than one might expect. . . . [One possible] explanation is that the threat of strategic behavior prevents parties from complex contracting. To create a tailored term requires disclosing information about one's interests and preferences. This again permits exploitation. In the absence of trust, parties may resort to a standard term to minimize this risk.

A mediator might . . . solicit and compare information from each side, potentially finding value-creating trades. The mediator might test the viability of various packages . . ., asking each side in confidence which of several sets of terms the party would accept, but not revealing the origin of the various packages. . . .

[Besides helping parties to overcome strategic barriers to transactions, mediators can also help them to overcome psychological barriers.] A neutral is in an ideal position to identify self-serving assessments by one or both parties. At a substantive level, if the neutral has sufficient expertise she can check each side's assumptions about "what's fair" and keep the parties from locking in to diverging stories about how a transaction should be priced or closed. Moreover, the mediator may be able to offer a neutral assessment or fair proposal that the parties will adopt. . . .

Negotiating parties must constantly assess information received from the other side. [A] neutral can help parties to overcome reactive devaluation in transactional bargaining by either adding noise to [that is, disguising the source of] the parties' communication or proposing solutions of her own. Adding noise may be as simple as raising Party A's proposed solution privately with Party B without telling B that the idea came from Party A. If B assumes that the idea originated with the neutral, B may be more willing to consider it on the merits.

A neutral may be less susceptible to the endowment effect than a partisan agent, and therefore able to help parties to overcome it. For example, a neutral may be able to provide both sides with market information against which they can test their (biased) evaluations. . . .

In strategic situations it is easy to assume that when the other bargainer "starts high" or "holds out," they do so because they intend to harm you or to treat you unfairly. Bargainers are less likely to attribute such actions to the exigencies of circumstance. By screening some overly opportunistic offers and at times sending fuzzy rather than clear information between the parties, a mediator can blunt such emotions and thereby keep the negotiations on track. Over time, avoiding emotional disagreements may help the parties to establish trust. This not only leads to more amiable negotiations, but also has serious substantive benefits. If the parties trust each other they may be better positioned to find value-creating solutions to their substantive differences. They may be able to rely more on informal agreements rather than contractual obligations and may be more flexible in the face of unexpected bumps in the road. Perhaps most importantly, they may avoid the destructive cycle of misattributions that can lead parties to "blow up" a deal or reach [an inefficient] agreement.

❖ **David A. Hoffman,** *Microsoft and Yahoo: Where Were The Mediators? They Help Countries and Couples, Why Not Businesses?*

Christian Science Monitor (May 12, 2008)

When Microsoft CEO Steve Ballmer met with Yahoo CEO Jerry Yang earlier this month, what kept them from making a deal? With Microsoft offering $33 per share for Yahoo's stock, and Yahoo willing to take $37, was there truly an unbridgeable gulf? The $4 gap seems trivial in comparison to the potential value of the deal. So did Microsoft and Yahoo walk away from a deal that would have made both sides better off? This type of bargaining failure is hardly rare — businesspeople frequently report deals that have come within inches of closing, only to slip away at the last moment, costing their companies plenty.

In the world of litigation, settlement gaps are routinely bridged with the help of mediators. In the world of foreign policy, mediation — sometimes called "shuttle diplomacy" — is used extensively to resolve conflict. Why, then, are business transactions rarely mediated?

One theory is that the functions that mediators perform are already handled by transactional lawyers and investment bankers who work hard — and are handsomely rewarded — to close deals. The problem with this theory is that the lawyers and investment bankers often approach the negotiation from a partisan perspective in order to prove their loyalty to their respective clients.

A more promising explanation is that when conflicts arise — as in a potential hostile takeover situation such as the Microsoft-Yahoo negotiations — the parties reject compromise because they see the world through a distorted lens. Conflict can cause "reactive devaluation" (a negative assessment of a proposal because it comes from an opponent). Neuroscientists tell us that conflict triggers some of our most primitive reactions — a fight-or-flight response — as opposed to the collaborative impulse required for dealmaking.

It's not surprising, then, that people — especially in business settings, where egos, competition, and high stakes collide — are unlikely to opt for mediation unless they are forced, or strongly urged, to do so. In the world of diplomacy, it is often the superpowers that intervene when smaller nations quarrel, and court cases are often mediated because a judge insists on it. Indeed, Microsoft mediated its antitrust dispute with the Justice Department only when the court ordered it. In the setting of mergers and acquisitions, however, the key difference is that there is no outside power that can insist on mediation. Accordingly, it is often up to boards of directors or shareholders to push management to mediation.

Dealmaking mediation has been used for years to create collective-bargaining agreements and to resolve impasses in the negotiation of major league sports contracts. . . . In the Microsoft-Yahoo negotiations, a mediator could have helped in several concrete ways.

First, since disagreements about the price of a company usually turn on financial predictions, mediators can help the parties structure creative options for mitigating their risks. Acquisition agreements often contain "earn-out" provisions that award benefits to the seller if the deal turns out to be a winner for the buyer. Without any investment in the outcome, mediators become "honest brokers" who can advance such ideas without the perception that they are seeking an advantage based on secret knowledge.

Second, a mediator can help the parties obtain neutral and independent opinions — as opposed to the potentially partisan opinions of the parties' hired experts, lawyers, and investment bankers.

Third, a "mediator's proposal" can test the waters of compromise. Let's say the mediator asks each side to tell the mediator — on a confidential basis — whether they would accept a deal at $35 per share. This protocol means the mediator will report the answers only if both sides say "yes." Thus, each side can take the risk of saying yes because the other side will never know unless they, too, have said yes.

When deals collapse, conflict often migrates to another venue. Yahoo is already defending lawsuits from disgruntled shareholders, angered by management's failure to accept Microsoft's offer. However, even if there were no possible zone of agreement in the Microsoft-Yahoo case, business managers in other deal negotiations might consider whether calling in mediators, when needed, might save them from bargaining failures and make both sides better off.

Questions

23. Why do you think Microsoft and Yahoo did not use mediation?
24. What problems might an inside counsel who suggested mediation in that situation have encountered

G. International Mediation

Until now we have discussed mediation as an almost entirely American phenomenon. In fact, however, people across the world and throughout recorded history have turned to third parties to assist them in resolving disputes. International mediation is best known in the context of disputes involving nation-states. Theodore Roosevelt, for example, won the Nobel Peace Prize for his work as mediator of peace talks between Russia and Japan, Jimmy Carter is remembered for facilitating the Camp David accords between Egypt and Israel, and former Senator George Mitchell played a key role in bringing peace to Northern Ireland.

Mediation can also be used, of course, in private disputes. There are two types of "international" private mediation, "domestic" and "cross-border." "Domestic" refers to use of mediation *within* another country, for example, to resolve a lawsuit pending in a British court between two English companies, or in India between Indian landowners. "Cross-border" mediation involves disputes between citizens of *different* countries, for example, between a U.S. and an Asian company over commercial contracts. We first focus on the use of mediation domestically within other countries, then on its use in cases arising from international transactions.

1. Mediation Within Foreign Legal Systems

The use of mediation varies greatly from country to country, and no single statement is possible about its prevalence. In countries with common-law legal systems, particularly Canada, Great Britain, and Australia, mediation has become relatively well known. In the civil-law countries of continental Europe, by contrast, it has not been applied broadly except in specialized areas such as family law, and the same is true of most of the rest of the world.

Michael McIlwrath, a manager of litigation for GE Power Systems and former Chair of the International Mediation Institute in the Hague, offers the following assessment of the use of mediation outside the United States.

❖ **Michael McIlwrath,** Can Mediation Evolve into a
Global Profession?

www.mediate.com (2009)

In many places around the world [commercial] mediation is struggling to gain any traction at all. It has gained a strong foothold in a few countries, such as Canada, the UK and the Netherlands, but in most places it is virtually unknown. It is rarely promoted and often misunderstood, causing lack of respect and acceptance.

In many legal environments, mediation has found itself in a bit of a rut, experiencing only very marginal growth. Where mediators are plentiful, they tend to be in chronic over-supply. In the view of many consumers of dispute services, this is not a problem of mediation but of the way it is presented within these particular markets.

Take the UK for example. Having developed initial techniques and training from the US, there are now thousands of trained mediators. However, it is claimed that only about 20 people practice as full time mediators, with perhaps 50 conducting 80% of the country's mediations. Thousands of others struggle to gain experience and practical skills. And this is in the one place in Europe where mediation is sometimes claimed to be "mature". . . .

Given that so many of us believe mediation represents a generally superior form of dispute resolution, we are bound to ask why it has not become more popular around the world. There may be many factors preventing a more rapid spread of the practice of mediation beyond its core jurisdictions.

One possibility is that the cost of litigation in North America, the UK, and Australia makes the search for an alternative that leads to settlement more pressing. That may certainly be the case, but it is not a completely satisfying explanation. [I]n Italy where I live, for example, court proceedings may cost the typical litigant a fraction of what a similar action would cost in the US, but the case will still take some years to work its way through the courts. Parties want resolution sooner rather than later, and one would think that inefficiency of dispute resolution would be a fertile environment for mediation. Yet it is little practiced here, despite efforts over the past decade to promote it, including legislation imposing an obligation to mediate certain types of disputes. And there are countries like India that make Italy a shining example of judicial efficiency, and where mediation is even less known and practiced.

So there must be other factors stalling the growth of mediation. One in particular appears to be variability in the quality of the services that are called "mediation" in different places. [McIlwrath goes on to argue that an essential prerequisite to the spread of mediation in other countries is a consistent method to certify the competence of mediators across borders. His proposed solution, the International Mediation Institute, is discussed in Chapter 14 in the context of mediator certification.]

2. Use in Cross-Border Disputes

Mediation can also be used to resolve disputes between citizens of different countries. Parties to international contracts are understandably reluctant to litigate in a foreign court system, and typically specify that disputes will be resolved by arbitration. In 2004, the European Commission issued a Directive endorsing the use of mediation in certain civil and commercial disputes, and has since promoted the process through publications and conferences. Advocates hope that this effort will spur the use of mediation in the European Union.

Although international business contracts rarely refer to mediation, international arbitrators have long followed the custom of seeking to "conciliate" cases. The following readings explore the different forms that these processes can take and what they mean when implemented by neutrals of different cultures.

❖ **Jeswald Salacuse,** *MEDIATION IN INTERNATIONAL BUSINESS*

Studies in International Mediation 213 (J. Bercovitch ed., 2002)

The International Deal: A Continuing Negotiation

All international transactions are the product of negotiation — the result of *deal-making* — among the parties. Although lawyers like to think that negotiations end when the participants agree on all the details and sign the contract, this view hardly ever reflects reality. In truth, an international deal is a *continuing negotiation* between the parties to the transaction as they seek to adjust their relationship to the rapidly changing international environment . . . in which they must work. . . . In the life of any international deal, one may therefore identify three distinct stages when conflict may arise and the parties rely on negotiation and conflict resolution to achieve their goals: *deal-making, deal-managing,* and *deal-mending*. Within the context of each of these three kinds of negotiation, one should ask to what extent third parties, whether called mediators or something else, may assist the parties to make, manage, and mend productive international business relationships. . . .

Deal-Making Mediation

The usual model of an international business negotiation is that of representatives of two companies from different countries sitting across a table in face-to-face discussions to shape the terms of a commercial contract. While many transactions take place in that manner, many others require the services of one or more third parties to facilitate the deal-making process. These individuals are not usually referred to as "mediators." They instead carry a variety of other labels: consultant, adviser, agent, broker, investment banker, among others. . . .

Although it could be argued that consultants and advisors should not be considered mediators since they are not independent of the parties, a close examination of their roles . . . reveals that they exercise a mediator's functions. . . . [I]n most cases, one of the principal assets of deal-making mediators is the fact that they are known and accepted by the other side in the deal.

Deal-Making Mediation in Hollywood

The acquisition in 1991 by Matsushita Electric Industrial Company of Japan, one of the world's largest electronics manufacturers, of MCA, one of the United States' biggest entertainment companies, for over $6 billion illustrates the use of mediators in the deal-making process. Matsushita had determined that its future growth was dependent upon obtaining a source of films, television programs, and music — what it termed "software" — to complement its consumer electronic "hardware" products. Matsushita knew that it could find such a source of software within the U.S. entertainment industry, but it also recognized that it was virtually ignorant of that industry and its practices. For Matsushita executives, embarking on their Hollywood expedition may have felt almost interplanetary. . . . They therefore engaged Michael Ovitz, the founder and head of Creative Artists Agency, one of the most powerful talent agencies in Hollywood, to guide them on their journey.

After forming a team to assist in the task, Ovitz . . . first extensively briefed the Japanese over several months, sometimes in secret meetings in Hawaii, on the nature of the U.S. entertainment industry, and he then proceeded to propose three possible candidates for acquisition, one of which was MCA. Ultimately, Matsushita chose MCA, but it was Ovitz, not Matsushita executives, who initiated conversations with the MCA leadership, men whom Ovitz knew well. Indeed, Ovitz assumed the task of actually conducting the negotiations for Matsushita. At one point in the discussions, he moved constantly between the Japanese team of executives in one suite of offices in New York City and the MCA team in another building, a process which one observer described as "shuttle diplomacy". . . . Although Matsushita may have considered Ovitz to be their agent in the talks, Ovitz seems to have considered himself to be both a representative of Matsushita and a mediator between the two sides.

Because of the vast cultural and temperamental differences between the Japanese and American companies, Ovitz's strategy was to limit the actual interactions of the two parties to a bare minimum. . . . He was not only concerned by the vast differences in culture between the two companies but also by the greatly differing personalities in their top managements. The Japanese executives, reserved and somewhat self-effacing, placed a high value on the appearance if not the reality of modesty, while MCA's president was an extremely assertive and volatile personality. Like any mediator, Ovitz's own interests may also have influenced his choice of strategy. His status in the entertainment industry would only be heightened by making a giant new entrant into Hollywood dependent on him and by the public image that he had been the key to arranging one of the biggest deals in the industry's history. . . .

Eventually the talks stalled over the issue of price, and meetings between the two sides ceased. At this point, a second deal-making mediator entered the scene to make a crucial contribution. At the start of the negotiation, Matsushita and Sony together had engaged Robert Strauss, a politically powerful Washington lawyer who had been at various times U.S. Ambassador to the Soviet Union and U.S. Trade Representative, as "counselor to the transaction." Strauss, a member of the MCA board of directors and a close friend of its chairman, was also friendly with the Matsushita leadership and did legal and lobbying work in Washington for the Japanese company. . . . Strauss' close relationship to the two sides allowed him to act as a trusted conduit of communication who facilitated a meeting between the top MCA and Matsushita executives . . . [H]e apparently gained an understanding of the pricing parameters acceptable to each side and then communicated them to the other party. . . . In the end, as a result of that meeting, the two sides reached an agreement by which Matsushita acquired MCA.

[A]lthough Matsushita did succeed in purchasing MCA, the acquisition proved to be troubling and ultimately a disastrous financial loss for the Japanese company. One may ask whether Ovitz' strategy of keeping the two sides apart during negotiations so that they did not come to know one another contributed to this unfortunate result. It prevented the two sides from truly understanding the vast gulf which separated them and therefore from realizing the enormity and perhaps impossibility of the task of merging two such different organizations into a single coordinated and profitable enterprise.

Other Deal-Making Mediators

An opposite mediating approach from that employed by Ovitz is the use of consultants to begin building a relationship between the parties *before* they have signed a contract and indeed before they have actually begun negotiations. When some companies contemplate long-term relationships . . . they may hire a consultant to develop and guide a program of relationship building, which might include joint workshops, get-acquainted sessions, and retreats, all of which take place before the parties actually sit down to negotiate the terms of their contract. . . .

. . . Sometimes persons involved in the negotiation because of their technical expertise or specialized knowledge may assume a mediating function and thus help the parties reach agreement. For example . . . local lawyers or accountants engaged by a foreign party to advise on law or accounting practices in connection with an international negotiation may assume a mediating role in the deal-making process by serving as a conduit between the parties, by suggesting approaches that meet the other side's cultural practices [or] by explaining why one party is behaving in a particular way. . . .

Deal-Managing Mediation

Once the deal has been signed, consultants, lawyers, and advisers may continue their association with one or both parties and informally assist as mediators in managing conflict that may arise in the execution of the transaction. . . . Once top management of the two sides have reached an understanding, they may have to serve as mediators with their subordinates to get them to change behavior and attitudes with respect to interactions at the operational level. . . .

Deal-Mending Mediation

The parties to an international business relationship may encounter a wide variety of conflicts that seem irreconcilable. . . . A poor developing country may stop paying its loan to a foreign bank. Partners in an international joint venture may disagree violently over the use of accumulated profits and therefore plunge their enterprise into a state of paralysis. Here then would seem ideal situations in which mediation by a third party could help in settling conflict. In fact, mediation is relatively uncommon once severe international business conflicts break out. To understand why, one must first understand the basic structure of international business dispute settlement.

International Commercial Arbitration

Nearly all international business contracts today provide that any disputes that may arise in the future between the parties are to be resolved by international commercial arbitration. . . . Thus in the background of virtually all international business disputes is the prospect of binding arbitration if the parties, alone or with the help of a third person, are unable to resolve the conflict themselves.

Arbitrating a dispute is not, however, a painless, inexpensive, quick solution. Like litigation in the courts, it is costly, may take years to conclude, and invariably results in a final rupture of the parties' business relationship. . . . [Arbitrators sometimes seek to play a mediating role. Their usual strategy] is to give the parties a realistic evaluation of what they will receive or be required to pay in any final arbitration award.

Mediation in International Business Disputes

Traditionally, companies engaged in an international business dispute have not actively sought the help of mediators. . . . With increasing recognition of the disadvantages of arbitration, some companies are beginning to turn to more explicit forms of mediation to resolve business disputes.

Conciliation

One type of deal-mending mediation used occasionally in international business is *conciliation.* . . . While the conciliator has broad discretion to conduct the process, in practice he or she will invite both sides to state their views of the dispute and will then make a report proposing an appropriate settlement. The parties may reject the report and proceed to arbitration, or they may accept it.

In many cases, they will use it as a basis for a negotiated settlement. Conciliation is thus a kind of non-binding arbitration. Its function is predictive. It tends to be rights-based. . . . Conciliators do not usually adopt a problem-solving or relationship-building approach. . . . The process is confidential and completely voluntary. . . . Thus far few disputants in international business avail themselves of conciliation. . . .

❖ **M. Scott Donahey,** *The Asian Concept of Conciliator/Arbitrator:*
Is It Translatable to the Western World?

10 Foreign Investment L.J. 120 (1995)

In various Asian countries, there is a profound societal and philosophical preference for agreed solutions.[19] Nevertheless, such generalizations are often necessary when comparing one cultural system to another. Rather than a cultural bias toward "equality" in relationships, there exists an intellectual and social predisposition towards a natural hierarchy which governs conduct in interpersonal relations. Asian cultures frequently seek a "harmonious" solution, one which tends to preserve the relationship, rather than one which, while arguably factually and legally "correct," may severely damage the relationship of the parties involved.

Where the Westerner will segregate the function of facilitator from that of decision-maker, the Asian will make no clear distinction. The Westerner seeks an arbiter that is unconnected to the parties to the dispute, one whose mind has not been predisposed by previous knowledge of the dispute or the facts which underlie it, a judge who is prepared to "let the chips fall where they may." On the other hand, many Asians seek a moderator who is familiar with the parties and their dispute, who will not only end their state of disputation but assist the parties in reaching an agreed solution, or, failing that, will find a position which will not only be one that terminates their dispute, but one that will allow the parties to resume their relationship with as little loss of "face" as possible. Thus, the distinction between the function of the arbitrator and that of the conciliator is blurred.

Clearly, as there is increased interaction in the forms of tourism and trade between the Western world and Asia, differences between the two cultures have diminished and will continue to diminish. We in the West tend to view this process as one in which the Asian countries are influenced by our economic and political systems and become more "Westernized." Our western pride and predispositions often do not permit us to recognize the degree to which we have been influenced and changed by the Asian cultures with which we have come in closer contact. . . .

Within the Confucian tradition, there is a concept known as "li," which concerns the social norms of behavior within the five natural status relationships: emperor and subject, father and son, husband and wife, brother and brother, or friend and friend. *Li* is intended to be persuasive, not compulsive and legalistic, a concept which governs good conduct and is above legal concepts in societal importance. The governing legal concept, "fa," is compulsive and punitive. While having the advantage of legal enforceability, *fa* is traditionally below *li* in importance. The Chinese have always considered the resort to litigation as the last step, signifying that the relationship between the disputing parties can no longer be harmonized. Resort to litigation results in loss of face, and discussion and compromise are always to be preferred. Over

---

19. [Footnote by the article's author] The author recognizes that the generalizations in which he engages tend to explain away the complexities and vast difference that exist in any nation or culture and [thus those generalizations] are inherently suspect.

time the concepts of *fa* and *li* have become fused, and the concept of maintaining the relationship and, therefore, face, has become part of the Chinese legal system. . . .

Adjudication is an act-oriented process. . . . In contrast, since conciliation/mediation is a "person-oriented" one, it is non-adversarial and set in a warm and friendly air of informality unbound by technical rules of procedure. Furthermore, while the nature of the adjudicative process requires that evidence and arguments presented by one party be made in the presence of the adverse litigant, separate conferences with the parties have been found to be an effective tool of conciliation. It is less important, in conciliation proceedings, to be accurate in finding the truth of the issues than to know what values are held by the parties so that a "trade-off" may be effected that will restore the disrupted harmonious relationship.

In Japan, as well, permitting a relationship to fall into a state of disharmony is culturally unacceptable: In Japan . . . the existence of a dispute may itself cause a loss of "face," and submission of a dispute to a third party may carry with it some sense of failure. . . . Thus, if there is one principle which can be said to lead to the combining of the role of arbitrator with that of conciliator it is that of preserving the harmonious relationship between the parties to the dispute. This principle is one that is frequently cited by Western arbitral institutions in promoting the use of commercial arbitration over litigation. . . .

Perhaps the foremost proponent of the practice of combining the role of conciliator and arbitrator . . . is the People's Republic of China. While no written rules have ever sanctioned or even described the practice, Chinese arbitrators and practitioners both practice and espouse the combination of mediation and conciliation: Arbitration and conciliation are interrelated and complementary with one another. They are not antagonistic and do not exclude each other. . . .

It is important to understand that the Chinese combination of arbitration and conciliation occurs during the ongoing process of arbitration. The arbitrator, after taking some evidence and hearing some witnesses, might attempt to conciliate the differences and, if efforts at conciliation fail, return to the receipt of evidence and the hearing of witnesses, ready to attempt conciliation again at an opportune time during the course of the proceedings. [I]t is unclear whether parties convey information to the arbitrators/conciliators in confidence during the conciliation phase, and, if so, how it is maintained. . . . This is different from the way that other Asian nations combine the functions of arbitrator and conciliator. . . .

The traditional Western view is that the conciliation process should be separate from the arbitration process and that the same persons who act as conciliators should not act as arbitrators in the same dispute. . . . However, the traditional Western view is changing, largely due to the influence of Asian cultures. . . . A combined conciliation and arbitration process offers significant advantages in reaching an agreed settlement and in preserving existing commercial relations between the parties. It is a system that apparently has worked well in Asia, and we in the West should not shrink from its use. . . .

Questions

25. What general approach would you expect from an Asian conciliator: facilitative or evaluative? Narrow or broad?

26. You are involved in an arbitration of a business contract dispute on behalf of a U.S. computer manufacturer who contracted with a Chinese firm to produce silicon chips, paid for and installed the chips in its products, and has since found out that they are unreliable, leading to serious repair costs and lost profits. Your client believes that the Chinese partner failed to comply with the quality requirements because it overstated its expertise in the area and simply did not understand them. The contract gives you the right to recover your damages, but it is not clear how you would enforce an award in arbitration against the supplier. If you know that the chair of the arbitration panel is a Chinese attorney,

   a. What, if anything, would you say to the neutral about the possibility of conciliation before the process begins?

   b. What instructions would you give your client about how to act during conciliation?

H. Online Mediation

One development in mediation does not involve a new subject area, but rather the use of technology to enhance its impact; it is online dispute resolution (ODR). ODR has two meanings. One is as a *method of communication*, as in negotiation or mediation conducted by e-mail. The other is as a *process managed electronically*, such as a program to manage monetary bidding.

ODR as a method of communication is a familiar concept. Lawyers have used electronic methods to negotiate since the invention of the telegraph and telephone, and e-mail and other electronic methods are conceptually not very different from a phone. Using a telephone provided bargainers greater efficiency but reduced their ability to observe and interact; e-mail and other electronic forms of communication have similar advantages and shortcomings. Technological developments are constantly changing how mediation can be conducted — video, for example, is now available to anyone with a laptop or smartphone.

ODR as a process managed electronically, however, is different. For one thing, it is asynchronous: Parties generally do not talk in "real time," as with cell phones and instant messaging, but rather exchange messages at their own pace, as with e-mail. Equally important, disputants do not meet face-to-face or even see each other by video. There are advantages and disadvantages to such methods. As a practical matter, however, parties to business disputes appear still to conduct almost all mediations through face-to-face meetings. It may be that the very cost of meeting someone in person — traveling to a site and remaining there for hours — demonstrates a mutual commitment to compromise and signals that the occasion is a "settlement event." It is also possible that lawyers and parties will become so comfortable with electronic media that they no longer will feel a need to mediate in person, or in real time.

As of now, ODR is not regularly used to conduct mediation except in disputes too small to justify the cost of meeting in person. For instance, eBay provides a system of computerized dispute resolution that permits buyers and sellers both to negotiate and mediate disputes. Companies that provide ODR services have sprung up and disappeared at a rapid pace in recent years, however, and customs of disputing may change rapidly.

Questions

27. A client bought an old mandolin on eBay for $250. On receiving the instrument she found that it was in much poorer condition than the seller had represented. She wants to return the mandolin and get her money back. Check eBay's Web site (*www.ebay.com*): What mediation options does eBay appear to provide for resolving her problem?

28. You are consulted by a business client who purchased a computer server system from an out-of-state supplier in a private transaction for $75,000. The system is dysfunctional, and the client believes that the seller defrauded him by not revealing that the system would function only with customized software, which would require an additional $15,000 to $20,000 to create. Even with this software, the client says, the system will not handle the volume of data that he has to process, contrary to assurances given during the sales process. He wishes to revoke the transaction. He has heard about the Cybersettle system (see *www.cybersettle.com*) and wonders if it would make sense to use it. What would you advise your client and why?

29. More generally, what seem to be the pluses and minuses of mediating through a computerized system using asynchronous communication conducted by e-mail?

CHAPTER
13

Court-Connected Mediation and Fairness Concerns

A. Court-Connected Mediation

Much of the early impetus for applying ADR in legal disputes came from judges concerned about overloaded dockets. It is not surprising, therefore, that courts throughout the United States have established dispute resolution programs and legislators have supported court-connected ADR. Modern ADR programs cover both general litigation and special categories such as divorce and small claims cases. Programs are most common at the trial level, but exist in appellate courts as well.

Congress required in the ADR Act of 1998, 28 U.S.C. §651(b), that every federal district court in the nation implement a dispute resolution program. Most federal courts allow litigants to choose among ADR processes, and mediation is the most popular option. A study of 49 federal district courts that received special ADR funding showed the following pattern (Stienstra 2005):

Federal Court Cases Referred to ADR Processes

Mediation	15,555
N.D. CA multi-option program (largely mediations)	3,317
Arbitration	2,588
Settlement conferences	1,608
Early neutral evaluation	1,332
Settlement week	296
Summary trials	6
Other	133
Total	24,835

The primary reason that state and federal courts have embraced mediation is to relieve their dockets of unwanted cases. In the words of one Texas judge, "I am interested in mediation because the cases settle earlier, and that gives me more time to be a judge, to spend that time I can gain improving the quality of justice in my court" (Bergman & Bickerman 1998).

Although their primary motivation is usually to reduce backlogs, courts divert cases to mediation for other reasons as well. Some cases involve continuing relationships, such as disputes between parents over visitation rights to their children. Adjudication is often ineffective to resolve such disputes, and litigation is beyond the financial means of many individuals. Court personnel also find some cases frustrating and personally demanding; family and neighborhood disputes, for example, often provoke raw emotions that defy rational analysis. Along with small claims and prisoners' rights suits, they also frequently involve pro se litigants who place extra burdens on court staff.

Court-connected mediation raises important policy issues, which involve designing programs not simply to yield the greatest benefit to the system but also to ensure fairness to participants. This section describes how court-connected programs are structured and explores the process issues they present.

B. Issues of Program Design

1. What Goals Should a Program Seek to Achieve?

What should be the purpose of a court-connected mediation program? Although many judges have embraced mediation as a means to reduce delay, the evidence that it accomplishes this is conflicting. For example, a study of six federal court programs that used mediation as one option did not find statistically significant evidence that the programs affected the duration of cases (Kakalik et al. 1996). On the other hand, studies of one federal and a group of state courts found that mediation programs did significantly reduce the length of cases, and a California study found similar results (Stienstra et al. 1997; Stipanowich 2004). (Summaries of numerous studies of court-related programs appear at *http://courtadr.org/files/MedStudyBiblio2ndEd2.pdf.*)

The differences in study results may owe to the great variations in how individual courts design and implement programs. Some courts, for example, do not send cases to mediation until after discovery is complete, greatly reducing their ability to cut cost or delay, and some courts have initial time frames for mediation as short as one or two hours, too little time to apply most of the techniques described in this book. Given these variations it is not surprising that results are mixed. But whether or not court-sponsored mediation consistently reduces delay, there may be reasons to support its use.

As a U.S. Magistrate Judge in California, Wayne Brazil has directed one of the nation's most innovative court-connected ADR programs. In this article he presents the rationale for a multifaceted approach.

❖ **Wayne D. Brazil,** *Why Should Courts Offer Non-Binding ADR Services?*

16 Alternatives 65 (1998)

[T]here is no one method of procedure that works best for resolving . . . every kind of dispute. . . . In some cases, the parties' dominating concern will be with trying to establish the truth. They will want to use the process that is most likely to generate historically accurate factfinding, regardless of other consider-ations. . . . Traditional adversarial litigation may well best meet the needs of such parties.

But for parties to whom other values or interests loom larger, other processes are likely to deliver more valued service — and are more likely to result in consensual disposition. . . . To some parties, relationship-building . . . may be of prime importance. . . . In some cases, what the parties care most about are feelings. . . . In some disputes, it is the quality and character of communication that matters most — or that holds the most promise of delivering constructive solutions. . . . It follows that if our judicial system is to be responsive to the full range of interests and needs that cases filed in our courts implicate, then the system cannot offer only one dispute resolution method. . . .

One role of public courts in a democratic society is to try to assure that it is not only the wealthy or the big case litigants who have access to appropriate and effective dispute resolution processes. Poor litigants, and parties to cases with-out substantial economic value, should not be relegated by our judicial system to the often-slow and disproportionately expensive procedures of traditional adversarial litigation. To force poor people and small cases into that system can be tantamount to denying them access to any system at all. . . .

A related consideration supporting court sponsorship of ADR begins with the observation that some litigants and lawyers might have greater confidence in the integrity of an ADR process and the neutral when the ADR services are provided or sponsored by a court than when they are provided in a wholly private setting. When the service provider is a public court, for example, there is no occasion for the concerns that have surfaced about the possible influence . . . of large companies that are current or potential sources of con-siderable repeat business. . . .

[In addition,] active participation in designing and implementing ADR programs provides courts with opportunities to gain insight that they can use to improve their handling of traditional litigation. [A] thoughtfully monitored ADR program can develop . . . insights into negotiation dynamics that can be shared with judges who host settlement conferences, enhancing the skills . . . that judges can bring to their work as settlement facilitators. . . .

Unhappily, there is a risk that courts could be tempted to permit institutional selfishness to infect the thinking that drives their program design. Some judges and judicial administrators, for example, might be attracted to ADR only or primarily as a docket reduction tool, [posing] serious threats to fairness or other values that ADR should be promoting. There also is a risk that some judges and administrators could try to use ADR programs as dumping grounds for categories of cases that are deemed unpopular, unimportant, annoying, or difficult.

Questions

1. Would a traditional, trial-oriented judge disagree with the arguments that Judge Brazil makes for court-connected mediation? Which ones?
2. Brazil promotes mediation as a means of securing justice for poor people. We will see that other commentators argue that ADR provides second-class justice to the disadvantaged. On what aspects of the process does each side focus?
3. One study found that attorneys permitted to choose from among several ADR processes were more likely than attorneys who did not have a choice to report that the ADR process lowered litigation costs, reduced the amount of discovery and number of motions, was fair, resulted in settlement, and had benefits that outweighed the costs (Stienstra et al. 1997). What downside might there be to permitting attorneys to choose among court ADR processes?

Professor Nancy Welsh has delved into some of the fairness concerns raised by Judge Brazil, focusing on what ordinary people mean by "justice" and whether court-connected ADR programs deliver it. In doing so, she distinguishes between "procedural" justice, which refers to disputants' feelings about process, and "distributive" justice, which focuses on their assessment of outcomes.

❖ **Nancy A. Welsh,** *Making Deals in Court-Connected Mediation: What's Justice Got to Do with It?*

79 Wash U. L.Q. 787 (2001)

Researchers have found that procedural justice matters profoundly. Disputants' perceptions of the justice provided by a procedure affect their judgments of the distributive justice provided by the outcome, their compliance with that outcome, and their faith in the legitimacy of the institution that offered the procedure. Disputants use the following indicia to assess procedural justice:

- whether the procedure provided them with the opportunity to tell their stories,
- whether the third party considered their stories, and
- whether the third party treated them in an even-handed and dignified manner.

The procedures used in socially-sanctioned dispute resolution processes assume such significance because disputants seek personal and pragmatic reassurance. Disputants need to believe that they are valued members of society and that the final outcome of a dispute resolution process will be based on full information. . . .

The Effects of Procedural Justice

Although issues of procedural justice often do not attract as much public attention as concerns about distributive justice, research has shown that when people experience dispute resolution and decision-making procedures, they pay a great deal of attention to the way things are done [i.e., how decisions are made] and the nuances of their treatment by others. . . .

Research has repeatedly confirmed that . . . [d]isputants who believe that they have been treated in a procedurally fair manner are more likely to conclude that the resulting outcome is substantively fair. In effect, a disputant's perception of procedural justice anchors general fairness impressions or serves as a fairness heuristic. Further, research has indicated that disputants who have participated in a procedure that they evaluated as fair do not change their evaluation even if the procedure produces a poor or unfair outcome.

The perception of procedural justice also serves as a shortcut means of determining whether to accept or reject a legal decision or procedure. Disputants who believe that they were treated fairly in a dispute resolution procedure are more likely to comply with the outcome of that procedure. This effect will occur even if outcomes do not favor the disputants or they are actually unhappy with the outcomes. . . .

Process Characteristics That Enhance Perceptions of Procedural Justice

Several rather specific process characteristics enhance perceptions of procedural justice. First, perceptions of procedural justice are enhanced to the extent that disputants perceive that they had the opportunity to present their views, concerns, and evidence to a third party and had control over this presentation ("opportunity for voice"). Second, disputants are more likely to perceive procedural justice if they perceive that the third party considered their views, concerns, and evidence. Third, disputants' judgments about procedural justice are affected by the perception that the third party treated them in a dignified, respectful manner and that the procedure itself was dignified. Although it seems that a disputants' perceptions regarding a fourth factor — the impartiality of the third-party decision maker — also ought to affect procedural justice judgments, it appears that disputants are influenced more strongly by their observations regarding the third party's evenhandedness and attempts at fairness.

. . . Concerns regarding the opportunity for voice apply in a variety of settings, including the courtroom, arbitration proceedings, contacts with the police, political decision making, and decision making in work organizations. Even in countries where the judicial systems typically use non-adversarial procedures, citizens often prefer procedures that allow a full opportunity for voice. Perhaps most surprisingly, both field and laboratory studies have demonstrated that the opportunity for voice heightens disputants' judgments of procedural justice even when they know that their voice will not and cannot influence the final outcome. . . .

Disputants' perceptions of procedural justice also are influenced by how the third party interacts with them on an interpersonal level. . . . For example, in one study comparing litigants' reactions to the third-party processes of trial, arbitration, and judicial settlement conferences, the litigants gave much higher procedural justice rankings to trial and arbitration, even though these proceedings required the litigants to surrender decision-making control. Most litigants perceived trial and arbitration as dignified and careful. In contrast, settlement conferences were more likely to strike litigants as undignified and contrary to the litigants' sense of procedural fairness.

Significantly, several studies have shown that disputants value these process characteristics as much as, or even more than, control over the final decision (also termed "decision control"). . . .

Ultimately, the procedural justice literature highlights the need to focus not solely on the fairness of outcomes, but also on the fairness of procedures. Further, the literature suggests that disputants are less concerned about receiving formal due process during their experiences with the courts than they are about being treated in a manner that is consistent with their everyday expectations regarding social relations and norms.

> **Questions**
>
> You are an advisor to a court seeking to design a mediation program for disputes in which only about half of the participants will be represented by a lawyer.
>
> 4. What do the procedural justice findings suggest about how the program should be designed in terms of structure — format, length of sessions, and physical facilities — and the selection and training of mediators?
> 5. Can you suggest specific problems the program should try to avoid?

2. How Should Services Be Provided?

The goals of promoting settlement and satisfying litigants' interests are not necessarily contradictory, but varying goals are likely to lead to different program designs. A program focused on stimulating settlements at minimal cost, on the one hand, might encourage participants to "cut to the chase." A program with a goal of addressing parties' underlying interests, by contrast, would be more likely to require longer sessions, probably increasing cost.

One key issue is who will mediate such cases. Most court programs rely on panels made up of neutrals with limited training and experience, usually practicing attorneys who often serve on a volunteer basis. This approach allows courts to offer ADR services at low cost and build support for mediation in the private bar. The services themselves, however, vary widely in quality. A second option is to create a roster of professional neutrals. Such panels are more consistently competent, but professionals are likely to require payment for their services. Some courts seek to achieve both goals by using professionals but requiring them to contribute some initial time without charge or to work at reduced rates. Finally, some courts, particularly in the federal and family court systems, use full-time employees as mediators, either exclusively or in combination with an outside panel. These neutrals may be lawyers, magistrates, senior judges, or lay personnel. Some have the advantage of receiving training and being able to devote substantial time to each case. However, the "full-time employee" model requires the court to bear most or all of the cost of providing neutrals and may make it difficult for litigants to avoid a mediator whom they consider ineffective.

Cases may be sent to court-connected programs by litigants, judges, or court screeners. Courts vary widely as to when they order or permit cases to go into mediation. Empirical research has not resolved whether earlier or later mediation is more effective in terms of settlement rate, but the general trend is to mediate disputes earlier in their lives.

Courts that offer mediation services face the following issues:

1. Will participation in the program be voluntary or mandatory?
   - If mandatory, will the mandate apply to all cases or only a subset of them?
   - If a subset, will it be defined by the type of case, the parties (for example, pro se versus represented litigants), the amount in controversy, or some other criterion?
   - If voluntary, will they enter by referral only, or will litigants be allowed to opt in?
2. How will neutrals be selected?
3. How much time will be allowed for the process? Can the time be extended?
4. How will program costs be covered?
   - Will neutrals be paid?
   - Will participants be charged? On what basis?
   - Will waivers be available to indigents?
5. What level of attendance will be required?
   - Will individual parties be required to attend in person?
   - Will corporate parties be required to send a representative with a specific level of authority (for example, "full authority")?
6. What level of participation will be required?
   - Will parties be either required or permitted to file written materials?
   - Will disputants be required to adhere to a standard of conduct (for example, to "mediate in good faith")?

These questions trigger others. If, for instance, parties are required to mediate in "good faith," what does this mean in practice? Should a court invade mediation confidentiality to gather evidence about what happened in the process? These and other legal questions are explored in Chapter 14.

Problem

Investigate a mediation program offered by your local courts. How does the program deal with the issues listed above?

Questions

6. A court has been requiring parties to participate in ADR for several years, and as a result the local bar has become very familiar with how mediation can be used to resolve disputes. The court has asked you whether as a matter of policy it should now drop its requirement and allow parties and lawyers to decide voluntarily whether to use ADR. What would you recommend? What factors or data might be important to your decision?

7. What are the potential pluses and minuses of using full-time court employees or judges, rather than a panel of trained lawyers, as the neutrals in a court-affiliated program?

3. *Appellate Mediation*

❖ **Dana Curtis & John Toker,** REPRESENTING CLIENTS IN APPELLATE
MEDIATION: THE LAST FRONTIER

1 JAMS Alert No. 3, 1 (December 2000)

These days mediation of disputes in trial courts is commonplace. Yet mediation of appeals is relatively rare, even though each circuit of the U.S. Court of Appeals has long maintained staffs of mediators and some state appellate courts have mediation programs. [In] the Ninth Circuit, the eight full-time . . . mediators helped parties settle over 600 cases last year. [And more] than forty percent of cases sent to mediation in [a California state court appellate program] have settled.

 . . . The introduction of mediation into the appellate process requires appellate lawyers to take on the role of counselor in the broadest sense. Lawyers must analyze cases not only from a *legal* viewpoint, but also from a *human* and *business* perspective. They need to help their clients make good decisions regarding not only whether, but also how, to proceed. The consideration of mediation should be part of that process. . . .

The similarities between mediation of appellate cases and other matters far exceed the differences. Nevertheless, understanding the distinctions will help you do a better job of representing your clients in appellate mediation.

1. *There's already a winner and a loser.* As counsel for the appellant, it may be that you have not considered mediation of appeals because it doesn't occur to you that the respondent, as the victor, would be willing to accept a compromise instead of an appellate decision. There are a number of reasons why a respondent may be willing to accept a compromise instead of [a] decision. Essentially, they boil down to a five little words: risk, cost, time, life, and gain.

 Risk Appellate courts can be unpredictable, even in cases that seem open and shut. Appeals from judgments entered as a matter of law, such as summary judgments . . . are particularly risky because the appellate court reviews these appeals de novo. The reversal rate in these cases is approximately 30 percent . . .

Cost Appeals can be very expensive. A five-day trial can translate into a $30,000 appeal with transcript production and briefing. If the appellate court reverses the judgment, the case may be remanded to the trial court for further costly proceedings. A reasonable compromise may be in the best interest of all parties.

Time It likely is in the interest of a respondent to have a judgment satisfied sooner rather than later. . . .

Life There comes a time for many litigants . . . when they just want to end the pain and get on with their lives.

Gain Mediation offers creative solutions outside of the litigation box. . . .

2. *The participants may be less optimistic about resolution.* Generally, parties in appellate mediation have had a number of failed negotiations and are therefore more discouraged about settlement than they were at the beginning of the dispute. And they also suffer from the skepticism discussed above, that is, why would the winner want to sit down at the mediation table?

3. *Paradoxically, the law and evaluation of the legal issues by the mediator may not be as important to settlement as it was before trial.* . . . Mediator evaluation of the merits of the case may not play an important role as it does in other litigated cases [because] parties have already had an evaluation by a judge or a jury, and at least one of them is not convinced it was right.

4. *The relationships between the parties may be more strained.* A contested trial court proceeding that has been resolved in favor of one of the parties never *enhances* the relationships between them. If they were antagonistic before litigation, parties often are bitter enemies by the time of the appeal. In selecting a mediator for an appeal, you'll need to consider the mediator's ability to manage high conflict and create a positive environment for problem solving.

5. *Lawyers and clients both have problems with cognitive dissonance* between their negotiating positions before and after the trial court decision. Failing to settle earlier for a greater/lesser amount before the court decision may make it more difficult for the client to enter into a settlement that differs greatly from the earlier offer or demand. You may also struggle with your failure to have settled for more/less before the decision. . . . If you can't put aside the previous settlement proposal, and your regret at having passed it up, you may not be able to advise your client rationally. . . .

Question

8. You are advising a legislative committee in your state that wishes to conduct a three-year project to test the usefulness of court-connected mediation. The committee has only enough funds to create pilot programs in two court departments. It must choose among the small claims, district (smaller cases), superior (larger cases), family, juvenile, and appellate courts. Which two departments would you advise the committee to select for funding? Why?

C. Policy Issues Regarding the Use of Mediation

An unstated assumption of the readings to this point is that settlement is desirable, and that because mediation assists parties to settle it is a good thing. But is this always true?

1. Should Some Cases Not Be Settled?

❖ **Owen M. Fiss,** AGAINST SETTLEMENT
_____

93 Yale L.J. 1073 (1984)

In a recent report to the Harvard Overseers, Derek Bok called for a new direction in legal education. He decried "the familiar tilt in the law curriculum toward preparing students for legal combat," and asked instead that law schools train their students "for the gentler arts of reconciliation and accommodation." He sought to turn our attention from the courts to "new voluntary mechanisms" for resolving disputes. In doing so, Bok echoed themes that have long been associated with the Chief Justice and that have become a rallying point for the organized bar and the source of a new movement in the law. . . .

The movement promises to reduce the amount of litigation initiated, and accordingly the bulk of its proposals are devoted to negotiation and mediation prior to suit. But the interest in the so-called "gentler arts" has not been so confined. It extends to ongoing litigation as well, and the advocates of ADR have sought new ways to facilitate and perhaps even pressure parties into settling pending cases. . . .

The advocates of ADR are led to support such measures and to exalt the idea of settlement more generally because they view adjudication as a process to resolve disputes. They act as though courts arose to resolve quarrels between neighbors who had reached an impasse and turned to a stranger for help.

Courts are seen as an institutionalization of the stranger and adjudication is viewed as the process by which the stranger exercises power. The very fact that the neighbors have turned to someone else to resolve their dispute signifies a breakdown in their social relations; the advocates of ADR acknowledge this, but nonetheless hope that the neighbors will be able to reach agreement before the stranger renders judgment. Settlement is that agreement. It is a truce more than a true reconciliation, but it seems preferable to judgment because it rests on the consent of both parties and avoids the cost of a lengthy trial.

In my view, however, this account of adjudication and the case for settlement rest on questionable premises. I do not believe that settlement as a generic practice is preferable to judgment or should be institutionalized on a wholesale and indiscriminate basis. It should be treated instead as a highly problematic technique for streamlining dockets. Settlement is for me the civil analogue of plea bargaining: Consent is often coerced; the bargain may be struck by someone without authority; the absence of a trial and judgment renders subsequent judicial involvement troublesome; and although dockets are trimmed, justice may not be done. Like plea bargaining, settlement is a capitulation to the conditions of mass society and should be neither encouraged nor praised.

The Imbalance of Power

By viewing the lawsuit as a quarrel between two neighbors, the dispute-resolution story that underlies ADR implicitly asks us to assume a rough equality between the contending parties. It treats settlement as the anticipation of the outcome of trial and assumes that the terms of settlement are simply a product of the parties' predictions of that outcome. In truth, however, settlement is also a function of the resources available to each party to finance the litigation, and those resources are frequently distributed unequally. Many lawsuits do not involve a property dispute between two neighbors, or between [a major corporation] and the government . . . , but rather concern a struggle between a member of a racial minority and a municipal police department over alleged brutality, or a claim by a worker against a large corporation over work-related injuries. In these cases, the distribution of financial resources, or the ability of one party to pass along its costs, will invariably infect the bargaining process, and the settlement will be at odds with a conception of justice that seeks to make the wealth of the parties irrelevant.

The disparities in resources between the parties can influence the settlement in three ways. First, the poorer party may be less able to amass and analyze the information needed to predict the outcome of the litigation, and thus be disadvantaged in the bargaining process. Second, he may need the damages he seeks immediately and thus be induced to settle as a way of accelerating payment, even though he realizes he would get less now than he might if he awaited judgment. . . . Third, the poorer party might be forced to settle because he does not have the resources to finance the litigation, to cover either his own projected expenses, such as his lawyer's time, or the expenses his opponent can impose through the manipulation of procedural mechanisms such as discovery. It might seem that settlement benefits the plaintiff by allowing him to avoid the costs of litigation, but this is not so. The defendant can anticipate the plaintiff's costs if the case were to be tried fully and decrease his offer by that amount. The indigent plaintiff is a victim of the costs of litigation even if he settles.

There are exceptions. Seemingly rich defendants may sometimes be subject to financial pressures that make them as anxious to settle as indigent plaintiffs. But I doubt that these circumstances occur with any great frequency. I also doubt that institutional arrangements such as contingent fees or the provision of legal services to the poor will in fact equalize resources between contending parties. . . .

Of course, imbalances of power can distort judgment as well: Resources influence the quality of presentation, which in turn has an important bearing on who wins and the terms of victory. We count, however, on the guiding presence of the judge, who can employ a number of measures to lessen the impact of distributional inequalities. He can, for example, supplement the parties' presentations by asking questions, calling his own witnesses, and inviting other persons and institutions to participate as amici. These measures are likely to make only a small contribution toward moderating the influence of distributional inequalities, but should not be ignored for that reason. Not even these small steps are possible with settlement. There is, moreover, a critical difference between a process like settlement, which is based on bargaining and accepts inequalities of wealth as an integral and legitimate component of the process, and a process like judgment, which knowingly struggles against those inequalities. Judgment aspires to autonomy from distributional inequalities, and it gathers much of its appeal from this aspiration. . . .

The Lack of a Foundation for Continuing Judicial Involvement

The dispute-resolution story trivializes the remedial dimensions of lawsuits and mistakenly assumes judgment to be the end of the process. It supposes that the judge's duty is to declare which neighbor is right and which wrong, and that this declaration will end the judge's involvement. . . . Under these assumptions, settlement appears as an almost perfect substitute for judgment, for it too can declare the parties' rights. Often, however, judgment is not the end of a lawsuit but only the beginning. The involvement of the court may continue almost indefinitely. In these cases, settlement cannot provide an adequate basis for that necessary continuing involvement, and thus is no substitute for judgment.

The parties may sometimes be locked in combat with one another and view the lawsuit as only one phase in a long continuing struggle. . . . This often occurs in domestic-relations cases, where the divorce decree represents only the opening salvo in an endless series of skirmishes over custody and support.

The structural reform cases that play such a prominent role on the federal docket provide another occasion for continuing judicial involvement. In these cases, courts seek to safeguard public values by restructuring large-scale bureaucratic organizations. . . .

The drive for settlement knows no bounds and can result in a consent decree even in the kinds of cases I have just mentioned, that is, even when a court finds itself embroiled in a continuing struggle between the parties or must reform a bureaucratic organization. The parties may be ignorant of the difficulties ahead or optimistic about the future, or they may simply believe that they can get more favorable terms through a bargained-for agreement. Soon, however, the inevitable happens: One party returns to court and asks the judge to modify the decree, either to make it more effective or less stringent. But the judge is at a loss: He has no basis for assessing the request. He cannot, to use Cardozo's somewhat melodramatic formula, easily decide whether the "dangers, once substantial, have become attenuated to a shadow," because, by definition, he never knew the dangers. . . .

Justice Rather Than Peace

The dispute-resolution story makes settlement appear as a perfect substitute for judgment, as we just saw, by trivializing the remedial dimensions of a lawsuit, and also by reducing the social function of the lawsuit to one of resolving private disputes. In that story, settlement appears to achieve exactly the same purpose as judgment — peace between the parties — but at considerably less expense to society. The two quarreling neighbors turn to a court in order to resolve their dispute, and society makes courts available because it wants to aid in the achievement of their private ends or to secure the peace.

In my view, however, the purpose of adjudication should be understood in broader terms. Adjudication uses public resources, and employs not strangers chosen by the parties but officials chosen by a process in which the public participates. These officials, like members of the legislative and executive branches, possess a power that has been defined and conferred by public law, not by private agreement. Their job is not to maximize the ends of private parties, nor simply to secure the peace, but to explicate and give force to the values embodied in authoritative texts such as the Constitution and statutes; to interpret those values and to bring reality into accord with them. This duty is not discharged when the parties settle.

In our political system, courts are reactive institutions. They do not search out interpretive occasions, but instead wait for others to bring matters to their attention. They also rely for the most part on others to investigate and present the law and facts. A settlement will thereby deprive a court of the occasion, and perhaps even the ability, to render an interpretation. A court cannot proceed (or not proceed very far) in the face of a settlement. To be against settlement is not to urge that parties be "forced" to litigate. . . . To be against settlement is only to suggest that when the parties settle, society gets less than what appears, and for a price it does not know it is paying. . . .

The Real Divide

To all this, one can readily imagine a simple response by way of confession and avoidance: We are not talking about *those* lawsuits. Advocates of ADR might insist that my account of adjudication, in contrast to the one implied by the dispute-resolution story, focuses on a rather narrow category of lawsuits. They could argue that while settlement may have only the most limited appeal with respect to those cases, I have not spoken to the "typical" case. My response is twofold.

First, even as a purely quantitative matter, I doubt that the number of cases I am referring to is trivial. . . .

Second, it demands a certain kind of myopia to be concerned only with the number of cases, as though all cases are equal simply because the clerk of the court assigns each a single docket number. All cases are not equal. The Los Angeles desegregation case, to take one example, is not equal to the allegedly more typical suit involving a property dispute or an automobile accident. The desegregation suit consumes more resources, affects more people, and provokes far greater challenges to the judicial power. The settlement movement must introduce a qualitative perspective; it must speak to these more "significant" cases, and demonstrate the propriety of settling them. . . .

[In] fact, most ADR advocates make no effort to distinguish between different types of cases or to suggest that "the gentler arts of reconciliation and accommodation" might be particularly appropriate for one type of case but not for another. They lump all cases together. This suggests that what divides me from the partisans of ADR is not that we are concerned with different universes of cases — that Derek Bok, for example, focuses on boundary quarrels while I see only desegregation suits. I suspect instead that what divides us is much deeper and stems from our understanding of the purpose of the civil lawsuit and its place in society. It is a difference in outlook.

Someone like Bok sees adjudication in essentially private terms: The purpose of lawsuits and the civil courts is to resolve disputes, and the amount of litigation we encounter is evidence of the needlessly combative and quarrelsome character of Americans. Or as Bok put it, using a more diplomatic idiom: "At bottom, ours is a society built on individualism, competition, and success." I, on the other hand, see adjudication in more public terms: Civil litigation is an institutional arrangement for using state power to bring a recalcitrant reality closer to our chosen ideals. We turn to the courts because we need to, not because of some quirk in our personalities. We train our students in the tougher arts so that they may help secure all that the law promises, not because we want them to become gladiators or because we take a special pleasure in combat.

To conceive of the civil lawsuit in public terms as America does might be unique. I am willing to assume that no other country — including Japan, Bok's new paradigm — has a case like *Brown v. Board of Education* in which the judicial power is used to eradicate the caste structure. I am willing to assume that no other country conceives of law and uses law in quite the way we do. But this should be a source of pride rather than shame. What is unique is not the problem that we live short of our ideals, but that we alone among the nations of the world seem willing to do something about it. Adjudication American-style is not a reflection of our combativeness but rather a tribute to our inventiveness and perhaps even more to our commitment.

Questions

9. Based on what you have learned, how would ADR advocates criticize Professor Fiss's arguments?
10. What kinds of cases does Professor Fiss think are especially inappropriate for ADR? Would you carve out certain areas, or types of disputes, as inappropriate for mediation?
11. If you would allow mediation in certain types of cases only if it is subject to special conditions, what conditions would you impose?

❖ **Richard Delgado,** *ADR AND THE DISPOSSESSED: RECENT BOOKS ABOUT THE DEFORMALIZATION MOVEMENT*

13 Law & Soc. Inquiry 145 (1988)

There are only a handful of basic ways in which our society responds to insoluble social problems — ones that, like blacks' demands for justice, women's claims for comparable worth, consumers' demands for well-made, reasonably priced goods, workers' demands for a larger share of the industrial pie, and everyone's desire for a safe, nonpolluted environment, cannot be solved at an acceptable cost.

If those agitating for reform are aroused and united, we cannot dismiss their problem as a nonproblem or the claimants as nonpersons (as we once did with slaves or do today with children and the insane). That would simply inflame them further. The only solution is to seem to be addressing the problem, but without doing anything that threatens the status quo too drastically. . . .

[One] approach is to enlarge the problem — to concede its existence but insist that it is much broader than most realize, that its solution entails expanding the context and taking account of a multitude of factors. . . . When "the problem" is transformed into something so complex and multifaceted that no simple legal formula can encompass it, it is also likely that no single remedy — such as an injunction or damages — can solve it. Instead, we must strive to avoid simplistic win-lose thinking and look for creative solutions that maximize many variables at once. Equally important, . . . [s]ince dozens, perhaps hundreds, of details are relevant to a case's resolution, the likelihood that identical cases will recur is remote. Therefore, we can dispense with stare decisis, the rule of law, written opinions, and judicial review. . . .

The movement toward alternative dispute resolution illustrates [this] approach. . . . It is an excellent way of seeming to be doing something about intractable social problems while actually doing relatively little. . . . [P]roblems are not faced, responsibility is diffused, grievants are cooled out, while everyone leaves thinking something positive has been done.

Some grievances will not succumb to burial. They will retain their sharp edges despite being embedded in a mass of extraneous detail. The grievant will decline ADR's demand for peace, for compromise, and insist that his or her problem be dealt with in accord with justice. In disputes of this type — ones that retain their initial polarity — a second problem with ADR emerges. . . .

Formal adjudication contains a multitude of rules and practices the effect, and sometimes intent, of which is to constrain bias and prejudice. These range from rules dealing with disqualification of judges and jurors for bias, to rules that protect the jury from prejudicial influence. . . . Moreover, studies indicate that simply becoming a member of a jury has a fairness-inducing effect on jurors, causing them to display a greater degree of impartiality and fairness than they ordinarily do in daily life. . . .

[P]rejudice is widespread in American society — surveys and polls indicate that most Americans harbor some degree of prejudice toward members of groups other than their own. . . . The expression of prejudice is far from simple, however, and certainly not automatic. . . . The formalities of a court trial are calculated to check prejudice. . . . [They] also encourage minority-race persons to press their claims more forthrightly. . . .

ADR can, by expanding disputes beyond recognition, cause them to lose their urgency and sharp edges. When ADR cannot avoid dealing with sharply contested claims, its structureless setting and absence of formal rules increase the likelihood of an outcome colored by prejudice, with the result that the haves once again come out ahead. . . .

Questions

12. In what types of cases is it most likely that the concerns set out by Professor Delgado would arise? Why?
13. Could mediation procedures be modified to take account of these concerns without losing the essential character of the process? How might this be done?

2. *Should Some Disputes Not Be Mediated?*

a. Issues of Gender, Ethnicity, and Culture

❖ **Michele Hermann,** NEW MEXICO RESEARCH EXAMINES IMPACT OF
GENDER AND ETHNICITY IN MEDIATION

1 Disp. Resol. Mag. 10 (Fall 1994)

Professors and students from the University of New Mexico Schools of Law and Sociology are collaborating on a research project . . . to study the effects of race and gender on mediation and adjudication of cases in Albuquerque's small claims court. This court, the Bernalillo County Metropolitan Court, is a non-record court with jurisdiction to hear civil cases in which the amount in controversy is $5,000 or less. All three judges are male; one is African American, one is Hispanic American, and one is European American. . . . The court contracts with a local mediation center to operate the court's mediation program, under which all civil filings are screened . . . and about one-third of the cases are referred to mediation.

The research project randomly assigned more than 600 cases to either adjudication or mediation, and tracked both the case results and the participants' reactions. . . . The study sought to evaluate results in mediation and adjudication by using two measures: (1) an objective formula for outcome . . . and (2) subjective measures of satisfaction. . . . Perhaps the most startling finding is that in the objective outcomes of both adjudicated and mediated cases, disputants of color fared worse than did white disputants. These disparate results were more extreme in mediated than in adjudicated cases. An ethnic-minority plaintiff could be predicted to receive eighteen cents on the dollar less than a white plaintiff in mediation, while an ethnic-minority respondent could be predicted to pay twenty cents on the dollar more.

When examining how the ethnicity of the co-mediators affected outcomes, the study found that when there were two mediators of color, the negative impact of the disputant's ethnicity disappeared. The ethnicity of the mediators did not change the objective outcomes of white disputants' cases.

The negative outcomes found for ethnic minority participants were not replicated when the data were analyzed for gender. For the most part, neither the gender of the claimant nor that of the respondent had a statistically significant effect on monetary outcomes in either adjudicated or mediated cases, except that female respondents did better in mediation than male respondents, paying less than their male counterparts.

The examination of procedural and substantive satisfaction produced interesting contrasts to the objective outcome analysis. Despite their disparately poorer outcomes, ethnic minority disputants were more likely to express satisfaction with mediation than were white disputants. Female disputants, on the other hand, were more likely to express satisfaction with adjudication. Indeed, white female respondents, who had the most favorable objective outcomes in mediation, reported the lowest level of satisfaction. Furthermore, compared to other mediation respondents, white women were less likely to see the mediation process as fair and unbiased. Women of color, on the other hand, reported the highest level of satisfaction with mediation, despite their tendency to fare the worst in objective outcomes as either claimants or respondents.

The evidence that disputants of color fare significantly worse in mediation than do white participants raises important questions about whether the traditional mediation process is appropriate in disputes involving ethnic minorities, as well as members of other groups who are traditionally disempowered in American society. . . .

It is far from clear, however, that bias, prejudice, and cultural blindness are the only explanation for the results of the UNM study. The underlying effects may be considerably more complex. . . . Similarly, the fact that white women fare well in small claims mediation does not dispel the concerns raised by scholars . . . about gender bias in other forums, such as family court. . . . In the meantime, mediation and other dispute resolution programs need to pay serious attention to the potential impact of power imbalances between and among parties who are in dispute, and should not assume that mediator neutrality will guarantee fairness.

Questions

14. If the conclusions of the New Mexico study are correct, can you think of safeguards that might reduce the risk of disparate results in small claims mediation? In mediation of family disputes?
15. Why might Latino disputants be more satisfied with mediation than Anglo disputants despite receiving less favorable results?
16. The federal courts for the District of Columbia and the Northern District of California have created panels of lawyers to represent pro se parties in ADR (Stienstra et al. 2001).
    a. Would providing legal representation in mediation resolve any of the issues identified by Delgado?
    b. Would it resolve the problems suggested in the New Mexico study?
17. Some courts will not refer pro se parties to mediation in situations in which the other side is represented by counsel. Do you agree with this policy? What are its advantages and disadvantages?

❖ **Sina Bahadoran,** *A Red Flag: Mediator Cultural Bias in Divorce Mediation*

18 Mass. Fam. L.J. 69 (2000)

Scenario One: An American wife and her Albanian husband are participating in divorce mediation. The couple shares a four-year-old daughter. During mediation, the wife alleges that her husband sometimes acts inappropriately with their daughter — one time fondling her genitalia. The mediator asks the husband about the wife's allegation and the husband responds that it is true.

Scenario Two: An American man and his Danish wife are involved in a divorce mediation. The couple shares a 14-month-old son. During mediation, the husband alleges that on several occasions his wife left their son outside in his stroller, while she went into diners to have lunch.

Scenario Three: An American woman and her Iraqi husband are participating in divorce mediation. The couple shares a nine-year-old daughter. During mediation, the wife accuses the husband of being violent and aggressive with their daughter. The wife also expresses fear over her husband's renewed interest in Islam.

In each of the above scenarios a mediator, as currently trained, would be unprepared to adequately handle these situations. In other words, mediation would be inappropriate. Scenario One is based on the incident involving Sadri Krasniqi of Plano, Texas. After fondling his daughter during a basketball match, Krasniqi was charged with sexual abuse and lost custody of his daughter. Eventually, five years later, charges against him were dropped after the prosecutors became aware that the idea of parent-child sex is so unimaginable in Albania that parental fondling is acceptable behavior.

Scenario Two is based on the case of Annette Sorenson, a Danish woman who left her 14-month-old daughter outside while she went into a diner to have lunch. Sorensen was jailed and charged with child endangerment. Only later was she freed after authorities learned that "parking," or leaving children in their strollers outside of stores, is common behavior in Denmark.

Scenario Three is a fictitious situation in which the foreign spouse would be just as disadvantaged as in the first two scenarios, not because of actual cultural differences, but rather because of perceived cultural stereotypes. . . .

American Collective Unconscious: Cultural Myths and Stereotypes

. . . A non-American spouse entering divorce mediation will face a great many cultural myths and stereotypes. . . . The cultural myths that surround people of various ethnicity and nationality vary greatly, but all are unified by a common theme: cultural inferiority.

. . . Parent-child suicide, religious fanaticism, barbarity, laziness, wife beating, forced marriage, and female genital mutilation are just some of the images associated with non-European immigrants. . . . Arab Muslims are seen as irrational beings, incapable of achieving cultural or intellectual success. . . . With Asian cultures, the myths take on a different quality. Asians are often seen as the "model minority." . . . Although intended to be complimentary to Asian-Americans, the "praise" can go too far. Most Asians are seen as being fungible. . . . In contrast to the "model" minority status associated with Asians, Latinos are often relegated to the bottom of the minority hierarchy: laziness, alcoholism, criminality, and gang culture are just a few of the myths. . . . [G]iven the cultural myths and stereotypes that pervade the American collective unconscious, the informal nature of mediation creates an atmosphere that is particularly prone to bias. . . .

Power and Danger of Narrative in Mediation

Much of the power of mediation comes from its opportunity for divorcing spouses to tell their own stories. Each spouse is the director, producer, and actor. . . . Despite the benefits of the narrative style, it is also at the center of the problems with mediation. Mediation is essentially a struggle between two opposing narratives. The prevailing narrative sets the context for all of the subsequent descriptions. Minority spouses will have more negative cultural myths aligned against them and will be disadvantaged in their ability to compete for narrative preeminence. . . .

Imagine a scenario where the Iraqi husband and his American wife are seeking mediation for their divorce. The couple has a nine-year-old daughter and is in a heated disagreement as to custody. One portion of the mediation revolves around an incident where the husband smacked their daughter's hand for misbehaving. In the wife's description, she will assign her husband the role of the violent, strict middle-easterner and herself and her daughter as the innocent victims of his rage. The husband will try and reconfigure the wife's "primary narrative." He will explain that the young girl had repeatedly misbehaved and that he lightly slapped her hand after several previous admonitions. In his narrative, the husband will assign himself the role of the "good" loving father and his wife as the unresponsive, distant mother who allows their daughter to be spoiled.

. . . Each spouse will attempt to manipulate the conversation by relying on as many positive cultural stereotypes about their identity group and negative ones about their spouse as possible. . . . The mediator sits in the middle of the competing stories as they circle around her. She must choose one. . . . Her choice will not be explicit, but she will offer more credence to one narrative over the other. The mediator enters mediation with his or her own selected conscious and unconscious cultural stereotypes. As the mediator listens to each spouse's perception of reality, she filters all of the narratives through her own individual (experiential) and cultural (identity group) filter. The effects of the narratives will be greater if they are of a subliminal rather than overt nature. . . .

Questions

18. Do you think that cultural myths are widespread enough to pose a serious problem in mediation? In what areas are problems most likely to occur?
19. You are the lawyer for a client from an Arabic culture who is involved in a parenting dispute that is going to mediation. How might you monitor whether your mediator is allowing stereotypes to influence her approach to the case? What could you do about it if she were?

b. Mandatory Mediation of Family Disputes

Many state court systems now require litigants to go through mediation before obtaining access to a judge, and the most popular area for mandatory mediation has been family disputes. Mandatory mediation raises special questions, however, particularly when intimate relationships are involved and the participants do not have lawyers. The following reading argues against the use of mandatory mediation in such situations. As you read it, ask yourself these questions.

Questions

20. To what extent would the concerns raised by Professor Grillo exist if mediation was voluntary?
21. To what extent do they exist if the parties have access to lawyers?
22. If parties to domestic relations cases are not required to mediate, what is likely to happen to them?

❖ **Trina Grillo,** *The Mediation Alternative: Process Dangers for Women*

100 Yale L.J. 1545 (1991)

There is little doubt that divorce procedure needs to be reformed, but reformed how? Presumably, any alternative should be at least as just, and at least as humane, as the current system, particularly for those who are least powerful in society. Mediation has been put forward, with much fanfare, as such an alternative. The impetus of the mediation movement has been so strong that in some states couples disputing custody are required by statute or local rule to undergo a mandatory mediation process if they are unable to reach an agreement on their own. . . .

[S]tudies have shown that mediation clients are more satisfied with their divorce outcomes than persons using the adversary system. Although there are significant methodological problems with each of these studies, the existence of substantial client satisfaction with some models of mediation cannot be completely discounted.

Nonetheless, I conclude that mandatory mediation provides neither a more just nor a more humane alternative to the adversarial system of adjudication of custody, and, therefore, does not fulfill its promises. In particular, quite apart from whether an acceptable result is reached, mandatory mediation can be destructive to many women and some men because it requires them to speak in a setting they have not chosen and often imposes a rigid orthodoxy as to how they should speak, make decisions, and be. This orthodoxy is imposed through subtle and not-so-subtle messages about appropriate conduct and about what may be said in mediation. It is an orthodoxy that often excludes the possibility of the parties' speaking with their authentic voices.

Moreover, people vary greatly in the extent to which their sense of self is "relational" — that is, defined in terms of connection to others. If two parties are forced to engage with one another, and one has a more relational sense of self than the other, that party may feel compelled to maintain her connection with the other, even to her own detriment. For this reason, the party with the more relational sense of self will be at a disadvantage in a mediated negotiation. Several prominent researchers have suggested that, as a general rule, women have a more relational sense of self than do men, although there is little agreement on what the origin of this difference might be. Thus, rather than being a feminist alternative to the adversary system, mediation has the potential actively to harm women.

Some of the dangers of mandatory mediation apply to voluntary mediation as well. Voluntary mediation should not be abandoned, but should be recognized as a powerful process which should be used carefully and thoughtfully.

Entering into such a process with one who has known you intimately and who now seems to threaten your whole life and being has great creative, but also enormous destructive, power. Nonetheless, it should be recognized that when two people themselves decide to mediate and then physically appear at the mediation sessions, that decision and their continued presence serve as a rough indication that it is not too painful or too dangerous for one or both of them to go on. . . .

The Rise of Mandatory Custody Mediation in California

The movement for voluntary mediation of divorce disputes began several decades ago as lawyers and therapists offered to help their clients settle their cases in a nonadversarial manner. . . . As mediation caught on, it began to be heralded as the cure for the various ills of adversary divorce. . . . Consumers, however, were not embracing the mediation cure. . . . In order to bypass this consumer resistance, some state legislatures established court-annexed mediation programs, requiring that couples disputing custody mediate prior to going to court. . . .

Local courts [in California] have the option of requiring mediators to make a recommendation to the court regarding custody or visitation. If the parties do not reach an agreement, the mediator may also make a recommendation that an investigation be conducted or mutual restraining orders be issued. More than half of California counties have opted to require mediators to make such recommendations. . . .

The Betrayal of Mediation's Promises: The Informal Law of Mediation

The good woman: She comes into mediation ready to be cooperative. She does not deny her feelings, but does not shift them onto her children. She realizes her problems are her problems, that she should not use the children as a way of solving them, and that it is critically important that her husband stay involved in the lives of the children. She does not play victim, but realizes what she is entitled to and insists on it calmly. She is rational, not bitter or vengeful, and certainly not interested in hurting her husband. She understands that she played a role in whatever harms he inflicted on her, since in a family no one person is ever at fault.

The bad woman: She is bitter and wants revenge for things that have happened to her in the past. She fights over the most trivial, petty things. She is greedy and ready to sacrifice her children as a tool against her husband. She is irrational and unwilling to compromise. When a specific, focused response is called for, she responds by bringing up a completely unrelated matter. It is hard to keep her on track. She keeps venting her anger instead of negotiating constructively.

In even the most mundane settings there develops a type of informal law, shared expectations that there is a right way of acting, that departures from this way are wrong, and that an offender should be sanctioned. . . . The norms that govern microlegal systems are unwritten and often not consciously perceived, but they are always present. . . . Persons in the midst of a divorce often experience what seems to them a threat to their very survival. Their self-concepts, financial well-being, moral values, confidence in their parenting abilities, and feelings of being worthy of love are all at risk. . . . They are especially vulnerable to the responses they receive from any professional with whom they must deal. Against this backdrop, mediation must be seen as a relatively high-risk process. [T]he parties are extremely sensitive to cues as to how they are supposed to act; they will look to the mediator to provide these cues. Mediators are often quite willing to give such cues, to establish the normative components of the mediation, and to sanction departures from the unwritten rules. The informal sanctions applied by a mediator can be especially powerful, quite apart from whatever actual authority he might have. These sanctions might be as simple as criticizing the client for not putting the children's needs first, or instructing her not to talk about a particular issue. . . .

The Promise to Contextualize Decisionmaking: Principles and Fault in Mediation

. . . The informal law of the mediation setting requires that discussion of principles, blame, and rights, as these terms are used in the adversarial context, be deemphasized or avoided. Mediators use informal sanctions to encourage the parties to replace the rhetoric of fault, principles, and values with the rhetoric of compromise and relationship. For example, mediators typically suggest that the parties eschew the language of individual rights in favor of the language of interdependent relationships. They orient the parties toward reasonableness and compromise, rather than moral vindication. The conflict may be styled as a personal quarrel, in which there is no right and wrong, but simply two different, and equally true or untrue, views of the world.

(1) Are All Agreements Equal? . . . Sometimes, however, all agreements are not equal. It may be important, from both a societal and an individual standpoint, to have an agreement that reflects cultural notions of justice and not merely one to which there has been mutual assent. Many see the courts as a place where they can obtain vindication and a ruling by a higher authority. It is also important in some situations for society to send a clear message as to how children are to be treated, what the obligations of ex-spouses are to each other and to their children, and what sort of behavior will not be tolerated. Because the mediation movement tends to regard negotiated settlements as morally superior to adjudication, these functions of adjudication may easily be over-looked.

(2) Conceptual Underpinnings: Family Systems and Circular Causality. On a more theoretical level, the reluctance to discuss principles is based on the view, held by most mediators, that the family is a self-contained system. Under this view, all parts of the family are equally implicated in whatever happens within it. Each part of this system is simultaneously a cause for, and an effect of, all the other parts. . . . Causality is circular; that is, "[n]o specific situation or person is considered the antecedent, cause, or effect of [the] problem. . . ."

Although this systems approach can be a useful one in understanding how families and other social organizations work, it has some serious shortcomings. Most critically, it obscures issues of unequal social power and sex role socialization. . . . It is typical for mediators to insist that parties waste no time complaining about past conduct of their spouse, eschew blaming each other, and focus only on the future. For example, one of the two essential ground rules mediator Donald Saposnek suggests a mediator give to the parties is the following:

> There is little value in talking about the past, since it only leads to fighting and arguing, as I'm sure you both know . . . Our focus will be on your children's needs for the future and on how you two can satisfy those needs. . . . [U]nless I specifically request it, we will talk about plans for the future. . . .

The Promise to Include Emotion and the Suppression of Anger

Another criticism of the traditional adversary method of dispute resolution is that it does not provide a role for emotion. . . . Although mediation is claimed to be a setting in which feelings can be expressed, certain sentiments are often simply not welcome. In particular, expressions of anger are frequently overtly discouraged. This discouragement of anger sends a message that anger is unacceptable, terrifying and dangerous. For a person who has only recently found her anger, this can be a perilous message indeed. . . .

At a recent meeting of a mediation group, a nationally known mediator was a moderator at a round table discussion. In the course of the discussion, a participant stated that she thought one of the problems that divorcing couples had was that they had never learned to fight with each other in a productive way. Several of those present, including the moderator, objected to the word "fight." The speaker tried to make her point more palatable by substituting the words "handle conflict." But this modification was not enough. There was general agreement that we should talk instead about "problem-solving." . . .

[T]here are other forces which may intensify this dynamic of suppression. Mediators working under time pressures recognize that it takes time to express anger, and its full expression might, indeed, jeopardize a quick settlement. More significantly, there are substantial societal taboos against the expression of anger by women, taboos which have particular force when the disputant is a woman of color. . . .

Mandatory Mediation and the Promise of Self-Determination . . .

Often, the time allotted to a mandatory mediation is short. Frequently, an entire mediation is expected to take place in an hour or less. Some take place in the hallways of the courthouse. Given these conditions, it is impossible for the state to ensure that an adequate process is being offered even in cases in which people have chosen it. Where the process is inadequate, its imposition is even more troubling.

Moreover, a person married to a liar or con artist knows that that person is often more persuasive than someone telling the truth. In a relationship in which the wife has been abused, for example, the abuser will often appear dominant, charming, agreeable, and socially facile in comparison to his less assertive wife. . . . Of course, liars show up in court, too; but in an informal process where nothing they say can be disproved, they are in a much stronger position. In sum, a person might decide against mediation because she knows the spouse is not capable of working honestly and productively within the process. Forcing mediation can produce a situation in which the parent with the fewest scruples wins.

A substantial proportion of women who file for divorce state that they do so, at least in part, because they have been the victims of domestic violence. . . . Mediation where abuse has occurred is troubling even when mediation is voluntary. Mandatory mediation programs, however, do not always permit abused parties to opt out. Moreover, even where such an exception to the mediation requirement exists, the abused spouse might have trouble showing she is entitled to it. . . .

Choice of Mediator: Partiality and Unacknowledged Perspective

Typically in mandatory mediation, the participants cannot choose their mediator or, at best, have a very limited choice of mediators. . . . Mediators, however, exert a great deal of power. . . .

Exclusion of Lawyers

In California, lawyers typically are excluded from mediation sessions, and the parties are required to speak for themselves, whether or not they wish to do so. Some argue that exclusion of lawyers contributes to client empowerment. In evaluating whether their exclusion actually furthers client empowerment, it is useful to consider the reasons why a person engaged in a divorce might want the services of a lawyer. . . .

Lawyers as Protectors of Rights. A lawyer who is excluded from the mediation sessions may be hampered in protecting her client's rights, particularly if custody is ultimately to be litigated in court. For example, privileged or irrelevant material, which the lawyer does not believe should be disclosed, may mistakenly be revealed in mediation. Once such privileged information is disclosed, it is often impossible to keep it out of a later court proceeding. . . .

Lawyers as Providers of Insulation. Lawyers serve another function in the divorce process, that of insulating the parties from the hand-to-hand combat and self-help that the rule of law is intended to avoid. The presence of a lawyer means that a party does not have to face his adversary directly if he does not wish to do so. Mediation is often put forward as a method of empowering the parties to a dispute, but the words "Don't call me, call my lawyer" are sometimes the most empowering words imaginable. Mandatory mediation, even absent the pressure to reach an agreement that exists when a recommendation to the court can be made, prevents lawyers from performing this protective function. . . .

There are, then, many good reasons why a party might choose not to mediate. While some argue that mediation should be required because potential participants lack the information about the process which would convince them to engage in it voluntarily, this is not a sufficient justification for requiring mediation. If the state were committed only to making sure that disputants become familiar with mediation, something less than mandatory mediation — such as viewing a videotaped mediation or attending an orientation program — could be required, and mediators would certainly not be permitted to make recommendations to the court. That more than the simple receipt of information is required under a statutory mediation scheme demonstrates a profound disrespect for the parties' ability to determine the course of their own lives. . . . The legislative choice to make mediation mandatory has been a mistake.

. . . The adversary system admittedly works poorly for child custody cases in many respects. There are, however, some ways to avoid damaging custody battles under an adversary system, such as enacting presumptions that make outcomes reasonably clear in advance, court-sponsored lectures on settlement, and joint negotiation sessions with lawyers and clients present. When in court, lawyers could be held to higher standards with respect to communicating with their clients, and judges could refrain from speaking to lawyers when their clients are not present. . . .

The only reason to prefer mediation to other, more obvious alternatives is that the parties may, through the mediation process, ultimately benefit themselves and their children by learning how to communicate and work together. Whether this will happen in the context of a particular mediation is something only the parties can judge. . . .

Notes and Questions

23. Your local family court has decided that it should impose protective rules to ensure that litigants are not subject to undue pressure to settle in its mandatory mediation program. It has asked you for advice:
    (a) In what situations should the rules apply?
    (b) What specific protections would you suggest?
24. Under California law, a divorce settlement that "advantages one spouse" gives rise to a presumption of undue influence. However, a California appellate court has ruled that such a presumption does not apply when settlements are reached through mediation. *In re Kieturakis*, 31 Cal. Rptr. 3d 119, 141 (Cal. App. 2006). Why might the court have ruled this way? Do you agree with the holding?

The issues raised by the use of mandatory mediation in domestic relations cases do not necessarily apply to other types of civil litigation. Thus Professor Roselle Wissler, for example, found in a study of two state court mediation programs that "the manner in which the case entered mediation produced few differences in parties' assessments of the mediator, the mediation process, and the outcome" (Wissler, 1997). See, to the same effect, Stienstra et al. (1997).

c. Domestic Violence Cases

Mediation, especially when mandated by a court, is particularly controversial when a case involves possible spousal abuse. Many, like Professor Grillo in the earlier reading, would object even to "voluntary" mediation in such cases. In the following reading, an experienced mediator presents a contrarian view.

❖ **Ann L. Milne,** *MEDIATION AND DOMESTIC ABUSE*

Divorce and Family Mediation 304
(J. Folberg et al. eds., 2004)

There are nearly 6 million incidents of physical assault against women reported every year, and 76% of these are perpetrated by current or former husbands, cohabiting partners, or dates. . . . Changes in the law and the increased media attention given to domestic abuse have sensitized the public to this formerly private issue. In contrast, the use of mediation has increased significantly as a less-public forum to resolve disputes between former spouses. Courts in at least 38 states have mandated that parents be referred to mediation when they are disputing custody or parental access schedules.

. . . The juxtaposition of strengthened court and legal interventions in domestic abuse cases with the expanded use of mediation has resulted in considerable controversy. . . . Current arguments about the use of mediation in domestic abuse cases . . . do not focus so much on the mediation process itself, but rather on the nature of domestic abuse and the concerns endemic to these cases. Mediators should take these public policy concerns seriously. . . .

Most mediation proponents agree with the following guidelines:

- Some cases involving domestic abuse are inappropriate for mediation.
- Screening is necessary to determine which cases are appropriate.
- Mediators must be well trained in the dynamics of domestic abuse.
- Participation in the mediation process must be safe, fair, and voluntary.
- Victims of abuse should not be required to mediate.

Given these guidelines, proponents of making mediation available in cases of domestic abuse generally start with the argument of the "BATMA": What is the couple's "best alternative to a *mediated* agreement"? . . . In short if mediation is not used, then what? It is argued by both social science experts and legal scholars that mediation is more appropriate and effective than the adversarial process, even in cases of domestic abuse. Some have said that the adversarial process exacerbates the dynamics between partners when abuse is a factor by escalating the conflict and reinforcing the power and control differential and the win/lose aspects of the relationship. . . . Few judges and lawyers have expertise in the subject of domestic abuse, whereas many mediators have had training in it. . . .

Reframing the Debate

. . . As in any conflict, the framing of the issues is critical. . . . Rather than framing the question, Should mediation be used in cases involving domestic abuse?, a more useful framing of the issue would be: What process can we develop that will best help individuals who have been involved in an abusive relationship address the issues between them, so that they can move on with their lives without violence and without the need for ongoing court and legal interventions? . . .

When providing mediation to batterers and victims, the following are excluded from the list of topics to be addressed:

- We are not mediating whether or not the abuse occurred. . . .
- We are not mediating reconciliation. . . .
- We are not mediating fault and blame. . . .
- We are not mediating punishment and consequences. . . .
- We are not mediating dropping of charges, protective orders, or restraining orders ("Do this, then she will drop the abuse charges.").
- We are not mediating contingencies or leveraging of issues. . . .
- We are not mediating court orders.
- We are not mediating threshold issues.

With the above procedural ground rules in place, the following areas can be effectively mediated:

Terms of Living Apart

Matters such as establishing a date for moving out, determining who is going to live where, division of household accessories, establishing a parenting schedule, and payment of household expenses are all day-to-day living arrangements that parties may need to address. The judge often does not have the time to take up each of these individual issues, and paying lawyers to negotiate them can be too costly for many. . . .

Property Division

Mediation can be a very helpful process for dividing up personal possessions such as furnishings, household supplies, photographs, books, tools, and all the other sundry things that family members need to manage their daily lives.

Financial Support . . . Use of Clothing and Toys . . . Activities with the Children

Mediation can be a very useful forum in which to share information about what activities the children would enjoy as well as to resolve disputes regarding activities of which a parent disapproves. Is it OK to take the children hunting? To a friend's home? To the corner tavern? . . .

School Contact

Is it OK for a parent to stop by the school to say hello to a child or to chat with the teacher? . . . Will both parents participate in children's sporting and other school events? . . .

Child-Care Arrangements

How will child-care decisions be made? . . . If a parent is called away from home, will the other parent be given the first opportunity to babysit? . . .

Research Findings

Quantitative longitudinal research on the impact of mediation in cases of domestic abuse is lacking. [S]tudies found that mediation was associated with a greater reduction in physical, verbal, and emotional abuse than lawyer-assisted settlement. . . . For the growing unrepresented or pro se population of litigants, mediation may be the only consumer support available, short of litigation. Outcome studies on the impact of precluding mediation would be very illuminating.

"Confessions of a Mediator"

I have been a mediator for more than 30 years and have worked in both a court-connected setting and a private practice. Over time I have come to several personal conclusions and observations about my own practices when mediating cases involving allegations or instances of domestic abuse:

I Am Far More Controlling of the Process

Whereas I normally espouse a mildly directive, facilitative style, when I am mediating in a case known to me to include allegations or instances of domestic abuse, I often find that I must be far more controlling of the process. . . . At the same time, I need to avoid becoming enmeshed in an arm-wrestling contest with the batterer, who may attempt to take over the process. . . .

Judgment Is Important

The role of the mediator is typically described as that of a nonjudgmental neutral party. . . . However, when mediating in cases of possible or known domestic abuse, . . . [t]he mediator must continually reevaluate whether this case is appropriate for mediation and whether he or she has the skills needed to work effectively with this couple.

Forget the Balancing Act

Terms such as maintaining balance, power balancing, and level playing field are often used when describing the mediation process. However, when mediating in a case involving issues of domestic abuse, I find that I am "off-balance" much of the time because I am challenged to keep control of the process.

The Process Is Less Collaborative and More of a Facilitated Negotiation

. . . The parties focus more on their separate interests and solutions rather than the mutual interests that I tend to focus on when abuse is not a factor.

Short-Term Agreements

One of the incentives to using mediation in cases involving concerns about domestic abuse is the ability to put in place agreements of a short-term nature and revisit and revise them as needs dictate. Predictability and steadfastness are not often present with these couples. Putting together agreements or court orders that apply over the long haul is often counterproductive. . . .

Need for Reliable Resources

The need to establish a scaffolding of support can be very important when mediating in domestic abuse cases. The support of the parties' attorneys, victim and batterer advocates, counselors, and a safety plan can all work together to facilitate the success of the mediation process.

Watch Your Language

Colloquialisms that I use in everyday speech can often take on unintended meanings with domestic abuse partners. Using expressions such as "Can you live with that?," "It strikes me that . . . ," or "Please cut that out," would be insensitive and inappropriate with couples who have abuse issues. . . .

Sweat Equity Is a Fact of Life

I usually tell my mediation students that I know something is wrong when I am working harder than the clients. I have found that, when mediating in cases where abuse concerns have been raised, my skills are challenged, there is a level of stress not found with non-abuse cases, and I work hard to ensure that the mediation process is serving the interests and safety of both parties.

Conclusions

The question of whether or not mediation is appropriate in cases of domestic abuse must be reframed to focus on finding an answer to the question of what kind of system we could design that would provide a safe and secure decision-making process for spouses and parents in dispute. Although a traditional mediation process may not offer the protection necessary in domestic abuse cases, dismissing mediation outright may also be a mistake. The development of hybrid mediation models that embody the self-determination principles of the mediation process while also addressing power, control, coercion, and safety issues must be the goal.

Questions

25. Does Ms. Milne's model accommodate Professor Grillo's concerns? Overall, which approach seems most appropriate?
26. Assuming Ms. Milne's model could work in the right circumstances, is it practical to implement in court programs, even on a voluntary basis? What assurances would you need to support such a program in your local family court?
27. If you favor excluding cases involving allegations of abuse from court programs, would you also favor barring such cases from going to private mediation on a voluntary basis?

d. Parental Rights

Mediation is also used to resolve disputes over parental rights, an area that also raises serious policy issues. Consider the following cases.

Note: A Student Mediates Access to Her Child[1]

Just after my eighteenth birthday I discovered I was pregnant with my daughter Emily. After carefully considering my options as an unwed, single mother without a college degree, I knew I could never provide Emily with the life I felt she deserved. In time, I accepted that I needed to explore alternatives to parenting and I chose to look at adoption. Through my research I learned about open adoption. Open adoption is an arrangement that allows for the birthmother to choose the couple who will parent her child and to work with them to design a plan for meaningful, ongoing contact throughout the child's life. Although it was the most painful choice I have ever made, I knew that choosing open adoption was in my daughter's best interest.

After almost five months of searching, I met my daughter's parents through an adoption agency in New York. At six months pregnant, I had reviewed countless profiles of prospective adoptive parents and was becoming discouraged by my inability to find the right couple. Clearly, this was not a situation where I could compromise — the "right couple" needed to have all of my predetermined qualifications. So after months of searching, I was overjoyed when I found David and Maureen, the couple that eventually became my daughter's parents.

For the remaining three months of my pregnancy, David, Maureen, and I essentially dated. We went out to dinner. I stayed over at their house. David called me every day to check in and demonstrated genuine concern for both me and the baby. In time, we agreed to maintain an extended family-type relationship after Emily's birth and pledged to always respect, value, and honor each other and the commitments that we had made. Unfortunately, everything changed as soon as Emily left the hospital with them.

The first year of her life was torturous for me. Despite what we had agreed upon, I never knew when I was going to see her, if I would hear from them, or whether or not it was even OK to contact them. When we did have visits, Maureen made it clear that I was not welcome and that this was simply something she "had" to do but certainly not something she wanted. Early on, I was not allowed to hold her for any extended period of time. After five minutes, she would always find a reason to take her back. Needless to say, this is not what I agreed to in the pre-birth discussions.

I felt devastated by the change in David and Maureen and eventually sought counsel to explore my rights. I thought very seriously about petitioning the court to overturn Emily's adoption based on fraud. However, the attorney I consulted (who I later learned was an adoptive parent of five children) told me the courts would never respect our agreement and that my only option was to work it out with them if I ever hoped to see my daughter. (I have since learned that that is not true.) Eventually, I requested that we enter mediation with the counselors at the agency that handled our adoption, and David and Maureen agreed.

At the time I entered mediation I knew nothing about the process. I had never been involved in anything like it before and I had serious doubts about the prospect of a positive result. I felt betrayed by both the agency and David

---

1. This is an account by a law student of the mediation of an actual dispute; identifying information has been changed to protect the privacy of the participants.

and Maureen, and I wasn't confident that the agency-provided mediator would help us come to an agreement that was binding. However, I didn't have any other options so I decided I had to try it.

Power played a huge part in our mediation. Neither side was represented by counsel, but David and Maureen are almost 20 years older than me, have advanced degrees, and are well-respected professionals in their respective fields. As an uneducated, single 19-year-old, I felt disadvantaged. Beyond the educational differences, I was plainly outnumbered. But most importantly, they had Emily, the seminal piece of the power puzzle. Because of that, I always felt like I was in a poor bargaining position. As the professional, our mediator should have done more to recognize and work around that imbalance of power. For example, by caucusing she could have buffered some of their posturing and helped diffuse a lot of the insecurity I felt as a (seemingly) powerless 19-year-old.

The mediator did not use caucusing. Rather, we had five 1-2 hour sessions together as a group. The first sessions were essentially extended opening statements, followed by the final sessions in which we attempted to talk to each other and develop a suitable visitation agreement.

I learned a lot about what not to do as a mediator through my experience. The mediator often cried, rubbed her chest in a circular motion, and expressed her desire to "honor our difficult work." I understand that she was attempting to be supportive but at the time, I thought she was ridiculous and inappropriate. Also, I couldn't stand it when I could express the incredible hurt, betrayal, and anger I felt about the situation and she would respond with "That sounds like it was really hard." Frequently, I wanted to scream *"No shit!"* because it felt so incredibly patronizing and condescending to me.

Finally, she never advised me to consult an attorney. I think that was because the agency had its own agenda for our sessions. It was in the agency's best interest to not have litigation spring from our troubled relationship. Therefore, I think the mediator's lack of neutrality affected the counsel she provided to all of us.

After almost 15 years, I am happy to report that I have a wonderful relationship with my daughter. The irony of our mediation result was that I left the state almost immediately after it was finalized because it was too painful to be so close to them, both physically and psychologically. However, after over a decade of living apart and seeing my daughter a couple of times per year, I am now back in Boston and visiting with her on a schedule that is based on our mediated agreement from so long ago. Thus, despite the problems with the process that I encountered, I still left with a legally enforceable agreement that protected my rights.

Questions

28. Should this dispute have gone to mediation at all? If it had not, what do you think would have happened?
29. Should it have gone ahead only with safeguards? What ground rules or procedures might have protected everyone's interests without overly burdening the process?

❖ *IN THE MATTER OF T.D., DEPRIVED CHILD v.*
STATE OF OKLAHOMA

2001 Okla. Civ. App. 92 (2001)

COLBERT, J.:

Mother, Pamela Dawn LaTray, appeals the district court's order terminating her parental rights in T.D. and awarding custody to Father, Sean Loftin. The issue on appeal is whether the district court erred in terminating Mother's rights based on the terms of a mediation agreement between Mother, Father, the District Attorney, and attorneys representing T.D.

Mother is the biological mother of T.D. . . . and Father is T.D.'s biological father. Although Mother and Father cohabited at the time of T.D.'s birth, they separated when T.D. was approximately 8 months old. Mother moved to Oklahoma with T.D., and Father was unable to locate them until T.D. was 3 years old. Mother subsequently married Damien C. LaTray, Sr., and T.D. lived in their home, along with LaTray's biological son. [In] 1997, the State of Oklahoma filed a petition seeking the adjudication of T.D. as deprived. The petition included allegations of physical abuse, exposure to sexual activity, domestic violence, and substance abuse. T.D. was removed from Mother's home and placed with Father and his wife. Mother stipulated to the allegations in the petition [and a few months later the] State filed an amended petition . . . seeking the termination of Mother's parental rights.

. . . Mother and her attorney met in mediation with Father, Father's attorney, an assistant district attorney, and three attorneys representing T.D. Following a full day of mediation, they executed an agreement in which Mother agreed to voluntarily relinquish her parental rights to T.D. on [several conditions. The] district attorney [also] agreed that "no act of omission or commission committed by" Mother or her husband occurring before the date of the mediation conference would be used as a basis for terminating their parental rights in [the Mother's second] baby. The district court accepted the mediation agreement . . . without comment. . . .

[A few months later] the Department of Human Services (DHS) filed a report with the district court recommending that T.D. remain with Father and his wife in their home and that Mother's parental rights be terminated. The report stated that efforts to reunite T.D. with his Mother had failed and that "[T.D.] continues to have behavioral problems associated with the abuse he has endured." The report included the following information: In the past, [Mother and her husband] have participated in swinger magazines and at the Centerfold Club. [They] also appeared on the Jerry Springer television program in the past displaying their untraditional lifestyle.

On February 25, 2000, the independent assessment of Karen S. Baumann, a psychologist, was filed with the district court in partial satisfaction of the mediation terms. Dr. Baumann reported that . . . "T.D. was diagnosed with post traumatic stress disorder, general anxiety disorder, and attention deficit disorder with hyperactivity. [Father and his wife] appear to be emotionally stable and loving parents."

Mother contends on appeal that the district court erred in enforcing the mediation agreement. . . . Certainly mediation is encouraged by Oklahoma courts. However, the use of mediation in a proceeding involving the termination of parental rights for cause has not been considered in any published Oklahoma case of which this court is aware.

. . . Oklahoma's legislature, in constructing the current statutory scheme, has not contemplated the use of mediation in the context of a state-initiated effort to involuntarily terminate parental rights, and this court is troubled by its use. *Parental rights are fundamental rights.* . . . The courts will apply the tests of strict judicial scrutiny to a state law which interferes with the exercise of fundamental rights and liberties explicitly or implicitly protected by the Constitution.

We have applied "strict judicial scrutiny" to this mediation process and find that it is seriously lacking in protecting the fundamental due process rights of an individual whose parental rights are in danger of termination. [T]his process lacked a significant procedural protection — that the trial court found a factual basis for its determination that Mother knowingly and voluntarily agreed to the *full and final* relinquishment of her parental rights in T.D. *One of our concerns with this mediation agreement is that it purports to release Mother from all accrued and future child support obligation. Such contracts have generally been held to be against public policy. Second, the terms of this agreement indicate that Mother was trying to protect her parental rights in a newborn baby. The idea of the district attorney trading the rights of one child to be raised in a safe and loving environment for the similar rights of another, younger child would seem to run counter to the public policy of this state.*

This also raises the question of Father's place in this proceeding. Oklahoma law *requires that the trial judge verify, on the record, that the relinquishing parent has been informed of the consequences of her action, answered certain required questions, and has agreed to the full and irrevocable relinquishment of her parental rights.* [Emphasis in original.]

There is nothing in the record before this court . . . to indicate that those procedural safeguards were observed in this case. Although Mother was represented by counsel . . . ultimately, Mother's full understanding and acceptance of the results of her agreement are not reflected in the record before us. They must be before this termination can be upheld. . . .

GOODMAN, P.J., dissenting:

I would not permit mediation of a non-voluntary proceeding by the State to terminate the rights of a parent to a child.

Questions

30. Should mediation be permitted at all in proceedings to terminate parental rights?
31. If so, are the procedural assurances suggested by the majority adequate? What would you require? If you conclude that mediation should not be permitted, would it change your opinion if studies showed that on average parents fared no better, and perhaps worse, in cases that were not mediated?

CHAPTER
14

The Law of Mediation

A. Confidentiality

One of the key attractions of mediation for both parties and lawyers is that the process is confidential. Participants in mediation regularly sign agreements in which they commit not to disclose to outsiders anything communicated during the process. In addition, states and the federal government have given mediation varying levels of confidentiality protection. Sometimes, however, participants in mediation seek to disclose, or outsiders attempt to discover, what occurred during the process.

Disputes over mediation confidentiality arise in three basic ways.

- Litigants sometimes attempt to take confidential information from the mediation process and use it in another context, usually in court. ("Isn't it true that in mediation you admitted that . . . ?"). We refer to these as *litigation* breaches.
- Disputants sometimes allege that the mediation process itself went awry ("Your Honor, I signed the agreement at 2 A.M. and wasn't thinking clearly. The mediator just wouldn't let me go home!"). This latter category can be thought of as *supervisory* intrusions, because confidentiality is being invaded allegedly to protect the mediation process itself.
- Parties may also disagree about whether they reached agreement during mediation and if so what the terms were, and call each other or the mediator to testify; often this occurs because, it is alleged, the process itself was flawed.

To understand how confidentiality issues may arise in practice, consider the following problems.

Problems

1. You represent a St. Louis company, Bates, Inc. Bates is a "headhunter" firm that fills executive positions for corporations. A year ago Bates

contracted with a Chicago software consultant, Alpha Websites, to develop a Web site for Bates. A key goal for Bates was that its clients be able to advertise openings without revealing their identity, and that candidates be able to input personal data online in confidence. One important function of the new software was to screen out conflicting requests (for example, an executive applying for an opening at a company where he is currently working). The site was to be developed over six months for a total fee of $150,000.

Bates reports that the transaction was a disaster. The developer took nearly a year to deliver the site, and the security provisions proved to be porous. Clients complained that candidates could determine who was advertising, and some found themselves applying to their current employer, causing embarrassment for all concerned. Bates estimates that it lost at least a million dollars in business as a result of the Web site problems.

You filed suit against Alpha in federal court and a few months later accepted an invitation from Alpha's counsel to go to mediation. The mediation was governed by a confidentiality agreement. After several hours of mediation you deadlocked, with your client at $350,000 and Alpha at $50,000. In an effort to break the impasse, the mediator offered both sides a tentative opinion that while Bates had a good case on the contract, the site was now up and running fairly smoothly, and that given the language of the contract he did not think the court would grant a recovery on the lost profits claim. He recommended a settlement at $125,000. You declined this proposal, feeling that the evaluation was unrealistic and that the neutral was "bending" his evaluation to produce a number that Alpha would accept.

Three months later, you are called into a status conference with the judge presiding over the case. He asks both sides if they have explored settlement. You mention the unsuccessful mediation. The judge asks if the mediator gave an evaluation of the case. You say that the discussions were confidential, but the Alpha lawyer says, "Yes, Judge. Do you want to know what it was?" The judge nods affirmatively.

    a. What should you do?

    b. Is there anything you could have done in advance to prevent this situation?

2. Assume that at a settlement conference in the Bates-Alpha case, the presiding judge suggests that the litigants participate in mediation. Bates is willing, but Alpha declines. The judge says that in his experience mediation is often beneficial, and exercises his authority to order the parties to mediate. Rules of the court's mediation program require that participants mediate "in good faith" and bring with them "full settlement authority." Three weeks later, Bates and Alpha appear before a court-appointed mediator. Bates is represented by its CFO and outside counsel, Alpha by an associate from its outside law firm. In its opening statement Bates indicates that while it believes strongly in its case, it is willing to consider a reasonable compromise. Alpha argues that there is no basis for liability and that Bates's damage claims are wildly inflated.

> After four hours of mediation, Bates, which entered the mediation demanding $750,000, has dropped to $450,000. Alpha, which had made no offer before the mediation, offers $5,000, then $10,000, and then refuses to move further. In a caucus discussion with the mediator, Alpha's counsel reveals that she has no authority to go beyond $15,000, and that any offer above $100,000 would have to be approved by the defendant's board of directors. Bates does not know about this conversation, but tells the neutral that it strongly suspects that Alpha never gave its negotiator "real" settlement authority.
>
> A week later, Bates files a motion for sanctions with the judge, charging that Alpha's conduct at mediation violated the court's ADR program rules. Bates subpoenas the mediator to testify at the hearing on its motion.
>
> a. How should Alpha respond to Bates's claim that it violated program rules?
>
> b. How should it respond to the mediator subpoena?

1. How Important Is Confidentiality to Mediation?

❖ *FRANCES LEARY & OTHERS v. FATHER JOHN J. GEOGHAN & OTHERS*

Single Justice, Mass. App. Ct. 2002

[People who had been sexually abused as children sued the priest who abused them and the Roman Catholic Archbishop of Boston, who they argued had failed to use reasonable care to prevent the abuse. After years of litigation the parties agreed to mediate and eventually announced a settlement.

A dispute soon arose, however, over its terms. The defendants argued that the settlement, which required the Church to sell real estate, was subject to review by the Archdiocese's financial council. The plaintiffs, however, maintained that the agreement was not subject to any such condition and called the mediator as a witness. The mediator objected and moved for a protective order barring him from testifying.]

COHEN, Single Justice[.]

[The plaintiffs] have represented . . . that their sole purpose in calling the mediator is to ask him whether a document that was drafted at the conclusion of the mediation contained all of the terms that the parties wished to include in an agreement to settle. . . .

. . . The [trial] judge construed the [state confidentiality] statute as not establishing an absolute bar to disclosure, but as creating a waivable privilege, belonging solely to the parties to the mediation and capable of being waived explicitly or by conduct. Because she found that the privilege was waived by both the plaintiffs and the supervisory defendants, she concluded that the statute created no impediment to the mediator's testimony. . . .

> . . . As mediation has gained popularity . . . virtually all states have promulgated statutes or court rules providing for varying degrees of confidentiality in mediation. . . . The underlying rationale of these statutes and rules is that confidentiality is crucial to the effectiveness of mediation. As one commentator has explained:

The willingness of mediation parties to "open up" is essential to the success of the process. The mediation process is purposefully informal to encourage a broad ranging discussion of facts, feelings, issues, underlying interests and possible solutions to the parties' conflict. Mediation's private setting invites parties to speak openly, with complete candor. In addition, mediators often hold private meetings — "caucuses" — with each of the parties. . . . Under such circumstances, mediation parties often reveal personal and business secrets, share deep-seated feelings about others, and make admissions of fact and law. Without adequate legal protection, a party's candor in mediation might well be "rewarded" by a discovery request or the revelation of mediation information at trial. . . . Participation will diminish if perceptions of confidentiality are not matched by reality. Another critical purpose of the privilege is to maintain the public's perception that individual mediators and the mediation process and neutral and unbiased. . . . [Kirtley 1995]

. . . There are those who have suggested that the need for strict confidentiality may be overstated. . . . However, our legislature has enacted a statute that plainly reflects a policy judgment in favor of confidentiality, and it is that statute and that policy judgment that dictates the result here. . . .

. . . I conclude that whether or not the parties have chosen to maintain the confidentiality of the mediation, [state law] does not permit a party to compel the mediator to testify, when to do so would require the mediator to reveal communications made in the course of and relating to the subject matter of the mediation. Compelling such testimony, even if potentially helpful to the motion judge's decision on the merits of the parties' dispute, would conflict with the plain intent of the statute to protect the mediation process and to preserve mediator effectiveness and neutrality. . . .

Questions

1. What kind of breach would this have been: litigation, supervisory, or enforcement?
2. How would you have ruled on the issue?

There is a consensus that some degree of confidentiality in the process is appropriate, but commentators do not agree on how strong the protection should be. In particular, some question whether mediation requires a formal legal privilege, whereas others argue that confidentiality protection should be stronger than a legal privilege, which is waivable. Consider the following article by a scholar who is skeptical of the need for confidentiality.

❖ **Scott H. Hughes, *A Closer Look: The Case for a Mediation Confidentiality Privilege Still Has Not Been Made***

5 Disp. Resol. Mag. 14 (Winter 1998)

Consider the case of the manipulating minister: At a small women's college, a minister with the campus ministry seduces a naive young coed into a sexual relationship. When she attempts to break off the relationship, the minister responds with harassment. She subsequently sinks into a deep depression and drops out after her first semester. Several months later, she confides in her sister, who promptly relays the sordid tale to their mother.

The family's attorney files suit and commences discovery, from which she learns about an earlier incident involving the same minister while at the college's sister institution. Finding that the previous dispute had been settled through mediation, the attorney issues a subpoena for the mediator and his notes. During a caucus with the mediator, it seems, the minister stated that his supervisors had been aware of his illicit urges for some time. The mediator, joined by the church and the minister, seeks to quash the subpoena by asserting the privilege contained in the state mediation act. Does the need to encourage settlement outweigh the victim's rights to this information? I think not.

[Or] consider the case of the disputant in duress: During a mediation, one party complains of chest pains and fatigue, only to be told by the mediator that he cannot leave the mediation session until a settlement has been reached. The disputant subsequently signs a settlement, but tries to have it set aside during a subsequent action for specific performance. The adverse party contends that the mediation privilege prohibits an examination of the communications that took place during mediation, preventing the assertion of such a defense. Mediation privileges would foreclose disputants from raising this or many other contract defenses. . . .

Over the past two decades we have witnessed a vast proliferation of mediation statutes throughout the United States, many of which contain privileges shielding the mediator and/or the parties from the disclosure of events that take place during mediation, thus shrouding mediation proceedings in a veil of secrecy. . . . Before rushing to create another privilege that may preclude the law's traditional right to "every person's evidence," we should take at least one more close look at the social and legal cost of such a privilege. If that important step is taken, it will become apparent that the benefit of the mediation privilege does not justify its cost.

To begin with, it should be noted that there is almost no empirical support for mediation privileges. For example, no data exists to show a difference in growth rates or overall use of mediation services between jurisdictions with privileges and those without such protections, or from within any jurisdiction before and after the creation of a privilege. . . . Moreover, there is no empirical work to demonstrate a connection between privileges and the ultimate success of mediation. Although parties may have an expectation of privacy, no showing has been made that fulfilling this expectation is crucial to the outcome of mediation. . . .

[T]o assess the overall value of mediation privileges, it is important to weigh any gains that would be attributable to mediation against their cost. Privileges sacrifice potentially important evidence for subsequent legal proceedings and restrict public access to information that may be necessary to a democratic society. Of course, finely detailed exceptions to a mediation privilege could be crafted that would help overcome many problems. However, numerous exceptions could well lead to an unpredictable privilege that would be more detrimental than no privilege at all.

Until [an] empirical connection can be made, the arguments in favor of mediation privileges should not overcome the historical presumption favoring the availability of "every person's evidence."

Questions

3. Who do you find more persuasive — Professor Kirtley, whose views are quoted in the *Leary* opinion, or Professor Hughes?
4. In the absence of a legal privilege, what can a lawyer do to increase the likelihood that mediation communications will be kept confidential?
5. Chapter 5 lists several ways in which a mediator can facilitate settlement, including:
   - Helping to ensure the presence of key decision makers at the table.
   - Allowing disputants to present arguments, interests, and feelings directly to their opponent.
   - Moderating negotiations, coaching bargainers, and reframing positions.
   - Assisting each side to reassess its litigation option.
   - Helping participants to focus on their underlying interests.

   For which of these functions is the assurance of confidentiality most significant?

2. Sources of Mediation Confidentiality

There are five primary sources of rules governing confidentiality in mediation:

- Rules of evidence
- Privileges
- Confidentiality statutes and rules
- Mediation agreements
- Disclosure statutes and rules

a. Rules of Evidence

Virtually every jurisdiction has adopted a rule of evidence to protect the confidentiality of settlement discussions. The key federal provision is Federal Rule of Evidence (FRE) 408.[1] Most states have evidentiary rules patterned on FRE 408 (Cole et al. 2008). The first point to note about FRE 408 is that it is a rule of evidence, not a guarantee of confidentiality. FRE 408 is intended to limit what litigants can offer in evidence in a court proceeding, not what parties or

---

1. The text of the rule is as follows:

Rule 408. Compromise and Offers to Compromise. Evidence of (1) furnishing or offering or promising to furnish, or (2) accepting or offering or promising to accept, a valuable consideration in compromising or attempting to compromise a claim which was disputed as to either validity or amount, is not admissible to prove liability for or invalidity of the claim or its amount. Evidence of conduct or statements made in compromise negotiations is likewise not admissible. This rule does not require the exclusion of any evidence otherwise discoverable merely because it is presented in the course of compromise negotiations. This rule also does not require exclusion when the evidence is offered for another purpose, such as proving bias or prejudice of a witness, negativing a contention of undue delay, or proving an effort to obstruct a criminal investigation or prosecution.

observers can disclose in any other context. The rule does not, for example, apply to discovery depositions, nor does it limit what a person can say in a conversation or a media interview. In addition, FRE 408 and its counterparts typically apply only to court proceedings, and may therefore not be effective in less formal forums such as administrative hearings and arbitrations; whether a mediation conversation will be admissible in another forum will depend on its rules and the philosophy of the presiding officer.

Even in court, FRE 408 may not prevent information about settlement discussions from being disclosed. The rule and its state counterparts cover only evidence that a person offered or agreed to accept "valuable consideration" to compromise a claim, not everything said in settlement discussions. Thus, for example, the rule does not protect a trade secret disclosed in mediation from being introduced into evidence unless it formed part of an offer to settle.

Indeed, even an offer of compromise is not necessarily sacrosanct under FRE 408, because the rule has many exceptions. The rule applies only if an offer of compromise is introduced for the purpose of proving "liability for or invalidity of the claim or its amount." Confidential information offered, for example, to show that a witness is biased or that a party did not bargain in good faith is not protected by the rule.

Other uncertainties arise from the fact that only the person against whom evidence is being offered can make an FRE 408 objection. The rule, in other words, is designed to prevent a party from being shot in court with a "gun" it provided to the other side during settlement discussions, not to help nonparties or mediators keep discussions confidential. Finally, a rule of evidence can often be hard to enforce, as parties who evade it ordinarily risk at most a judicial reprimand.

b. Privileges

Roughly half the states now have statutes that apply generally to mediation, and every state has a law covering the use of mediation in specific types of cases or settings, such as environmental disputes or court-connected programs. Of the states with general statutes, most have created formal legal privileges.

It is important to bear in mind the following distinction: Although a privilege bars evidence from being admitted in adjudication, it does not bar persons from disclosing the same information outside a court proceeding. *The fact that a matter is "privileged," therefore, does not necessarily guarantee that it will be kept completely confidential.* A privilege alone may therefore not bar persons from disclosing the information in non-court settings, such as over the Internet. By contrast, a statute providing "confidentiality" ordinarily bars the release of information in all contexts. The terminology can be confusing, however: The lawyer-client privilege, for example, does bar disclosures in all circumstances, in and out of court, unless waived by the client who is the "holder" of the privilege.

A privilege is less subject to evasion than an evidentiary rule such as FRE 408 because privileges bar the admission of evidence regardless of the purpose for which it is offered. Violations of privileges may also give rise to a cause of action for damages. To understand the level of protection offered by a privilege in any particular setting, consider the following issues:

- What privilege applies to the process?
- What does it cover? Testimony in litigation only, or disclosure in any context?
- In what phases of the process does the privilege apply?
- Who can invoke it?
- Is it subject to exceptions or exclusions?

What privilege applies?

Courts almost always apply their own rules of evidence, but this is not true of privileges. Thus, if a mediation takes place in State A but the case later goes to trial in State B, which state's privilege will be applied will depend on choice-of-law principles, making the outcome hard to predict. As Professor Ellen Deason has commented, "Mediation confidentiality would make an ideal poster child for the shortcomings of choice-of-law" (Deason, 2002b).

A few federal courts have recognized a mediation privilege as a matter of federal common law, but there is no general mediation privilege in federal proceedings. FRE 501 authorizes courts to apply either state or federal privilege rules in a federal case, making it difficult to predict how confidential communications will be treated in federal court.

What is covered? In what phases of the process?

As we have noted, some privileges apply only to testimony given during litigation, whereas other privileges impose confidentiality in non-court settings as well. A particular privilege may, for example, apply only to the mediation session itself, but not to conversations and e-mails between counsel and the neutral before and afterward. The rule on what phases of the mediation process are covered by privilege varies from state to state and is sometimes poorly defined.

Who "holds" the privilege?

Only persons designated as "holders" of a privilege are entitled to invoke it. Typically the parties to a case hold a mediation privilege and thus can prevent disclosures. The mediator, however, may not be entitled to use the privilege as a shield, just as lawyers are not usually permitted to invoke the attorney-client privilege unless their client elects to do so. Thus, if a neutral is called to testify about what occurred during a mediation he may have to ask a party to protect him from testifying. In Hauzinger v. Hauzinger, 892 N.E.2d 849 (N.Y. App. 2008), for example, a New York appellate court ruled that when both parties in a divorce case waive a right to confidentiality granted by state law and the mediation agreement contemplates possible disclosure, a court can order the mediator to testify.

By contrast, in the *Leary* sex abuse case, the judge barred the mediator's testimony even though both sides had waived their objections. The Uniform Mediation Act (UMA), discussed below, similarly grants mediators the right to prevent disclosure of their own mediation communications (UMA §4).

California's law is even stronger: The consent of the mediator and the parties is needed for anyone to testify as to the content of a mediation, and mediators may not testify at all (Cal. Evid. Code §§1122, 703.5).

Is the privilege qualified or absolute? What exceptions apply?

Some states have adopted mediation privileges that are absolute, meaning that they contain no exceptions. The UMA allows disclosure and other statutes require disclosure in certain situations, for example, to report evidence of a felony, threats of harm to children, perjury, and other matters. Even when a privilege is absolute on its face, courts sometimes create exceptions as a matter of common law.

c. Confidentiality Statutes and Rules

As noted, roughly half of the states have enacted statutes governing mediation. Many of these go beyond establishing an evidentiary privilege to make the entire mediation process confidential. A Massachusetts statute, for instance, states that any communication during a mediation, as well as the mediator's work product, "shall be confidential," as well as inadmissible in adjudication, and California statutes similarly provide that the mediation process shall be "confidential." (See Mass. Gen. Laws ch. 233, § 23C; Cal. Code §§1115-1128.)

Neither Congress nor the federal courts have provided any general guarantee of confidentiality to mediation. Confidentiality provisions exist, however, in specific federal statutes, such as the Administrative Dispute Resolution (ADR) Act of 1996, 5 U.S.C. §574, which provides that neutrals and parties in mediations of administrative cases "shall not voluntarily disclose or through discovery or compulsory process be required to disclose any dispute resolution communication." The ADR Act of 1998, 28 U.S.C. §652(d), requires that federal district courts adopt local rules to provide for the confidentiality of ADR processes that occur within their court-connected programs. As a result, parties are more likely to find confidentiality protected in federal cases if they mediate under the aegis of a court ADR program than if they go to a private mediator.

State court and private mediation programs also typically provide that mediations held under their auspices will be confidential. The rules of such programs often do not specify, however, what is meant by confidentiality. In one sense a party's incentive to comply with the rules of a court-affiliated program is strong, because litigants may be concerned that if they violate a rule they will incur the wrath of the judge who will hear their case. This is not to say, however, that a party will have a legal cause of action or other remedy if an opponent does violate a confidentiality rule.

d. Mediation Agreements

Mediation agreements offer the best opportunity for a lawyer to tailor confidentiality protections to the needs of particular clients. A mediation agreement is a contract, however, and thus is subject to the limitations inherent in any contractual undertaking. First, agreements bind only those who enter into them, not nonparties. In the case of mediation, this means that outsiders to the process, such as third-party litigants, are not bound by agreements between parties to maintain confidentiality. Second, if a breach does occur, the only remedy is usually to sue for monetary damages, which rarely can be proved. Even in the unusual situation in which a litigant knows of an impending violation and is able to seek a court order to prevent it, a judge may refuse to act out of concern that a contract not to provide evidence in court violates public policy. This said, however, practicing neutrals report few complaints from parties to commercial mediation that an opponent agreed to confidentiality and then violated it.

Parties also often contract for confidentiality as part of settlement agreements. Such agreements typically provide that the terms of settlement shall remain confidential and sometimes specify liquidated damages for any breach.

e. Disclosure Statutes and Rules

Public policy sometimes weighs against secrecy concerning settlement negotiations. Many states, concerned that secret settlements have operated to hide serious social problems from officials and society, have considered statutes that would bar courts from ordering certain kinds of settlements sealed.

Some states also have decisional law or statutes that require persons who become aware of certain offenses to report them to authorities. Thus, for example, some jurisdictions require therapists to report potential physical harm that they learn about from clients (see Tarasoff v. Regents of Univ. of Cal., 17 Cal. 3d 425 (1976)), and many states require mediators to report instances of child abuse.

Finally, individual states and the federal government have enacted "sunshine laws," which require that certain meetings involving government officials be open to the public. As a result, when government officials participate, the mediation process may have to be open to outside observers.

3. Examples from Practice

As we have discussed, most attempts to penetrate the confidentiality of mediation occur because a litigant is seeking to use information revealed in mediation to bolster its case, because a participant is alleging that the process itself was defective, or as proof of what was agreed to. We consider each category in turn.

a. Use of Mediation Information in Litigation

❖ *ROJAS v. SUPERIOR COURT OF LOS ANGELES COUNTY*

33 Cal. 4th 407 (2004)

CHIN, J.:

We granted review in this case to consider the scope of Evidence Code Sec. 1119(b), which provides: "No writing . . . that is prepared for the purpose of, in the course of, or pursuant to, a mediation . . . is admissible or subject to discovery. . . . "

Factual Background

Julie Coffin is the owner of an apartment complex in Los Angeles that includes three buildings and a total of 192 units. In 1996, Coffin sued the contractors and subcontractors who built the complex . . . alleging that water leakage due to construction defects had produced toxic molds and other microbes on the property. . . . In April 1999, the litigation settled as a result of mediation. . . .

In August 1999, several hundred tenants of the apartment complex filed the action now before us against [Coffin and] numerous . . . entities that participated in development or construction of the complex. Tenants alleged that defective construction had allowed water to circulate and microbes to infest the complex, causing numerous health problems. They also alleged that all defendants had conspired to conceal the defects and that they (Tenants) had not become aware of the defects until April 1999. Tenants served [a] request for production of all photographs . . . taken . . . during the underlying action. . . . Coffin asserted that, under section 1119, the requested documents were not discoverable. . . .

[The trial judge] denied Tenants' motion . . . explaining: "The plaintiffs say that they need these photos and there's no other evidence of the conditions as they were at that time and in those places, and defendants are saying these photographs were created for mediation purposes. . . . They're clearly protected by the mediation privilege. This is a very difficult decision . . . because it could well be that there's no other way for the plaintiffs to get this particular material. On the other hand, the mediation privilege is an important one, . . . and if courts start dispensing with it by using the . . . test governing the work product privilege, . . . you may have people less willing to mediate."

[The intermediate court of appeal reversed the trial court.]

Discussion

As we recently explained, implementing alternatives to judicial dispute resolution has been a strong legislative policy since at least 1986. Mediation is one of the alternatives the Legislature has sought to implement. . . . One of the fundamental ways the Legislature has sought to encourage mediation is by enacting several mediation confidentiality provisions. [C]onfidentiality is essential to effective mediation because it promotes a candid and informal exchange regarding events in the past. This frank exchange is achieved only if participants know that what is said in the mediation will not be used to their detriment through later court proceedings and other adjudicatory processes.

The particular confidentiality provision at issue here is section 1119(b) [of the California Code], which provides: "No writing . . . that is prepared for the purpose of, in the course of, or pursuant to, a mediation or a mediation consultation, is admissible or subject to discovery, and disclosure of the writing shall not be compelled, in any . . . noncriminal proceeding. . . ." The Court of Appeal's holding directly conflicts with the plain language of these provisions. . . .

[Section 1120 of the Code] does not, as the Court of Appeal held, support a contrary conclusion. As noted above, section 1120(a), provides that "[e]vidence otherwise admissible or subject to discovery outside of a mediation . . . shall not be or become inadmissible or protected from disclosure solely by reason of its introduction or use in a mediation. . . ." Read together, sections 1119 and 1120 establish that a party cannot secure protection for a writing — including a photograph, a witness statement, or an analysis of a test sample — that was not "prepared for the purpose of, in the course of, or pursuant to, a mediation" simply by using or introducing it in a mediation. [The statutory scheme] prevents parties from using a mediation as a pretext to shield materials from disclosure.

. . . More broadly, the Court of Appeal's construction is inconsistent with the overall purpose of the mediation confidentiality provisions. . . .

For all of the above reasons, we conclude that the Court of Appeal erred in holding that photographs, videotapes, witness statements, and "raw test data" from physical samples collected at the complex — such as reports describing the existence or amount of mold spores in a sample — that were "prepared for the purpose of, in the course of, or pursuant to, [the] mediation" in the underlying action are . . . discoverable "upon a showing of good cause.". . .

Questions

6. The California Supreme Court in *Rojas* refused to allow judicially created exceptions to the state's mediation privilege statute. Suppose, however, that you were a legislator considering the issue. Would you support a law giving materials prepared for mediation absolute protection, or the narrower protection available under the "work product doctrine" that governs materials lawyers create in preparation for trial? Why?

7. Can you think of other situations in which the interest in mediation confidentiality should give way to the needs of the justice system or other social needs?

8. Is the effect of the *Rojas* decision that the defendant Coffin, having created the photographs, can use them but the plaintiffs cannot? If so, is that fair? If not, should she be permitted to do so? Why?

9. If you conclude that *Rojas* bars all parties to a case from introducing data created for a mediation in court, how would you handle this situation: The plaintiff lawyer in a California personal injury case creates a video that shows a "day in the life" of his seriously handicapped client to dramatize the extent of the plaintiff's injuries to the insurer and the neutral in a mediation process. The mediation, however, is not successful. The plaintiff later seeks to introduce the same video at trial. The defense objects, citing the statute at issue in *Rojas*. Assuming that a video is a "writing" for purposes of the statute, how should the court rule? Is your result fair? Can you suggest any changes to the statute to deal with this issue?

10. In the mediation of more than 500 civil cases alleging priest abuse, the Archdiocese of Los Angeles offered to prepare written summaries or proffers of the personnel files of more than 100 priests who had been identified by private plaintiffs as molesters, to deal with the issue of whether the Archdiocese had notice of an accused priest's propensities before the alleged misconduct took place. After the Archdiocese indicated its intention to make the proffers public, 26 priests named in the proffers objected. An appellate court ruled that under the *Rojas* rule the proffers could not be made public, although nothing prevented the Archdiocese from releasing the underlying information from which they were prepared. Doe 1 et al. v. Superior Court, 34 Cal. Rptr. 3d 248 (2005).

11. An insurance company mediated a Delaware medical malpractice case in which liability was conceded. It settled the case for $945,000, based on the plaintiff's representations that the medical error had left her with "immediate, chronic and unrelenting nerve pain in her right neck, jaw, shoulder, and arm [and an inability to] employ her arm for lifting even light objects. For example she is unable to hold a can of soda. . . . " The plaintiff talked at her deposition of having "good days" when she had "a lot of energy and I try to do some stuff . . . a little laundry . . . and then I tend to end up paying for that for the next two or three days."

The day after the mediation, the defendant's lawyer saw the plaintiff dancing at a fundraiser for local cheerleaders while holding a beer with her injured arm. He got a video camera and secretly videotaped her. The insurer then moved to rescind the settlement alleging fraud, and in support of its request asked the court to allow the mediator to testify that the video was inconsistent with his understanding of the plaintiff's claims, or his statement to the defense during the mediation that he thought the plaintiff would be a good witness. The court denied the motion. Princeton Ins. Co. v. Vergano, 883 A.2d 33 (Del. Ch. 2005). Was *Vergano* a stronger or weaker case for disclosure than *Rojas* or *Doe*? Why?

For a discussion of cases and principles concerning mediation confidentiality, see Widman (2008).

One of the strongest arguments for allowing a party to disclose information revealed in mediation in a subsequent proceeding involves criminal law enforcement. The following case illustrates one way that the issue can arise.

❖ Byrd v. The State

367 S.E.2d 300 (Ga. App. 1988)

[Byrd was accused of stealing property from Graddy. He participated in pretrial mediation and agreed to pay $800 in restitution. When Byrd failed to make the payments required by the mediated settlement, criminal charges were reinstated and he was convicted. Byrd appealed on the ground that statements he had made during mediation were introduced against him at trial.]

BEASLEY, J.

. . . Appellant alleges error [by the trial court] in allowing evidence concerning a mediation proceeding. . . . [T]he parties were directed to the Neighborhood Justice Center of Atlanta, Inc., by the state court before which the criminal charge was first pending. The purpose was to facilitate a civil settlement for the dispute by way of the mediation process provided by that agency. The criminal charge, brought by warrant, remained pending, to await the outcome of the settlement efforts. If they were successful, the state court would entertain dismissal of the criminal charges. If not, the latter would proceed. After about eight months elapsed without appellant's compliance with the mediated agreement, he was indicted and bound over to superior court for trial.

By allowing this alternative dispute resolution effort to be evidenced in the subsequent criminal trial, the trial court's ruling eliminates its usefulness. For no criminal defendant will agree to "work things out" and compromise his position if he knows that any inference of responsibility arising from what he says and does in the mediation process will be admissible as an admission of guilt in the criminal proceeding which will eventualize if mediation fails . . . Federal Rule of Criminal Procedure 11(e)(6) . . . protects statements and conduct made in negotiations and plea bargains in criminal cases except in very limited circumstances. . . .

In the instant case, as is standard in these referrals, defendant's mediation-related statements and actions were not made with any warning of rights against self-incrimination, and yet they were prompted by court action, itself creating a close procedural tie. A serious Fifth and Fourteenth Amendments *Miranda* problem is created by the admission of the objected-to evidence. This differs from the situation in *Williams v. State*, 342 S.E.2d 703 (Ga. App. 1986), in which a privately-negotiated agreement, not instigated at court direction during criminal proceedings, was ruled admissible.

Just as a withdrawn plea of guilty "shall not be admissible as evidence against [a defendant] at his trial," so too must be the words and actions which defendant undertakes in an effort to comply with the court's direction that mediation be pursued to resolve the pending criminal matter.

A new trial is required because we cannot conclude that the inadmissible evidence did not contribute to reaching the verdict. . . . Judgment reversed.

SOGNIER, J., dissenting:

I respectfully dissent. "Any statement or conduct of a person, indicating a consciousness of guilt, where such person is, at the time or thereafter, charged with or suspected of the crime, is admissible against him upon his trial for committing it." . . . The mediation proceedings in this case occurred while appellant was under criminal charges, and his conduct in signing a mediation agreement acknowledging his liability is conduct indicating a consciousness of guilt. Hence, under the rule . . . the evidence was admissible as bearing on appellant's guilt or innocence. Accordingly, I would affirm appellant's conviction. . . .

Questions

12. Do you agree with the majority or the dissent in *Byrd*? Does it make a difference that Byrd failed to comply with the agreement he made in mediation?

13. Would it be better policy to give a *Miranda*-type warning to all defendants in such mediations, then to permit the use of any statements that they make?

14. The court says that an admission by someone in Byrd's situation presents different issues from one made by a party in a private mediation process. Should a defendant's admissions during a non-court-sponsored process be admissible?

15. If a defendant cannot be "hoisted with his own petard" by using statements he makes in mediation against him, is it also improper to invade confidentiality when it is the defendant who asks for disclosure? In one case a defendant charged with attempted murder claimed that he had acted in self-defense. To support his defense he sought to introduce into evidence threatening statements made by the alleged victim during the mediation of an earlier altercation between them. Should defendants be barred from using such evidence? (See State v. Castellano, 400 So. 2d 480 (Fla. App. 1984).)

Problems

3. Assume that you are counsel for the defendant Alpha in the Alpha-Bates case mentioned at the start of this chapter. In the course of mediation you argued that Bates should accept a reasonable settlement, because as a practical matter your client could never pay a six-figure judgment. In response to a request for substantiation, you provided the mediator with an asset-liability statement for Alpha. The mediation failed and the parties returned to court. Two days later, Bates moves for a $250,000 attachment against Alpha's bank account, including with its motion copies of the asset-liability statement that your client provided in mediation.
   a. How should you respond on behalf of Alpha?
   b. Is there anything that you could have done, before or during the process, to make admission less likely?

4. Seven years ago you represented a young man, James Connor, who said that he had been sexually abused ten years before by the minister of his church. The abuse occurred when your client was 12 years old, during outings of the church's youth group. It appeared to be a difficult case to prove because of the absence of objective evidence and the time that had elapsed since the incidents, but you gave notice of your intent to sue the minister and the church official who oversaw his work. Shortly afterward the church agreed to mediate the matter. In the course of the mediation, the supervisory official offered your client a heartfelt apology and swore that this kind of abuse would never happen again. The church made what you thought was a good monetary offer; however, it was conditional on Connor signing a confidentiality clause that barred him from ever discussing the case. Connor decided to accept the offer, and the settlement was finalized.

Over the past month your local newspaper has published a series of dramatic stories alleging a widespread pattern of sexual abuse by clergy. One of the stories said that the same minister who abused your client had been sued several other times, and that two months after the settlement in your case the church had transferred him to a different community, where he continued his pattern of abuse. Connor has just called you. He is outraged by the stories, and even more so by the church's violation of its promise to him. He wants to talk to a reporter about what happened in his case, including the promise he was given in mediation.

a. What advice should you give to Connor? What are the potential consequences of his talking with the reporter?

b. Assume that your client has said nothing yet, but that a lawyer has subpoenaed him to testify at a deposition in another case brought against the same minister. The lawyer plans to ask about what occurred during Connor's mediation. What advice should you give Connor?

c. If Connor refuses to answer questions at the deposition and the lawyer seeks a court order compelling him to testify, how should the court rule?

b. Supervisory Intrusions into the Process

To this point we have focused on the confidentiality issues that arise when a litigant discloses confidential mediation information for an ulterior purpose — usually to support a position in court. Another major category of confidentiality disputes involves claims that the mediation process itself went awry. In these situations a litigant is typically alleging either that mediation was thwarted because an opponent did not participate in good faith or the process itself was badly flawed. This kind of claim poses a conflict between a court's need to gather evidence to supervise the process and the interest in preserving confidentiality. In the following case, Judge Brazil, known for his commitment to ADR, grapples with these issues.

As you read the case consider these questions:

Questions

16. Are you persuaded by the decision? What factors seem most significant to it?

17. If you were a lawyer practicing in the court that decided *Olam*, would the decision affect the advice you gave to clients about what to say or do during mediation?

18. Would the decision affect your willingness to recommend that a client enter the court's mediation program?

❖ *Olam v. Congress Mortgage Co.*

68 F. Supp. 2d 1110 (N.D. Cal. 1999)

Brazil, United States Magistrate Judge:

The court addresses in this opinion several difficult issues about the relationship between a court-sponsored voluntary mediation and subsequent proceedings whose purpose is to determine whether the parties entered an enforceable agreement at the close of the mediation session. As we explain below, the parties participated in a lengthy mediation that was hosted by this court's ADR Program Counsel — an employee of the court who is both a lawyer and an ADR professional. At the end of the mediation (after midnight), the parties signed a "Memorandum of Understanding" (MOU) that states that it is "intended as a binding document itself. . . . " Contending that the consent she apparently gave was not legally valid, plaintiff has taken the position that the MOU is not enforceable. She has not complied with its terms. Defendants have filed a motion to enforce the MOU as a binding contract. One of the principal issues with which the court wrestles, below, is whether evidence about what occurred during the mediation proceedings, including testimony from the mediator, may be used to help resolve this dispute. . . .

Facts

The events in the real world out of which the current dispute arises began unfolding in 1992, when Ms. Olam applied for and received a loan from Congress Mortgage in the amount of $187,000. The 1992 loan is secured by two single-family homes located in San Francisco and owned by Ms. Olam. Eventually she defaulted. Thereafter, Congress Mortgage initiated foreclosure proceedings. [Mrs. Olam later sued the mortgage company, alleging violations of state and federal consumer laws, and the case went through discovery.]

At the final pretrial conference, the court asked plaintiff's counsel whether there was any meaningful possibility that a mediation would be useful. [Both sides subsequently agreed to mediate.] The mediation continued throughout the day and well into the evening. Sometime around 10:00 P.M. [the mediator and counsel went into another room] to type up what they believed were the essential terms of a binding settlement agreement. At approximately 1:00 A.M., when the mediation concluded, Ms. Olam and her lawyer, and [the defendant] signed the MOU.

[Later on the same day, counsel confirmed the settlement with the court.] At approximately 1:45 P.M. [that day], plaintiff telephoned my chambers. She was referred to the mediator. . . . [M]ore than seven months after the mediation, defendants filed a Motion to Enforce the Original Settlement. . . . Ms. Olam, through [a] new attorney, filed her "Opposition" to the defendants' motion to enforce. [One ground] for opposition was that at the time she affixed her name to the MOU (at the end of the mediation) the plaintiff was incapable (intellectually, emotionally, and physically) of giving legally viable consent. Specifically, Ms. Olam contended that at the time she gave her apparent consent she was subjected to "undue influence" as that term is defined by California law.

[P]laintiff alleges that at the time she signed the MOU she was suffering from physical pain and emotional distress that rendered her incapable of exercising her own free will. She alleges that after the mediation began during the morning of September 9, she was left *alone* in a room *all* day and into the early hours of September 10, while all the other mediation participants conversed in a nearby room. She claims that she did not understand the mediation process. In addition, she asserts that she felt pressured to sign the MOU — and that her physical and emotional distress rendered her unduly susceptible to this pressure. As a result, she says, she signed the MOU against her will and without reading and/or understanding its terms.

[The court determined that California law, rather than federal law, governed the issue of mediation confidentiality.] California has offered for some time a set of strong statutory protections for mediation communications. If anything, those state law protections might be stronger than the [federal] protections offered through the relevant local rule of the Northern District of California or through any federal common law mediation privilege that might have been emerging when the mediation took place in this case.

As we noted earlier, the plaintiff and the defendants have expressly waived confidentiality protections conferred by [California law.] Both the plaintiff and the defendants have indicated, clearly and on advice of counsel, that they want the court to consider evidence about what occurred during the mediation, including testimony directly from the mediator. . . .

The Mediator's Privilege

[U]nder California law, a waiver of the mediation privilege by the parties is not a sufficient basis for a court to permit or order a mediator to testify. Rather, an independent determination must be made before testimony from a mediator should be permitted or ordered.

. . . First, I acknowledge squarely that a decision to require a mediator to give evidence, even *in camera* or under seal, about what occurred during a mediation threatens values underlying the mediation privileges. [T]he California legislature adopted these privileges in the belief that without the promise of confidentiality it would be appreciably more difficult to achieve the goals of mediation programs. While this court has no occasion or power to quarrel with these generally applicable pronouncements of state policy, we observe that they appear to have appreciably less force when, as here, the parties to the mediation have waived confidentiality protections, indeed have asked the court to compel the mediator to testify — so that justice can be done.

. . . [O]rdering mediators to participate in proceedings arising out of mediations imposes economic and psychic burdens that could make some people reluctant to agree to serve as a mediator, especially in programs where that service is pro bono or poorly compensated. This is not a matter of time and money only. Good mediators are likely to feel violated by being compelled to give evidence that could be used against a party with whom they tried to establish a relationship of trust during a mediation. . . . These are not inconsequential matters.

. . . But the level of harm to that interest likely varies, at least in some measure, with the perception within the community of mediators and litigants about how likely it is that any given mediation will be followed at some point by an order compelling the neutral to offer evidence about what occurred during the session. . . . [T]his case represents the first time that I have been called upon to address these kinds of questions in the more than fifteen years that I have been responsible for ADR programs in this court. [M]y partially educated guess is that the likelihood that a mediator or the parties in any given case need fear that the mediator would later be constrained to testify is extraordinarily small.

The magnitude of the risk to values underlying the mediation privilege that can be created by ordering a mediator to testify also can vary with the nature of the testimony that is sought. [E]vidence about what words a party to the mediation uttered, what statements or admissions that party made . . . could be particularly threatening to the spirit and methods that some people believe are important both to the philosophy and the success of some mediation processes.

[W]e turn to the other side of the balance. The interests that are likely to be advanced by compelling the mediator to testify in this case are of considerable importance. Moreover, as we shall see, some of those interests parallel and reinforce the objectives the legislature sought to advance by providing for confidentiality in mediation. The first interest we identify is the interest in doing justice. Here is what we mean. For reasons described below, the mediator is positioned in this case to offer what could be crucial, certainly very probative, evidence about the central factual issues in this matter. There is a strong possibility that his testimony will greatly improve the court's ability to determine reliably what the pertinent historical facts actually were [and to do justice].

. . . In sum, it is clear that refusing even to determine what the mediator's testimony would be, in the circumstances here presented, threatens values of great significance.

[The Court decided that the mediator's testimony might be sufficiently important to justify an *in camera* exploration of what he would say. After the hearing, the Court decided] that testimony from the mediator would be crucial to the court's capacity to do its job.

The Evidentiary Hearing

The court held the evidentiary hearing. We heard testimony and considered documentary evidence about Ms. Olam's medical conditions, the events of September 9-10 . . . and various post-mediation events related to the purported settlement. All the participants in the mediation testified, as did the physician who was treating plaintiff during the pertinent period. We took [the mediator's] testimony.

Conclusion

Because plaintiff has failed to prove either of the necessary elements of undue influence, and because she has established no other grounds to escape the contract she signed . . . the court GRANTS defendants' Motion to Enforce the settlement contract that is memorialized in the MOU.

Questions

Recall that in *Rojas v. Superior Court,* the California Supreme Court rejected a litigant's effort to intrude into the mediation process for purposes of discovery.

19. Which do you think is more likely to promote effective mediation, the approach adopted by the court in *Rojas* or the one favored by the *Olam* judge?
20. Would the *Olam* decision make you, as a California lawyer, more or less likely to advise clients to participate in mediation?
21. Other courts have, like *Olam*, invaded mediation confidentiality to determine whether participants were competent to make settlement decisions. See, e.g., Wilson v. Wilson, 282 Ga. 728 (2007) (court may call mediator to testify concerning his general impression of competence of unrepresented party who claimed he lacked the capacity to agree to a divorce settlement due to depression, exhaustion, and effect of medication).

Another kind of supervisory issue arises when parties disagree about whether they reached agreement, or what they agreed to do. A few states bar the introduction even of signed agreements reached in mediation if they do not meet specified conditions. A California statute, for instance, requires that for evidence of a mediated agreement to be admissible over objection, the document must either state that it is admissible or intended to be enforceable or binding, or words to that effect, or be offered to show illegality (Cal. Evid. Code § 1123(b)).

The issue of invading confidentiality to establish an agreement arises most often, however, when one party alleges that disputants reached an oral meeting of the minds. An example is the *Leary* sexual abuse case at the start of this chapter. Some laws contain exceptions to permit introduction of evidence of oral settlements, and other statutes, although absolute on their face, have been interpreted to permit such testimony. In many states, however, it is not clear whether disputants may testify about the existence of an oral settlement, or whether the mediator can be called as a witness on the issue.

Sections 4(a) and 6(a) of the UMA, discussed below, prevent participants from testifying about agreements reached in mediation, but allow the introduction into evidence of accords that are signed and in writing or electronically recorded. The effect of the UMA is to bar enforcement of purely oral settlements, but permit enforcement of written or recorded ones.

Questions

22. Is the UMA provision allowing the introduction of evidence about written or recorded settlements, but not oral ones, justified? Why or why not?
23. Do you agree with the California rule on admission of mediated agreements?

4. Confidentiality in Caucusing

So far we have discussed confidentiality in terms of disclosures that are made to persons outside the mediation process or the courts. In caucus-based mediation, however, there is an additional layer of privacy: Mediators typically assure disputants that if they request that information disclosed in a caucus be held in confidence, the mediator will not disclose it to their opponent. As we have seen, however, one of a mediator's key functions is to facilitate communication between parties to a dispute. What is the appropriate balance between confidentiality and communication in caucus-based mediation? Consider how you would respond to the following situations, drawn by Professor Marjorie Aaron from actual cases.

Problems

5. You are plaintiff's counsel in the mediation of a commercial contract case. After hours of bargaining, the parties are stuck, with the plaintiff at $240,000 and the defendant at $90,000. The mediator proposes to play "confidential listener," and asks for the absolute lowest dollar number that you would accept to settle the case. The mediator also asks you for a "public" offer that he can convey to the other side. You tell the mediator that your client will never accept less than $150,000 to settle, and authorize him to communicate to the other side a new demand of $225,000.

   When the mediator conveys the $225,000 figure, the other side expresses frustration. "They've hardly moved at all," says counsel. "It looks like they won't go any lower than $200,000 to settle, and we're just not going to go that high. The very most this case is worth is $150,000. We'd be prepared to go to $100,000 at this point, but it's probably a waste of time. I hate playing games — what will it take? Should we just pack up and leave?"

   a. The mediator says to the defense, "I think I can get them to $150,000, if I can tell them that that will truly settle it — Are you saying that $150,000 would do it?" Has he broken his pledge of confidentiality to you?

   b. Suppose you had told the mediator that your bottom line was $175,000, but the mediator suspects from observations of your client's body language that he would in fact go as low as $150,000. Can the mediator say, "They're hanging tough at $225,000, but I think I can get them to $150,000. If I can do that, will it settle the case?" Does it depend on whether the mediator "read" your client's intentions correctly?

6. You are representing the complainant in the mediation of a discrimination case. After the legal arguments have been aired in joint session, the mediator moves both sides into private caucusing. The mediator spends a great deal of time with you and your client, who is decidedly "dug in" and unwilling to see any weakness in his case or the need to lower her settlement expectations. Although you are well known as a zealous advocate, in this case you see reasons to reach a reasonable settlement.

In a hallway conversation you indicate to the mediator that you are aware of the problems in the case and support his efforts to bring your client into a zone of reality.

In the mediator's caucus with the defense side, counsel expresses frustration at the lack of progress. "I bet the problem is the lawyer here. I've litigated with her before," he complains. "She is just hell-bent on getting a high number. This is a political cause for her, but we're not going to cave to meet her agenda." His anger toward you seems to be driving his resistance to further movement.

What, if anything, can the mediator appropriately say about your or your client's attitude toward the case?

5. A Movement Toward Consistency: The Uniform Mediation Act

The current state of protection

How serious is the problem of mediation confidentiality in practice? From the discussion above and the varying responses of courts, it is plain that many gaps and ambiguities exist in mediation's "confidentiality safety net," and there is disagreement about how much confidentiality protection the process needs. Although court cases over confidentiality issues exist, they appear to represent only a tiny fraction of all disputes mediated. Commercial mediators report, for instance, that they rarely hear parties complain about breaches of confidentiality, and the judge in *Olam* commented that he had never before encountered a case in which parties sought a mediator's testimony.

Confidentiality cases do arise, however: Over a seven-year period between 1999 and 2005, for example, researchers at Hamline University identified nearly 250 reported decisions that dealt with mediation confidentiality. See *www.law.hamline.edu/adr/mediation-case-law-database*. Some scholars cite this as evidence that "misuse of mediation communications is common" (Cole et al. 2008). At the same time, such a number amounts to less than one reported case per year per state, in an environment where courts in states such as Florida send more than 100,000 cases a year to mediation (Press 1998).

Why do disputes over confidentiality not arise more often? For one thing, a large majority of mediated cases reach agreement, and even those that do not settle in mediation are very unlikely ever to go to trial. If a case is never adjudicated, the parties have less reason to breach confidentiality. It also appears that when people enter into a clear commitment to keep information confidential, they honor their agreement. And, as we have seen, when the mediation process focuses on distributive bargaining, disputants are less likely to reveal sensitive information in the first place. Finally, we should bear in mind that to the extent that mediation brings a sense of peace to a situation, the process itself may induce participants to treat rules with respect. Whatever the cause, parties' compliance with confidentiality obligations appears to be higher than a purely tactical analysis would suggest.

Reported cases involving confidentiality arise largely in the context of court-connected mediation. This may be because parties are often compelled to participate in court programs, whereas they usually enter private mediation voluntarily. A person unhappy to be in a process is probably less likely to respect its rules. Also, litigants are probably more apt to complain, and judges to impose sanctions, when a problem arises in a court-affiliated setting. That said, "courts rarely punish parties who misuse mediation communications" (Cole et al. 2008). It is rare for parties complaining about confidentiality abuses to sue for damages, perhaps because it is so difficult to prove that an ascertainable monetary loss resulted from the alleged breach (Moffit 2003b).

A response

What level of protection should be given to confidentiality in mediation? Assuming that confidentiality is necessary, the lack of uniformity among jurisdictions, and the resulting uncertainty about what rule will apply to a given mediation, is troublesome. One possibility is for states to adopt a uniform confidentiality statute. To this end the National Conference of Commissioners on Uniform State Laws has proposed a Uniform Mediation Act. (For the complete text of the UMA, see the Web Appendix.)

The Act states that communications made during mediation are not "subject to discovery or admissible in evidence" in a legal proceeding (§4(a)). The UMA thus prevents parties from using mediation communications in adjudicatory proceedings. It leaves them free, however, to make disclosures outside litigation, for example, in conversations or media interviews, unless they agree not to do so. (See comments to UMA §8.) Disputants in UMA jurisdictions who wish mediation communications to remain confidential in all circumstances must therefore enter into confidentiality agreements. Samples of such agreements appear in the Web Appendix.

The UMA contains exceptions to its bar on disclosure in legal proceedings. Sections 5 and 6(a) of the Act permit a court to order disclosure of mediation communications about:

- Agreements signed by all parties.
- Documents required to be kept open to the public.
- Threats to commit bodily injury or crimes of violence.
- Plans to commit or conceal an ongoing crime.
- Information needed for a mediator to respond to claims or charges against him.
- Situations involving child abuse and neglect.

Section 6(b) of the UMA creates an additional exception to confidentiality in situations where a tribunal finds that a party has shown that:

- Evidence is not otherwise available,
- There is a need for the evidence that substantially outweighs the interest in protecting confidentiality, and
- The mediation communication is sought or offered in a court proceeding involving a felony or litigation over a contract reached in mediation (but in the latter situation the mediator cannot be compelled to testify).

The UMA has provoked disagreement within the mediation community. Some commentators argue that its provisions are inadequate because they do not cover out-of-court disclosures, and others consider the UMA's restrictions excessive. In addition, some mediators and lawyers who practice in states with stronger confidentiality rules object to "watering down" their protections in the interest of national uniformity. If the UMA is enacted on a widespread basis, confidentiality rules will become more uniform from one state to another, and the likelihood that federal courts will develop a uniform rule may also increase. As of this writing ten states have adopted the UMA, but it is not yet clear whether it will achieve nationwide acceptance.

B. Enforcement of Participation in Mediation

1. Agreements to Mediate

Parties entering into relationships, particularly ones that are lengthy or complex, are increasingly likely to include in contracts a clause obligating them to mediate any disputes that may arise in their interactions. Businesses entering into commercial supply agreements or divorcing parents with young children, for instance, can expect to encounter changes in circumstances over the term of their agreement and would benefit from a process to address such changes. Commitments to mediate are also required by law in some states; Arizona and Washington, for example, require divorcing couples who seek court approval of joint custody or other parenting arrangements to include an ADR provision in their plan (Cole et al., 2008).

The first question raised by a mediation clause is whether a court will enforce it. In early cases defendants objected successfully to enforcement, arguing that it would be impossible to determine whether a party was in compliance or to supervise participation. "Until the mid-1980s, courts refused to enforce mediation . . . agreements on the theory that a court would not use its equity powers to order a 'futile gesture' . . . [but] enforcement is gradually becoming routine, and little is heard today about futile acts, vain orders, or the problem of adequate remedies" (Katz, 2008a).

California residential real estate purchase contracts, for example, permit the prevailing party in litigation to recover attorneys' fees, but deny recovery to parties who fail to mediate before suit. Applying this language, courts have refused to grant fees to prevailing parties who refused to mediate. Frei v. Davey, 124 Cal. App. 4th 1506 (2004). Another enforcement option is to dismiss complaints filed by parties who have failed to comply with an obligation to mediate. See Halcomb v. Office of the Senate Sergeant-at-Arms of the U.S. Senate, 205 F. Supp. 2d 175 (D.D.C. 2002).

Parties who have the right to compel mediation may decide not to enforce it, on the theory that a forced process would be meaningless. At the same time, a party who is opposed to mediation but subject to a requirement may decide that it is easier to go through a mediation session than to litigate over it. Still, between 1999 and 2005, the Hamline mediation case law project identified nearly 500 reported court decisions that dealt with parties' duty to mediate.

One commentator has suggested the following guidelines for drafting an enforceable obligation to mediate:

- Keep the language simple,
- Avoid ambiguity; in particular keep commitments to mediate separate from obligations to arbitrate,
- Include specific reference to sanctions and other consequences for breach, for example, dismissal of the claim or imposition of attorneys fees, and
- Make the process fair, given the context of the contract (Katz 2008b).

Questions

In the early 1990s, a large California bank instituted a multistep ADR program for many of its customers, which required consumers to mediate any dispute they might have with the bank. Under the program, professional mediators would be provided through either of two prominent ADR organizations. Many of these mediators charged hundreds of dollars per hour for their time. Consumers were obligated to pay half of the cost of mediation, although the program allowed them to apply for an exemption from the obligation to pay. The plan also stated that neither party could leave mediation until the mediator had made a finding that there was "no possibility of resolution without pursuing the adjudicatory phase."

24. If you were a customer with a claim against the bank, would you challenge this program? What grounds might there be to do so?
25. Is the program likely to create practical problems for the mediators?
26. Two parties mediate, sign a term sheet with the expectation of drafting a formal settlement document later, and send e-mails informing the court that the matter has been settled. They then fall into disagreement over what terms should appear in the final document. Are the parties bound by their e-mails? What factors should determine the outcome? Compare Delyanis v. Dyna-Empire, Inc., 465 F. Supp. 2d 170 (E.D.N.Y. 2006), with DeVita v. Macy's East, Inc., 828 N.Y.S.2d 531 (2d Dept. 2007).

Problem

7. An owner of land and a general contractor enter into a contract to build a shopping center. The contract includes a clause requiring the parties to mediate all disputes that arise during the project, to come to mediation with "full settlement authority," and to mediate "in good faith." The project is seriously delayed by the discovery of bedrock during excavation, and a dispute arises over who should bear the cost of the delay and extra work. One side seeks mediation and the other objects, saying that mediating would be a waste of time and money. How could a supervising court determine whether the parties:

> a. Participated in mediation?
> b. Came with full settlement authority?
> c. Mediated in good faith?

2. *Mandates to Mediate*

a. Issues of Court Authority

As we saw in Chapter 13, many court systems, impressed with the potential of mediation, have decided to make participation in the process mandatory. Courts sometimes do so in the belief that disputants and counsel are unfamiliar with the benefits of mediation and need to be compelled to "try some." Or they may impose mediation out of concern that the very parties most in need of the process, or most likely to consume judicial resources unnecessarily, will not enter mediation voluntarily. Thus, for example, many states require parents involved in child visitation or custody disputes to mediate before seeking a court order.

Early in the development of court-connected mediation commentators were concerned that for a court to order parties into ADR might be unconstitutional — for instance, that such requirements might interfere with state constitutional provisions that give citizens a right to free access to justice. Courts have upheld mediation mandates against arguments that they violate constitutional guarantees, probably because participation is inherently no more burdensome than other steps in the litigation process, such as compelled appearance at depositions (Golann 1989).

The fact that mandatory ADR is constitutional, however, does not mean that a particular court has the authority to order it. Courts ordinarily derive their authority from specific statutes and rules. Many federal courts, for example, base orders compelling litigants to mediate on plans and rules adopted pursuant to the Civil Justice Reform Act of 1990 or the ADR Act of 1998. The 1998 Act, in particular, bars federal courts from forcing parties to arbitrate but says nothing about whether disputants can be required to mediate, which some courts have interpreted to mean that they can adopt rules requiring mandatory mediation.

Can a federal court that has not adopted a rule nevertheless order parties to mediate as a matter of "inherent judicial power"? The Court of Appeals in In re Atlantic Pipe Corp., 304 F.3d 135 (1st Cir. 2002), confronted the issue in a complex construction dispute with many parties. It confirmed the inherent power of a trial judge to order mediation over a party's objection, to require an objector to pay part of the cost, and to name as a mediator a private neutral nominated by one of the parties. The appeals court nevertheless expressed concern over the lack of any conditions on the appointment, particularly in light of the fact that the mediator charged $9,000 per day, and remanded the case to the trial court to enter additional orders.

Courts in other jurisdictions have reached contrary results. In Jeld-Wen v. Superior Court, 146 Cal. App. 4th 536 (2007), for example, an appellate court found that although California courts have the statutory power to order smaller civil cases to mediation processes whose cost is paid for by the state, they could not order parties to attend and pay for private mediation.

b. Good-Faith Bargaining Requirements

If a court has the power to order disputants to mediate, should it require them to satisfy any minimum standard of conduct? If the adoption of rules is any guide, the answer is plainly yes. Professor John Lande found that at least 22 states have "good-faith bargaining" requirements for mediation, and that many federal district and state trial courts have local rules imposing such duties on disputants, usually in connection with a court-related ADR program. The problem is that virtually none of these rules defines what "good faith" means. According to Professor John Lande, the reported cases on good-faith obligations break down as follows:

- Failure to attend mediation at all.
- Failure to send a representative with adequate settlement authority.
- Failure to submit required memoranda or documents.
- Failure to make a suitable offer or otherwise participate in bargaining.
- Failure to sign an agreement.

In practice courts have found it easiest to sanction objective acts, such as a party's failure to appear or file a statement. They have found it much more difficult to assess subjective matters, such as whether a party's offer was adequate in the circumstances. Apart from having to define amorphous concepts such as good faith, courts would usually have to take evidence about what occurred in the mediation process, raising confidentiality concerns. Only a few decisions to impose sanctions based on a trial judge's subjective conclusions about mediation misconduct have been upheld on appeal (Lande 2002).

Even if enforcement is feasible, good-faith bargaining requirements arguably conflict with a key value of mediation, self-determination. The first principle in the Model Standards of Conduct for Mediators states that "Parties may exercise self-determination at any stage of a mediation, including . . . participation in or withdrawal from the process." Under this standard, can a court order parties into mediation or compel a specific level of participation? Suppose, however, that one party in a compelled process expends substantial resources to participate — should an adversary be permitted to frustrate the effort by failing to prepare or refusing to bargain? The following questions illustrate the issue.

    a. If applicable rules require that the parties "bargain in good faith," has Alpha complied?

    b. Does anything else that Alpha did or failed to do in that process strike you as "bad faith"?

29. Consider the situation of defense counsel in the following case: A court-appointed master ordered the parties to engage in a five-day mediation of a complex construction defect claim. Knowing that such claims necessarily involve expert testimony, the neutral instructed each side to bring its experts to the process. The neutral's charges and the plaintiff's cost for assembling its experts for mediation totaled nearly $25,000. Defense counsel, however, arrived 30 minutes late for the first session and appeared alone. Asked about his failure to bring his client or his experts, he said, "I'm here, you can talk to me." See *Foxgate Homeowner's Association, Inc., v. Bramlea California, Inc., et al.,* 25 P.3d 1117 (Cal. 2001).

    a. Did the defense counsel's actions constitute bad faith? Why, exactly?

    b. The mediator in *Foxgate* reported to the court that defense counsel took this approach because he believed that his pending motion for partial summary judgment would substantially reduce the value of the plaintiff's claims. Does this justify the lawyer's strategy?

    c. The neutral also reported that, in his opinion, the defendant had sufficient time to present the motion before the mediation but had not done so. How relevant is the mediator's opinion on this issue? Should the mediator have offered it?

The fact that mediation often leads people to change their minds makes it particularly important that the persons who attend have the authority to adopt new positions. If a negotiator ultimately decides that a difficult compromise is appropriate, for example, he needs the authority to implement his judgment. Recognizing this, mediation agreements and program rules usually require that if a party does not appear personally — which is not possible for a corporation — it must send a representative who has "full" or "adequate" settlement authority. This raises similar issues to the problem of defining good faith. As you read the following case, ask yourself these questions.

Questions

30. If the authority that the defendant brought to this mediation was not adequate, what would have been sufficient?

31. If you were counsel to a corporation whose business required it to mediate cases around the country, what practical problems might the court's ruling present for you?

❖ *NICK v. MORGAN'S FOODS OF MISSOURI, INC.*

270 F. 3d 590 (8th Cir. 2001)

Gee Gee Nick, a Kentucky Fried Chicken employee, filed a district court complaint against her employer, Morgan's Foods, alleging sexual harassment. Following a scheduling conference, the parties were ordered to participate in the federal court's Alternative Dispute Resolution ("ADR") process pursuant to its local rules, which provided in part: "Duty to Attend and Participate: All parties, counsel of record, and corporate representatives or claims professionals having authority to settle claims shall attend all mediation conferences and participate in good faith." (Court rules also required that each side file a memorandum with the mediator in advance, but Morgan's Foods's lawyer did not do so because, the court said, he "believed it was unnecessary and a waste of time.")

The mediation conference was attended by Nick, her court-appointed counsel, Morgan's Foods's outside counsel, and the local regional manager. The manager's settlement authority was limited to $500. Any decision to change the company's settlement position had to be made by its general counsel, . . . who was in Connecticut and only available by telephone. During the mediation, Nick twice made offers of settlement that were rejected without counteroffers. The mediation was terminated shortly thereafter. The neutral informed the district court of the minimal level of Morgan's Foods's participation in the ADR process. In response, the trial court . . . sanctioned Morgan's Foods $1,390 [in costs], . . . its outside counsel $1,390 [as well, and] ordered the company to pay a $1,500 fine. . . . In its Memorandum and Order, the Court explained why personal attendance at a mediation session is a sine qua non:

"For ADR to work, the corporate representative must have the authority and discretion to change her opinion in light of the statements and arguments made by the neutral and opposing party. Meaningful negotiations cannot occur if the only person with authority to actually change their mind and negotiate is not present. Availability by telephone is insufficient because the absent decision-maker does not have the full benefit of the ADR proceedings, the opposing party's arguments, and the neutral's input. The absent decision-maker needs to be present and hear first-hand the good facts and the bad facts about their case."

"Instead, the absent decision-maker learns only what his or her attorney chooses to relate over the phone. This can be expected to be largely a recitation of what has been conveyed in previous discussions. Even when the attorney attempts to summarize the strengths of the other side's position, there are problems. First, the attorney has a credibility problem: the absent decision-maker wants to know why the attorney's confident opinion expressed earlier has now eroded. Second, the new information most likely is too much to absorb and analyze in a matter of minutes. Under this dynamic it becomes all too easy for the absent decision-maker to reject the attorney's new advice, reject the new information, and reject any effort to engage in meaningful negotiations.

"It is quite likely that the telephone call is viewed as a distraction from other business being conducted by the absent decision-maker. . . . [The] easiest decision is to summarily reject any offer and get back to the business on her desk. . . .

"Morgan's Foods's lack of good faith participation in the ADR process was calculated to save Morgan's Foods a few hours of time in preparing the mediation memorandum and to save its general counsel the expense and inconvenience of a trip to attend the mediation. The consequence of Morgan's Foods's lack of good faith participation in the ADR process, however, was the wasted expense of time and energy of the Court, the neutral, Nick, and her court-appointed counsel. If Morgan's Foods did not feel that ADR could be fruitful and had no intention of participating in good faith, it had a duty to report its position to the Court and to request appropriate relief. Morgan's Foods did not do so and sanctions are appropriate to remedy the resulting waste of time and money."

[The court affirmed the sanctions ordered by the trial judge.]

Questions

32. You are counsel to Morgan's Foods. Another employee has filed a claim similar to Nick's, and it has been referred to the same mediation program. What do you need to do to comply with the court's rule?

33. In a case involving an East Coast computer company's claim that a Silicon Valley firm had improperly "stolen" its development team, the defendant's general counsel refused to travel to a mediation session in New York. At the mediator's request, however, she did agree to be present on a conference call during all of the joint meetings and throughout each caucus that the mediator held with her side. Does that form of participation meet the objections of the *Nick* court? What are the potential drawbacks to such an arrangement?

34. Florida, one of the most active states in promoting court-related ADR, requires litigants to appear at mediation, and defines appearance to mean that: "[The] party or a representative with full settlement authority is present along with the party's counsel, if any, and a representative of the insurance carrier with full authority to settle up to the plaintiff's last demand or policy limits, whichever is less. . . . "

   Assume that you are the national litigation counsel for a Fortune 500 company with operations in Florida that occasionally result in cases being filed against your company, and you are required to mediate under this rule.

   a. Could your local outside counsel appear at a court-connected mediation in Florida without a company representative, if he had full authority to bind your company?

   b. What practical problems would this rule create for you? Can you think of any steps that would lessen them?

_____

In response to the difficulty of defining and enforcing "good-faith" requirements, some have argued that such rules should be discarded entirely. Professor Lande, for example, warns that

Sanctioning bad faith in mediation actually may stimulate adversarial and dishonest conduct. . . . [It] might also encourage surface bargaining. . . . Because mediators are not supposed to force people to settle, participants who are determined not to settle can wait until the mediator gives up. . . . Similarly, tough mediation participants could use good-faith requirements offensively to intimidate opposing parties. . . . [Innocent] participants may have legitimate fears about risking sanctions when they face an aggressive opponent. . . . [In addition, a] good-faith requirement gives mediators too much authority . . . to direct the outcome in mediation.

He has proposed that litigants instead be given education about the value of interest-based processes, and that courts limit themselves to enforcing objective standards of conduct, for example, that parties appear at mediation for a minimum period of time (Lande, 2002).

Problems

8. Two companies are in mediation. In the underlying lawsuit, the plaintiff has alleged that the defendant knowingly violated a franchise agreement. The "hard" damages in the case, computed on the basis of the franchisee's minimum purchase requirements, are about $100,000. However, the plaintiff has also claimed $500,000 in lost profits and made an initial settlement demand of $600,000. It appears to the franchisee's lawyer that her client has about a 50-50 chance of being found liable under the contract and having to pay the hard damages, but that the risk that her client will be liable for lost profits is virtually nil. Applying the 50-percent risk factor to the hard damages, the defense therefore assesses the value of the case at $50,000. The parties agree to mediate.

9. In a first caucus meeting with the mediator, the plaintiff's lawyer says that while its demand is "negotiable" it will not make any concessions until the defense puts a "significant offer" on the table. The defense lawyer informs the neutral that he will not make any offer at this point because the plaintiff is "on another planet." He tells the mediator that it's his job first to bring the plaintiff into a zone of reality, and $600,000 is not it. The mediation agreement commits the parties to "engage in good-faith bargaining." Is either the plaintiff or the defendant violating its obligation? If so, why?

3. Enforcement of Mediated Settlements

Mediation is a voluntary process, but if it is successful then the parties usually enter into a binding contract — a settlement agreement. Even settlements, however, may provoke new controversies over issues such as the following:

- Did the parties actually reach a final agreement? If so, what were its terms?
- Should the agreement be invalidated on grounds such as duress, mistake, unconscionability, or lack of authority?

We have seen that such issues provoke disputes over confidentiality, as courts are asked to take testimony about what occurred in the process. Apart from confidentiality concerns, however, there are substantive questions: What is required to make a settlement binding? And how much deviation should courts permit from an "ideal" process before overturning its result?

a. The Existence of an Agreement

Good practice calls for parties who settle in mediation to memorialize their agreements in writing. To ensure that this occurs, mediation texts counsel neutrals, however late the hour or strong the settling parties' wish to depart, to push the disputants to sign a memorandum that summarizes the settlement before they leave. Sometimes, however, the parties do not execute an agreement, or it is attacked as, or alleged to be, incomplete.

Most courts test mediated settlements by the standards that apply to contracts generally. If an agreement is oral, the first issue is whether it complies with the applicable statute of frauds. Courts in several states have held oral mediated settlements to be enforceable contracts, and although there are few reported cases it appears that federal common law also permits enforcement of oral settlements. Where a court has refused to enforce an oral agreement reached in mediation, it has usually been because state law imposes procedural rules more severe than the requirements of the common law of contracts. Florida and Texas, for example, mandate that pending court cases may be settled only through a written document signed by the parties or their counsel (Cole et al. 2008).

Another possibility is that the parties sign an agreement but one side later argues that the writing is incomplete, as in the *Leary* case at the start of this chapter. Such claims raise issues under the Parole Evidence Rule and other evidentiary standards, as well as concerns about invading confidentiality.

b. Grounds for Invalidation

Suppose, following a successful mediation process, the lawyers draw up an agreement and the parties sign it. Is that enough to ensure that a settlement will be enforced? Generally the answer is yes, but not always. Again there are potential concerns. Some of these are formal in nature. First, settlement agreements must contain the essential terms of the parties' bargain. If, for example, a settlement provided that "the parties shall exchange mutual releases," a court would probably find the language sufficient to form a binding agreement. If, however, a settlement stated that a defendant would make payments "in installments" but did not specify a schedule, a challenge would be more likely to succeed. A few jurisdictions also require that mediated settlements of pending litigation be approved by a court.

The most serious basis for invalidating a mediated settlement is a substantive one: that the process of mediation itself was so deficient that any resulting agreement is invalid. On the one hand, the presence of a neutral person would seem to make it less likely that a "bad" settlement would result. On the other hand, aspects of the process that are intended to push litigants to confront unpleasant realities can also create stress that inhibits good decision making. An example is the *Olam* case, above, in which an individual who agreed to a settlement in the early morning hours later claimed that she did so under duress.

Questions

35. Are there particular circumstances in which a mediated settlement should be subject to special scrutiny? When, for example, might this be true?
36. When a mediated agreement is challenged on grounds such as duress or misrepresentation, should the court apply a different standard than it would to a settlement reached through direct negotiation? Why or why not?

❖ *CHRISTIAN COOPER v. MELODIE AUSTIN*

750 So. 2d 711 (Fla. App. 2000)

HARRIS, J.:

Cooper appeals a final judgment which adopted a mediation agreement Cooper alleges was obtained by extortion and was the basis for [a] contempt citation. . . . During the course of a lengthy mediation, it is undisputed that the wife sent Cooper the following note:

> If you can't agree to this, the kids will take what information they have to whomever to have you arrested, etc. Although I would get no money if you were in jail — you wouldn't also be living freely as if you did nothing wrong.[‡]

Relatively soon thereafter, the parties "settled" their property matters. . . . In the midst of extended negotiations before the mediator, the wife sent the husband a note that constituted classic extortion. However, the wife convinced the [trial] judge that the note was merely a "wake-up" call and did not influence the agreement subsequently reached. The court relied on two established facts to reach this conclusion. First, the husband did not immediately accede to the wife's demands but continued to negotiate for a period thereafter. Second, the husband did not seek relief from the extortionate agreement until after his efforts to reconcile with the wife failed. Even accepting these facts as true, we cannot agree that they negate the effect of extortion when reviewing the remainder of the record.

---

‡. [Footnote to court opinion] The crime threatened to be reported by the wife was Cooper's photographing a nude, underage girl. Cooper, who had experienced firsthand the law's disapproval of this practice on an earlier occasion, was aware that in going through his property, the wife's children had found a photograph taken by him of a young woman who indeed looked under age. It was not until shortly before this action for relief from judgment was filed that Cooper tracked down the woman and verified she was "of age" at the time the photograph was taken.

The husband testified, without contradiction, that the result of the mediated agreement was that the wife received $128,000 in marital assets while the husband received $10,000. . . . This grossly unequal distribution speaks volumes about the effect of the extortionate note sent by the wife. . . .

In this case, the wife's "wake-up call," which demanded the husband either give in to her demands or go to jail, was clearly extortionate and her presentation of the extorted agreement to the court was a fraud on the court making the trial court an instrument of her extortion. Mrs. Cooper should not profit from her actions. Nor should this Court, or any court, ignore them.

GRIFFIN, J., dissenting:

This is not the first time an appellate court has been unable to overcome the urge to trump factual findings of a trial judge with which the panel violently disagrees, nor will it be the last. But it is awkward when it happens. . . . *How*, the majority asks incredulously, could the trial judge have allowed himself to be hoodwinked in this fashion? After reading the transcript of the hearing, it is clear to me that Judge Hammond simply did not believe Mr. Cooper. This is important because there are only three items of evidence to support Mr. Cooper's claim of duress: (1) the threat; (2) the apparent uneven distribution of assets; and (3) Mr. Cooper's testimony that the reason he entered into the agreement was because of the threat.

The lower court so much as said it did not find Mr. Cooper to be credible. First of all, Mr. Cooper, who has a bachelor's degree and a master's degree in business, both from Duke University . . . testified repeatedly that he had no idea of the value of the marital assets. [T]he evidence, in fact, showed that he had a very good idea of what the marital assets were. . . .

There was direct conflict between Mr. and Mrs. Cooper concerning Mr. Cooper's response to her threat. She testified that his response was that he was not scared, that the kids did not "have anything" and that he knew that he "owed it to her to put her through school." . . . As the lower court succinctly said: "The former husband knew that the photographs in his possession were not illegal."

There is also the fact that Mr. Cooper, his free will forborne due to his "fear of arrest," continued to negotiate the agreement for another two and one-half hours[, securing substantial changes in the terms of a promissory note to the wife]. . . . The fact that he received all of the benefits of the mediation agreement as adopted by the Final Judgment, made all alimony payments . . . , received back all of the personal property he was concerned about, [and] continued his pursuit of the Former Wife are not the actions of a man who was subject to extortion, coercion or duress. . . . We should affirm.

Question

37. If Mr. Cooper's counsel thought that his client was feeling extorted during the mediation, what should he have done?

C. Certification

It might surprise you to hear that mediators, unlike many professionals, do not need a license to practice — there is no equivalent to bar membership, or even a driver's license, for mediators. A child can act as a mediator, and in fact some schools encourage students to mediate peer disputes. This reflects the history of modern mediation, which was fueled in large measure by frustration with the litigation system and peoples' wish to find new ways to approach disputes. The idea of creating a licensing system for mediators, with the need for an official body to define and test "good" practices and exclude and perhaps sanction those who do not qualify, strikes many in the field as antithetical to its basic values.

There is more of a debate over whether mediators should be certified. Certification is less centralized and has less restrictive impact than licensing and is carried out by a variety of private and public organizations rather than a single government agency. While lack of certification prevents people from working in situations in which it is required, it does not foreclose them from mediating generally.

Certification does, however, allow mediators to indicate that they have been "certified by" a particular organization. Professional associations of mediators, for instance, have established membership requirements and certification schemes to encourage quality mediation and allow members to indicate that they have been "certified" by the organization. In the domestic relations field, for example, Family Mediation Canada has created a private certification scheme that includes videotaped mediations observed and evaluated by experienced mediators and a written examination; those who pass the test can advertise that they are certified by the organization.

Another form of certification involves imposing requirements on mediators who wish to participate in a program. Thus professionals who want to be listed on court-connected mediation panels are often required to meet specific criteria, reflecting the view that a court, as a branch of government, should take responsibility for the quality of those who practice under its aegis. Florida was the first state to establish qualifications for court-connected panelists and other states have followed; California, for example, recently adopted "Model Qualification Standards" for mediators recommended, appointed, or compensated by its courts. There is no uniformity in the standards applied by court mediation programs, however, and admission to a court's program does not ordinarily authorize a mediator to say that she has been "certified" by the court.

The absence of any general system of state regulation or certification of mediation is not for lack of proposals. In California alone, hundreds of bills have been introduced to control or regulate mediation, and the American Bar Association and many state bar associations have worked to formulate policy proposals on the issue.

Why have these efforts met resistance? George Bernard Shaw is credited with saying that any effort to professionalize services is a conspiracy against the public, and this cynical note may have relevance to efforts to certify mediators. Although mediation is now widespread in the United States, consumers have not come forward to register frequent complaints or make claims of being damaged by non-certified mediators. This may reflect the fact that in commercial cases at least, parties are usually represented by counsel who are well-positioned to select, assess, and — through their control over hiring — exclude neutrals who are ineffective. Indeed most of the push for certification and licensing has come from mediators wanting the field to have the status of a distinct profession rather than from parties or lawyers.

Even assuming some public benefit in certifying mediators, the question remains whether it would create more problems than it resolved. Certification raises questions about diversity and exclusion, defining competence, squelching creativity, increasing costs, encouraging misplaced reliance, and deciding who to make the gatekeeper. One example of the divisiveness that can be created by the issue is the debate regarding what is "real" mediation. If, for example, a gatekeeper believed that mediation must be facilitative, then mediators who help parties evaluate outcomes would be disqualified and consumers deprived of a choice of styles. If, on the other hand, evaluative mediators dominated the process, purely facilitative approaches might be excluded.

Most court systems and private organizations that offer mediation do, however, impose standards for admittance to their panels. The effect is that certification standards have become widespread, especially in connection with court-connected mediation programs. The popularity of certification in this setting probably reflects the view that courts, as official institutions, should take responsibility for the quality of mediators who practice under their aegis. However there is no national, or in many cases even statewide, uniformity in the standards for certification even where they exist. The following articles discuss whether a wider, more consistent system for certifying mediators should be created.

❖ Juliana Birkoff & Robert Rack, with Judith M. Filner,
POINTS OF VIEW: IS MEDIATION REALLY A PROFESSION?

8 Disp. Resol. Mag. 10-21 (Fall 2001)

[T]here has been a push for quality assurance by developing credential programs for mediators. Skeptics have said that the drive toward credentials comes from the desire of some practitioners to reduce competition. Others have urged resistance to this impetus to create qualifications, claiming it is elitist and exclusionary. Some further assert that creating qualifications will limit the diversity of the field. Advocates, however, perceive a need and responsibility to protect consumers from incompetent mediators, to enhance the credibility and status of the field, and to address the need for agencies, courts, and other referral sources to assure the quality of the services provided.

Skeptics and advocates alike puzzle over how qualifications can be related to performance, whether credential programs assure quality, and whether or not the field of mediation is sufficiently mature to define what mediation is, what mediators do, and what they have to know to serve competently. While the discussion continues, various states and agencies are, in fact, establishing qualifications and standards. And, the field is maturing . . . The interview that follows . . . frames the quality assurance discussion.

JMF: So . . . is mediation a profession?

JB: Yes, I think mediation is a profession or is becoming a profession. When I began my research, I did not expect to find [this]. . . .

BR: I certainly think most mediators are professional in the sense that they are committed to their work. . . . But I think mediation is bigger than a profession and I resist the temptation to try to capture and contain it. We've seen mediation explode in use throughout society. . . . I see it as a broad social movement. . . .

JMF: . . . If mediation is a profession, how do we, as a field, as practitioners, as program directors, assure quality or address issues of quality practice?

JB: Credentialing is a way that professionals try to define what they do and distinguish it from what other professions or occupations do. For me, it is not so important to look at credentialing. Rather, it is important to look at the body of knowledge that a mediator uses to do the work, to practice. . . .

BR: . . . I see the heart of good mediation as skillfully facilitating communication and effectively infusing strained relationships with goodwill. The most essential "knowledge" for a mediator seems to me to be an understanding of human nature and human behavior, especially under stress and in conflict. That knowledge can be largely intuitive, and developed through experience. We may one day have such a precise understanding of human behavior that we can write it down and require mediators to commit it to memory, like biology, laws, and accounting rules for doctors, lawyers, and accountants. And we might then be able to measure a mediator's ability to apply that knowledge. But I doubt that will happen anytime soon.

JB: Let me clarify; mediators do not develop their unique knowledge by studying literature. This is why so few mediators find that going to M.S. or Ph.D. programs improves their skills as mediators. Mediators develop their knowledge by doing the work. . . .

BR: The first thing I look for in new mediator candidates is a kind of life stance — an inclination to see the validity in apparently conflicting points of view and to seek synthesis, rather than domination by any one of those views. The second thing I look for is experience that demonstrates a skillful articulation of that inclination . . . So I'd say that mediation is a life skill first. . . . Daniel Bowling and David Hoffman published an article [excerpted in Chapter 5] in . . . which they concluded that a mediator's mere "presence" is a major ingredient in the mediation dynamic . . . I completely agree. Now, how do we "credentialize" that?

JB: While I understand where Bob is coming from, it sounds like he believes that being artistic and creative has no place in a profession. . . . Professional knowing is not only tacit theory but also the intuition, skill, and experience of trained and talented individuals who know how to apply that knowledge. . . .

JMF: One of the reasons mediators talk about assuring quality is that there is poor practice out there. . . .

JB: I guess I would ask what proof exists, besides rumors and anecdotes, that there is a need to protect the public. This is often an argument that beginning professions use to protect their insecure control of their work . . . However, I do believe that the mediation organizations should promote standards of practice and require a commitment from members to abide by the standards of practice.

BR: I agree with almost everything Juliana has said. If participants understand the very basics of mediation, it's really pretty hard for a mediator to do
much harm . . . I believe the focus and responsibility for resolution should
remain on the parties and there already is a tendency for many disputants to
hand over that responsibility to the mediator. I hate to give any more authority
or stature to the mediator than is absolutely necessary. . . .

JMF: Finally, I see a strong, albeit disorganized and informal, move toward
credentialing. . . .

JB: It is significant that people are representing themselves as professional
mediators. . . . This says more about the ways we as a society judge the effectiveness of lawyers and therapists than it does about the benefits of having a
conflict resolution profession.

BR: I understand the disdain for charlatans, the frustration over not being
able to do anything about incompetent people in our field, and the feeling of
responsibility for assuring quality. It's just that we have no reason at this time to
believe we know how to legislate for the selection of good mediators and the
screening out of bad ones. . . . There are things that can be done to advance the
quality ball without legislating requirements for everyone. First, let's . . . let
[private associations] experiment with qualifications and see if they can find
some that really make a difference. . . . This field is still hot and is still evolving
rapidly. My vote remains that we not try to freeze it with mandatory qualifications or performance standards until we know it will make a significant and
positive difference.

❖ **James E. McGuire,** CERTIFICATION: AN IDEA WHOSE TIME HAS COME

10 Disp. Resol. Mag. 22 (Summer 2004)

Is mediation a profession? If it is, what are the requirements to be a professional
mediator? Who should do the certifying? These seemingly simple questions
have been part of the mediation dialogue in the United States for more than 25
years. . . .

Why Certify Any Mediator?

Mediators not only want to be competent, they want to be perceived as
competent. Currently, mediators do so by collecting credentials: training programs taken, panels joined, articles written, and for those with actual experience, number of cases mediated. While not ensuring competence, credentialing
creates a competitive advantage for a mediator.

In order to secure the credential of participating on a panel, taking the
sponsor's training course is often a prerequisite. Training programs can be a
major source of revenue for the sponsor and a significant burden for potential
mediators. Moreover, multiple, repetitive, mandatory entry-level training programs exist within most states and practice areas. Certification may provide an
answer to the frustration these duplicative requirements present. . . .

As legislators begin to codify mediation confidentiality . . . some are asking
the basic hard questions: Who are these mediators? How do they get trained?
What safeguards exist to ensure that the mediators are trustworthy? An additional reason for considering voluntary mediator certification is recognition

that if mediators do not create a certification process, others will and it may not be as voluntary or nuanced and flexible as the field would desire. . . .

How to Become Certified

. . . A likely model is [a] two-step process . . . : preparation and submission of a "portfolio" . . . . The portfolio is a paper submission documenting . . . hours of training and relevant course work [and experience] as an active mediator. . . . Letters of recommendation, evidence of professional liability insurance, and disclosure of disciplinary matters complete the portfolio requirements.

A candidate with an acceptable portfolio would then take a written examination. . . . The exam is intended to test awareness of mediation principles, approaches, and relevant techniques. [T]here is likely to be no provision for reviewing an actual demonstration of mediation skills. Such live evaluations are difficult to develop and expensive to administer. This is especially true where the goal is to avoid having certification itself become an economic barrier to entry into the mediation field.

Who Certifies?

The development and successful implementation of certification standards is most likely to succeed if it is a multi-organizational effort. . . . [N]either lawyers nor the ABA "own" the mediator certification process. . . . Though there can be no guarantee of success, any other approach may well be a guarantee of failure.

Questions

38. Assume that you wish to become a mediator and can meet the qualifications described by Mr. McGuire. Would you prefer to have your state adopt a credentialing program like the one he outlines, or take a "hands-off" approach?
39. What is gained or lost if regulation of mediators is limited to certification, rather than a licensing system like bar membership?
40. As noted in Chapter 12, the International Mediation Institute in the Hague, in response to complaints by large companies that they are unable to verify the competence of mediators to mediate cross-border commercial disputes, has created a certification program intended to provide a roster of qualified mediators. The Institute requires the following of persons wishing to be certified: (1) An application describing in detail the applicant's background and experience, (2) evidence that the applicant has taken a 40-hour training program from a training program approved by the Institute, and (3) letters of recommendation from five persons who have mediated cases with the applicant, either as parties or attorneys.
41. The Institute has asked you to critique its program: Does it provide adequate assurances that its certified mediators are competent? Do you have any suggestions as to how the program could be improved? Why do you think your suggestions have not been implemented already?

CHAPTER
15

Ethical Issues for Advocates and Mediators

Lawyers may engage in mediation either as advocates or as neutrals. Some attorneys play both roles, maintaining an active law practice and also acting as a mediator. The ethical issues for each role are different and we discuss them in turn.

A. Advocates in Mediation

We have seen that advocates in mediation act primarily as negotiators. The rule that governs lawyers as negotiators is ABA Model Rule 4.1, which does not mention mediation at all. Several years ago the ABA proposed changes to the Model Rules through its Ethics 2000 (E2K) Commission. The E2K recommendations changed lawyers' obligations in the arbitration process by defining an arbitrator as a "tribunal" to which counsel owe a heightened duty of candor. (See E2K Report, Rules 1.0(m), 3.3, in the Web Appendix.)

The proposed changes did not, however, grant similar status to mediators. Neither current ethical rules nor the E2K revisions require attorneys to be more truthful with mediators than with opponents in direct negotiation. See Formal Opinion 06-439, ABA Standing Committee on Ethics and Professional Responsibility ("the same standards that apply to lawyers engaged in negotiations must apply to them in the context of caucused mediation"). In the view of Dean James Alfini, the effect of the E2K changes is that mediation

> would appear to fall into a gap (or black hole) between the formal proceedings contemplated by Rule 3.3 [Candor Toward the Tribunal] and the informal settings contemplated by Rule 4.1 [Truthfulness in Statements to Others]. . . . Thus, lawyering activities in mediation would appear to be governed by the permissive Rule 4.1 . . . which provides an inadequate ethics infrastructure to support the settlement culture that has developed over the past 20 years. . . . The rules should be re-drafted to hold lawyers to a higher standard of conduct [in mediation]. . . . (Alfini 2001)

Professor Cooley similarly has written that "As long as there are not uniform ethical standards defining truthfulness in mediation, lawyer-mediators and mediation advocates will have the unfettered capacity to practice their show-manship and produce their 'magic' effects by any method they wish" (Cooley 1997).

Although the Model Rules do not impose any special standards on mediation, other rules may. For one thing, many court-connected ADR programs impose standards of conduct on participants, such as the obligation to mediate in good faith, and lawyers who engage in private mediation often sign agreements that commit them to similar conduct. Finally, advocates may voluntarily observe standards higher than the minimum imposed by law, either because of their personal values or for practical reasons we explore below. Special issues do arise, however, when advocates bargain in the context of mediation, and are discussed below.

1. Candor Toward the Mediator

We saw in Chapter 12 that bargaining in mediation is unique because it is often three-sided. At times disputants are negotiating directly with their opponent, using the mediator simply as a channel of communication ("Tell them that we won't move into six figures until . . ."), but attorneys adopting a competitive approach also negotiate with the neutral. Here are two examples:

Mediator: "I understand that your current offer is $10,000, but can you give me a private indication of where you'd be willing to go if the plaintiff dropped its demand?"
Lawyer: "Well, if they drop to six figures, I would recommend. . . ."
Mediator: "I am going to ask each side to tell me confidentially how far they would go to get a final settlement in this matter. . . ."
Lawyer: "The bottom dollar we can take is. . . ."

Should lawyers be more candid with a mediator than with an adverse party? Although there is no legal obligation to bargain differently, there are practical reasons to do so. To begin with, an attorney, sensing that a mediator is acting in an impartial and cooperative manner, might feel a natural inclination to reciprocate. A lawyer might also opt to treat a mediator well in the hope that she would reciprocate by exercising influence over the process to the attorney's benefit.

Problems

1. You represent the employer in a bitterly contested case involving an executive fired from a Silicon Valley company. The parties have bargained fiercely for several hours. For the past hour they have been at an impasse. The mediator now makes a mediator's proposal in an effort to break the deadlock. You ask for a few minutes to confer privately with your client, the company's CEO. After batting the proposed number back and forth, the CEO says, "I don't think we can live with that, but let's say 'yes' and see if the plaintiff bites. Nothing's final until it's signed anyway." You fear that the CEO is simply testing the waters and will renege if the employee accepts the deal.

    a. Can you indicate that your client assents to the proposal? Would doing so violate the Model Rules?

    b. Suppose that the CEO's tactic will achieve her goal, but will impair your credibility with the mediator in future cases. Does this change the analysis?

    c. Under the law of confidentiality in your jurisdiction, can anyone be compelled to testify concerning your client's response to the mediator's proposal?

2. Assume the same facts, except that the CEO thinks that the plaintiff's entire case is bogus. She does not authorize you to make any settlement offer, and tells you to go to mediation "just to see where they're coming from." The CEO has given no indication that she will authorize you to make a settlement offer, but it is possible.

    a. If the mediation agreement commits the parties to bargain "in good faith," is your client violating it?

    b. Do you owe the mediator or the other party any obligation to disclose your situation?

    c. If you disagree with this approach, how would you explain your viewpoint to the client?

2. Obligations to Other Parties

We have seen that the Model Rules of Professional Conduct impose few obligations on a lawyer vis-à-vis an adversary when negotiating, and that an attorney's obligations are no higher in mediation than in direct bargaining. Still, the structure of the process can create unique issues for lawyers. Consider these problems.

Problems

3. You are a lawyer preparing for mediation with mediator Alvarez, who began her practice as a neutral about a year ago, after a long career as a civil litigator. She had an excellent reputation as a lawyer and did well with a small personal injury case that you mediated with her six months ago. You ran into Alvarez on the street a few weeks ago, and she mentioned her interest in doing another case with you. A long-term client, a casualty insurer, has asked you to mediate a major tort case. You recommended Alvarez as a possibility, and it appears that she would be acceptable to the plaintiff's counsel. As you are preparing to call the mediator to make final arrangements, your contact at the insurer calls and says, "Tell her we're a major player in the market. If she gets a good result on this one, we'll think strongly about sending her more cases."

    a. Under the Model Rules, the sample commercial mediation agreement in the Web Appendix, or any other applicable standard, is it improper for you to pass along this comment to Alvarez? Why or why not?

b. If you say something to the mediator, how will you phrase it? If not, what if anything will you say to the adjuster?

4. You practice as a litigator in a small firm and are representing a plaintiff in an automobile tort case. The defendant is insured by a major insurance company. Given the market power of the insurer, you are concerned that the mediator might be less than fully neutral. Is there anything that you can do to alleviate your concern? Is there any risk to your proposed course of action?

3. The Duty to Advise Clients About ADR

An increasing number of jurisdictions require lawyers to advise clients about the nature of alternative dispute resolution and the potential for using it in their dispute. For example, Colorado (via the bar association), Arkansas (by statute), and Ohio, New Jersey, and Massachusetts (through court rules), each require attorneys to give such advice. Several federal and state courts have adopted similar rules. Comments to the ABA's Ethics E2K proposals also mention ADR, stating that, "In general, a lawyer is not expected to give advice until asked by the client, . . ." but going on to say that "[W]hen a matter is likely to involve litigation, it may be necessary . . . to inform the client of forms of dispute resolution that might constitute reasonable alternatives to litigation . . ." (E2K Report, Comments to Rule 2.1).

Questions

1. The Colorado Bar's Code of Ethics states that lawyers should "advise the client of alternative forms of dispute resolution that might reasonably be pursued to attempt to resolve the legal dispute or to reach the legal objective sought." Draft the key points you would mention about ADR if you were meeting with a secretary at a local manufacturing company who had just retained you to sue the company for sexual harassment that created a hostile work environment, forcing her to leave her job

2. What, in practical terms, does the Colorado rule require an attorney to do? Could a lawyer comply with the rule by giving a one-sentence definition of mediation and saying that it would be a waste of time in this particular case? If so, does the rule have any value?

B. Concerns for Mediators

There is no empirical evidence that mediators often engage in misconduct. Professor Michael Moffit conducted a survey of cases filed against mediators and concluded that: "Despite the thousands, if not millions of disputants who have received mediation services, instances of legal complaints against mediators are extraordinarily rare" (Moffit, 2003b). His survey yielded only one reported case in the past quarter-century in which a verdict had been entered against a mediator for improper conduct, and that result was overturned on appeal. The cost of mediator malpractice insurance is also very low. As of 2009, for example, a leading insurer of mediators was offering a malpractice liability policy in most states that provided $300,000 in coverage for a premium of less than $300 per year. Such rates could not be offered if there were a significant number of claims requiring a defense, much less a money payment.

The rarity of lawsuits against mediators does not necessarily mean that they do not commit misconduct, however. Many neutrals operate under immunity conferred by court-sponsored programs or mediation agreements and even if a mediator is not immune from suit, a plaintiff would find it very difficult as a practical matter to prove a causal connection between a mediator's misconduct and an ascertainable monetary loss (Moffit, 2003b). How could a complainant show, for example, that a mediator's misconduct caused it to settle for a specific amount more or less than if the mediator had acted competently?

Even allegations of mediator misconduct are relatively unusual. In Florida during the late 1990s, for example, state courts were sending more than 100,000 cases per year to mediation. Although Florida maintains a board to investigate complaints against court-certified mediators, over its first eight years of operation it received an average of only six complaints per year (Bergman & Bickerman 1998). Formal complaints against mediators thus appear to be infrequent — although this is admittedly only a minimal measure of ethical behavior.

The absence of any system of licensing means that mediators are not subject to any binding system of rules akin to the canons of ethics for lawyers. Nor do the Model Rules for Professional Conduct impose a higher duty on lawyers when they act as mediators. For example, the ABA Standing Committee on Ethics and Professional Responsibility has opined Model Rule 8.4(c), which bars lawyers from engaging in dishonesty or misrepresentation and does not impose higher obligations on lawyers acting as mediators than their obligations under Model Rule 4.1 (ABA Formal Opinion 06-439, at 6 n.19).

In the interest of advancing the field and recognizing the value of self-regulation, however, three organizations — the American Arbitration Association, American Bar Association, and Association for Conflict Resolution — have jointly promulgated an ethical code known as the Standards of Conduct for Mediators (Model Standards). Specialty organizations have created similar ethical codes for mediators in fields such as family mediation. In addition, the UMA contains a requirement that mediators disclose conflicts of interest, and both courts and private ADR organizations like JAMS and CPR impose ethical rules on mediators on their panels.

The American Bar Association maintains a clearinghouse with a searchable database of state and local opinions on mediation ethics at *www.abanet.org/dispute/clearinghouse.html*, and the ABA Section on Dispute Resolution has a Mediator Ethical Guidance Committee that issues opinions in response to requests. The Model Standards, the UMA, and other prominent ethical standards for mediators appear on the companion Web site to this book.

Excerpts from the some of the most important ethical standards appear below. They are followed by problems drawn from actual practice.

❖ **Excerpts from** *MODEL STANDARDS OF CONDUCT*
FOR MEDIATORS **(2005)**

Standard I: Self Determination

A. A mediator shall conduct a mediation based on the principle of party self-determination. Self-determination is the act of coming to a voluntary, uncoerced decision in which each party makes free and informed choices as to process and outcome. Parties may exercise self-determination at any stage of a mediation, including mediator selection, process design, participation in or withdrawal from the process, and outcomes. . . .

1. Although party self-determination for process design is a fundamental principle of mediation practice, a mediator may need to balance such party self-determination with a mediator's duty to conduct a quality process in accordance with these Standards.
2. A mediator cannot personally ensure that each party has made free and informed choices to reach particular decisions, but, where appropriate, a mediator should make the parties aware of the importance of consulting other professionals to help them make informed choices.

B. A mediator shall not undermine party self-determination by any party for reasons such as higher settlement rates, egos, increased fees, or outside pressures from court personnel, program administrators, provider organizations, the media or others.

Standard II: Impartiality

A. A mediator shall decline a mediation if the mediator cannot conduct it in an impartial manner. Impartiality means freedom from favoritism, bias or prejudice.
B. A mediator shall conduct a mediation in an impartial manner and avoid conduct that gives the appearance of partiality. . . .

Standard III: Conflicts of Interest

A. A mediator shall avoid a conflict of interest or the appearance of a conflict of interest during and after a mediation. A conflict of interest can arise from involvement by a mediator with the subject matter of the dispute or from any relationship between a mediator and any mediation participant, whether past or present, personal or professional, that reasonably raises a question of a mediator's impartiality.
B. A mediator shall make a reasonable inquiry to determine whether there are any facts that a reasonable individual would consider likely to create a potential or actual conflict of interest for a mediator. . . .
F. Subsequent to a mediation, a mediator shall not establish another relationship with any of the participants in any matter that would raise questions about the integrity of the mediation. . . .

Standard IV: Competence

A mediator shall mediate only when the mediator has the necessary competence to satisfy the reasonable expectations of the parties. . . .

Standard V: Confidentiality

A. A mediator shall maintain the confidentiality of all information obtained by the mediator in mediation, unless otherwise agreed to by the parties or required by applicable law.

B. A mediator who meets with any persons in private session during a mediation shall not convey directly or indirectly to any other person, any information that was obtained during that private session without the consent of the disclosing person. . . .

Standard VI: Quality of the Process

A. A mediator shall conduct a mediation in accordance with these Standards and in a manner that promotes diligence, timeliness, safety, presence of the appropriate participants, party participation, procedural fairness, party competency and mutual respect among all participants. . . .

1. The role of a mediator differs substantially from other professional roles. Mixing the role of a mediator and the role of another profession is problematic and thus, a mediator should distinguish between the roles. A mediator may provide information that the mediator is qualified by training or experience to provide, only if the mediator can do so consistent with these Standards.

Standard VII: Advertising and Solicitation

A. A mediator shall be truthful and not misleading when advertising, soliciting or otherwise communicating the mediator's qualifications, experience, services and fees. . . .

Standard VIII: Fees and Other Charges

A. A mediator shall provide each party or each party's representative true and complete information about mediation fees, expenses and any other actual or potential charges that may be incurred in connection with a mediation. . . .

B. . . . A mediator should not enter into a fee agreement which is contingent upon the result of the mediation or the amount of the settlement. . . .

Standard IX: Advancement of Mediation Practice

A mediator should act in a manner that advances the practice of mediation. . . .

❖ **Excerpt from the** *UNIFORM MEDIATION ACT*

Section 9. Mediator's Disclosure of Conflicts of Interest, Background

(a) Before accepting a mediation, an individual who is requested to serve as a mediator shall:

(1) make an inquiry that is reasonable under the circumstances to determine whether there are any known facts that a reasonable

individual would consider likely to affect the impartiality of the mediator . . . and

(2) disclose any such known fact to the mediation parties as soon as is practical before accepting a mediation.

(b) If a mediator learns any fact described in subsection (a)(1) after accepting a mediation, the mediator shall disclose it as soon as is practicable.

(c) At the request of a mediation party, an individual who is requested to serve as a mediator shall disclose the mediator's qualifications to mediate a dispute. . . .

[*Note:* UMA Sections 4–8 contain substantive prohibitions on a mediator disclosing confidential information, violation of which would be an ethical breach. — EDS.]

❖ **Excerpt from** *DELAWARE LAWYERS' RULES OF PROFESSIONAL CONDUCT*[*]

Rule 1.12 Former . . . Mediator or Other Third-Party Neutral

(a) Except as stated in paragraph (d), a lawyer shall not represent anyone in connection with a matter in which the lawyer participated personally and substantially as a . . . mediator . . . unless all parties to the proceeding give informed consent, confirmed in writing.

(b) A lawyer shall not negotiate for employment with any person who is involved as a party or as lawyer for a party in a matter in which the lawyer is participating personally and substantially as a judge or other adjudicative officer or as an arbitrator, mediator or other third-party neutral. . . .

(c) If a lawyer is disqualified by paragraph (a), no lawyer in a firm with which that lawyer is associated may knowingly undertake or continue representation in the matter unless:

(1) the disqualified lawyer is screened from any participation in the matter and is apportioned no part of the fee therefrom; and

(2) written notice is promptly given to the parties and any appropriate tribunal to enable them to ascertain compliance with the provisions of this rule. . . .

Questions

3. Any standard of conduct embodies a vision of what the mediation process should be. Can you classify the vision implicit in the Model Standards in terms of mediator styles — broad or narrow? Facilitative or evaluative/directive?
4. Do the Model Standards appear to discourage any particular approach to mediation?

---

* The Delaware Lawyers' Rules of Professional Conduct parallel the ABA Model Rules of Professional Conduct.

The Model Standards embody core values of mediation and for that reason are fairly noncontroversial. This does not mean, however, that they are easy to apply in practice. Ethical codes are clear about what a mediator must do in egregious situations, such as when she discovers that a case involves a close friend. Good mediators, however, have little difficulty deciding how to handle such situations. The more difficult problems arise when two ethical principles, each valid in itself, come into conflict and there appears to be no way to satisfy both of them. To understand how this can occur, consider the following problems.

1. Issues of Fairness

Among the most serious problems are issues of fairness. They arise most often in cases in which the disputants are proceeding pro se. Such situations present a tension between Sections I, II, and VI of the Model Standards.

Problems

5. In a private mediation of a divorce case, the husband appears without a lawyer and the wife has counsel. As the process goes forward, the husband becomes progressively more upset, sometimes making illogical arguments and reversing decisions that he had previously made. The mediator suggests to the husband that the mediation be adjourned so that he can rest and consult a lawyer, but the husband expresses a strong wish to "get it over with." He tells the mediator privately that "outside factors" make it important that he resolve the case quickly. The husband will not explain what they are, but the mediator suspects that he has formed a new relationship and is anxious to get out of his old one. The wife's counsel, sensing this, drives a very hard bargain, demanding that she receive 50 percent more alimony than court guidelines would suggest and 75 percent of the marital estate. The process continues for several hours. The husband becomes increasingly upset but refuses to stop. At one point, late in the afternoon during a private caucus, he says to the mediator in an agitated tone, "This can't go on any longer! I guess I've got to take their offer."

   How should the mediator respond? What problems could arise if the husband signs an agreement?

6. Professor Timothy Hedeen has noted numerous cases in which parties later sought to overturn mediated settlements on the ground that they were incompetent to bargain. He cites a case in which a plaintiff "who was on heart medicine tried to set aside a mediation settlement agreement by claiming that despite chest pains and fatigue he was told that he would have to continue in the mediation session until he was willing to reach agreement." [*Wilson v. Wilson*, 282 Ga. 728, 731-32 (2007)] Given the experiences of disputants in this case and cases such as *Olam*, he asks whether mediation requires advisory packaging such as

Warning: This dispute resolution process may involve long hours, many in small rooms alone (while the mediator meets with other parties) and without obvious opportunity to obtain food, drink or even necessary medications. (Hedeen 2009)

The suggestion was delivered with tongue in cheek, but what should a mediator who uses such techniques tell an unrepresented party? Draft a short disclosure or explanation.

7. A volunteer mediator is handling landlord-tenant cases in a community mediation program. A case is referred over by a court clerk. The defendant is a tenant facing eviction who is proceeding pro se. The landlord is a corporation represented by counsel. The tenant seems to have little understanding of what will happen in court if he does not settle. At one point shortly before lunch, the landlord offers a "final deal": He will allow the tenant two more months' occupancy, provided that all past rent is paid, the future rent is put into escrow, and the tenant agrees now to the entry of judgment for eviction at the end of the two months. The landlord's representative states that if the defendant does not accept the offer by 2 P.M., he will go back to court and ask the judge to rule on his request that the tenant be ordered to vacate the premises within seven days.

The tenant is unsure what to do, and in a private caucus asks the mediator, "Are they right about the law here? What do you recommend?" The mediator privately believes that if the tenant offers to pay rent into escrow, it is very likely that the court will give him at least six months to move, although for a judge to grant the landlord's request is not inconceivable.

a. What do the Model Standards counsel the mediator to do?
b. Does it make a difference that this case was referred to mediation by a court? Why?

2. Questions of Competence

Mediators sometimes encounter cases in areas in which they have not practiced or previously mediated — indeed, if their practices expand then such situations are quite likely. What obligation does a mediator have to disclose her lack of expertise to disputants? Article IV of the Model Standards and §9 of the UMA each deal with this issue.

Problem

8. You are a litigator with ten years of experience who occasionally acts as a mediator. You have handled a total of 15 mediations as a neutral and participated in dozens more as an advocate. You have been asked to mediate a bitter employment dispute involving an employee who says that she was sexually harassed by her supervisor and that management knew of the problem but "swept it under the rug." You do not handle employment

cases and have never mediated one, but you do read summaries of decided cases that are printed in your local legal newspaper, and these include court decisions in employment cases, among others.

   a. Do the Model Standards or the UMA require you to make any disclosure?

   b. Draft an outline of what you would tell the parties if you do make a disclosure.

   c. Does it make a difference if the parties are represented by counsel?

3. Repeat-Player Concerns

To be successful as a mediator one must have clients, and busy neutrals rely on repeat business. One national organization of mediators estimates, for example, that two thirds of the revenue of their successful panelists comes from cases involving lawyers who have mediated with that neutral at least three times during the past year. When does repeat business create unhealthy dependence? Sections II and III of the Model Standards and §9 of the UMA may apply to a mediator in such situations; other standards may apply to advocates.

Problem

9. Assume that you are a mediator and have mediated three cases involving Attorney Okawa. In each case the result was a settlement satisfactory to both sides, and at least one of the opposing lawyers in those other cases has selected you as a neutral again. Okawa now calls and asks you to mediate another case. He says that he has just about persuaded the other party to use you, but has not mentioned to them that he has previously mediated with you because it would require discussing the earlier cases, which his clients strongly want to be kept confidential. He asks that you not mention the prior mediations to the other party.

   a. What do the Model Standards require?

   b. What should you do?

4. Differences Between Attorney and Client

At times a mediator is dealing with people who are on the same side of a dispute but have widely divergent viewpoints. An attorney, for example, may not appear to be "on the same page" as her client about the risks of litigation or whether to take an offer. Ethical standards for both lawyers and mediators state that in such situations the client's wishes govern. However, parties often hire lawyers in part because they have more experience and are thought to have better judgment in highly charged situations, and many lawyers feel that clients sometimes become too emotional to make good decisions. And, it should be noted, commercial mediators know that attorneys, not clients, are their primary source of referrals. Sections I, III, and VI of the Model Standards for Mediators and §1.2 of the Model Rules for lawyers may apply to such situations.

Problems

10. Two parties have gone through nine hours of difficult mediation in a product liability case. The plaintiffs have alleged that their infant daughter died because of defects in a baby carriage manufactured by the defendant. The plaintiff couple is represented by experienced counsel and has held up well to the stress of the process. The maker of the carriage is represented by its CFO and outside counsel. The mediator's impression is that the CFO is being unrealistic about the company's legal exposure. The mediator has tried to bring other company officials into the case, but without success.

At 6 P.M. the mediator brings another offer to the defense, which is promptly rejected. At this point the neutral says to the defense team that although she's willing to keep talking, they appear to be close to deadlock and it may make sense to adjourn for the day. As the neutral leaves the room, defense counsel says she's going to the restroom. In a private conversation in the hallway, she asks the mediator to "get tough" with her client. The CFO, she says, has a visceral dislike of the plaintiff's lawyer. He is letting his determination to beat the other guy lead him into a position that is against the company's best interests. This is her firm's first case with this client, and she does not have the clout to make him listen to advice herself.

The neutral respects counsel's reputation as an advocate and privately agrees with her assessment of the situation. On her return she asks the defense team if it would be helpful for her to give her impressions of how a court would view the case if it had to be tried. The defense lawyer promptly responds that they would welcome her thoughts. The mediator delivers a hard-hitting evaluation that represents her honest assessment, emphasizing some jury sympathy factors that she believes the CFO is ignoring. The CFO does not respond to the mediator's comments, but appears to be a bit taken aback. The bargaining process resumes, and the disputants continue without a dinner break, munching on fast food. At 9:30 P.M., after several lengthy caucuses, the CFO agrees to essentially the same proposal that the mediator had brought to him at 6 P.M.

a. Did the lawyer act unethically in saying what she did to the mediator?

b. Did the mediator act improperly in her response? Why or why not?

11. Assume the same situation as in the prior problem, but that the reason for the CFO's refusal, in counsel's judgment, is that he is seriously overconfident about the company's chances of prevailing in litigation. The lawyer again meets the mediator in the hallway. She says that she selected the neutral, a retired judge, primarily for her credibility on legal issues and asks her to "bring out your gavel" and give her client a "hard" evaluation of the company's chances of success in court. It is clear to the mediator that the counsel wants her to give a reasoned evaluation, but also to strongly emphasize the risks of continuing in litigation. Would such a request be more or less troublesome than the prior problem?

5. Improper Conduct by Litigants

Ethical standards instruct mediators to support the parties' right to self-determination. But what should a mediator do if she learns that one party is acting improperly vis-à-vis another party, or that both parties are considering terms that appear likely to harm the interests of a person not represented in the process? Family mediators may find, for instance, that parents seek to satisfy other goals by agreeing to a visitation arrangement likely to create serious difficulties for their children. In commercial mediation the problem is more likely to arise when disputants create value for themselves by cheating an outsider — often the Internal Revenue Service. Mediators may not be asked to contribute ideas in such situations, but they are typically called on to carry proposals back and forth, advocate their acceptance, and act as scribes to memorialize dubious arrangements.

Problems

12. You are mediating a divorce case in which the parents are negotiating over custody and visitation of their two young children. As is common in family mediation, the process is occurring entirely in joint session, and lawyers are not present. You have stated that you will not talk with a party unless the other is present. However, after one session the wife returns to pick up a hat that she had left behind and, as she is leaving, mentions, "You know, I've just gotten a really attractive job offer, so I'm going to move out of state in two months. But I can't tell Jim — we've almost agreed on everything. If he knows I'm moving 2,000 miles away it'll blow everything up. Let's just work out the custody and visitation and all, and then I'll deal with it."

    Your impression is that the husband is conceding much more than he otherwise would on issues such as support, and has agreed to grant the wife sole legal custody of the children, in return for her agreement to generous visitation arrangements.
    a. What should you do in this situation?
    b. Does it matter if the mediation is being conducted under the auspices of a court-connected ADR program?
13. You are mediating a family dispute in which one of the spouses is self-employed. As part of the process the parties are mediating alimony, support for their seven-year-old child, and a division of assets. You have asked each spouse to prepare a financial statement, which they have exchanged. As the mediation goes forward, stray comments by the husband make you strongly suspect that he is hiding substantial cash income that is not reflected on his financial statement. What should you do?
14. A terminated executive has been mediating with his former employer for ten hours. After fierce bargaining in which the mediator has used her entire "bag of tricks," the defense has come painfully to a final offer of $180,000, but the plaintiff refuses to accept less than $200,000. A

key issue, from the plaintiff's perspective, is that he needs to come out of the process with $100,000 in the bank, net of his attorney's one-third contingency fee. Because the primary claim is for lost pay, however, any settlement will be treated by the company as back pay and therefore will be subject to payroll withholding. The effect is that the plaintiff would net only about $70,000, well below his minimum requirement. The plaintiff also has asserted a vague claim for emotional distress, but federal law bars plaintiffs from receiving settlement money tax-free unless an injury is physical in nature. "Mere" emotional distress is not sufficient to avoid a tax bite.

Suddenly the plaintiff attorney asks the mediator to take an idea to the defense: In a spell of depression caused by the firing, the plaintiff now remembers, he suffered from erectile dysfunction. Counsel didn't make it an explicit part of the claim because of the embarrassment factor, but it's there and it was a physical injury. The lawyer, with her client's approval, proposes allocating most of the settlement to this injury, allowing the plaintiff to receive his $100,000.

a. Is there a problem for the mediator in presenting this idea to the defense?

b. Assume that the mediator does so. Defense counsel laughs and says that this is the first she's heard about this malady, but if the plaintiff says he's dysfunctional, that's his problem. She says the proposal is OK with her client, as long as the plaintiff certifies the condition and assumes any risk that the IRS will contest it. The lawyers ask you to write down the terms they dictate summarizing the deal. Does this pose a problem?

c. Model Rule of Professional Conduct for Lawyers 8.3 states that "a lawyer who knows that another lawyer has committed a violation of the Rules of Professional Conduct that raises a substantial question as to that lawyer's honesty . . . shall inform the appropriate professional authority. . . ." Is it a violation of Rule 8.3 for a lawyer-mediator in the circumstances of Problem 13 not to report an apparent tax violation? For an argument that it is, see Rubin and Spector (2008).

C. Combining Practice as an Advocate and a Mediator

Experienced lawyers increasingly seek to combine their practices as litigators with work as mediators. Experienced attorneys find it refreshing to take on new roles, and if a lawyer is thinking of changing careers, this allows her to explore being a neutral without "quitting her day job." Even if an attorney decides to continue to practice law, experience as a mediator is likely to enhance her effectiveness as an advocate in the process.

1. Conflicts of Interest

One major issue for lawyers who alternate between the roles of advocate and neutral is the potential for conflicts of interest — the possibility that a party in a mediated case will be a past or future legal client of the mediator-lawyer or his firm. This is a particular concern in large law firms, where a single modestly compensated mediation can disqualify the entire firm from representing a party in a much more lucrative litigation matter.

Standards for neutrals call for disclosure in such situations. Model Standard III requires disclosure of "all actual and potential conflicts that are reasonably known to the mediator and could reasonably be seen as raising a question about the mediator's impartiality." If the conflict "might reasonably be viewed as undermining the integrity of the mediation," the Standards require a mediator to recuse himself.

The UMA also relies on disclosure: Section 9(a) requires a neutral "to make an inquiry . . . to determine whether there are any known facts that a reasonable individual would consider likely to affect the impartiality of the mediator [including] an existing or past relationship with a mediation party or foreseeable participant. . . ." If such facts exist, the UMA requires the neutral to disclose them. The UMA does not impose disqualification on the lawyer or his firm for violating this rule, but §9(d) does bar violators from asserting the mediation privilege.

The ABA's E2K Report deals explicitly with conflicts between roles, stating that "a lawyer shall not represent anyone in connection with a matter in which the lawyer participated personally and substantially as a . . . mediator. . . . " The rule goes on to provide that "If a lawyer is disqualified . . . no lawyer in a firm with which that [lawyer-mediator] is associated may knowingly undertake or continue representation in that matter." However, the firm may represent a mediator's client if the lawyer-mediator is screened from knowledge or fees associated with the case and the parties to the mediation are notified of the situation (E2K Report, §1.12 [a, c]). The issue is also addressed by other codes of ethics, in particular the CPR-Georgetown Rule (on the companion Web site to this book).

Question

5. A lawyer-mediator has no current or past attorney-client relationship with the parties in a case she is mediating, but she knows that lawyers in another department of her firm have approached the defendant in the case about serving as outside counsel. The firm has never received a case from the defendant but hopes to represent it in the future.
   a. What do the above standards require of the lawyer?
   b. Must she disqualify herself as mediator?
   c. If she mediates the case, is her firm disqualified from representing the party as counsel?

2. Role Confusion

The very fact that a mediator is an attorney may lead pro se litigants to believe that the neutral will provide them with legal advice. The E2K report proposed the following rule to deal with this issue:

> *Rule 2.4(b)* . . . A lawyer serving as a third-party neutral shall inform unrepresented parties that the lawyer is not representing them. When the lawyer knows or reasonably should know that a party does not understand the lawyer's role in the matter, the lawyer shall explain the difference between the lawyer's role as a third-party neutral and a lawyer's role as one who represents a client.
>
> *Comment:* . . . Where appropriate, the lawyer should inform unrepresented parties of the important differences between the lawyer's role as third-party neutral and a lawyer's role as a client representative, including the inapplicability of the attorney-client evidentiary privilege. . . .

Questions

6. In what types of disputes is the danger of confusion between the role of counsel and mediator likely to be greatest?
7. Assume that you are a lawyer who has agreed to mediate a dispute between a quarry and neighbors who are complaining about noise and dust from its operations. The company is represented by its business manager, the neighbors by a committee of three laypeople.
   a. Draft a statement that you could make to the participants to explain your role.
   b. When and how would you deliver it?
8. Consider these situations:
   a. Lawyer-mediator Garcia successfully mediates a case in which Allen sued Thompson. A month later, Allen approaches Garcia and asks her to represent her in a matter not related to the dispute that was mediated. Can Garcia accept the case? Must she follow any special procedure? Does it matter whether the matter, although unrelated in terms of subject matter, involves Thompson in any way?
   b. Suppose that Allen instead approaches Garcia's law partner, Black, to represent her in the new case. What, if anything, is required then?
   c. What if Thompson asks Garcia to represent her in pursuing a third-party defendant in the *Allen v. Thompson* dispute? The activities of the third party were discussed during the mediation, but the third party was not involved in the mediation process. Does Allen have to consent? If so, why?
   d. Lawyer-mediator Horwitz conducts a one-hour orientation session about the mediation process for a couple who are considering divorce, but they decide not to go ahead with the mediation. Two months later, the wife asks one of Horwitz's partners to represent her in the divorce, which is contested. Is the lawyer disqualified from doing so? Should she be? (See Bauerle v. Bauerle, 615 N.Y.S.2d 954 (1994), *later opinion* 616 N.Y.S.2d 275 [1994].)

The role of a mediator is inherently somewhat ambiguous, in that she has obligations toward both sides in disputes as well as to the process itself, and ethical standards for mediators tend to be quite general. This leaves even conscientious neutrals in doubt about what to do in particular situations. We hope to have convinced you that being an ethical mediator or lawyer is a process of continuing self-examination rather than simply a matter of learning a set of rules, and that you will continue to explore these issues for the rest of your professional life.

CHAPTER
16

Mixed and Changing Roles

Thomas J. Stipanowich

A. The Use of Mixed Processes: Med-Arb

Suppose that mediation does not produce a settlement. Is the only alternative to abandon settlement efforts and enter a separate adjudicatory process — either court or arbitration? Or is there a third way? In fact, disputing parties sometimes opt for a format in which a single neutral plays more than one role in a dispute, first nonbinding, but if that fails, a binding one. The most common mixed process is known as "med-arb." Here a person acts as mediator in the usual manner but, if the process fails to achieve a settlement, then "morphs" into the role of arbitrator in a binding, adjudicatory proceeding.

It is worth taking a moment to consider the vast difference between the roles of mediator and arbitrator. Although the parties may circumscribe an arbitrator's powers by agreement, in the typical commercial case the arbitrator is in effect a private judge. As a result, for the same person to act both as a mediator and arbitrator requires her to assume, successively, very different, almost contradictory mindsets toward a case. It is also important to appreciate the finality of the arbitration process. Students are often surprised to learn that except in extraordinary cases, proof that an arbitrator has misinterpreted the law or misunderstood the facts is *not* adequate grounds for a court to overturn the decision. As a result, successful appeals from arbitrators' decisions, or "awards," are quite rare.

There are nevertheless situations in which experienced litigators opt to have one person take on both roles. Indeed, mixing processes is quite common in other cultures: Recall, for example, how Asian arbitrators routinely interrupt arbitration processes to attempt to mediate disputes, returning to their arbitral role if conciliation is not successful.

Although commentators have expressed concerns about neutrals wearing multiple hats, the reality is that a significant percentage of active arbitrators and mediators sometimes serve in roles very different from the ones to which they were initially appointed. A few years ago a group of 128 commercial and employment mediators was queried about how frequently they change hats. They responded as follows:

When initially appointed as a mediator, I have arbitrated issues at the request
of the parties when mediation failed to resolve them:

Always	Often	About half the time	Occasionally	Never
1	3	0	45	78

I have mediated issues at the request of the parties even though I was initially
appointed as arbitrator:

Always	Often	About half the time	Occasionally	Never
1	3	3	46	69

Attorneys representing clients in mediation or arbitration are likely to be confronted with the option of employing a neutral in multiple roles, either as a matter of initial planning or midway through the course of a proceeding. It is therefore important to understand the relevant practical, legal, and ethical concerns raised by the use of the med-arb process.

1. Concerns About Med-Arb

Some neutrals regularly employ med-arb to resolve contractual disputes, and some institutional sponsors of ADR offer med-arb procedures. Advocates of such approaches argue that having a single neutral serve in both roles avoids the necessity of having to educate two separate neutrals about the same case, saving time and money. They also reason that if the parties are aware that their mediator will render a final and binding decision if a dispute is not settled, they will be encouraged to resolve the matter in mediation.

Despite the arguments put forward in favor of med-arb, many lawyers oppose mixing these roles. They argue, first, that the approaches of mediators and arbitrators are fundamentally incompatible: The arbitrator's interaction with the parties is confined to adversary hearings in which parties present and contest evidence. By contrast, mediation usually involves extensive ex parte communications with disputants. Parties who know that their mediator will become the ultimate decision maker should mediation fail may be less candid in communicating with her, undermining an important feature of the process. Moreover, there is always the possibility that the mediator-turned-arbitrator's view of the issues will be affected by information imparted confidentially that has never been subjected to cross-examination or rebuttal. Another concern is that the "big stick" wielded by a mediator-arbitrator will undermine party self-determination, especially if the intervener "telegraphs" her own views of the issues in dispute. Finally, many mediators have little or no experience conducting an arbitration hearing and may not be competent to take on this role.

If parties do wish a neutral to serve in mixed roles, they must address waiver issues, in particular the right of a party to challenge an arbitration award on the ground that the neutral had ex parte contacts with the other litigant. Otherwise, a med-arb arrangement may simply set the stage for a later motion to disqualify the arbitrator or vacate the arbitration award.

The difficulty of managing roles is exemplified by Township of Aberdeen v. Patrolmen's Benevolent Association, 669 A.2d 291 (N.J. S. Ct., App. Div. 1996), a decision regarding a med-arb arrangement in a public employment contract. When negotiations over a new collective bargaining agreement between the township and the police officers' union reached an impasse, the union petitioned for the initiation of arbitration. Prior to the start of hearings, the parties agreed to have the arbitrator attempt to mediate the dispute. When mediated negotiations fell apart, the case went to arbitration. The arbitrator rendered an award in favor of the union, largely on the basis of the township's shifting positions during mediation.

Although state law permitted med-arb, the court struck down the award on the basis that the arbitrator had improperly relied on information gained during the course of mediation and not presented in the arbitration hearing. The court reasoned that "parties should feel free to negotiate without fear that what they say and do will later be used against them," and that "[m]ediation would be a hollow practice if the parties' negotiating tactics could be used against them by the arbitrator in rendering the final decision." For the same reason that "it would be unthinkable for a trial court to base its decision on information disclosed in pretrial settlement negotiations," the court ruled that mediated negotiations preceding arbitration should be protected.

With these concerns in mind, consider your approach to the following scenarios based on actual cases.

Problems

1. You are representing a party in an arbitration proceeding before a panel of three neutral arbitrators in a significant commercial case. During a break in the prehearing conference that arbitrators typically hold with both sides, the chair states her sense that the circumstances might lend themselves to mediation. You would rather not mediate, because the strength of your case lies in your witnesses, and mediation will not allow them to be presented to full advantage. The other lawyer says, "That sounds like an excellent idea, Your Honor." What should you say or do?

2. You have been appointed to arbitrate various issues associated with a corporate "divorce." After several arbitration sessions have been held, the parties jointly inform you that they have discussed settlement and believe it would be productive to mediate. Given your familiarity with the issues and their comfort with you as a neutral, they ask you to act as mediator. What will you do?

2. The Need for Precision in Specifying Roles

Efforts to structure a workable and enforceable ADR agreement are sometimes undermined by a lack of precision. Such issues are particularly acute when a single individual is assigned multiple roles, or when the neutral's role may be characterized in more than one way.

These concerns are illustrated by *Ex parte Industrial Technologies*, 707 So. 2d 234 (Ala. 1997), a case in which a bank filed suit on a promissory note, and the borrower counterclaimed for conversion of certain equipment taken by the bank during collection efforts. Prior to trial the parties agreed to refer the matter to an out-of-court process, described as "mediation or arbitration," with a retired circuit judge named Snodgrass as "mediator/arbitrator." After the parties had engaged in settlement negotiations supervised by Snodgrass, they announced to him that they had entered into a "stipulation of agreement." The agreement acknowledged that the bank had converted the borrower's equipment, called for appraisers to determine the fair market value of the converted property, and provided for Snodgrass to determine the lost rental value of the property during the time it was improperly held by the bank.

Snodgrass subsequently issued an "Order" that directed the bank to pay the lost value of the property during the conversion period, plus the difference between the fair market value of the equipment at the time it was converted and its salvage value at the time of return. The borrower sought to enforce the outcome, which it termed a "binding arbitration order." The bank, however, argued that the proceeding was merely a mediation and that Snodgrass had no authority to issue the order.

The Alabama Supreme Court determined that both the parties' agreement and the subsequent process were fatally flawed. First of all, it was impossible to determine the precise character of the process agreed to by the parties, only that they apparently intended for Snodgrass to determine damages based on an agreed formula. Unfortunately, the court concluded, there was never a meeting of the minds about whether Snodgrass was empowered to award damages, other than to determine the lost rental value of the property. While the lack of precision in tailoring the original ADR agreement might have been overcome by the participants in their subsequent "stipulation of agreement," the second document merely exacerbated their mistakes.

Question

1. The borrower in the Snodgrass case has approached you, asking how it should draft an ADR clause in the future so as to avoid the problems identified by the *Industrial Technologies* court. What suggestions can you offer?

B. Changing Roles

We conclude with a look at important opportunities and challenges confronting lawyers as problem solvers today and in the future. After more than a quarter century of efforts to develop different and more effective ways of managing conflict, lawyers have the opportunity to approach the litigation experience in a wholly new way and achieve more satisfactory results for their clients. As advisors they are ideally poised to bring about a wholesale change in the culture of disputing. Understanding the value of mediation, they can pioneer interventions "upstream," such as the mediation of deals and the facilitation of long-term relationships. As citizens, they can play a leading role in creating a society that is transformed by the application of problem-solving and meditative approaches to individual disputes. As neutrals and as consumers of dispute resolution services, they must also face the challenges of an expanding and increasingly competitive field.

Throughout this book we have noted the primary role that judges have played in reordering the litigation landscape. Here, U.S. Magistrate Judge Wayne Brazil considers how, with a different mindset, a well-known legal case might have taken a very different path.

❖ Hon. Wayne Brazil, *ADR IN A CIVIL ACTION: WHAT COULD HAVE BEEN*
Disp. Resol. Mag. 25 (Summer 2007)

While there may be a dearth of ADR portrayed in recent fiction and nonfiction, it is not hard to imagine scenarios in which ADR could have drastically altered the stories we read. Jonathan Harr's book *A Civil Action* is just one example where wise counsel grounded in problem-solving approaches may have made for a happier ending for everyone involved. . . .

The litigation pitted 33 individual plaintiffs against large corporations. The plaintiffs alleged that by contaminating the local public water supply the defendants were responsible for the deaths of five children and for serious injuries and illnesses suffered by many other people.

After following a notoriously tortured course that included enormously expensive discovery and motion work, and a fractured, frustrating, highly publicized trial that was followed by visits to the court of appeals, the matter slid over a period of years toward a settlement that satisfied no one and did no real good. . . .

Many of the plaintiffs in *A Civil Action* had suffered in the most severe of ways, physically and emotionally. They felt both afraid and angry. They wanted answers. They wanted help dealing with the consequences of their tragedies. They wanted restoration of their community.

Lawyers with insufficient vision would have said that the plaintiffs were naive to think that they could achieve these kinds of ends through the legal system. Certainly the system as it was used in this litigation delivered precious little toward these ends. The transaction costs, not counting a dime of the settlement money that eventually was paid, appear to have been well above $15 million. But that huge investment of money and the eight years of the parties' time that the case consumed yielded a judgment and a settlement that brought no answers to the biggest questions, no emotional healing, no restoration of community, and no repair of severely damaged good will.

Instead of compounding the real-world tragedy with a litigation tragedy, a truly wise counselor would have helped the defendants understand, shortly after the severity of the harms became clear, that the circumstances presented an opportunity to build — to use ADR to create new, long-range value of great significance. Even if the only value that really mattered to defendants was profit, a good lawyer would have advised them to move in a very different direction, and to use ADR to do so. What could such a lawyer have helped his clients see?

Defendants knew that the Environmental Protection Agency had designated the area as a Superfund site and had been investigating the extent and sources of the obvious contamination for some time before the lawsuit was filed. Defendants knew that they were required by law to cooperate fully with the EPA investigation. Defendants knew that there was a substantial possibility that the EPA would order them to contribute toward the cost of clean up. The defendants knew that the U.S. Geological Survey also was studying contamination in the area. And defendants knew that if they were not truthful with federal authorities, the Department of Justice might well intervene. In fact, the Justice Department ultimately indicted one of the corporate defendants for just such untruthfulness, and that defendant ultimately pleaded guilty.

Defendants also could foresee that a case like this would generate a great deal of press coverage and that the defendants would not be favored in the sympathy slant; 77 percent of people polled in surveys taken as the trial date approached believed that the corporate defendants were responsible for the deaths of the children. Moreover, two of the three companies that ended up being pulled into the case knew they would remain in the community, employing local workers, working with local politicians, and needing local services.

Given these circumstances, a good lawyer would have counseled his client to use an ADR process early in the pretrial period, well before most of the litigation transaction costs were incurred and before the litigation process further alienated the plaintiffs and rigidified their positions. The goal would be to use ADR to explore what was most important to the plaintiffs themselves, as opposed to their lawyers, to un-demonize the defendants, and to reach out to the plaintiffs in a constructive and civic spirit that might make it possible to work out a settlement that would simultaneously save the defendants some money and yield potentially huge public relations benefits.

A good lawyer would have urged each corporate defendant to send its chairman or its CEO as its principal representative to the ADR session to demonstrate graphically that the company understood the gravity of the losses that plaintiffs had suffered. Direct participation by the highest level corporate officers was fully justified by financial considerations alone and could have considerably improved the odds that the companies' proposals would elicit favorable responses from the plaintiffs.

Good lawyers would have advised their companies' representatives to listen actively to the plaintiffs before making any statements of their own. After listening, each CEO or chairman would seek an opportunity to speak directly to the plaintiffs in the presence of their lawyers and the neutral. He or she would communicate, with compassion and concern, the following messages and proposals.

The company's representative would begin by telling the plaintiffs how sorry he or she and the company were about what had happened to them. The representative would acknowledge, directly and without qualification, that the plaintiffs had suffered severe losses, and that he or she was not about to claim that he or she could fully understand the pain they had experienced. Then, the speaker would say that he or she doesn't understand what the causes were of these tragedies, but he or she really wants to. The representative would explain that the scientists who advise him or her do not think that chemicals associated with the company's operations reached the wells or caused the illnesses, and he or she would emphasize that the company never would have permitted the operations to proceed if they had known that such tragic consequences would ensue. But he or she would concede that no one knows enough about the sources of these kinds of illnesses to be completely sure, so one of the representative's goals will be to support the effort to learn from these tragedies.

The representative would propose doing that in two ways. First, by cooperating fully with the EPA and all other governmental agencies who are investigating these matters. He or she would promise that his company would open its records and provide the authorities promptly with all the information and other forms of assistance they might seek. The second way his company, along with the other defendants, would support the search for answers would be to contribute several million dollars directly to support independent research into the possibility that there are environmental causes of leukemia.

In making these proposals, the spokesman for the company would emphasize that many of his or her valued and long-time employees live here, so it is partly on their behalf that she wants to help find out why this happened. But the representative also would emphasize that the company wants to be a responsible and valued member of this community and thus wants to identify with certainty any aspects of its operations that might cause harm to any other members of the community.

Next, the CEO or chairman would commit the company to contribute its full fair share to the cost of cleaning up the contaminated area. He or she would say that even though it is not clear that the contamination that has been found caused the cancer, it is clear that the contamination is a legitimate source of concern and must be removed. So the company, he or she would say, stands ready to pay toward the cost of the clean-up whatever share the government scientists conclude is appropriate. The representative also would say that the company would do everything it can to speed up the process of making that determination and to press for completion of the cleanup work on as fast a timetable as possible.

To evidence his or her good faith, the representative then would say that none of the commitments just described are contingent on the case settling. The company intends to go forward with them, including the commitment to support the cancer research, even if the parties cannot reach an agreement that would end the litigation.

Finally, on behalf of all defendants, the representative would offer money to help the plaintiffs meet the needs that the situation has created. He or she would start by acknowledging that no amount of money could adequately compensate for the personal losses that have been suffered. But he or she would also emphasize that the tragedies have had real and damaging consequences that require resources. The defendants collectively would like to provide some of those resources, and toward that end they would like to offer the plaintiffs, as a group, $10 million.

Making a package of proposals like this early in the pretrial period would have encouraged a perception that defendants were sincerely sorry about the plaintiffs' losses and wanted to act as responsible and engaged members of a shared community. The likelihood that the plaintiffs would not have responded positively to such an offer is small. With acceptance of this offer, defendants would have saved considerable money. They also would have generated considerable positive press and good will and avoided the years of bad press, to say nothing of the criminal indictment, that accompanied the protracted litigation. Moreover, they would have distinguished themselves from their competitors, encouraging investors to perceive them as possessing especially acute business judgment and thus being worthy of investment confidence.

There is a real chance that a scenario like the one just described could have occurred. That real possibility demonstrates that breadth of "solution-vision" can be an essential tool even in pursuing client interests that are limited to money. A lawyer who cannot help her client explore problem-solving solutions simply cannot be considered a wise counselor.

> Question
>
> 2. Do you think Judge Brazil's advice is realistic? What barriers might there be — on the defendants' side, the plaintiffs' side, or elsewhere — to successfully executing the scenario he contemplates?

C. Challenges Facing Lawyers as Neutrals

As we noted in Chapter 15, many lawyers have become increasingly active as mediators and arbitrators. Their activities are a natural outgrowth of the expanding use of ADR in the management of conflict in many different settings — trends that have fueled a growing debate over the need for credentialing mechanisms for those offering ADR services in public and private contexts. In the following excerpt a longtime leader in the ADR field offers reflections on trends and challenges facing lawyer-neutrals.

❖ Linda R. Singer, *The Lawyer as Neutral*

19 Alternatives 40 (January 2001)

For lawyers, a refreshing outcome of the increased use of ADR is the diversity of roles now available. From the role of zealous advocate in negotiation or litigation have evolved the roles of settlement counsel and advocate in a variety of forums. But what has most captured the imagination and enthusiasm of many lawyers is the role of neutral dispute resolver.

In the 1960s and 1970s, lawyers serving as neutrals were a fairly new phenomenon, and those of us who did had to struggle for acceptance. Most lawyers and judges then did not even know the difference between mediation and arbitration. Gradually, we caught the attention of a few courts, legislatures and agencies that were brave enough to experiment with alternative processes. Now, primarily as mediators, but possibly as arbitrators or case evaluators, neutral lawyers are likely to be a permanent fixture of the legal landscape.

The increased popularity of this field, however, means that it has attracted a large number of unevenly qualified entrants. As a result, a number of experienced practitioners have become concerned about whether the increased number of persons calling themselves ADR professionals has the necessary training and experience to do the job well. Legislators worry about the dearth of standards to protect the public from inferior services. Legal academics and bar associations question whether mediation or case evaluation constitutes the practice of law and thus, by implication, should be engaged in only by lawyers. Ethicists raise questions about rules — or the lack of all but the most primitive guidelines — and practitioners worry about ensuring the quality of services into the 21st century.

As a result of these often competing pressures, over the next 20 years the field will receive greater emphasis on credentialing, regulation, specialization and commercialization. . . .

In addition to enhanced credibility, one positive effect of specialization is the neutral's ability to ask probing questions and assist in developing sophisticated solutions in disputes in his or her specialized field.

The negative effect is more subtle. Lost may be the freshness, the tendency to question broadly and the lack of attachment to any particular option that a generalist can bring to a particular dispute because of his or her distance and objectivity. There also is the concern that substantive experts' knowledge can overwhelm the parties' ability to make their own choices, a feature that always has been a source of enhanced public confidence in the ADR process. Despite these concerns, retired judges may be the only group of generalists that remains into the next generation. I, for one, would consider such a swing toward specialization a loss.

Another result of a maturing profession is bound to be greater commercialization. As with the legal profession as a whole, some dispute resolution practices are being run like the businesses they have become. Advertisements and marketing seminars no longer are a rarity. For those of us who consider the profession a calling, this is a difficult adjustment. Although there still remain think tanks and nonprofits that are oriented toward community and public policy conflicts, the dominant mode of professional practice is likely to become a commercial enterprise. We must be on alert that a trend toward commercialization does not detract from the public's and institutions' confidence in the process.

Some lawyer-neutrals increasingly are applying their skills to streams of disputes, rather than to individual cases. Increasingly, our task is to design systems to resolve the multiple conflicts of large organizations and to resolve class actions by separating individual claims from issues of more general applicability and creating claims processes to negotiate mediate and/or arbitrate each claim when needed. . . . Some of us have begun to focus on the issues such processes raise, such as benchmarking, or creating settlement standards, while balancing the goal of efficiency (sometimes needing to resolve thousands of longstanding claims) against the goal of providing access to meaningful processes for people who are one-time players in a system in which everyone else (attorneys, institutional representatives, and mediators) is a repeat player.

From peace in the Middle East and Northern Ireland to huge class actions and the Microsoft Corp.'s antitrust suit, judges and politicians, as well as disputants, are growing ever more ready to consider settlement negotiations assisted by neutrals. This development, together with the teaching of conflict resolution in the schools, should lead to greater public awareness of what we do. . . .

Efficiency remains the value that accounts for much of the interest of advocates, the courts and the general public in our processes. At the same time the values of access, preserving relationships, individualizing processes and solutions, party participation, and the opportunities for us to apply our own creativity are what attracted most of us to neutral lawyering in the first place and what will keep our practices vibrant in the coming years.

Questions

3. Can lawyers bring value to resolving tensions among peoples of different races, religions, cultures, and genders? What skills or knowledge might be useful before tackling such types of conflicts? Jay Rothman suggests that identity-based conflict is particularly delicate because people draw meaning, safety, and dignity from their identities (Rothman 1997). Clearly, identity-based conflict is not something "resolved" once and for all with a peace treaty; it requires resources for continued dialogue and community building (Schneider 2006).
4. The South African Truth and Reconciliation Commission granted amnesty to certain offenders who acknowledged past crimes and allowed victims to confront their persecutors. If you were designing a post-war restorative justice system, what would your goals be? Would you try to promote accountability, punishment, healing, financial redress, community norm-affirmation, or other goals (Waldman 2004)?

D. Transforming the Community

Lawyers can apply meditative skills to serve their clients, their profession, and their community as peacemaking leaders. In the 1850s, Abraham Lincoln wrote:

> Discourage litigation. Persuade your neighbors to compromise whenever you can. Point out to them how the nominal winner is often a real loser, in fees, expenses, and waste of time. As a peacemaker the lawyer has a superior opportunity of being a good man. There will still be business enough.

Former Attorney General Janet Reno extols below the value lawyers add to society when they serve as peacemakers and problem solvers.

❖ **Hon. Janet Reno,** *Promoting Problem Solving and Peacemaking as Enduring Values in Our Society*

19 Alternatives 16 (January 2001)

[T]here is an understandable sense of accomplishment and pride within the dispute resolution community. We have witnessed significant growth in the use of dispute resolution by courts, corporations, government bodies, schools and communities. There is much to celebrate. There is also vast, untapped potential for appropriate dispute resolution in so many aspects of society. There are so many ways that dispute resolution can help to improve society's response to conflict. We must all learn how to be effective dispute resolvers and peacemakers. Indeed, our challenge for the 21st century is to make certain that dispute resolution becomes an enduring, ingrained value that is promoted and endorsed in all aspects of our society.

We begin this task by shedding the notion that "cookie-cutter" justice is sufficient, that one size or one process fits all when we deal with disputes. It is neither possible nor appropriate for the courts to serve as the single mechanism for resolving the many kinds of disputes that arise in this complex, busy age. Instead, we need to establish a range of options and processes to resolve disputes.

[The Association for Conflict Resolution has] adopted guidelines for organizations wishing to design integrated conflict management systems. These guidelines emphasize two important points. First, effective integrated systems provide multiple options for addressing conflict, including some processes that are rights-based and others that are interest-based. Second, the goal of these systems is to empower people by making them more competent to resolve their own disputes and to offer assistance, rather than decision-making, when direct negotiations are difficult.

I think we need to build on this splendid work by committing ourselves to create an integrated conflict management system for society as a whole. At one end of the spectrum, we must make sure that people have the skills to negotiate disputes one-on-one without intermediaries. In the middle, we need more skilled people to provide an entire spectrum of dispute resolution processes. Here, people can tailor the process to suit the dispute. Finally, we need to ensure that there is adequate access to courts and that our judiciary has the resources to resolve disputes that they are best suited to address. In a sense, this means that we must encourage all elements in our society to identify the best process to resolve their dispute, before moving to the substance of the dispute. This would allow us to be less adversarial at the outset. By using the techniques and skills of the mediator, we can be better listeners, more creative problem solvers and better able to have those difficult conversations with one another. In this manner, we can avoid some disputes and resolve others much earlier.

Our challenge, then, is to engage all sectors of the public in dispute resolution, and to obtain society's recognition that dispute resolution is a necessary life skill at which we should all be proficient, just like math, reading, and spelling. To reach this goal, there are several steps that we must take. First, we must begin with the formal, structured means for resolving conflict in our society, and make sure that the courts have programs to divert those cases into dispute resolution that can and should benefit from facilitated negotiation. We must make the Multi-door Courthouse a reality to ensure appropriate access for all and greater respect for our system of justice.

Second, governments, law firms, and frequent litigants should have programs in place to avoid litigation by using dispute resolution at the earliest possible time. . . . I hope that the efforts now being made by the federal government also will contribute to the growing recognition that dispute resolution is a vital skill every lawyer and senior manager must have.

Third, we need to do more with our law schools to promote problem solving in legal education. Our young lawyers need to be educated to recognize that even if the outcome of litigation is relatively certain, there is not always just one right answer to a problem. Our lawyers need to be educated in how not only to root out the facts of a problem, but to understand the context in which the problem arose. We should work with law schools to encourage curricula that include an expanded approach to traditional casebook study of appellate decisions, exposure to interdisciplinary insights, as well as academic courses and clinics that promote crosscutting skills such as negotiation, mediation, and collaborative practices.

Fourth, the use of these skills should not be limited to a select segment of our society. Our schools should teach our children skills in dispute resolution. Through such training, our children can participate in peer mediation programs and, we hope, carry these skills with them to use through later life. It is my vision that every teacher, every school administrator, and every community police officer who comes in contact with young people will be trained in mediation skills to deal with disputes that involve our youth. It is so exciting to see what is going on in schools all across the country when young people gain insight and confidence into genuine, nonviolent problem solving. It truly makes a difference in their lives.

Fifth, we should make use of dispute resolution concepts in creating community courts where justice is approached from a problem-solving perspective, and all relevant players participate in the resolution of a dispute. At the Midtown Community Court in Manhattan, the building contains not only courtrooms but also a social services center, a community service program with mediators, community probation officers, and other services. Local residents, community prosecutors, businesses, and social service providers collaborate with the criminal justice system to provide swift, visible justice that is augmented by drug treatment, health care, employment counseling, education, and other services. By holding defendants immediately accountable for their crimes while, at the same time, addressing the underlying problems that contribute to crime, we improve the community and free other courts to prosecute more serious crime.

Sixth, we must work hard at developing mechanisms that address the impact of technology in conflict resolution. We are communicating ever so rapidly; our economy is truly global, and the possibilities for new types of disputes have expanded exponentially. We must find ways to use these technologies to resolve conflict and to address those types of conflicts that would not have occurred in an earlier age. Each of these steps represents a formidable undertaking. But we know the way, because substantial progress has been made in every one of these areas. What is needed now is the commitment to see all of this as integrated and effective conflict management for our society, where dispute resolution skills for everyone — participants, neutrals, and bystanders — are valued because of their contribution to the overall health of our institutions, organizations, and communities.

Conclusion

As this final chapter has suggested, the revolution in approaches to legal conflict that inspired the writing of this book continues apace. It will become progressively more important that lawyers provide their clients with the full benefit of a range of tools for resolving disputes, in particular mediation. This is true for attorneys who advise or advocate on behalf of businesses and government institutions, as well as those representing domestic partners, employees, or consumers and those who take on formal roles as mediators.

We hope this book has provided you with the fundamental understanding of one of the most important new tools that lawyers can use to serve clients and promote justice. If we have not led you to all of the answers, we hope we have equipped you to ask the right questions.

APPENDIX

The appendix to this book is entirely Web based and is shared with Resolving Disputes: Theory, Practice, and Law, Second Edition. This makes it possible for students and teachers to have access to more resources and download and edit materials to meet their individual needs. To access the combined Appendix, enter the following URL:

www.aspenlawschool.com/books/folberg_resolvingdisputes

The contents of the Appendix, which will be updated from time to time, include the following :

Negotiation

- Ethical Guidelines for Settlement Negotiations (ABA)
- Federal Rule of Civil Procedure 68
- Model Rules of Professional Conduct (ABA)

Mediation

- Legislation
  - ADR Act of 1998
  - Uniform Mediation Act (NCCUSL)
- Rules
  - Commercial Mediation Procedures (AAA)
  - CPR Mediation Procedure (CPR)
  - Ethics 2000 ("E2K") Report (ABA)
  - Model Rule of Professional Conduct for the Lawyer as Third-Party Neutral (CPR-Georgetown)
  - 2005 Model Standards for Mediators (AAA, ABA, and ACR)
  - Model Standards of Practice for Family and Divorce Mediators (ACR)
  - Sample Mediation Agreements

Arbitration

- Legislation
  - Federal Arbitration Act
  - Convention on the Recognition and Enforcement of Foreign Arbitral Awards

- Model Legislation for Potential State Adoption
  - Uniform Arbitration Act (1956)
  - Revised Uniform Arbitration Act (2000)
  - Revised Uniform Arbitration Act with Commentary
- Rules
  - Code of Ethics for Arbitrators in Commercial Disputes (AAA and ABA)
  - Commercial Arbitration Rules and Mediation Procedures (AAA)
  - Arbitration Appeal Procedure (CPR)
  - Comprehensive Arbitration Rules (JAMS)
  - Optional Appeal Procedure (JAMS)
  - Principles for ADR Provider Organizations (CPR-Georgetown)
  - Rules for Non-Administered Arbitration (CPR)
  - Rules of Arbitration (ICC)
  - Streamlined Arbitration Rules (JAMS)
- Protocols
  - Consumer Due Process Protocol (AAA)
  - Consumer Arbitration Minimum Standards (JAMS)
  - Employment Minimum Standards (JAMS)

BIBLIOGRAPHY AND REFERENCES

BOOKS AND ARTICLES

The titles of books are in italics and the titles of articles are in quotes.

Aaron, Marjorie Corman (1995) "The Value of Decision Analysis in Mediation Practice," 11 *Negot. J.* 123.

Aaron, Marjorie Corman (2009) "Merits Barriers: Evaluation and Decision Analysis" in D. Golann, *Mediating Legal Disputes* 145

Aaron, Marjorie Corman, & David P. Hoffer (1996) "Decision Analysis as a Method of Evaluating the Trial Alternative," in D. Golann, *Mediating Legal Disputes* 307. Boston: Aspen Publishing.

ABA Sub-Committee on Alternative Means of Dispute Resolution (1986) "The Effectiveness of the Mini-Trial," in *Resolving Complex Commercial Disputes: A Survey.* Chicago: American Bar Association.

Abramson, Harold I. (2010) *Mediation Representation: Advocating in a Problem-Solving Process.* Notre Dame, Ind.: NITA.

Adamowicz, Viktor L., et al (1999) "Experiments on the Difference Between Willingness to Pay and Willingness to Accept," 69 *Land Econ.* 86.

Adler, Robert S. (2005) "Flawed Thinking: Addressing Decision Biases In Negotiation," 20 Ohio St. J. on Dispute Reol. 683.

Adler, Robert S., & Elliot M. Silverstein (2000) "When David Meets Goliath: Dealing with Power Differentials in Negotiations," 5 *Harv. Negot. L. Rev.* 1 (Spring).

Albrecht, Karl & Steve Albrecht (1993) *Added Value Negotiating: The Breakthrough Method for Building Balanced Deals.* Homewood, Ill.: Irwin.

Alexander, Janet Cooper (1991) "Do the Merits Matter? A Study of Settlements in Securities Class Actions," 43 Stan. L. Rev. 497.

Alfini, James J. (1999) "Settlement Ethics and Lawyering in ADR Proceedings: A Proposal to Revise Rule 4.1," 19 *N. Ill. Univ. L. Rev.* 255.

Alfini, James J. (2001) "Ethics 2000 Leaves Mediation in Ethics 'Black Hole,' "7 *Disp. Resol. Mag.* 3 (Spring).

Alfini, James J., & Eric R. Galton, eds. (1998) *ADR Personalities and Practice Tips.* Washington, D.C.: ABA Section of Dispute Resolution.

Ambrose, Stephen E. (1996) *Undaunted Courage.* New York: Touchstone Books.

Arnold, Tom (1995) "Twenty Common Errors in Mediation Advocacy,"13 *Alternatives* 69.

Arnold, Tom (1999) "Client Preparation for Mediation," 15 *Corporate Counsel's Q.* 52 (April).

Arrow, Kenneth J. et al., eds. (1995) *Barriers to Conflict Resolution.* New York: W.W. Norton.

Austin, Elizabeth and Leslie Whitaker (2001) *The Good Girl's Guide to Negotiating: How to Get What You Want at the Bargaining Table.* Boston: Little, Brown.

Austin, William (1980) "Friendship and Fairness: Effects of Type of Relationship and Task Performance on Choice of Distribution Rules," 6 *Pers. & Soc. Psychol. Bull.* 402.

Axelrod, Robert M. (1984) *The Evolution of Cooperation.* New York: Basic Books.

Ayres, Ian (1991) "Fair Driving: Gender and Race Discrimination in Retail Car Negotiations," 104 *Harv. L. Rev.* 817.

Ayres, Ian (1995) "Further Evidence of Discrimination in New Car Negotiations and Estimates of Its Cause," 94 *Michigan L. Rev.* 109.

Ayres, Ian, & Barry J. Nalebuff (1995) "The Role of Fairness Considerations and Relationships in a Judgmental Perspective of Negotiation," Kenneth Arrow, et al., eds. *Barriers to Conflict Resolution.* New York: W.W. Norton.

Ayres, Ian, & Barry J. Nalebuff (1997) "Common Knowledge as a Barrier to Negotiation," 44 *U.C.L.A. L. Rev.* 1631.

Babcock, Linda, & Sara Laschever (2003) *Women Don't Ask: Negotiation and the Gender Divide.* Princeton, N.J.: Princeton University Press.

Bahadoran, Sina (2000) "A Red Flag: Mediator Cultural Bias in Divorce," 18 *Mass. Fam. L.J.* 69.

Baird, Douglas G., Robert H. Gertner, & Randal C. Picker (2002) *Game Theory and the Law,* Cambridge, Mass.: Harvard University Press.

Bartos, Otomar (1978) "Simple Model of Negotiation," William Zartman, ed. *The Negotiation Process.* Thousand Oaks: Sage.

Baruch Bush, Robert A. (1984) "Dispute Resolution Alternatives and the Goals of Civil Justice: Jurisdictional Principles for Process Choice," 1984 *Wis. L. Rev.* 893.

Bazerman, Max H., & Margaret A. Neale (1992) *Negotiating Rationally.* Free Press.

Bennett, Mark D., & Michele S.G. Hermann (1996) *The Art of Mediation.* Notre Dame, Ind.: NITA.

Bentham, Jeremy (1996) *An Introduction to the Principles of Morals and Legislation.* Oxford: Oxford University Press.

Bercovitch, Jacob (2002) *Studies in International Mediation.* New York: Palgrave Macmillan.

Berger, Vivian (2003) "Employment Mediation in the Twenty-First Century: Challenges in a Changing Environment," 5 *U. Pa. J. Lab. & Empl. L.* 487 (Spring).

Bernard, Phyllis, & Bryant Garth, eds. (2002) *Dispute Resolution Ethics: A Comprehensive Guide.* Washington, D.C.: ABA Section of Dispute Resolution.

Berryman-Fink, Cynthia, & Claire C. Brunner (1985) "The Effects of Sex of Source and Target on Interpersonal Conflict Management Styles," 53 *S. Speech Comm. J.* 38.

Bingham, Gail (2002) "The Environment in the Balance: Mediators Are Making a Difference," 2 *ACResolution* 21 (Summer).

Birke, Richard (1999) "Reconciling Loss Aversion and Guilty Pleas," 1999 *Utah L. Rev.* 205.

Birke, Richard (2000) "Settlement Psychology: When Decision-Making Processes Fail," 18 *Alternatives* 203 (December).

Birke, Richard, & Craig R. Fox (1999) "Psychological Principles in Negotiating Civil Settlements," 4 *Harv. Negot. L. Rev.* 1 (Spring).

Birkoff, Juliana, & Robert Rack, with Judith M. Filner (2001) "Points of View: Is Mediation Really a Profession?" 8 *Disp. Res. Mag.* 10 (Fall).

Bleemer, Russell, ed. (2005) *Mediation: Approaches and Insights.* New York: Juris Publishing.

Bohnet, Iris, & Bruno S. Frey (1999) "The Sound of Silence in Prisoner's Dilemma and Dictator Games," 38 *J. Econ. Behav. & Org.* 43.

Bordone, Robert C. (1998) "Electronic Online Dispute Resolution: A Systems Approach — Potential, Problems, and a Proposal," 3 *Harv. Negot. L. Rev.* 175

Bowling, Daniel, & David Hoffman (2000) "Bringing Peace into the Room: The Personal Qualities of the Mediator and Their Impact on the Mediation," 16 *Negot. J.* 5.

Bowling, Daniel, & David Hoffman, eds. (2003) *Bringing Peace into the Room.* San Francisco: Jossey-Bass.

Brams, Steven J. & Alan D. Taylor (1996) *Fair Division: From Cake-Cutting to Dispute Resolution.* Cambridge, England: Cambridge University Press.

Brams, Steven J., & Alan D. Taylor (2000) *The Win-Win Solution: Guaranteeing Fair Share to Everybody.* New York: W.W. Norton.

Brazil, Wayne D. (1998) "Why Should Courts Offer Non-binding ADR Services?" 16 *Alternatives* 65.

Breslin, J. William, & Jeffrey Z. Rubin, eds. (1991) *Negotiation Theory and Practice.* Cambridge, Mass.: Program on Negotiation.

Brett, Jeanne M. (2000) "Culture and Negotiation," 35 *Intl. J. Psychol.* 97, 273, Collected References.

Brett, Jeanne M., Zoe I. Barsness, & Stephen B. Goldberg (1996) "The Effectiveness of Mediation: An Independent Analysis of Cases Handled by Four Major Service Providers," 12 *Negot. J.* 259 (July).

Buhring-Uhle, Christian (1996) *Arbitration and Mediation in International Business.* Boston: Kluwer Law International.

Bunker, Barbara Benedict, & Jeffrey Z. Rubin, eds. (1995) *Conflict Cooperation & Justice: Essays Inspired by the Work of Morton Deutsch.* San Francisco: Jossey-Bass.

Burton, Lloyd et al. (1991) "Feminist Theory, Professional Ethics, and Gender Related Distinctions in Attorney Negotiation Styles, 1991 *J. Disp. Resol.* 199.

Bush, Robert A. Baruch, & Joseph P. Folger (2004) *The Promise of Mediation: The Transformative Approach to Conflict.* San Francisco: Jossey-Bass.

Bush, Robert A. Baruch, & Sally Ganong Pope (2004) "Transformative Mediation: Principles and Practice in Divorce Mediation," in J. Folberg, et al., eds., *Divorce and Family Mediation.* New York: Guilford Press.

Camp, Jim (2002) *Start With No.* New York: Crown Business.

Carroll, Eileen, & Karl Mackie (2000) *International Mediation — The Art of Business Diplomacy.* The Hague: Kluwer Law International.

Carter, Jimmy (1982) *Keeping Faith: Memoirs of a President.* New York: Bantam Books. Carter, Jimmy (2003) *Negotiation: The Alternative to Hostility.* Macon, GA: Mercer Univ. Press.

Chester, Ronald (1999) "Less Law, But More Justice?: Jury Trials and Mediation as Means of Resolving Will Contests," 37 *Duq. L. Rev.* 173 (Winter).

Chew, Pat K., ed. (2001) *The Conflict & Culture Reader.* New York: New York University Press.

Cialdini, Robert B. (2001) "Persuasion," 284 *Scientific American* 76.

Cialdini, Robert B. (2001) *Influence: Science and Practice* (4th. ed.). Allyn & Bacon.

Cloke, Kenneth (2000) *Mediating Dangerously.* San Francisco: Jossey-Bass.

Cobb, Sarah, & Janet Rifkin (1991) "Practice and Paradox: Deconstructing Neutrality in Mediation," 16 *Law & Soc. Inquiry* 35.

Coben, James and Thompson, Peter (2006) "Disputing Irony: a Systematic Look at Litigation About Mediation," 11 Harv. Neg.L.Rev 43.

Cohen, Herb (2003) *Negotiate This!: By Caring, But Not That Much.* New York: Warner Business Books.

Cohen, Jonathan (2001) "When People are the Means: Negotiating with Respect," 14 *Geo. J. Legal Ethics* 739.

Cohen, Jonathan R. (1999) "Advising Clients to Apologize," 72 *S. Cal. L. Rev.* 1009.

Cohen, Jonathan R. (2000) "Apologizing for Errors," *Disp. Res. Mag.* (Summer).

Cohen, Raymond (1999) *Negotiating Across Cultures: International Communication in an Interdependent World.* Washington, D.C.: United States Institute of Peace.

Cole, Sarah R., Craig McEwen, & Nancy H. Rogers (2001) *Mediation: Law, Policy & Practice.* St. Paul, Minn.: West Publishing..

Cole, Sarah Rudolph (2000) "Managerial Litigants? The Overlooked Problem of Party Autonomy in Dispute Resolution," 51 *Hastings L.J.* 1199.

Colosi, Thomas R. (2001) *On and Off the Record: Colosi on Negotiation* (2d. ed.). New York: American Arbitration Association.

Condlin, Robert J. (1992) "Bargaining in the Dark: The Normative Incoherence of Lawyer Dispute Bargaining Role, 51 *Md. L. Rev.* 1.

Contuzzi, Peter (2000) "Should Parties Tell Mediators Their Bottom Line?" 8 *Disp. Res. Mag.* 30 (Spring).

Cooley, John W. (2000) *The Mediator's Handbook.* Notre Dame, IN: NITA.

Cooley, John W. (2002) *Mediation Advocacy.* Notre Dame, Ind.: NITA.

Cooper, Christopher (2000) "Police Mediators: Rethinking the Role of Law Enforcement in the New Millennium," 7 *Disp. Res. Mag.* 17 (Fall).

Cooter, Robert, et al. (1982) "Bargaining in the Shadow of the Law: A Testable Model of Strategic Behavior," 11 *J. Legal Stud.* 225.

CPR Institute of Dispute Resolution (2001) *Into the 21st Century: Thought Pieces on Lawyering, Problem Solving, and ADR.* New York: CPR Institute.

Craver, Charles B. (1997) "Negotiation Ethics: How to Be Deceptive Without Being Dishonest/ How to Be Assertive Without Being Offensive," 38 *Tex. L. Rev.* 713.

Craver, Charles B. (2001) *Effective Legal Negotiation and Settlement* (5th. ed.). Newark: LEXIS.

Craver, Charles B., & David W. Barnes (1999) "Gender, Risk Taking, and Negotiation Performance," 5 *Mich. J. Gender & L.* 299.

Creo, Robert A. (2001) "Emerging from No Man's Land to Establish a Bargaining Model," 19 *Alternatives* 191 (September).

Cronin-Harris, Catherine (1997) *Building ADR into the Corporate Law Department: ADR Systems Design.* New York: CPR Institute.

Croson, Rachel, & Nancy Buchan (1999) "Gender and Culture: International Experimental Evidence from Trust Games," 89 *Am. Econ. Rev.* 386.

Crystal, Nathan M. (1998) "The Lawyer's Duty to Disclose Material Facts in Contract or Settlement Negotiations," 87 *Ky. L. J. 1055.*

Curtis, Dana (1998) "Reconciliation and the Role of Empathy," in J. Alfini & E. Galton, eds., *ADR Personalities and Practice Tips.* Washington, D.C.: ABA Section of Dispute Resolution.

Curtis, Dana, & John Toker (2000) "Representing Clients in Appellate Mediation: The Last Frontier," 1 *JAMS Alert.* 3 (December).

Dauer, Edward A. (1994) *Manual of Dispute Resolution.* San Francisco: Shepard's/McGraw-Hill.

Dauer, Edward A. (2000) "Justice Irrelevant: Speculations on the Causes of ADR," 74 *So Cal. L. Rev.* 83.

Dauer, Edward A. (2005) "Apology in the Aftermath of Injury: Colorado's 'I'm Sorry' Law, "34 *COLAW* 47.

Davis, Benjamin G. (2005) "International Commercial Online and Offline Dispute Resolution: Addressing Primacism and Universalism," 4 *J. Amer. Arb.* 79.

Davis, Morton D. (1997) *Game Theory: A Nontechnical Introduction.* Mineola, N.Y.: Dover.

Dawson, Roger (2001) *Secrets of Power Negotiating* (2d. ed.). Franklin Lakes, N.J.: Career Press.

Deason, Ellen E. (2001) "Enforcing Mediated Settlement Agreements: Contract Law Collides with Confidentiality," 35 *U.C. Davis L. Rev.* 33 (November).

Deason, Ellen E. (2002) "Predictable Mediation Confidentiality in the U.S. Federal System," 17 *Ohio. St. J. on Disp. Resol.* 239.

Deason, Ellen E. (2005) "Procedural Rules for Complementary Systems of Litigation and Mediation — Worldwide," 80 *Notre Dame L. Rev.* 553.

Deaux, Kay (1976) *The Behavior of Women and Men* Monterey, CA: Brooks/Cole Publishing.

Delgado, Richard (1988) "ADR and the Dispossessed: Recent Books About the Deformalization Movement," 13 *Law & Soc. Inquiry* 145.

Deutsch, Morton (1973) *The Resolution of Conflict.* New Haven, CT.: Yale University Press.

Deutsch, Morton, & Peter T. Coleman, eds. (2000) *The Handbook of Conflict Resolution.* San Francisco: Jossey-Bass.

Dixit, Avinash K., & Barry J. Nalebuff (1991) *Thinking Strategically: The Competitive Edge in Business, Politics, and Everyday Life.* New York: W.W. Norton & Co.

Donahey, M. Scott (1995) "The Asian Concept of Conciliator/Arbitrator: Is It Translatable to the Western World?" 10 *Foreign Inv. L. J.* 120.

Dore, Laurie Krath (1999) "Secrecy by Consent: The Use and Limits of Confidentiality in the Pursuit of Settlement," 74 *N.D. L. Rev.* 283.

Dunnigan, Alana (2003) "Comment — Restoring Power to the Powerless: The Need to Reform California's Mandatory Mediation for Victims of Domestic Violence," 37 *U.S.F. L. Rev.* 1031.

Eckel, Catherine & Philip Grossman (1996) "The Relative Price of Fairness: Gender Differences in a Punishment Game," 30 *J. Econ. Behav. & Org.* 143.

Eckel, Catherine, & Philip Grossman (1998) "Are Women Less Selfish Than Men?: Evidence from Dictator Experiments," 108 *Econ. J.* 726.

Edwards, Harry, & James J. White (1977) *The Lawyer as Negotiator.* St. Paul: West.

Edwards, T. Harry (1986) "Alternative Dispute Resolution: Panacea or Anathema?" 99 *Harv. L. Rev.* 668 (January).

Epstein, Lynn A. (1997) "Post-Settlement Malpractice: Undoing the Done Deal," 43 *Cath. U. L. Rev.* 459 (Winter).

Erickson, Stephen K., & Marilyn S. McKnight (2001) *The Practitioner's Guide to Mediation: A Client Centered Approach.* San Francisco: Jossey-Bass.

Fairhurst, Gail T., & Robert A. Sarr (1996) *The Art of Framing.* San Francisco: Jossey-Bass.

Fazzi, Cindy (2005) "The Five Golden Rules of Dispute Resolution: Gain the Edge!" 59 Disp. Resol. J. 88.

Fehr, Ernst, & Simon Gachter (2000) "Fairness and Retaliation: The Economics of Reciprocity," 14 *J. Econ. Persp.* 159.

Felder, Raoul (2004) *Bare-Knuckle Negotiation.* Hoboken, N.J.: John Wiley & Sons.

Findings and Proposals," 26 *U.S.F. L. Rev.* 343.

Fisher, Roger (1991) "Negotiating Power: Getting and Using Influence," William J. Breslin, & Jeffrey Z. Rubin, eds. *Negotiation Theory and Practice.*

Fisher, Roger, & Danny Ertel (1995) *Getting Ready to Negotiate: The Getting to Yes Workbook.* New York: Penguin.

Fisher, Roger, & Scott Brown (1988) *Getting Together: Building a Relationship that Gets to Yes.* Boston: Houghton Mifflin.

Fisher, Roger, & William J. Ury, with Bruce Patton (1991) *Getting to Yes* (2d ed.). New York: Penguin.

Fisher, Roger, et al. (1994) *Beyond Machiavelli: Tools for Coping with Conflict.* Cambridge, Mass.: Harvard University Press.

Fisher, Tom (2001) "Advice by Any Other Name," 29 *Conflict Resol. Q.* 107.

Fiss, Owen M. (1984) "Against Settlement," 93 *Yale L.J.* 1073.

Fobia, Cynthia S., & Jay J. Christensen-Szalanski (1993) "Ambiguity and Liability Negotiations: The Effects of the Negotiator's Role and the Sensitivity Zone," 54 *Org. Behav. & Hum. Decision Proc.* 277.

Folberg, Jay (1982) "Divorce Mediation: The Emerging American Model," paper presented at the Fourth Ann. Conf. of the Int'l Socy. for Family Law, Harv. U (June).

Folberg, Jay (1985) "Mediation of Child Custody Disputes," 19 *Colum. J.L. Soc. Probs.* 413.

Folberg, Jay (1996) "Certification of Mediators in California: An Introduction," 30 *U.S.F. L. Rev.* 609 (Spring).

Folberg, Jay (2003) "The Continuing History of Conflict Resolution Practice," *ACR Res.*

Folberg, Jay, & Alison Taylor (1984) *Mediation: A Comprehensive Guide to Resolving Conflicts Without Litigation.* San Francisco: Jossey-Bass.

Folberg, Jay, Ann L. Milne, & Peter Salem (eds.) (2004) *Divorce and Family Mediation — Models, Techniques and Applications.* New York: Guilford Press.

Folberg, Jay, Joshua Rosenberg & Robert Barrett (1992) "Use of ADR in California Courts:

Frascogna, Jr., X.M., & H. Lee Hetherington (2001) *The Lawyer's Guide to Negotiation: A Strategic Approach to Better Contracts and Settlements.* Chicago: ABA.

Freedman, Lawrence R., & Michael L. Prigoff (1986) "Confidentiality in Mediation: The Need for Protection," 2 *Ohio St. J. on Disp. Resol.* 37.

Freund, James C. (1992) *Smart Negotiating: How to Make Good Deals in the Real World.* New York: Simon & Schuster.

Friedman, Gary and Jack Himmelstein (2008) *Challenging Conflict: Mediation Through Understanding.* Chicago: American Bar Association.

Fuller, Lon (1971) "Mediation: Its Forms and Functions," 44 *S. Cal. L. Rev.* 305 (February).

Fuller, Lon (1978) "The Forms and Limits of Adjudication," 92 *Harv. L. Rev.* 353.

Galanter, Marc & Mia Cahill (1994) "Most Cases Settle: Judicial Promotion and Regulation of Settlements," 46 *Stan. L. Rev.* 1339.

Galanter, Marc (1983) "Reading the Landscape of Disputes: What We Know and Don't Know (and Think We Know) About Our Allegedly Contentious and Litigious Society," 31 *UCLA L. Rev.* 4 (October).

Galanter, Marc, & Joel Rogers (1991) *The Transformation of American Business Disputing: Some Preliminary Observation.* Madison, WI: University of Wisconsin Law School.

Galton, Eric (1994) *Representing Clients in Mediation.* Dallas, Tex.: American Lawyer Mediation.

Gelfand, Michele J., & Sophia Christakopoulou (1999) "Culture and Negotiator Cognition: Judgment Accuracy and Negotiation Processes in Individualistic and Collectivistic Cultures," 79 *Org. Behav. & Hum. Decision Proc.* 248.

Geronemus, David (2001) "The Changing Face of Commercial Mediation," 19 *Alternatives* 38 (January).

Gifford, Donald G. (1989) *Legal Negotiation: Theory and Applications.* St. Paul: West.

Gilligan, Carol (1982) *In a Different Voice: Psychological Theory and Women's Development.* Cambridge: Harvard University Press

Gilson, Ronald J. (1984) "Value Creation by Business Lawyers: Legal Skills and Asset Pricing," 94 *Yale L. J.* 239.

Gilson, Ronald J., & Robert H. Mnookin (1995) "Disputing Through Agents: Cooperation and Conflict Between Lawyers in Litigation," 94 *Colum. L. Rev.* 509.

Goh, Bee Chen (1998) "Sino-Western Negotiating Styles," 7 Canterbury L. Rev. 82.

Golann, Dwight (1989) "Making Alternative Dispute Resolution Mandatory: The Constitutional Issues," 68 *Or. L. Rev.* 487.

Golann, Dwight (1996) *Mediating Legal Disputes: Effective Strategies for Lawyers and Mediators.* New York: Aspen Publishing.

Golann, Dwight (2000) "Variations in Style: How — and Why — Legal Mediators Change Style in the Course of a Case," 2000 *J. Disp. Resol.* 40.

Golann, Dwight (2001) "Cognitive Barriers to Effective Negotiation, 6 *ADR Currents* 6 (September).

Golann, Dwight (2002) "Is Legal Mediation a Process of Reconciliation — Or Separation? An Empirical Study, and Its Implications," 7 *Harv. Negot. L. Rev.* 301.

Golann, Dwight (2004) "Death of a Claim: The Impact of Loss Reactions on Bargaining," 20 *Negot. J.* 539.

Golann, Dwight (2004) "How to Borrow a Mediator's Powers," 30 *Litig.* 41 (Spring).

Golann, Dwight (2009) *Mediating Legal Disputes: Effective Strategies for Neutrals and Advocates.* Chicago: American Bar Association.

Golann, Helaine, & Dwight Golann (2003) "Why Is It Hard for Lawyers to Deal with Emotional Issues?" 9 *Disp. Res. Mag.* 26 (Winter).

Goldberg, Stephen B. (2005) "How Interest-based, Grievance Mediation Performs Over the Long Term," 59 *J. Disp. Resol.* 8.

Goldberg, Stephen B. (2006) "Mediating the Deal: How to Maximize Value by Enlisting a Neutral's Help At and Around the Bargaining Table" 24 Alternatives 147.

Goldberg, Stephen B. and Margaret L. Shaw (2008) "Further Investigation into the Secrets of Successful and Unsuccessful Mediators," 26 *Alternatives 149.*

Goleman, Daniel (1996) *Emotional Intelligence.* Vancouver: Raincoast.

Goodpaster, Gary (1993) "Rational Decision-Making in Problem-Solving Negotiation: Compromise, Interest-Valuation, and Cognitive Error," 8 *Ohio St. J. on Disp. Res.* 299.

Goodpaster, Gary (1997) *A Guide to Negotiation and Mediation.* Irvington-on-Hudson, N.Y.: Transnational.

Grant, Malcolm J., & Vello Sermat (1969) "Status and Sex of Other as Determinants of Behavior in a Mixed-Motive Game," 12 *J. Personality & Soc. Psych.* 151.

Green, Eric (1986) "A Heretical View of the Mediation Privilege," 2 *Ohio St. J. on Disp. Resol.* 1.

Green, Eric, & Jonathan Marks (2001) "How We Mediated the Microsoft Case," *The Boston Globe* A23 (November 15).

Green, Stuart (2005) "Theft by Coercion: Extortion, Blackmail, and Hard Bargaining," 44 *Washburn L. J.* 553.

Grillo, Trina (1991) "The Mediation Alternative: Process Dangers for Women," 100 *Yale L.J.* 1545 (April).

Gross, Samuel R., & Kent D. Syverud (1991) "Getting to No: A Study of Settlement Negotiations and the Selection of Cases for Trial," 90 *Mich. L. Rev.* 319.

Guernsey, Thomas F. (1982) "Truthfulness in Negotiation," 17 Univ. Rich. L. Rev. 99.

Guernsey, Thomas F. (1996) *A Practical Guide to Negotiation.* South Bend, In.: NITA.

Guthrie, Chris (2003) "Panacea or Pandora's Box?: The Costs of Options in Negotiation." 88 *Iowa L. Rev.* 601.

Guthrie, Chris, & James Levin (1998) "A 'Party Satisfaction' Perspective on a Comprehensive Mediation Statute," 13 *Ohio St. J. on Disp. Resol.* 885.

Guthrie, Chris, & James Levin (1998) "A 'Party Satisfaction' Perspective on a Comprehensive Mediation Statute," 13 *Ohio St. J. on Disp. Resol.* 885.

Hall, Lavinia, ed. (1993) *Negotiation: Strategies for Mutual Gain,* Newbury Park, Ca.: Sage.

Halpern, Richard G. (1998) "Settlement Negotiations: Taking Control," 34 *Trial* 64 (February).

Hammond, John S. (1999). Ralph L. Kenney, &

Hartman, Raymond S., et al. (1991) "Consumer Rationality and the Status Quo," 106 *Q. J. Econ.* 141.

Hartwell, Steven, et al. (1992) "Women Negotiating: Assertiveness and Relatedness," Linda A.M. Perry, et al., *Constructing and Reconstructing Gender.* Albany, NY: State University of New York Press.

Haydock, Roger S., et al (1996) *Lawyering: Practice and Planning.* St. Paul: West.

Haynes, John (1989) *Mediating Divorce: Casebook of Strategies for Successful Family Negotiations.* San Francisco: Jossey-Bass.

Hazard, Geoffrey (1981) "The Lawyer's Obligation to Be Trustworthy When Dealing With Opposing Parties," 33 *S.C. L. Rev.* 181.

Hedeen, Timothy (2009) "Mediation as Contact Sport?," _____ Disp. Resol. Mag. 23.

Hensler, Deborah R. (2003) "Our Courts, Ourselves: How the Alternative Dispute Resolution Movement is Reshaping Our Legal System," 108 *Penn St. L. Rev.* 165.

Herman, G. Nicholas (2005) "10 Tools for Mediation Cases," 41 *Trial* 66.

Hermann, Michele (1994) "New Mexico Research Examines Impact of Gender and Ethnicity in Mediation," 1 *Disp. Res. Mag.* 10 (Fall).

Herring, Victoria L. (2004) "Creative Advocacy in Voluntary Alternative Dispute Resolution," 40 *Trial* 40.

Hetherington, H. Lee (2001) "The Wizard and Dorothy, Patton and Rommel: Negotiation Parables in Fiction and Fact," 28 *Pepperdine L. Rev.* 289.

Hindrey, Leo, & Leslie Cauley (2003) *The Biggest Game of All: The Inside Strategies, Tactics, and Temperaments that Make Great Dealmakers Great.* New York: Free Press.

Hirshleifer, Jack (2001) "Game-Theoretic Interpretations of Commitment," Randolph Nesse, ed., *Evolution and the Capacity for Commitment.* New York: Russell Sage Foundation Publications.

Hodges, Ann C. "Mediation and the Transformation of American Labor Unions," 69 *Mo. L. Rev.* 365.

Hoffman, David A. (2008) "Microsoft and Yahoo: Where Were The Mediators? They Help Countries and Couples. Why Not Businesses?," *Christian Science Monitor* (May 12)

Hoffman, Elizabeth & Matthew L. Spitzer (1985) "Entitlements, Rights, and Fairness: An Experimental Examination of Subjects' Concepts of Distributive Justice," 14 *J. Legal Stud.* 259.

Hoffman, Elizabeth, et al. (1994) "Preferences, Property Rights, and Anonymity in Bargaining Games," 7 *Games & Econ. Behav.* 346.

Honeyman, Christopher (1990) "On Evaluating Mediators," 6 *Negot. J.* 23.

Howard Raiffa, *Smart Choices: A Practical Guide to Making Better Decisions.* Cambridge, Mass.: Harvard University Business School.

Hughes, Scott H. (1998) "A Closer Look: The Case for a Mediation Confidentiality Privilege Still Has Not Been Made," 5 *Disp. Res. Mag.* 14 (Winter).

Hyman, Jonathan M. (2004) "Swimming in the Deep End: Dealing With Justice in Mediation," 6 *Cardozo J. of Conflict Res.* 19.

Issacs, William (1999) *Dialogue and the Art of Thinking Together.* New York: Doubleday.

Izumi, Carol L., & Homer C. La Rue (2003) "Prohibiting 'Good Faith' Reports Under the Uniform Mediation Act: Keeping the Adjudication Camel Out of the Mediation Tent," 2003 *J. Disp. Resol.* 67.

Jandt, Fred E., with Paul Gillette (1985) *Win-Win Negotiating: Turning Conflict Into Agreement.* New York: John Wiley & Sons.

Johnston, Jason S. & Joel Waldfogel (2002) "Does Repeat Play Elicit Cooperation? Evidence From Federal Civil Litigation," 31 *J. Legal Stud.* 39.

Jones, Ashby (2004) "House Calls," *Corporate Counsel* 4 (October)

Kahneman, Daniel & Amos Tversky (1979) "Prospect Theory: An Analysis of a Decision Under Risk," 47 *Econometrica* 263.

Kahneman, Daniel, & Amos Tversky (1984) "Choices, Values, and Frames" 39 *Am. Pyschologist* 341.

Kahneman, Daniel, & Dale T. Miller (1986) "Norm Theory: Comparing Reality to Its Alternatives," 93 *Psychol. Rev.* 136.

Kahneman, Daniel, Jack L. Knetsch, & Richard H. Thaler (1990) "Experimental Tests of the Endowment Effect and the Coase Theorem," 98 *J. Pol. Econ.* 1325.

Kahneman, Daniel, Paul Sovic, & Amos Tversky (1982) *Judgment under Uncertainty: Heuristics and Biases.* Cambridge: Cambridge University Press.

Kakalik, James, et al. (1996) *An Evaluation of Mediation and Early Neutral Evaluation Under the Civil Justice Reform Act.* Santa Monica, Calif.: RAND Corp.

Kaplow, Louis, & Steven Shavell (2004) *Decision Analysis, Game Theory, and Information.* New York: Foundation Press.

Katsh, Ethan, & Janet Rivkin (2001) *Online Dispute Resolution — Resolving Conflicts in Cyberspace.* San Francisco: Jossey-Bass.

Katz, Lucy V. (2008a) "Getting to the Table, Kicking and Screaming: Drafting an Enforceable Mediation Provision," 26 *Alternatives* 183.

Katz, Lucy V. (2008b) "Keep It Simple: Developing the Legal Lessons for More Effective Mediation Enforcement," 26 *Alternatives* 2006.

Keating, Michael (1996) "Mediating in the Dance For Dollars," 14 *Alternatives* 71 (September).

Kennedy, Gavin (1994) *Field Guide to Negotiation: A Glossary of Essential Tools and Concepts for Today's Manager.* Boston: Harvard Business School Press.

Kheel, Theodore W. (1999) *The Keys to Conflic Resolution: Proven Methods of Settling Disputes Voluntarily.* New York: Four Walls Eight Windows.

Kichaven, Jeffrey G. (1999) "How Advocacy Fits In Effective Mediation," 17 *Alternatives* 60.

Kimmel, Melvin J., et al. (1980) "Effects of Trust, Aspiration and Gender on Negotiating Tactics," 38 *J. Pers. & Soc. Psychol.* 9.

Kimmel, Paul R. (1994) "Cultural Perspectives on International Negotiations," 50 *J. Soc. Issues* 179.

Kirtley, Alan (1995) "The Mediation Privilege's Transition from Theory to Implementation: Designing a Mediation Privilege Standard to Protect Mediation Participants, the Process and the Public Interest," 1995 *J. Disp. Resol.* 1.

Kloppenberg, Lisa A. (2002) "Implementation of Court-Annexed Environmental Mediation: The District of Oregon Pilot Project," 17 *Ohio St. J. on Disp. Resol.* 559.

Knetsch, Jack L., & J.A. Sinden (1984) "Willingness to Pay and Compensation Demanded: Experimental Evidence of an Unexpected Disparity in Measures of Value," 99 *Q. J. Econ.* 507.

Koh, Hea Jin (2004) "Yet I Shall Temper So Justice with Mercy: Procedural Justice in Mediation and Litigation," 28 *Law & Psychol. Rev.* 169.

Kolb, Deborah M & Judith Williams (2000) *The Shadow Negotiation: How Women Can Master the Hidden Agendas that Determine Bargaining Success.* New York: Simon & Schuster.

Kolb, Deborah M. & Judith Williams (2003) *Everyday Negotiation: Navigating the Hidden Agendas in Bargaining.* San Francisco: Jossey-Bass.

Kolb, Deborah M. et. al. (1994) *When Talk Works — Profiles of Mediators.* San Francisco: Jossey-Bass.

Korobkin, Ruseell, & Chris Guthrie (1997) "Psychology, Economics, and Settlement: A New Look at the Role of the Lawyer," 76 *Tex. L. Rev.* 77.

Korobkin, Russell (1998) "Inertia and Preference in Contract Negotiation: The Psychological Power of Default Rules and Form Terms," 51 *Vand. L. Rev.* 1583.

Korobkin, Russell (2000) "A Positive Theory of Legal Negotiation," 88 *Geo. L. J.* 1789.

Korobkin, Russell (2002) "Aspirations and Settlement," 88 *Corn L. Rev.* 1.

Korobkin, Russell (2002) *Negotiation Theory and Strategy.* New York: Aspen.

Korobkin, Russell, & Chris Guthrie (1994) "Opening Offers and Out of Court Settlement: A Little Moderation Might Not Go a Long Way," 10 *Ohio St. J. on Disp. Res.* 1.

Korobkin, Russell, & Chris Guthrie (1994) "Psychological Barriers to Litigation Settlement: An Experimental Approach," 93 *Mich. L. Rev.* 107.

Korobkin, Russell, Michael Moffett, & Nancy Welch (2004) "The Law of Bargaining" 87 Marq. L. Rev. 839.

Kovach, Kimberlee K. (1997) "Good Faith in Mediation — Requested, Recommended, or Required? A New Ethic," 38 *S. Tex. L. Rev.* 38.

Kovach, Kimberlee K., & Lela P. Love (1998) "Mapping Mediation: The Risks of Riskin's Grid," 3 *Harv. Negot. L. Rev.* 71.

Kramer, Roderick M., et al. (1993) "Self-Enhancement Biases and Negotiator Judgment: Effects of Self-Esteem and Mood," 56 *Org. Behav. & Human Dec. Proc.* 110.

Kremenyuk, Victor A., ed. (1991) *International Negotiation: Analysis, Approaches, Issues.* San Francisco: Jossey-Bass.

Kressel, Kenneth, & Dean G. Pruitt (eds.) (1989) *Mediation Research: The Power and Effectiveness of Third-Party Intervention.* San Francisco: Jossey-Bass.

Kritek, Phyllis Beck (2002) *Negotiating at an Uneven Table: Developing Moral Courage in Resolving Our Conflicts* (2d ed.). San Francisco: Jossey-Bass.

Kritzer, Herbert M. (1991) *Let's Make a Deal: Understanding the Negotiation Process in Ordinary Litigation.* Madison: University of Wisconsin Press.

Kritzer, Herbert M., "Fee Arrangements and Negotiation," 21 L. & Soc. Rev. 341 (1987)

Krivis, Jeffrey (2006) *Improvisational Negotiation.* San Francisco: Jossey-Bass.

Krolb, Deborah M. & Gloria Coolidge (1991) "Her Place at the Table: A Consideration of Gender Issues in Negotiation," in J. William Breslin & Jeffrey Z. Rubin, eds., *Negotiation, Theory and Practice.* Cambridge, MA: Program on Negotation.

Laborde, Genie Z. (1987) *Influencing with Integrity.* Palo Alto, Ca.: Syntony.

Laflin, James, & Robert Werth (2001) "Unfinished Business: Another Look at the Microsoft Mediation," 12 *California Tort Reporter No. 3*, 88 (May).

Lande, John (2002) "Using Dispute Systems Design Methods to Promote Good-Faith Participation in Court-Connected Mediation Programs," 50 *UCLA Law Rev.* 69 (October).

Lang, Michael D., & Alison Taylor (2000) *The Making of a Mediator: Developing Artistry in Practice.* San Francisco: Jossey-Bass.

Lawrence, James K.L. (2003) "Collaborative Lawyering: A New Development in Conflict Resolution," 17 *Ohio St. J. on Disp. Res.* 431.

Lax, David & James Sebenius (1992) "Thinking Coalitionally: Party Arithmetic, Process Opportunism, and Strategic Sequencing," H. Peyton Young, ed., *Negotiation Analysis.* UMP.

Lax, David A., & James K. Sebenius (1986) *The Manager as Negotiator: Bargaining for Cooperation and Competitive Gain.* New York: Free Press.

Levi, Deborah (1997) "The Role of Apology in Mediation," 72 *N.Y.U. L. Rev.* 1165.

Levinson, Jay Conrad, Mark S. A. Smith, & Orvel Ray Wilson (1999) *Guerilla Negotiating: Unconventional Weapons and Tactics to Get What You Want*. New York: John Wiley & Sons.

Lewicki, Roy J., David M. Saunders, & John W. Minton (2006) *Negotiation* (5th. ed.). New York: McGraw-Hill/Irwin.

Lewicki, Roy J., et. al. (2004) *Essentials of Negotiation* (3d. ed.). Chicago: Irwin.

Lewis, Michael (1995) "Advocacy in Mediation: One Mediator's View," 2 *Disp. Res. Mag.* 7 (Fall).

Lieberman, Jethro K. (1991) *The Litigious Society*. New York: Basic Books.

Lieberman, Jethro K., & James F. Henry (1986) "Lessons from the Alternative Dispute Resolution Movement," 53 *U. Chi. L. Rev.* 424.

Liebman, Carol B. & Chris S. Hyman (2004) "A Mediation Skills Model to Manage Disclosure of Errors and Adverse Events to Patients," 23 *Health Affairs* 22.

Lipsky, David B., & Ronald L. Seeber (1998) *The Appropriate Resolution of Corporate Disputes: A Report on the Growing Use of ADR by U.S. Corporations*. Ithaca, NY: Cornell/PERC Institute on Conflict Resolution.

Lipsky, David B., & Ronald L. Seeber (1999) "Patterns of ADR Use in Corporate Disputes," 54 *Disp. Res. J.* 66 (February).

Little, J. Anderson (2007) *Making Money Talk: How to Mediate Insured Claims and other Monetary Disputes* Chicago: American Bar Association

Locke, Edwin A, & Gary P. Latham (1990) *A Theory of Goal Setting and Task Performance*. Englewood Cliffs, N.J.: Prentice-Hall.

Loder, Reed Elizabeth (1994) "Moral Truthseeking and the Virtuous Negotiator," 8 *Geo. J. Legal Ethics* 45.

Loewenstein, George F., et al. (1989) "Social Utility and Decision Making in Interpersonal Contexts," 57 *J. Pers. & Soc. Psychol.* 426.

Loewenstein, George, et al. (1993) "Self-Serving Assessments of Fairness and Pretrial Bargaining," 22 *J. Legal Stud.* 135.

Longan, Patrick (2001) "Ethics in Settlement Negotiations: Foreward," 52 *Mercer L. Rev.* 810.

Love, Lela P. (1997) "The Top Ten Reasons Why Mediators Should Not Evaluate," 24 *Fla. St. U. L. Rev.* 937.

Lowry, L. Randolph (1997) "To Evaluate or Not — That Is Not the Question!" 2 *Resolutions* 2 (Pepperdine University School of Law).

Lubet, Steven (1996) "Notes on the Bedouin Horse Trade or 'Why Won't the Market Clear, Daddy?'" 74 *Tex. L. Rev.* 1039.

Luce, R. Duncan, & Howard Raiffa (1989) *Games and Decisions: Introduction and Critical Survey*. Mineola, NY: Dover Publications.

Luskin, Frederic, & Dana Curtis (2000) "The Power of Forgiveness," *Cal. Lawyer* (December).

Lynch, Hon. Eugene F., et al. (1992) *California Negotiation and Settlement Handbook*. Rochester, NY. Lawyers Co-operative.

Maccoby, Eleanor Emmons, & Carol Jacklin (1974) *The Psychology of Sex Differences*. Palo Alto: Stanford University Press.

Madoff, Ray D. (2002) "Lurking in the Shadow: The Unseen Hand of Doctrine in Dispute Resolution," 76 *S. Cal. L. Rev.* 161.

Matz, David E. (1999) "Ignorance and Interests," 4 *Harv. Negot. L. Rev.* 59.

Max, Rodney A. (1999) "Multiparty Mediation," 23 *Am. J. Trial Advoc.* 269.

McCarthy, William (1985) "The Role of Power and Principle in Getting to Yes," 1 *Negot. J.* 59

McEwen, Craig (1998) "Managing Corporate Disputing: Overcoming Barriers to the Effective Use of Mediation for Reducing the Cost and Time of Litigation," 14 *Ohio St. J. on Disp. Resol.* 1.

McGuire, James E. (2004) "Certification: An Idea Whose Time Has Come," 10 *Disp. Res. Mag.* 22 (Summer).

McIlwrath, Michael (2009) "Can Mediation Evolve into a Global Profession?" *Mediate.com*.

McKean, David, & Douglas Frantz (1995) *Friends in High Places: The Rise and Fall of Clark Clifford*. Boston : Little, Brown & Co.

Menkel-Meadow, Carrie (1984) "Toward Another View of Legal Negotiation: The Structure of Problem-Solving," 31 *U.C.L.A. L. Rev.* 754.

Menkel-Meadow, Carrie (1991) "Pursuing Settlement in an Adversary Culture: A Tale of Innovation Co-Opted of 'the Law of ADR,'" 19 *Fla. St. U. L. Rev.* 1.

Menkel-Meadow, Carrie (1999) "Do the 'Haves' Come out Ahead in Alternative Judicial Systems?: Repeat Players in ADR," 15 *Ohio St. J. on Disp. Resol.* 19.

Menkel-Meadow, Carrie (2000a) "Teaching About Gender and Negotiation, Sex., Truth, and Videotape," 16 *Negot. J.* 357.

Menkel-Meadow, Carrie (2000b) "When Winning Isn't Everything: The Lawyer as Problem Solver," 28 *Hofstra L. Rev.* 905.

Menkel-Meadow, Carrie (2001) "Ethics in ADR: The Many 'Cs' of Professional Responsibility and Dispute Resolution," 28 *Fordham Urban L. J.* 979.

Menkel-Meadow, Carrie (2003) *Dispute Processing and Conflict Resolution*. Burlington, VT.: Ashgate.

Menkel-Meadow, Carrie, & Elizabeth Plapinger (1999) "Model Rules Would Clarify Lawyer Conduct When Serving as a Neutral," 6 *Disp. Res. Mag.* 20 (Summer).

Menkel-Meadow, Carrie, & Michael Wheeler, eds. (2004) *What's Fair: Ethics for Negotiators*. San Francisco: Jossey-Bass.

Miller, Geoffrey P. (1987) "Some Agency Problems in Settlement," 16 *J. Legal Stud.* 189.

Miller, Lee E.,& Jessica Miller (2002) *A Woman's Guide to Successful Negotiating:How to Convince, Collaborate, & Create Your Way to Agreement.* New York: McGraw-Hill.

Milne, Ann L. (2004) "Mediation and Domestic Abuse," in J. Folberg, et al., eds., *Divorce and Family Mediation.* New York: Guilford Press.

Mnookin, Robert H. (1993) "Why Negotiations Fail: An Exploration of Barriers to the Resolution of Conflict," 8 *Ohio St. J. on Disp. Res.* 235.

Mnookin, Robert H. (2003) "Strategic Barriers to Dispute Resolution: A Comparison of Bilateral and Multilateral Negotiations," 8 *Harv. Negot. L. Rev. 1.* (Spring).

Mnookin, Robert H., & Lawrence E. Susskind, eds. (1999) *Negotiating on Behalf of Others.* Thousand Oaks: Sage.

Mnookin, Robert H., & Lewis Kornhauser (1979) "Bargaining the in Shadow of the Law: The Case for Divorce," 88 *Yale L. J.* 950.

Mnookin, Robert H., & Ronald J. Gilson (1994) "Disputing Through Agents: Cooperation and Conflict Between Lawyers in Litigation," 94 *Colum. L. Rev.* 509.

Mnookin, Robert H., Scott R. Peppet, & Andrew S. Tulumello (1996) "The Tension Between Empathy and Assertiveness," 12 *Negot. J.* 217.

Mnookin, Robert H., Scott R. Peppet, & Andrew S. Tulumello (2000) *Beyond Winning: Negotiating to Create Value in Deals and Disputes.* Cambridge, Mass.: Harvard University Press.

Moffit, Michael (2003) "Suing Mediators," 83 *B.U. L. Rev.* 147.

Moffit, Michael (2003) "Ten Ways to Get Sued: A Guide for Mediators," 8 *Harv. Negot. L. Rev.* 81.

Moffitt, Michael L. & Robert C. Bordone, eds. (2005) *The Handbook of Dispute Resolution,* San Francisco: Jossey-Bass.

Moore, Christopher (2004) *The Mediation Process: Practical Strategies for Resolving Conflict.* San Francisco: Jossey-Bass.

Mosten, Forrest S. (1996) *The Complete Guide to Mediation: The Cutting-Edge Approach to Family Law Practice.* Chicago: ABA Section of Family Law.

Murnighan, J. Keith (1992) *Bargaining Games.* New York: W. Morrow.

Murray, John S. (1986) "Understanding Competing Theories of Negotiation," 2 *Negot. J.* 179.

Nadler, Janice (2001) "In Practice: Electronically Mediated Dispute Resolution and E-Commerce," 17 *Negot. J.* 333.

Nelken, Melissa L. (2001) *Understanding Negotiation.* Cincinnati: Anderson.

Niemic, Robert J., Donna Stienstra, & Randall E. Ravitz (2001) *Guide to Judicial Management of Cases in ADR.* Washington, D.C.: Federal Judicial Center.

Nierenberg, Gerald I. (1981) *The Art of Negotiating* New York: Pocket Books.

Nolan-Haley, Jacqueline (1996) "Court Mediation and the Search for Justice Through Law," 74 *Wash. Univ. L. Q.* 47.

Nolan-Haley, Jacqueline (1998) "Lawyers, Clients, and Mediation," 73 *Notre Dame L. Rev.* 1369.

O'Connor, Kathleen M., & Peter J. Carnevale (1997) "A Nasty but Effective Negotiation Strategy: Misrepresentation of a Common-Value Issue," 23 *Personality & Soc. Psychol. Bull.* 504.

O'Hara, Erin Anne, & Douglas Yarn (2002) "On Apology and Concilience," 77 *Wash. L. Rev.* 1121.

Ochs, Jack, & Alvin E. Roth (1989) "An Experimental Study of Sequential Bargaining," 79 *Am. Econ. Rev.* 335.

Olson, Walter (1991) *The Litigation Explosion.* New York: Penguin Books.

Ordover, Abraham P., & Andrea Doneff (2002) *Alternatives to Litigation: Mediation, Arbitration, and the Art of Dispute Resolution.* Notre Dame, Ind.: NITA.

Owen, Rebecca M. (2005) "In re Uncertainty: A Uniform and Confidential Treatment of Evidentiary and Advocacy Materials Used in Mediation," 20 *Ohio St. J. on Disp. Resol.* 911.

Parks, McLean, et al. (1996) "Distributing Adventitious Outcomes: Social Norms, Egocentric Martyrs, and the Effects of Future Relationships," 67 *Org. Behav. & Human Decision Proc.* 181.

Peppet, Scott R. (2002) "Mindfulness in the Law and ADR: Can Saints Negotiate?" 7 *Harv. Negot. L. Rev.* 83 (Spring).

Peppet, Scott R. (2004) "Contract Formation in Imperfect Markets: Should We Use Mediators in Deals?" 38 *Ohio St. J. on Disp. Resol.* 283.

Perry, Linda A.M., et al., eds. (1992) *Constructing and Reconstructing Gender.* Albany, NY: State University of New York Press.

Perschbacher, Rex R. (1985) "Regulating Lawyers' Negotiations," 27 *Ariz. L. Rev.* 75.

Peters, Geoffrey M. (1987) "The Use of Lies in Negotiation," 48 *Ohio St. L. J.* 1.

Picker, Bennett G. (1999) "New Roles: Problem Solving ADR: New Challenges, New Roles, and New Opportunities," 72 *Temple L. Rev.* 883 (Winter).

Picker, Bennett G. (2003) *Mediation Practice Guide: A Handbook for Resolving Business Disputes.* Washington, D.C.: ABA Section of Dispute Resolution.

Picker, Bennett G. (2008) "Navigating Relationships: The Invisible Barriers to Resolution," 2 *Amer. J. of Mediation* 41.

Pinkley, Robin L., et al., "The Impact of Alternatives to Settlement in Dyadic Negotiation," 57 Org. Behav. & Human Decision Proc. 97 (1994)

Polythress, Norman G. (1994) "Procedural Preferences, Perceptions of Fairness and Compliance with Outcomes: A Study of Alternatives to the Standard Adversary Trial Procedure," 18 *L. & Hum. Behav.* 361.

Polzer, Jeffrey T., et al. (1993) "The Effects of Relationship and Justification in an Interdependent Allocation," 2 *Group Decision & Negot.* 135.

Press, Sharon (1998) "Florida's Court-Connected State Mediation Program," in Edward J. Bergman & John G. Bickerman, eds., *Court-Annexed Mediation: Critical Perspectives on State and Federal Programs*. Washington, D.C.: ABA Section of Dispute Resolution.

Price, Marty (2000) "Personalizing Crime: Mediation Produces Restorative Justice for Victims and Offenders," 7 *Disp. Res. Mag.* 8 (Fall).

Priest, George, & Benjamin Klein (1984) "The Selection of Disputes for Litigation," 13 *J. Legal Stud.* 1.

Rachlinski, Jeffrey J. (1996) "Gains, Losses, and the Psychology of Litigation," 70 *S. Cal. L. Rev.* 113.

Raiffa, Howard (1982) *The Art and Science of Negotiation*. Cambridge, Mass.: Harvard University Press.

Raiffa, Howard (1985) "Post-Settlement Settlements," 1 *Negot. J.* 9.

Raiffa, Howard (2002) *Negotiation Analysis: The Science and Art of Collaborative Decision Making*. Cambridge, Mass.: Harvard University Press.

Raitt, Susan E., et al. (1993) "The Use of Mediation in Small Claims Courts," 9 *Ohio St. J. on Disp. Resol.* 55.

Reichert, Klaus (2005) "Confidentiality in International Mediation," 59 *J. Disp. Resol.* 60.

Reno, Janet (2001) "Promoting Problem Solving and Peacemaking as Enduring Values in Our Society," 19 *Alternatives* 16.

Resnik, Judith (1995) "Many Doors? Closing Doors? Alternative Dispute Resolution and Adjudication," 10 *Ohio St. J. on Disp. Res.* 211.

Riskin, Leonard (1993) "Mediator Orientations, Strategies and Techniques," 12 *Alternatives* 111.

Riskin, Leonard (1996) "Understanding Mediator's Orientations, Strategies, and Techniques: A Grid for the Perplexed," 1 *Harv. Negot. L. Rev.* 7 (Spring).

Riskin, Leonard (2003) "Decision-Making in Mediation: The New Old Grid and the New New Grid System," 79 *Notre Dame L. Rev.* 1 (December).

Riskin, Leonard (2003) "Retiring and Replacing the Grid of Mediator Orientations," 21 *Alternatives* 69.

Robbennolt, Jennifer K. (2003) "Apologies and Legal Settlement: An Eupirical Examination," 102 *Michigan L. Rev.* 460.

Robinson, Peter (1998) "Contending with Wolves in Sheep's Clothing: A Cautiously Cooperative Approach to Mediation Advocacy," 50 *Baylor L. Rev.* 963.

Robinson, Robert J. (1995) "Defusing the Exploding Offer: The Farpoint Gambit," 11 *Negot. J.* 277.

Rogers, Joshua S. (2004) "Riner v. Newbraugh: The Role of Mediator Testimony in the Enforcement of Mediated Agreements," 107 *W. Va. L. Rev.* 329.

Rose, Carol (1995) "Bargaining and Gender," 18 *Harv. J. L. & Pub. Pol'y.* 547.

Rosenberg, Joshua D., & Jay Folberg (1994) "Alternative Dispute Resolution: An Empirical Analysis," 46 *Stan. L. Rev.* 1487.

Rosengard, Lee A. (2004) "Learning From Law Firms: Using Co-Mediation to Train New Mediators," 59 *Disp. Resol. J.* 16.

Ross, David (2000) "Strategic Considerations in Choosing a Mediator: A Mediator's Perspective," 2 *J. Alt. Disp. Res. in Empl.* 7 (Spring).

Ross, Lee (1995) "Reactive Devaluation in Negotiation and Conflict Resolution," Kenneth Arrow, et al., eds., *Barriers to Conflict Resolution*. New York: W.W. Norton.

Ross, Lee, & Andrew Ward (1995) "Psychological Barriers to Dispute Resolution," 27 *Advances Experimental Soc. Psychol.* 255.

Roth, Bette J., Randall W. Wulff & Charles A. Cooper (1993) *The Alternative Dispute Resolution Practice Guide*. Scarborough: Carswell.

Rubin, Jeffrey Z. (1991) "Some Wise and Mistaken Assumptions About Conflict and Negotiation," William J. Breslin & Jeffrey Z. Rubin, eds., *Negotiation Theory and Practice*. Cambridge, MA: Program on Negotiation.

Rubin, Jeffrey Z. (1993) "*Conflict From a Psychological Perspective*," in Laviria Hall, ed., Negotiation Strategies for Mutual Gain. Newbury Parle, CA: Sage.

Rubin, Jeffrey Z., & Bert R. Brown (1975) *The Social Psychology of Bargaining and Negotiation*. New York: Academic Press.

Rubin, Jeffrey Z., & Frank E.A. Sander (1991) "Culture, Negotiation, and the Eye of the Beholder," 7 *Negot. J.* 249.

Rubin, Melvin A. and Spector, Brian F. (2008) "Ethical Conundrums for the 21st Century Lawyer/Mediator," 2 *Amer. J. Mediation* 73.

Rubin, Michael H. (1995) "The Ethics of Negotiation: Are There Any?" 56 *La. L. Rev.* 447.

Rule, Colin (2002) *Online Dispute Resolution for Business: B2B, Ecommerce, Consumer, Employment, Insurance, and Other Commercial Conflicts* San Francisco: Jossey-Bass.

Rummel, R.J. (1991) *The Conflict Helix*. New Brunswick, NJ: Transaction.

Salacuse, Jeswald (2002) "Mediation in International Business," in J. Bercovitch, ed., *Studies in International Mediation*. New York: Palgrave Macmillan.

Salacuse, Jeswald W. (1988) "Making Deals in Strange Places: A Beginner's Guide to International Business Negotiations," 4 *Negot. J.* 5.

Salacuse, Jeswald W. (1998) "Ten Ways That Culture Affects Negotiating Style: Some Survey Results," 14 *Negot. J.* 221.

Salacuse, Jeswald W. (2003) *The Global Negotiator: Making, Managing, and Mending Deals Around the World in the Twenty-First Century*. Hampshire, UK: Palgrave Macmillan.

Salem, Richard (2003) "The Benefits of Empathic Listening," Conflict Research Consortium, University of Colorado, *http://www.crinfo.org*.

Scanlon, Kathleen, ed. (1999) *Mediator's Deskbook*. New York: CPR Institute.

Schelling, Thomas C. (1960) *The Strategy of Conflict*. Cambridge, Mass.: Harvard University Press.

Schmitz, Suzanne J. (2001) "What Should We Teach in ADR Courses?: Concepts and Skills for Lawyers Representing Clients in Mediation," 6 *Harv. Negot. L. Rev.* 189.

Schneider, Andrea Kupfer (2000) "Perceptions, Reputation and Reality: An Empirical Study of Negotiation Styles," 6 *ABA Disp Res. Mag.* 24 (Summer).

Schneider, Andrea Kupfer (2002) "Shattering Negotiation Myths: Empirical Evidence on the Effectiveness of Negotiation Style," 7 *Harv. Negot. L. Rev.*, 143 (Spring).

Schon, Donald (1983) *The Reflective Practitioner*. New York: Basic Books.

Sebenius, James K. (2002) "Caveats for Cross-Border Negotiations," 18 *Negot. J.* 122.

Senger, Jeffrey M. (2002) "In Practice: Tales of the Bazaar — Interest-Based Negotiation Across Cultures," 18 *Negot. J.* 233 (July).

Senger, Jeffrey M. (2004) *Federal Dispute Resolution: Using Alternative Dispute Resolution with the United States Government*. San Francisco: Jossey-Bass.

Seul, Jeffrey R. (1999) "How Transformative Is Transformative Mediation?: A Constructive-Developmental Assessment," 15 *Ohio St. J. on Disp. Resol.* 135.

Shapiro, Ronald M., & Mark A. Jankowski, with James Dale (2001) *The Power of Nice* (2d. ed.). New York: John Wiley & Sons.

Shell, G. Richard (1988) "Substituting Ethical Standards for Common Law Rules in Commercial Cases: An Emerging Statutory Trend," 82 *Nw. Univ. L. Rev.* 1198.

Shell, G. Richard (1991) "Opportunism and Trust in Negotiation of Commercial Contracts: Toward a New Cause of Action," 44 *Vand. L. Rev.* 221 (1991)

Shell, G. Richard (1999) *Bargaining for Advantage: Negotiation Strategies for Reasonable People*. New York: Viking.

Sherman, Edward F. (1988) " From 'Loser Pays' to Modified Offer of Judgment Rules: Reconciling Incentives to Settle with Access to Justice," 76 *Tex. L. Rev.* 1863.

Silbey, Susan S. (2002) "The Emperor's New Clothes: Mediation Mythology and Markets," 2002 *J. Disp. Resol.* 171.

Simon, William H. (1988) "Ethical Discretion in Lawyering," 101 *Harv. L. Rev.* 1083.

Singer, Linda (1994) *Settling Disputes: Conflict Resolution in Business, Families, and the Legal System*. Boulder, CO: Westview.

SiSjöstedt, Gunnar (2003) *Professional Cultures in International Negotiation: Bridge or Rift?* Lanham, MD: Lexington Books.

Slaikeu, Karl A. (1996) *When Push Comes to Shove: A Practical Guide to Mediating Disputes*. San Francisco: Jossey-Bass.

Slavitt, Evan (2006) "Using Risk Analysis as a Mediation Tool," 2006 *Disp. Resol. J.* 18.

Smith, Pam (2006) "Separating Opponents Key to JAMS Neutral's Success," *The Recorder* 4 (June 20)

Smith, Robert M. (2000) "Advocacy in Mediation: A Dozen Suggestions," 26 *S.F. Att'y* 14 (June/July).

Spegel, Nadja M., Bernadette Rogers, Ross P. Buckley (1998) *Negotiation: Theory and Techniques*.

Sperber, Philip (1985) *Attorney's Practice Guide to Negotiations*. Wilmette, Ill.: Callaghan & Co.

Spolter, Jerry (2000) "A Mediator's Tip: Talk to Me!" *The Recorder* 4 (March 8).

Stallworth, Lamont E., et al. (2001) "Discrimination in the Workplace: How Mediation Can Help," *Disp. Res. J.* 35.

Starr, V. Hale (1999) "The Simple Math of Negotiating," 22 *Trial L.* 5 (January — February)

Stempel, Jeffrey W. (1997) "Beyond Formalism and False Dichotomies: The Need for Institutionalizing a Flexible Concept of the Mediator's Role," 24 *Fla. St. U. L. Rev.* 949.

Stern, David M. (1998) "Mediation: An Old Dog with Some New Tricks," 24 *Litigation* 31.

Sternberg, Robert J., & Diane M. Dobson (1987) "Resolving Interpersonal Conflicts: An Analysis of Stylistic Consistency," 52 *J. Pers. & Soc. Psychol.* 794.

Sternberg, Robert J., & Lawrence J. Soriano (1984) "Styles of Conflict Resolution," 47 *J. Pers. & Soc. Psychol.* 115.

Stienstra, Donna (1998) "Demonstrating the Possibilities of Providing Mediation Early and by Court Staff: The Western District of Missouri's Early Assessment Program," *Court-Annexed Mediation: Critical Perspectives on State and Federal Programs* 251.

Stienstra, Donna, Molly Johnson, & Patricia Lombard (1997) "Report to the Judicial Conference Committee on Court Administration and Case Management: A Study of the Five Demonstration Programs Established Under the Civil Justice Reform Act of 1990." Washington, D.C.: Federal Judicial Center.

Stipanowich, Thomas J. (2001) "Contracts Symposium: Contract and Conflict Managment," 2001 *Wis. L. Rev.* 831.

Stipanowich, Thomas J. (2004) "ADR and 'The Vanishing Trial': What We Know – and What We Don't," *Disp. Res. Mag.* (Summer).

Stone, Douglas, Bruce Patton, & Sheila Heen (1999) *Difficult Conversations: How to Discuss What Matters Most.* New York: Penguin Books.

Strudler, Alan (1998) "Incommensurable Goods, Rightful Lies, and the Wrongness of Fraud," 146 *U. Pa. L. Rev.* 1529.

Stulberg, Joseph (1981) "The Theory and Practice of Mediation: A Reply to Professor Susskind," 6 *Vt. L. Rev.* 85.

Stulberg, Joseph (1997) "Facilitative Versus Evaluative Mediator Orientations: Piercing the 'Grid' Lock," 24 *Fla. St. U. L. Rev.* 985.

Sumner, Anna Aven (2003) "Is the Gummy Rule of Today Truly Better Than the Toothy Rule of Tomorrow? How Federal Rule 68 Should be Modified," 52 Duke L. J. 1055.

Susskind, Lawrence (1981) "Environmental Mediation and the Accountability Problem," 6 *Vt. L. Rev.* 1.

Susskind, Lawrence, et al., eds. (1999) *The Consensus Building Handbook: A Comprehensive Guide to Reaching Agreement.* Thousand Oaks, Calif.: Sage.

Symposium (2001) "ADR and the Professional Responsibility of Lawyers," 28 *Ford. Urb. L. J.* No. 4. Taft, Lee (2000) "Apology Subverted: The Commodification of Apology," 109 *Yale L. J.* 1155.

Technology Mediation Services (2004) "High Tech and Intellectual Property Disputes," *www.technologymediation.com/hightech.htm.*

Temkin, Barry R. (2004) "Misrepresentation by Omission in Settlement Negotiations: Should there Be a Silent Safe Harbor?" 18 Geo. J. Legal Ethics 179.

Tesler, Pauline H. (2001) *Collaborative Law.* Chicago: ABA Section on Family Law.

Tesler, Pauline H. (2003) "Collaborative Law Neutrals Produce Better Resolution," 21 *Alternatives* 1.

Thaler, Richard H. (1988) "Anomalies: The Ultimatum Game," 2 *J. Econ. Persp.* 195.

Thompson, Leigh & Reid Hastie (1990) "Social Perception in Negotiation," 47 Org. *Beh. & Human Dec. Processes* 98.

Thompson, Leigh (2001) *The Mind and Heart of the Negotiator* (2d. ed.). Upper Saddle River, N.J.: Prentice-Hall.

Thompson, Leigh L., et al. (1999) "Some Life it Hot: The Case for the Emotional Negotiator," Leigh L. Thompson, et al. *Shared Cognition in Organizations: The Management of Knowledge.* Mahwah, NJ: LEA.

Thompson, Leigh, & Janice Nadler (2002) "Negotiating Via Information Technology: Theory and Application," 58 *J. Soc. Issues* 109.

Thompson, Peter (2004) "Enforcing Rights Generated in Court-Connected Mediation — Tension Between the Aspirations of a Private Facilitative Process and the Reality of Public Adversarial Justice," 19 *Ohio St. J.Disp. Resol.* 509.

Trachte-Huber, E. Wendy & Stephen K. Huber (1999) *Mediation and Negotiation: Reaching Agreement.* Cincinnati: Anderson.

Tversky, Amos, & Daniel Kahneman (1992 "Advances in Prospect Theory: Cumulative Representation of Uncertainty," 5 *J. Risk & Uncertainty* 297.

Uelmen, Gerald F. (1990) "Playing 'Godfather' in Settlement Negotiations: The Ethics of Using Threats," *Cal. Litigation* 3 (Fall).

Ury, William (1993) *Getting Past No: Negotiating Your Way From Confrontation to Cooperation.* New York: Bantam Books.

van Dijk, Eric, & Daan van Knippenberg (1996) "Buying and Selling Exchange Goods: Loss Aversion and the Endowment Effect," 17 *J. Econ. Psych.* 517.

Wade, John (2004) "Representing Clients Effectively in Negotiation, Conciliation and Mediation of Family Disputes," 18 *Austl. J. Fam. L.* 283.

Waldman, Ellen A. (2004) "Healing Hearts or Righting Wrongs?: A Mediation on the Goals of 'Restorative Justice,'" 25 *Hamline J. Pub. L. & Pol'y* 355.

Walton, Richard E., Joel E, Cutcher-Gershenfeld, & Robert B. McKersie (2000) *Strategic Negotiations: A Theory of Change in Labor-Management Relations.* Ithaca: Cornell University Press.

Wangerin, Paul T. (1994) "The Political and Economic Roots of the 'Adversary System' of Justice and Alternative Dispute Resolution," 9 *Ohio St. J. on Disp. Res.* 203.

Ware, Stephen J. & Sarah Rudolph Cole (2000) "Introduction: ADR in Cyberspace," 15 *Ohio St. J. on Disp. Res.* 589.

Ware, Stephen J. (2001) *Alternative Dispute Resolution.* St. Paul: West.

Watkins, Michael, & Susan Rosengrant (2001) *Breakthrough International Negotiations.* San Francisco: Jossey-Bass.

Watkins, Normal J. (1999) "Negotiating the Complex Case," 41 *For the Defense* 36 (July).

Watson, Carol (1994) "Gender versus Power as a Predictor of Negotiation Behavior and Outcome," 10 *Negot. J.* 117.

Weinstein, John (1996) "Advocacy in Mediation," 32 *Trial* 31.

Welsh, Nancy A. (2001) "Making Deals in Court-Connected Mediation: What's Justice Got to Do With It?," 79 *Wash. Univ. L.Q.* 787 (Fall).

Welsh, Nancy A. (2004) "Remembering the Role of Justice in Resolution: Insights from Procedural and Social Justice Theories," 54 *J. Legal. Educ.* 49.

Wetlaufer, Gerald B. (1990) "The Ethics of Lying in Negotiation," 76 *Iowa L. Rev.* 1219.

Wetlaufer, Gerald B. (1996) "The Limits of Integrative Bargaining," 85 *Geo. L. J.* 369.

White, James J. (1980) "Machiavelli and the Bar: Ethical Limitation on Lying in Negotiation," 1980 *Am. Bar. Found. Res. J.* 926.

White, James J. (1984) "Essay Review: The Pros and Cons of 'Getting to Yes;'" Roger Fisher, "Comments on White's Review," 34 *J. of Legal Educ.* 115.

Widman, Stuart M. (2008a) "The Protections and Limits of Confidentiality in Mediation," 24 *Alternatives* 167.

Widman, Stuart M. (2008b) "More Mediation Confidentiality Limits: What the Court May Allow In to Establish a Settlement Agreement," 24 *Alternatives* 179.

Wilkinson, John H., ed. (1990 and annual supplements) *Donovan Leisure Newton & Irvine ADR Practice Book*. New York: Wiley Law Pulbications.

Williams, Gerald R. (1983) *Legal Negotiation and Settlement*. St. Paul: West.

Williams, Gerald R. (1996) "Negotiation as a Healing Process," *J. of Disp. Res.* 33.

Wissler, Roselle L. (2001) "To Evaluate or Facilitate? Parties' Perceptions of Mediation Affected by Mediator Style," 7 *Disp. Res. Mag.* 35 (Winter).

Wissler, Roselle L. (2002) "Court-Connected Mediation in General Civil Cases: What We Know from Empirical Research," 17 *Ohio St. J. on Disp. Resol.* 641.

Wissler, Roselle L. (2006) "The Role of Antecedent and Procedural Characteristics in Mediation: A Review of the Research," in Margaret S. Hermann, *The Blackwell Handbook of Mediation*. Malden MA: Blackwell Publishing Ltd.

Wittenberg, Carol, Susan Mackenzie, & Margaret Shaw (2009) "Employment Disputes," in D. Golann, ed., *Mediating Legal Disputes: Effective Strategies for Neutrals and Advoacates* Chicago: American Bar Association

Zitrin, Richard A. (1999) "The Case Against Secret Settlements" 2 *J. Inst. For Study of Legal Ethics* 115.

Zitrin, Richard, & Carol M. Langford (1999) *The Moral Compass of the American Lawyer*. New York: Ballantine Books.

WEB SITES

American Bar Association Section of Dispute Resolution, *http://www.abanet.org/dispute/home* (Professional association of lawyers and law students interested in mediation and other forms of ADR).

Association for Conflict Resolution, *http://www.spidr.org* (Professional association for lawyers, law students, and nonlawyers interested in mediation and other forms of ADR).

Center for Analysis of Alternative Dispute Resolution Systems, *http://www.caadrs.org* (Abstracts of empirical studies of court-related ADR programs).

Center for the Study of Dispute Resolution, University of Missouri, *http://www.law.missouri.edu/csdr/adr* (References to information and other academic ADR Web sites).

Centre for Effective Dispute Resolution, *http://www.cedr.co.uk* (Information on British and European use of ADR in commercial disputes).

Conflict Resolution Information Source, Conflict Research Consortium, University of Colorado, *http://www.crinfo.org* (Information and referral sources on a wide variety of ADR issues).

Court ADR Across the U.S., *http://courtadr.org/court-adr-across-the-us/*.

CPR Institute of Dispute Resolution, *http://www.cpradr.org* (Information concerning use of ADR in commercial disputes).

Federal ADR Network, *http://www.adr.af.mil./general/guide_adr.doc* (a comprehensive list of ADR Web sites).

VIDEOTAPES AND DVDS (ALL ARE VIEDIOTAPES, UNLESS OTHERWISE NOTED)

Representing Clients

Golann, Dwight (2000) "Representing Clients in Mediation: How Advocates Can Share a Mediator's Powers," *http://www.abanet.org/cle* (Unscripted examples of advocates using mediators to advance bargaining goals).

Phillips, John (2003) "Mediation Madness," *http://www.abanet.org/dispute/videos.html* (Examples of good and bad mediation advocacy).

Mediation Skills

Aaron, Marjorie Corman, & Dwight Golann (2004) "Mediators at Work: A Case of Discrimination?" *http://www.pon.org* (Unscripted mediation of an age discrimination case).

CPR Institute for Dispute Resolution (1994) "Mediation in Action," *http://www.cpradr.org* (Mediation of international contract dispute).

CPR Institute for Dispute Resolution (2003) "Resolution Through Mediation," *http://www.cpradr.org* (Mediation of international trademark case).

Golann, Dwight, & Marjorie Corman Aaron (2009) "Skills of a Mediator" (JAMS Foundation 2009) (Mediation of American-Indian commercial dispute) (also available with D. Golann, Mediating Legal Disputes (ABA 2009))

Golann, Dwight, & Marjorie Corman Aaron (2009) "Mediators at Work: Breach of Warranty?" *http://www.pon.org* (Unscripted mediation of commercial contract dispute).

Himmelstein, Jack, & Gary Friedman (2001) "Saving the Last Dance: Mediation Through Understanding," *http://www.pon.org* (No-caucus mediation of a manager-organization dispute).

JAMS Foundation (2003) (DVD) "Mediating A Sexual Harassment Case: What Would You Do?" *http://www.jamsadr.com* (Vignettes of challenging situations for a mediator).

TABLE OF CASES

Principal cases are indicated by italics.

INDEX